Shakesqueer

Edited by Michèle Aina Barale,
Jonathan Goldberg, Michael Moon,
and Eve Kosofsky Sedgwick

Shakesqueer

A Queer Companion to

the Complete Works of Shakespeare

Edited by **MADHAVI MENON**

DUKE UNIVERSITY PRESS DURHAM AND LONDON 2011

© 2011 Duke University Press
All rights reserved
Printed in the United States
of America on acid-free paper ∞
Designed by Amy Ruth Buchanan
Typeset in Monotype Dante
by Keystone Typesetting, Inc.
Library of Congress Cataloging-
in-Publication Data appear on the
last printed page of this book.

CONTENTS

ACKNOWLEDGMENTS

This book has been a labor of love that has accrued various and immense debts. It is my pleasure to record them here.

At American University, I would like to thank, first, my students. The idea for *Shakesqueer* was born as an idea for a class in which I could more fully integrate Shakespeare and queer theory. My colleagues Keith Leonard, Mandy Berry, Richard Sha, Despina Kakoudaki, Linda Voris, and Richard McCann have helped this project along pleasurably and immeasurably. And the Dean's office of the College of Arts and Sciences—especially Kay Mussell, Peter Starr, and Thomas Husted—gave me several grants that allowed me to complete the work on this volume.

Also at American University, I have had the help of the incomparable Melissa Yinger, who has been my research assistant and general factotum for this volume. Thanks also to Jessie Rutland, Tara Schupner, and Cathy Johnson for providing formatting services in many tense situations!

I would like to register my deep thanks to Ken Wissoker at Duke University Press for his intelligent skepticism and earnest enthusiasm. Without his suggestions, this book would not be as strong. The two anonymous readers, who read both the prospectus and the finished product, were astonishing in the acuity and generosity of their suggestions. They will see several of those suggestions manifested in the pages that follow. My thanks to them for their insights.

Also at Duke, I had the good fortune of landing Mandy Earley as my editor during the early part of assembling this book, and Mark Mastromarino during the later stages. They have both been patient, good-humored, and encyclopedic in their knowledge, which is more than anyone can ask for from one's editors. Scott Smiley has made the index as exciting as the volume, and for that amazing feat, I thank him.

Ellis Hanson and the English Department at Cornell University held a conference based on the volume that brought many of the contributors face-to-face with one another for the first time. It was a queer couple of days in

x

Ithaca in September 2008, and the excitement at the conference only proved that the volume was onto something big.

And that something big, of course, has been provided by all the contributors to *Shakesqueer*, who have been unrelentingly fun to work with. They have written surprising essays, pushed themselves out of their comfort zones, and played with the governing rubric of the book in ways that I would not have imagined possible. They have even adhered to deadlines. My deep, abiding, and heartfelt thanks to them all.

Shakesqueer would have been impossible without the good wishes, sage advice, and loving ministrations of Lee Edelman, Joseph Litvak, Stephen Guy-Bray, Jonathan Goldberg, Ellis Hanson, Judith Brown, A. T. Shelden, Kathryn Schwarz, and Bill Cohen. Ken Reinhardt organized a talk for me to air *Shakesqueer* at UCLA, and I also presented a version of the introduction at an MLA session organized by Henry Turner; my thanks to them both.

As always, there is a circle of family and friends that has had less to do with the book itself and more with the well-being of its editor: Mohan and Indira Menon, Kalyani Menon, Kevin Schjerning, Mango Menon (may his love of books be fed by this one), Stella, Norman, and Miriam Harris, Asma Barlas, Ulises Mejias, Suparna Sharma, Samit Tandon, Nandini Gopinadh, Anupama Chandra, Shikha Behl, Shweta Kumar, Shruti Devi, Rashmi Nair-Ripley, Kripa Amritanand, and Ritin Rai.

Neither *Shakesqueer* nor I would be here without Gil Harris.

Queer Shakes

MADHAVI MENON

When I first decided to title the introduction to this volume "Queer Shakes," a friend pointed out that "Queer Shakes sounds a bit like a libertine's pathology." He offered, by way of example, the following sentence: "After decades of too many cocks and too many cocktails, Wilde was afflicted with the Queer Shakes." I found this sense of affliction fortuitous: it positions *Shakesqueer* as a germ infecting the ways in which we do queer business. While Shakespeare scholarship has for years been flirting with queer theory, the relationship between the two is less reciprocal than we might expect, and queer theory rarely resorts to Shakespeare as a ground for its formulation. The reason for this one-sided relationship is twofold. First, in its institutionalized avatar, queer theory takes as its ambit a historical period after 1800; since Shakespeare died in 1616, his texts are not generally understood to be proper subjects of queer theory as we know it today. And second, the reason this historical date of, or around, 1800 is important is that it is believed to mark the institutionalization of homosexuality and heterosexuality. Despite its suspicion of institutional constraints, then, queer theory has set up two strong institutional boundaries of its own, accepting as its proper domain a historical period in which queerness comes to be understood as homosexuality. The convergence of these two boundaries—the one temporal and the other identitarian—ensures that a queered Shakespeare is never a queer Shakespeare. Instead, it allows us to fix the place of Shakespeare and queer theory both in themselves and in relation to each other and gives us able-bodied monoliths instead of libertines with the queer shakes.

Oddly, this fixed Shakespeare conjured by an institutional queer theory resembles nothing so much as the canonical figure we have inherited as the privileged signifier of the literary and the human. Deemed by the cult of canonicity to be "not of an age but for all time," Shakespeare has enjoyed the kind of status that no other author has inside or outside the academy; this is why Derek Jarman remarked ruefully, after his *Tempest* failed in the United States, that in America "messing with Will Shakespeare is not allowed."[1] But privilege is not all that it appears to be, and being canonized also deprives a text of agency, containing what is potentially too disturbing to be contained. It is in this way that queer theory's refusal to engage Shakespeare as queer becomes indistinguishable from the far from queer worship of the canonizers. The conservative impulse to venerate Shakespeare stems from the same source as the desire to ignore his queerness. Both involve circumscribing him as untouchable: if we mount him, it can only be behind glass. While the canonizers make him "our" author who transcends time, the queer theorists use him to confirm who we are *not* by placing him squarely in his "own" historical moment. Either way, Shakespeare is not allowed to unsettle our sense of ourselves. Indeed, if canonizing Shakespeare protects our idea of ourselves, then not engaging the canonical Shakespeare allows that protection to continue unimpeded. Thus, even as Eve Kosofsky Sedgwick's engagement with the Sonnets was an early example of queer theory's interaction with Shakespeare, it has become increasingly impossible to cross the temporal boundaries within which the institutionalized version of queer theory has bound itself. It is only by allowing Shakespeare to break out of the boundaries within which he has been confined, though, that we take away from him the burden of being the "inventor" of the human and the privileged signifier of the literary. Equally, by reading the textual Shakespearean body as queer, we interrupt and disrupt queer theory as we know it today, expanding the parameters within which it has confined itself. For this to happen, it is not enough simply for Shakespeare to be queered: queer theory, too, needs to be Shaken.[2]

There are thus two assumptions that we need to rethink to formulate the possibility of Shakesqueer. The first is the idea that queerness has a historical start date. The second is that queerness is a synonym for embodied homosexuality.

In his challenge to the first assumption—the limits of chronological thinking—Slavoj Žižek famously proposed *Richard II* as a text that "proves beyond any doubt that Shakespeare had read Lacan."[3] The queerness of this statement depends on a number of confusions: a temporal confusion that positions the twentieth-century psychoanalyst Jacques Lacan as temporally prior to the sixteenth-century playwright William Shakespeare; a causal confusion that posits cause as supposed effect—Shakespeare has read Lacan rather than Lacan has read Shakespeare; and an epistemological confusion that "proves beyond any doubt" the problematic nature of proof itself. These unexpected moments of dislocation are the characteristic features of a Shakesqueer that does not abide by the law of chronology and that insists, in a major academic Shake-up, on redrawing, if not collapsing, the temporal divide between the sixteenth century, when Shakespeare lived and wrote, and the twentieth century, when queer theory was first formulated as such. This insistence is also characteristic of an academic theory that is not dutiful, good, or proper and that refuses to buy into the "institutional domestication of queer thinking."[4]

Such a refusal has serious ramifications for the institutional structures within which we do our work. After all, a challenge to chronology is also a challenge to periodicity. Where and what would we be if we were not modernists or medievalists or eighteenth centuryists? Hitching queer theory to Shakespeare forces us to consider the posts we currently occupy: if ideas can be brought together over the centuries, then what is the locus standi of the centuries themselves? What would we be if we had to dislocate who we are and what we do—if we had to, that is, queer ourselves? Currently, the understanding of scholarly "expertise" is located squarely in the realm of historical specificity rather than methodological modes of reading and thought; it is considered more legitimate to speak of queerness in texts and bodies after the nineteenth century, no matter whether one reads these texts and bodies as psychoanalytic, Marxist, deconstructive, or feminist, critics. *How* one reads has becomes less important than the historical period within which one reads. And so, even as "Queer Theorist" has recently begun to be advertised as an academic position in its own right, the disciplinary straightness of the position is amply demonstrated in the descriptions that accompany the advertisements. Inevitably, they ask for the queer theorist to be "located" in nineteenth-century or twentieth-century literature. Such an insistence on location chronologically orients the very theory that seeks to be disorienting. If Shakespeare were to be considered queer, that would change the ways in which we advertise our jobs, undertake our dissertations, theorize queerness, and carve out our identities.

Shakesqueer thus reformats the historical date we currently attach to the idea of the queer. And since this grafting of queerness onto time pivots crucially on the so-called emergence of the gay body, *Shakesqueer* also asks us to reevaluate the relationship between queerness and homosexuality. Most studies deemed legitimately queer focus on post-nineteenth-century literature and cultures, after "the homosexual" is understood to be in the domain of public legibility. Thus, no matter how great their variety, and how dazzling their intelligence, queer studies of the Renaissance tend to wrap themselves in an armature of apology for their work because they are scared to term as "queer" a time "before" the homosexual. Here are two random, though typical, examples of such apologia: "Were there homosexuals in early modern Europe? Did men who had sex with each other in this period regard their behaviour as determining their identity?"[5] And again: "We all know that there were no early modern heterosexuals, homosexuals, lesbians, gays, or bisexuals. There were also no early modern queers."[6] The difficulty for *Shakesqueer* rests precisely in the coils of this thorny question: if no homosexuals existed in the Renaissance, then did queerness? Thus formulated, the query collapses homosexuality and queerness so that the queer is grounded in specific bodies and acts. Homosexuality and its historical placement become synonymous with the queer. In such a schema, the acceptable face of Shakespearean queerness becomes the project of locating characters in the poems and the plays— Antonio in *The Merchant of Venice* and Viola in *Twelfth Night*, for example—and suggesting that they might be proto-homosexuals.[7]

But *Shakesqueer* does not accept as its basis the identification of queerness with specific bodily practices. Instead, this volume asks whether we are still able to read *The Merchant of Venice* and *Twelfth Night* as queer texts without also assuming that they are either homosexual or proto-homosexual documents. This disorienting experience—when we queer texts that have no gays in them —takes queerness away from its primary affiliation with the body and expands the reach of queerness beyond and through the body to a host of other possible and disturbing configurations. Even as queerness is informed by its historical association with sexual irregularities, it cannot be reduced to or located in their embodiment. Indeed, one reason Shakespeare is a prime candidate for the expansion of queer theory is that queerness as homosexuality deems him to be such an unlikely candidate. If we extend queerness beyond the body, then Shakespeare—as Virgil before him and Milton after—is as queer as, say, Elizabeth Bishop and Derek Jarman. He is not a post-nineteenth-century homosexual, and he never comes out as gay—or, rather, we cannot tell, and that is what makes him so queer.

So Who or What Is Queer?

In my description for a Modern Language Association (MLA) roundtable on Shakesqueer in December 2007, I provided the following rationale: "Intervening in an academic culture in which queerness is largely considered a post-nineteenth-century phenomenon, Shakesqueer insists on destabilizing that chronological certainty. Shakespeareans have often arrived at queerness, but this panel suggests it is time also for queerness to come to Shakespeare. Shakesqueer will intervene critically in both Shakespeare studies and queer theory, highlighting not only the many ways in which Shakespeare can be queered, but also the many ways in which Shakespeare can contribute to the process and assumptions of queering itself." After the session, there was time for only one question, and it was the following: "While it is clear that queer theory can help us read Shakespeare in ways that change our understanding of Shakespeare's texts, is it possible for Shakespeare's texts to help us formulate and animate queer theory? Is the relationship between 'Shakes' and 'queer' an equal one, or are we simply dignifying Shakespeare by assuming he has as much to offer queer theory as queer theory has to offer him?" As formulated, the question goes to the very heart of this project: can Shakespeare be regarded as a queer theorist, or is he always the object on which queer theory acts in a one-sided relationship?

The question assumes both that Shakespeare is not a queer theorist and that queer theory can be recognized as an entity in and of itself. We who know queer theory know what it can do, and we who know queer theory are not certain how an alliance with Shakespeare can add to its many theoretical riches. Shakespeare can be queered because the project proves so irresistible, but the theoretical traffic cannot move in both directions, because queerness —here conflated with homosexuality—is a post-nineteenth-century phenomenon. Clearly, if the panel had been about queer Whitman or queer Woolf or queer Jarman, the question of equality and reciprocity would not have emerged, because the assumption is that both partners in the relationship are working with the same vocabulary. Shakespeare, unfortunately for him, lies beyond the pale of acceptable chronology, so to extend queerness to him is to play fast and loose with academic credibility.[8]

I want to address these legitimate concerns by asking a slightly different question: Where does queer theory come from? If we can be fairly sure that it does not come from Shakespeare—or any other author and text before the nineteenth century—then from where does it emerge? Which texts generate queer theory? Can we have a queer theory that strays from the path of periodization? If my experience with putting together this volume is anything to go by, then the answer to that last question is "no." In a significant phenomenon that may be termed "Shakesfear," many of the queer theorists I approached said—in the nicest possible way—that even though they loved the sound of the project, they could not do it because it was scary to write something about Shakespeare. People confessed to ignorance of Shakespeare, to having failed exams on Shakespeare, to fear of the Bard, to hesitation about what for them lay so manifestly beyond their abilities. This phenomenon puzzled me extremely, not because I thought everyone would say yes to the project, but because it suggested the fact that Shakespeare does not generally count as queer, and so writing on Shakesqueer seemed to be a turn away from queer business as usual, a turn away from queer theory. Even though I had assured them in emails soliciting their participation that "the goal [of the volume] is to gather the most provocative queer theorists together to engage whatever issues interest them by way of reference, in each case, to a specific Shakespeare text," the very idea of an intersection between the queer work of "now" and the Shakespeare of "then" was sufficient to give people pause. Again, this is not to say that Shakesfear is not a legitimate phenomenon and that people should not be scared of the very thing they are expected to revere, but as with the question from the MLA roundtable, this is a phenomenon whose fears are extremely instructive for the project of *Shakesqueer*. It assumes that while it is worthwhile to queer Shakespeare, the reciprocal movement—Shaking queer theory—is simply an alien concept.

What is this queer theory that is nervous about being Shaken, and where does it come from? To what and to whom does it belong? Even though Lauren Berlant and Michael Warner argue that "it is not useful to consider queer theory a thing,"[9] that is precisely what we do. We further conclude that this thing has a referent that can be explained. Several answers are offered to the question of what constitutes the queerness theorized by queer theory, and here are two random examples. For the first commentator, "Queer designates a range of acts, identities, propensities, affectivities, and sentiments which fissure heteronormativity."[10] For the second commentator, queer refers to "the open mesh of possibilities, gaps, overlaps, dissonances and resonances, lapses and excesses of meaning when the constituent elements of anyone's gender, of anyone's sexuality aren't made (or can't be made) to signify monolithically."[11] But surely this "open mesh of possibilities," Sedgwick's resonant description of the term "queer," necessitates an openness not only to sexual and gendered possibilities, but also to chronological, national, racial, philosophical, and animal choices; to texts and ideas that address questions of sameness across times, the non-coincidence of the same with itself, and the vexed relation between sameness and difference?

In addition to widening the horizon of queer possibility, then, we need to leach the term of a certain sentimentality that has become attached to it, in which "queer" automatically means "good." In the academy, queer theorists are often accused of being hip and fashionable simply for the sake of it, and worse, of not having a coherent object for our analysis. Our defensive comeback is to assure our detractors that what we do is good and right and will go a long way in enabling a brave new world; even better, we assure them that queerness is a clear and recognizable thing worthy of our attention. But the characteristic of queer theory that makes it at once attractive to theorists and vulnerable to critics is that it can never define the queer. Rather than attaching to specific times and authors, queerness allows us to encounter the violence of specificity itself by being excluded from its ambit. Lest we conclude from this that queerness can mean anything at any time and in any place, let me hasten to add that queerness cannot "mean" in any final sense of that word. If queerness can be defined, then it is no longer queer—it strays away from its anti-normative stance to become the institutionalized norm. Queerness is not a category but the confusion engendered by and despite categorization.[12] Queer theory deals with an excess that renders undefinable the very thing it might have been brought in to define. Queerness "is," inasmuch as it can be said to "be" anything, nothing that can fully be contained in a volume of essays or an orgy of leather.[13] It recognizes the absurdity of limits and interrupts the ways in which we live our lives and write our texts, but it cannot be contained by how we live and what we write.

One might ask at this point how queer theory is different, say, from poststructural thought in general, and deconstruction in particular? And what is the relation between queerness and sexuality if the term "queer" is being expanded so far beyond embodied desire? Both of these questions respond to a possible lack of boundaries with a desire for the assertion of boundaries. It is all very well to say that queer theory recognizes the absurdity of limits, but really, where *does* one draw the line?

As this volume makes clear, that line is very difficult to draw. Queerness is bodily and that which challenges the limits of what we understand as the body. It expands its ambit to include discussions of the universe, animals, and rationality. While sexual desire sometimes lurks in the background or looms in the foreground, it is not always recognizable as desire. For instance, a play on language might be as sexual as a kiss, or a tussle with authority can become as intense as sex. In keeping with its challenge to temporal and identitarian boundaries, then, this volume also suggests that queerness is everywhere. It cannot be confined to what we think of as same-sex sexuality. Indeed, queerness here might not be recognizable as adult same-sex desire, but equally it provides more arenas within which to get one's kicks. It expands the ambit of the sexual rather than being restricted by it. Such an expansion is very much in keeping with our lived experiences of desire and sexuality. Do any of us really stay within the boundaries that a particular terminology delimits? Do we not—even the most high-minded of us—stray in our desires? *Shakesqueer* treats the strayness of desire as crucial to queerness and follows its thread to the very unraveling.

The unraveling of what appears to be a tight-knit concept is very much the legacy of deconstruction. With its suspicion of absolutes and its conviction that the center cannot hold, deconstruction, especially in its de Manian and Derridean forms, insists on the fragility, and therefore the malleability, of texts and all the life forms associated with texts, especially the human. But while this expansion of the text to humans, and then animals, is the legacy of the later Derrida, queer theory has always been invested in humans and animals. If anything, deconstruction moved to where queer theory has always already been: the intersection between life and death, text and pleasure, sex and politics, human and animal. In an essay on irony in *Aesthetic Ideology*, Paul de Man gestures toward the presence of the sexual in philosophy, only to reject that imbrication as being, surely, unthinkable:

> There is in the middle of [Friedrich Schlegel's short novel] *Lucinde* a short chapter called "Eine Reflexion," which reads like a philosophical treatise or argument, but it doesn't take a very perverse mind, only a slightly perverse one, to see that what is actually being described is not a philosophical argument at all but is—well, how shall I put it?—a reflection on the very physical questions involved in sexual intercourse. Discourse which seems to be purely philosophical can be read in a double code, and what it really is describing is something which we do not generally consider worthy of philosophical discourse, at least not in those terms—sexuality is worthy of it, but what is being described is not sexuality, it's something much more specific.
>
> It's not just that there is a philosophical code and then another code describing sexual activities. These codes are radically incompatible with each other. They interrupt, they disrupt, each other in such a fundamental way that this very possibility of disruption represents a threat to all assumptions one has about what a text should be.[14]

Returning to the same passage later, de Man asserts: "You are [at one moment] writing a splendid and coherent philosophical argument but, lo and behold, you are describing sexual intercourse."[15] Deconstruction's brilliance lies in its ability to see that every text is interrupted from within, that coherence is a projection and not a truth. Indeed, de Man here has a strong hunch that this particular disruption may threaten all assumptions within which we read, write, and live. But even as de Man seems surprised by this *particular* eruption, queer theory would not be surprised in the least; indeed, it sees sex and desire and sexuality where others may not. At one level, this difference marks the difference between deconstruction and queer theory. While deconstruction at first primarily challenged philosophy's claim to transcendence, queer theory has always been interested in the larger lived realities of desire. But it also points to the interrelatedness of, and therefore the lack of absolute difference between, deconstruction and queer theory. Often based on an analysis of language and the insufficiency of terms to embody what they claim to represent, queer theory has insisted on the contaminating effects that desire can exert on ideas of purity. De Man's point in this passage, after all, is that the language of philosophy is, fascinatingly and disturbingly, *infected* by the language of sex.

The same mutuality can be said to mark queer theory's relation to Marxism in their joint investigation into structures of power; to feminism in their exploration of gender; to critical race theory in their consideration of interwoven social, legal, and cultural tales; and to postcolonialism in their analysis of hybridity, temporality, and mimicry, to name only a few. In this sense, queer theory may be considered a hybrid, an amalgamation of several different theories and texts that thwarts our desire to pin down its essence. It is in conversation with other theories, but equally, these conversations change the shape of what queer theory "is." Indeed, it would be counterproductive for queer theory to insist on its inviolable grounding in homosexual bodies and desires because this would attribute fixed contours to those bodies and desires. As with the relation between institutionalized queer theory and Shakespeare, this insistence would be inseparable from the homophobic belief in the transparent legibility of the homosexual body and the ease with which it may be punished. To the question, "What does a homosexual look like?," queer theory's answer is, "I do not know." Equally, to the question, "What is queer theory?," the answer is, "All things that militate against the obvious, the settled, and the understood—in other words, nothing that may be fully or finally grasped." Queer theory *returns* us to the question of desire. But its strength lies in being able to re-turn almost anything to that question while continuing to retain it as a question rather than an answer.

It is often argued that the term "desire"—inflected as it is by psychoanalysis—itself has a historical starting date and therefore limits the ambit of queer theory. Thus, to speak of desire in relation to Shakespeare is not only anachronistic, but also universalizing. Scholarship has already addressed this very question (see, for instance, Valeria Finucci's and Regina M. Schwartz's collection *Desire in the Renaissance*), but what makes it persist as a question is our continued fascination with mapping sexuality onto chronology. While terms such as "power," "domination," "subversion," "class," and "race," to name only a few, repeatedly have been transported into chronological realms in which they did not originally exist, the desire to historically police "desire" has been more fierce. Ironically, this desire to police desire is the very thing against which queerness militates, even as it has become the very thing that marks the institutionalization of queer theory.

What are the consequences of policing the one term that is arguably most resistant to the law? Even more urgent, what are the implications for the field when *queer theory* itself polices the range of its subject? I want to join these two paragraphs. For one, accepting that texts before the nineteenth century can be queer would be tantamount to accepting that queer theorists have existed for a longer time than we have thus far been willing to accept, that Shakespeare as much as Sedgwick is a queer theorist. Since it is not a matter of self-aware terminology—after all, Freud did not call himself a queer theorist, but several strands of queer theory openly acknowledge their Freudian genealogy—this expansion is potentially endless and underscores the fact that period studies should not be considered part of queer studies. One is not queer by acts and chronologies alone. One cannot be queer while insisting on barricading queerness. One cannot be queer and not be Shaken.

Thus, if it is a truth universally acknowledged that a single man in possession of a literary reputation must be in want of some queering, then that queering itself is in need of being queered. To think of Shakespeare as a queer theorist involves throwing into doubt all our pieties about his universality, and his invention of the human. As Lee Edelman has taught us to see, Shakespeare the humanist—who produces order out of chaos—also evinces the antihuman cacophony of voices that is the shadow or *sinthome* within the humanist project. Indeed, what we understand by "Shakespeare" needs to be shaken up rather than being taken for granted. Is "Shakespeare" the author of his works? The effect generated by those works? The body of literature independent of an author? A fragmented set of texts put together hastily by sycophantic editors? A pseudonym for a cabal of impoverished writers? None of the above? If queer theory is the theory of no one thing, then Shakespeare is the not-single author of a set of diversely fragmented texts. One of the reasons queer theory is reluctant to extend its reach backward in time is that it is—understandably—wary of entering into systems of literary and cultural production that seem so alien from our own. But equally, reading Shakespeare as a queer theorist disrupts what we think we understand as *our* systems of literary and cultural production—it expands the definitions within which we think. Shakesqueer throws into doubt not only our relation to queerness, but also the very idea of Shakespeare, rhyming him out of the sublime by letting him chime with the queer. Even as queer theory brings all of its force to bear on questions of desire, power, and sexuality, it also needs to dispense with a historical trajectory that distinguishes between unified, self-identical humanity, on the one hand, and chaotic medieval fluidity, on the other. If Shakespeare were to be considered a queer theorist, then not only would he not look like anything we might expect, but he would equally change the way that we look (in both senses of the term). My proposal for a queer Shakes thus is nothing less than a proposal to dissolve the boundaries between the two entities—not so they can indulge in free love while seeking the meaning of the universe, but precisely to undermine the monolithic nature of the *universe* as we think we understand it today. Shakesqueer ruthlessly destroys the very idea of a singular identity—his and our own—that has thus far kept Shakespeare away from the queer party.

Shakesqueer

Allowing Shakespeare to attend the queer party may seem like the ultimate capitulation. Not only has Shakespeare been credited with the invention of the human, but he is now also being crowned the Queen of queer theory. There is some truth to the fact that Shakespeare is frequently brought in as the crutch to support any and every point of view—he has even been invoked to justify the abolition of the death tax in the United States.[16] But such a formulation—"allowing Shakespeare to attend the queer party"—also suggests that his attendance is something about which we have a choice. I want to argue, *au contraire*, that Shakespeare has always already been Shakesqueer; that queer theory as we know it today is already Shakespearean, and the time has arrived for us to acknowledge that fact.

In claiming that Shakespeare is a queer theorist, and that Shaking queer theory is a phenomenon whose time has come, I do not mean to suggest that we need Shakespeare to legitimate queer theory. Rather, I intend my claims to be far more radical. First, Shakespeare is queer even though neither he nor a single one of his characters is historically homosexual.[17] And second, Shakespeare is already embedded within a queer theory that nonetheless exorcises Shakespeare by distancing itself from him institutionally. To adduce only two examples of this claim, Rene Girard's theorization of homosocial triangulation, which forms the basis of Sedgwick's hugely influential—indeed, foundational—queer text, *Between Men: English Literature and Male Homosocial Desire*, derives its energy from Shakespeare's *Troilus and Cressida*. Sedgwick's book also begins with a famous essay on Shakespeare's sonnets.[18] To cite a more recent occurrence, Elizabeth Freeman's introduction to a special double issue of *GLQ* on "Queer Temporalities," begins with an invocation and analysis of Hamlet's pronouncement that "the time is out of joint."[19] Shakespeare is a specter haunting queer theory—our ideas of normativity and desire owe a debt to Shakespearean ideas and language that we have been strangely unwilling to pay. Instead, we banish him to the realm of the pre-queer, where he is sometimes considered worthy as an object of queer theoretical attention but is rarely recognized as having provided, to a significant extent, the very vocabulary for that theory. Indeed, the invocation of "Shakespeare" by queer theory is always a contradictory call. On the one hand, it is the hyper-canonical Shakespeare that queer theory sees as the opposite of queerness. In this scenario, asserting Shakespeare's queerness is tantamount to making Shakespeare the transcendent signifier of all things, including the queer. On the other hand, the demonization of Shakespeare's hyper-canonicity disavows the ways in which queer theory is and always has been informed, enabled, and identified by its Shakespearean cadences.

Shakespeare is a queer theorist, then, not because he has written essays with the word "queer" in the title, but because his work already inhabits the queer theory we occupy today. It also challenges many of the limits beyond which queer theory currently refuses to stray. Reading Shakespeare as queer rather than queered challenges the rule of chronology and identity that has thus far kept his poems and plays from exercising queer agency. To look at some concepts that deeply inform current queer theory in a Shakespearean light, therefore, is to challenge the monolithic conception of Shakespeare that is the legacy of the canonical, as well as to examine the chronological and identitarian blind spots that prevent queer theory from being Shaken. I want to pay attention to three particular areas to which Shakespeare's texts and queer the-

ory insistently return: language, identity, and temporality. All of them allow us
to reconsider the parameters within which we contain queer theory today.

Language

Queer theory has an ambivalent relationship to language.[20] On the one
hand, given its deconstructive lineage, queer theory is deeply invested in the
shape of words, but on the other hand, given its activist component, queer
theory has at times ignored the shape of words and focused on their content.
Early queer theorizations of language have included, most importantly, the
work of Eve Kosofsky Sedgwick, whose analyses are indebted to a structural-
ist understanding of language and its discontents, while working also with
J. L. Austin's theorization of performative language. This investment in the
shaping power of language—that "bodies forth / The forms of things unknown"[21]—later routed itself through a psychoanalytic framework in which
Freudian and Lacanian theories provided the ground for thinking about how
language creates, and not merely represents, bodies and desires. As Theseus's
quote makes clear, Shakespeare is invested in the link between linguistic and
bodily registers. In his essays in *Homographesis*, Lee Edelman teases out the
peculiar strictures of legibility under which gay bodies are placed. Gayness is
considered that which can be *read* (on the body), but equally, the anxiety
about homosexuality often pivots on the fear that it might prove to be *unread-
able*, thus throwing into disarray the relation between legibility and identity.
The identifications created by language—whether by descriptive terminology or derisive slurs—have been crucial in theorizing queer theory's relation
to desire. Like bodies and objects, words too have *orientations*, and the orientation of desire, as Sara Ahmed has teased out that term, brings together
queer theory's geopolitical dimensions and its textual interests.

While projects of queering Shakespeare have focused fruitfully on plot
details, generic problems, and sexual disguise, the question of language has
tended to be contained in both historical and political terms. Studies of Shakespearean language often deal with the "early modern" meanings of words
that render them queer, sometimes in contradiction to our own current definitions. As important as such historical contextualization no doubt is, the
queerness of Shakespeare's language lies in much more than the meanings of
words or in their cultural specificity. It lies in their very texture and sound, in
the Os that Joel Fineman follows in his analysis of desire in *Othello*, and the
"R"s that Jonathan Goldberg excavates in the relationship between Romeo

and Mercutio in *Romeo and Juliet*. Shakespeare uses, for instance—infrequently but always with devastating effect—the metrical foot called the trochee, a combination of one stressed syllable followed by an unstressed one; it is the opposite of the iamb, which, with its combination of one unstressed and stressed syllable, is supposedly the language of everyday speech. The trochee is not everyday speech—it is the odd one out, the uncommon one, the queer one. The word "ho / mo" is a trochee. If divided into two syllables, then so is the word "que / er." The trochee is a metrical foot that literally goes nowhere: Rather than rising to greater heights, it falls off with its unstressed syllable. It trails off instead of punctuating, inverting the teleological imperative of progress that has shaped so much heterosexuality. Precisely because it is used so furtively in Shakespeare, its deployment stands out as a queer event that "bodies forth / The forms of things unknown."

One such event, staged by arguably the most famous spouters of the trochee in English literature, involves the Weird Sisters as they brew their poisonous potion:

> *Second Witch*: Fillet of a fenny snake
> In the cauldron boil and bake;
> Eye of newt, and toe of frog,
> Wool of bat, and tongue of dog. . . .
> *All*: Double, double toil and trouble;
> Fire burn and cauldron bubble. (*Macbeth*, 4.1.12–15, 20–21)

The perfect trochees in these lines achieve the intended incantatory effect as the Weird Sisters prepare the brew from which Macbeth will be shown his future. Described by them as a "deed without a name" (4.1.49), this activity is queer in the very etymological sense of being "strange, odd, [and] peculiar."[22] The weirdness of the Weird Sisters derives from their semantic closeness to the queer, since weird means "strange, unusual, . . . odd."[23] The Queer Sisters perform a deed without a name from which spouts double toil and trouble. The hags, who are indeterminately male and female—"You should be women, / And yet your beards forbid me to interpret / That you are so" (1.3.45–7), says Banquo when he first meets the witches—speak a queer language that makes them queer, otherworldly outcasts doomed to doom the straightforward order of things in Duncan's Scotland.

Indeed, Shakespeare seems to reserve his trochees for weird characters and fairies. The other great exponent of the trochee in Shakespeare is Puck,

also known as Robin Goodfellow, in *A Midsummer Night's Dream*. The only
character in the Shakespearean corpus to have a simultaneous double name
(Viola / Cesario in *Twelfth Night* comes close, but her name changes depending on the clothes he wears, so it is never simultaneous), Puck / Robin is the
general factotum and troublemaker in the play. As Oberon's right-hand man,
Puck is sent to gather the Flower of Love with which to sow concord among
the four Athenian lovers; predictably, he sows discord instead. Less predictable, however, is his language, which is frequently trochaic:

> *Puck*: Through the forest have I gone,
> But Athenian found I none. . . .
> Night and silence! who is here?
> Weeds of Athens he doth wear.
> (*A Midsummer Night's Dream*, 2.2.66–67, 70–71)

This fairy's talk is not only punctuated with a queer metrical footprint; it also
wanders about without being able to settle on the object of its choice. Like
the queer in person, the queer here is difficult to locate in language. Since
Puck only speaks frequently, and not exclusively, in trochees, is he queer? His
sporadic, odd meter certainly points in that direction, but even more, its
language suggests that queerness cannot easily identify bodies or be identified *as* a body. Puck / Robin looks for a body and finds the wrong one. Meanwhile, the fairies do not know whether to call him Puck or Robin. For Puck, as
for the Weird Sisters, queerness is largely traced in and as a verbal outline,
even as the words themselves can only offer us the specter of its shadow.

Identity

The potentially infinite multiplication of identity—Puck is both Puck and
Robin, the witches in *Macbeth* mysteriously expand from women to men—
makes the trochee move assiduously away from a notion of stable identity.
Long the keyword in queer theory, "identity" allows for an easy conflation
between homosexuality and queerness. It identifies bodies that then go on to
bolster the very idea of identity. However, queer theory has moved away from
an exclusive interest in embodiment toward questions about the limits of
ethical, ethnic, human, and psychic integrity. The queer self presumably anchored by the gay body is no longer predominant in theorizations of queerness. This means, however, less a replacement of the gay body than a shift in
emphasis from sex acts to more wide-ranging issues of non-normativity and

non-coincidence. Such a movement can be traced from the work of Michel Foucault—sometimes considered the main voice of and in queer theory—to that of Judith Butler and, more recently, José Esteban Muñoz.

For Foucault, the gay body is a created rather than a given body. To this extent, he is in agreement with those who rely on language and psychoanalysis to gain access to bodies and desires. However, for Foucault psychoanalysis is one of the major discourses by means of which homosexuality is created and then demonized. Interestingly, even as Foucault largely ignores language, this does not mean he focuses exclusively on the body. Indeed, he insists, in works such as *The History of Sexuality, Volume I* and *Madness and Civilization*, that there is no such thing as a body that is not the effect of discourse. For him, desires are never given. They are only created differently at different historical moments using different cultural and political mechanisms. In *Gender Trouble* and *Bodies that Matter*, Butler picks up on this argument to insist that the delineation of what counts as the "natural" body should never be taken for granted. Equally, Butler insists that the ways in which our bodies are circumscribed have significant consequences for how we live and are perceived in the world. Butler's work focuses on the body but attempts also to retheorize what we mean by the bodily, emphasizing always the role of psychic and social performativity in the creation of bodily identity. The field of performance studies has developed this observation while thinking about sexual and ethnic bodily identity, notably in the work of Muñoz (*Disidentifications*), which has expanded the field of queer theory to include considerations of race and queers of color. His work explores the schism between a seemingly wholesome, natural norm and the copies that set themselves against it, thereby splitting apart also what we think of as the norm.

Like Foucault's, Butler's, and Muñoz's characters, the Shakespearean self is never identical with its self. Shakespearean protagonists have money, horses, kingdoms, power, and even children, but selves they never have, and this is what renders queer even their most earnest quests for selfhood. Thus, the deposed Richard II, when asked whether he is "contented to resign the crown," speaks to this queer idea of a self that seems always out of reach of itself:

> Ay, no; no, ay; for I must nothing be;
> Therefore no, no, for I resign to thee. (*Richard II*, 4.1.201–2)

The *Tragedy of King Richard the Second* does not lie primarily in the fact that he has lost his kingdom, but that he does not have a self. Critics have argued that

Richard's self is so closely tied to his kingdom that the loss of the latter signifies as the loss of the former. But if that is the case, then it is puzzling that Richard seems to care so little for his kingdom—unless, of course, that means he cares so little for himself. No stirring speeches of patriotic fervor are assigned to this king, nor is he depicted as having a plan for his future as monarch. Rather, his self remains oddly nebulous, associated most fully with his male favorites, Bushy, Bagot, and Green, whose murders seem to hurt Richard more deeply than even the loss of his crown. Richard's assertion that he "must nothing be" does not amount to a cancellation of the self, however, so much as a puzzlement with the very concept of selfhood. A play with two nominated kings—Richard II and Henry IV—in its text, *Richard II* insists on thinking through the relation among names, bodies, and identities. It also asks about the politics of reproduction, making clear that the king who loses the crown has no offspring, while the king who gains the crown has both an heir and a spare. Richard is placed outside the reproductive mainstream even as he is divested of royalty. The living embodiment of the trochee, Richard starts out strong but does not swell to royal and reproductive heights. Instead, he resigns himself to resigning his self, and the text unravels any sense of a fixed identity in relation to power. This unraveling becomes the play's queer disidentification.

Neither king nor villain by the end of his play, Richard in his lack of identity comes to resemble Coriolanus, another center of power who struts about in an eponymous play before being destroyed. Indeed, the most significant feature of *Coriolanus* is that Coriolanus does not occupy his title for long. He begins the drama under a different name—Caius Martius—and is later named Coriolanus when he defeats Corioles in battle against Rome. He is then stripped of his title when he becomes an ally of Corioles against Rome. At various points in the text, then, before and after becoming Coriolanus, Coriolanus is out of step with himself. For instance, in Act 4 Scene 5 of the play, when the now-banished Roman warrior seeks refuge with his former enemy, the latter repeatedly asks him who he is:

> *Aufidius*: Whence com'st thou? What wouldst thou? Thy name?
> Why speak'st not? Speak, man. What's thy name?
> *Coriolanus* [*unmuffling his head*]: If, Tullus,
> Not yet thou know'st me, and seeing me dost not
> Think me for the man I am, necessity
> Commands me name myself.

> *Aufidius*: What is thy name?
>
> *Coriolanus*: A name unmusical to the Volscians' ears
>
> And harsh in sound to thine.
>
> *Aufidius*: Say, what's thy name?
>
> Thou hast a grim appearance. . . .
>
> What's thy name?
>
> *Coriolanus*: Prepare thy brow to frown. Know'st thou me yet?
>
> *Aufidius*: I know thee not. Thy name?
>
> *Coriolanus*. My name is Caius Martius. . . .
>
> My surname Coriolanus. . . .
>
> Only that name remains. (*Coriolanus*, 4.5.52–59, 61–64, 67, 72)

Coriolanus wants his name to be self-evident, but Aufidius underscores that it is not. Despite the "unmuffl[ing] of [Coriolanus's] head," Aufidius steadfastly refuses to recognize the enemy until his name is spoken between them. This elaborate dance around the name of Coriolanus emphasizes its hollowness—Coriolanus promises to deliver it several times and fails each time until the end. When he finally owns up to his name, it is only with the recognition that the name by which he is known in the present is already in the past, while what was once his future—the surname of Coriolanus—is the only thing that remains in his present. Despite the confusion surrounding his name, and the shame and anger that he feels about it, Coriolanus nonetheless wants "Coriolanus" to be filled with self-evident meaning; he wants to be thought of as "the man I am." But Aufidius demands to know his visitor's name six times in the space of eight lines, an insistence that hysterically draws attention to itself. The name of Coriolanus is at stake in this conversation, yet it is a thing without any face value, which is why it goes unattributed even when Coriolanus unmuffles his face. At the start of the play, then, there is a name without a man, and at the end of the play, a man without a name. The very name of Coriolanus, deriving as it does from Corioles (pronounced cor-eye-o-lees) accords an exaggerated sense of importance to the diminutive "i." But *Coriolanus* arrives before its hero, and Coriolanus runs out of time before the end of his text. The time of the title is not coincident with the identity of its hero, and arguably, this is the play's tragedy in real time.

Temporality

The challenge to identity thus seems crucially to be a question of time. If *Coriolanus* articulates a tragedy of time, then it also asks us to think of queerness as a phenomenon out of time. *Shakesqueer* is an instance of this lack of temporal propriety. After all, even as we speak of the ways in which Shakespeare theorizes queer language, and queers identity, we need to grapple with the fact that he never uses the word "queer" in his texts. Are we, therefore, retrospectively exporting current queer terminology back to Shakespeare? This would seem to be the gist of the question posed at the MLA panel that asked how Shakespeare could possibly formulate or affect queer theory except as a subject of queer theory's ministrations. The obverse side of this question may be: Is it Shakespeare who has initiated these terms—fairy, weird —that we, oblivious of their etiology, now use as queer terms? Is Shakespeare the precursor of the languages and sensibilities we inhabit today? Is he the recipient or antecedent of queer theory? Both versions of this question depend on a chain of causality between two objects presumed to be fixed in their own sphere; equally, both versions presume that Shakespeare and queerness are somehow separated in time. But if our formulations of queerness depend crucially on things being out of joint, unhinged rather than straight, then why should we not theorize our relation to time? What if we were to dispense with a model of temporal linearity that translates also into causal linearity? What if time itself were to be queered?

Indeed, it has been. Perhaps the most exciting development in queer theory in the past few years has been a consideration of temporality in relation to issues of reproduction, lineage, power, and ethnicity. Annamarie Jagose thinks through the question of sequence in relation to lesbian desire; Elizabeth Freeman focuses on the relation between queer temporalities and histories; and Judith Halberstam has done powerful work on uncovering the normatizing routine of the biological "clock" or the teleological time line that normal lives are meant to follow.[24] This trend in queer theory has proved to be one of the most promising developments in the field, even as it has insufficiently questioned the parameters of its own constitution. Queer theory has done tremendous work in thinking through what constitutes heteronormativity in terms of time and, increasingly, in addressing the specter of homonormativity in which homosexuality models itself along the lines of heterosexuality to be more acceptable. However, studies of what makes queerness normative also need to take into consideration the question of periodization and the ways in which the academy organizes itself and its studies. We need to push Carolyn Dinshaw's "queer historical impulse . . . toward making connections across time" and Carla Freccero's violently slashed juxtapositions to grapple with institutionalized queer theory's chronological Bantustans.[25]

Shakespearean texts not only theorize the relation between temporality and desire (for instance, in the Sonnets). They also think through the question of chronological periodization. In *Pericles*, for instance, the text imports a fourteenth-century poet into a seventeenth-century play simultaneously to open up the boundaries of the chronological and the sexual:

> To sing a song that old was sung,
> From ashes ancient Gower is come, . . .
>
> If you, born in these latter times,
> When wit's more ripe, accept my rimes . . .
> I life would wish, and that I might
> Waste it for you like taper-light. (*Pericles*, 1.1–2, 11–12, 15–16)

Gower, the medieval poet who has come before, now comes after to pander to an audience described as having riper wits than his original audience had. These riper wits would appreciate Gower more than his own period did, which makes him wish he had been brought back to life in "these latter times"—which, of course, he has. This riddling play between *then* and *now* blurs distinctions premised on chronology alone and places this blurring in the service of a play plagued with riddles and seething with sexual deviance. Twisting time opens up the text to a host of non-normative configurations. Not only does Gower present a play about sexual deviance, but the text also seems unable to remain within generic bounds. It begins as a romance, then doubles as a tragedy, only then to triple as a comedy. Although *Pericles* is not even regarded conventionally as a "problem play," the question of time becomes a question of genre becomes a question of organization becomes a question of deviance becomes a question of the norm becomes a question of desire. *Pericles* consists of one long metonymic slide, and every twist in its tale has to do with non-normativity; every seemingly acceptable end to a romantic tale is riddled through with incest and violence.

Indeed, the very anti-category of "problem play" qualifies Shakespeare to be the Queen of the Queers. He famously deviates from chronological history in the history plays, but he also dispenses with temporal linearity in other texts, several of which posit a relation between before and after only to show us the pleasures of upsetting the two fixed poles as fixed poles. One such play is *All's Well That Ends Well*, in which the very title presumes a temporality leading to a happy ending. The climax is meant retrospectively to justify and extol its precursor events, implying a parallelism that makes story and conclusion balance each other—except that the two, story and conclusion, as well as the two parts of the title, do not balance each other. Indeed, the end of the play, in which an uneasy Bertram is blackmailed into accepting his relationship with Helena, has made many critics term this a problem play. Far from justifying the difficulties in the text, then, the end only compounds them. And the title, which seems at first the image of harmony and perfection, betrays its queer underbelly even before we start reading the play. If "All's Well" is meant to balance and be balanced by "Ends Well," then what do we do with the queer excess that attaches to the first part of that equation? "All Is Well" has one syllable more than its counterpart in "Ends Well," even as this extra syllable is truncated to fit a punctuation mark—an apostrophe that stands in for the missing letter. But is this apostrophe in the title a missing letter or an anal fistula? I ask this perhaps surprising question because the play suggests in its very opening scene that it is the latter: The king is close to death because of an excess, an extra syllable, that threatens the balance of his health. This excessive growth is simultaneously an abscess, identified as an incurable fistula in a privy place that will determine the future of the kingdom even though it will never be fully visible. It threatens the well-being promised by the "All's Well" of the title and has to be cured for things to end well. This cure, however, can never be full or final. Even as Helena heals the king early in the text, the fistula's deathlike effects, calling into question the play's investment in reproductive heterosexuality, linger in a tale in which anality, temporality, virginity, and deception are closely and claustrophobically intertwined. In the title itself, this anal fistula lingers as the apostrophe—contained but irrevocably infectious, present only as a potent absence.

This cankerous apostrophe forces us to reformulate the relation between Shakespeare and queerness. Does Shakespeare theorize language and identity and temporality? Do these theorizations count as queer, or is queerness a retrospective attribute we give to Shakespeare? If queer theory rigorously addresses the question of non-coincidence—between a name and a body, between a body and desire, between gender and sexuality, between title and text, between a norm and itself—can this queerness extend also to thinking about and acknowledging its own debt to Shakespeare, to thinking about the non-coincidence of canon and text, time and identity? These are questions that necessitate a complete overhaul of the ways in which we think. They also are all questions that Shakespeare asks repeatedly. If queer theory chafes against containment by and in the norm, then Shakespeare provides another norm to resist—his own non-acknowledgment as queer. The attraction of Shakesqueer is that it gives queer theory the Shakes and forever disrupts its containment in the period after the nineteenth century. It also disrupts the conflation between queerness and homosexuality. Instead, it insists on thinking through the Shakespearean texts of queerness—those that have explicitly informed queer theorization and those that haunt queer theory spectrally by informing our ideas of the normative and the deviant. We have spent so much time keeping different times and desires distinct from each other that we forget the deeply unsettling characteristics of queerness. If we are not prepared to be shaken in our theoretical convictions, then we are not queer. If we are not thrown into doubt by queerness's propensity to turn up in the most unexpected places and at the most surprising times, then we are not Shakespearean. If queerness is to be a line of inquiry, a horizon of impossibility that stretches forward and backward and sideways, then it is also an idea that refuses to settle into any single orthodoxy, be it authorial or theoretical. No matter how embarrassing, debilitating, and unwieldy it might be, then; no matter how much a sign of the libertine and the rake; no matter where it has been acquired, and no matter how painful and impossible the symptoms; it is time for us to own and enjoy our Queer Shakes, allowing it, as Hamlet says, "to horridly . . . shake our disposition / With thoughts beyond the reaches of our souls" (*Hamlet*, 1.4.36–37).

Queer Designs

Queer theory is not the theory of anything in particular, and
has no precise bibliographic shape. —Lauren Berlant and
Michael Warner

Shakesqueer seems such an institutionally inexplicable phenomenon that its listing in the November 2007 issue of *PMLA* was extremely instructive.[26] The roundtable did not appear in the section under panels on "Shakespeare"; nor was it visible under "Drama" or "Medieval and Renaissance." Rather, we were assigned to panels on "Literary Criticism and Theory," presumably because the roundtable had been sponsored by the Division of Gay Studies. It seemed as if now that we were "Theory," we had ceased to be "Shakespeare."

As for the aegis under which we appeared, Shakesqueer was the first session dealing with pre-nineteenth-century literature that the Division of Gay Studies in the MLA had sponsored. Indeed, a quick search revealed that only a single pre-nineteenth-century paper—dealing with the Castlehaven scandal—had made it to any of the sessions sponsored by the division over the past ten years. This is not to suggest that the *PMLA* needs to update its classificatory scheme or that the Division of Gay Studies has been remiss in its intellectual efforts. It is to underscore that the neologism of Shakesqueer seems comprehensible only in one category or another. While Shakesqueer could possibly be (mis)taken for "Shakespeare"—it looks the same and has the same number of syllables—that "mistake" ultimately seems impossible to accommodate, and so Shakesqueer is removed from the list of panels on the Bard. Shakesqueer departs from what we understand as the Shakespearean.

Organizing the contents of *Shakesqueer* thus poses a double challenge. The volume needs to be recognizable as a text on Shakespeare, but it also needs to be estranged from what we think we understand as Shakespearean. Most editions of Shakespeare's complete works are organized chronologically according to date of textual composition. The Oxford edition, on which the influential *Norton Shakespeare* is based, is organized according to this principle. By anchoring texts in fixed dates, however, such chronological ordering repeats the methodological problems against which *Shakesqueer* works even as it replaces the older mode of organization, familiar from the printing of the First Folio in 1623, of grouping texts by genre. The *Norton Shakespeare* in fact provides two tables of contents, one organized according to conjectured date of composition and the other more conventionally by genre, within which texts are arranged according to date of composition. The *Riverside Shakespeare* edition follows this latter mode of chronological organization and provides only a single table of contents. (In its categorization by genre, the First Folio does not list its texts by chronological date of composition.)

In contrast, *Shakesqueer* prints essays according to the alphabetical order of the play or poem. As such, *All Is True* (*Henry VIII*) appears first on the list, even though it would be the penultimate play if we adhered to date of composition. *The Winter's Tale*, which generally appears as the sixth play from the end of the table of contents, appears here as the last essay.[27] Such an arrangement allows for an unconventional juxtaposition of texts—the late *Tempest* is close to the early *Titus Andronicus*, while the comic *Much Ado about Nothing* abuts the tragic *Othello*. Our most common preconceived modes of organization—chronology and genre—are turned inside out in this volume, even as *Shakes-*

queer remains confined by the ordering of the English alphabet.[28] An interesting offshoot of this alphabetical organization by title is that Shakespeare's history plays now appear in their "proper" chronological position: The *Henry IV* cycle precedes the *Henry VI* cycle, even though it was written after it. The table of contents in this instance has the bizarre effect of straightening out Shakespeare's queer ordering of history.

This volume also includes essays on "nonexistent" plays such as *Cardenio* and *Love's Labour's Won*. Both of these texts are grouped under a section on "Lost Plays" in the table of contents arranged according to genre in the *Norton Shakespeare*; both receive a one-page historical introduction and brief plot summary from the editors. The *Riverside Shakespeare* mentions neither text. Including these "lost" plays in *Shakesqueer* seems particularly fitting, not just for the sake of capaciousness (although had we pursued this directive faithfully, we might also have included an essay on *Edward III*), but also to highlight the idea on which this volume is based: that the object of queerness is not always known or recognizable or identifiable. In addition to having separate essays for both of these "Lost Plays," *Shakesqueer* has separated "A Lover's Complaint" from its frequent association with the Sonnets and elevated "The Phoenix and Turtle" from the pool generally described as "Various Poems." Thus, forty-six Shakespearean texts are featured in *Shakesqueer*, in contrast to forty-four in the Norton edition (this number includes three versions of *King Lear*) and forty-seven in the Riverside edition (including the now discredited "Funeral Elegy," the miscellany of verses called "The Passionate Pilgrim," and *The Reign of King Edward the Third*, not generally included under Shakespeare's name). The number of essays in *Shakesqueer*, however, exceeds the number of Shakespearean texts because it features three essays on the Sonnets. When it comes to queerness, more is more, and nothing quite adds up.

In keeping with the volume's emphasis on Shaking queerness, most of the contributors to *Shakesqueer* self-identify as queer theorists rather than as Shakespearean and Renaissance scholars. A quick count reveals that of the volume's forty-eight contributors, exactly two-thirds, or thirty-two contributors, work in periods other than the Renaissance, while sixteen consider their work as being based primarily in Renaissance literature, both English and continental. All scholars have been absolved from the responsibility of providing an overview of literature already published on their texts; interested readers may refer to the bibliography at the end of the volume for such details. The focus in this volume is on exploring what is odd, eccentric, and unexpected in the canonical Shakespeare, but equally, not to reveal a queerness

that can be limned or known in advance. Given the eclectic cast of its contributors—the volume features at least three generations of scholars—*Shakes-*
queer showcases varied ideas on queerness, engaging not just sexual identities,
but also race, temporality, performance, adaptation, and psychoanalysis.
Non-Renaissance scholars have been asked not to sound "Shakespearean,"
and Renaissance scholars have been told not to feel constrained by considerations that might otherwise matter in a straightforward collection on Shakespeare. The point of this volume is not to provide queer "readings" of Shakespeare texts. It is, instead, to bring queerness into varied engagements with
those texts without chronological or conceptual privilege. *Shakesqueer* is neither exclusively Shakespearean nor recognizably queer: It will make neither
camp happy, but in the process, it may make the camp happy. The variety
generated by the punning fecundity of *Shakesqueer* both earns this volume an
invitation to the queer party and allows it to throw that party wide open, not
just to any one age, but for all time.

Notes

1. Jarman, *Dancing Ledge*, 206.
2. Even as many forays into queer waters have been pioneered by scholars of
medieval and Renaissance studies—one might think of Burger and Kruger, *Queering
the Middle Ages*; Dinshaw, *Getting Medieval*, Fradenburg and Freccero, *Premodern Sexualities*; and Shannon, *Sovereign Amity*—and even as they have sought to scrutinize
both sides of the relationship between premodernity and queerness, this has nonetheless not dented the ways in which we do queer theory. The assumption still very
much is that queer theory is a "thing" that we can export back to premodern texts;
the commensurate move to export premodern texts out to our present moment is
always accompanied with great skepticism, as is the attempt to push open the
boundaries of nominations like the premodern, early modern, and postmodern.
3. Žižek, *Looking Awry*, 9. In a different context, Žižek glosses King Richard's line
as:

> This apparently confused reply to Henry's request relies on a complex reason-
> ing, based on a brilliant exercise in what Lacan called *lalangue* (a neologism
> which some translate as "language": language as the space of illicit pleasures
> that defy any normativity: the chaotic multitude of homonymies, word-plays,
> "irregular" metaphoric links and resonances). It plays with three different
> ways to write (and understand) what we pronounce as "Ay, no; no, ay." Rich-
> ard's words can be read simply as a redoubled refusal, accompanied with the
> exclamatory "ay." Or, if we understand "ay" as "I," they can also be read as a
> refusal, but this time based on a denial of the very existence of the I, a con-

densed form of "I (say) no (because there is) no I to do it." This same point can be made also in the third reading, which understands it as (a homophony of) "I know no I": "You want me to do it, but since you want me to be nothing, to totally undo myself, who am I to do it? In such a situation, there is no I to do it, to give you the crown." (Slavoj Žižek, "Troubles with the Real: Lacan as a Viewer of *Alien*," available online at http://www.lacan.com/zizalien.htm).

Marjorie Garber's early and fabulous book, *Shakespeare's Ghost Writers*, makes a similar move in relation to the Freudian understanding of the uncanny and the uncanniness with which Shakespeare surfaces in the texts of modern and postmodern theory.

4. Butler, "Against Proper Objects," 21.

5. Betteridge, *Sodomy in Early Modern Europe*, 1, quoted in Stanivukovic, "Between Men in Early Modern England," 233.

6. Jankowski, "Pure Resistance," 218.

7. See, e.g., Traub, "The Homoerotics of Shakespearean Comedy."

8. I must add that the question, as articulated at the MLA panel, was neither hostile nor dismissive. If anything, it challenged us to articulate the assumptions on which a queer Shakespeare rested, and for that challenge I am grateful.

9. Berlant and Warner, "What Does Queer Theory Teach Us about *X*?," 343.

10. O'Rourke, "Introduction," xxvi.

11. Sedgwick, *Tendencies*, 25.

12. I owe the latter formulation to the insightful Asma Barlas.

13. It is useful here to consider Jacques Derrida's account of the dangers posed by the supplement. "Why is the surrogate or supplement dangerous? It is not, so to speak, dangerous in itself, in that aspect of it that can present itself as a thing, as a being-present. In that case it would be reassuring. But here, the supplement is not, is not a being (*on*). It is nevertheless not a simple nonbeing (*me on*) either. Its slidings slip it out of the simple alternative presence / absence. That is the danger": Derrida, "Plato's Pharmacy," 109.

14. De Man, "The Concept of Irony," 169.

15. Ibid., 181.

16. *Congressional Record*, June 9, 2000, available online at http://wais.access.gpo .gov (accessed August 2001).

17. This part of the argument forms the basis for several queer studies of the Renaissance, including those by Stephen Orgel (*Impersonations: The Performance of Gender in Shakespeare's England*, 1996), Bruce R. Smith (*Homosexual Desire in Shakespeare's England*, 1995), and Valerie Traub (*The Renaissance of Lesbianism*, 2002), among others.

18. Sedgwick, *Between Men*.

19. Freeman, "Queer Temporalities," 159.

20. After all, like many words, "queer" has multiple grammatical positions. It can be a verb, "to queer"; an adjective, "a queer fish"; and a noun, "Is there a queer in this text?" The word straddles registers of grammar in the same way that Shake-

speare converts "boy" in *Antony and Cleopatra* from being only a noun (the young of one particular gender) to also being a verb (Cleopatra complains that a Roman child actor will boy—with a pun on "buoy"—her greatness on stage).

21. *A Midsummer Night's Dream*, in Greenblatt et al., *The Norton Shakespeare*, 5.1.14–15. Citation in parentheses are to this edition.

22. Simpson and Weiner, *The Oxford English Dictionary*, s.v, "queer."

23. Ibid., s.v. "weird."

24. Jagose, *Inconsequence*; Freeman, "Queer Temporalities"; Halberstam, *In a Queer Time and Place*.

25. Dinshaw, *Getting Medieval*, 1; Freccero, *Queer / Early / Modern*.

26. The quotation in this section's epigraph is from Berlant and Warner, "What Does Queer Theory Teach Us about *X*?," 344.

27. The *Arden Shakespeare Complete Works* (1998), in one volume, is the only edition I know of that houses its entries alphabetically by title. But this alphabetical ordering also gives in to some generic impulse: First the poems are listed without being separated as poems, then the list continues with the plays from the beginning of the alphabet.

28. Jeffrey Masten provides some suggestions for alternative configurations of tables of contents. "You could print the essays alphabetically by play title, but provide (à la Oxford and Norton) multiple tables of contents, according to different modes of organization: alphabetical by first word, alphabetical by last word (hysteron pro teron), alphabetical by essay author, according to date of essay composition": Masten, private correspondence, August 2008.

All Is True (Henry VIII)

The Unbearable Sex of Henry VIII

STEVEN BRUHM

> If I see a man that is Hot, Hairy, high-coloured, with a black
> thick curled head of haire, great veines, & a big voice, I dare be
> bold to say, that that man hath a hot and dry Liver, and his
> Generative parts are also of the same Temper; & that
> consequently he is inclined to lustfull desires.
>
> —James Ferrand, *Erotomania*, 170

Hot, hairy, and big. Were it not for the archaic language and suspicion of "lustfull desires," this passage from James Ferrand's treatise *Erotomania* (1645) could come from hairyboyz.com or any website devoted to "bears"—those chubby, bearded, and hirsute gay men who constitute a significant modern subculture. Nor was Ferrand the only premodern writer to figure an erotic—or is it a pornographic?—of pogonotrophy. Clement of Alexandria had argued that God adorned man "with a beard like a lion, making him tough, with a hairy chest, for such is the emblem of strength and empire."[1] Marcus Ulmus contended in 1603 that "Nature gave to mankind a Beard, that it might remaine as an Index in the Face, of the Masculine generative faculty."[2] In a similar vein, John Bulwer argued in *Anthropometamorphosis* (1654) that "shaving the chin is justly to be accounted a note of Effeminacy."[3] Indeed, according to Will Fisher, the clean-shaven man in early modern England "quite literally becomes 'lesse man' or even a 'woman,'"[4] a prejudice Fisher finds in Phillip Massinger's play *The Guardian* (1658). Massinger suggests that a husband without a beard is worse than an adulterer because the former risks being considered sodomitical; lacking facial hair, he was supposed incapable of sexual regeneration.[5] And in the opinion of Johan Valerian (1533), the shaven face ranks its holder among "chyldren" and "gelded men"[6]—that is, the smooth, shaved, barely adolescent twink that is the current front-runner of gay desire.

For the contemporary bear lover, though, the happy hunting grounds that extend to the Lone Star Bar find a particularly rich den in early modernism. After a centuries-long chaetophobia inspired by the early Christian conviction that body hair was the mark of the Beast on fallen man, the fur flew back onto the faces of the sixteenth-century man. In English culture, the papa of these bears is Henry VIII, as shown most readily in Hans Holbein's famous portrait of him of 1540 (figure 1). Here Henry's face offers immediate satisfaction to the beard lover, both for what is there and for what is to come. Thanks to Henry's introduction of the beard to the English court, English Renaissance portraiture from Holbein on would be dominated by bearded figures. Bearded and bearish: The corpulent body in Holbein's canvas at least whets the appetite for the hairy chest that is metonymically suggested by the ermine draping over the king's shoulders and down across his nipples. The sashes under the belly, the sweep of the costume toward the remarkably genital knot of the belt, the right arm directing our gaze down across the stomach to the left hand placed tantalizingly on the hilt of a dagger—all of this leads viewers so inclined to fantasize about how long that dagger really is and what it might prick. With a remarkable and pointed clarity, the filigree of Henry's *costume* images his actual bodily *flesh*, a Henry stripped bare to become Henry the bear (figure 2).

Such a perverse reading of His Majesty's magisterial body is not beside the point in early modern figurations of Henry. Shakespeare opens *Henry VIII* with the spectacle of not one but two big, hurly, kingly bodies on display. Moreover, Shakespeare gives them an erotic dynamism that the Holbein portrait can only hint at. The Duke of Norfolk begins the play by describing to Buckingham the famous summit at the Field of the Cloth of Gold in which Henry meets the equally large (and equally hirsute) King Francis I:

> I was then present, saw them salute on horseback,
> Beheld them when they lighted, how they clung
> In their embracement as they grew together,
> Which had they, what four throned ones could have weighed
> Such a compounded one?
>   . . . Men might say
> Till this time pomp was single, but now married
> To one above itself.[7]

This is the play's first spectacle of huge bodies growing together, melding or "marrying" into an undifferentiated one—the first, but certainly not the only. During Anne Boleyn's coronation in Act 4, we read that

FIGURE I. Henry VIII, in the manner of Hans Holbein, circa 1540

FIGURE 2. Photographed by Wayne Brereton; modified by Sue Healy

> Great-bellied women,
> That had not half a week to go, like rams
> In the old time of war, would shake the press,
> And make 'em reel before 'em. No man living
> Could say "This is my wife" there, all were woven
> So strangely in one piece. (4.1.78–83)

And at the baptism of the baby Elizabeth, we have the crowds turning the court into a version of Paris Garden ("a park for bear- and bull-baiting") to catch sight of the child, as if "some strange Indian with a great tool [has] come to court " (5.3.32–33). "Bless me," cries the Porter, "what a fry of fornication is at the door! On my Christian conscience, this one christening will beget a thousand. Here will be father, godfather, and all together" (5.3.33–36). If the great bellies of Act 4 vie for space with the great tool of Act 5, the effect is merely to embroider on the play's indulgence in swollen bodies entering strangely into one piece—women like phallic rams, great tools and great bellies producing many papas. Papas, and Papa *Bears*, for while the marriage of pomp and circumference at the Valley of the Cloth of Gold does not mention hair, we know it is covered in the stuff: Francis was one of the first European heads of state to sport a beard (figure 3), in defiance of medieval Christian practice, and Henry, in imitation (in identification? in desire?) of Francis, quickly followed suit, bringing the hirsute home to England. In this sense Shakespeare's play opens with something of a girth-and-mirth orgy, where "two kings" become "but one" (1.1.28–32) to beget a thousand beards across the English landscape.

If the invocation of two beefy, hairy men embracing each other into one-ness makes my bear-loving imagination run wild, it also brings it up short. I remember, of course, that Henry VIII is the story of a man who marries six different women to produce a kingly heir, and that two of these women end up on the chopping block. When Henry VIII wants someone to give head, he does not have my sort in mind. Moreover, I remember that the gropefest at the Valley of the Cloth of Gold failed to produce any stable and meaningful allegiance between its two monarchs; this particular love story was doomed to failure. But it is precisely these two "failures" to produce a future that cement for me the necessity of reading Henry within the discourses of queer temporality and corporality. Henry's large, fecund body, his beard figuring the seminal overflow of his generative parts,[8] his lustful desires, the sexual and political prowess that adheres to his regal body all figure impotence and cas-

FIGURE 3. Francois Clouet, Francis I, circa 1520

tration, an inability to live up to the normative promises that Henry's body makes. How then might *Henry VIII* bear up under a sustained queer reading of its bearishness? How might those simultaneous signifiers of phallic excess and phallic failure help us to read an unregenerate queerness in Shakespeare's play? Let us begin again, with another bearish characteristic: fatness.

In an essay on fat children, ghosts, and animals, Kathryn Bond Stockton teaches us how to read for "sideways growth"—that is, how queer bodily contours and queer bodily acts often register a refusal to grow "up" (into normalcy, singularity, legibility) while nevertheless insisting on growing "out," "around," or "across" sites of meaning.[9] Contemporary society, she contends, does not yet know what to do with the fat body other than to incorporate it into a pathologizing discourse of unsuccessful human development. Queers would do well, she suggests, to consider how sideways growth can figure a refusal of the strictures of normative development. Cast in other terms (those of Gilles Deleuze and Félix Guattari), sideways growth may signal the significatory excesses of the rhizomic body, one that does not or will not align itself with the dictates of Oedipal health—that is, the imperative to grow *up*, straight and tall, with all the rights and normalcy pertaining thereto. While Stockton's preferred site for analysis of this anti-Oedipal, sideways growth is the fat child and the dog-loving lesbian, I suggest we consider the *ursine* as well. Given that the first English law prohibiting sodomy took effect under the reign of Henry VIII, and that it named as a crime the "abhomynable vice of buggery commyttid with mankynde or beaste,"[10] let us consider how mankind as beast—as bear—refuses to keep *Henry VIII* straight.

The list of male bodies that grow sideways in *Henry VIII* is as imposing as the bodies themselves. There is Henry of course, and his symbiotic Francis; but there is also Cardinal Wolsey, that "keech" (suet, "hunk of fat"; 1.1.55) with "unbounded stomach" (4.2.34) who "can, with his very bulk, / Take up the rays o' th' beneficial sun, / And keep it from the earth" (1.1.55–57); and from whose "ambitious finger" "No man's pie is freed" (1.1.52–53). Sexually speaking, the pie that receives Wolsey's ambitious finger is doubtless female, but his clean-shaven face, in obedience to a century of papal dictates, telegraphs a celibacy bordering on the catamitic or the gelded. And if a fat *hairless* body is not condemning enough, let us fantasize hair onto it, as Buckingham and Norfolk do, to complete his moral degradation. Wolsey is a "fox, / Or wolf, or both," says Buckingham (1.1.158–59), animal hair acting as metaphor for bestial, degraded behavior. What is most interesting for my purposes, though, is how Wolsey's courtly ambitions also get figured in terms of sideways growth: not just a horizontal bear body for our Wolsey, but also a sideways *political* growth that bespeaks lack of proper allegiance to the Oedipal, filial, class-based inheritance that constituted Tudor aristocratic propriety. Norfolk's chief complaint about Wolsey is that his power, in addition to being pernicious, is undeserved by someone of his class. This "keech" is, after all, the son of a butcher, and

> There's in him stuff that puts him to these ends [political ambitions].
> For being not propped by ancestry, whose grace
> Chalks successors their way . . .
>   [he] gives us note
> The force of his own merit makes his way—
> A gift that heaven gives for him which buys
> A place next to the King. (1.1.58–66)

Not a proper Oedipal lineage propped by ancestry, then, but a sideways acquisition. The gifts of his own merit place Wolsey next to (not beneath) the
king. Little wonder, then, that Wolsey should figure his undoing in terms of
physical shrinkage and deflation. He has "ventured, / Like little wanton boys
that swim on bladders, / . . . far beyond my depth" (3.2.359–62) and just as his
"greatness is a-ripening, [Fortune] nips his root, / And then he falls" (3.2.358–
59). But it is not Fortune that nips this boy's root, it is Papa Bear. *Henry* breaks
the wanton Wolsey's bladder, removing a "load," a "burden / Too heavy"
from the cardinal's shoulders (3.2.384–86). A grandeur gained sideways has
been too much for Wolsey's king to bear.

   This anti-Oedipal charge bears weight elsewhere in *Henry VIII*. As Wolsey
levels against his successor, Thomas Cranmer, the accusation that Cranmer
has not risen to his position of power so much as he "hath crawled into the
favor of the King" (3.2.104), we get a sense of the potbelly calling the kettle
black. And according to the (possibly fallacious) testimony brought against
the Duke of Buckingham, such sideways acquisition may also characterize
Buckingham's pretensions to the throne should Henry "without issue die"
(1.2.135). But perhaps the most notable sideways growth, the most anti-Oedipal position in the play, belongs to Henry himself. In a passage that would
make psychoanalytic readers of *Hamlet* green with envy, Henry decries his
almost-but-not-quite Oedipal union with Katherine, the princess "dowager, /
Sometimes our brother's wife" (2.4.177–78). "My conscience first received a
tenderness, / Scruple, and prick," the king tells Wolsey, when the Bishop
of Bayonne wonders whether Henry's daughter, Mary, is the legitimate offspring of a man married to his brother's wife (2.4.167–68). Is Henry properly a
father (and Mary his direct, vertical descendent), or is he more like an uncle,
constituted by a sideways relationship to his own brother's wife?

> This respite shook
> The bosom of my conscience, entered me,
> Yea, with a spitting power, and made to tremble
> The region of my breast. (2.4.178–81)

Let us leave aside the entering, pricking, and spitting, the shaking bosoms and
trembling breasts, to focus instead on what gets accomplished by this entrance into Henry's already capacious and sensitive body (at least according
to the logics of Shakespeare's history play). From this anti-Oedipal union
comes not only a crisis of sexual subjectivity but also a new marriage, the
birth of Elizabeth I, the reformation of Catholicism's hold over the English

monarchy, and the eventual establishment of the Church of England. That is quite a growth to come from the failure of reproduction—or, rather, from a reproduction that fails to authorize itself as legitimate.

Reading for bears in *Henry VIII*—that is, reading for masculine sexuality that refuses the ideological stabilizing of futurity—is ultimately to read for the ways in which sideways growth thwarts the normalizing fictions of heterosexual reproduction, the way it disfigures the Oedipal linearity of family power. Such lack of linearity takes us, richly and paradoxically, to the play's end, where the birth of Elizabeth I replicates the circular—or is it circumferential?—patterns I have been locating in the body of the bear. In the economy of the Tudor court, Elizabeth is both blessing and curse, an heir who should have been a boy and a virgin who should have been a mother. Yet while she is a female in name, she seems to be a male metonymically. At the moment of Elizabeth's birth, the old lady perversely announces to a panting father that Anne has been delivered

> of a lovely boy. The God of heaven
> Both now and ever bless her! 'Tis a girl
> Promises boys hereafter. Sir, your queen
> Desires your visitation, and to be
> Acquainted with this stranger. 'Tis as like you
> As cherry is to cherry. (5.1.165–70)

Elizabeth signifies as girl only to the degree that she promises boys, a reproductive futurity that empowers the court's masculine and misogynistic qualities, to be sure, but that also re-produces the same-sex economies of desire with which the play opened. Given the play's emphasis on sideways growth around or beyond the strictures of the Oedipal, it is not for nothing that the promise of boys hereafter is precisely the promise that Jacobean audience members at the time of the play's debut would have recognized not to have been honored. It is not for nothing that Elizabeth as metonymic boy is also Elizabeth as *metaphoric* boy, being as like to her father as cherry is to cherry. And it is not for nothing that her own succession, predicted metaphorically in Cranmer's famous speech of Elizabeth as a "maiden phoenix" who will "create another heir" out of her own ashes (5.4.40–41), produced no heirs at all. Rather, she proceeded by way of horizontal accommodation in the appointment of James I to the throne. (Plenty of boys hereafter in James's court perhaps, but not necessarily of the type Cranmer was forecasting.) What a delight, then, that *Henry VIII* stands as the last of Shakespeare's history plays, since it not only dramatizes so profoundly how the story of this history reproduces the failure to reproduce but, in so doing, produces multiple other histories of queer cathexes, narcissistic pleasures, anti-linear interventions that must be read alongside, but are not equal to, its tyrannies and violence.

It is not for nothing, finally, that "bear" is a homograph—and, indeed, the first example of the trope to appear, innocently but fortuitously, in Lee Edelman's discussion of "homographesis." The homograph, we remember, is that singular signifier that collects different and unrelated meanings to it according to its different etymological histories.[11] In this sense, it goes to the heart of queer inscription, as it allegorizes the inscription of the queer: Given that the queer body must be read not just for its difference but for its difference masquerading as sameness, Edelman argues, normative masculinity must always

> *perform* its self evidence, must represent its own difference from the derivative and artificial "masculinity" of the gay man. The homosexual, in such a social context, is made to bear the stigma of writing or textuality as *his identity*, as the very expression of his anatomy, by a masculinist culture eager to preserve the authority of its own self-identity through the institution of a homographesis whose logic of legibility, of graphic difference, would deny the common "masculinity," the common signifying relation to maleness, of gay men and straight men alike.[12]

Henry VIII does not as a rule set masculine men against feminine men (the starting point for Edelman in his discussion of the twelfth-century sodomite as effeminate), but that is precisely my point. In a queerly anachronistic reading, Shakespeare's play exploits the homograph of the bear as it plays the sexualized body type (Old English *bera*: "a heavily-built, thick-furred plantigrade quadruped") against the imperatives to carry or support and to produce or give birth to (Old High German *ber-an*). Given the unstoppable play of expansion and explosion in *Henry VIII*, of hetero-sexed bodily demarcations that insistently turn back onto (or into) the erotic registers of sameness, and of a reproductive futurity rendered unbearable by the bear's bodily excesses, *Henry VIII* might well offer us ways to reconfigure the contemporary bear as the masculinity that is not one, but that nevertheless troubles the structures of the two.

> *Exit pursued by a bear.* (*The Winter's Tale*, 3.3.57)

Notes

1. Reynolds, *Beards*, 8.

2. Fisher, "The Renaissance Beard," 174.

3. Ibid., 179.

4. Ibid., 168.

5. Ibid., 177.

6. Ibid., 179.

7. *All Is True (Henry VIII)*, in Greenblatt et al., *The Norton Shakespeare*, 1.1.9–21. Citations in parentheses are to this edition.

8. Fisher, "The Renaissance Beard," 174.

9. Stockton, "Growing Sideways, or Versions of the Queer Child," 279.

10. Goldberg, *Sodometries*, 3.

11. Edelman, *Homographesis*, 13.

12. Ibid., 12.

All's Well That Ends Well

Or, Is Marriage Always Already Heterosexual?

JULIE CRAWFORD

I propose in this essay that the dominant formal claims we make about Shakespearean comedies—that they plot a heterosexual love story (that is also the guiding logic for social order) and that they end in marriage—are intimately caught up with the formal and teleological expectations, the dominant storylines, we have about sexuality and its workings.[1] This formalism, whether based in psychoanalytic theories (the Oedipal drama) or anthropological ones (the traffic in women) structures much criticism of Shakespearean comedy. To take two key examples, critics frequently insist, even in the face of contradictory evidence, that the fulfillment of desire in heterosexual marriage is comedy's dominant telos, and that homoeroticism registers in the plays primarily in its (adolescent) passing or foreclosure in the face of marriage.[2] These readings are informed by, and conceptually map onto, the dominant structures— the lifecycle narratives—through which modern critics understand human sexuality. Both sexuality and comedy may have pleasures of various kinds along the way, that is, but they both end in heterosexuality.

Elsewhere I asked something I believe is only seemingly counterintuitive. What if marriage in the early modern period was not the end of homosocial structures and homoerotic desires but, instead, an enabling condition for their continuation?[3] Marriage in the period, and in Shakespeare's comedies, is as much about the suturing and reconfiguring of economies, households, and relationships as it is about a putatively heterosexual and dyadic culmination. In two kinds of relationships in which I am particularly interested, those between childhood friends and those between attending gentlewomen and their mistresses, women often retain their bonds with each other *through* marriage. This multiplying and complicatedly *systemic* and *contingent* (as opposed to teleological) notion of marriage is particularly true, as I will show, in *All's Well That Ends Well*, and the play thus encourages us to question the generic and sexual stories we think we know.

With Judith Butler's work on kinship in mind, I also want to reconsider how we read the complex familial and erotic nominations that both begin and characterize *All's Well* (son as husband, and, later, among many others, mistress as mother and virgin as bride). In querying the putative heterosexuality of kinship, Butler revisits the assumption that the incest taboo not only precludes illicit, but necessarily delimits and structures *licit* forms of sociality and sexuality. "From the presumption that one cannot—or ought not to—choose one's closest family members as one's lovers and marital partners," she writes, "it does not follow that the bonds of kinship that *are* possible assume any particular form."[4] An "invariant social organization of sexuality," she suggests, does not necessarily follow from prohibitive law. If we suspend our belief in universal and transcendent formalizations of sexuality, the hybrid nominations of *All's Well* allow us to see a broader range of kinship relations and affective bonds than those we can conceive under formal models of the "sex / gender system." These bonds are structured less by the law of the father or the traffic in women than by affective and economic interdependence in both the material and social senses. They are also gestured at by a language that cannot quite define them but nonetheless registers their existence and meaningfulness. More specifically, the familial-like nominations and complex structures of desire and affiliation that accumulate and transform as the play progresses—relations that simply cannot be articulated according to formally normative structures of incest taboo-driven heterosexuality—give us a hint of the possibilities the play imagines in these semi-articulated and formally unaccounted-for bonds that are so central to its plot. The relationships between the Countess of Roussillon and Helen, and, in the second half of the play, between Helen, the Widow, and her virgin daughter Diana are certainly formed in full consciousness of the incest taboo and via marriage, but those structures neither produce nor conclude the relationships' configurations in any programmatic or teleological sense. Kinship is not always already heterosexual, in other words, and marriage is rarely the end of anything.[5]

The Story We Think We Know, Part I: Helena and Bertram

My reading of *All's Well That Ends Well* begins with a reconsideration of the (generic and sexual) way we read its marriage plot.[6] When the play's main character, Helen, weeps at the beginning of the play, she claims it's because "there is no living, none, / If Bertram be away."[7] This line and the next, "Twere all one / That I should love a bright particular star / And think to wed it, he is so above me," are often taken as testament to the depth of Helen's love for Bertram, a claim that fits the expected telos for both heterosexuality and romantic comedy. Yet much of this first soliloquy is also concerned explicitly with social ambition. After commenting on Bertram's bright particular starriness, Helen says further that "in his bright radiance and collateral light / Must I be comforted, not in his sphere. / The ambition in my love thus plagues itself" (1.1.86–88). Helen's investment in "collateral" spheres—a term that means both "descended from the same stock, but in a different line" and "ranking side by side"—testifies to the complexity of her feelings for Bertram, as well as to the extent to which they are caught up in familial and socioeconomic ("ambitio[us]") considerations.

Helen's and Parolles's famous debate on virginity highlights their mutual awareness of the strategic value of sexuality. Helen's ultimate question about virginity, "How might one do, sir, to lose it to her own liking?" (1.1.147) has, along with other signs of her "efficient" and "predatory" nature, offended generations of critics with its violation of the idealized logic of comic romance.[8] It disrupts, that is, a strongly held belief in a heterosexual development narrative driven solely by love or erotic desire (or, at least, by the relative passivity of the woman) by suggesting instead that the story is driven by a desire for which sexual congress may be a means rather than the sole end. Helen herself identifies that desire as "her own liking."

When Helen tells Parolles that she wishes Bertram "well," she then proclaims it a pity

> that wishing well had not a body in't,
> Which might be felt; that we, the poorer born,
> Whose baser stars do shut us up in wishes,
> Might with effects of them follow our friends. (1.1.177–80)

"Wishing well"—in a play called *All's Well That Ends Well*—is identified as a desire one wants to make material. It is a pity, Helen asserts, that wishing well is not the same thing as making things well—that it is not, in other words, the same thing as achieving one's desired ambition. And this is in fact what Helen does in the course of the play—she makes her wish have a body: Bertram's. It would be a mistake to think—or, rather, to presume as axiomatic—that her wishing is motivated solely by heterosexual desire rather than to equally consider the socioeconomic ambition to which it also clearly refers. Helen's expressed desire is as concerned with "follow[ing] . . . friends" whose status is higher than her own as it is with (hetero)sexual congress. Sexuality, as Michael Lucey points out, can be a ruse of inheritance structures—or put more baldly, sexual desire can follow from or serve material desire.[9] Our reading of Helen's desire is determined by which structure of desire we presume is a priori. In the last line of the play's first scene, Helen states that her "intents are fix'd and will not leave me" (1.1.225), but it does not follow that marriage to Bertram *as an end in itself* is her final intention. The way we understand the telos of the play is thus also a question of how we understand the relationships—the "friends" she seeks to "follow"—that Helen's desire to marry Bertram formalizes.

The Story We Think We Know, Part II: Helen and the Countess

While Bertram insists that the Countess is his mother and Helen's mistress, the Countess is considerably less clear on the matter. When her steward claims that the Countess "love[s her] gentlewoman entirely," the Countess expounds on the nature of this love: "Faith, I do: her father bequeathed her to me; and / she herself, without other advantage, may lawfully / make title to as much love as she finds" (1.3.95–99). When she learns that Helen loves her son, the Countess both empathizes with her feelings and inaugurates a dialogue with Helen that simultaneously interrogates and reconfigures the bonds they have with each other. "You know, Helen," the Countess begins, "I am a mother to you." When Helen demurs with, "Mine honourable mistress," the Countess pushes her:

> Nay, a mother:
> Why not a mother? When I said "a mother,"
> Methought you saw a serpent. What's in "mother,"
> That you start at it? I say, I am your mother;
> And put you in the catalogue of those
> That were enwombed mine. 'Tis often seen
> Adoption strives with nature and choice breeds
> A native slip to us from foreign seeds. (1.3.133–41)

It is certainly possible to read this exchange merely as the Countess's attempt to out Helen's love for her son and to reconfigure herself as her mother(-in-law). Yet the incest taboo that keeps Helen from calling the Countess her mother—a nomination that would make Bertram her brother and therefore unavailable as her husband—does not necessarily delineate the contours of the relationship between the two women. It forecloses, in other words, but it does not clearly produce. The Countess registers her affection for Helen with a nomination that is closer to mother than either mistress or mother-in-law but cannot be easily reduced to any one term. In the face of the incest taboo, Helen accepts the appellation daughter-in-law even as she becomes something more than that in both affectionate and socioeconomic terms. The Countess has already said that Helen might have "lawful title" to any love she might have "without other advantage," and we know that Helen is pursuing her "advantage" with great intensity of purpose. Their incest-navigating dialogue thus highlights the inextricable connections between love and inheritance and between status and desire that characterize their bond.

The two women's battle over terminology culminates in the following exchange. The Countess asks Helen, "Love you my son?" When Helen responds, "Do not you love him, madam?," the Countess dismisses her question with impatience. "Go not about," she says, "my love hath in't a bond, / Whereof the world takes note" (1.3.182–84). The love of a mother for her son, in other words, is a socially recognizable script; Helen's feelings for Bertram must be of a different order. Yet the attestations of desire the Countess solicits from Helen—"Come, come, disclose / The state of your affection" (1.3.184–85)—sound a lot like those Helen has already expressed. I love him, she says, but "I follow him not / By any token of presumptuous suit; / Nor would I have him till I do deserve him" (1.3.192–94). Once again, the telos of this line is one of meritorious ambition—"*till* I do deserve him"—and the union devoutly to be wished is inextricable from the socioeconomic, familial, and affective support of her mistress-mother.

If the Countess had initially and suggestively given Helen "lawful title" to her love, she now gives her a more tangible set of tools: "Thou shalt have my leave and love, / Means and attendants and my loving greetings / To those of mine in court" (1.3.246–48). "What I can help thee to," she concludes, "thou shalt not miss" (1.3.51). Here, the Countess's ends are certainly marriage, but the enabling of marriage is manifestly not the straightforward enabling of heterosexual desire. The familial, socioeconomic, and affective bonds that the Countess and Helen entrench and forge, in light of incest and via marriage, cannot be deduced from any single desire and cannot be reduced to any single nomination. Indeed, it would take a great deal of heteronormative and genre-straightening effort to see them as motivated solely or primarily by the pursuit of Helen's heterosexual desire for Bertram.[10]

The Story We Think We Know, Part III:
Helen, the Widow, the Virgin, and Her Friend

While Helen's marriage to Bertram is facilitated by his mother's love and money, it is consummated with the help of another woman: the virgin Diana. Critics presume that the chaste Diana functions as the binarized other to Helen's heterosexually desirous Venus. Together, they symbolize and bring about the play's marriage.[11] Yet the figure of "Dian" also invokes female alliances, and the flesh-and-blood Diana in *All's Well* comes with just such an alliance: her widowed mother and her friend Mariana. As they do for Helen, however, critics frequently chart a startlingly heterosexual (not to mention extra-dramatic) story for Diana. They point out that the king offers to dower her at the end of the play, suggesting that the story—a complex one, certainly, but one nonetheless centered on a virtuous virgin's marriage to a man—will begin again, reinitiating the whole cycle of heterosexual courtship and marriage that is, in that most overly enunciated formulations of Shakespeare criticism, the driving force of comedy.[12]

What these critics ignore, however, is that Diana has already been given a dower much earlier in the play, that it was given to her by Helen, and that she has sworn two things in response: first, that she will remain a virgin and, more interestingly, that she "is" Helen's. Helen begins her relations with the women by offering to "bestow some precepts on this virgin / Worthy the note" (3.5.99), a gesture that invokes the valuable "prescription[s]" or "receipt[s]" her own father left her and that she used to great advantage in saving the king and thereby getting his blessing to marry Bertram (1.2.250, 1.3.227). Helen later promises the Widow that, after Diana has invited Bertram into her bed and then allowed Helen to take her place, "To marry her, I'll add three thousand crowns / To what is passed already" (3.7.34–35). It sounds, at first, as if Helen is offering to marry Diana herself. Yet the enormous sum Helen offers "to marry" Diana is a portion or dowry, money that will enable Diana to marry (someone else). And, indeed, Helen later explains her gift in this way, telling the Widow that "Heaven / Hath brought me up to be your daughter's dower" (4.4.18–19).

Yet if Helen is more endower than husband, it does not necessarily follow that there will be an actual husband. A woman's dowry, in other words, does not prescript a heterosexual marriage. Diana has already sworn that she will "live and die a maid" (4.2.74), and when she learns of Helen's dower, she vows to Helen, much as one does when one marries, "I am yours" (4.4.28). As Theodora Jankowski has pointed out, virginity is defined not by the absence of desire or sexual pleasure but by the absence of sexual congress with a man. As is the case for Diana, virginity can also be understood as a vow made *between* women—a vow cemented through her inheritance of a "dowry." In the early modern period, women earned their marriage portions in multiple ways, including through inheritance from other women. Virgins' portions, moreover, did not always work in the direct service of marriage. Single women often used their portions to make money by lending out the money at interest. Indeed, Florence, where Helen finds Diana and her all-female community, was famous for its *monte delle doti*, or bank of dowries.[13] Rather than merely a precursor to marriage, then, the dowry was often a means to entrench women's independence and socioeconomic mobility and to forge networks of female support and community. Far from inaugurating the supra-patriarchally mandated traffic in women, Diana's dowry testifies to the complex relationships between marriage and women's homosociality and socioeconomic power.

By providing Diana with a portion—money that Helen obtained through a combination of service and (female) inheritance—Helen sutures Diana and her kin group into the socioeconomic and affective bonds she has forged with the Countess. Diana's dowry may well start "the story" over again, but that story, like Helen's, may not be the heterosexual telos on which critics so frequently insist. Much like the Countess does in the first part of the play, Helen extends kinship and socioeconomic interdependence, creating new same-sex bonds via both marriage itself and its mechanics (in this case, the dower).

My point is not that these are fully egalitarian or loving relationships. When Diana tells Helen, "I am yours," it is followed by a statement about her obligation to suffer for her, and Helen makes it clear that the rooted nature of her love is contingent on the woman's continual service. Instead, I want to highlight the multiply influenced and systemic nature of the familial, socioeconomic, and affective same-sex bonds so central to marriage in Shakespeare's play. In *All's Well That Ends Well*, both sexuality and desire are provisional and context-dependent, enmeshed in material and social realities—such as marriage—that are less delimiting and more productive than we often presume. The marriage that ends the play is not the single-minded triumph of heterosexuality critics so often strain to see it as. Indeed, this strained insistence exposes the work it takes not only to script a heterosexual telos for human sexuality and for the genre of comedy but also to make them map so tidily onto one another. The stories we think we know, in other words, may be nothing of the sort.

Notes

1. Frye, *The Anatomy of Criticism*, 163–86, famously charted the affinities between marriage and comic structure. On genre in general, see Rosalie Colie's argument that genres are lenses of interpretation, "frames or fixes on the world": Colie, *The Resources of Kind*, 8.

2. The former comment is central to almost all criticism of Shakespearean comedy; the latter has been nuanced differently by those interested in tracking the history of homoeroticism rather than simply accepting it as the (sometimes) necessary past of a happy heterosexual arrival. For readings informed by and sympathetic to queer studies, see Valerie Traub, who focuses her attention on plays "where female affections and bonds are not so much marked by invisibility and silence as harnessed to a dramatic trajectory that renders them simultaneously crucial and insignificant to their romantic plots": Traub, *The Renaissance of Lesbianism in Early Modern England*, 164.

3. Crawford, "The Homoerotics of Shakespeare's Elizabethan Comedies," 137–58. Mario DiGangi has begun the work of "Queering the Shakespearean Family," but looks at marriage primarily in relationship to relations between men: see DiGangi, "Queering the Shakespearean Family," and *The Homoerotics of Early Modern Drama*. On marriage as the end of women's same-sex relationships, see Traub, *The Renaissance of Lesbianism in Early Modern England*, 181.

4. Butler, *Antigone's Claim*, 66.

5. My phrasing here comes directly from Butler, "Is Kinship Always Already Heterosexual?"

6. John F. Adams, to take an example, summarizes the plot this way: Helen is "a virtuous woman whose aim in the play is to fulfill her function of procreation by losing her virginity through marriage to a man who pleases her" (cited in Ranald, "The Betrothals of *All's Well That Ends Well*," 180). I am particularly interested in the ways in which critics willfully read the play as a story of naturalized heterosexual development and successful marital closure. In his introduction to his edition of *All's Well*, for example, Alexander Leggatt quotes Robertson Davies's claim that when Bertram "is ready for the kind of woman that Helen is, Helen is waiting for him": Leggatt, "Introduction," 26.

Some feminist critics also insist on this telos. Carol Thomas Neely argues that "Bertram is not yet even at the beginning of the journey toward sexual maturity that Helen is already embarked on": Neely, *Broken Nuptials in Shakespeare's Plays*, 70. On the most tenuous of grounds, the heavily mediated ending of the play is, in turn, willfully read as a celebration of mutual love. Barbara Hodgdon, for example, claims that Helen's and Bertram's "commitment to their shared sexuality becomes hesitantly apparent, more in silence than through extravagant speech or romantic gestures, as the possibility of kindness and love": Hodgdon, "The Making of Virgins and Mothers," 67. Perhaps the most willful of these readings is that of Gerald Gross, who insists that Bertram must possess "some quality which inspires such devotion" in Helen; that "his speech patterns, despite their brevity, have a ring of sincerity." He asks, finally, why we should not expect "that they will be happy?": Gross, "The Conclusion of *All's Well That Ends Well*," 265, 270. It is clearly the expectation that comedies end in happy marriages that drives Gross's reading, even as he acknowledges that "the quickness with which Helena turns from Bertram to the Countess [at the end of the play] says little for the capability of Bertram to hold her attention": Gross, "The Conclusion of *All's Well That Ends Well*," 271. His reading, in other words, is dictated by formal ideas about both sexuality and genre even as he sees the dramatic and affective importance of the bonds between women.

7. Hunter, *All's Well That Ends Well*, 1.1.82–83. Citations in parentheses are to this edition.

8. Arthur Quiller-Couch famously concluded that Helen "is perhaps too efficient to engage our complete sympathy": Quiller-Couch, "Introduction," cited in Schwarz, "'My Intents Are Fix'd,'" 206. David Scott Kastan describes Helen as possessing "a tenacity too nearly predatory to be completely attractive or satisfying": Kastan, "*All's Well That Ends Well* and the Limits of Comedy," 579. In perhaps the best line of all, E. K. Chambers claimed that in Helen, Shakespeare turned "man's tender helpmate . . . into the keen and unswerving huntress of man": Chambers, *Shakespeare*, 203.

9. Lucey, *The Misfit of the Family*, xxix

10. Even at the point of her reunion with the formerly estranged Bertram at the end of the play—and its culmination in marriage—Helen's joy is reserved for the Countess. When Bertram attests to his loyalty to Helen in the concluding scene, she replies that if it proves untrue, "Deadly divorce step between me and you!" (5.3.315). Her attention is reserved for the Countess. "O my dear mother," she says, "do I see you living?" (5.3.308).

11. See Snyder, "Naming Names in *All's Well That Ends Well*," *Shakespeare Quarterly*, 43.3 (Autumn 1992), pp. 265–79. Yet as the play insists in many registers, any reference to the goddess of women's chastity evokes single-sex female communities, the privileging of women's choices, and women's desire qua desire rather than vis-à-vis or always already directed toward men. On Diana and female same-sex relations, see Berry, *Of Chastity and Power*; Jankowski, *Pure Resistance*; Shannon, *Sovereign Amity*, esp. 69–81; and Traub, *Renaissance of Lesbianism*.

12. The king says, "If thou be'st yet a fresh uncropped flower, / Choose thou thy husband, and I'll pay thy dower" (5.3.321–22). See, e.g., Bennet, "New Techniques of Comedy in *All's Well That Ends Well*," 355; Hodgdon, "The Making of Virgins and Mothers," 66; Kastan, *All's Well That Ends Well* and the Limits of Comedy," 579–80; Neely, *Broken Nuptials in Shakespeare's Plays*, 82; Snyder, "Introduction," 52.

13. On loaning dowries, and not marrying, see Erickson, *Women and Property in Early Modern England*, 81–85 and Spicksley, "To Be or Not to Be Married," 91–95. On the *monte delle doti*, see Erickson, *Women and Property in Early Modern England*, 81.

Antony and Cleopatra

Aught an Eunuch Has

ELLIS HANSON

"What's your Highness' pleasure?" the eunuch Mardian asks of his mistress Cleopatra.[1] Good question! Does he ever get an answer? He sounds like a modern-day bartender, as the queen elbows up first to Charmian's bar and then to Mardian's in search, she says, of some sleepy draught of mandragora to soothe the "great gap of time" (1.5.5) while her Antony is away. Cleopatra is defined by her gaps. Her demands only perform them, announce them, widen them with words, and here she seems neither to receive nor even particularly to insist on the things she claims to wish. Her gaps occupy her, they interrupt her lines with a dash, they even trail in her wake as if by some languorous reverberation of feminine lack. If it were possible, she would leave a very "gap in nature" (2.2.224) as she passes on her barge and the crowds desert Antony and the marketplace to gape at her. In this play, where every sauce is cloyless, sharpening the appetite it feeds, all feast is famine and every presence an absence (and vice versa), and so there may well be mystification on either side of the bar at this pressing question of the queen's pleasure—or, for that matter, anyone else's. Not even the oblivion of the mandragora would give much respite if it is true that her "oblivion is a very Antony" (1.3.90), as she has said, or that she sleeps only to dream of "such another man" as he (5.2.78). Does Antony ever satisfy her desire, or does he merely help her to sustain it better?

In Cleopatra's first exchange with Mardian, female lack consults with male lack, mistress with eunuch, and the result is a series of vague locutions that, understandably, beg the initial question of pleasure. The queen seizes the occasion for her usual flirtatious jesting with him. Because she finds herself once again the other woman to Antony's wife, she teasingly interviews Mardian for the job of the other man for her own use, all the while assuming that he does not have whatever it takes to fill her gap:

Cleopatra: Not now to hear thee sing; I take no pleasure
In aught an eunuch has: 'tis well for thee,
That, being unseminar'd, thy freer thoughts
May not fly forth of Egypt. Hast thou affections?
Mardian: Yes, gracious madam.
Cleopatra: Indeed!
Mardian: Not in deed, madam; for I can do nothing
But what indeed is honest to be done:
Yet have I fierce affections, and think
What Venus did with Mars. (1.5.9–17)

What exactly did Venus do with Mars in Mardian's imagination, or Mars with Venus? What, indeed, is honest to be done by a eunuch whose primary purpose in the plot is to tell Antony a lie? What is this unspecified "aught" that an eunuch has? Would it fill a gap in time—or any other gap the queen would care to see occupied? I want to dilate on this queer figure of the eunuch, unsexed and thereby oversexed, so sexually overdetermined that in this play of phallic jesting and jousting, his marginality cannot help but to feel central. He is an allegorical figure for the gap not in woman but in man, a castration universal to men, a masculine ardor of fierce but languorous affections that enjoy sex, even deify it, precisely by not having it. He may be "unseminar'd" in the testicular sense, as Cleopatra notes, and therefore chaste and honest indeed, but he is obscene by virtue of his imagination, a tendency he has in common with his mistress, whose pleasure onstage is mostly in pining about what she is not getting.

Through her bawdy banter, Cleopatra does take pleasure in aught an eunuch has, even as she disavows it. What abundance, what lack, renders him so attractive, so amusing, yet so troubling an ornament to an Egyptian palace, a Jacobean stage, or a queer critique? She wants, of course, the inches that he lacks, and as Iras explains, it is not on a man's nose one hopes to find them. Later, in her ongoing inches envy, Cleopatra finds she cannot always get them from Antony when she wants them: "I would I had thy inches thou shouldst know / There were a heart in Egypt" (1.3.40–41). This line must have sounded amusing coming from the actor called on to boy her greatness and refer repeatedly to his own cross-dressed feigning of genital lack. What of Mardian's wit, his music, his affection? The queen seems to occupy herself with all three, as if to admit implicitly that to lack a prick is not necessarily to lack a point. She refers specifically to Mardian's singing voice, since he is evidently her musician, and his music might serve like mandragora to fill the gap of time with a pleasant substitute for Antony. The music, like her own frequent exposition on her desire, is inherently melancholic, her very longing given a certain perfection of form. Mardian instantly appears when she calls for "music, moody food / Of us that trade in love" (2.5.1–2). Her every orgy, her most voluptuous spectacles, all of them offstage, are enacted only in the mode of such music, descriptive lines of poetry on the lips of some soldier engaged in no more fleshly pastime than conversation with another man. The pleasure she gives, no less than the pleasure she demands, is transcribed into song and rendered achingly eternal. Fierce affections are left to the imagination. When Enobarbus evokes Cleopatra on her barge, it is to seduce another man with ear-kissing descriptions. Like Mardian, these men here merely think what Venus did with Mars, and so do we. The theater makes eunuchs of as all.

We are an affectionate priesthood, nevertheless. Cleopatra dwells on the sacredness of her desire in a blasphemous conceit about the "unseminar'd" Mardian. The punning neologism presumably means he cannot come, has no semen to offer—or even mandragora—but the word would also have evoked the Roman thoughts of a later era: those of the Roman Catholic seminary. Desire goes to church in this phrase, it even goes to school, and the sexual relation between a man and a woman becomes a sacred ritual, some religious discipline from which Mardian's thoughts—not to mention his body and his music—have been freed. Cleopatra accuses Mardian of being a freethinker, to use a term that would gain popularity later in the seventeenth century. She deems him a kind of atheist, unschooled, unseminar'd in the gospel of love. His freedom leaves him paradoxically moored to worldly things and incapable of grasping what we might, suitably enough in this context call the world to come. Here we see the martyr in Mardian, at once freed and imprisoned by his castration. Unlike Antony, he is allegedly not distracted by his affections, or even by Roman thoughts of any description, and he is therefore much more attentive to his mistress, despite his shortcomings. But Mardian points up the failure in the logic of her pun when he notes that his thoughts do fly from Egypt and the body precisely by dwelling on them. They imagine the perfection of pleasure in such randy deities as Venus and Mars and make a religion of desire rather than its fulfillment. Even in Shakespeare's England, the sacred status of the eunuch musician would have been evident, if perhaps a scandal, as a newly emergent figure in Roman Catholic ritual: the castrato in the choir, a dubiously foreign invention, at once seminar'd and unseminar'd. A figure like Mardian would most likely have been a foreigner castrated when he was sold into slavery, and yet eunuchs throughout the ancient world became courtiers, royal servants, teachers, priests, even generals, such as the eunuch Photinus, who is said to have led Cleopatra's armies. In other words, aught a eunuch had was often something to covet. The eunuch here is a queer figure of paradox, desexualized but obscene, the freethinker serving as high priest, the outsider as insider, the castrato as ideal lover.

Later in the play, casting about her for a partner at a curiously anachronistic game of billiards, Cleopatra says, "As well a woman with an eunuch play'd / As with a woman" (2.5.5–6). Oddly, onstage she plays with a woman or a eunuch more often than she plays with Antony. There are forty-two scenes in *Antony and Cleopatra*, but in fewer than a quarter of them do Antony and Cleopatra address each other, and even then it is frequently what he calls "wrangling" or "conference harsh" (1.1.45–48). Roland Barthes once wrote that the lover is the one who waits, and by this definition, Cleopatra is a lady-in-waiting even more than her own attendants. In the meantime, we see her talk to those attendants, to Iras and Charmian, to Mardian and Alexas, to various messengers and guards, to a clown—she even talks lovingly to the asps as they poison her. Why are these interludes with her partners in waiting more engaging than her conversations with Antony? How might we theorize their often queer eroticism, not quite sexual, not quite chaste, not quite hetero, not quite homo, that the word "friend" or "lover" or "servant" fails to grasp?

Cleopatra and her eunuchs make me think of a particular kind of woman and her gay entourage, one quite numerous here in New York—or, at any rate, at certain Zip codes on the Upper East Side of Manhattan. They are regal ladies of a certain age, their apartments palatial, their brown hairs mixed with gray when not dyed gold, their pleasures frequently in excess of their pedigree, and their wealthy lovers or wealthy husbands, like Antony, conspicuously absent—with the other woman, or at the office, or in the grave. Age cannot wither them, nor custom stale their infinite variety. Every modern Cleopatra has at least one Mardian in her life. The modern world has denied these women proper eunuchs, but supplied them, instead, with gay men of a sensitive and artistic disposition. We find this queer couple delightfully evoked in queer modernist fiction if not in queer theory, in the writings of Marcel Proust, Ronald Firbank, Noel Coward, Cecil Beaton, Truman Capote, and other urbane literary luminaries—or in the backroom of Swifty's on Seventy-second Street and Lexington Avenue (and I use the term "backroom" advisedly, so busy is it with gay men). These ladies-who-lunch dine not with husbands or lovers but with more reliable and affectionate company, with other ladies-in-waiting, with their Irases and their Charmians or with the gay men who design their dresses, the gay men who decorate their duplexes, the gay men who dance with them at AIDS benefits, the gay men who are their confidantes and partners in gossip—the gay men, in short, who rescue them from the tedium of having married well. Promiscuous though these Mardians may be offstage, whether in thought or in deed, their erotic function in any heterosexual twosome is attendant. They are a good example of what Roland Barthes called the *Neutre*, the Neutral—or suitably enough in this context, the Neuter, that deconstructive *tertium quid* that attends any opposition as a non-combatant, an alternative not in contention with a central problem but, rather, occupying the vanishing point of its logic, playing at its margins, in its midst, insistently, hauntingly, peacefully, ineffectually, creatively, eternally. He is not another lover, but somehow he completes the triangle of this elegantly sustained impossibility, this romance of Venus and Mars—and himself.

But sirrah, mark how Mardian participates in an elaborate punning that links his name not only with Mark Antony and Mars, but also with marriage and the marketplace elsewhere in this play of "Making and marring fortunes" (3.11.65). Mars may be the god of war, but "mars" is also something the devil does to women: as the clown informs us, for every ten women the gods make, "the devil mars five" (5.2.277). Frequently, something has gone awry with gender, even when the making and marring is martial or maritime. Amid much marching, we find a messenger curiously painted "one way like a Gorgon, / The other way's a Mars" (2.5.116–117); we learn that when soldiers go to war on horses and mares, the horses are lost (3.7.6–7); Cleopatra is "marble-constant" as any soldier when, improbably, she endeavors to have nothing of woman in her (5.2.240); and when the soldier's pole is fallen, there is nothing left "remarkable" beneath that reliable sign of feminine inconstancy, the visiting moon (4.15.67). As for marriage, we might as well call it war, for no one is resigned to it peacefully, even in the prognostications of the soothsayer. As for the marketplace, it is the stuff of bad theater, where public performance and ostentation typically go amiss. The lover in Antony mars the soldier and the soldier mars the lover in a manner that transgresses the elaborate and relentless division of labor that gender is expected to perform in the play—as in, for example, that delicious erotic game where we find Cleopatra putting her "tires and mantles on him" whilst she wears "his sword Philippan" (2.5.22–23). The mark of this marring is already inherent in Antony's name, not to mention in the names of the odd Marcus or Marcellus, each of them luckless in love or war. Amid all of this punning and trading of genders, Mardian emerges as a symbol of a masculinity made and marred at once through its symbolic and even literal castration.

What do we make of the frequent comparisons of Antony to eunuchs? Would his marring make him less masculine or more? Is there such a thing as masculinity without castration? From the opening scene, Antony is scarcely distinguishable from the eunuchs fanning Cleopatra as they first arrive on-stage, and Philo, Antony's aptly named friend, deems him merely "the bellows and the fan / To cool a gipsy's lust" (1.1.8–9). When Antony is angry at Cleopatra for what he sees as her betrayal of him, she charges Mardian with a message for him that she has died with the mark of Antony on her lips. To recall the Clown's phallic jests about the woman and the worm, Mardian is a very honest eunuch, but something given to lie, as a eunuch should not do but in the way of honesty. He tells an important truth by telling a lie that redeems the queen but casts Antony into fatal despair. As the queen's messenger, Mardian repairs a romance and disrupts it in the same gesture. When he arrives, Antony cries out at him, "O! thy vile lady! / She has robb'd me of my sword" (4.14.22–23). Whose vile lady? Is Mardian his castrated mirror image, one strumpet's fool addressing another? With lines such as this one, we could easily reduce the play to a conservative, misogynistic reading, a moral plati-tude about masculine duty compromised by lust—the paradoxical effeminacy of a man's loving a woman too much. Yet the play undermines such a reading at every turn, rendering Antony most attractive when he is least Roman and rendering the dutiful Romans sterile and unremarkable. We might well agree with Cleopatra that, with Antony's death, the world has lost a noble standard for manhood, not least because "his delights / Were dolphin-like; they show'd his back above / The element they lived in" (5.2.88–90). This odd image of Antony as phallic and transcendent precisely because he arches his backside in the air exemplifies the persistent erotic ambiguity of his appeal. This belief in a transcendent masculinity, which refuses to choose between pleasure and duty, renders his death all the more tragic. Why should masculinity assume an impossible disavowal of the very phallic pleasure that defines it in the first place? In the no-win logic of this play, if you do not use it, you lose it, but, unfortunately, even if you do use it, you lose it. Every honorable man despises the eunuch he cannot help resembling. In the sustained violence of this irony, the play seems to charge Mardian with a very different message, to tell us that it is not Antony's pleasure, but masculinity itself, that is the real tragedy.

How does Mardian figure in this tragedy in the end? Shakespeare is often thought to have marred his own text by including the redundant Mardian in the stage directions for the final scene. Just as the nameless eunuchs in the first scene are, like the audience, mere fans of the queen who silently watch the drama of her self-dissolution, Mardian apparently observes the action of the final scene without speaking or affecting its course. He is her greatest fan. This castrated member of the cast is finally cast adrift as an audience with nothing to say and nothing to do, and no one even addresses him or seems to notice he is there. Is his silent presence here a lingering question? A spectral marker for the absent and silenced corpse of Antony? A gap in the text? An authorial error? Does the eunuch outlive the Venus and Mars he contemplates—or, perhaps, in his final witnessing does he define them and perform by his silent presence the truth that their sexual relation does not exist? "O, couldst thou speak" (5.2.306), Cleopatra exclaims to an asp, and she might as well address the same question to Mardian in this scene. If we were to take the stage directions at their word, we should puzzle over his mute attendance, silent as the audience, silent as the asps, silent but for his music, perhaps, which may or may not attend with its moods the passing of his mistress, that final sleep in the gap of an unfinished question: "What should I stay—"

Note

1. *The Tragedy of Antony and Cleopatra*, in Greenblatt et al., *The Norton Shakespeare*, 1.5.8. Citations in parentheses are to this edition.

Fortune's Turn

VALERIE ROHY

Everyone talks about Rosalind. "Of all Shakespeare's cross-dressed heroines," Marjorie Garber writes, "it is Rosalind who is almost always chosen as the normative case."[1] And why not? For queer and feminist readers in particular, she represents a bold swerve from the normative, a heroine who assumes, along with Ganymede's male attire, a host of new erotic possibilities.[2] When I first encountered *As You Like It* in a high-school English class, I, too, was fascinated by Rosalind's queer potential. Then, liking the play meant seeing in it a likeness of myself, forging an identification through whose alchemy I became "Rosalind" and my best friend "Celia" in countless notes passed between us. At the time, there was no question of which roles we would play: having invented the game, and being "more than common tall," I took the better part for myself. Although in time I would come to "suit me all points like a man," in time I also guessed that the parts had been miscast.[3] I wanted to be like witty, boyish Rosalind, but in liking girls, I was more like Celia, who, after all, likes Rosalind long after her fickle friend starts liking a likely young man.

There are, of course, complex homosexual energies surrounding Ganymede, Phoebe, Orlando, and Rosalind, not least in the play's teasing epilogue. But as the story advances, Celia persists in another sort of same-sex love, protected by the gender normativity that screens it from view—or rather, allows it to hide in plain sight.[4] In the first act, Charles hints that Rosalind remains at court because "the Duke's daughter her cousin so loves her, being ever from their cradles bred together, that she would have followed her exile, or have died to stay behind her," for "never two ladies loved as they do" (1.1.93–95, 97). Le Beau notes that their "loves are dearer than the natural bond of sisters" (1.2.242–43). And pleading against Rosalind's banishment, Celia says as much:

> We still have slept together,
> Rose at an instant, learned, played, eat together,

And wheresoe'er we went, like Juno's swans
Still we went coupled and inseparable. (1.3.67–70)

She tells her father "I cannot live out of her company" (1.3.80) and assures Rosalind that "thou and I are one" (1.3.97) before faithfully escorting her companion into Arden.

By the play's end, however, Celia will agree to wed Orlando, in a change of character so profound as to earn the name "conversion." The marital denouement of *As You Like It* depends on three unlikely reversals, among them Oliver's and Duke Ferdinand's turn from villainy to good. Saved by his brother from a rampant lion, Oliver hardly knows himself:

'Twas I, but 'tis not I. I do not shame
To tell you what I was, since my conversion
So sweetly tastes. (4.3.134–37)

And Duke Ferdinand, we are told, ventures into Arden in pursuit of his brother, but

meeting with an old religious man,
After some question with him was converted
Both from his enterprise and from the world. (5.4.149–51)

The language of conversion is striking in a play so profoundly concerned with mutability. As the Oxford English Dictionary notes, the Latin *convertre* means "to turn about, turn in character or nature, transform, translate." That usage pervades the play: Rosalind calls Silvius "a fool . . . turned into the extremity of love" (4.3.23–24), and Celia vows her love for Rosalind, saying "When I break that oath, let me turn monster" (1.2.21–22). But in her own last-act conversion, Celia will forswear her oath and turn her attention to Oliver. Her last lines in the play, addressed first to the fainting Rosalind, show little regard for the young man and even less hint of what will follow: "Come, you look paler and paler. Pray you draw homewards. Good sir, go with us" (4.3.177–78). Turning, it seems, extends to the realm of love, where what turns one's head is apt to turn one's nature. Two scenes later, Orlando enters marveling at Celia's and Oliver's successful speed dating: "Is't possible that on so little acquaintance you should like her? That but seeing, you should love her? And loving, woo? And wooing, she should grant?" (5.2.1–3). "Is it possible?" indeed.[5] In *As You Like It*, love is always the impossible, the inexplicable. Like Oliver and Duke Ferdinand, the villains improbably changed for the better,

Celia undergoes what we might call a conversion experience, turning if not into a monster, at least, *mutatis mutandis*, into a bride.

The notion of conversion presumes that some aspects of character are inessential and impermanent—that is, contingent. As it happens, *As You Like It* has something to say about contingency, albeit in other terms. In the play's first act, Rosalind and Celia idly compare fortune and nature, Celia proposing to "mock the good housewife Fortune from her wheel" (1.2.31–32) and Rosalind noting that "Fortune reigns in gifts of the world, not in the lineaments of nature" (1.2.35–36). We could read fortune, then, as a name for contingency, and nature as its antithesis, an essential substance of character. Fortune, as Fluellen puts it in *Henry V*, is "turning and inconstant and mutability and variation"—a largely antagonistic force whose vicissitudes individuals must suffer or overcome.[6] A common trope since the Middle Ages, it would have been familiar to Renaissance audiences, as would its moral valence. John Shaw notes that "from classical times it was felt that when a conflict between Fortune and Nature occurred, wisdom or character, the gifts of Nature, would prevail." Thus, he argues, in *As You Like It* the enduring good character —or, rather, good nature—of Rosalind, Celia, the Duke Senior, and Orlando enables them to withstand their transitory bad fortune.[7] But although Renaissance authors typically placed nature above fortune, *As You Like It* suggests that where love is concerned, fortune reigns supreme. Perhaps there is always something sexual about contingency, a term derived from "touching together," but what is contingent about sexuality? Particular loves can be arbitrary and impermanent, as we all know, but if Celia's change of heart is commensurate with Oliver's and Duke Ferdinand's conversions, *As You Like It* presumes the contingency of desire *as such*. From the shallowest play-acting to the deepest propensities, nothing is immutable, nothing sure. In a persuasive reading of the play, Valerie Traub associates both Ganymede and Rosalind's famous epilogue with "erotic contingency," predicated on "a simple conjunction: 'if.'" As Traub notes, rather than "being" homosexual, "characters temporarily inhabit a homosexual position of desire"—a formula that usefully uncouples Shakespeare from today's identity politics.[8] We might ask, however, whether heterosexuality is itself a temporary "position of desire." If sexuality is subject to the whims of fortune, would that allow an endless turning? What, finally, does it mean that the play's matrimonial conclusion depends on the radical contingency of desire?

The effects of desire's contingency in the play range from indeterminacy to conversion, from the demonstrably queer to the decisively otherwise: Rosalind's bold ventures are made of the same stuff as Celia's conventional fate. In fact, the mutability that enables the queerest moments of As You Like It—including the homoerotic play attending Rosalind's turn as Ganymede—is the same logic through which, today, the eradication of homosexuality is often imagined. As a form of sexual conversion, Celia's fate recalls the language of today's noxious "conversion therapy," by whose lights she might (if anachronistically) seem "ex-gay."[9] One proponent of "conversion therapy" or "reparative therapy," Exodus International, insists that "reorientation of same sex attraction is possible," as is "growth towards Godly heterosexuality."[10] In response to this virulent notion of sexual contingency, queer communities have denounced as biased any theory that would make same-sex love arbitrary and mutable rather than biological and essential. Though hardly universal, the claim is widespread: we are "born gay," as the title of a 2004 book proclaims, or "born different," in the words of a 2006 media campaign.[11] At stake in both queer and anti-gay claims is the possibility of desire's contingency; for both, the definition of desire as anything *other than* nature opens up the (threatening or promising) prospect of homosexuality's end. So if contingency at its logical extreme approaches conversion, what are the politics of sexual fortune, of desire's precipitous turns?

I want to suggest that the uncomfortable proximity of contingency and conversion in As You Like It and in right-wing rhetoric stems not from desire's contingency but from the narrative fantasies it is made to serve. Conversion is contingency subordinated to narrative—that is, to the determinist structuring of specific ideological formations. Although they seem to divorce desire from nature, in other words, those who promote today's hetero-turning marriage plots also refuse fortune. The notion of straightening conversion offends not because it *assumes* desire's contingency, but because, seeking to subordinate eros to an intentional narrative of sexual orthodoxy, it *denies* that endless turning. The problem lies in any narrative (whether of Shakespearean comedy or of "ex-gay ministries") that can have only one conclusion—marriage and the reconstitution of social order—in pursuit of which it both promotes and effectively denies desire's contingency. This paradox of determinism and possibility resembles what Žižek calls "the empty gesture," whereby "the subject is ordered to embrace freely, as the result of his choice, what is anyway imposed on him." His formula for this gesture is: "I offer you X . . . on the condition that you reject it."[12] In narrative terms, and with As You Like It in mind, we might rewrite his statement as: "Anything can happen, as long as it is what *must* happen."[13] Now, "choice" and contingency are by no means identical (explosive though both are in questions of queer etiology), so my revision of Žižek's axiom necessarily bends it awry. But both choice and contingency imply an openness, as opposed to the narrative inevitability with which each axiom concludes. Rather than granting too much scope to fortune, both *As You Like It* and today's anti-gay views of sexual contingency do not grant nearly enough. The narrative that *can* take any possible shape but also *must* conform to conventional genders and desires sustains itself by representing as chance what is more accurately called certainty.

In short, the notion of desire's contingency does not *in itself* perform a heteronormalizing function, as both "ex-gay" and "born gay" voices would insist. One need not accept the religious right's notion of sexual orientation as "chosen" to hold a more nuanced view of sexual contingency—which means to question the prevalent queer notion in which the imputation of homosexuality to *anything but* nature can only be homophobic. Instead, detached from heteronormative narrative ends, the notion of contingency may offer some purchase on the deadlock between gay activists' deterministic insistence on nature and the religious right's notion of sexual orientation as fundamentally volitional. Returning to the dictionary, we find that contingency is double-edged: "the condition of . . . being open to the play of chance, or of free will" but also the "condition of being subject to chance and change, or of being at the mercy of accidents." Both glosses turn on chance, then diverge, toward "free will" on the one hand, and on the other, toward a radical lack of agency ("being subject to" and "at the mercy of"). Suspended between agency and determinism, contingency has the potential to become a third term defined by neither voluntarism nor subjection. That potential, however, can never be taken for granted, for we can no more find a contingency outside the exigencies of narrative than we can locate a discourse outside the forces of ideology. The knot of this dilemma anchors, among other things, the tension between an academic queer theory indebted to poststructuralist notions of contingency and a broader queer community that largely construes homosexuality as biologically essential. Although queer theory seems the servant of fortune, it, too, may err on the side of nature by accepting the poststructuralist thesis in which nature is, in a sense, always already fortune. Traub's discussion of "erotic contingency" in *As You Like It* is eloquent and insightful, but its poststructuralist contrast between hegemonic fixity and a resistant openness is also by now familiar. Since the publication of Traub's essay, a certain reading of contingency has become academic orthodoxy; from queer readings of Shakespeare to attempts to describe queer theory as such, contingency indicates a liberating play of sexual meaning.[14] Queer theory has itself narrativized contingency, including its own. While in such contexts contingency does not mean conversion, as it does in anti-gay discourse and in the last act of *As You Like It*, it has become something less than contingent; yoked to a foregone conclusion, it risks calcifying into another "empty gesture."

What, then, would constitute a more contingent view of contingency? What would such a reading turn toward, or turn into? In "Nothing Fails like Success," Barbara Johnson suggests that the reader's openness to an encounter with otherness is the only way "to avoid becoming too comfortable in the abyss"—too comfortable, we might say, with contingency's own abyssal potential. She writes: "The one imperative a reading must obey is that it follow, with rigor, what puts in question the kind of reading it thought it was going to be."[15] I thought this essay was going to be the kind of reading that turned on difference—between past and present, Celia and Rosalind, liking and likeness, nature and fortune. Who wouldn't want to move beyond a naïve high-school reading of *As You Like It*? But that "movement beyond" imposes a narrative of intellectual progress on a relation to the play that was both a lucky accident and a stubborn refusal of story. Indeed, how I liked *As You Like It* shows how profoundly interwoven contingency and narrative can be. My early reading of the play was defined by its willful elision of everything that failed to strengthen my teenage cathexes: not only did it banish the male players far beyond Arden, but its juvenile Rosalind and Celia never left the first act, after which Rosalind, "dear coz," would cozen her cousin to aid her romance.[16] Instead, suspended in time, they lingered in the simultaneity of two who "have slept together, / Rose at an instant" (1.3.67–68), exempt from the narrative traction of Shakespeare's marriage plot. Yet even my denial of narrative had its own narrative insistence. As I was telling another Rosalind recently, *As You Like It* became a part of my own queer story: a tutelary volume in my library of same-sex love, an instrument of lesbian self-making. In that story, chance sets in motion a plotting that chance cannot help but complicate, and it is precisely this play of contingency and purpose—the good fortune of finding such a text and the inescapable narrative torsion in and around it— that returns me again to *As You Like It*.

Notes

I thank Alison Bechdel, Matthew Bell, and Madhavi Menon for their generous comments during the long writing of this short essay.

1. Garber, *Vested Interests*, 72.

2. See Garber, *Coming of Age in Shakespeare*, 140–41; Traub, "The Homoerotics of Shakespearean Comedy," 135–60; idem, "The Renaissance of Lesbianism in Early Modern England," 255–57.

3. *As You Like It*, in Greenblatt et al., *The Norton Shakespeare*, 1.3.115–16. Citations in parentheses are to this edition.

4. Traub, "The Renaissance of Lesbianism in Early Modern England," 256.

5. Granted, love comes quickly to Rosalind, too, and in nearly identical language. In Act I, Celia asks Orlando, "Is it possible, on such a sudden, you should fall into so strong a liking?" (1.3.26–28). For Rosalind, however, "impossible" love is not unmotivated. Before Orlando appears, she has decided to fall in love with a man. When Celia fails to divert her from her father's banishment, Rosalind proposes other distractions ("What think you of falling in love?" [1.2.25]), although her friend is less keen on the idea: "I prithee, do, to make sport withal. But love no man in good earnest" (1.2.27).

6. *Henry V*, in Greenblatt et al., *The Norton Shakespeare*, 3.6.31–32.

7. Shaw, "Fortune and Nature in *As You Like It*," 46. For a contrasting view, in which Fortune is aligned with the natural world against human nature, see Frye, "The Tragedies of Fortune and Nature."

8. Traub, "The Homoerotics of Shakespearean Comedy," 141.

9. See Erzen, *Straight to Jesus*.

10. "Policy Statements," Exodus International. http://exodus.to/content/view/34/61/ (accessed July 1, 2008).

11. Wilson and Rahman, *Born Gay*. The "Born Different" Internet, print, and television campaign ran in the United States in 2006: see the website at http://www.borndifferent.org/home.html (accessed December 9, 2007).

12. Žižek, *The Plague of Fantasies*, 27.

13. Ibid., 30.

14. In *Queer Theory*, Jagose posits "queer" as an indefinable term in constant mutation, 129–31.

15. Johnson, *A World of Difference*, 15.

16. Shakespeare knew the pun well: see *Richard III*, in Greenblatt et al., *The Norton Shakespeare*, 4.4.221.

Cardenio

"Absonant Desire": The Question of *Cardenio*

PHILIP LORENZ

No more than an interesting curiosity.
> —Stephen Greenblatt, et al., eds., *The Norton Shakespeare:*
> *Based on the Oxford Edition*, 1997, 3109

One of the most fascinating and baffling of literary problems.
> —Walter Graham, ed., *Double Falsehood*, 1920, 24.

The Golden Fleece of Literature.
> —Charles Hamilton, *William Shakespeare and John Fletcher—*
> *Cardenio—or—The Second Maiden's Tragedy*, 1994, 1.

As if a master of language airily made believe he wasn't
touching any of it. And by the way, is he doing it on purpose?
Or is he letting a treacherous symptom show an obsession too
strong to be dominated or formalized? A dread that is within
language before it haunts an individual subject?
> —Jacques Derrida, *On Touching—Jean-Luc Nancy*, 60

There is no *Cardenio*. No manuscript survives of a play registered as either
Cardenno or *Cardenna*, based on a character from Cervantes's *Don Quixote*,
that was performed at the court of King James I during the Christmas festivities of 1612–13.[1] What remains are traces of a lost text, records of payments
and performances, adaptations and rewritings, including Lewis Theobald's
Double Falsehood from the eighteenth century, as well as the recent co-produc-
tion by Charles Mee and Stephen Greenblatt.[2] What also remain are competing claims for attribution to a play most scholars now believe was co-written
by Shakespeare and John Fletcher, the continuing pursuit of which has been
likened to a "detective story."[3]

A source, a copy, a reception history—and no play. The situation puts scholars in an odd position, leaving them speculating, reconstructing, and, above all, *desiring* to know what may have been Shakespeare's.[4] The question of *Cardenio* thus not only presents us with a mystery—what Greenblatt reportedly referred to as the "Holy Grail" of Shakespeare's theatrical oeuvre[5]— but also with a question: something itself Adam Phillips calls a "queer species of prediction."[6] To see what we can find out about the missing *Cardenio*, then, we have to perform a double operation, moving backward and forward at once, between copy and source, Theobald and Cervantes, *Double Falsehood* and *Don Quixote*.

Despite—or perhaps because of—its absence, *Cardenio* continues to provoke a wider scholarly desire to discover, beneath *Double Falsehood*'s "layers of rewriting," Shakespeare's hand.[7] In 1994, the handwriting expert Charles Hamilton claimed to have solved the three-century mystery of the "Golden Fleece of Literature." He discovered *The Second Maiden's Tragedy* in the British Museum Library, a play usually attributed to Thomas Middleton but that Hamilton "authenticates" by finding in it the very mark of the Master himself: Shakespeare's handwriting, "identical down to the very dots on the *i*'s with the script in Shakespeare's holograph will."[8] Although the notion of locating individuality in handwriting runs counter to an entire tradition of Renaissance education, which, as Jonathan Goldberg has shown, "does not seem to place any particular value on the spelling of the proper name or on the hand in which it is written," and despite the fact that Hamilton's discoveries have proved dubious at best, the desire to find Shakespeare's hand in the lost *Cardenio* is nevertheless not restricted to the quirky pursuits of "forensic cryptographers."[9]

Given the absence of an actual Shakespeare–Fletcher text, some scholars have turned toward historical context instead, hoping to find there the clue that solves the mystery of the missing *Cardenio*. Arguing that the authorship debate has obstructed a "historicist reading," Richard Wilson situates the play in relation to events surrounding its first known performance—specifically, the death and funeral of King James's son Prince Henry and the precipitate marriage arrangements for his daughter Princess Elizabeth. It is a moment marked by a pronounced and complex duality: divided between Catholic and Protestant factions, mourning and celebration, tragedy and comedy, tears and "unseasonable laughter."[10]

While this social, sexual, and geopolitical context is surely an important part of the mystery of *Cardenio*, it nevertheless cannot bring us fully into contact with the lost play, even by decoding Theobald's text as a veiled key to the royal deaths, marriages, and scandals that presumably constitute its historical moment of 1612–13. *Cardenno*—or *Cardenna*—continues to slip out of our hands. It remains a question and a possibility as much as a solution to Jacobean intrigues and Shakespeare's Catholic politics. Any consideration of the missing play, then, must proceed historically and obliquely at once, taking con-text as at least as much of a problem as a solution.

What we see, in critics such as Hamilton and Wilson, are different responses to the desire to *know* Shakespeare, to touch his hand (in Hamilton's case) or attach his name to history (in Wilson's). As different as their work is methodologically, both Hamilton's cryptography and Wilson's historicism are themselves symptomatic of a wider literary-historical problem the question of *Cardenio* raises. Both wish to fill the gap in our knowledge about the lost play with their own hands.

As a hole in the *body* of the playwright's works, *Cardenio* presents several tantalizing reasons for scholars to imagine a literary history other than the conventional one that situates Shakespeare as a model of universal values, within a nationalist framework with, at best, an eye to his Italian sources. For one, the prospect of a Shakespearean (and Fletcherian) *Cardenio* raises the possibility of a relation and historical collaboration with that other great writer of the period, Miguel de Cervantes, who already is so often associated with Shakespeare by, among other obvious reasons, the peculiar coincidence of their death dates (not days) and whose hand provides Shakespeare and Fletcher with their source. It tempts us to imagine those hands touching, working together, Shakespeare's reshaping of Cervantes's writing for the theater, as Cervantes himself so famously "failed" to do. It makes visible a series of movements and relations, textual as well as sexual, between a critical-historical desire to *authenticate* (to touch) Shakespeare's hand, under the layers of *Double Falsehood*, to find in that hand another that is held, incorporated, and theatricalized by it—*and* a corresponding desire, marked by a movement *away* from the desired object, the textual body, and the sense of *touch*. It is the question of desire itself, insofar as desire has been understood, from Plato through Freud and Derrida, to consist of contradictory movements produced in relation to an inaccessible object.[11] Desire is always at least a question, and a *relation*, if not the question of a relation. In the case of *Cardenio*, the relation is that between desire and knowledge, and the question is why might *Cardenio*'s absence be *queer*? And why might our own relation to this question be a *queer* one?

Two of the thinkers who have taught us the most about the relationship between desire and knowledge are Michel Foucault and Jacques Lacan. But as Tim Dean points out, it is precisely the question of the relationship between desire and knowledge that distinguishes Foucault's understanding of sexuality in terms of an *epistemophilia*, or a desire to know, from Lacan's view of an unconscious governed by a "will *not* to know."[12] If Foucault's *La volonté de savoir* situates sexuality in relation to a will to know, then the ontological truth of sexuality (if one can put it that way) for Lacan is that "being, *by speaking*, enjoys," and, he adds, "*wants to know nothing more about it.*"[13] For Lacan, "there is no sexual relation, insofar as it would be conceptualized."[14] Like subjectivity itself, which in psychoanalytic formulations is nothing if not disharmonious, this relation is less a *thing*, or a knowable concept, than a *movement* away from reason and a certain conceptual sounding out.

This movement itself is at the center of Theobald's tragicomic adaptation *Double Falsehood, or The Distrest Lovers* (1728). Like *Don Quixote*, as we shall see, *Double Falsehood* figures the connection between desire and knowledge as a question of sense and touch (especially by the hand).[15] In the first act of *Double Falsehood*, in a passage many scholars regard as having "a significant Shakespearean ring,"[16] one of the story's two wronged heroines, Violante (Dorotea in *Don Quixote*), attempts to rebuff the sexual advances of the licentious Henriquez (Don Fernando in *Don Quixote*) by appealing to the order of sense:

Home my Lord,
What you can say, is most unseasonable; what sing,
Most absonant and harsh. Nay, your Perfume,
Which I smell hither, cheers not my Sense
Like our Field-violet's Breath.[17]

If Theobald's play is based on a lost Shakespeare-Fletcher original, it also introduces its own complications to the question of *Cardenio*. Despite his enormous vocabulary, Shakespeare never uses the word "absonant."[18] Yet the term is particularly suggestive, not only for thinking about the unwelcome words of the false lover, but also for the wider relations of desire the question of *Cardenio* raises. From the Latin "*absonus*" (*ab* 'off, away from' plus sonant-*em* sounding, 'harsh, inharmonious; discordant or abhorrent to reason and nature'), "absonant" refers, on the one hand, to the harshness, discord, and disharmony of, in this case, the bad Henriquez's words (desire). It names a movement *away from* reason and harmony. Its cognate terms, including "absence," "abstinence," "sonar," and even, with a wave of the hand, the Spanish "*soñar* (to dream),'" all invoke different aspects of the problem concerning the relation between desire and knowledge that the missing play presents. If the literary-historical problem of *Cardenio* is that of its absence and the critical desire for the authorial hand it provokes, then the sexual-theoretical one has to do with the anxiety raised by the possibility that the scholar (especially the Shakespeare scholar), too, may never fully touch the object of his or her desire.

As in *Double Falsehood*, the desires—literary-historical as well as sexual-theoretical—unleashed by our relation to *Cardenio* thus perform a double and somewhat tragicomic operation, moving simultaneously toward and away from fulfillment. If the search for Shakespeare's authorial hand looks backward, like tragedy, toward sources and origins, then it also looks forward, like comedy, toward copies and reproductions. At this point, absonant desire resembles but remains distinct from the desire of attribution, which as the term (from *ad-* 'to' plus *tribuere* 'assign') suggests, refers to a movement toward the assignment of a name—in this case, "Shakespeare." Like Hamilton's "authentication" of Shakespeare's hand, attributive desire moves toward its object, wanting to *know* it, *touch* it, and conceptualize it based on its tangibility. Absonant desire, on the other hand, marks a more contradictory movement that proceeds both toward and away from its object at the same time. That is, if attribution figures the relation between desire and its object as a movement toward touch, motored by a desire to know (Foucault's epistemophilia), then absonant desire more closely resembles Lacan's view of a sexuality that moves away from conceptualization while simultaneously embracing absence or negation.[19] If attribution looks backward toward sources, absonance turns away. If the first movement implies the possibility of *knowing*, the second resists knowledge. The two "models," attribution and absonance, suggest different relations of desire to knowledge, different kinds of *touch*. Containing both movements, the question of *Cardenio* makes visible different manners of figuring our own relation to Shakespeare.

The surviving texts themselves stage the dual movement between attribution and absonance as a series of touches and desires interrupted. If Theobald's adaptation is *Cardenio*'s most tangible remainder, it is also notable for its various changes to the original and at least one glaring absence: there is no "Cardenio" in *Double Falsehood*.[20] Instead, *Double Falsehood* presents the story of Julio, who, like Cardenio, is wronged by a socially superior "friend," Henriquez (Don Fernando in *Don Quixote*), who attempts to steal away his beloved via a forced marriage. In Theobald's rewriting of this scene, *Double Falsehood* notably departs from *Don Quixote*. At the climactic moment where Leonora

(Lucinda in *Don Quixote*) must respond to Henriquez's (Don Fernando's) marriage proposal, Julio bursts in just in time to halt the forced ceremony:

> *Jul.* Hold, *Don Bernard*,
> Mine is the elder Claim.
> *D. Bern.* What are you Sir?
> *Jul.* A Wretch, that's almost lost to his own Knowledge,
> Struck thro' with Injuries.
> *Henr.* Ha! *Julio!*—Hear you,
> Were you not sent on our Command to Court?
> Order'd to wait your fair Dismission thence? . . .
>
> *Jul. Ungen'rous* Lord! The Circumstance of things
> Should stop the Tongue of Question.—You have wrong'd me;
> Wrong'd me so basely, in so dear a Point,
> As stains the cheek of Honour with a blush;
> Cancells the Bonds of Service; bids Allegiance
> Throw to the Wind all high Respects of Birth,
> Title, and Eminence; and, in their Stead,
> Fills up the panting Heart with just Defiance.
> If you have Sense of Shame, or Justice, Lord,
> Forego this bad Intent; or with your Sword
> Answer me like a man, and I shall thank you.[21]

Moving from the law, authority, and questions of priority or primogeniture—("Mine is the elder claim")—through the problem of knowledge, *Double Falsehood* restores a relation between acts and their imagination—figured as a "marriage" in Cervantes's text—that *Don Quixote* "pathologically" crosses.[22] "Almost" lost to his own knowledge," Theobald's *re-touched* Cardenio recovers his senses just in time to (re)act "like a man" and interrupt a bad wedding. Yet when we turn back to the "original" Cardenio, what we see is that answering "like a man" is more closely related to wishes, absences, and failed interruptions than successful acts. Moving from Theobald's play, and its obsession with securing the marital hand (and the violence that attends it), to the authorial hand of the source from which Shakespeare and Fletcher presumably worked, Cervantes's *Cardenio* presents a different relation between desire and touch.

In *Don Quixote*, when the priest asks Lucinda if she will take Don Fernando as her husband, Lucinda falls to the ground in a swoon—not, however, before first answering, "I do (*sí, quiero*)" and thus completing the wedding that is interrupted in *Double Falsehood*. At this point, Cardenio is aroused to the point of madness. In Shelton's translation (which was available to Shakespeare), the passage reads:

> I thrust out all my head and neck out of the tapestry, *and with most attentive ears* and a troubled mind, settled myself to hear what Lucinda answered, expecting by it the sentence of my death or the confirmation of my life. *O, if only I had dared to sally out at that time, and cry with a loud voice,* "O Lucinda! Lucinda! see well what thou doest; consider withal what thou owest me! Behold how thou art mine, and that thou canst not be any others; Note that thy saying of Yea and the end of my life shall be both in one instant. O traitor, Don Fernando, robber of my glory! death of my life! what is this thou pretendest? What wilt thou do? Consider that thou canst not, Christian-like, achieve thine intention, seeing Lucinda is my spouse, and I am her husband." *O foolish man! now that I am absent, and far from the danger, I say what I should have done, and not what I did.*[23]

In his retelling of the tale to Don Quixote and Sancho, Cardenio addresses himself in terms of his own absence, structuring his speech according to a wish logic ("O, *if only*"): "O foolish man! now that I am absent, and far from the danger, I say what I should have done, and not what I did."[24] At the time that Cardenio actually witnesses all this from behind the curtains, however, his response is quite different. Vowing to avenge Don Fernando's and Lucinda's betrayal, he determines to turn his vengeance not on them but, instead, on himself

> and execute in myself the pain which they deserved, *and that perhaps with more rigour* than I would have used toward them if I had slain them at that time, seeing that the sudden death finisheth presently the pain; but that which doth lingeringly torment, kills always, without ending the life.[25]

Because of Cardenio's desire for a more rigorously executed pain and a "lingering torment," Cervantes scholars have seen in him elements of masochism as well as narcissism.[26] As Nicolás Wey-Gómez points out, Cervantes's description of Cardenio's reaction neatly corresponds with Freud's theory of delusional jealousy in which, "in some cases, the jealous male even consciously imagines himself to be in the position of the faithless woman."[27]

In this view, Cardenio both identifies with Don Fernando and imagines himself in the "female" position of the faithless Lucinda to punish himself *as*

Lucinda. If, as Eve Kosofsky Sedgwick, following Roland Barthes, has shown, the "female position" has historically been figured as one of absence, then Cervantes's Cardenio performs a complex repositioning of the object of desire, which ultimately ends up pointing either to himself or to an absence—or to himself *as an absence*.[28]

Returning to our own relation to the missing Shakespearean *Cardenio*, we can see that the scholarly pursuit of the lost play similarly puts "Shakespeare" in the "female position," the place where, in this case, the curiously repositioned "Master" is courted, wooed, and offered an authoritative hand. Prompted by its absence, the scholar's relation to the body, or, rather, to both "bodies"—the body of "Shakespeare" and the "body" of knowledge—becomes an erotic one, filled with a desire to heal the gap with a touch.[29]

Yet for Cervantes's Cardenio, this touch could be nothing other than failure. Cervantes stages the scene of Cardenio's knowledge as an act of repeated disappointment. Cardenio not only does not act; he compulsively repeats and reenacts his failure as a failed scene of mastery and authorship: "O, *if only* . . ." *If only* I had said, *if only* I had acted." It is both the failure of his desire of, and for, Lucinda *and* the failure of desire for the Master. Cardenio queers the very figure or the very fact of desire itself. For him, desire is "absonant" not because it is "delusional" or "irrational," but because it moves toward and away from its object at once, failing and repeating its failure to touch, to act.

In this regard perhaps the most significant re-touch of Theobald s adaptation, which critics have not noticed, has to do with the figure of Don Quixote himself. In the novel, Cardenio and the others all tell their stories to Don Quixote, who responds with his own brand of mimetic desire for authorial control. *Double Falsehood*, by contrast, excises the title character altogether, placing the spectator instead in the "Don Quixote" position. *Double Falsehood* in effect makes Don Quixotes of us all, which is a queer position to be in with regard to desire and control, touch and absence.[30]

What survives of Cardenio, in the form of *Double Falsehood*, then, is the trace of both what is *absent* and, at the same time, curiously resonant with the desire not only to authenticate and to know, but also to *have* a certain *relation* to Shakespeare—to "touch" him in one way. "Absonant desire" is what makes Shakespeare queer—if by that, one means resistant to identification (Hamilton's) and the kind of historical allegorization (Wilson's) that domesticates, conventionalizes, or solves the mystery of our own desire by turning what is not there into an identity. This desire has been part of the "detective story" from the start.[31] Yet isn't desire always *absonant*, insofar as its object's very inaccessibility is also its occasion and its stage? What we see in this movement between attribution and absonance, then, is the queerness of desire itself, its drive to know, and resistance to being sounded out, contained, and / or conceptually captured.

Notes

1. *Cardenio*, in Greenblatt et al., *The Norton Shakespeare*, 3109.

2. Produced in association with the Joseph Papp Public Theater, New York, May 10–June 8, 2008, Loeb Drama Center, Cambridge, Mass.

3. Frazier, *A Babble of Ancestral Voices*, 22. For a summary of the current scholarly consensus, see Metz, *Sources of Four Plays Ascribed to Shakespeare*, 283.

4. See ibid., 283, 289.

5. See Sam Allis, "Dramatic License," *Boston Globe*, May 11, 2008, available online at http://www.boston.com / ae / theater_arts / articles / 2008 / 05 / 11 / dramatic_license / ?page=full (accessed May 14, 2010).

6. Phillips, *Terrors and Experts*, 4.

7. Bate, *Genius of Shakespeare*, 81.

8. Hamilton, *William Shakespeare and John Fletcher*, 2.

9. Goldberg, *Shakespeare's Hand*, 129. On the contingency of the Shakespeare canon, as well as the scholarly desire for the "singular text," see ibid., 105–31, 270. As Irvin Leigh Matus puts it, Hamilton persists "undaunted by the virtually unanimous dismissal of his assertion by Shakespearean scholars": Irvin Leigh Matus, "A Forced Marriage," *Times Literary Supplement*, August 5, 1994, 20.

10. See Wilson, "Unseasonable Laughter."

11. See, e.g., the exchange between Socrates and Agathon in Plato, *The Symposium*, 200a–201d.

12. Dean, "Lacan and Queer Theory," 242.

13. Lacan, "Seminar on the Purloined Letter," 104–5.

14. Ibid., 114.

15. I am much indebted to Jacques Lezra's brilliant reading of this section of *Don Quixote*. "When Cervantes reflects upon what forces or allows stories to *make sense*, he *goes to the hand*: he interrupts and figures interruption, he writes upon and about what the hand bears, what is written on and by it": see Lezra, "Cervantes' Hand," esp. 198–256; emphasis is in the original.

16. Metz, *Sources of Four Plays Ascribed to Shakespeare*, 282.

17. Graham, ed., *Double Flasehood*, 44. Subsequent to writing this essay I learned that Arden is releasing a new edition (2010) of *Double Falsehood*, edited by Brean Hammond.

18. Muir, *Shakespeare as Collaborator*, 158.

19. See Dean, "Lacan and Queer Theory," 242–251.

20. The three main changes *Double Falsehood* makes to *Don Quixote* occur in its

treatment of the marriage ceremony; its insertion of a hearse in Henriquez's abduction of Lucinda from the convent from which she escapes; and, finally, its resolution, which in *Don Quixote* takes place without the lovers' parents but that in *Double Falsehood* heavily depends on the intervention of fathers: see Metz, *Sources of Four Plays Ascribed to Shakespeare*, 287.

21. Graham, ed., *Double Falsehood*, 60.

22. Lezra, "Cervantes' Hand," 249.

23. Shelton, *Don Quixote of the Mancha*, 260–61; emphasis added.

24. Ibid., 260–61.

25. Ibid., 262; emphasis added.

26. "By turning his impotent rage and spite against himself . . . Cardenio may merely demonstrate who has been the real object of his love all along": Quint, *Cervantes' Novel of Modern Times*, 31.

27. "The substitute formula of the jealous male, particularly of the male who suffers from what Freud termed delusional jealousy, is this: '*I* do not love him, *she* loves him!'": Wey-Gómez, "The Jealous and the Curious," 172–73.

28. See Barthes, *A Lover's Discourse*, 13–14, quoted in Sedgwick, *Between Men*, 32.

29. On the emptying and filling of the body as an erotic act, see Plato, *The Symposium*, 186d.

30. If, as Lezra has shown, to be in the "Don Quixote position" means to have an authoritative relation to lost or antiquated texts and their interpretation, on the one hand; then on the other hand it also means to be quite literally left hanging, bound (and shortly) bellowing, in a curiously absonant relation to the object of desire: Lezra, *Unspeakable Subjects*, 187–256.

31. Frazier, *A Babble of Ancestral Voices*, 22.

The Comedy of Errors

In Praise of Error

LYNNE HUFFER

To err: to go astray in thought or belief; be mistaken; be
incorrect.
ME *erren* OF *errer* L *errare*.
queer: strange or odd from a conventional viewpoint; oblique,
cross, adverse.
G *quer*.
— *The Oxford English Dictionary*. 2d ed. 1989

Why did Western culture expel to its extremities the very
thing in which it might just as easily have recognised itself—
where it had in fact recognised itself in an oblique fashion?
—Michel Foucault, "Madness, the Absence of an Oeuvre" (1964),
in *History of Madness*, 541.

Michel Foucault published *History of Madness* in 1961, 367 years after the first
performance of Shakespeare's play *The Comedy of Errors*. Both are early works
in their creators' careers; both gave birth to authors we now recognize as
famous. If Foucault gave us the stuff that became queer theory, we now use
that theory to make Shakespeare queer precisely because of his canonical
status. We do not queer the creations of unknown scribblers. It is the sacred
texts of Authors we are after.

But, famously, what is an Author?

Shakespeare's comedy about misrecognition might serve to remind us of
this Foucauldian cliché: The coherence of identity—and therefore of authorship—is a fragile creation. Thematizing the mismatch of the self with self,
Shakespeare dramatizes identity's rupture from the very first scene of the
play. The comedy opens with the tale of a ship "splitted in the midst."[1] This
"unjust divorce of us" (1.1.104) symbolically repeats a prior double birth that, a

few lines earlier, had produced two sets of "twins both alike" (1.1.55): two masters (the Antipholuses) and two bondsmen (the Dromios). Bought by the masters' father, Egeon, the Dromios join with the Antipholuses, their unity secured as a happy family. But in the second birth of the shipwreck scene, "a mighty rock" (1.1.101) re-splits the twins, along with mother and father, into the initial configuration of fractured doubles. The twins are twinned once again. This doubling of a double nativity scene sets in motion a dizzying series of further doublings, replications, and displacements that seem ready made for queer theory. Indeed, it is tempting to read the play's extravagant display of self-splitting subjects as a premodern Lacanianism gone wild.

Such a psychoanalytic take on the *Comedy*'s mad doublings could certainly fuel at least a few pages of academic prose. But if we follow Foucault, as I propose to do, the play's split subjects may describe something other than a psychoanalytic linguistic structure. As Foucault puts it, alluding to the Lacanian unconscious, the doubling of the subject "is not a question of installing, as people say, another scene."[2]

Lacan's other scene, like the Freudian play from which it borrows, is an ahistorical structure. But for Foucault, as for Shakespeare, time matters. Time is "in debt" (4.2.57) and "a thief too" (4.2.59). "Have you not heard men say," Dromio asks, "that Time comes stealing on by night and day?" (4.2.60). Similarly, Foucault describes the temporality of history as indebted, "fallen time."[3]

If time did not matter, I would be happy to call *The Comedy of Errors* queer. Queerness and the *Comedy* seem made for each other. To err—to deviate, to go astray—is not unlike queering: cross, transverse, oblique. To queer is to err is to be mad, to wander off the path of the straight and narrow. From that perspective, Shakespeare's premodern twins seem to be waiting in the wings, ready to perform on *our* stage in the contemporary drama of queer theory. Indeed, all of the play's characters—from the "horn-mad" (2.1.58) Antipholus, "mad as a buck" (3.1.72), to the "mountain of mad flesh" (4.4.154) that is Dromio's kitchen maid—seem to enact not only mental but also queer bodily forms of error. Living in a world that "sorcerers inhabit" (4.3.11), they "wander in illusions" (4.3.43): "possessed" (4.4.92), "lunatic" (4.3.93), consumed by "mad jealousy" (2.1.116), and universally "past thought of human reason" (5.1.189).

But Foucault's histories—especially *History of Madness*—refract the queer through the prism of time. Foucault's mad split subjects, from the "senseless cargo" of the Renaissance ship of fools to the convulsing hysterics on Charcot's stage,[4] are both doubled and divided not by that a-temporal other scene, the psychoanalytic unconscious, but by the temporal force we call history.

Foucault's historical subjects are not intelligible to us except as ghosts, doubles, and *Doppelgängers* of "a thing that we can no longer apprehend."[5] The cataclysmic event in Foucault's story—the event that produces the split between before and after, between the premodern dialogue of reason and madness and the modern exclusion of madness as mental illness—comes after Shakespeare, in the "strange coup" of the Cartesian cogito in the seventeenth century.[6] René Descartes's *Meditations* mark the advent of an age that splits the mind from the body and captures the self by exiling madness from the reasoning subject and the rationalist moralities of modern humanism.

Descartes taught us well not to go astray, not to misrecognize ourselves or others, as Shakespeare's characters did, for something we are not:

> Unless perhaps I think that I am like some of those mad people whose brains are so impaired by the strong vapour of black bile that they confidently claim to be kings when they are paupers, that they are dressed up in purple when they are naked, that they have an earthenware head, or that they are a totally hollowed-out shell or are made of glass. But those people are insane, and I would seem to be equally insane if I followed their example in any way.[7]

Of course, even Descartes allowed for some mental deviation. "My mind likes to wander and is not yet willing to stay within the boundaries of the truth," Descartes admits in the Second Meditation. "Let it be," he calmly counsels himself, "and allow it once again to be completely unconstrained." But this lack of constraint in the *Meditations* is not the mad errancy of Shakespeare's twins. It is, rather, a step in the protocols of systematic doubt to prepare the self for reason's ultimate triumph when, with Descartes at the end of the *Meditations*, we can declare ourselves "completely free from error."[8]

This seems to leave no room, post-Descartes, for any light-hearted living as a *Comedy of Errors*. Rational moralism is a serious affair, and even laughter in modernity reinforces exclusion. So is the queer the force that thwarts the rigid divisions between truth and error that define our rationalist modern world? As Eve Kosofsky Sedgwick first argued, following Foucault, the regime of knowledge that defines truth and error is central to homophobic oppression in our contemporary age.[9] To jam the machinery of that regime of knowledge is to rupture self-identity and therefore, surely, to challenge a post-Cartesian "monologue by reason *about* madness."[10]

Might we then say that Shakespeare's Renaissance madness dramatizes precisely the ludic, lustful, erotic confusions that queer theory so insistently seeks for healing our own "merciless" time?[11] Does Shakespeare stage an ethics of the self that Foucault will articulate, not only in *Madness* but also, more famously, in the last two volumes of *The History of Sexuality*, as an erotic freeing of the self from itself? At the end of the *Comedy*, Dromio says to Dromio, that "sweet-faced" other of himself, "I see by you I am a sweet-faced youth" (5.1.421). Does queering Shakespeare mean that the modern "I" comes to love his own queer beauty, as Dromio does, in the beautiful face of his Renaissance beloved?

Not if time matters. The queer search for a mirror in the writings of the past must always be interrupted by the temporal fracture that governs the telos of history. Foucault's story of queer madness is the story of a split not within a timeless subject who is simply there waiting to be analyzed, but within a temporal emergence whose before and after produces a subject in time. As an emergence in time, the subject will be fractured not like an analysand but, rather, like a succession of actors, the thespian doubles of Shakespeare's twins that, over the centuries, emerge and disappear as shadows of a past that can never catch up with its own future. Shakespeare's split subjects thus dramatize the non-coincidence of before and after that defines the limits of our historical knowledge and, correspondingly, of the subject itself. Alluding to Foucault's *The Order of Things*, Gilles Deleuze reminds us: "We must take quite literally the idea that man is a face drawn in the sand between two tides: he is a composition appearing only between two others, a classical past that never knew him, and a future that will no longer know him."[12]

The subject we know in the modern era is not the subject of *The Comedy of Errors*. This means that Shakespeare's subject cannot be queer (indeed, cannot be a subject) except as a modern creation that "imposes silence on [the] thing that we can no longer apprehend." In queer theory's contributions to the "great *oeuvre* of the history of the world," the naming of queer subjects "renews . . . at every instant" what Foucault calls "the absence of an *oeuvre*." Queer theory, as a discourse in history, "is only possible against the backdrop of the absence of history."[13]

We queer theorists belong to a world and a time that stole the premodern ship of fools—a *theatrum mundi* "filled with the senseless"[14]—and left in its place regimes of exclusion, confinement, and disciplinary biopower that Foucault calls power-knowledge. Like Foucault, we might lament the loss of Shakespeare's wacky Renaissance world where reason and unreason "are still on speaking terms" and "all that are assembled . . . sympathize . . . error" (5.1.399–400). But because the queer, like madness, "is the constitutive moment of an abolition" in time—"an absolute rupture of the oeuvre"—we can discern only its "outer limit, the line of its collapse."[15] As historical alterity, the queer cannot be made intelligible *for us*.

We who live in this post-cogito time have learned to exclude, manage, or analyze the queer historical "thing that we can no longer apprehend."[16] If the queer names "all that we experience today as limits, or strangeness, or the intolerable," the formation of a field (queer power-knowledge) suggests that the queer "will have joined the serenity of the positive" in a knowledge formation we inherited from nineteenth-century science.[17] For Foucault, that positivist structure culminates in Freud and his descendants: a modern *psyche-logos* we still inhabit.

Still, there is something more to say here than simply what I have said: that time passes, that the past is not the present, and that now we are stuck in a scientistic regime of the psyche that started with Cartesian reason. All that is true, and yet: Time is not linear. As Deleuze reminds us, there is *"an emergence of forces which doubles history."*[18] If time plods on as that course of change we call History, events also repeat themselves, although always with a difference.

So we might still ask of the queer what Foucault asks of madness: "What place could [it] have in becoming?"[19] If Foucault's madness is not the madness of Shakespeare, might we find a place for it not as an object of knowledge but in the form of a renewed dialogue between reason and unreason? In an interview in 1961, Foucault affirmed that "madness can not be found in its raw state" but "only exists in society." Thus, he continued, "in the Renaissance, madness was present on the social horizon as an aesthetic or daily fact; then in the 17th century—starting with confinement—madness experienced a period of silence, exclusion. It lost its function of manifestation, of revelation, that it had during the time of Shakespeare and Cervantes."[20] For example, he adds, "Lady Macbeth begins to tell the truth when she goes mad."[21]

This power of revelation in the Renaissance sounds to me like a celebration of madness. So I want to ask, along with Foucault's interviewer in 1961, "Is madness then worth more than reason?"[22]

And Foucault might respond again, smiling as he did then, *"ever so indulgently"*:

> One of the objections of my dissertation jury [to *History of Madness*] was that I had tried to do a remake of *In Praise of Madness*. No, I meant, however, that madness has only become an object of science to the extent that it has been robbed of its ancient powers. . . . But as far as making an

apology for madness, in and of itself, no. Each culture, after all, has the madness it deserves.[23]

I would like to know: What is the madness *our* culture deserves? And what place might it have in becoming? If madness has lost its powers of revelation, what powers are left to it? What powers beyond biopower are left *to us*?

Perhaps in our age, the queer powers of madness can function only as an assault on the rationalist knowledge that "expel[s] to its extremities the very thing in which it might just as easily have recognised itself" and that queer theory then recognizes "in an oblique fashion."[24] The scene has shifted since Shakespeare's age from an enchanted Ephesus to an academic battle site that pits the purveyors of reason against the feebleminded. As Richard Wolin puts it in a fairly typical recent polemic against the seductions of unreason:

> *Let there be no mistake*: the claims Foucault makes against 'knowledge' are simply astonishing. To characterize knowledge as such . . . as 'malicious,' to argue, presumably in good faith (by what standard, one would rightfully demand to know), that it is 'something murderous, opposed to the happiness of mankind,' is dishonest and, ultimately, anti-intellectual. This claim, gleefully parroted by numerous American acolytes, has in its various versions and forms probably wreaked more intellectual havoc, has been responsible for more pseudo-scholarly *feeblemindedness*, than one could possibly recount.[25]

"Let there be no mistake": No error will be allowed after Descartes, which means, of course, no "feeblemindedness," a term that brings together, as well as any, the collapsing of the mad and the perverted. Would Wolin dare to launch a similar polemic against Shakespeare's *The Comedy of Errors*? Would he write, as he does about Foucault, that the claims Shakespeare makes against knowledge in his staging of madness are simply astonishing?

Probably not. Shakespeare belongs, for the enemies of the feebleminded, to reason's arsenal. Let there be no mistake: He is the canonical Author par excellence, everyone's known object.

Here is my truth: I long for a comedy of errors for our present biopolitical age. I long for a different voice, preferably anonymous, in praise of error and the feebleminded.[26] Perhaps I will hear it as a "masked philosopher" speaking anonymously to an unknown bard whose words hold a power of revelation—not master to master but Dromio to Dromio, the masked philosopher might say to the playwright:

Long after I'm gone, people will entomb me as part of the canon. I dread that future: my consecration as an object. They have been doing it to you, dear Will, for centuries. When I saw the first folio of your plays in a climate-controlled room at the British Library, I thought you looked sad, pinned down under glass like some dead butterfly. I know you and I are different in our madness. Madness in your time is not madness in mine. But there is something we share: our praise of error. In that, my dear Will, "methinks you are my glass." Not a queer glass, exactly, but a different mirror, "both utterly real and utterly unreal."[27] You are my heterotopia, a "sweet-faced youth" who becomes "to the world . . . like a drop of water, that in the ocean seeks another drop . . . Unseen, inquisitive" (1.2.35–36, 38), a shadow cast as a ship of fools disappears over the edge of history's horizon.

Notes

1. *The Comedy of Errors*, in Greenblatt et al., *The Norton Shakespeare*, 1.1.101–3. Citations in parentheses are to this edition.

2. Foucault, *Abnormal*, 15.

3. Idem, *History of Madness*, xxxi.

4. Ibid., 9.

5. Ibid., xxxi.

6. Ibid., 44; trans. modified.

7. Descartes, *Meditations and Other Metaphysical Writings*, 19.

8. Ibid., 27, 70.

9. Sedgwick, *Epistemology of the Closet*.

10. Foucault, *History of Madness*, xxviii.

11. Ibid., xxvii.

12. Deleuze, *Foucault*, 89.

13. Foucault, *History of Madness*, xxxi.

14. Ibid., 11.

15. Ibid., xxviii, 536.

16. Ibid., xxxi.

17. Idem, "Madness, the Absence of an Oeuvre," 541.

18. Deleuze, *Foucault*, 85.

19. Foucault, *The History of Madness*, xxxi.

20. Lotringer, *Foucault Live*, 8–9. Foucault describes Don Quixote as a border figure between the Renaissance episteme of resemblance and the Classical episteme of representation. As such, Don Quixote is both a madman ("the disordered player of the Same and the Other" who, like Descartes's madman, "takes things for what they are not") and "the poet" who "strains his ears to catch that 'other language'" of the Renaissance: Foucault, *The Order of Things*, 49–50.

21. Lotringer, *Foucault Live*, 9.

22. Ibid.

23. Ibid.

24., Foucault, "Madness, the Absence of an Oeuvre," 541.

25. Wolin, *The Seduction of Unreason*, 42; emphasis added.

26. As Walt Whitman put it in the preface to the first edition of *Leaves of Grass*, published in 1855, "Give alms to every one that asks, stand up for the stupid and crazy." Whitman reworked this line in a poem added to subsequent editions of *Leaves of Grass*. "I have given alms to every one that ask'd, stood up for the stupid and crazy": "By Blue Ontario's Shore," in Whitman, *Leaves of Grass*, sec. 14, line 240. I thank Michael Moon for bringing this reference to my attention.

27. "The mirror functions as a heterotopia in the sense that it makes this place I occupy at the moment I look at myself in the glass *both utterly real*, connected with the entire space surrounding it, *and utterly unreal*": Foucault, "Different Spaces," 179; emphasis added.

Coriolanus

"Tell Me Not Wherein I Seem Unnatural": Queer Meditations on *Coriolanus* in the Time of War

JASON EDWARDS

A Covering My Ass(es) Preface, or, Why It is Important to Know Your Arses, Plural, from Your Elbows

It is the fall of 1990. I have just turned nineteen. My father is somewhere in the Gulf, and I am having my first paranoia-inducing, degree-level encounter with Shakespeare, my supervisor having set a sonnet as a practical criticism exercise. At the group tutorial a week later, I am not the only person who, precociously proud of his legally themed reading, is mortified to discover that he remained oblivious to the poem's apparently obvious erotic subtext regarding the differences between vaginal and anal sex. More than one of us, it seems, was just not getting it. It is all a bit humiliating.

Looking back now, I can understand what happened that day with more compassion. My militaristic, very late-Victorian, Section 28–era boarding-school education had not exactly emphasized Shakespeare's queerer tendencies.[1] And two summers later, I came across Eve Kosofsky Sedgwick for the first time in person, then posing the still unimaginable-to-me question of whether the rectum was straight, and whose broader queer oeuvre subsequently opened me up conceptually and corporeally, finger's breadth by finger's breadth, in ways I could not have foreseen.[2] Sadly, however, Sedgwick came too late for the potential couple *manqué* that was Shakespeare and me, since by this point I completely avoided the Bard, another painful more or less "ex."

Our final autobiographical tableau takes place decades later. It is the wet summer of 2007. Having become a professional queer-theory art historian and an early-stage initiate in the pedagogies of Buddhism and object-relations psychoanalysis, I receive an unexpected e-mail encouraging me to be part of this project. Flattered by the suggestion that *Shakesqueer*'s "fabulousness" will depend, at least in part, on my presence in the text; reassured that I was not expected to be an expert on Shakespeare and his commentators; and delighted potentially to be working alongside the other, more obviously qualified and worldly contributors, I agree to write a chapter by return of post. On the advice of Victoria Coulson, who believes the play will be right up my alley, I opt for *Coriolanus*, sight unseen, and having been gaily allocated the text by Madhavi, I get down to reading it the following day, knowing little about it except the old joke Victoria told me about New Historicists being the scholars who put the anus back into *Coriolanus*, the knickers back into *Titus Andronicus*.[3]

Keeping that potential comic insight in mind, I read the text repeatedly over the coming weeks and, boy, is the experience reparative—an excitingly insistent, regularly repeated, ultimately relaxing reminder, should any be needed, of Shakespeare's endlessly queer generativity, of that occasionally reassuring interpretive experience of not always having to read outside the canon, against the grain. Indeed, rather than feeling viscerally ashamed of my own ungainly adolescent flat-footedness, as I had in 1990, I find myself, in my mid-thirties, like Danaë, deliciously embarrassed at the hermeneutic anal and erotic riches Shakespeare showers down on and in me.

I differentiate anal and erotic here, not because I seek, repressively, to diminish the idea or experience of anal eroticism, which could not be more intellectually, imaginatively, and corporeally germane to me. I do so, rather, because where Jonathan Goldberg and his queer-theory peers were understandably keen in 1993–94, in the context of the related pandemics of AIDS and homophobia, to return anal eroticism to center stage, as a differently queer thinker writing in the midst of the "war on terror," and having been deeply affected by Sedgwick's itself-queer move away from the topics of anal eroticism and the hermeneutics of suspicion toward Buddhist, Kleinian, and other strategies of reparation, I wanted to consider *Coriolanus* in the light of another paradigm of mostly pleasurable intersubjective anality that came to prominence in 1993: the object-relations theorist and analyst Michael Eigen's account of a potentially more meditative and respiratory, although still relaxed and open, sphincter. Thus, if Eigen is fully cognizant of the Kleinian topos of fecal spoiling, because the asshole also permits "greater ambiguity than either oral or genital models with reference to self-other differentiation," as well as to apparent opposites such as active–passive, top–bottom, and in–out, then his oeuvre seeks to open a potentially utopian understanding of the anus's liberatory possibilities from the travails of identity within those varieties of Buddhism in which meditation gurus recommend that we try the experience of calmly "breathing from" our anuses.[4] It is this meditative, respiratory, and potentially utopian intersubjective understanding of anality that I want to bring in relation to *Coriolanus* and to which I return in the final part of this essay.

Putting (Ano)the(r) Anus Back into *Coriolanus*

In the midst of the apparently never-ending war on terror, how might we understand *Coriolanus* to be a queer play? What, in the text's phraseology, is "clean kam"—and, in the Arden edition's accompanying gloss "absolutely perverse"—about it and what is depressingly familiar?[5] Why might we want to put the anus back into both Shakespeare's tragedy and our own?

During the summers of 2007 and 2008—the two periods I was writing this essay—the "coalition forces" of the United Kingdom and the United States continued relentlessly with their murderous foreign policies in Afghanistan and Iraq, policies accompanied by increasing clampdowns on civil liberties at home. (I say "the United Kingdom and the United States" although, as a nominally British citizen, these actions were not performed with my democratic consent.) Unable to keep these quotidian acts of terrorism from my mind, much about *Coriolanus* felt uncannily familiar. After all, the play features a supposedly democratic, ruling political and military elite with a fearful contempt for the people; a government whose budgets suffer the populace to famish while their storehouses are "crammed with grain"; and leaders who "repeal any unwholesome act established against the rich" while providing "more piercing statutes [to] chain up and restrain the poor" (1.1.80–84). The text also reveals the surprising longevity of the parasitic, self-serving, democracy-damaging spin classes in the form of the tribunes of the people and depicts the political and personal tragedy awaiting those, like its eponymous hero, who seek to remain outside of the cultures of spin. In addition, and like much contemporary "coalition" rhetoric, *Coriolanus* features the poignant image of significant numbers of people imagined to have "no more soul nor fitness for the world [than] camels in their war" (2.1.247–49).

The play also depicts a fast-changing political scene, not unlike our own, in which leaders such as Coriolanus and Aufidius—former enemies who become unexpected allies, and vice versa—and an army in which Coriolanus, like many contemporary generals, has to humiliate and terrorize his subordinates into action. Finally, both the text and its eponymous hero pose as central, still pressing questions: whether generals make good democratic political leaders, and what the tragic costs are for populations "bred in broils" (3.2.81), whether victims or victors "i' th' wars" (3.1.317). Reading the text in 2007–2008, I also understood why Bertolt Brecht was so fond of *Coriolanus*. After all, centuries before *Mother Courage*, Shakespeare had already made explicit the use of war as social Darwinism—a "means to vent / Our musty superfluity" (1.1.224–25)—and a way to quiet a people perceived to be mutinous or sexually licentious. For example, Aufidius's cynical servant observes that peace is a "getter of more bastard children [than] war's a destroyer of men" (4.5.231–32).

However, seen from another, Sedgwickian angle, the play resonates as queer in a number of ways. For instance, *Coriolanus* is explicit about the male homosocial desire that binds military corpuses together and its tragic costs. Thus, Cominius wants to "clip" Coriolanus in "arms as sound" as when he first "woo'd" his wife, when their "nuptial day" was nearly done and "tapers burned to bedward" (1.6.29–32). Aufidius similarly longs to meet Coriolanus "beard to beard," admits that Coriolanus is "mine, or I am his," and wants to "potch"—which is to say, jab or poke—"at him some way" (1.10.11–15). In his famous soliloquy, meanwhile, Aufidius hopes to "twine" his arms about Coriolanus's body and to "contest" as "hot and nobly" with his "love" for Coriolanus as "ever in ambitious strength" as he contended against Coriolanus's "valour." Echoing Cominius's sentiments, on seeing Coriolanus in person, Aufidius acknowledges that his "rapt heart . . . more dances" than when he first his "wedded mistress saw." Aufidius also recalls that "nightly since" he and Coriolanus last fought, he has dreamed of "encounters 'twixt thyself and me, . . . down together" in his sleep, "unbuckling helms" and "fisting each other's throat," only to wake "half dead with nothing" (4.5.107–27).[6] Such intense homosociability, of course, requires scapegoats of various kinds, most obviously in the form of women. Thus, in a too evident triangulation, Coriolanus promises his men that they will beat their enemies to their wives (1.4.41), while Aufidius repeatedly attacks Coriolanus's womenfolk for coming between the two men and "unmanning" Coriolanus.

The play is perhaps also queer, however, in a second, less familiar and more recent way, in that it displaces from center stage the notion of *sexual identity*.[7] *Coriolanus* does so, first, by imagining desire as only one gravitational pull within a much richer, queerer, ever altering early modern constellation of, in the text's richly diverse terms, pleasures, activities, personal qualities, dispositions, wits, wills, virtues, inclinations, humors, souls and

spirits, plots, issues, ideas, merits, spices, hopes and memories, natures, projects, designations, reasons, affects, more or less cardinal or deadly sins, and
aches, pains, and diseases, environmental and congenital, passing and fatal.
The intensely homosocial play also challenges models of intersubjectivity
imagined to be ideally and primarily predicated on the genital desire of one
person for another because it almost entirely fails to mention the genitals or
ass, even though it refers to the body more than two hundred and fifty times,
on almost every page, and in spite of its Petrarchan pleasure in pinpointing
nearly fifty separate body parts. On the head, these include the hair, pate,
forehead, face, cheeks, mouth, nose, palate, lips, tongue, teeth, chin, and
beard; within the internal organs, the spleen, womb, lungs, stomach, and
brain; on the extremities, the head, neck, hands, fingers, thumbs, knees,
thighs, heels, and feet; and within the trunk, the veins, bosom, breast, shoulder, back, and navel.

Indeed, despite the play's dominant phallic economy of armored bodies akin
to a sculptural "mould" (3.2.103) or inhuman bell, "engine," or "battery" (5.4.19–
21), a metaphoric penis seems to emerge only once in the form of the possible
allusion to how Aufidius, hearing of Coriolanus's banishment, "thrusts forth"
into the world his "previous inshell'd" horns, a slimy and curiously divided
invertebrate image that is anything but monolithic or erectile-phallic (4.6.43–
45). The buttocks and anus, meanwhile, appear just three times. Meninius mentions them twice in short succession: first, in the bawdy metaphoric form of his
being better acquainted with the "buttock of the night" than the "forehead of
the morning." Then, in an extended metaphor satirizing the tribunals' responsiveness to the whims of the populace, he caricatures Brutus and Velutus as
being characteristically "pinched with the colic," making "faces like mummers"
and "roaring for a chamber-pot," into which they dismiss each "controversy
bleeding, the more entangled" by their hearing (2.1.51–52, 74–77). Volumnia,
meanwhile, later describes how Coriolanus risks "tearing / His country's
bowels out" (5.3.102–3).

Aside from these brief, crucial images of painful anal voiding and violation, the apparent absence of the anus in Coriolanus is, perhaps, particularly
surprising both because of the famous pun on the second part of the eponymous hero's name and because of the text's obsession with other bodily
orifices, with Shakespeare referring to the mouth and nose nearly fifty times
and to open wounds of various descriptions nearly forty times. None of these
are, however, "lov'd" as a "most dear particular," in the play's terms (5.1.2–3).
Instead, they are the sources, almost without exception, of bad odor, wound-

ing, suffering, infection, infantilization, and emasculation, which, in turn, stand as the play's tragic models for sociability.

Thus, in the text's models of almost exclusively agonistic, contra- rather than inter-, subjectivity, intimacy is imagined as assault or defense, in the imagery of fight or Machiavellian flattery: of following your enemy into a "fiery gulf" or "flatter[ing] him in a bower" (3.2.91–92). The stench of the people, and particularly their reeking breath, is also proverbial in the play, apparently representing democratic exchange (see, e.g., 2.1.234, 5.1.31–32). Through the agency of the wind, and therefore presumably up the mouth and nose, sociable bodies are also repeatedly infected, more or less metaphorically, with measles (3.1.77), typhus (4.1.13), cankers (4.5.92), carbuncles (1.4.55), and boils and plagues (1.4.31), while in battle and elsewhere bodies are additionally imagined or experienced as being broken "ope" like "locks" and "peck[ed]" at by birds (3.1.137–38); "bruis'd" (4.1.47), "mark[ed]" (3.3.111), "flay'd," "stretch'd," and "scratche[d] with briars" (3.3.52); and "cut i' th' middle" by other people (4.5.203). Coriolanus, meanwhile, has a nose that bleeds (1.9.47) and some "two-dozen odd" (2.3.127), "unaching" (2.2.148) ear-like wounds and scars that "smart" again to "hear themselves remember'd" (1.9.28–29) and that he would sooner reopen than "hear say how" he got them (2.2.69–70).

If this image cluster suggests that listening and talking to other people, like smelling and fighting them, are potentially unpleasant, scarring, and painful, if not fatal, activities, Meninius encourages the people to turn their eyes toward the napes of their necks so that their "proud, violent, testy" inner "magistrates" can make an "interior survey" of their "good selves" (2.1.38–39), suggesting further, painful bodily openings than those individuals are commonly born with. The people also fear that if Coriolanus shows them his mouth-like wounds and tells them of his deeds, they will be forced to put their "tongues into those wounds, and speak for them" (2.2.6–8), an image that further suggests the potentially wounding nature of seeing, hearing, and speaking, as well as the distasteful character of kissing, rimming, and cunnilingus.

In the play, sores are also "tent[ed]" open (3.1.234)—that is, treated with a roll of linen to stop them from scabbing or healing over—and bodies and spaces are forcefully opened up and out in various other painful ways. For instance, bodies are "grief-shot" with "unkindness" (5.1.44), and Coriolanus can apparently "tear with thunder the wide cheeks o' th' air" and charge his "sulphur with a bolt" that "rive[s] an oak" (5.3.150–53). Finally, rather than being conjoined or affiliated more pleasurably or profitably, sociability in the play is figured as an emasculating, infantilizing return to a paranoid, night-marish, pre-Oedipal dependence on an apparently all-powerful, potentially murderous mother (4.6.67, 76). Thus, Meninius refers to an "unnatural dam [who] should now eat up her own" (3.1.290–91); Volumnia describes herself as Coriolanus's "wife," "son," "senators," and "nobles" in one (3.2.65); and the eponymous hero admits that no man in the world is more bound to his mother. Seeing himself being persuaded by his family, meanwhile, reduces Aufidius's erstwhile martial ideal to a mummy's "boy of tears" (5.6.100), "small as a eunuch," or to a "virgin voice" that "lull[s]" babies "asleep" (3.2.114–15).

Now, *Coriolanus* is, of course, a tragedy. Its hero gets a fatal and martial, not a happy, marital ending, whether with Virgilia or Aufidius. But because all of our bodies are inextricably in "the weal" (2.3.179), and because one cannot, as the play insists, be entirely the author of one's self and know "no other kin" (5.3.36–37), we might want to use *Coriolanus* as an opportunity to explore its unspoken, imagined, comic opposite—an alternative, possible, queerly uto-pian model of sociability to the phobic, militaristic, homosexually panicked one still experienced by many of Shakespeare's audience. With that in mind, in concluding I want to bring back into relation to the play Eigen's seductive account of the anus. After all, if the text only explicitly imagines the anus within the terms of the potentially painful, reeking, wounding, humiliating, or even fatal scene of defecating, pre-potty training, anal rape, and battlefield disemboweling, we might need to be reminded that, in less tragic contexts than its own and our own, orifices, like the asshole, might open up to or soften around some potentially more queer pleasures. These might include the idea that bodies of both genders can be pleasurably penetrated with things other than painful infections or fatal weapons and the possibly produc-tive sense of being uncertain around, rather than scared or scarred by—or sphincterally defended against—the blurred conceptual and experiential lines between inhalation and exhalation, mastery and passivity, topping and bot-toming, adult and infant; curiosity, shame, repudiation, and desire; and in the midst of the rhythmic alternations of up and down, taking in, expelling out.

If more of us could develop a taste for these queer possibilities, if more of us were, unlike Coriolanus, able to understand part–part and part–whole relations in desirable, democratic, intersubjective terms, rather than as dis-gusting or the inevitably degenerative interplay of mutually "monstrous members" (2.3.13) in "mutinies and revolts" (3.1.124), there might be the hope of a happier ending. We would have to risk opening ourselves up in spite of the fear, reality, and proximity of infection, impingement, bombardment, and the often toxic nourishment provided by other people. We would have to risk being "infant-like" again in not "doing much alone" (2.1.36–37). We would have to seek alternatives to only "com[ing] off . . . aidless" or "strik[ing]" each other with fists, bombs, or "like a planet" (2.2.112–14).[8] And rather than trying to defend and deny them as a "kind of nothing," we would have to be prepared to keep as open questions: What are the "nature of our seats" (3.1.135)? "What are . . . our o[rif]fices" (3.1.34)?

How do yours feel right now? How might they feel different in the future? And what range of politically and pleasurably productive things might they be used for? After all, there are other options than the coalition's bleakly reductive and extremist alternatives of bombing and terrified introspection, of Coriolanus's "Think upon me?" or "Hang 'em!" (2.3.58); a queerer global democracy and ecology in which an individual, general, prime minister, pope, president, or species might not have to "depopulate" a "city" to "be every man himself" (3.1.262–63). There may be a more difficult, fragile, democratic, humane, pleasurably soft, better lubricated, open-ended, and less bloody way. We might be able to keep things open even if the "end of it" is "unknown to the beginning" (3.2.325–26). We might imagine a global ecology based on the sense, hope, and knowledge that "I shall be lov'd" even, and perhaps especially, where and "when I am lack'd" (4.1.15).

"Tell me not," then, that "I seem unnatural" but, rather, that I breathe out deeply and relax (5.3.83–84). Inhale and exhale, slowly, with your asshole and other orifices in mind. Think, feel, and imagine what, who, and where you might next want to let in, out, go, or off the hook. Keep breathing, feeling, softening, and listening. Birds and women are singing.

Notes

Dedication: For Victoria Coulson.

1. Enacted on May 24, 1988, Section 28 of the Local Government Act stated that local authorities could not "intentionally promote homosexuality," "publish material with the intention of promoting homosexuality," or "promote the teaching in any maintained school of the acceptability of homosexuality as a pretended family relationship." The result, in fear of losing state funding, was that many educators became anxious about teaching texts, having discussions with students, or facilitating groups that portrayed gay relationships as anything other than abnormal. Section 28 was repealed on June 21, 2000, in Scotland and in November, 2003, in the rest of the United Kingdom.

2. Sedgwick was not the only queer theorist then dilating on the question of anal eroticism. Following from the earlier (ahem) *anus mirabilis* of 1987, which witnessed the publication of Bersani, "Is the Rectum a Grave?," and Sedgwick, "A Poem Is Being Written," the early to mid-1990s saw the publication of Edelman, *Homographesis*, and Sedgwick, *Tendencies*, and the republication of Hocquenghem, *Homosexual Desire*. Perhaps most relevant here, however, was Goldberg, "The Anus in *Coriolanus*," first given at the Shakespeare Association in 1994, to which I shall happily return.

3. It is hard to know who is ultimately responsible for this joke, since, as Goldberg reveals, if Shakespeare owed to Plutarch the name of his titular hero, Burke, *Language as Symbolic Action*, certainly recognized that Coriolanus's name was "tonally suggestive" in the "context of Freudian theories of the fecal nature of invective." By 1993, Burke had been joined by Paster, *The Body Embarrassed*, which defiantly asserted that it was time to "stop protecting Shakespeare from anal contamination" and to "open up the question of anal erotics" in the Bard's oeuvre. It was, however, perhaps Goldberg himself who, like Titania, most delighted in the love of ass and articulated most deliciously the "'rightness' of the anus in *Coriolanus*" when he suggested that the asshole was a *"productive* site for the character of the play" outside of the "Freudian trajectories of shame and sublimation": Goldberg, "The Anus in *Coriolanus*," 260–61, 264–65, 268.

4. Eigen, *The Electrified Tightrope*, 194–95 and *passim*.

5. Brockbank, *Coriolanus*, 3.1.301. Citations in parentheses are to this edition.

6. According to Goldberg, Aufidius's "scene of fisting," like many moments in the play in which "oral and anal exist in a substitutive relationship," must be "read as a displacement of anal sex to the mouth": Goldberg, "The Anus in *Coriolanus*," 263, 267.

7. For a range of positions in relation to this potential displacement, see the special "After Sex" issue of *South Atlantic Quarterly* (Summer 2007).

8. In making these particular, intersubjective suggestions, I am not, however, seeking to demonize the potentially liberatory queer and trans- pleasures and possibilities of Internet subjectivities and eroticisms, which are again very germane to me. I was put in mind of these by Goldberg's earlier suggestion that Coriolanus's "career of attempted self-authorship represents a desire to become a machine, to 'live' in some realm that is not the biological" and by his concluding argument that the play perhaps "imagines an 'inhuman' sexuality that would not be subject to betrayal," a dream that "may be Shakespeare's too": Goldberg, "The Anus in *Coriolanus*," 268–69.

desire vomit emptiness:
Cymbeline's Marriage Time

AMANDA BERRY

Sharing their will to discipline the Bard into speaking "true English," Shakespeare's early-eighteenth-century editors exchanged numerous informational, opinionated, and at times erotic letters, an example of which, from 1729, was written by Lewis Theobald to William Warburton:

> I agree with you, Cymbeline is a most corrupt play, and I have a great number of corrections upon it: you say, you have 30 stable ones in store. I wish earnestly I could be favoured with them, if possible by the next post. . . . You bring back to my mind the times of a love-correspondence; and the expectations of every fresh letter from you is the joy of a mistress to me.[1]

Even the formidable Samuel Johnson was unable to separate the queer from the Bard. His sense of the corruption in *Cymbeline* was more broadly understood, and more intensely felt, expressed in lieu of a Romantic interlocutor with whom to savor it. Indeed, Dr. Johnson's response to *Cymbeline* enacts a rhetorical and affective flourish worthy of the paranoid revulsion—and concomitant astute analysis—performed by Jerry Falwell when he called Tinkywinky the gay Teletubby:

> To remark the folly of the fiction, the absurdity of the conduct, the confusion of the names, and manners of different times, and the impossibility of the events in any system of life, were to waste criticism upon unresisting imbecility, upon faults too evident for detection, and too gross for aggravation.[2]

Folly, the confusion of names, faults flaunted openly, and waste! One begins to wonder if it might ever be possible to *un*-queer Shakespeare.

British Romantic readers tried. Against the eighteenth-century reception of *Cymbeline* as a problem play among problem plays, the Romantics ennobled *Cymbeline*, singling it out as their favorite among Shakespearean drama. John Keats, who looked "upon fine phrases," including Shakespeare's, "as a lover,"[3] borrowed heavily from *Cymbeline* in his own poetry, and William Hazlitt praised the "tender gloom" that "o'erspreads the whole,"[4] deeming *Cymbeline* Shakespeare's only true romance. Specifically, Romantic readers exalted the play by identifying and canonizing its main character, Imogen, as the consummate female heroine. For Hazlitt, Imogen figured the perfect woman: beautiful, "tender and artless," delightfully incredulous in response to her husband's plot to murder her, and later full of pardon both for her murderous husband and for the play's intended villain, who attempts to rape her and ruin her marriage. Hazlitt forgot to mention that Imogen also stands by her father after he exiles her husband, likes to read, and spends a disproportionate amount of time sleeping. If there is a prescriptive misreading in Romantic celebrations of the play, it is not the interpretation of Imogen as a paragon of normative femininity, but the resolute insistence that *Cymbeline* is centrally a play about *her*.

As is evident, the play and the flawless Imogen never achieved the emphatic popularity Romantic readers championed. Much later, Swinburne squelched the possibility of the play's heteronormative reception most decidedly. He loved the play, and in doing so reinvested it with a distinctly queer, somewhat NAMBLA, sensibility: "The play of plays, which is 'Cymbeline,' remains alone to receive the last salute of all my love I think, as far as I can tell, I may say I have always loved this one beyond all other children of Shakespeare."[5]

To agree with Dr. Johnson, *Cymbeline* is a staggeringly excessive play: its chaotic self-stuffing effects an uncontainable atmosphere queered by its own insatiable appetite for excess, filled with multiple plot lines, countless referential flashpoints, time-and-space networks that defy science fiction, and the layered inclusion of every possible generic storytelling mode. Moving swiftly through affective registers, *Cymbeline* careers from tragedy to comedy to tragedy and back again. Self-consciously, campily even, the play presents characters who announce their motivations and plans through liberal use of expository asides that produce competing revelatory whispers from character to reader. The chaos of the drama is also attended, not unreasonably, by a growing worry in its reader that the various strands of plot may refuse tying together, that the Bard, in this version of the late plays / last plays / Romances, may not be able to pull himself off. Plot trajectories reproduce to such a state of entangled multiplicity that, in the penultimate scene, the Roman god Jupiter descends from the sky, throws a thunderbolt, and gives the play, and its ostensible hero Posthumous, a coded message that signals the reassurance that he, and the drama, will escape their predicament intact. Jupiter's moment, which is itself as confusing as it may be consoling, prefigures the way in which the mythic Bard, like Imogen, will wake up and close the play, in a dizzying final act stuffed with drastic, blunt plot remedies, an ending described by George Bernard Shaw, who rewrote it, as "an unpardonable stupidity."[6]

In other ways, too, as with the hyperbolic intervention of Jupiter, *Cymbeline* deploys its excesses self-consciously. After the hero Posthumous sails to Italy, his wife, Imogen, imagines watching herself watching the departure of her husband. The wicked queen fools the doctor who fools her in return and so himself avoids being fooled by the plot from *Romeo and Juliet* by giving her a sleeping potion rather than poison. The kidnapped sons of the king live happily in a cave with a kind woodsman they know as their father, wander the pastures, and pontificate to each other about both their innate simplicity and their shared will to learn new things, a desire that inexplicably makes them feel like "prisoned birds."[7] Well before the play's midpoint, after the dramatic action has split across an ocean and has already produced a secret marriage, a wicked stepmother, a wannabe-heir, a denunciation and exile, a symbolic rape, an oath of deadly revenge, and the procurement of fake poison, an ambassador from Rome at the beginning of Act 3 politely tells the British king (Cymbeline) that the two countries are now enemies: "Receive it from me, then: war and confusion" (3.1.70). The text confirms that the promise of war as an additional plot concern is more chaos for the play itself, a promise underscored later by King Cymbeline, who announces: "We fear not / What from Italy can annoy us, but / We grieve at chances here" (4.4.41–43).

King Cymbeline has been grieving from the start of the play. In fact, grieving—the "tender gloom" Hazlitt perceived in the play—is the standard mode of operation in *Cymbeline*. The main source of the play's grief is a marriage, the union between the king's daughter, Imogen, and her husband, Posthumous. Their marriage, which occurs before the play begins, is the anterior fact that drives the play and characterizes the state of being that organizes *Cymbeline*'s atmospheric queer present. The remarkable first eighty lines of the play, spoken by two anonymous gentlemen, explain the prehistory of the drama that situates its both doleful and wacky present. The pertinent fact of the marriage is announced immediately: King Cymbeline's daughter, Imogen, has recently married a "poor but worthy" man. As a result, "All is outward sorrow." The remainder of the otherwise unwritten prequel reports a slew of losses and hardships that, although not all caused directly by the wedding, proceed under its sign. King Cymbeline, "touched at very heart," has banished the husband, Posthumous, and imprisoned the wife, Imogen. In addition, King Cymbeline's first wife, Imogen's mother, is dead, and his two sons, Imogen's long-lost brothers, have been missing for twenty years. Gutted of nearly all its rightful inhabitants, the domestic landscape of *Cymbeline* has been replenished by dynamic and spectacular double substitutes. The desolate space of loss is also the receptacle for mimetic excesses that fail to console: King Cymbeline's toxic new wife and her clownish, ineffectual son Cloten who, at his mother's insistence, means to procure Imogen and therefore the kingdom.

From first report, and then throughout the play, there is something curious about the existential status of the Imogen–Posthumous marriage. In announcing it, First Gentleman says: "She's wedded, / her husband banished, she imprisoned" (1.1.8–9). Discursively, the monolithic states of being fall like dominoes: The wedding precedes, and presumably causes, banishment for husband and imprisonment for wife. But when the report of the prequel ends, and the play's present action begins, the banished Posthumous, still in Britain, leisurely readies for his departure, and the imprisoned Imogen roams freely at court. Soon, he leaves for Italy and she returns alone to her room, but the gap in time between the past act of banishment and the present not-consequences of it characterizes the work of marriage time throughout *Cymbeline*, a temporality produced between performative utterance and the state of being that utterance presumably confers. Imogen and Posthumous are married to the degree that news of their wedding spurs a series of undoings in the play; at the same time, their marriage fails to signify as a contract or a stipulation. The play's characters simultaneously feel the effects of the marriage and proceed as though it is a trauma that has not yet happened and can be avoided. Marriage in *Cymbeline* guarantees none of the expected effects of marriage at the level of either the plot or the drama's structure. Indeed, the actions set into effect by Imogen's and Posthumous's wedding—a series of profound misrecognitions—fail to operate according to any of the normative guarantees conferred by the state of marriage. For a moment in time—the moment during which *Cymbeline* exists—marriage as yet has no authority to marry. To suggest that *Cymbeline* produces a purposive engagement with the ideology of marriage is simultaneously to recognize that the marriage in the play is not merely troubled by the father / king's disapproval, but that marriage itself is troubling thematically, architectonically, and temporally. Marriage in *Cymbeline* produces loss (not reproduction), separation (not union), frustration (not bliss), and, importantly, behavior that presumably corresponds to a state of *un-marriage*. In other words, marriage engenders a queer time inside which actions fail to enact the conferral of the very meanings for which they exist.

After the fact of his banishment, and after having promised complete fidelity to his wife, during which he beseeches her to stop crying lest he be "suspected of more tenderness / Than doth become a man" (1.1.108–9), Posthumous goes to Italy. In an unaccountably perverse act of attempting to cuckold himself, he immediately accepts a wager from the villain Iachimo. Posthumous risks his wife and the diamond ring that represents her in a bet that Iachimo will not succeed in seducing Imogen. Posthumous, having learned nothing from *Othello*, seals the wager with Iachimo through "lawful counsel" and a "covenant" (1.4.173–75), an authorial contract, and an utterative performance that far outweighs and outdoes his marriage bond. Iachimo, like his homonymous familiar, Iago, plans to convince Posthumous that Imogen has been unfaithful and to win the bet regardless of whether he seduces Imogen or not. Rebuffed by Imogen, Iachimo hides in her bedroom overnight inside some luggage and stages a symbolic seduction by looking at her while she sleeps, seeing "On her left breast / A mole cinque-spotted" (2.2.41–42), then stealing the bracelet Posthumous gave her as a parting "manacle of love" (1.1.143). When he returns to Italy, Iachimo reports to Posthumous, produces the evidentiary bracelet, and describes Imogen's mole, which he relocates from "on her left breast" to "under her breast," convincing Posthumous that his wife has sexually betrayed him. Until the wager begins, Posthumous is described as a noble man worthy of Imogen's "referral," but from beginning to end, the gambling scheme confirms that he is as unsuitable as the king believes him to be, though for entirely different reasons. In a spectacular rendering of logic between men, Posthumous berates Imogen and all women:

> Is there no way for men to be, but women
> Must be half-workers? We are all bastards,
> And that most venerable man which I
> Did call my father was I know not where
> When I was stamped. Some coiner with his tools
> Made me a counterfeit; yet my mother seemed
> The Dian of that time; so doth my wife
> The nonpareil of this. O, vengeance, vengeance!
> Me of my lawful pleasure she restrained
> And prayed me oft forebearance. (2.5.1–10)

Posthumous seems to be having some difficulties coming to terms with his marriage, which is not unreasonable in the context of *Cymbeline* and is never unreasonable in Italy, from which so much perversion has been exported to Britain. The logic here that completes his mercurial conversion from noble, faithful husband to misogynistic, murderous husband is worth considering. The trouble for Posthumous, and for all bastards and counterfeits, is not that fathers, who are anyway interchangeable, go missing, but that those fathers and all men need women as "half-workers" to be, and do, anything: get born, have sex, reproduce. Women are evil in multiple and unsurprisingly contra-dictory ways. Women are sexual creatures who hunt for men, fuck them, and then reproduce bastards and counterfeits. Women, at the same time that they are unabashed whores, are also prudes: They refuse to have sex with the very men to whom they are married and should rightfully give "lawful pleasures."

At the simplest informational level, Posthumous's confession that he has never had sex with Imogen sheds light on Iachimo's shifting description of the location of Imogen's mole. Whether Iachimo has seen Imogen's mole and whether Imogen possesses an identifying mole—or, indeed, any literal body at all—are beside the point of Iachimo's rhetorical trickery. The mere invoca-tion of a female breast between Iachimo and Posthumous confers the pri-macy of their aleatory bond against the marriage between Posthumous and Imogen. Women are literally impossible. In *Cymbeline*, under the sign of the queerness of marriage, this is one way in which "homosexual" happens. Post-humous's relationship with Iachimo is determined, and intensified, by the same marriage it works to undermine.

Posthumous's relationship to the villain Iachimo rivals his relationship to his clownish rival, Cloten. A fair description of the relationship between Im-ogen's husband and her ridiculous suitor results from the tension between Imogen, who has already chosen—and married—Posthumous, and her step-mother, who wants Imogen to marry Cloten. Imogen likens Cloten to a put-tock, a lowly grasping bird of prey, compared with her husband, whom she deems an eagle. In return, the queen describes Posthumous as "a thing that leans" (1.5.67), anticipating Freud's rendering of narcissistic desire propped up on another person, signaling immaturity. When Posthumous sails for Italy, Cloten remains at court, celebrating a fleeting encounter with Posthumous during which he believes he has scared Posthumous. Cloten heaps praise upon himself for his bravery while his attendants laugh and berate him in asides that undermine his masculinity and, at the same time, confirm his (homo)sexual aggression: "His steel was in debt; it went o'th' backside of town" (1.2.12–13).

After Posthumous has cuckolded himself and decried the impossibility of women, Imogen's "half-work"—which signifies both her part in her marriage and the ambiguous halfness of her marriage itself—leads to her profound misrecognition of her husband's body. A merciless accumulation of plot twists results in Imogen's waking from the effects of the sleeping potion to find a headless dead body laid out next to her. What she beholds is not her dead husband but Cloten's decapitated corpse dressed in Posthumous's clothing. Tragicomically, the play lingers on Imogen's encounter with the body:

> A headless man? The garments of Posthumous?
> I know the shape of 's leg. This is his hand,
> His foot Mercurial, his Martial thigh,
> The brawns of Hercules; but his jovial face—
> Murder in heaven! How? 'Tis gone. . . .
>
> O Posthumous, alas,
> Where is thy head? Where's that? Aye me, where's that? (4.2.381–94)

The careful procedures by which Imogen identifies the corpse weigh heavily against the error they produce. She figuratively dismembers the body, traversing a disordered map from leg to hand to foot to thigh to an allusive generalization of his build, "the brawns of Hercules" (4.2.384). Though she comically mourns the loss of the head, Posthumous's face is not required to satisfy her self-assured recognition. Here Posthumous's words ring true: In *Cymbeline*, marriage fails to confer unique identities; all men are counterfeits and, as counterfeits, interchangeable. Marriage time subvents both a mutual illegibility between husband and wife and a significant corporeal bond between husband and villain (Iachimo) and husband and clown (Cloten).

Part of the title of this essay, "desire vomit emptiness," means to propose a generative, mobile heuristic taken directly from *Cymbeline* in lines spoken to Imogen by the villain Iachimo during his attempt to seduce her. Iachimo says, "Sluttery to such neat excellence opposed / Should make desire vomit emptiness, / Not so allured to feed" (1.6.49–51). While Iachimo offers the words as a lecherous backhanded compliment, and Imogen pretends not to hear them, they signify the alterity of normative forms of desire in *Cymbeline*, which most consistently generates unexpected relational effects detrimental to, and running interference in and around, any heteronormative marriage ideal. "Desire vomit emptiness," then, is an encapsulation of the process through which *Cymbeline* figures marriage time as a queer and queering temporality; acts of desire produce nothing other than, or outside, themselves. Vomiting is vomiting without the production of vomit, just as marrying is marrying without the production of marriage. *Cymbeline* begins with the same marriage with which it ends, and queer marriage time draws to an end at the end of the play when King Cymbeline speaks the magical incantation that closes the space between performative utterance and effect: "son-in-law."

At the same time, *Cymbeline*'s queer reception time seems never to end. Despite his florid refusal to "waste criticism" on *Cymbeline*, Dr. Johnson was drawn to the phrase "vomit emptiness." It troubled him so much that he edited—which is to say rewrote—it, inserting a comma between the words "vomit" and "emptiness:" "Sluttery to such excellence opposed / Should make desire vomit, emptiness / Not so allured to feed."[8] Johnson opposed "vomit emptiness" and therefore grammatically occluded the otherwise indecent personification by cutting the phrase in half. Never one to let well enough alone, he could not resist further explaining his emendation and, in the process, transforming his sense of the vulgar bodily trope of dry heaving with which he wanted to dispense into the vulgarly queer bodily trope of either interrupted or premature ejaculation with which he leaves *Cymbeline*: "This is not ill-conceived. But I think my own explanation right. *To vomit emptiness*, is in the language of poetry, to feel the convulsions of eructation without plenitude."[9] In Dr. Johnson's world, vomiting produces vomit, as playwrighting produces plays and marrying produces marriages. But in the world of *Cymbeline*, marriage time, rather than containing or resolving queer possibility, staves off its own desultory result for as long, and as largely and as wildly, as it can.

Notes

1. Moulton, *The Library of Literary Criticism of English and American Authors*, 536.
2. Ibid., 538.
3. Rollins, *The Letters of John Keats 1814–1821*, 139–40.
4. Moulton, *The Library of Literary Criticism of English and American Authors*, 537.
5. Ibid. NAMBLA is the acronym for the North American Man / Boy Love Association.
6. Shaw, *Two Plays by Bernard Shaw*, 116.
7. Mowat and Werstine, *Cymbeline*, 3.3.47. Citations in parentheses refer to this edition.
8. Eccles, *Cymbeline: A Tragedy*, 62.
9. Ibid.

Hamlet's Wounded Name

LEE EDELMAN

When Hamlet, in his best-known speech (whose first six words survive among literature's most recognized quotations), confronts the requirement of the Symbolic order that everything, as Jacques Lacan writes,"must be *or* not be in a particular place," he does so by engaging what troubles a universe organized by "or": the excess inherent in the signifier that disorients the *order* it ordains.[1] Less a philosopher, then, than the manifestation of the "supra-cognitive" surplus an anti-philosophy would propound[2]—a personification of too-much-ness beyond the grasp of philosophy's reason—Hamlet cannot stop fingering the various stops of rhetoric's flute, neither for nor even *in* death, as if he were seized by some ruthless machine of which he catches a glimpse when he writes of "this machine [that] is to him" in a letter to Ophelia.[3] His final, virtually posthumous words (after acknowledging, "I am dead" [5.2.322]), address themselves to the paradox of what remains in the wake of those words. "The rest is silence" (5.2.347), he declares at the end, thus imprinting himself on that silence, identifying it as *Hamlet*'s silence and making it his remainder. The rest of the world, what rests in the world, is now what rests of him, for the whole world speaks his silence, and in that silence he rests, he remains. Horatio, himself enjoined to survive to tell his prince's story, immediately tries to limit the sense of "rest" to final repose, the better to forestall the prospect of Hamlet's spectral circulation: "Good night, sweet Prince, / And flights of angels sing thee to thy rest" (5.2.348–49). But this lyric vision of death as rest ignores life's restless remnant (though it has haunted the play from the outset), denies the "something after death" (3.1.78), the excess beyond death's "bourn" (3.1.79) that scorns the "or" whose border determines life or death: "to be, or not to be" (3.1.56).

The specters that cross that border (and thus make it spectral, too) frequent the work of Jacques Derrida throughout his long career. Not two full months before his death, in an interview published first in *Le Monde* and then as *Apprendre à vivre enfin*, Derrida reflected on the place of survival and spectrality in his thought:

> I have always been interested in this thematic of survival, whose meaning
> is not something that adds itself to living and to dying. It is originary: life *is*
> survival. To survive in the current sense means to continue to live, but also
> to live *after* death. With regard to translation, Benjamin underlines the
> distinction between *überleben*, on the one hand, to survive death as a book
> can survive the death of its author or a child the death of its parents, and,
> on the other hand, *fortleben*, *living on*, to continue to live. All the concepts
> that have helped me to work, notably those of the trace and the spectral,
> were bound up with "to survive" (*survivre*) as a structural and rigorously
> originary dimension. It doesn't derive from either to live or to die.[4]

Neither supplementary to living or dying nor derived from one or from the
other, survival precedes and determines both, according to Derrida, unsettling from the outset every attempt to distinguish between the two. As primal
trace, as originary writing, survival survives by precipitating the differential
*or*der it refuses. It occasions and requires a conceptual geography where everything "must be *or* not be," such that even non-being would inhabit a place,
would assume the signifiable form that turns it into a one. In short, survival
determines the Symbolic as the *or*der *of* survival, giving rise, at the moment
when immortality and "a sense of posterity" conjoin, to what I called in *No
Future* reproductive futurism.[5]

Consider in this regard Derrida's account of Benjamin's two senses of
survival. If *überleben* pertains to the traces that are left in the wake of someone's death and *fortleben* to whatever successfully eludes the grip of death in
the first place, then Derrida's chosen examples of the former may point to an
opening that troubles the border he cites them to define. The book that
survives an author's death, whether it names that author or not, allows its
readers, by virtue of narrative, genre, rhetoric, and style, to generate an account of the author, if not of the person, who produced it. *Hamlet* tells more
about the author called "Shakespeare" than Shakespeare does about Hamlet.
But if Hamnet, Shakespeare's biological child, had lived instead of the fictional character who survives, some have said, in his place, he would have
little to tell about the author of the plays who, as "Shakespeare," left Shakespeare behind. The child whom its *parents* leave behind is not, like a book, the
product of a system we can figure through an author's name, but rather a

living organism endowed with such agency as that entails, shaped by and carrying the genetic materials in which its parents *live on.*[6] At the crossing of *überleben* and *fortleben*, then, those genetic materials, which precipitate the child, constitute the site where residual trace and the thing itself coincide, where the very inscription of what is dead throbs with life and life takes its cue from a code, calling into question the distinction between living after and living on.[7]

Because such genetic "living on" can offer by itself no assurance of survival in and as cultural memory, the child as biological survivor (*fortleben*) needs an educational supplement to make its survival similar to that of a book (*überleben*), a supplement that renders the biological organism a support for the ghostly imperative that Hamlet's father intones: "Remember me" (1.5.91). Internalizing that injunction, Hamlet depicts his brain as a book that bears his father's words, thus realizing a mode of survival that makes of the prince the specter's specter, much as Hamlet will make of the world, when he finally leaves it, his specter in turn:

> Remember thee?
> Yea, from the table of my memory
> I'll wipe away all trivial fond records,
> All saws out of books, all forms, all pressures past
> That youth and observation copied there,
> And thy commandment all alone shall live
> Within the book and volume of my brain,
> Unmixed with baser matter. (1.5.95–102)

Taking writing as the figure of knowledge—and so, by extension, of education—Hamlet associates its materiality with "trivial . . . records" that he disdains, with the lifeless copies of "pressures past" that his hand can "wipe away." By contrast, "the book and volume of [his] brain" will hold only his father's "commandment," free of the material excrescence of writing, "unmixed with baser matter" such as writing might convey. If Hamlet enacts what Jonathan Goldberg aptly describes as a "scene of writing," he seems to know, as Goldberg puts it, that for "memory to be supplemented, it must also be supplanted." The "trivial" or merely mechanical supplement to memory's vital self-presence destroys its spontaneous agency, leaving it just as empty as writing itself and as easily "wipe[d] away."

But Hamlet nonetheless avows that his father's words "shall live" in his brain, enjoying the vital presence denied to mere records or representations. The paternal commandment must escape, in his mind, the triviality pertaining to the copy and endure instead as a pressure *not* past, a pressure like that of a drive that does not remind so much as insist. Hamlet in consequence becomes a sort of appendage to this living book, the material substrate of a survival that lives, in more than one sense, in his place. Goldberg evokes this perfectly when he notes that "Hamlet voices his father's text."[8] Child and book exchange properties once the son becomes a repository to house the father's word: the former acquires the status of memorial, while the latter attains to the presence of life. And survival depends on preserving, as an archive anticipating a future that the act of anticipation ironically prevents, an *or*der kept in motion through persistent repetition. "Order is a kind of compulsion to repeat," Freud remarks in *Civilization and Its Discontents*, a normalizing practice of "regularization" that determines "when, where and how a thing shall be done, so that in every similar circumstance one is spared hesitation and indecision."[9] One is spared, that is, an encounter with life by the automatic, machinelike response that obviates "hesitation and indecision." If these words seem resonant in relation to *Hamlet*, that resonance may express the impossible tension in the fantasy of the living book, of the spontaneously present archive, the fantasy that underwrites the *or*der of survival through reproductive futurism. That tension, moreover, inheres in every affirmation of the *or*der of survival as something inherently resistant to, or in conflict with, the repetition compulsion as the agency of the death drive.

Hamlet, however, speaking on behalf of a futurism he virtually initiates, denies the *universal* incompatibility of the archive with "anamnesis as spontaneous, alive and internal," to quote from Derrida.[10] While admitting that the hypomnemic supplement, the externalized remainder essential to the archive as site of consignation, can indeed be "wipe[d] away," Hamlet evokes his brain as a "book" in which his father's commandment, fully present, both lives on and lives after. Equally invested in the violence constitutive of cultural transmission, Derrida, especially in *Archive Fever*, posits the archive as memorializing the "spontaneous" memory it annihilates, but he shares with Hamlet a messianic belief that the archive can nonetheless quiver with life through its opening onto the future.

Although the archive's *or*der of memory always pledges itself to this future, Derrida perceives within that archive (and within that future, as well) something at odds with real openness to the unknown of the "a-venir." With regard to the commandment to remember, he writes:

It orders to promise, but it orders repetition, and first of all self-repetition, self-confirmation in a *yes, yes*. If repetition is thus inscribed at the heart of the future to come, one must also import there, *in the same stroke*, the death drive, the violence of forgetting, . . . in short, the possibility of putting to death the very thing, whatever its name, which *carries the law in its tradition*.[11]

The "yes" that Derrida refers to here acknowledges survival as the privilege of the One by affirming submission to the archive's conflation of the future with repetition. Like Hamlet's thrice-repeated response to his father's "Remember me"—"Ay," "Yea," and "Yes, by heaven" (1.5.96, 98, 104)—the *"yes, yes"* cited by Derrida strategically performs, in the name of remembrance, a forgetting of the Lacanian Thing and so a negation, in affirmation's guise, of the object-less act of remembrance silently entrusted to the death drive alone. "Yes, yes" affirms, in the name of the future, an identity—precisely that of the One, of the archive as consignation and as law—that obliges the future to conform to the past, to affirm itself as survival within an economy of reserve. The archive, after all, like the specter—and so like the ghost of the dead King Hamlet—evinces that reserve whose survival produces the future *as its own*. However much it presents itself, then, as life in its infinite openness to something yet to come, this future, like the "yes" by which archivization would affirm it, performs a compulsory return to the One of the law and of the father. Futurism, the horizon of the human in the world to which *Hamlet* might be said to give birth, emerges as proleptic behindsight: the father's insistent penetration from behind, from the back, of what thus gets conceived as the future in an act of self-affirmation by which the Child, like Hamlet, gets screwed.

But *Hamlet* remains a question posed to this concept of the human whose normative shape it nevertheless imposes on us all. Let us call it, then, a "questionable shape" (1.4.43), this human that emerges from the putative inwardness of Hamlet's habitual questions, his restless returns to the site of non-knowledge where obsession, perhaps even madness, becomes the template for human consciousness and the human becomes the ghost of a query—"to be, or not to be"—between whose terms it finds itself poised and by which it finds itself poisoned. The venom in its ears is "or," which bestows on Hamlet's most famous oration a ration of Horatian rationality that aims, by means of scholastic dispute, to establish a ground to stand on through the logical parsing and limitation of terms that distinguishes one from another. But in Hamlet's world, in Elsinore, there is something else in "or": a fetishization of difference to which the prince of puns is heir, a primal irrationality lodged at the origin of "or," something as fully *unheimlich* as Hamlet, who is blind to it in himself but spots it at once in the gravedigger's reasoning, that mode of perverse literality so clearly the double of Hamlet's own. "How absolute the knave is! We must speak by the card, or equivocation will undo us" (5.1.128–29), Hamlet exclaims.

The "or" of categorical thinking aims to forestall equivocation by installing instead the logic that distinguishes Hyperion from a satyr, preserving the *or*der of nature from threats of monstrosity and confusion, from "uncle-father" and "aunt-mother" (2.2.366–67), from incestuous ecstasy and corruption, from the lust that occasions everything "carnal, bloody, and unnatural" (5.2.370). To affirm this order of "or" that keeps what is from being undone, the dead king's spirit walks by night, enlisting his son as a soldier pledged to defend the sexual norm: "Let not the royal bed of Denmark be / A couch for luxury and damned incest" (1.5.82–83) is the injunction he imparts. And Hamlet understands full well, like any moral zealot, that he is charged to treat more than the symptom. He must wipe out the very disease. "The time is out of joint. O cursèd spite, / That ever I was born to set it right!" (1.5.88–89). And "set it right" means nothing less for Hamlet than "set it straight," since "out of joint," as the Oxford English Dictionary notes, while referring to this line, bespeaks a state "disordered, perverted, out of order, disorganized," like the "unweeded garden / That grows to seed" (1.2.35–36) in an earlier soliloquy, or like Hamlet himself when Ophelia, making use of a horticultural metaphor after Hamlet has called her a whore, paints him as the "feature and form of blown youth, / Blasted with ecstasy" (3.1.160).

Made by paternal command a sort of disease to assail the diseased—"like the hectic in my blood he rages" (4.3.65), Claudius muses to himself—Hamlet may be the "mould of form" (3.1.153) for the modern human being but only insofar as the human, like Hamlet, is a monster of normativity, incapable, for all the self-consciousness that we, as his scions, grant him, of seeing how much he gets off on the luxury of his anti-luxurious discourse. Repelled not just by "country matters" (3.2.111) but also by matter as such, he looks to master matter by riding a raging torrent of words through which his passion —out of joint, displaced, made spiritual or intellectual—comes in hot and steady bursts condemning passion's slaves. Laced with a rancid misogyny, Hamlet's outbursts vilify sex with a prurient intensity. He links the unkemptness of "grow[ing] to seed," the moment of reproductive possibility, to the condition of being possessed, taken over, by things that are "rank and gross"

(1.2.136). Even this, however, seems anodyne when compared with his acid precision in evoking what he calls "compulsive ardour" (3.4.87): "to live / In the rank sweat of an enseamèd bed / Stewed in corruption, honeying and making love / Over the nasty sty" (3.4. 92–95).

Disdaining the putrid carrion as which he recognizes flesh, Hamlet dismisses life and sex as equally excremental. "We fat ourselves for maggots" (4.3.22–23), he notes and traces the course of Alexander's dust to find "it stopping a bunghole" (5.1.192). He may pray for sublimation, "O that this too too sullied flesh might melt, / Thaw, and resolve itself into a dew" (1.2.129–30), and imagine himself as standing apart from any earthly appetite—"I eat the air" (3.2.90–91), he jests—but his mind is drawn to dirt and stench with what we must call a vengeance. His revulsion in the face of embodiment, redoubled at the very thought of sex, leads him beyond the paternal charge to root out "damned incest," even to the point of decrying conception and demanding "no more marriage" (3.1.147). Fanning the flames of Hamlet's loathing for all that "flesh is heir to" (3.1.63), the ghost, to which Hamlet is heir, as well, leaves Hamlet, as son, asunder, torn between the enforcement of sexual norms to repair what is out of joint and the extravagance of his passion for enforcing those norms, which exceeds all normative bounds. By being too much his father's child, he would have no children be fathered; defending too well the institution of marriage, he would have no marriage at all.

Stricken by this excess of filial passion for the reassertion of norms, Hamlet is truly "too much in the sun" (1.2.67), or too much his *father's* son, for his brief against breeding not to breed, as he claims the sun does, maggots—the maggots, I mean, that taint his mind as it feasts on decay and corruption, leaving Hamlet as much out of joint as the time, as perverse as his father's restless ghost that refutes by its presence the order of "or" it returns from the grave to defend, mocking the very distinction pronounced in "to be, or not to be." The inwardness, construed as psychic depth, for which Hamlet provides the model, responds therefore to the impossible task he confronts as his father's child: to live from the outset an afterlife as ambassador of the dead without, in the process, becoming merely an ambassador of death.

But Hamlet learns that success in the one means failure in the other. In accepting the duty to set time right, he keeps it out of joint, becoming thereby the prototype of the modern subject as Child whose efforts to make present a ghostly past in the space of an infinite future produce instead the emergent order of hetero-temporal repetition. If the Child thus effectively *keeps* time out of joint, how can Hamlet hope to put time to rights without putting an end to the Child? "Why would'st thou be a breeder of sinners?" (3.1.121–22), Hamlet inquires of a startled Ophelia, who seems to intuit that breeding as such is what Hamlet seeks to prevent. And he does so because he knows full well, as a subject in the form of the Child, that breeders of life prevent life, too—and literally, by coming before. "Remember me" is the fatal text the past inscribes on the Child, preventing the Child from living a life *not* out of joint with time. This out-of-jointedness positions Hamlet between two versions of generational succession: an older model of heroic, because unfathered, subjectivity (whose final exemplar may be Fortinbras) and that of the Child commanded by the father to preserve this older model but unable, because *subservient* to the force of that command, ever to fulfill it. No wonder the question of Hamlet's age exerts such fascination; something keeps him from ever escaping the role of his father's son.

In Hamlet, Shakespeare names that something and bequeaths it to us all. Beckoned to follow his father's ghost but held back by Marcellus and Horatio, Hamlet cries out: "By heaven, I'll make a ghost of him that lets me!" (1.4.85). Playing on the double sense of "let"—to permit or allow, on the one hand, and to hinder or prevent, on the other—these words free Hamlet to follow his father, the "ghost of him that lets me"; the ghost of him who gave life and preempts it; the ghost who confirms, in more ways than one, that time is out of joint; the ghost whose example dooms Hamlet at once to be *and* not to be— that is, to be and not to be "Hamlet," the name by which he is prevented from being what it gives him leave to be. But that, of course, is what Hamlet means, perhaps even literally: "[I] am let." It is also what normativity means in the world we inherit from Hamlet: to be let, constrained, or prevented by the power that gives us permission to be, even while it incites, perversely, our passion to constrain what appears as perverse. "Let not the royal bed of Denmark be / A couch for luxury and damned incest," the ghost enjoins his son. And by way of "let not," Hamlet is let and left in the knot of his name, which he, though left without children, must leave to the world he leaves behind, affirming a hetero-temporal subjectivity so deeply in debt to the dead that it needs to invent the future to pay off what is mortgaged to the past.

When Horatio therefore proposes to die like a Roman by his dying friend's side, Hamlet, assuming his father's place—"I am dead," he twice exclaims— prevents him by imposing, as his father did, the obligation to memory, the obligation to which Hamlet has yielded his life and by which he still hopes to survive: "O God, Horatio, what a wounded name, / Things standing thus unknown, shall live behind me! / If thou didst ever hold me in thy heart, /

Absent thee from felicity awhile, / And in this harsh world draw thy breath in pain, / To tell my story" (5.2.333–38). Hamlet, the name of an unhealed wound for the sake of which blood must be let, cannot let the lack of a name-sake leave his wounded name drenched in blood. Charged with its restoration, Horatio, too, must "live behind," a phrase that perfectly captures the temporal order we inherit from *Hamlet*. He must live, that is, in perpetual arrears, in the indistinction of future and past, in the endless out-of-jointedness that marks the time of the Child and fuels the machinery of the death drive at work in the secularized messianicity of reproductive futurism. If the order of "or" impels that machine and conjures its spectral future in the name of survival, of life against death, then the question of *Hamlet* may not be Hamlet's "to be, or not to be," but rather, how to resist survival's archive, its consignation, by becoming what lets the future be and by being what lets the future.

Notes

This essay is excerpted from "Against Survival," forthcoming as a chapter in my book in progress, *Bad Education*.

1. Lacan, "Seminar on the Purloined Letter," 39.

2. "Supra-cognitive" is the term Alain Badiou applies to anti-philosophy in his account of Giles Deleuze, cited in Hallward, *Badiou*, 20.

3. *Hamlet*, 2.2.124, in Harbage, *William Shakespeare*, 933–74. All citations in parentheses are to this edition.

4. Derrida, *Apprendre à vivre enfin*, 26.

5. See Lefort, "The Death of Immortality?," 267, cited in Copjec, *Imagine There's No Woman*, 20.

6. Elsewhere Derrida notes that "one can sign neither a child nor a work": Derrida and Ferraris, *A Taste for the Secret*, 29.

7. See Turner, *Shakespeare's Double Helix*, for a compelling reading of literary and genetic codes in the context of Shakespeare's *A Midsummer Night's Dream*.

8. Goldberg, *Shakespeare's Hand*, 45.

9. Freud, "Civilization and Its Discontents," 21:93.

10. Derrida, *Archive Fever*, 11.

11. Ibid., 79.

Henry IV, Part 1

When Harry Met Harry

MATT BELL

Henry IV, Part 1 does nothing so well as to solicit our appreciation of its capaciousness. Shakespeare's text surveys an expansive dramatic terrain that contains settings from court to battlefield, characters from robber to royal, and language from commonest prose to rarest poetry. The play's dazzling variety has earned the admiration of most recent commentators, one of whom succinctly observes, "The range of the play is as wide as the early modern world itself."[1] Indeed, its production of such an impression of comprehensive inclusion remains its most striking *coup de théâtre*, the mark of its distinction among other, more narrow-minded examples of Elizabethan drama; the play inspires the fantasy that nothing exists outside its limitless reach, and it invites in return a suitably universal applause.

In characterizing *Henry IV, Part 1* this way, I mean to emphasize the ambition it shares with the field of scholarship that we have lately learned to call either LGBT studies or, as I will refer to it here, queer studies. A term that means to encompass innumerable projects across the disciplines, queer studies houses not only its brainy predecessor, queer theory, but also, potentially, every other scholarly endeavor we might construe as relevant to marginalized sexuality, now or in the future. The historical shift in name from queer theory to queer studies tells a story of geometric progression that leaves no minor plot or character out. The emergence of queer studies as a more or less agreed-upon name for the field surely follows the liberal-humanist doctrine of the various civil-rights movements that seek continually to broaden the category of personhood. Queer studies seems to aspire in kind to make room for all people and all projects.[2]

For both Shakespeare's play and queer studies, however, the movement toward expanded capacity entails the exclusion of a certain sameness. A representative instance of this exclusion within queer studies appears in the special issue of the *South Atlantic Quarterly* called "After Sex? On Writing since Queer

Theory" (2007). In her contribution to the issue, while endorsing a "proliferation of projects" in the field, Ann Cvetkovich remarks, "It has been extremely important for queer studies to move across historical and geographic boundaries, away from the recent history of gay and lesbian identities and communities in the Western metropolis."[3] I take Cvetkovich's comment to be indicative of a common understanding in queer studies of an academic and ethical responsibility to extend the field's domain beyond established limits. Insofar as it expresses a goal of historical, humanist, and geographical expansion by rejecting ostensibly well-known times, people, and territories, however, the statement exemplifies how an intolerable familiarity motivates this rhetoric of expansion. Even as the sentiment affirms an additive conception of queer studies, it expresses the field's objective to dislodge the familiar in the terms of a zero-sum game. Changing the subject of queer studies keeps us from indulging the bad habit of pursuing the same thing.

For the sake of queer scholarship, then, no small part of the value of revisiting *Henry IV, Part 1*—one of the central texts in the oeuvre of the most canonical author in the English language—will be to test the validity of undertaking a project that some critics would regard as yet another iteration of the same thing. Such critics would want to point out not only that this play has enjoyed the privilege of a reverent critical tradition but also that at least one brilliant and thoroughgoing queer analysis of it has already appeared in print.[4] Why should the queer critic bother to come back to this play, and why now? Returning to *Henry IV, Part 1* affords the opportunity to scrutinize its false front of capaciousness and, in turn, to think through the problems inherent in adopting capaciousness as an ideal either for the local practices of individual queer scholars or for the conceptualization of queer studies as an academic institution. In my reading, the play's effort to conscript us within an ideology of pluralist expansion, to earn our assent for its program of inclusion, allegorizes the will to expand queer studies exactly insofar as this effort veils and displaces the play's uneasy fascination with a pair of characters whose sameness grounds its action.

After all, Shakespeare's history play, which is based on chronicles of the Battle of Shrewsbury in 1403, accomplishes its greatest dramatic effect through the invention of a fictitious climactic meeting between two men called Harry: Prince Henry Monmouth, also known as Hal, who is firstborn son to King Henry IV and heir apparent, and Henry Percy, the rebel leader commonly identified as "Hotspur." *Henry IV, Part 1* represents the battle as a struggle between competing visions of England's future—one of a nation unified by its monarchy; one of a land divided by regional factions—and Shakespeare personifies this polarity in the two Harrys, characterizing the prince as the force of unification and Hotspur as the force of division. The play's repeated insistence on their nominal identity, however, belies this narrative difference. Increasingly, as the play moves forward, its language suggests instead a mirroring relationship between Hal and Hotspur, most emphatically in a couplet voiced by Hotspur himself on the eve of battle: "Harry to Harry shall, hot horse to horse, / Meet and ne'er part till one drop down a corse."[5] For the present discussion, the resonance of these lines lies in their conjunction of non-differentiation between the two men with the assertion of their mortal competition. Though Hotspur's couplet distinguishes two Harrys syntactically ("Harry to Harry"), we cannot discern which Harry is which, and just at this moment, when the distinction between Harry and Harry founders in nominal sameness, Hotspur declares their relationship one of mutual exclusion. Perhaps because they are identified in duplicative, redundant terms here, a second Harry becomes not merely superfluous but more exactly, in the economy of Hostpur's thinking, intolerable.

For plot coherence, Hotspur's couplet constitutes a narrative promise that Shakespeare fulfills when, in the penultimate scene of Act 5, Hotspur and Prince Hal at last appear together onstage. Because the play has foreshadowed but long delayed this moment, it arrives as the most thrilling of what Marjorie Garber calls the play's "uncanny" structural effects.[6] If we draw on Freud's classic gloss of "the uncanny" as a disquieting "recurrence of the same thing,"[7] Garber's suggestion about this play's form becomes all the more pertinent in this context: the play's production of sameness, both in character and in narrative design, signifies most forcefully not the pleasing consonance or unity that critics like to ascribe to it, but the revelation of eerily familiar content. In Freud's discussion of the uncanny, returning to "the same thing" represents no deliberate act of self-protection within the insular safety of convention but the startling disclosure of a purposeful repetition that operates against our will. Of course, we should not construe as uncanny all instances of foreshadowing or of promise keeping. In Shakespeare's play, though, when the foreshadowed event takes place, when Harry meets Harry, it produces an uncanny effect because the narrative repetition itself doubles the nominal identity of the two men. In other words, the play's fulfillment of Hotspur's promise transcribes the mimetic stasis of sameness, through repetition, into a temporal register, mirroring its doubled characters in a doubled narrative form. Designating the climactic encounter in *Henry IV, Part 1* as *uncanny* involves a certain critical conceit, of course, but this conceit allows the connection of this play to other literary forms, such as Gothic fiction, through the conflicts of which critics have more traditionally elaborated Freud's thought. One pertinent example, Edgar Allan Poe's short story "William Wilson," pairs its title character with an antagonist who bears exactly the same name, and the story ends when the narrator William Wilson murders his alter ego William Wilson.[8]

The play's uncanny historiography, more exactly, confronts us with repressed sameness, and I call the climactic moments of this play uncanny to sharpen our awareness of the play's negation of the specific sameness that we call homosexuality. We should not take the negation of homosexuality to mean Shakespeare's failure to entertain it conceptually. On the contrary, that negation brings homosexuality into relief as a relentless shadow of the play's action. It should not go without saying, moreover, that *Henry IV, Part 1* also makes ample room for readings that would attend to positive representations of same-sex desire, readings that might take up Falstaff's affection for his "sweet wag," the prince (e.g., 1.2.16), or Hotspur's homophobic account of having been "pestered with a popinjay" (1.3.29–69). My subject, by contrast, is not the presence in the play of love between men but the trace of repression that occasions the uncanny shiver we might feel when Harry meets Harry, the shadowy counterpart of love that I prefer to call *love's likeness*. Among its meanings, this term registers at once the commonplace image of homosexuality as insubstantial artifice and the force that that image disavows, the substantial dread signified by repressed homosexuality's return. From the perspective of heteronormativity, homosexuality figures love's *mere* likeness, a false derivative or funhouse mirror image of real (heterosexual) love; as a haunting recurrence of the same thing, however, the homosexual uncannily insists on love's fundamental likeness, reminding us emphatically that all love is predicated on likeness.[9] I proffer the term "love's likeness" in the context of *Henry IV, Part 1* to capture the powerful burlesque of heterosexuality embodied in the two Harrys: their pairing is simultaneously an impossible absurdity and a creepy disruption. Although we cannot designate the relationship between Hal and Hotspur homosexual in any positive sense, this relationship crystallizes suggestively around the negation of love. In this light, the violence promised in Hotspur's fantasy of their engagement nonetheless fails to obscure the nearly matrimonial aspect of their mutual devotion: "Harry to Harry shall

. . . meet and ne'er part till one drop down a corse." The couplet speaks not love, but love's likeness. The very negation of love invokes it ironically, preventing us from properly distinguishing love from its negative image.

The tropology of same-sex desire between Harry and Harry, the figurative activity that I call love's likeness, presents not simply an inversion of normative heterosexuality but also, and more important for the play, a negative image of the play's urgent narrative movement toward capaciousness. The play ultimately yields a martial rather than a marital victory, and this victory is a victory for an ideology of unification. The king, after all, will close the play with words that propose to continue the project of overcoming discord:

> Rebellion in this land shall lose his sway,
> Meeting the check of such another day,
> And since this business so fair is done,
> Let us not leave till all our own be won. (5.5.41–44)

As Shakespeare's final pun suggests, to win means to make one, to remedy rebellion in a colonial act of totalization. Because the uncanny climactic meeting of Harry and Harry represents the last stand of Percy's rebellion, the play invites us to imagine the two men's meeting, the coming together of same terms, as a structural impasse in the coming together of a nation of differences. The moment functions as the necessary narrative ground for the unification toward which the king will gesture in his final lines. Shakespeare emphasizes the sameness of their names when they finally encounter each other on the battlefield. Though the two have never met, Hotspur greets Hal familiarly. "If I mistake not, thou art Harry Monmouth," he says, adding, "My name is Harry Percy" (5.4.59, 61). Hal's reply—"Why then, I see / A very valiant rebel of the name" (5.4.61–62)—insists on Hotspur's imposture, on his usurpation of the name Harry. The language Hal uses to confront Hotspur here notably draws on Hotspur's logic of mutual exclusion earlier in the play:

> Two stars keep not their motion in one sphere,
> Nor can one England brook a double reign
> Of Harry Percy and the Prince of Wales. (5.4.63–67)

In addition to its suggestion of a divided kingdom, the intolerable notion of a "double reign" means simply the existence of one Harry too many, an excess tantamount to the production of the same thing.

The play generally, and Prince Hal more locally, vanquishes the disturbance brought about by the doubling of Harry and Harry by incorporating it.

As we have already seen, Hal imitates Hotspur's logic in Act 5, and he takes Hotspur's place in language more literally and brutally when, having mortally wounded him, Hal completes his last words. Hotspur begins,

> O, I could prophesy,
> But that the earthy and cold hand of death
> Lies on my tongue. No, Percy, thou art dust,
> And food for— (5.4.83–86)

"For worms," Hal says, as Hotspur dies. At last Hal violently takes his place as the proper speaker of Hotspur's words, doing away with his double by taking his tongue. Hal elaborates the implications of this particular subordination of the uncanny same in the eulogy that follows:

> This earth that bears [thee] dead
> Bears not alive so stout a gentleman.
> If thou wert sensible of courtesy,
> I should not make so dear a show of zeal;
> But let my favors hide thy mangled face,
> And even in thy behalf I'll thank myself
> For doing these fair rites of tenderness. (5.4.92–98)

Hal withholds his "courtesy" toward Hotspur until the moment when he has at last contained him within his own magnanimous capacity, until the moment, in other words, when he can direct his courtesy not to the strange, unsettling double embodied in an antagonist who bears his own name but, instead, to himself as incipient king, one whose "favors" can "hide" the face of excessive sameness. In a deft ventriloquism, he briefly plays Hotspur, using Hotspur's voice to thank himself. The logic of exclusion that the play initially attributes to Hotspur's thinking—it is he who has vowed that one of the two Harrys must die—is the very logic that structures the play's climax, projecting intolerance and exclusion onto Hotspur so that the prince, and the play in general, might appear to be the force of inclusion. As a result, the seductive pull of historical "inevitability" might invite a celebratory reading of this scene: it takes a necessary step toward the unification of England under the monarch Henry V. The invention of this scene, highlighted by Hal's testament of affection for his vanquished double, however, functions as a stunning elegy for sameness, for the impossible "double reign" of Harry and Harry.

The capaciousness imagined by *Henry IV, Part 1* thus comes at a revealing cost: it can contain anything so long as it contain two of nothing. More accurately: It can contain two Harrys, but their doubling provides the very motivation for a narrative project of expansion that will ultimately exclude— by incorporating—the excessive same. The play fantasizes and then evades the trouble of uncanny masculine doubling, and it is this evasion I have in mind when I mention the expansive ambitions of queer studies. Quite simply, I want to call into question the motivation to broaden queer studies ever outward to contain differences. Why does the field have an urgent drive to account for an always displaced other, in such forms as the racial, the multicultural, the heterosexual, the bisexual, the transgender, the transatlantic, the global, the obscure, and the historically remote? If the example of Shakespeare will serve, it seems that this ideology that valorizes endless expansion to account for difference is not merely the product of recent academic fashion. Just as we ought to recognize the contributions of individual scholars who have pushed at the boundaries of queer studies, we ought to attempt to answer the following question: by seeking to expand and to include the differences of various people, places, and times, what subject matter does queer studies insistently avoid? A tentative reply would be "homosexuality," or even "male homosexuality," but even this answer strikes me as insufficient.[10] My reading of *Henry IV, Part 1* ultimately presents a great structural challenge to queer studies, a challenge to treat sameness with the kind of force that the field has increasingly brought to difference. After all, sameness in its many forms—not only homosexuality, but also consistency, doubling, insularity, separatism, paranoia, narrowness, inversion, refusal, obviation, ignorance, and narcissism—continues to be the uncanny subject for us that it was for Shakespeare. We may seek to change this subject, to get over it or to move beyond it, but it will continue to haunt us.

Notes

For their invaluable suggestions, I thank Gregory Chaplin, James Crowley, Jeffrey Masten, Valerie Rohy, John Sexton, and Madhavi Menon.

1. Garber, *Shakespeare after All*, 315. Stephen Greenblatt argues that the play's model of power is so compelling because it deploys and contains its own subversion: Greenblatt, "Invisible Bullets."

2. A nuanced genealogy of the terms used to name this field would take up a lengthy study. The present discussion concerns the shift from "theory" (queer theory) to "studies" (LGBT studies or queer studies), a shift that aims for wider disciplinary range and greater accessibility, rejecting simultaneously a narrowly specified and supposedly elitist "theory." Major projects that have adopted the term "queer stud-

ies" since the mid-1990s include Foster et al., *The Gay '90's*; the "Black Queer Studies in the Millennium" conference in 2000 at the University of North Carolina, Chapel Hill, which yielded Johnson and Henderson, *Black Queer Studies*; and Eng et al., "What's Queer about Queer Studies Now?"

3. Cvetkovich, "Public Feelings," 463.

4. Goldberg, "Desiring Hal," 145–75.

5. *Henry IV, Part 1*, in Evans et al., *The Riverside Shakespeare*, 4.1.122–23. All citations in parentheses are to this edition.

6. Garber uses the word "uncanny" twice, first to evoke how the play anticipates our era's understanding of the political grooming process, and second to describe the "dramatic correspondences" of the play's doubled plot lines: Garber, *Shakespeare after All*, 314, 317.

7. Freud, *The Uncanny*, 142.

8. Poe, "William Wilson."

9. From the great canon of philosophical writings that argue for the priority of sameness in the etiology of love, consider Winthrop, "A Modell of Christian Charity," which uses two same-sex biblical couples (Jonathan and David, Ruth and Naomi) to emblematize love. See also Shannon, *Sovereign Amity*.

10. I have in mind Richard Rambuss's persuasive case for studying what he calls "male masculinity": Rambuss, "After Male Sex," 585

The Deep Structure of Sexuality:
War and Masochism in *Henry IV, Part 2*

DANIEL JUAN GIL

One could perhaps speak of three waves of Renaissance queer studies. The first wave sought to recover lost "gays": Shakespeare himself was gay or some of his characters were gay. This approach was displaced by a second wave that dispensed with the notion of gays as a timeless category of people that could be recovered in the past. Instead, the second-wave approach argued that same-sex sexuality was intertwined with and inextricable from seemingly non-sexual relationships between men. This second wave was aligned with two theoretical models: Michel Foucault's critique of the notion of sexual identity (heterosexual / homosexual) and Eve Kosofsky Sedgwick's concept of the "homosocial" as a category that encompasses both sexual and social desire.[1] The second wave represented a considerable expansion of the field of sexuality studies to encompass all social relationships and the ways they are suffused with currents of sexual desire. But while this second-wave approach made clear how central sexuality was to early modern social and textual life, it also made it difficult to identify sexuality as a distinct phenomenon within the constellation of interpersonal ties that define social life. In that sense, the second-wave approach sometimes had the (paradoxical) effect of desexualizing sexuality studies.

At its most sophisticated, however, the second-wave approach spawned a dialectical partner that tried to pry sexuality out of its homosocial cover, so to speak, by theorizing the ways that Renaissance sexuality differed from other kinds of interpersonal practice. We might call this dialectical partner the third wave of Renaissance sexuality studies.[2] Leo Bersani has played an especially important role in this third wave because he offers a definition of sexuality as a distinct social and psychological phenomenon without reducing it to a sexual identity. Bersani argues that sexuality is sparked when the human infant is

confronted with an external world of overwhelming power and symbolic
complexity and learns to take a kind of protective pleasure in the possibility of
having its as yet weakly consolidated self overwhelmed and shattered.[3] Bersani claims that this adaptive form of masochistic pleasure forms the blueprint for the later "adult" sexuality in which a more fully formed ego again
gives itself up to the pleasure of being unsettled or overwhelmed. Thus, Bersani defines sexuality as the expression of a core of masochism—a desire for
self-shattering—that persists at the very heart of the self.[4]

But if we say, with Bersani, that the deep structure of sexuality is masochism, then we must take stock of the fact that the early modern period lacked
the ready-made concept of "masochism" along with the word. In these pages,
I suggest that Shakespeare uses a queer version of "war" to fill the discursive
gap created by the absence of the concept of masochism. I will suggest that
Shakespeare uses war to conceptualize a masochistic core in the self and
in the self's relationship with others, and that the masochistic impulse that
"war" reveals is the blueprint for sexuality as Shakespeare understood it.

In *King Henry IV, Part 2* (as well as in many other plays), Shakespeare
represents war as an interpersonal practice that reveals the vulnerable, fleshly
body beneath the socio-symbolic armor of personhood. Thus, Morton tells
Northumberland that when he sent his son, Hotspur, to war, he should have
taken account of his physical vulnerability: "You were advised his flesh was
capable / Of wounds and scars."[5] In this play, even as war drives characters to
inflict "wounds and scars" on their enemies and thus reduce them to vulnerable flesh, it also drives them to use the fleshly wounded bodies of their
enemies as a means to discover and even to take pleasure in the fleshly vulnerability of the self. In fact, what we find again and again in the play's discourse of war is a pattern in which a character reduces his enemy to physically
vulnerable flesh, only to then identify with his victim and thus enter into a
vicarious experience of being vulnerable, too. In that sense, Shakespeare uses
war to point to the coincidence of an impulse to build up the self (as van-
quisher) with a deep impulse to humiliate and even shatter the self, an impulse that Bersani sees as the distinguishing characteristic of sexuality *as such*.[6]

The basic pattern appears, for example, in the forestalled "battle" of Gaultree. This episode—in which Lancaster dupes his enemies into dismissing
their army, only to then send them "to present execution" (4.3.72)—reduces
war to something like a sadistic practical joke, and like all sadistic practical
jokes it is shot through by a masochistic impulse to identify with the victims
of the joke. Though Lancaster and his fellow loyalists take obvious pleasure in

having power over their victims, the extent to which they savor the humiliation they plan to inflict also suggests a kind of erotic identification with their
victims. Westmoreland (ironically) promises that "my love to ye / Shall show
itself more openly hereafter" (4.2.75–76), and the deal itself is sealed with a
bout of drinking and Lancaster's hope that "we shall lie tonight together"
(4.2.97). If it is a form of love that drives Lancaster and Westmoreland, then it
is a love whose chief expression is the desire to humiliate the other in order to
share vicariously in that humiliation. And if Lancaster and Westmoreland's
willingness to identify with their victims is safely confined to the realm of
fantasy, the practical joke nevertheless has real effects of humiliation in the
honor economy of the play, in which Lancaster's social and symbolic reputation takes a hit when he shows himself willing to impugn "the honor of my
blood" (4.2.55) by lying not only to his enemies but also to the theater audience, which is not in on the joke.

Although Gaultree is a sort of aborted war, it nevertheless hints at a deep
masochistic impulse that often drives Shakespearean war, and Falstaff's battlefield "capture" of the rebel Sir John Coleville in the next scene seems to codify
the dynamic of humiliating the victim, only to experience a vicarious humiliation of the self. When Coleville encounters Falstaff on the battlefield, he
surrenders as soon as he identifies Falstaff:

> *Coleville:* Are not you Sir John Falstaff?
> *Falstaff:* As good a man as he, sir, whoe'er I am. Do ye yield, sir, or shall I
>   sweat for you? If I do sweat, they are the drops of thy lovers, and they
>   weep for thy death. Therefore rouse up fear and trembling, and do
>   observance to my mercy.
> *Coleville:* I think you are Sir John Falstaff, and in that thought yield me.
>   (4.3.10–17)

Falstaff's odd threat, "If I do sweat, they are the drops of thy lovers, and they
weep for thy death," suggests that Coleville's "lovers" are somehow inside
Falstaff, which is to say that Falstaff feels a kind of love for Coleville—a love
whose chief expression is the desire to capture Coleville and send him to his
death, which Falstaff does. Yet Falstaff's desire to humiliate Coleville is inextricable from his own humiliation, for Falstaff himself notes that the contrast
visually, on the stage, between the two will only highlight his own body and
the pleasure-loving gluttony it advertises. In the chagrined prose soliloquy
that follows the "capture," he says: "I have a whole school of tongues in this
belly of mine, and not a tongue of them all speaks any other word but my

name" (4.3.18–20). Taking Coleville only highlights Falstaff's own fleshy body
—a belly with tongues, as he puts it. When Falstaff hands Coleville over to
Lancaster he sings his own praises: "[I] have, in my pure and immaculate
valor, taken Sir John Coleville of the dale, a most furious knight and valorous
enemy. But what of that? He saw me, and yielded, that I may justly say, with
the hook-nosed fellow of Rome, their Caesar, 'I came, saw, and overcame'"
(4.3.37–42). But Falstaff can hardly expect this hyperbolic self-praise to be
taken seriously and, in a sense, he is only setting himself up for the fat joke
that Lancaster duly obliges him with, along with his dismissive: "It was more
of his courtesy, than your deserving" (4.3.43). Like the Gaultree episode, this
sequence seems to posit a deep-seated desire for humiliation of self that is
coincident with (and even drives) a desire to flatter the self by triumphing
over the enemy. In both sequences, Shakespeare uses war to designate a psychological dynamic that we, in our very different conceptual universe, can
readily term "masochism."

The master narrative of the *Henry IV* plays frames war as the epically
serious alternative to the sexualized dalliance of the tavern world. But if we
read backward, as it were, from war to tavern, we come to see that the
currents of desire that flow through the tavern are decisively structured by the
masochistic impulse that the war lays bare. Whereas second-wave critics have
focused on the sexual frisson that runs through the homosocial bonding of
Hal and Poins and Falstaff, reading the tavern scenes in light of the war scenes
uncovers a sexuality that is structurally distinct from conventionally (and
comfortingly) eroticized male–male camaraderie.

One example of a relationship whose sexual charge seems to lie in its
masochistic structure is the farewell between Doll and Falstaff (who is about
to head off to war) while Poins and Hal, disguised as lowly tapsters, look on.
The whole scene is bathed in the light of the coming war. Doll tells Falstaff,
"Come, I'll be friends with thee, Jack. Thou art going to the wars and,
whether I shall ever see thee again or no, there is nobody cares" (2.4.64–66). As
ever, war introduces the possibility of reducing Falstaff to vulnerable flesh;
Doll seems to think it quite likely that he will die. In relation to Doll, however,
Falstaff seems to embrace the possibility of being made vulnerable in the body,
for he systematically humiliates Doll as a means to humiliate himself. Falstaff
begins by calling Doll a syphilitic whore (2.4.37–46), only subsequently to beg
her to pretend she loves him as though he were not paying for her services.
Doll reciprocates with the loving abuse that can only answer to a masochistic
drive: "Ah, you sweet little rogue, you!," Doll says after Falstaff beats Pistol.

"Alas, poor ape, how thou sweatest! Come, let me wipe thy face; come on, you whoreson chops. Ah, rogue! i' faith, I love thee. Thou art as valorous as Hector of Troy, worth five of Agamemnon" (2.4.213–18). Like Falstaff's self-praise after capturing Coleville, Doll's exaggerated praise of Falstaff only highlights his flesh, as with her emphasis on his sweating body and her reference to him as a "whoreson little tidy Bartholomew boar-pig" (2.4.227).

Viewed through the eyes of Hal and Poins as they spy on Falstaff and Doll, the entire scene seems engineered (and who has engineered it if not Falstaff?) to highlight Falstaff's age and presumed impotence. Hal observes, "Look, whether the withered elder hath not his poll clawed like a parrot" (i.e., his head scratched), to which Poins responds, "Is it not strange that desire should so many years outlive performance?" (2.4.258–59). Poins's comment suggests that there is a kind of sexuality at play in the scene that is not genital, since he thinks Falstaff is impotent. In fact, Poins, like Bersani after him, seems to identify humiliation itself as the essence of sexuality. Poins proposes to Hal that they respond to the scene by giving Falstaff a humiliating beating: "Let's beat him before his whore" (2.4.255). It may be the very thing Falstaff is (secretly or not so secretly) aiming for. Moreover, when Hal reveals himself to humiliate Falstaff, Hal also exposes himself to a rebound of humiliation, since he has disguised himself as a lowly tapster to spy on Falstaff. It is a disguise that Hal found beneath him earlier in the play ("From a prince to a prentice? A low transformation!" [2.2.167–68]) and that he compared to the bestial transformations Jupiter's erotic desires led him to adopt: "From a God to a bull? A heavy decension! It was Jove's case" [2.2.166–67]. Hal's comment suggests that, as with Jove's taking the form of a bull to seduce Europa, his own disguise as a tapster is driven by a kind of desire, but a desire whose chief expression is aiming to humiliate Falstaff to then share his humiliation. Indeed, Hal ends the scene by wondering whether he is the one who has lost face: "By heaven, Poins, I feel me much to blame," Hal says, "So idly to profane the precious time" (2.4.358–59). If it is a desire for humiliation that structures the sexuality that joins Falstaff and Doll, then it appears that a very similar structure of desire also drives Hal into Falstaff's arms.[7]

Indeed, having moved from Shakespeare's representation of war as structured by masochistic drives backward to the masochistic love of Falstaff for Doll, it is possible now to move forward again to the most famous scene of *Henry IV, Part 2*: the rejection of Falstaff at Hal's coronation. When Falstaff hears that Hal is king, he claims to believe that his influence with Hal will make him a great man in the kingdom, and he promises offices to his various

hangers-on. But since Falstaff must know exactly what is in store for him
when Hal becomes king (at least since the play-within-the-play of *Henry IV,
Part 1*), Falstaff's rushing to throw himself on Hal at his public coronation
("stained with travel, and sweating with desire to see him" [5.5.24]) must be
understood as another instance of his engineering a scene of humiliation for
himself, and on the biggest and most public stage possible. While Hal is
obviously serious about asserting his new social authority as king, he nevertheless notes that humiliating Falstaff is inseparable from a kind of humiliation of himself. His goal, after all, is to make "the world perceive, / That I
have turned away my former self" (5.5.57–58). Humiliating Falstaff, in other
words, allows Hal to humiliate himself, which suggests that even as they are
breaking up, Falstaff and Hal nevertheless join each other one last time on the
sexual terrain defined by the quest to humiliate in order to be humiliated.[8]

   On the one hand, there is no doubt that the rejection scene represents the
definitive "reformation" that Hal had long promised. But on the other hand,
from the perspective of the hard school of Gaultree and the structure of
masochistic desire it makes visible, it is possible to catch in this scene a funny
mirror reflection of a relationship founded on the sexual terrain of humiliating
the other to humiliate the self. Seen in this light, the rejection scene takes its
place in Shakespeare's oeuvre as one instance among many in which Shakespeare tries to point toward a sexuality that is neither the basis for a "gay"
identity nor the byproduct of a comforting male–male camaraderie. Instead,
it is a distinctive form of interpersonal bonding founded on the historically
"missing" concept of masochism.

Notes

   1. Sedgwick's theoretical paradigm obviously worked in lockstep with Alan
Bray's groundbreaking study of "friendship" as a category that encompasses social
and sexual forms of desire: see Bray, *Homosexuality in Renaissance England*.
   2. I view Jonathan Goldberg's *Sodometries* as the text that codified second-wave
criticism even as it also articulated the beginning of what I am calling the third-wave
approach. Goldberg's methodology allowed him to identify the complex ways sexuality could inhabit, but also complicate, conventionally social circuits of interaction
and thereby draw attention to itself as a specific form of social experience. The
historical trajectory of Renaissance sexuality studies that I am sketching here was
therefore prefigured in this inaugural book.
   3. See Bersani, *The Freudian Body*, 39.
   4. Several critics have identified this account of sexuality as a powerful tool for

investigating Renaissance culture: see esp. Marshall, *The Shattering of the Self*. Bersani's assumptions about the self are obviously not the same as those of Renaissance culture insofar as the well-defined, well-defended adult ego that he sees as the subject of a pleasurable self-shattering is not something that could be taken for granted in the early modern era. In *Before Intimacy*, I attempted to transpose Bersani's account of sexuality as a (non-historically specific) failure of a well-fashioned self into a (historically conditioned) failure of the functional social ties that define early modern society. I argued that at its core, early modern sexuality was a compensatory experience that allowed people to take pleasure in the experiences of social fraying and contradiction that were the inevitable accompaniment of the birth of the modern world. In this essay I offer a less sociologically contextualized, more symptomatic response to the same historiographical problem: Gil, *Before Intimacy*.

5. Humphries, *Henry IV, Part 2*, 1.1.172–73. Citations in parentheses are to this edition.

6. One reason that Shakespeare consistently uses "war" as the occasion to highlight a sexuality founded on humiliation of the self is that on the Shakespearean stage war is so unrealistic and therefore so insistently theatrical and performative. For Shakespeare, war is an interpersonal practice that *performs* the death of the self, as it were, without anybody actually dying. It is this theatrical *performance* of the death of the self that seems to point to sexuality as Shakespeare (and Bersani after him) understand it.

7. In understanding the conclusion of this scene as an explosion of polymorphous masochism that joins Hal and Falstaff as much as it joins Falstaff and Doll, I am drawing on Orson Welles's brilliantly queer film *Chimes at Midnight*, which I examine more fully in Gil, "Avant-garde Technique and the Visual Grammar of Sexuality in Orson Welles's Shakespeare Films."

8. The coincidence of humiliation with Hal's rise to power is prefigured in the ritual abasement Hal performs in relation to his father after Hal tries on the crown in Act 4, Scene 5.

Scambling Harry and Sampling Hal

DREW DANIEL

Sounding the resonant space of a hole, the text of *Henry V* begins with a startling evocation of pseudo-embarrassment at the promiscuity of a mathematical "cipher," an open gate built out of a numerical nothing through which a potentially infinite range of content is free to pass:

> Oh, pardon! Since a crooked figure may
> Attest in little place a million;
> And let us, ciphers to this great account,
> On your imaginary forces work.[1]

Imagining the architectural space of theater as an empty placeholder that expands and expounds and simulates through the productive void of its signifying "O," this invocation cues a curiously anachronistic proximity with the technological present.[2] The prologue's opening hymn to the signifying powers of zero commences what one might now recognize as a distinctly digital poetics.

What are the preferred reproductive techniques of this digital "O"? What exactly might pass in and out and through this textual opening? If pardons are being handed out, I ask you to forgive some impertinent questions: What might a queer digital poetics contribute to our dramatic experience of *Henry V*? More specifically, how might King Henry's practices of appropriation, mimicry, disguise, and simulation within this history play constitute an early modern practice of digital "sampling"?[3] What drives Harry to take, store, reprocess, and then erase the content of others, ceaselessly in search of new territory, new terrain?[4] Is there not something rather queer about this promiscuity, this discursive restlessness, the itchy wanderlust that drives Harry to sidle up to others in disguise and attempt to "blend in," to slink alongside them, to ape their manners by sounding like them, to mirror and deceive his company with a series of passable approximations, imitations, and feints? If

King Harry extracts "samples" of the behavior, habits, and sounds of others and willfully transforms them for his own use, what do his choices, his filters, the contours of his processing of information tell us about his desire and how it functions?

Obviously, to call Harry's desires to critical account is hardly new. In the wake of Jonathan Goldberg's first turn of the screw in 1992, and Richard Corum's renewed assault four years later, one could be forgiven for thinking that the topic of desire—and of queer desire, in particular—in relation to Prince Hal / King Henry / "Harry" was all shagged out.[5] By now this "dried neat's tongue" has cottonmouth. Arriving a generation too late to be a part of queer theory's first-wave "band of brothers," I might simply rest content in admiring those brandishing the scars they nobly won in long-ago critical battles for the existence of sodomitical readings of Shakespeare and Shakespearean scannings of sodomy. But the economic scarcity of the academic labor pool has made the exclusive thrust of the phrase "we happy few" seem ever chillier and more distant in this context. With all the goodwill in the world, the entrenched vanguard of queer theory may not have room for even one more.

All the same, "once more into the breach"—but this time with our eyes closed. The optical regime of historical hermeneutic encounter as a visual matter of "seeing clearly" into the past or "projecting" onto its defenseless surface might itself benefit from a queer reorientation toward audio as an alternative modality. We can shut our eyes but not our ears, and this constant open-ness to sound, this endless receptivity that precedes "consent" and with it, the possibility of egoic regimes of aversion, self-control, and "looking away," founds the sonic on a queer passivity of listening that is both ravenous and orthogonal to desire and self. What might happen when we stop scanning experience for its legibility and the visual politics of "cultural visibility" and start queering our hearing? Sound that cannot be located spatially has a curious capacity to "distract" or "upstage" other phenomena and thus to upset the priority of the visual and its signifying regimes of "same" and "different." Invoking a different set of muscular, neural, and cognitive spectra of segregation and ambiguity, sounding drama rather than watching it might reduce the eyestrain of wide-eyed presentism, and the pronounced squint of various historicisms, and introduce us to a new set of problems altogether. Specifically, what would the deliberately anachronistic projection of today's sampling practices—shorthand for a range of techniques to manipulate digital audio and video whereby content is captured, stored, transformed, filtered, and re-synthesized—permit us productively to misrecognize within the sexual poetics of Shakespeare's text?

The sampler can be portably defined as an electronic device for the storage and manipulation of audio signals. Sounds are taken in, remembered, and re-presented, permitting a range of playback conditions, from precise capture and replay to highly distorted and estranged transformations of the original signal. Functionally, the initial purpose of the sampler was to "trick" the ear into believing that a particular signal was not an electronic mirage but an acoustically immediate moment of original material presence—that is, not a digitally stored playback of a clarinet but the real thing. What the grapes of Zeuxis are to visual representation, the sonic deceptions of sampling are to acoustic instruments. Samplers are engineered to permit a *"trompe l'oreille"* effect of artificial substitution, and it is no accident that, before the play is through, one of Henry's savviest auditors will exclaim in shock at the seductive effect of his impostures, *"Oh, bon Dieu! Les langues des hommes sont pleines de tromperies"* (5.2.117).

The capacity for cloaking, mimicry, and imitation through specifically sonic pathways is fundamental to Harry's capacity to charm and astonish his admirers. His chameleon-like tendencies are savored and celebrated by the Archbishop of Canterbury before he has even arrived onstage:

> *Canterbury*: Hear him but reason in divinity,
> And, all-admiring, with an inward wish
> You would desire the King were made a prelate.
> Hear him debate of commonwealth affairs,
> You would say it hath been all in his study.
> List his discourse of war, and you shall hear
> A fearful battle rendered to you in music. (1.1.39–45)

Hear . . . Hear . . . List . . . Music . . . One is so seduced by the sonic experience of these impersonations that the distinct tunings of divinity, governance, and war become transposed to a single chord of confident oration delivered with a timbral authority whose persuasive eloquence self-verifies in the archbishop's gushed declaration of surrender. The fearful battle rendered in music indexes the material rattle of thunder sheets, the Foley and fakery of the company at work backstage but, more fundamentally, our lived experience of Harry within the play as at once a con artist and a "sound artist," pleasing his audience with cunning impersonations of expertise and command. If the chorus fitfully warns us, "Yet sit and see / Minding true things by what their mockeries be" (4.0.52–53), the experience of the pleasing sound of Harry's voice as it produces the martial music of war and the amorous music of flirtation with an equally relentless success rate produces a gradual dulling of our vigilance on the boundary between "true things" and their representations.

Such reports of Harry's silver-tongued success feed forward into his own firsthand technical demonstrations of the impact of sound. Listen to the first speech at the siege of Harfleur:

Once more unto the breach, dear friends, once more,
Or close the wall up with our English dead!
In peace there's nothing so becomes a man
As modest stillness and humility.
But when the blast of war blows in our ears,
Then imitate the action of the tiger:
Stiffen the sinews, conjure up the blood,
Disguise fair nature with hard-favored rage. (3.1.3–8)

As with Harry's conjuring of legal expertise and religious piety, the trigger for this military technology of affect is sound. The blast blows through the ears, and this war signal, repeated in a "once more" that instantly summons its own reinforcement, cues up a wave of somatic posturing poised between animal instinct and theatrical artifice. The soldier's body becomes a machine for replication and imitation, and Harry's rhetoric consists of a "sample bank" of materials from which to put together in a collage the hardened and threatening aspect of war: tiger, cannon, cliff, ocean. Such a response is "becoming" in a double sense: "becoming" as behavior that is masculine and "appropriate," but also "becoming" in the sense of a poetic "becoming animal / mineral / liquid." Harry's war machine disguises nature with the found materials of nature now reconfigured as rhetorical effects, outward shows, synthetic postures. Each soldier is instructed to "Be copy now to men of grosser blood / And teach them how to war" (3.1.24–25). Harry at once discursively samples and poetically reassembles military history into a synthetic narrative and instructs others on the battlefield in this same mimetic art. "Copying to others" names the fraught process of performance, storage, and reproduction by which one simultaneously verifies and exports one's national identity and family honor: One can "attest / that those whom you called fathers did beget you" (3.2.22–23) only by "begetting" virtual imitations and copies, battlefield *Doppelgängers* who act as compatible "back-ups" that can run the same sequencing program.

This fundamental concern with the reproduction of a soldierly identity that is neither fully organic nor fully artificial carries over from the rhetoric of war to the rhetoric of seduction, when the victorious king claims his French princess: "If ever thou be'st mine, Kate, as I have a saving faith within me tells me thou shalt, I get thee with scambling, and thou must needs therefore prove a good soldier-breeder" (5.2.204–7). Here Hal would seem to gearshift from the synthetic practice of "sampling" to the physical activity of "scambling": struggle, violence, shoving one's way forward through the world. But the "scam" at the core of such boudoir "scambling" is not an alternative to, but an example of, Hal's prior practice of "sampling." Patching images of war through a filter of seduction, he is crafting the "fearful battle rendered in music" already praised by the Archbishop of Canterbury, now re-keyed to the Lydian mode. Here amorous Hal samples warlike Harry in order to sample and hold Kate.

Cross-fading "scambling" into "sampling" in such a manner courts the accusation of anachronistic projection, a presentist misprision that any of a number of ready-to-hand historicisms stand poised to correct and rebuke. The Oxford English Dictionary forbids it. The word "sampler" triggers a polysemous historical medley: needlework, catechism, chocolate box, electronics. In the early modern period, the needlework definition predominated: One finds in Thomas Blount's *Glossographia* "Samplar (a corruption from Examplar)[,] a pattern or copy to imitate, an extract or draught; most used for a pattern of several sorts of needlework."[6] But in practice, one encounters the term used as a moralizing metaphor to refer to exceptionally beautiful or virtuous people. If its definition as a demonstrative exercise in needlework suggests typological exemplarity, its subsequent redefinition as a chocolate box of options (the proverbial Whitman's Sampler) suggests its generatively nonspecific capacity to group together a casual assemblage of disparate cases. "Samplers" and "samplars" both represent exemplary content; they also run the risk of leveling content down. Like the empty cipher of the "O" in which an infinite range of behavior can be multiplied and imitated, the promise and the threat of this technical practice is that *anything* can be routed through a blank pathway.

Sampling in the sense of a digital synthetic function of "sample and hold" entered the English language in the mid-1960s, during the Golden Age of modular synthesis. "Sampling" in the sense of the digital appropriation and collage of a sound signal had to wait until the late 1970s for the introduction of the Fairlight and its poetically named, if cheaper, competitor, the Emulator, a few years later.[7] But such commercially available technology, far from naming into being a heretofore unthinkable artistic practice, itself constitutes poetic condensations of artistic habits that are distinctly early modern in their genesis. Consider Francis Bacon's eerily prophetic imagination of contemporary studio practices of sound manipulation, distortion, storage, and relay:

> We have also sound-houses, where we practise and demonstrate all sounds, and their generation. We have harmonies which you have not, of quarter-sounds, and lesser slides of sounds. Divers instruments of music likewise to you unknown, some sweeter than any you have; together with bells and rings that are dainty and sweet. We represent small sounds as great and deep; likewise great sounds extenuate and sharp; we make divers tremblings and warblings of sounds, which in their original are entire. We represent and imitate all articulate sounds and letters, and the voices and notes of beasts and birds. We have certain helps which, set to the ear, do further the hearing greatly. We have also divers strange and artificial echoes, reflecting the voice many times and, as it were, tossing it; and some that give back the voice louder than it came; some shriller, and some deeper; yea, some rendering the voice differing in the letters or articulate sound from that they receive. We have also means to convey sounds in trunks and pipes, in strange lines and distances.[8]

In an instrumentalizing fantasy of control that should be familiar to historians of early modern science, the relay of sound, the management of scale, and the construction of sonic networks of transmission are all forecasted in a manner that suggests the sonic as a flexible perceptual pathway through which to further the ongoing project of the capture and subjection of the natural world. But Bacon's "sound-houses" also open up the potential for a mimetic practice that would prosthetically extend (and thus disrupt) the acoustic immediacy of natural sound, including the privileged sound of the human voice, not only mirroring the world but adding new hybridities, new glides and "lesser slides" of pitch that move beyond known practices of Western scales and notation. Baconian sound practice registers a queer difference from the givenness of the natural world in a trembling, warbling, "differing," sliding practice that can "toss" the voice outside of its body of origin, critically estranging it in the process.

If Bacon's imagined sound houses startlingly resemble contemporary electronic production techniques, the practices of appropriation and collage that we associate with the formal outcome of "sampling" as a compositional practice also have early modern analogues in literature and music. The construction of a work of art out of fragments of the work of others arguably underwrites the continental practice of the "cento" and the authorial bricolage of commonplace books by individuals, families, clusters of intimate friends, and unknowably anonymous others.[9] Early modern textuality hinged on collective acts of collage and assemblage: Manuscripts and commonplace books were circulated, embroidered on, added to, redacted, and reconstituted through relentless creative reuse of verbal and graphic palimpsests in which distinctions between "author" and "end user" are porous. Raw material was excerpted, personalized, recirculated, commented on, and parodied in a manner whose disorienting resemblances to contemporary information landscapes go far beyond the scope of this essay. These practices have their mirrors in the musical compositions of early modernity. Replete with macaronic and mashed-up medleys of folk forms, religious subjects, intellectual disputation, and "wraggle taggle" nonsense, in the sixteenth-century *ensaladas* of Mateo Flecha and the *quodlibet* tradition of Wolfgang Schmeltzl and Ludwig Senfl and in the compositions of Orlando Gibbons, we see culture crafted into cut-ups—four hundred years before the appearance of *musique-concrete*. Their deliberately loose formal assemblage and relentlessly unified functional imperative are implicit in their name: *Quodlibet* simply means "what pleases." Collaging together aureate speech for the nobles and tavern talk for the churls and affected warrior "plain speaking" for the ladies, convolving a self out of Hal and Henry Plantagenet and Harry Le Roy, Harry's own audio subjectivity obeys the same functional imperative: He is an identity sampler, a "queer assemblage" who speaks "what pleases" to whoever happens to be in earshot.

If such citational practices mark his sample speeches as persistently derivative and heterogeneous, and never more so than when they recursively play back their "own" prior content, this risks an embarrassingly circular and perhaps unanswerable final question: could we ever have heard the sound of Hal's *own* voice? To draw an analogy from drama to music, one might compare this theoretical possibility with the sonic practices of "no input sampler players" such as the Japanese sound artist Sachiko Matsubara, a key player in the *"onkyo"* movement of phenomenologically oriented improvisers and experimental musicians who work at the edges of perceptible audio signals. "Auto-sampling" in a radically anorexic manner, Sachiko crafts work out of only the resonant sixty-cycle hum and inner digital signal processing artifacts of commercial samplers, trying to sharpen the contrast on the fingerprint whorls of an allegedly transparent technological interface between digital storage media and an analogue world of external content.

Sachiko is not soliloquizing when she does this. The dramatic model for how a self might run on / to itself when cut off from the opportunity to bounce dialogically off of others cannot be analogically captured in this manner. Soliloquies and asides, however privileged as moments of access to an inaccessible interiority, are to the purpose nothing when the topic is sonic experience. Short of the direct stimulus of the auditory nerve (entirely possible given existing cochlear implant technology), there is no such thing as a purely "inner" sound or a purely "dry" sound that would not be sound vibrating across and through a space. Sound and (social) space are a manifold, and every sound Hal makes is thus "for us," marked, productive, available to us, and thus never "inward" at an acoustic level.

Nor is Hal ever truly "alone." In ceaselessly bouncing his audio signal off others, Hal needs listeners to whom to playback his samples as much as he needs source material to sample. If the confident declaration "I know you all" (1.2.189) from *King Henry IV, Part I* sets in motion a fantasy of universally comprehensive ambition, it also ricochets uncomfortably onto the audience, sounding their cohabiting presence in the wooden "O" as the viewers / listeners whose presence ratifies his reformation. Hal as sampler might be another way to understand Harry as "cipher," a desiring machine whose curious movement from sadistic fantasy (in the "babies spitted upon pikes" speech) to modest pleading (in the courtship of Kate) works on our "imaginary forces" by producing in us as listeners a perverse fantasy of negation: the desire that we might somehow hear the sounds this machine could make when it stops working fluently and flawlessly. What would this play sound like if King Henry *didn't* "know us all"? What is he when all his banks have been emptied out?

Stanley Kubrick's film *2001: A Space Odyssey* familiarized the listening public with the queer audio phenomenon of a beguiling simulacrum achieved entirely through an artificial voice, a machine intelligence whose power failure and resulting system death consolidated this antihero's ironic position on the outer boundary of bare life. In a manner that conveys the fragility of sonic illusion, this "digital" voice was never more—and never less—"human" than when it became, through the digitally stepped tics of slurred and sloweddown speech synthesis, most audibly "humanoid." This eroded machine voice makes audible what Roland Barthes only framed as a hypothetical possibility: "There is no human voice in the world which is not the object of desire—or of repulsion: there is no neutral voice—and if occasionally this neutrality or blankness of the voice occurs, it constitutes a great terror, as if we were to frightfully discover a petrified world, where desire would be dead."[10] Barthes's thought experiment inadvertently summons for me what I imagine the voice of "Harry the Sampler" might sound like were it to speak without any front-loaded "samples" to work on, finally, having seduced all comers and won every battle, exhausting itself in shutdown, becoming dead to its own desire, consuming itself. Sounding the "cipher" of a machine voice that both recalls Barthes's affectless zombie and Shakespeare's victorious Plantagenet prince, Kubrick's queer machine generated a sound that should be uncannily familiar by now. It is the quietly commanding voice of "Hal."

Notes

1. *The Life of King Henry the Fifth*, in Bevington, *The Complete Works of Shakespeare, Portable Edition*, 15–18. Citations in parentheses refer to this edition.

2. Compare this with Polixenes's statement in *The Winter's Tale*, "Therefore, like a cipher / Yet standing in rich place, I multiply / With one 'We thank you' many thousands more / That go before it" (1.2.55–58). *The Winter's Tale*, in Wells and Taylor, *William Shakespeare: The Complete Works*, 1101–31.

3. This question was posed to me by Madhavi Menon. Answering it has forced a shaky truce between two identities (the electronic musician and the academic) that tend to take turns saying "I know thee not, old man," to each other.

4. I intend to remain consistently inconsistent on the matter of the name of this particular dramatic persona as a graphic means of representing his character as on assemblage.

5. Goldberg, "Desiring Hal"; Corum, "Henry's Desires."

6. Blount, *Glossographia*, "SA," 242.

7. Théberge, *Any Sound You Can Imagine*, 82.

8. Bacon, *New Atlantis*, 34–35.

9. Moss, *Printed Commonplace-Books and the Structuring of Renaissance Thought*.

10. Barthes, "La musique, la voix, la langue," 247.

Henry VI, Part 1

"Wounded Alpha Bad Boy Soldier"

MARIO DIGANGI

According to Shakespeare's contemporary Thomas Nashe, Elizabethan play-goers were collectively and irresistibly moved by the spectacle of heroic death. In a much quoted passage most likely referring to Shakespeare's *Henry VI, Part 1*, Nashe describes the overwhelming emotional response to the on-stage demise of the fifteenth-century English hero John Talbot:

> How would it have joyed brave Talbot (the terror of the French) to think that after he had lain two hundred years in his tomb, he should triumph again on the stage and have his bones new embalmed with the tears of ten thousand spectators at least (at several times), who, in the tragedian that represents his person, imagine they behold him fresh bleeding![1]

While the very early and "dazzlingly unformed" *Henry VI, Part 1* has long existed on the margins of the Shakespeare canon,[2] Nashe's resonant passage has drawn renewed critical attention to the play's engagement with early modern discourses of nationalism, subjectivity, and masculinity.[3] Yet what remains to be considered is the possibility that Nashe's account of playhouse dynamics serves a normalizing function in turning a queerly passionate en-counter between male bodies into a "straight" tableau of masculine virtue.

With good reason, critics such as Andrew Gurr, Jean Howard, and Phyllis Rackin have understood Nashe to be articulating the dominant ideology of early modern masculinity. Gurr cites Nashe to demonstrate that "the minds of men in company at plays in the 1590s needed stronger meat for their affec-tions" than the romantic drama of the 1580s had supplied. This hardier man's meat consisted not only in the greater "realism" of stage representation, but also in the focus on "masculine affairs of war and military history" in plays such as *Henry VI, Part 1*.[4] Howard and Rackin include Nashe among the Eliz-abethan apologists for the theater who celebrated history plays for "preserving the memory of English heroes" and "encouraging patriotic feelings in spectators."⁵ In history plays, Nashe explains:

> Our forefathers' valiant acts, that have lain long buried in rusty brass and worm-eaten books, are revived, and they themselves raised from the grave of oblivion, and brought to plead their aged honours in open presence: than which, what can be a sharper reproof to these degenerate effeminate days of ours?⁶

Reviving valiant deeds, the memorials of which have long decayed in old armor and neglected books, the English history play also reproves contemporary spectators who have degenerated from a bygone ideal of masculine valor. In such passages, Howard and Rackin argue, Nashe articulates an English nationalism that "associated the foreign with the female" and "helped to determine the marginal locations of female characters in Shakespeare's English histories."⁷

Building on the gender critique of Howard and Rackin, I suggest that Nashe's masculinist rendering of audiences' response to *Henry VI, Part 1* can be read to reveal queer affects centered on the body of the wounded hero. Before proceeding, it needs to be said that it would be wrongly positivistic for a queerly oriented criticism to assert absolutely that the passage from Nashe refers to *Henry VI, Part 1*. For my argument, it will be enough to suggest that (1) since *Henry VI, Part 1* is the only English Renaissance play we know with a character named "Talbot," Nashe most likely was referring to it; (2) it is worth pursuing the connection between the passage from Nashe and Shakespeare's play to dislodge the way they have been connected in the critical tradition; and (3) queer criticism is well suited to an analysis of texts that might have only an oblique relationship of referentiality or affiliation to each other.

In Eve Sedgwick's resonant formulation, "queer" signifies "the open mesh of possibilities, gaps, overlaps, dissonances and resonances, lapses and excesses of meaning" when the "constituent elements" of gender or sexuality cannot be made "to signify monolithically."⁸ Critics of *Henry VI, Part 1* have productively located queer possibilities and dissonances in Joan la Pucelle's subversive gender and sexual performances.⁹ Nashe's account of audiences' response to *Henry VI, Part 1* erases altogether the threatening figure of Joan, but in its attempt to laud the heroic figure of Talbot, it makes available queer excesses of same-sex passion.

We can begin to get some queer purchase on Nashe's account by under-standing its function not as reporting but as normalizing the intensely emo-tive interaction of male bodies. Early moderns typically regarded weeping as a feminine trait: A man who cries might well be accused of effeminate soft-ness.[10] In Nashe's account, however, "Weeping is no longer a sign of feminine weakness but a patriotic virtue."[11] Defending the theater as a virtuous institu-tion that redeems "these degenerate effeminate days of ours," Nashe imag-ines playgoers as sacramental figures positioned above the prone figure of Talbot, "embalming" his bleeding body with their falling tears.[12] To borrow Sara Ahmed's terminology, Nashe here produces a collective and normative *orientation* of male bodies: "The normative can be considered an effect of the repetition of bodily actions over time, which produces what we can call the bodily horizon, a space for action. . . . The normative dimension can be redescribed in terms of the straight body, a body that appears 'in line.'"[13] For Ahmed, the straight line represents the normalizing imperatives of reproduc-tive heterosexuality. In sixteenth-century England, before the historical emer-gence of "heterosexuality" as the ideological foundation of domestic life, the normative might be better described as male homosociality, which encom-passed both affective male bonds and family formation. By orienting male spectators above the body of Talbot, Nashe advances the normalizing work of early modern homosociality.

Imagining that thousands of playgoers at "several" performances of the play have collectively embalmed Talbot's body with their pious tears, Nashe imposes a phenomenological norm that regularizes the emotional and cor-poreal dispositions of playgoers as well as players. In the actual playhouse, of course, some playgoers would have been seated in the galleries looking down on or horizontally across at the actors, while others would have been standing in the yard looking up. Nashe's fantasy reduces male playgoers' various dispo-sitions—topographical as well as affective—into a collective body that "lines up" with the prone body of the actor playing Talbot and with the theatrically represented corpse of the historical Talbot (whom playgoers imagine they behold "fresh bleeding"). Nashe thus appears to echo the famous scene earlier in *Henry VI, Part 1* in which Talbot outfoxes the Countess of Auvergne by claiming that, in capturing him, she has taken possession only of his "shadow," for his true "substance"—his "sinews, arms, and strength"—resides in the English army.[14] Embodying the nation, Talbot identifies himself with "a col-lective project" of English manhood.[15] Nashe's fantasy of uniformly oriented male bodies similarly advances a collective nationalism that redeems playgoing from its stigmatized association with the "extreme" pleasures available to London men: "gaming, following of harlots, drinking, or seeing a play."[16]

We can see further normalization at work in the way Nashe's account closes off the open mesh of gender and sexual possibilities that surrounds Talbot's death in *Henry VI, Part 1*. At the moment of Talbot's death, another bleeding male body is on stage: that of Talbot's son, also named John Talbot. Young John's death troubles Nashe's tableau of corporate masculinity in several ways. First, the death of this young man emphasizes the terrible price of war in disrupting what Lee Edelman calls the "reproductive futurism" that bolsters "heteronormativity."[17] Urging John to flee, Talbot complains: "In thee thy mother dies, our household's name, / My death's revenge, thy youth, and England's fame" (4.6.38–39). If Talbot's investment in "our household's name" represents an early modern form of "heteronormativity," then John's death might indicate that the project of reproductive futurism, of "fighting for the children," has been jeopardized by the masculine ethos of military honor that requires children to fight.[18]

Moreover, much like the death of Young Siward in *Macbeth*, John's death places older soldiers in the potentially embarrassing situation of expressing intense feelings for someone in a liminal stage of manhood—namely, the state of blossoming adolescence that so often provokes homoerotic affect in the period's comedies. In the last scene of *Macbeth*, the surviving warriors debate how much emotional capital to spend over the death of a soldier who has just reached the cusp of manhood. Young Siward, who, according to Ross, "only lived but till he was a man," died like a man by facing his foe bravely and receiving his wounds "on the front."[19] Although old Siward refuses to grieve for a son who died so honorably, Malcolm disputes this reasoning: "He's worth more sorrow, / And that I'll spend for him" (5.11.17). In *Henry VI, Part 1*, there is no debate over how much grief the young soldier's death requires; rather, Talbot volubly emotes over his son's bleeding body. Unlike the stoic Siward, who wants only to know whether his son was wounded while charging or fleeing the enemy, Talbot vividly recounts how the Duke of Orleans penetrated his son's body, thus taking "the maidenhood / Of [his] first fight" in an overt metaphor of sexual intercourse (4.6.17–18). A young "blossom" cut down "in his pride" (4.7.16), John is presented to us as an object not only of mourning, but also of aesthetic and erotic appreciation—perhaps even of sodomitical pleasure, if we credit those Elizabethan anti-theatricalists who loudly railed against the same-sex allure of the popular stage.[20]

Erasing the death of young John, Nashe normalizes the scene of male passion in *Henry VI, Part 1* by focusing on the self-sacrifice of the national hero. But if "bodies are sexualized through how they inhabit space,"[21] then even Nashe's "straightened" account of Talbot's death betrays alternative possibilities of male–male relations that belie the pious metaphors of "embalming" and filiation.[22] To begin with, embalming is a rather troubling metaphor for describing playgoers' intimacy with their fantasized object of devotion. In the early modern period, as Susan Zimmerman explains, the corpse was perceived as "semianimate" and still possessed of some form of "personhood."[23] Consequently, the "temporary staunching of the process of putrefaction" through embalming "succeeded only in extending the liminal power of the corpse"—namely, its "power to pollute and also to torment the living."[24] Moreover, anatomical theories of blood as a nurturing fluid and as the substance from which semen was concocted meant that the blood of a corpse "signified past and future potencies."[25] "Embalming" the imagined corpse of Talbot, washing its blood with their tears, the playgoers in Nashe's account might be understood to engage in intercourse with a dangerously liminal body: a living body representing a dead body that, through its ability to elicit playgoers' embalming tears, seems not quite dead.[26]

Since we have no record of what actual playgoers might have found attractive, empathetic, or unnerving about Talbot, we can only speculate, along with Nashe, about how this imposing historical figure might have organized their desires and identifications. But if "queering history" involves rejecting the normative protocols of traditional historiography,[27] then one avenue of speculation might lead us to note how Talbot's embodiment of wounded masculinity resembles that of the hero of the contemporary romance novel. In her classic study *Reading the Romance*, Janice Radway finds that "the terrorizing effect" of the romance hero's "exemplary masculinity" is "always tempered by the presence of a small feature that introduces an element of softness into the overall picture."[28] According to the female readers Radway interviewed, the ideal hero typically combines a "self-protective aggressiveness" with a "fleeting revelation of his underlying capacity for gentleness."[29] This description is not so far from Shakespeare's Talbot. On the one hand, Talbot is the "terror of the French," a ferocious warrior who readily degrades Joan la Pucelle as a whore; on the other hand, he is a civilized nobleman, gentle enough to enjoy "cates" with a countess and to cradle his dying son in his arms (2.4.79). A reader of contemporary romances might appreciatively describe Talbot as a "wounded alpha bad boy soldier."

I came across this definition of the ideal romantic hero on the Write-

Minded blog for fans of romance novels. In a post in August 2006, the host, Jan, solicited definitions of the ideal hero in terms of antithetical character-istics: "What type of character is your favorite hero? Alpha or beta male? Wounded hero or geek? Soldier or bad boy?" Many of the respondents to the post, however, conflated and combined characteristics of the hero in ways that undermine binary taxonomies. One might argue that the romance blog constitutes a potentially queer space in which desire is communally expressed and is detached from identifiably gendered / sexed bodies (since the actual identities of the bloggers are occluded).[30] Nonetheless, the bloggers tend to agree with one another—and with Radway's findings—in defining their fa-vorite type of hero as a wounded alpha male:[31]

> *Little Lamb Lost*: Wounded alpha bad boy soldier.
>
> *Cherie Japp*: Alpha, wounded hero, bad boy. The three is an awesome com-bination.
>
> *Yolanda*: sucker for the alpha bad boy. . . .
>
> *Crystal B.*: Alpha wounded hero bad boy. Great combination. :)
>
> *Angie T*: I am such a huge fan of men in uniform and especially [S]pecial [F]orces types. I love them alpha males with just a little touch of beta so they are not total a-holes!!!
>
> *Danny*: My favorite hero is an Alpha with a tiny touch of Beta. I love wounded / tortured heroes. Both soldiers and bad boys have their ad-vantages. The combination is Alpha / wounded bad boy.
>
> *Minna*: I love them all.
>
> *Sherry Hobbs*: I love alpha male, wounded hero, bad boy and soldiers. But the [m]ilitary stories are always my favorite.
>
> *cathy*: My favorite hero these days is an alpha soldier with some bad boy thrown in. Give him a sense of humor and I am sold.
>
> *MelJ*: . . . I'd say alpha with some beta thrown in for good measure. Soldier? Yes, please! Bad boy? Yes, please!
>
> *Bonnie Ferguson*: Alpha heroes are my favorite.
>
> *Rosie G.*: I love alphas and bad boys.
>
> *May*: Alpha male. Preferably wounded, or shaken in some way.
>
> *Pat L.*: Bad Boy of Course; alpha with a hint of beta.
>
> *ellie*: Alpha male, hero with a snippet of beta and definitely wounded bad boy.
>
> *joelle*: Alpha male wounded bad boy but with a smattering of beta for sure.
>
> *Sarah Lehan*: beta bad boy.

> Pam P: I am a sucker for that alpha wounded bad boy, but I like them [all?], including those geeky professors. I really like a combo—alpha with a bit of beta.
>
> Dena: . . . I like the Alpha hero with some kind of quirk, he has to have some kind of imperfection that is endearing and that draws me to him.

No matter how exotic, fantastic, or hyperbolically masculine the alpha romance hero might be, these readers use the familiar domestic idiom of cooking to describe the "little touch," "tiny touch," "hint," "snippet," or "smattering" of gentleness "thrown in for good measure" that saves the alpha hero from being "a total a-hole." The language of cooking signals the bloggers' desire to fashion a fantasy hero whose "beta" qualities are indications not of weakness but of an "endearing" femininity that draws the reader closer in an act of identification as well as desire.

Nashe's account of impassioned male playgoers suggests that they, too, might have been drawn in by both the "masculine" aggression and the "feminine" tenderness of Shakespeare's wounded alpha male. Yet Nashe's overt admiration for the Elizabethan history play's nationalist agenda in reviving "our forefathers' valiant acts" indicates that he understands Talbot's wounded body primarily as the sign of a historical trauma. Here Nashe takes his cue from *Henry VI, Part 1*, which insistently marks and mourns this trauma as the collective betrayal of an ethos of self-sacrificing chivalric masculinity by an emergent courtly masculinity centered on self-promotion. Thus, the Duke of Gloucester accuses the Bishop of Winchester of manipulating the passive King Henry VI: "None do you like but an effeminate prince, / Whom like a schoolboy you may overawe" (1.1.35–36). If Henry is imagined as a schoolboy, the bishop might be imagined as a stereotypically perverse pedant who likes to beat his pupils.[32] In this scenario, the properly civic, pedagogical aims of corporal punishment have yielded to the schoolmaster's self-serving pleasures. The inverted emblem of the sodomitical bishop "on top" of the "overawed" king indicates that, in the world of the play, England's decline into what Nashe calls "these degenerate effeminate days of ours" has already begun.

When Nashe describes Talbot's imagined joy at witnessing his valiant acts and his pitiful death reenacted on the Elizabethan stage, he renders the historical trauma of betrayed masculinity in terms of the ghostly return. Existing in "an ambiguous state of being, both present and not, past and not," the ghost embodies a traumatic past that queerly continues to exert an "ethical imperative" on the present.[33] If we approach the Elizabethan history play from

Nashe's perspective, we might well conclude that Talbot's ghost, "raised from the grave of oblivion," would regard playgoers' tears as signs of shamed self-recognition at being the heirs of his betrayal. But those tears, as we have seen, participate in a much messier drama of same-sex empathy, affiliation, identification, and desire. Whatever his own motives, when Nashe describes the long dead Talbot as "triumph[ing]" again on the Elizabethan stage, he encourages us to understand the Shakespearean playhouse as a queer place in which past and present bodies intermingle in an impassioned dynamic of commemoration and disavowal, of intimate connection and alienating loss.

Notes

1. Nashe, *Pierce Penniless His Supplication to the Devil*, 113.
2. Pye, *Vanishing*, 19.
3. Although they use Nashe in very different ways, Jean Howard and Phyllis Rackin, *Engendering*; Brian Gibbons, "Romance"; Andrew Gurr, *Playgoing*; Martha Kurtz, "Tears"; and Christopher Pye, *Vanishing* all cite this passage to bolster arguments about the cultural impact of *Henry VI, Part 1*.
4. Gurr, *Playgoing*, 135, 137.
5. Howard and Rackin, *Engendering*, 18
6. Nashe, *Pierce Penniless His Supplication to the Devil*, 113.
7. Howard and Rackin, *Engendering*, 51.
8. Sedgwick, *Tendencies*, 8.
9. Jankowski, *Pure Resistance*, 1–4; Schwarz, *Tough Love*, 81–91.
10. Kurtz, "Tears," 163–64.
11. Ibid., 176.
12. In his study of early audience responses to Renaissance drama, Charles Whitney writes that Nashe's "defense of plays also emphasizes how moral implications can stem from emotional abandon": Whitney, *Early Responses to Renaissance Drama*, 36.
13. Ahmed, *Queer Phenomenology*, 66. Karma Lochrie vigorously critiques the scholarly tendency to define heterosexuality as the "norm" of premodern societies, a critique with which I am sympathetic: Lochrie, *Heterosyncrasies*, xii–xxv. In this essay, I am using "normalization" in a non-universalizing sense, as the effort to bring erratic or abject elements (such as effeminacy in men) into line with dominant ideologies. In the seventeenth century, "normal" had meaning only as a geometrical term: "standing at right angles, perpendicular" (Lochrie, *Heterosyncrasies*, 3). What it might mean to speak of a "normalizing" impetus in the early modern period, before the modern notion of the statistical "norm" had arisen (Lochrie, *Heterosyncrasies*, 1–25), should, I think, remain an open question.
14. *Henry VI, Part 1*, in Greenblatt, ed., *Norton Shakespeare*, 2.3.62–63. Citations in parentheses refer to this edition.

15. Howard and Rackin, *Engendering*, 57. Here Ahmed's thoughts on racial and national orientations are also relevant: Ahmed, *Queer Phenomenology*, 109–56.

16. Nashe, *Pierce Penniless His Supplication to the Devil*, 112.

17. Edelman, *No Future*, 2.

18. Ibid., 3.

19. *Macbeth*, in Greenblatt, ed., *Norton Shakespeare*, 5.11.6, 13

20. I am not claiming that Talbot is aware of homoerotic connotations in his expressions of paternal love, for his overt aim is clearly to memorialize his son as one of "Two Talbots" whose valiant deeds, enrolled in the chronicles, will "escape mortality" (4.7.21–22). In other words, Talbot wishes to see his son as a perfect copy of himself: see Kahn, *Man's Estate*, 52–54.

21. Ahmed, *Queer Phenomenology*, 67.

22. "The boy 'appears' in line by being seen as reproducing the father's image and is even imagined as a point in another line, one that has yet to be formed, insofar as he may 'become a father' to future sons": Ahmed, *Queer Phenomenology*, 83. Nashe's placing of male playgoers above the body of Talbot might suggest that they are his metaphorical sons, especially if we remember that Renaissance genealogical charts sometimes employed the visual metaphor of the tree: the origin of the family line was placed below at the root, and descendants were placed on the various branches spreading above.

23. Zimmerman, *Early Modern Corpse*, 130, is citing Park, "The Life of the Corpse," 116.

24. Ibid., 131, citing Park, "The Criminal and Saintly Body," 6; idem, "The Life of the Corpse," 116.

25. Ibid., 131–32.

26. Richard Rambuss demonstrates in *Closet Devotions* that even the sacramental can have erotic, and homoerotic, implications.

27. Freccero, *Queer / Early / Modern*, 80.

28. Radway, *Reading the Romance*, 128.

29. Ibid., 129.

30. It would be naïve, however, to ignore the conservative elements of the blog, not least its celebration of traditional male gender roles. As Radway argues, the romance as a genre might be considered "fundamentally conservative on the one hand or incipiently oppositional on the other": ibid., 209.

31. An illuminatingly blunt celebration of the dominant virility of the "alpha male" can be found at the website "The Modern Male," by Dan Bacon. In Bacon's polarized gender ideology, alpha and beta males are completely distinct beings: by purchasing Bacon's self-help book, a beta male can become an alpha male, but one cannot simply be—nor would one want to be—an alpha-beta male.

32. Stewart, *Close Readers*, 84–121.

33. Freccero, *Queer / Early / Modern*, 85; cf. Pye, *Vanishing*, 37.

The Gayest Play Ever

STEPHEN GUY-BRAY

Henry VI, Part 2 is not gay in the sense of being concerned with intense same-sex bonds (it does not consist of five acts of hot earl-on-earl action, for instance), but it is gay in the pejorative sense popular with young people today of being weak: The play does not have many of the qualities now called Shakespearean and has thus suffered in comparison with most of the other history plays (while admittedly being more popular than poor *King John*). For one thing, the demands the play makes on the spectator's knowledge of English history are considerable and arguably greater than the demands made by *Henry IV, Part 1* or *Richard II*, to name two of the really popular history plays. Moreover, the action of the play is confusing: Much of *Henry VI, Part 2* presents the various transformations of the play's various characters, and it is not always clear from one scene to the next who is in charge in the kingdom or in the hierarchical relationships on which the kingdom depends: the relationships, for instance, between governor and governed, upper class and lower class, husband and wife. Nor, on the whole, does the play give us the memorable characters and poetic speeches that are the hallmark of what we have been taught to see as Shakespearean drama. Instead, *Henry VI, Part 2* focuses on the fluidity of identity and the power of performance. Also, in focusing on the power and intelligence of women and in allotting a considerable amount of stage time to a peasants' rebellion, the play gives us the materials with which to mount a critique of the hierarchies on which the world of the play and of Shakespeare's history plays in general depend. For these reasons, we could see the play as being gay in the sense of queer—perhaps not least in the fact that, if we think the play is good, and I do, we might be led to question the dominant views of Shakespeare's achievement, views that are really only based on the plays (perhaps as little as a quarter of the plays he wrote) that are currently in favor.

The idea that identities of all sorts are fluid and determined by performance has become one of the central concepts of much queer theory. In the play, the typical form this performance takes is substitution. The substitutions begin even before the first act with the play's title, and many of the play's substitutions are onomastic. In most editions of Shakespeare, the play is called *Henry VI, Part 2*, a title that derives from the Folio of 1623; however, in 1594, when the play was first published, it was called *The First Part of the Contention of the Two Famous Houses of York and Lancaster*, and this name is used in some editions, as it is in the Norton. Once the play begins, we soon learn that names, even at the highest level—or, rather especially at the highest level—are no guarantee of order or meaning. In the first few lines of the play, for instance, Suffolk refers to Margaret as a princess and to himself as a marquis, when in fact she is already a queen and he will soon be a duke.[1] These examples should remind us that fifteenth-century English society was characterized in some ways by change (and often by violent change) rather than by stability. This is certainly the vision of the play presented by the title *The First Part of the Contention of the Two Famous Houses of York and Lancaster*, which calls attention to conflict and to the substitution of members of one branch of the royal family for another.

On the other hand, to call the play *Henry VI, Part 2* is to stress continuity, despite Henry's own weakness. If there is a Henry VI, there must be a Henry V (and, as English history tells us, a Henry VII and a Henry VIII); if there is a part 2, there must be a part 1 (and, as literary history tells us, a part 3). These two kinds of continuity (historical and dramatic) are not so much related or similar as interdependent or even identical: Of all kinds of literature, a history play is perhaps most susceptible to being understood narratively. A narrative is, in effect, a machine for producing meaning and for transmitting information. In this context, our contemporary understanding of information is genetic information, the DNA that we fondly hope will explain everything. In Shakespeare's time, the information in question was more likely to be the name or title that placed a person and that explained his or her relation to the world. The action of the play demonstrates the instability of names and titles, but the title of the play as a whole might serve as a useful corrective to any vision of general instability. The power of narrative—of the narrative of the history plays and of the narrative of English history—ultimately turns out to be too great to be defeated by all the performances set in motion by the play itself.

It might be most accurate to say that *Henry VI, Part 2* performs the power of performance without finally endorsing it. For instance, the play opens when the Marquis of Suffolk reports to the king on his mission to France,

telling Henry that he went "to marry Princess Margaret for your Grace"
(1.1.4). Suffolk says that the marriage took place in the "presence of the Kings
of France and Sicil" (1.1.6) and that he carried out his "task and was espoused"
(1.1.9). Of course, Suffolk also makes it clear that he was acting as Henry's
proxy and that his mission has now ended with the safe arrival of Margaret at
the English court. Crucially, he speaks of Henry's hands as "the substance /
Of that great shadow I represent" (1.1.13–14). But while this image is most
obviously intended as a comment on the restoration of the real state of affairs,
throughout the play it is often difficult to determine in any particular case
which is the substance and which is the shadow. In this case, Suffolk's marriage to Margaret is only a performance of marriage that stands in for her real
marriage to Henry, but for much of the play it is really Suffolk who functions
as Margaret's mate. Shakespeare's confusion of shadow and substance here is
typical of his approach throughout the play, and I shall look at some other
examples of this approach, but it is still clear overall which is which. Within
the dramatic narrative, Suffolk is beheaded; Margaret is punished for her
audacity; and Henry's weakness is shown to be an insurmountable problem.
Within the historical narrative, the upheavals of the middle of the fifteenth
century lead to the establishment of the Tudor dynasty and the triumphs of
the sixteenth century. Shadow and substance turn out to be distinguishable
after all.

The impression of reading or seeing the play is typically one of instability,
however. Shakespeare demonstrates instability in a variety of ways, one of
which is clothing. Early in the play, Margaret asks Suffolk, "Is this the fashions
in the court of England" (1.3.47) and goes on to ask, "Am I a queen in title and
in style, / And must be made a subject to a duke?" (1.3.53–54). If kingship is no
longer fixed, then identity as a whole becomes provisional in the world of the
play and—in a way that now seems to us to be distinctively queer—both
selves and names become to some extent fictitious. We might also identify as
queer the focus in these lines on fashion and style; while these words have
multiple meanings, and the obvious ones in this speech are respectively "way
of acting" and "mode of address," the sartorial meanings were available to
Shakespeare. What is more, I would argue that the idea of identity as a garment that can be put on and taken off (and put on and taken off by anyone) is
especially apposite in *Henry VI, Part 2*. At the very center of the play and of the
world in which it is set is, of course, the royal crown of England itself, which
often seems throughout the history plays to be merely a garment that anyone
might wear, the accessory that makes the (royal) outfit.

Still, Shakespeare demonstrates that things are not quite that fluid. An especially clear example of the limits of what we could call the sartorial theory of identity comes at the beginning of the Act 2, when the mayor of St. Albans presents Simpcox, a poor man who has miraculously regained his sight, to the court. Gloucester questions the man by asking him to identify the colors of the garments worn by some of the courtiers. Simpcox identifies red, green, yellow, and black, but when he is unable to name three successive people to whom Gloucester points, he is declared to be

> the lying'st knave
> In Christendom. If thou hadst been born blind
> Thou mightst as well have known our names as thus
> To name the several colours we do wear. (2.1.129–32)

Simpcox is indeed lying about having been blind, but his responses make perfect sense nonetheless. While the garments do have particular colors, and while garments do appear to constitute identity in the world of *Henry VI, Part 2*, the connection between the name and the individual has already been shown to be unstable—not only in this play but in the history plays as a whole. For instance, while "King Henry" and "the Duke of Gloucester" are both stable as names, over the course of the history plays these names refer to different people. In this play, for instance, the Duke of Gloucester is Humphrey, the younger son of Henry IV, but the spectators would know that Richard of York, who also appears in the play, will be Duke of Gloucester before becoming King Richard (the third of that name). Simpcox's apparent confusion over names is shared by most of the history plays' viewers and readers and is an entirely explicable problem. Nevertheless, the fact that Simpcox is unable to profit from this instability draws attention to the limits of performative power in the play.

In *Henry VI, Part 2* and, to some extent, in the history plays as a whole, it seems that names and titles—even royal titles—can be put on and taken off just like clothes, and in this play, the instability of names among the royalty and high nobility of England is complemented by a similar instability in gender. For instance, Simpcox's wife is given considerable prominence, and in the scene of the conjuration, it is the witch Margery Jordan who predominates. Most obviously, of course, each of the two royal couples in the play—the king and queen and the Duke and Duchess of Gloucester—is composed of a bold and daring woman and a mild-mannered man, and each woman is impatient with her husband's gentleness. It could be said that these gender reversals are onc of the distinctive features of the Henry VI plays. In addition to the unusual power and ferocity of Queen Margaret in this play and in the third part of the trilogy, there is, of course, also the figure of Joan of Arc in the first part. As was the case with Simpcox, however, Shakespeare draws our attention to these apparent exceptions to the rule only to reinforce the rule: These women ultimately are all punished.

It turns out that the undermining of stable identities and the emphasis on identity as a function of performance are not only masculine privileges but also the privileges of the upper class. When Gloucester orders the arrest of Simpcox and his wife, who have attempted a minor transformation that would have yielded a moderate reward, the wife says, "Alas, sir, we did it for pure need" (2.1.157). In a way that is instructive for our own thinking about contemporary queerness, performance is not equally open to all classes. Jack Cade's rebellion is a good illustration of this point. His self-presentation is marked by substitutions (4.2.33–107). He presents himself as a Mortimer, says that his mother is a Plantagenet and his wife, a Lacey, and, in what may be the play's most marked performance of identity, declares himself a knight. The initial success of the rebellion seems to indicate that Cade's transformation has worked, but this is qualified by the fact that before we saw Cade, the Duke of York told the audience that he had

> seduced a headstrong Kentishman,
> John Cade of Ashford,
> To make commotion, as full well he can,
> Under the title of John Mortimer. (3.1.356–59)

Despite his power, then, Cade is himself ultimately only a substitute for one of the powerful nobles who rule the world of the play, and the failure of his rebellion and his un-heroic death suggest that transformations of identity may only be temporary.

Cade's fall resembles the fall of the Duchess of Gloucester in that both serve to point out the limits of substitution. I shall look at her fall first. The Duchess is consistently associated with substitution: of her husband for his nephew and of herself for the queen. In fact, when the Duchess dreams that she is crowned in Westminster Abbey, she underlines this substitution by referring to the queen as "Dame Margaret" (1.2.39); the title of "dame" was reserved for English women who were not of noble birth—like the Duchess herself. When the Duchess is disgraced, Henry summons her as "Dame Eleanor Cobham, Gloucester's wife" (2.3.1). Not only does he thus strip her of her married name and end her ambitions, he also proclaims the fixity of her identity in its earlier form as the daughter of an English gentleman. The Duchess herself appears to endorse the idea of a fixed identity in her final lines in the play. After performing the penance in which she had to walk through London in her shift, she is sent to the Isle of Man as a prisoner. The governor of the island points out that as her penance has been done she can change out of her shift, to which the Duchess says, "My shame will not be shifted with my sheet" (2.4.108), making a distinction between clothing, which can be altered at will, and identity and reputation, which are now seen as fixed. The Duchess's play on the two meanings of "shift" may hint that play is really only permissible in language, but that in the social sphere identities are not infinitely malleable. The Duchess is forced to learn the limits of what I have called the sartorial theory of identity, as well as the limits of women's power.

When Cade last appears, he is a hunted man, driven to risk his life by coming into the open because of his hunger, a variety of the "pure need" mentioned by Simpcox's wife and thus a reminder of the extent to which the lives of the poor are less malleable than the lives of the rich. Unfortunately for him, Cade turns up in the garden of Alexander Iden, a Kentish squire who kills him and takes his head to the king. On the one hand, this action represents the restoration of order after the chaos of the rebellion; on the other, the parallels between Cade and Iden serve to draw our attention to the limits of play and mobility. For one thing, the characters enter the scene by uttering similar platitudes. Cade says, "Fie on ambitions" (4.9.1), and Iden says, "Lord who would live turmoil'd in the court / And may enjoy such quiet walks as these?" (4.9.14–15). Although Iden initially appears to pity Cade, he eventually kills him; when the dying Cade reveals his identity, Iden strikes off his head and takes it to the king, who is pleased by this thoughtful present and knights him (5.1.76–77). This is a new version of the seventh scene of the Act 4, when the heads of Lord Saye and Sir James Cromer were displayed with considerable merriment for Cade's benefit. A further parallel is that both Cade and Iden seek promotion. The play as a whole could be taken to demonstrate that to advance from being a peasant to being a ruler is impossible and that a man who seeks to make this change must be presumptuous and ridiculous. Nevertheless, the less drastic change from country gentleman to knight that Iden accomplishes is possible.

Both Cade's fall and the Duchess's should remind us that the social acts as a limit to what is possible. Another limit is the body, and the decapitated heads in the second half of the play—including Suffolk's head, which makes it into two scenes (a Shakespearean record, I believe)—are a particularly vivid illustration of the power of the social. While the play begins in a welter of narratives and the play as a whole seems never quite to cohere, the confusion of the play is more apparent than real, and the action of the play as a whole is underwritten by the dominant narrative of royal power. The substitutions of the play turn out not to matter so long as there is a strong hierarchy. After all, royal power is premised on substitution, as the saying "The king is dead, long live the king" demonstrates. The play creates a space in which play and experimentation are possible, but this space is circumscribed, as nothing is allowed to interfere with political continuity for very long. The substitutions and instabilities of the play recall (or anticipate) our contemporary idea of queerness, but the play's ultimate focus on the limits of substitutions and instabilities should remind us that performance is not action. Performance could be seen to function in *Henry VI, Part 2* as the mechanism by which queerness is tolerated in a way that will not make any real difference. Still, the play's focus on political instability, its demonstration that people do not always conform to their social and gender roles, and its depictions of pure need may lead us to question both our sense of how politics does and should work. And in being minor, peripheral, marginal, and not what people mean when they speak and write of Shakespeare as the greatest writer of all time, but still very much worthwhile for all sorts of reasons, *Henry VI, Part 2* may be gayer than we thought.

Note

1. *Henry VI, Part 2*, in Greenblatt et al., *The Norton Shakespeare*, 1.1.4, 15. Citations in parentheses are to this edition.

Henry VI, Part 3

Stay

CARY HOWIE

Henry VI, Part 3 is a play in a hurry. It is, of course, many other things, as well. It might seem more sensible, in a volume like this one, to address the gender inversions and anxieties that permeate its world. After all, Queen Margaret is repeatedly compared to an Amazon; her husband, Henry, to the goddess Diana. Time after time, the various noblemen fighting for York or Lancaster describe one another—particularly in their neglect of fraternal or filial duty— as unnatural. Richard of Gloucester is a hunchback and, in Henry's estimation, a scatological "lump," "indigested and deformed."[1] But nothing—not even gender, not even the shape of a bent body—seems to return, undigested and insistent, with the frequency of this play's preoccupation with abridged time, its repeated refusal, in its own words, to stay. Nonetheless, by staging a nearly universal refusal to stay or stand or linger or wait, *Henry VI, Part 3* also raises the complicated question of how gender effects may be articulated temporally: It shows the queer stakes—in the most violent sense possible—of cutting to the chase.

Henry's haste is not limited to any one of its warring factions. The play's action—the fifteenth-century houses of York and Lancaster literally duke it out over competing claims to England—implicates both sets of contenders in a surprisingly symmetrical set of gestures. Margaret and Clifford, on the Lancastrian side, theatrically stab the Duke of York at the end of Act 1; Gloucester and Clarence, on the Yorkist side, return the favor to Margaret's son, Prince Edward, in the play's final act. Everyone accuses everyone else of usurping the throne; everyone's claims are articulated almost exclusively in terms of filial succession. But more striking even than these symmetries is the vocabulary of speed and impatience: If George can say, "Forslow no longer, make we hence amain" (2.3.56), Edward can equally observe how "haste is needful in this desperate case" (4.1.128). There are, to be sure, moments of invoked pause—Edward, like York before him, will take time to breathe (2.6.30)—but

Somerset's words in Act 4 are more representative of the play's overall frenzy: "Come therefore, let's about it speedily" (4.6.102).

What is the gender—or, for that matter, the sexuality—of speed? Somerset's exhortation, after all, could apply as easily to the bedroom as to the battlefield. What, in other words, are the erotic (but also, of course, the political) consequences of refusing to stay? The Earl of Oxford speaks explicitly of a "policy"—and therefore a politics—of haste when he describes Edward this way: "It is his policy / to haste thus fast to find us unprovided" (5.4.62–63). Haste is not just the impulsive, if inevitable, result of an escalation of armed conflict; it is a "policy," a strategic decision and, perhaps, a matter of political principle. Edward's is a hurried politics, in Oxford's estimation, to be contrasted—we might infer—with the relative slowness of his rival Henry's contemplative inclinations. Edward's erotics, for its part, is no less hurried. When, in Act 3, he flirts with Lady Grey, who has come to ask for her dead husband's land, she innocently declares, "Right gracious lord I cannot brook delay" (3.2.18), and Edward ironically grants her wish. He cuts short their discussion of Lady Grey's reluctance to sleep with (and ultimately to marry) him by commanding, "Answer no more, for thou shalt be my queen" (3.2.106). Haste, here, takes the form of the imperative not to answer as well as the form of absolute—and absolutely foreclosed—futurity: "Thou *shalt* be my queen." The erotics of haste, then, demands a future whose determination is already done; a future of refused response, whose political equivalent in the play is Edward's declaration that "they shall have wars" (4.1.114); where the certainty of what is to come confirms its tyranny and its despair. The world in which wars and marriage are inevitable—and, more than inevitable, to be hastened toward—is a world in which it is difficult to think otherwise, a world in which it is difficult to imagine other times or other logics than those of succession and usurpation, coercion and refusal.

Edward is not alone in his impatience; nor is he alone in inflecting that impatience erotically. Margaret, his enemy, who will be called "an Amazonian trull" by York later in Act 1 (1.4.114), also insists that patience is no virtue. In the very first scene, having accused her husband of "unnatural[ly]" disinheriting his son in a bid to placate his Yorkist rivals (1.1.219), she responds in these terms to Henry's demand for patience:

Henry: Be patient, gentle queen, and I will stay.
Margaret: Who can be patient in such extremes? (1.1.215–16)

Patience, here, is incommensurate with extremity (and, one might also observe, with gentleness). Its temporality—of "stay[ing]," which is to say, of endurance and, perhaps, deferral—is resolutely *between* those ends of things that extremity presumes to mark and know. Margaret will go on to accuse her husband of untimeliness, as if it were bound up with (and perhaps analogous to) the unmanliness elsewhere ascribed to him (e.g., 1.1.187): "What is it [relinquishing his title to York] but to make thy sepulcher / And creep into it far before thy time?" (1.1.237–38). She then turns to her son and says, at this point unsurprisingly, "Come son away, we may not linger thus" (1.1.264).

Whereas Henry's lingering implies the threatening interstices of a premature death and, just as important, a spatialized (which is to say, a literally entombed) time, Margaret prefers the clarity of extremes. Faced with the ambiguities of staying, she chooses to leave. It is, however, telling that the very demand she refuses here—Henry's demand to stay—is one that she will take up with Edward, to no avail, a little later in the play:

> *Margaret*: Stay, Edward.
> *Edward*: No, wrangling woman, we'll no longer stay.
> These words will cost ten thousand lives this day. (2.2.175–77)

Margaret finds herself requesting the very patience that she has just denied. In doing so, she foregrounds both the reversibility and the communal implications of staying: The demand to stay is always, in other words, a demand to stay *with* someone, to keep someone company, to inhabit a shared time or sense of time. To refuse this demand is to refuse what could be said to be common, a refusal highlighted by Edward's ironic "we": togetherness, the acknowledgment that the first person plural binds us somehow, is what persists "no longer," to the extent, in fact, that it will take the hyperbolic form of the loss of "ten thousand lives." Moreover—but what, really, does "more" say, in the horizon of such horribly enumerated death?—Margaret's request for patience is explicitly inscribed as feminine: To stay is to acquiesce to the demands of a "wrangling woman," and the suture torn open by Edward's refusal, therefore, is not only between singularities and the "we" (royal or not) through which they are collectively spoken; nor is it only between the living and the dead; but it is also, more concretely, between men and women, which is to say, between bodies authorized and unauthorized to wrangle.

Warwick, one of Edward's close allies who will eventually join the Lancastrians, similarly aligns femininity with standing still:

Why stand we like soft-hearted women here,
Wailing our losses while the foe doth rage,
And look upon as if the tragedy
Were played in jest by counterfeiting actors?
Here on my knee I vow to God above
I'll never pause again, never stand still
Till either death hath closed these eyes of mine
Or fortune given me measure of revenge. (2.3.25–32)

Coming hard on the heels of Edward's dismissal of Margaret, standing becomes, in Warwick's formulation, what women do, women who are, here, not wrangling but "soft-hearted." In fact, standing is accompanied by "wailing," with the implication that this show of grief—which is also a show of the soft heart, a particular kind of cardiac display –would be explicitly and effeminately theatrical. But what seems crucial to me is not the (often remarked) *mise en abîme* of war and theater but, instead, something simpler and more damning—namely, the temporal foreclosure of Warwick's double refusal: "I'll never pause again, never stand still." This repeated "never" occurs in an analogously double horizon: that of death, on the one hand, and fortune, on the other. Nonetheless—like the absolute future of Edward's "thou shalt" and "they shall have"—Warwick's double "never" is recklessly certain, literally cavalier, in relation to its own future, to the sorts of possibility and impossibility that death and fortune might otherwise seem to mark as precisely unknowable. (It is not coincidental that Warwick will both switch allegiances and die before the play is over.) And the standstill that Warwick refuses is also, once again, the site of a crisis in community, in the pronouns through which community articulates itself. "Why stand *we*" gives way to "*I'll* never stand still": the ties that bind us—which is to say, the ties that bind *me* to *us*—seem to require some kind of pause.

What would it mean, in this light, to stay together? *Henry VI, Part 3* shows how even King Henry's contemplative response is inadequate to the question. Within the economy of the play, Henry comes closest, to be sure, to standing still. In Act 2, he yearns nostalgically for the life of the shepherd who, in Henry's words, would spend his days "carv[ing] out dials quaintly" and "see[ing] the minutes how they run" (2.5.24–25). But this task—which Henry also calls "divid[ing] the times" (2.5.30)—is a fundamentally solitary one. It does not solve the problem of the social; it avoids the social altogether. Pastoral time, in other words, does not mend, or attempt to mend, the double rift (within the temporal and the social) spoken by Warwick's double negation. Rather, it consists of the fantasy of a pure time—the fantasy of a solitary relation to time in the abstract, a time thought outside of the constraints it imposes on others, a time, in fact, that has, properly speaking, no outside, but is merely internally divisible ad nauseam (or really *ad mortem*). To stay would be to remain with the *indivisible*, with what is stubbornly beyond quantification, with what threatens—but also, always, promises—to be more than it is. In contrast, Henry's pastoral reverie is, for all his talk of piety, a resolutely *immanent* fantasy: the fantasy of a time that is no more than it is; a time that will fail to surprise.

And this is where *Henry IV, Part 3* may speak to queer theory—not just because the primary ways of thinking eroticized temporalities seem to have narrowed in recent years, in certain circles, to the choice or refusal of a future (a future that, chosen or refused, never ceases, like Warwick's, to be ultimately knowable and, therefore, unsurprising), and not just because standing still might be one strategy of resistance among the many that have been ascribed to, and embraced by, people and objects variously described as queer, but, just as important, because the problem of our staying, the problem of *our* pause, in the strongest sense, is one in which the time of our sexed, gendered, and desiring bodies is inseparable from the thought of who *we* are, whoever we are. That is, there may be as much, or more, compressed within this slight, slow imperative—*stay*—as within any explicit account of what bodies do with their extremes.

To stay with a text like *Henry VI, Part 3* is also, then, to stay with one another, to acknowledge patiently what happens in the middle of things, where we are reading and living, singularly and in common, but also writing and fighting and waiting and dying; where one of the hardest things to do, but also one of the most necessary, is to resist the impulse to say what we will or will not become. But the alternative to this is not retreat. It is not Henry's pastoral withdrawal. Instead—and whether this is queer or not is, really, beside the point—it may be a question of learning to be more gentle, especially if, as Henry implies when he speaks to Margaret, gentleness may align itself with patience. What would a gentle criticism look like? Could it disrupt the violence that so often attends this play's staging of the body in haste? Could it even disrupt—in the most literal sense of disruption, and, with all due respect to Toni Braxton, could it *unbreak*—the brokenness, the ungentle extremes, of our critical habits, accustomed as we so frequently are to the form and the fantasy of disputation? How can we begin to treat our texts and one another more gently? *Henry IV, Part 3* provides us with at least one gesture toward a response. It invites us to stay here. Stay longer. Wait a while. Something or someone may still—may even, and this is the most shocking thing, *gently*—take us by surprise.

151

Note

1. Martin, *Henry VI, Part 3*, 5.6.51. Citations in parentheses are to this edition.

Julius Caesar

Thus, Always: *Julius Caesar* and Abraham Lincoln

BETHANY SCHNEIDER

Forward

I began thinking about the queerness of Shakespeare's *Julius Caesar* by thinking about the three Booth brothers. The Booth brothers were American actors. One, John Wilkes Booth, assassinated Abraham Lincoln. Another, Edwin Booth, became the greatest American tragedian of the nineteenth century and an important interpreter of *Hamlet*. The third was named (after his father) Junius Brutus Booth. His name underlines the fact that these three brothers, and their relationship to *Julius Caesar*, political assassination, and repetition, was—to put it mildly—overdetermined. In 1864, five months before John killed Lincoln, these three brothers performed *Julius Caesar* together to a packed house at New York's fabulous Winter Garden Theater. It would have been cool if John, the future assassin, had played Brutus, but in fact he took the role of Marc Antony. Edwin was Brutus, and Junius was Cassius.

There is certainly something queer—or maybe it's just plain gay—about three handsome brothers (people said John was the handsomest man in America) acting together, in togas. Then, five years after Lincoln was assassinated, Edwin staged a spectacular and long-running production of *Julius Caesar* in the new Booth Theater in New York. He played, in succession, Brutus, then Cassius, and finally Marc Antony. There is *really* something queer about the fact that Americans flocked to see John Wilkes Booth's brother kill Caesar as Brutus, then kill Caesar as Cassius, and finally mourn Caesar as Marc Antony. Perhaps it is the prurience of it and the proliferation of Edwin's performances sideways into multiple political "brothers" (Americans) whose actions swarm around the figure of Caesar (Lincoln). Certainly you get to feel all sorts of things—some naughtier than others—about political brotherhood and about your dead political daddy if you see his assassin's real flesh-and-blood brother act out all three of those roles. And that, in a nutshell, is how I started thinking about the queerness of *Julius Caesar*. What follows is the end of that train of thought.[1]

Plutarch and Lincoln

Sometime in the late winter or early spring of 1865, Abraham Lincoln had a dream. He relayed the dream to his friend, Ward Hill Lamon, who wrote it down:

> There seemed to be a death-like stillness about me. Then I heard subdued sobs, as if a number of people were weeping. I thought I left my bed and wandered downstairs. There the silence was broken by the same pitiful sobbing, but the mourners were invisible. . . . I kept on until I arrived at the East Room, which I entered. There I met with a sickening surprise. Before me was a catafalque, on which rested a corpse wrapped in funeral vestments. Around it were stationed soldiers who were acting as guards; and there was a throng of people, gazing mournfully upon the corpse, whose face was covered, others weeping pitifully. "Who is dead in the White House?" I demanded of one of the soldiers. "The President," was his answer; "he was killed by an assassin." Then came a loud burst of grief from the crowd, which woke me from my dream. I slept no more that night; and although it was only a dream, I have been strangely annoyed by it ever since.[2]

The most obvious thing about this dream, in retrospect (and retrospect came very quickly, for Lincoln was shot on Good Friday, April 14, 1865), is the fact that several elements of Lincoln's dream "came true." Not only was Lincoln assassinated, but the long drama of Lincoln's funeral procession across the United States began with his body laid out for viewing upon just such a catafalque—the plinth on which a coffin is displayed—in the East Room, where it was viewed by many mourning Americans (see figure 1). Of course Lamon may well have made up or embellished aspects of the dream. Perhaps he thought that Lincoln needed signs and portents (after all, "When beggars die there are no comets seen; / The heavens themselves blaze forth the death of princes").[3] Perhaps he added some frills and furbelows to a dream that wasn't quite so . . . screamingly portentous. Or perhaps Lamon is an utterly reliable narrator and Lincoln could indeed see the future. Why not?

If the dream is prophetic, it is also a repetition of—or, at least, it shares

FIGURE 1. President Abraham Lincoln's funeral service
at the White House, *Harper's Weekly*, May, 1865

some interesting generic elements with—Plutarch's account of Julius Caesar's assassination. Here is Sir Thomas North's translation from *Parallel Lives*,
the source Shakespeare used for his drama:

> Men reporte also, that Caesar did still defende him selfe against the rest,
> running everie waye with his bodie: but when he sawe Brutus with his
> sworde drawen in his hande, then he pulled his gowne over his heade, and
> made no more resistaunce, and was driven either casually, or purposedly,
> by the counsel of the conspirators, against the base whereupon Pompeys
> image stoode, which ranne all of a goare bloude, till he was slain. Thus it
> seemed, that the image tooke just revenge of Pompeys enemie, being
> throwen downe on the ground at his feete, and yelding up his ghost there,
> for the number of wounds he had upon him.[4]

In Lincoln's dream, the face of the corpse is already covered; Plutarch's Caesar
covers his own face. In both cases, the head of the assassinated leader ends up
shrouded. Both Lincoln and Caesar have a moment of revelation; each recognizes and accepts the reality of his assassination through the words or actions

of a soldierly figure. In Caesar's case, the young man, Brutus, is beloved, perhaps (some say) an illegitimate son. In Lincoln's case, the young man is generically beloved, a symbolic son, a sort of universal Union soldier chosen to guard the president's body.

Both Caesar and Lincoln were killed in theaters: Caesar in Pompey's Theater in Rome, where the Senate was meeting on that Ides of March while the Senate building itself was being renovated, and Lincoln in the Ford Theater in Washington, where he was attending a Good Friday performance of *Our American Cousin*. Of course when Lincoln dreamed his dream, that death in the theater was in the future. But for the sake of argument, and because it is fun, let us accept that Lincoln dreamed exactly as Lamon reports and that he was dreaming the future. Lincoln's actual death was literally and hyperbolically theatrical. If you are going to have a scary prophetic dream of your own death, why not foresee that moment when, while watching a play, you are shot from behind? If ties to Caesar's assassination entwine your dream, why not foresee that you will be shot by an actor who fancies himself a modern-day Brutus and who famously acted in *Julius Caesar* just a few months earlier? Why not dream him hollering *"sic semper tyrannis?"* It is not from Shakespeare or Plutarch, but it is Latin, and it does suggest that no assassination is singular ("thus always to tyrants"). Honest Abe was, however, subtler than that. He does not dream his own death in a theater, but he still dreams of theater. He encounters the East Room as a stage with performance in full swing, complete with actors and audience and set. He is woken by the audience ("crowd") reaction. The weeping, like applause, awakens him to the realization that he has also been an audience to a drama that is not real (though it will be).

Sic semper is the point. Thus, always. Assassinations are always repetitions, and we should not be surprised by their sameness. And yet, that doubled theater of assassination is pretty damn uncanny—more so when you realize that it is not only doubled, but that each iteration is nested with repetition, with literal stages within stages. Both Plutarch's and Lamon's theatrical scenes have, at their center, a plinth. When the dreaming Lincoln enters the East Room, he is confronted by something that makes him feel "sickening surprise." Eventually he learns that the president lies dead. But it is not that revelation that first nauseates him. It is the sight of the ceremonial plinth on which a coffin is displayed: "Before me was a catafalque." Plutarch is also interested in a plinth. Caesar, in his agonies, could have expired anywhere in the room but finally dies against the base of Pompey's statue. What is so creepy, so fateful, so overwhelming about a *plinth*? These two—the catafalque

and the statue's base—are stages within stages and uphold the constancy of
the past and the sameness of the future in the midst of the volatile passing
moment. Dramatic action, live, real, swirls around them—murders!—but on
these pedestals dead fathers are held up in their permanency, blindly over-
looking the very assassinations that, in toppling them, constitute them again.
A statue made of stone and a corpse pumped full of preservative chemicals
reside, eternal, ossified, elevated, above the seemingly singular live action of
assassination. Both dying Caesar and dreaming Lincoln are still (barely) alive
in these scenes. Dreaming and dying—each is brought up short by his own
imminent monumentality. They stumble (die, begin to wake to a consciousness of impending death) against a plinth.

Rebecca Schneider (yes, she is my sister, and yes, that is a bit awkward in an
essay partly about murderously reenacting siblings) has this important element to add to the old story of sons killing fathers—the importance of the
monument to the scene:

> Patricidic Culture is culture that depends on the production of Dead Dads
> —dads must die to insure that dead dads remain. Patricidic Culture is a
> culture invested in insuring that the dead remain, and the live pass by. . . .
> The drama of brothers and fathers in opposition to others is horrifyingly
> playing out, performed, across monuments again and again.[5]

The moment that the soon-to-be-dead dad confronts the plinth, he confronts
not his own end but his own transformation from an actor / brother into the
immortality of dead, monumental paternity. This patriarchal futurity, centered by the monument, depends, as Rebecca Schneider argues, "on the production of dead fathers, killed for safekeeping into the interest of brothers."[6]
Caesar and Lincoln each have a plinth embedded in the theatrical scene in
which they come to understand their own assassination. They share it, because *what* they must understand in that moment is their own imminent
monumentality, a sort of dead immortality that is reconstituted through repetition. And assassination, like all good queer performance, is "a kind of imitation for which there is no original."[7]

Plutarch sees Caesar as already a variation on a theme, pairing him with
Alexander the Great in the very structure of *Parallel Lives*. He also doubts the
singularity of Caesar's assassination. He is suspicious of the drama of the death
against the plinth, wondering whether the senators drove the dying man
against the statue "casually, or purposely." That "purposely" suggests that
Caesar's death was a literary as well as a political plot. In its theatricality, the

assassination is already generic, already a repetition—and Plutarch knows it *because* of that plinth. As for Lincoln, his assassination is old hat before it even occurs. And if Lincoln dreams the future, he also dreams *from* the future. The dream begins with "deathlike stillness"—he is already dead when he dreams his own future death. When he learns of his death from the soldier, he learns of its immediate multiplicity. "Who is dead in the White House?" he asks, and the answer is not "Abraham Lincoln," but "the President." There is always a king ("The king is dead, long live the king"), and there is always a president. Lincoln's "two bodies"—one spectrally dreaming; the other shrouded and dead—confront each other in the dream.[8] Lincoln's assassination doubles (perhaps infinitely multiplies) him into "the President." Our generation knows that Lincoln's assassination was merely the first of many attempted and successful assassinations of presidents, but his generation also experienced his assassination as multiple, already a repetition. Here is Walt Whitman in 1879:

> How the imagination—how the student loves these things! America, too, is to have them. For not in all great deaths, not far or near—not Caesar in the Roman senate-house . . .—outvies that terminus of the secession war, in one man's life, there in our midst, in our own time—that seal of the emancipation of three million slaves—that parturition and delivery of our at last really free Republic, born again, henceforth to commence its career of genuine homogeneous Union, compact, consistent with itself.[9]

The eternal repetition of assassination (*"sic semper tyrannis"*) is, indeed, in the service of patricidal sons. The very fact that Lincoln's death is a more glorious copy of Caesar's proves for Lincoln's generation the monumental immortality of the dead dad, under whose stony eye brothers can continue to make beautiful patriarchy together. It is homosocial reproductivity at its best, that "parturition and delivery of our at last really free Republic, born again," in which braces of patricidal sons are begotten en masse by dead dads upon symbolic women. Or do patricidal sons give birth backward in time to dead dads? Assassination proposes a homosocial eternity of dead dads and patricidal sons over against the linear teleology of heterosexual reproductive futurity (see figure 2). It is no accident that only women—Calphurnia in Shakespeare's *Julius Caesar*, and Mary Todd Lincoln in rumors about the aftermath of Lincoln's dream—think that their husbands can *avoid* their fate and settle down to normal, presumably progenerative, Mr. and Mrs. status.

Laying aside Whitman's elegiacs, and more recent scholarship suggesting

FIGURE 2. J. A. Arthur, *Washington and Lincoln*
(Apotheosis), Philadelphia, 1865

that Lincoln had homosexual relationships—laying aside (reluctantly) the issue of the *Weekly World News* that claimed Lincoln was a woman and Booth
his jilted lover (see figure 3)—we can still say that Lincoln had a queer eye for
reproduction.[10] The generative power of relations between men was a life-
long fascination for Lincoln. As a teenager, Lincoln wrote a poem about two
boys named Billy and Natty getting married. The marriage could work, he
thought, but he was not sure the offspring of such a union could survive:

> So Billy and Natty agreed very well
> And mama's well pleased at the match

FIGURE 3. "Abraham Lincoln was a Woman!"
Weekly World News, January 22, 2002

The egg it is laid but Natty's afraid
The Shell is So Soft that it never will hatch.[11]

By 1863, Lincoln had decided that the egg was viable. In a speech his eulogist, Senator Charles Sumner, called "monumental," Lincoln laid out his case (a case Whitman would repeat).[12] "Four score and seven years ago our fathers brought forth on this continent, a new nation, conceived in Liberty, and dedicated to the proposition that all men are created equal." Not only can dead dads lay hatchable eggs, but while dedicating a cemetery (a site of monumentality par excellence), Lincoln is able to argue that patricidal brothers die into immortal paternity: "We here highly resolve that these dead shall not have died in vain—that this nation, under God, shall have a new birth of freedom."[13]

Julius Caesar

Which brings me, finally, by way of Plutarch and Lincoln, the first century and the nineteenth century, to William Shakespeare's sixteenth-century play *Julius Caesar*. I have gestured toward the queerness of a few of the play's nineteenth-century productions. The homosocial structures of the play itself have been ably argued by Coppelia Kahn, Barbara L. Parker, and others.[14] It is a fin-de-siècle (1599) play famously occupied with time and repetition. As David Daniell reminds us in his introduction to the Arden edition, Shakespeare is concerned that England is out of sync with Europe's adoption of the "New Style" calendar and that the English, by staying with the old Julian calendar, remain literally and politically in the time of Caesar. For example, the famous "mistake" of the clock striking in a Rome that preceded the invention of clocks can be read as a purposeful fold in time in which Shakespeare's be-clocked London is double exposed with Caesar's Rome—because they are, in fact, reduplications.[15]

So rather than reinvent the wheel (others before me have pointed out that this is a queer play about time and repetition), I will take us right to the plinth. Plutarch's anxiety over whether Caesar's death against the plinth happened "casually, or purposedly" becomes, in Shakespeare's hands, a problem encompassing the vast scope of repetitive time. After they have killed Caesar, Cassius and Brutus wash their hands in Caesar's blood and discuss what kind of immortality they have made for Caesar and themselves:

> *Cassius*: Stoop, then, and Wash. How many ages hence
> Shall this our lofty scene be acted over
> In states unborn and accents yet unknown?
> *Brutus*: How many times shall Caesar bleed in sport
> That now on Pompey's basis lies along,
> No worthier than the dust? (3.1.130–35)

Exultant Cassius and ambivalent Brutus have just assassinated the ruler of a vast empire. But with Caesar's blood wet on their hands, that singular murder has already shattered into countless reenactments across human history. On that they are agreed. They disagree over whether the repetitions will be "lofty" or "base." It is a divide between kinds of memory: high and low; purposeful and casual; political and theatrical. Cassius's "lofty" ignores the now ominous plinth on which monumental memory is always staged. Brutus insists on the plinth, pointing out that it *is* a stage, and argues that Caesar's death will return not in the political sphere but in the endless nested iterations of theater. Caesar died against a stage prop, Brutus argues. He will bleed in sport in future, because he bleeds in sport now. *Julius Caesar* was probably the play that opened the Globe Theater. Its first audience knew that England was one of the unborn states Cassius predicted, but what they *saw* was Caesar bleeding in sport, his death giving birth not to a new nation, but to a new theater.

What both Cassius and Brutus admit in this exchange is that the purported goal of their actions—saving Rome—is already lost. If "this our lofty scene" is to "be acted over / In states unborn and accents yet unknown," and if Caesar is to become a mere stock character in future theatricals, then Rome itself— the Eternal City—must disappear to make way for new, post-imperial (imperial again) states. Cassius and Brutus assassinate Caesar to save Rome and thereby immortalize Caesar into monumentality and kill Rome. But the assassination will repeat in "states unborn," states of patricidal brothers whose very birth depends on the violent monumentalizing death of fathers. It is the *brotherhood* that must survive. States and theatricals—the specifics do not matter. As Cassius says in complacent response to Brutus's vision of theatrical repetitions of Caesar's death,

> So oft as that shall be,
> So often shall the knot of us be call d
> The men that gave their country liberty. (3.1.17–19)

Eternal, reproductive brotherhood is assured by the reiterative death and monumentalizing of the dad. It is assured even—perhaps especially—if that death is only in sport, played out again and again against the plinth. And so Rome returns, as England, as the United States, "that parturition and delivery of our at last really free Republic, born again."

Notes

1. There are as many publications about John Wilkes Booth and Abraham Lincoln as there are stars in the sky, including a recent biography of Booth handily entitled *American Brutus*. But I relied heavily on Furtwangler, *Assassin on Stage*. I am also grateful to Nora Johnson for sharing a chapter in progress: Johnson, "Shakespearean Melodramas."

2. Lamon, *Recollections of Abraham Lincoln, 1847–1865*.

3. Daniell, *Julius Caesar*, 2.2.30–31. Cites in parentheses are to this edition.

4. Plutarch, *Plutarch's Lives of the Noble Grecians and Romans*, 68.

5. Schneider, "Patricidal Memory and the Passerby."

6. Ibid.

7. Butler, "Imitation and Gender Insubordination," 21.

8. See Roach, *Cities of the Dead*, 73–118.

9. "Death of Abraham Lincoln: Lecture deliver'd in New York, April 14, 1879—in Philadelphia, '80—in Boston, '81," in Whitman, *The Collected Writings of Walt Whitman*, 508.

10. See Cavitch, *American Elegy*, 233–85; Tripp, *The Intimate World of Abraham Lincoln*. See also "Abraham Lincoln Was a Woman!" *Weekly World News*, January 22, 2002.

11. Herndon, *The True Story of a Great Life*, 55.

12. Sumner, *The Promises of the Declaration of Independence*, 40.

13. Lincoln, "Address at the Dedication of the Gettysburg National Cemetery."

14. See Kahn, "Passions of Some Difference," 271–83; Parker, "The Whore of Babylon and Shakespeare's Julius Caesar," 251–269.

15. David Daniell, "Introduction," in idem, *Julius Caesar*.

Queer Futility:
Or, *The Life and Death of King John*

KATHRYN SCHWARZ

In a discussion of the authorship controversies surrounding *Henry VI, Part 1*, E. M. W. Tillyard writes, "Apart from the queer reluctance to allow Shakespeare to have written ill or like other dramatists when he was immature, the chief reason why people have been hostile to Shakespeare's authorship is the way he treats Joan of Arc. That the gentle Shakespeare could have been so ungentlemanly as to make his Joan other than a saint was intolerable. This is precisely like arguing that Shakespeare could not have written *King John* because he does not mention Magna Carta."[1] I have always thought of this as a provocative comment on *Henry VI*. It also, however, involves a rather odd assumption about *King John*.

Why is *King John* safe from interrogation? It is easy to dispute the analogy —misogyny is not, after all, quite the same thing as Magna Carta—but it is perhaps more interesting to consider the underlying premise. What makes this comparatively obscure play a touchstone for the silliness of the authorship question? Could we refute an absurd proposition by saying, "That's like believing that Shakespeare didn't write *King John*?"

It might be easy to claim *King John* for Shakespeare precisely because disclaiming it wouldn't rock our world. If a hard-core Shakespearean could do a deal with a diehard Oxfordian, trading uncontested rights to *King John* for those to, say, *King Lear*, I suspect the deal would get done. There has been much good scholarship on *King John* but little sign of a general and passionate proprietary desire. Yet there has also been little evidence of aversion, of the kind of disavowal that has trailed *Titus Andronicus* or, indeed, *Henry VI, Part 1*. If Shakespeare's Joan precipitates, in Tillyard's evocative phrase, a queer reluctance, Shakespeare's John has been met with what I would venture to call a queer acceptance. The failure to question may be less indifference than symptom: if we feel we need not ask, it is perhaps because the play itself informs us that to tell, to declare legitimacy, is a perfectly counterproductive exercise. *King John* posits a radical failure of connection between assertion and authenticity. It presents a history unmoored, set adrift from fixed positions of consequence and cause. To put this in terms of an aptly improper temporality, its performative practice cites queer theory.

I want, then, to consider two obvious propositions from this play's eccentric point of view. The first such proposition is that men, as sovereign subjects, reproduce themselves by way of women. The second is that death makes history. Each of these natural laws has been interrogated and transformed by recent scholarship, and *King John* makes its own contribution to that project. Because my reading cannot queer this play, but traces a queer process already at work, I have imagined that theories of performativity and historiography might function as intertext and even play-text—not as retrospective analyses, but as parallel articulations; not as correctives, but as stage direction, character, or chorus. In what follows, italicized theoretical interjections appear in such roles.

Bastard Sentiments

"A strange beginning: 'borrowed majesty,' " the king's mother says at the start of *King John*.[2] That one line dismantles a two-step truism: history plays follow the links of authorized patrilineality, and patrilineal connections rest on bodies they claim not to need. Forged in the fantasy of autonomous replication, those connections represent symbolic power, which, as Pierre Bourdieu writes, "is defined in and through a given relation between those who exercise power and those who submit to it, i.e. in the very structure of the field in which *belief* is produced and reproduced."[3] For a structure of credible perpetuation to produce and reproduce itself, the connections among men must be at once substantiated by and phantasmatically independent of the interventions of women. The system remains self-evident and self-assured to the degree that it remains silent, complacently sustained by a founding illogic that defies articulation and forecloses the space of question. "Don't ask, don't tell" is the contract of presumptive legitimacy.

King John violates that contract. Tillyard's comment, which highlights resistance to a mean-spirited Shakespeare but accepts a Shakespeare who forgot Magna Carta, implies that affect trumps history. If in a general way this cannot be true, it might be true of *King John*. In this play sentiment endorses legitimacy, and destroys the project it pursues. As Elinor defends John against the challenge to his rule, she reveals his dependence on maternal devotion. Constance, the play's most notoriously outspoken figure, gives exclusive priority to her own attachment: "O Lord, my boy, my Arthur, my fair son! / My life, my joy, my food, my all the world! / My widow-comfort, and my sorrows' cure!" (3.4.103–5). She trusts the words of her bond to be entirely sufficient, to such an extent that she puts paternal identity in question. "My boy a bastard? By my soul I think / His father never was so true begot" (2.1.129–30). The voice of maternity contradicts the politics of reproduction: as Elinor says to Arthur, "There's a good mother, boy, that blots thy father" (2.1.131). *How could one take the* other *"side," when taking any side at all necessarily constrains one to take the side* of, *by virtue of taking a side* within, *a political order that returns to the Child as the image of the future it intends?*[4] Constance compromises the future by reimagining the past; in the context of a contested sovereign line, her affective compositions have the effect of erasure. This, I suggest, is the larger argument of *King John*, which models a queer sentimentality that displaces—literally, takes the place of—patrilineal history.

Queer sentimentality is a socially coded and at the same time anarchic mode of annexation, deployed toward targets that lose their autonomy to the power of its demand. It attaches a conventional sentiment to an appropriate object, but in so doing, it rewrites the relationship between agency and value implicit in that contract. Constance's speech, with its reiterative "my," is generative rather than reflective; her statements do not echo an immanent truth but make and own a desirable artifact. The relational frame of the transaction is less a mirror than a mirror stage through which response to an object creates the illusive integrity of a subject, only to mediate that integrity through a contingent and coercive desire. Instead of compulsively reinforcing prescribed formations—patrilineal legitimacy, for example, or conjugal duty, or filial obedience, or any other social imperative—queer sentimentality displays the constitutive but also devastating force of investment. It is in this sense a dynamic of appropriative affirmation, which reveals the extent to which the ordered relations of history are both made and unmade by the energy of proprietary affect.

This might explain the response to what Herschel Baker terms "this appalling woman's rhetoric."[5] Everyone wants Constance to stop talking: "Women and fools, break off your conference" (2.1.150); "Bedlam, have done" (2.1.183); "Peace, lady, pause, or be more temperate" (2.1.195); "I do beseech you, madam, be content" (3.1.42); "Lady Constance, peace!" (3.1.112); "O fair affliction, peace!" (3.4.36). *The offensive call runs the risk of inaugurating a subject in speech who comes to use language to counter the offensive call.*[6] Repudiating these demands, Constance imagines her rhetoric as a kind of natural disaster: "No, no, I will not, having breath to cry. / O that my tongue were in the thunder's mouth! / Then with a passion would I shake the world" (3.4.37–39). Or perhaps this is a natural disaster of kind, for articulate sentimentality disrupts the logic and obscures the meaning of heterosocial reproduction; it is, in the fully adversarial sense, a dangerous supplement. If patrilineal order confirms itself by foreclosing the need for confirmation—if its stability inheres in an Althusserian obviousness that is also and inextricably an Althusserian silence—then Constance's explicit insistence is precisely as destructive as it is redundant. Maternal passion, as affective excess, does shake the world, that historical world in which silent transmission is the only firm ground. King Philip describes Arthur in terms of such transmission, inscribing a conservative teleology that reasons seamlessly from what has been to what must be: "This little abstract doth contain that large / Which died in Geffrey; and the hand of time / Shall draw this brief into as huge a volume" (2.1.101–3). *This move bolsters the failing family, and hides the workings of power beneath the register of the sovereign, the father in all his guises.*[7] But when Philip says to Constance, "You are as fond of grief as of your child," she replies, "Grief fills the room up of my absent child" (3.4.92–93). Arthur is not yet dead, but her desolation at his loss means that he *is* lost, at least to patrilineal narrative. Grief takes the place of its object.

If Arthur is undone by the defense of his identity, Faulconbridge emerges from the loss of his name. Repeatedly described as the play's only man of action, he derives that potency from his mother's illegitimizing voice. He poses the question that no son should think to ask and no mother should need to answer: "Good my mother, let me know my father; / Some proper man, I hope. Who was it, mother?" (1.1.249–50). Inspired by his mother's account of adultery, Faulconbridge chooses a father who violates the contractual past and erases the foreseeable future. Elinor asks, "Hadst thou rather be a Faulconbridge, / And like thy brother, to enjoy thy land; / Or the reputed son of Cordelion, / Lord of thy presence and no land beside?" (1.1.134–37). *King John* animates the fantasy that in matters of paternity, what you want is what you get—or, rather, what you want got you. *What is transmitted in the cohabitation of ghostly past and present is related to survival, to "living well," and to the "pleasures of mortal creatures," survivals and pleasures that have little to do with normative understandings of biological reproduction.*[8] As desire displaces knowledge ("Ay, my mother, / With all my heart I thank thee for my father!" [1.1.269–

70]), Faulconbridge wills himself into another name: Bastard. Arthur echoes this revisionism when he appeals to his jailer: "Is it my fault that I was Geffrey's son? / No indeed is't not; and I would to heaven / I were your son, so you would love me, Hubert" (4.1.22–24). *These roles are played in signs themselves and not in ontologies.*[9] Caught up in a power game, the rightful heir to an exalted patriline prefers an affective guarantee. Fathers in this play inhabit a contingent temporality; they are necessities born of invention, expedient effects of sentimental impersonation.

Counterfactual Desires

I have little space for death, but then, so does the play. As if exhausted by the affect they have inspired and deployed, the central figures of *King John* simply vanish, their curiously unevocative absence breaking even that tenuous link between a past they have unremembered and a future they cannot ordain. *In such a world, chronology does not determine teleology, and teleology does not govern desire.*[10] Deaths appear as asides, bracketed by offstage dissolution and secondhand report. King John (or so we hear) is poisoned by a monk; Arthur jumps off a wall and dies, vanishing in two lines and a stage direction [*Fuck the social order and the Child in whose name we're collectively terrorized*].[11] The play's mothers disappear in a brutal synopsis: "The first of April died / Your noble mother; and as I hear, my lord, / The Lady Constance in a frenzy died / Three days before" (4.2.120–23). Death is closed off from the processes of consequential continuity: understated, offhand, anticlimactic, and barely told, it is an afterthought to an already vitiated teleology. The voices that linger in this play are not historical but counterfactual, their articulations taking the wistfully resistant forms of "if only" and "if not." *Any number of voices, now, could find themselves in the open space of implicit rejoinder.*[12] Counterfactuals are queer locutions, at odds with and even hostile to a dominant narrative. Here, in the failure of any such narrative, they make the condition of being at odds at once non-referential and self-sufficient. The Oxford English Dictionary cites two enigmatic uses of the term: "The analysis of counterfactuals should parallel that of 'fugitive propositions,'" and "Counterfactuals constitute an irreducible form of statement."[13] Parallel to (but never touching) an idea of ordered time rendered fugitive by alternative propositions, counterfactuals haunt the seductively incoherent space between event and desire.

History, too, dies as an afterthought, eclipsed by that fugitive and irreducible longing. It is not surprising that the Bastard, who gives up his father's name, takes the last word. He has often been construed as quintessentially English, and such a reading queers national history not only in the loose and useful sense of disengaging it from itself—the English, one might say, truly become Angles—but in the more particular sense of altering the relationship between past and future. When the Bastard speaks last, nationalist sentiment fully displaces patrilineal inheritance.

> This England never did, nor never shall,
> Lie at the proud foot of a conqueror,
> But when it first did help to wound itself.
> Now these her princes are come home again,
> Come the three corners of the world in arms,
> And we shall shock them. Nought shall make us rue,
> If England to itself do rest but true. (5.7.112–18)

The Bastard has words to die for, to be sure. But what relation exists between the dead who are afterthoughts of the past and the deaths that will secure the future? Who populates this narrative, and on what temporal or ontological terms? And what can nationalism promise when its demand is founded in the sacrifice of name? Dislocated from history by a bastard's sentimental "if," the play's ending is less a conquest narrative than a wish yoked to a risk. *Their futures can be imagined according to logics that lie outside of those paradigmatic markers of life experience—namely, birth, marriage, reproduction, and death.*[14]

King John is a bastard play. It tells a story in which every gesture toward authority exposes insufficiency and irrelevance, in which legitimacy kills. As a chronicle play, it stages the byproducts of futility: a contested throne gained by neither claimant; a war indistinguishably international and civil but irredeemably inept; a dynastic marriage that endures for two scenes; a royal heir, the image of his father, who falls off a wall and dies. As a history play, it is sterile, with neither prequels nor sequels, and it has only an uneasy and tenuous relationship to its more established siblings, none of whom shares its name. As a character study, it is most notorious for giving free rein to the high camp histrionics of the stage mother. As a literary child, it inherits only an awkward place in the family album (*Henry, Henry, Henry, Richard. John. Richard, Henry, Henry, Henry*). If we were looking for canon fodder, we would hardly start here. But if we are looking for queer history—for a history hostile to idealized reproduction; haunted by impious ghosts; skeptical of identities and subjectivities; radically disruptive of category, authority, causality, and futurity—we might do worse. *King John* argues that to speak for normalcy or conformity, for linearity or teleology, is to utterly unmake the illusive security of those terms. Through a series of falls off the narrative wall, the play shows that the only traces of a functional history are the broken bits left behind. In the non-place of such history, it sets the ruinous sentimentality of that counterfactual "if."

This play takes place and makes time in the interstices of historical continuity: we know what has happened and what must happen, but we know from an unsituated location in which such certainties have neither firm foundation nor fixed meaning. The representational practice of *King John* is a theory of mimetic rupture through which the past must produce the future, and the future reproduce the past, across an alienated moment of non-presence. As it undoes the systems that order time toward conservative ends, the "now" of this play exists only as a disavowal of the "then" of history and futurity. It is in this sense something like the "now" of our own queer historiography, which repudiates the mastery of linear progress. In interweaving the play's methodologies with our own, I do not mean to make a case for Shakespeare's precedence or prescience. I hope instead to emphasize the productive perversion of estranged recognition, to highlight a twisted logic by which intertextuality might take place not across time but through a counterfactual alterity that unravels such constructions. In "Queering History," Jonathan Goldberg and Madhavi Menon write, "Reading unhistorically cannot take the object of queering for granted and should be open to the possibility of anachronism. . . . In keeping alive the undecidable difference between difference and sameness it would refuse what we might term the compulsory heterotemporality of historicism, whether it insists on difference or produces a version of the normative same."[15] The canonicity of the Shakespearean text, when it asserts both a transcendent sameness to itself and a privileged difference from others, stands at odds with the project of queering—and, indeed, stands in for the substantial complacencies against which queer theory defines its work. But it seems worth wondering what happens to that relation if Shakespearean canonicity is at odds with the Shakespearean text, a tension made acute when the text itself deracinates truth claims. Recognizing *King John* not only as anachronism but as iconoclasm—not only as object, but as process—crosses the signals of practice and theory. It is at the very least suggestive that Magna Carta, that notorious trace of a moment at which a king was forced to make history, has no place in *The Life and Death of King John*.

Notes

1. Tillyard, *Shakespeare's History Plays*, 162.

2. *The Life and Death of King John*, in Evans et al., *The Riverside Shakespeare*, 1.1.5. Citations in parentheses are to this edition.

3. Bourdieu, "On Symbolic Power," 170.

4. Edelman, *No Future*, 3.

5. Baker, "Introduction," 766.

6. Butler, *Excitable Speech*, 2.

7. Goldberg, "The History that Will Be," 9.

8. Freccero, *Queer / Early / Modern*, 80.

9. Case, "Toward a Butch–Femme Aesthetic," 304.

10. Menon, *Unhistorical Shakespeare*, 26.

11. Edelman, *No Future*, 29. The stage direction is more commonly transcribed as "[dies]."

12. Goldberg, "The History that Will Be," 4.

13. Simpson and Weiner, *The Oxford English Dictionary*, s.v. "counterfactual."

14. Halberstam, *In a Queer Time and Place*, 2.

15. Goldberg and Menon, "Queering History," 1616.

Lear's Queer Cosmos

LAURIE SHANNON

"The Universe," the flamboyantly atheist evolutionary biologist Richard Daw-kins proposes, is "too queer" for us to understand.[1] Dawkins argues that *Homo sapiens* and all other creatures evolved within an earthly scale (what he calls the "middle world") will have perceptual and cognitive capabilities de-signed to function *at that scale*. The incommensurate and even contradictory cosmic fictions that each creature will create are thus never enough for the cosmos, but always (roughly) enough for the creature. In asserting the queer-ness of the universe—indeed, its "increasing queerness"—Dawkins, Oxford's first Charles Simonyi Professor in the Public Understanding of Science (also known as Darwin's Rottweiler), retransmitted the earlier cadences of another bioscientist, the British geneticist J. B. S. Haldane.[2]

In likewise positing an oppositional relationship between queerness and positive knowledge in 1928, Dawkins's predecessor in queer cosmography invoked Shakespeare. Haldane amplified Hamlet's lines in a way Renaissance rhetorical scientists surely would have appreciated: "Now, my own suspicion is that the Universe is not only queerer than we suppose, but queerer than we *can* suppose. . . . I suspect that there are more things in heaven and earth than are dreamed of, *or can be dreamed of*, in any philosophy."[3] By "philosophy," Shakespeare had meant "natural philosophy," a precursor of modern science but one with less homogeneous protocols. Indeed, Renaissance ideas of coex-isting but incommensurate spheres (above and below the moon, for example) accepted a relativity principle that would make a twentieth-century (re)ap-pearance, and the "lower world" of Elizabethan thought seems akin to Daw-kins's "middle world." By what survival mechanism, genetic inheritance, or other relay might the four-hundred-year-old words of Shakespeare voice twenty-first-century skeptical science? And what might usefully be "queer" about that? This is also to ask whether queerness is conceptually limited to human-exceptionalist applications. Like notions of the soul, reason, language, or tool use, *does such queerness as we are capable of supposing pertain only in a human domain?*

This exploration of *King Lear* concerns science, in its capacious historical sense: knowledge "before" techno-science. It asks how anti-identitarian trajectories of queerness—brilliantly elaborated around (overwhelmingly human) questions of gender, sexuality, and desire—might broadly address cosmography or even describe that cosmos "itself," whether speaking of its moving parts or systemic operations. What might queer studies and criticism's "scientific turn," together, suggest for new historiographies of the contested grounds of knowledge itself? After all, the modern modalities of identitarian subjectivity and techno-science arise in tandem, and *cogito ergo sum* may be their common ancestral organism.

Queer Rain

King Lear troubles the terms and conditions of knowledge, charting for early modernity the then nightmare that would become what Dawkins calls its "increasingly queer" truth. Either *Lear*'s cosmos is unhinging or the unfixity of its parts is becoming perceptible. Early modern "things" (from basic elements of earth, water, air, and fire to the larger, assembled bodies they compose) do have describable "natures" in that they have individuated and generally operative characters, especially from the limited vantage of what early moderns would call our "sublunary" view. But insofar as those natures are enacted only in the unsettling contexts of a performance that is always open to waywardness, accident, and invention, those natures do not govern things securely. In other words, "Nature" does not preside in the evenly homogeneous, unbroken manner attributed to such legal fictions as "the Law of Nature," which conventionally grounds and encompasses the possible—and thus should be impossible to violate or exceed.

In a bedrock iteration of natural law orthodoxy, Richard Hooker's *Laws of Ecclesiastical Polity* (1593) defends political order by means of the divine dispensation apparent in the natural world. As familiar as this passage is, I offer it less to stand in for an Elizabethan ideology of microcosm and macrocosm than to highlight the persistent anxiety dogging even this magisterial articulation of it. "As it cometh to pass in a kingdom rightly ordered, . . . so . . . it fareth in the natural course of the world"; God, Hooker expounds, "made a law for the rain" and decreed "unto the sea, that the waters should not pass his commandment." Given this edict settling the world into limiting identities, Hooker offers a long rhetorical question: "*If nature should intermit her course, and leave altogether . . . the observation of her own laws*: If those principal . . . elements . . . whereof all things in this lower world are made, should lose the qualities which they now have; if the frame of that heavenly arc erected over our heads should loosen and dissolve itself; if the celestial spheres should forget their wonted motions and . . . turn themselves any way as it might happen"; if the sun "which now . . . doth run his unwearied course" should "stand and rest himself; if the Moon should wander from her beaten way," what then? And "what would become of man himself, whom [following Genesis] these things do now all serve?" For Hooker, the divine settlement (the "establishment of nature's law") provides "*the stay of the whole world.*"[4]

In *Lear*, the whole world is *unstaid*. The implicit answer to the questions Hooker poses with such grandiloquence—that a dissolving, relativistic, non-identitarian, or errant cosmos is impossible—is exposed as a local, single-species fiction. Groping with questions of scale and science in a kind of field test on the heath, Lear tries to take a measure of the "*extremity of the skies*" (3.4.101; emphasis added). Considering "unaccommodated man" and embracing that unaccommodation, Lear puts off the comfort of Hooker's fiction exactly as he sheds his clothes ("Off, off you lendings! Come, unbutton here") to expose his body to a tempest that unsettles the elements themselves (3.4.105–8). Even if there were any natural law in *Lear*, its hold is revealed to be startlingly *intermittent*; nature "intermit[s] her course," in Hooker's parlance. This suspension is no act of state but an initiative within the dispersed sovereignties of things themselves. Wonted motions, unwearied courses, beaten ways: each of Hooker's formulations connects natural law to movement, but all are subject to the persistent fantasy that those motions will stray and the "stays" of "obedience" in objects and creatures will unravel. In a play populated not only by characters, but also by a host of non-human creatures and the "elemental actors" of storm and heath, *Lear* calls the questions Hooker tried to contain rhetorically. In the *Lear* cosmos, *everything is queer*—not just certain (human) affinities, desires, or motions that stray from a prescriptive order otherwise known as natural.[5]

The play thus enacts Hooker's notionally impossible fantasy of the "heavenly arc" over our heads loosening and dissolving. Lear directly summons the elements, addressing infectious "airs," the "vengeances of heaven," "nimble lightnings," and "fen-sucked fogs" (2.4.162–67). He "abjure[s] all roofs" (2.4.209). Nature strikes *against* the "roofs" and edifices of ordered law rather than reinforcing them metaphorically: "Blow, winds, and crack your cheeks!

Rage, blow! / You cataracts and hurricanoes, spout / Till you have drenched our steeples, drowned the cocks!" (3.2.1–3). With churches drowned and barn-topping weathercocks underwater, an elemental surge upends the sheltering fictions of human knowledge. Water submerges the church steeple as heavenly marker, and the device designed to measure vectors of wind direction spins meaninglessly, instead, in flooding currents. But nature's representatives share the fate of those icons of human culture. Lear calls on thunder to "Strike flat the thick rotundity o' th' world! / Crack nature's moulds, all germens spill" (3.2.7–8). Sweeping from the earth's sphere to its globelike microcosm in seeds, "thick rotundities" are to be crushed in a complex anti-reproductive gesture, consistent with the play's vision of evil children and conjuring the false cosmography of a flat earth. Splicing theological skepticism with an epistemological one, *Lear* refutes the Cartesian sequence (from doubt through reason to faith) *avant la lettre*. The play enacts a cosmically queer science instead: a searing vision of the fictionality of order—not only in cultural contexts (which is to be expected) but in nature itself.

Despite Hooker's incantations about "a law for the rain" that restrains it to acting like normal rain, this rain (not a "hundred-year storm," but maybe a "ten-thousand-year storm") is like no rain to be found in the scaled fictions of human memory. The fool implores Lear to go inside, arguing that "court holy water [flattery; i.e., part of the edifice Lear is rejecting] in a dry house is better than this rainwater out o' door" (3.2.10–11). Kent marvels that he can "never / Remember to have heard" in his lifetime "such sheets of fire, such bursts of horrid thunder, / Such groans of roaring wind and rain." He asserts that *"Man's nature cannot carry / The affliction"* (3.2. 46–49; emphasis added). The play knows water is a solvent. Nature (the flexing cosmos) afflicts or cracks nature (the more fragile natures of beings in Dawkins's "middle world"). Queerness here is not only a particular departure from fictions about the natural but also a focal condition precipitated by the collision of incommensurate perspectives "in" and on nature. *Lear*'s "uncorrected" split focus registers the local fiction called natural law worked up by beings of an earthly scale for their use but simultaneously reaches toward the minimally scrutable workings of elements arrayed in maximal cosmic dimensions. The precipitation of this dilemma of scaled perspectives—an "afflicting" double vision that the human apparatus "cannot carry"—makes Lear's rain *queer*.

The Bias of Nature

I have come this far—to asserting queer rain in *King Lear*—without specifying in advance the relevant mechanisms of significance for the term "queer." As the critical prehistories that enable this volume witness, Shakespeare has been an epicenter for research on the history of sexuality and the querying of present dispensations. The alterity of early modernity as a time "before" an identity politics of desire and yet a place where same-sex affects could, under certain conditions, be perfectly "normative" grounds much of this work. Building on the research of many, many others,[6] I have described the cultural centrality of a "like seeks like" principle as "Renaissance homonormativity."[7] This homonormativity pertains not only onstage but also in the rangier contexts of elements, creatures, and other natural bodies; principles of motion display it (attraction, propulsion, direction, tendency, intention, deviation, aversion). Things have qualities or natures that are expressed through characteristic movements. This sense structures commonplaces about "nature taking its course." How did Shakespeare visualize the unfolding trajectories of "the *course* of nature"? Here the wily relativizing adjectives "straight" and its most precise opposite, "queer," come into play.

Conceptions of "nature's bias" recur in Renaissance literature, referring to the game of bowls, in which a ball contains a lopsided weight—the "bias"— which gives the natural course of each particular ball a signature swerve. "Nature's bias" or route, then, is specifically not straight.[8] Even when nature is prevailing in things and governing their operations, varied arcs are expressed "in the course of nature," charted by the obscurely autonomous weight inside the body of the ball. For Montaigne, illness and medical treatment *both* knock the author "cleane out of my right bias."[9] A "bias" can be "right," but exorbitant nature can still depart from it. Nature loosens its stays; it swerves. When Francis Bacon charts the domains of natural history, he classifies this power of vagary or wandering. In *The Advancement of Learning* (1605), he describes natural history writing as "of three sorts: of nature in course; of nature erring or varying; and of nature altered or wrought."[10] While "wrought" nature refers to the impact of human arts and sciences, nature on its own is either "in course" or "erring or varying." In either case, it is dynamic; it migrates; it has a trajectory.[11]

Thus, when Gloucester lists the strange cosmic effects under way in *Lear*, his connection of "late eclipses in the sun and moon" with mishaps in the affairs of human culture does more than invoke the microcosmic and macrocosmic analogies understood to traverse cosmic distances in period thought. He also posits a world in which "nature varying" has become perceptible. Gloucester describes the alienation between Lear and Cordelia, saying, "The King falls from [the] bias of nature" (1.2.114). To fall or err from the arc of the bias is to swerve in some extravagant way from the so-called ordinary course. Since nothing exceeds Bacon's three "Natures," nature includes what middle-world fictions exclude. Thus, Lear's super-swerve itself *is* nature.[12] As Gloucester reports, "Though the wisdom of nature can reason it thus and thus, yet nature finds itself scourged in the sequent effects" (1.2.107–9). Torsions of sequence within nature make nature vary.

Natural errancy likewise appears in Brabantio's horror when his unexpectedly autonomous daughter desires Othello; he seeks out what caused "nature so *preposterously* to err."[13] As queerly philological research on preposterousness shows, such period terms richly support queer reading.[14] Patricia Parker suggests that preposterousness is "a more revealing term than sodomy" because "it links something represented as sexual inversion with the whole range of recto and verso, front and back, before and behind."[15] For purposes of "nature's course" here, a preposterous flipped sequence, reversing before and behind, indexes an unsettled law that nevertheless is nature's. Nature is sufficiently free to move "preposterously." In a helpful gloss in 1611, Randall Cotgrave gives this chain of synonyms: "arseward, backward, preposterously, oblikely, awry, overthwartly, quite contrary, full *against the course*, wool, or hair."[16] As these adverbs suggest, and as Hooker's passage insisted, vectors or moving trajectories—not just static hierarchies—underwrite period understandings of both order and departures from it.

In one of the great freaks of nature for commentary, "queer" makes no appearance in Shakespeare's queer prolixity. But etymologically, the "bias" in "queer" shows the same tendency to directional movement as Cotgrave's gloss. The Oxford English Dictionary describes the origin of "queer" as uncertain but suggests the "German *quer*[:] transverse, oblique, crosswise, at right angles, obstructive, . . . going wrong . . . peculiar . . . directed sideways . . . at odds with others (see *thwart adv.*)."[17] Whatever is queer stands (or moves) at an angle to something else; it encodes a relationality that, as such, precipitates a perspectival dilemma between two moving points. The Oxford English Dictionary carefully tracks discontinuities between historical (and historically British) senses of the term "queer" and its U.S. anti-identitarian (yet more human-centered) peregrinations in contexts of sexuality, even including entries for "queer theory" and "queer theorist." And surely no U.S. scientist would call the universe "queer." Yet thinking queerness beyond the parameters of the human, transatlantic resonances do coincide, insofar as phenomena that unsettle cultural fictions of natural law yield dilemmas of perspective, normality, and scale. *Being only human* (and beneath the moon), we cannot say whether the queerness of nature—its obliqueness—stems from its powers to wander "preposterously" or from its capacity to "afflict" or "crack" our nearsighted fictions of stability. Either way, what Lear grasps as the *"extremity* of the skies" is queerer than we have dared suppose.

Notes

1. "Universe 'Too Queer' to Grasp," BBC News, July 12, 2005, available online at http://news.bbc.co.uk/2/hi/science/nature/4676751.stm (accessed May 10, 2010), reporting on Richard Dawkins, "The Universe Is Queerer Than We Can Suppose," paper presented at the Technology, Engineering, Design Global Conference, Oxford, July 2005, available online at http://www.ted.com/index.php/talks/view/id/98 (accessed May 10, 2010).

2. Thomas Henry Huxley was called "Darwin's bulldog" in the 1860s; Charles Simonyi, the Microsoft executive who endowed the Oxford chair, intensified the moniker for Dawkins: Robert Downey, "Darwin's Rottweiler, Perhaps," *Eastsideweek*, December 11, 1996.

3. Haldane, *Possible Worlds and Other Essays*, 286; second set of italics added, varying Hamlet's "There are more things in heaven and earth, Horatio, / Than are dreamt of in your philosophy"; *Hamlet*, 1.5.175–76, in Bevington, *The Complete Works of Shakespeare* (5th ed.). *King Lear* citations in parentheses refer to this edition.

4. Hooker, *Of the Laws of Ecclesiastical Polity*, 60; emphasis added.

5. This recalls Jonathan Goldberg's claim that "sodomy is the name for all behavior in" Marlowe's *Edward II*: Goldberg, *Sodometries*, 123. For a consequential account of the emergence of "the normal" as a statistical or universalizing structure, see Traub, *Mapping Embodiment in the Early Modern West*.

6. I mention, with appreciation, four brilliant jewels in this research. Each specifically brings the dilemmas of historical double vision into critical focus: Bray, "Homosexuality and the Signs of Friendship in Elizabethan England"; De Grazia, "The Scandal of Shakespeare's Sonnets"; Goldberg, "Sodomy and Society"; Sedgwick, "Swan in Love."

7. Shannon, "Nature's Bias"; idem, *Sovereign Amity*, 19–23. A comparison with Lisa Duggan's contemporary critical objects suggests the difference historical context makes, even for critical terms: Duggan, "The New Homonormativity."

8. For a fascinating, related account of Lucretian atomism, see Goldberg, "Lucy Hutchinson Writing Matter."

9. Montaigne, "Of Experience," 977.

10. Bacon, *The Advancement of Learning*, Book 2, chap. 1.

11. "Erring" is not "making a mistake" but "errancy" or roaming; it preserves a "wandering" sense from the Latin *errare*, derived from Indo-European (*ers*, "to go").

12. See Polixenes's speech, "This is an art / Which does mend nature—change it rather—but / The art itself *is nature*": *The Winter's Tale*, 4.4.95–97, in Bevington, *The Complete Works of Shakespeare* (5th ed.); emphasis added.

13. *Othello*, 1.3.64, ibid.; emphasis added.

14. As Jeffrey Masten has elaborated its practice, queer philology investigates the etymology, circulation, transformation, and constitutive power of key words within early modern discoures of sex and gender: Masten, *Spelling Shakespeare, and Other Essays in Queer Philology*,(forthcoming). See also Freccero, "Practicing Queer Philology with Marguerite de Navarre."

15. Parker, *Shakespeare from the Margins*, 27. See also idem, "Preposterous Events"; Goldberg, *Sodometries*, 181.

16. Cotgrave, *A Dictionarie of the French and English Tongues*, unpaginated, entry for "rebours"; emphasis added.

17. *Oxford English Dictionary*, Internet ed., s.v. "queer."

Learning How to Love (Again)

ASHLEY T. SHELDEN

William Shakespeare's "A Lover's Complaint" bristles with queerness, but after my first reading of the poem, if you had asked me to identify the locus of this queerness, I could not have. All I had then was a feeling, non-knowledge. My task became to interpret this feeling, which I could not separate from a certain uncanniness. Though I was encountering this poem for the first time, I sensed that I had read it before. I soon realized that my experience of déjà vu had to do with the fact that this poem is indeed an instance of repetition. "A Lover's Complaint" tells one of my own narratives: the story of how queer theory seduced me.

Seduction

Consider it: Shakespeare's poem gives an account of a young woman's attraction to a beautiful, androgynous, and deceitful youth; her moral abasement at his—apparently, very talented—hands; and their breakup. The poem ends with her assertion that after everything, if given the opportunity, she would give in to the temptation for him again. Just as Shakespeare's maid falls for the dubious (but very sexy) youth, so did I fall for queer theory. My seducer dressed in drag: The figure with whom I first came—indirectly, flirtatiously, serendipitously, but not, luckily for me, cautiously—to queer theory was Shakespeare. Though he looked as straight as the Shakespeare that I had heard about, he sounded unmistakably queer. And in "A Lover's Complaint," the young man fools the maid, just as Shakespeare fooled me: "Deceits were gilded in his smiling . . . vows were ever brokers to defiling . . . characters and words merely but art, / And bastards of his foul adulterate heart."[1] Deceitful smiles, defiled vows, bastard words, and impure hearts feed, and feed on, queer theory.

To read Shakespeare's poem as a repetition of my own romance with

queer theory suggests, in part, a potentially reductive allegorical interpretation. The young woman stands in for me, and the beautiful youth holds the
place of queer theory. But if one characterizes the young man as an allegorical
placeholder, then this placeholder troubles the ideas of both allegory and
place holding because the androgynous youth refuses to retain any one form:

> In him a plenitude of subtle matter,
> Applied to cautels, all strange forms receives,
> Of burning blushes or of weeping water,
> Or swooning paleness; and he takes and leaves,
> In either's aptness, as it best deceives,
> To blush at speeches rank, to weep at woes,
> Or to turn white and swoon at tragic shows
>
> That not a heart which in his level came
> Could scape the hail of his all-hurting aim. (302–10)

What does Shakespeare describe here if not the most aggressive charisma, the
most successful sort of attraction? The gorgeous youth in Shakespeare's
poem beguiles the maid because he thrives on self-difference. Just as the
identity of Shakespeare's enticing youth depends on shape shifting, so, too,
does the identity of queer theory (if it could be said to have one at all) emerge
out of non-identity.

In Shakespeare's poem, the youth's non-identity relates directly to his androgyny. Both masculine and feminine, the youth registers as both man and
woman and neither man nor woman simultaneously. Shakespeare describes
him as having little facial hair—"Small show of man was yet upon his chin"—
suggesting his femininity, which is also borne out by his being "maiden-
tongued" (92, 100). Nevertheless, he rides a horse with expertise that other
men admire: "Well could he ride, and often men would say / 'That horse his
mettle from his rider takes'" (106–7). Not unlike the "master mistress" of
"Sonnet 20," who is a "man in hue" with "a woman's gentle heart," the youth
in "A Lover's Complaint" is nothing if not ambiguously gendered, enabling
him to seduce men and women alike.[2] Shape shifting, being particularly inflected by the question of gender, makes the youth appealing to everyone:
"He did in the general bosom reign / Of young, of old, and sexes both enchanted" (127–28). No one is immune to the young man's charm. Like a virus,
it spreads to all who see him: "Each eye that saw him did enchant the mind"
(89). Queer theory has a similarly viral quality. It infects everything by virtue

of its ability to take any form, to be fundamentally different from itself. Nothing appeals to me more than queer theory's ability to make any sort of appeal, which is precisely what its non-self-identity enables.

Queer theory has many guises, some of which undoubtedly are incompatible with one another despite the fact that all of these forms fall under the same rubric. The critique it offers penetrates multiple aspects of experience. Queer theory can look more like "Shakespeare," "history," or "film" than itself. This plurality, the ability to take almost any form or to have multiple forms at once, makes it so easy to fall head over heels in love. Like a lovesick girl, I see queer theory everywhere I go.

Falling in Love

Given this multiplicity, one might ask: What would it mean for queer theory to look "like itself"? Or, even more to the point, if one falls in love with queer theory, and if queer theory is not like itself, then, one might ask: What defines the object of this love? What *is* queer theory? Queer theory, I submit, can be characterized as the masochistic compulsion to learn, teach, or think what cannot be learned, taught, or thought. Indeed, Shakespeare describes such an enterprise as "suffering ecstacy" (69). In my own romance, this compulsion manifests in not so much the ease with which I fell in love as the difficulty of *not* falling. Queer theory tantalized me with a lesson about desire, a concrete message concerning sexuality. It drew me in at first because it promised to teach me something, but the seduction really took hold of me when I found out that queer theory has nothing to teach. I must continually learn that I can learn nothing about desire, that the only way to learn about desire is, in effect, not to learn. If I ever seem to grasp the lesson of this nothing, then in the moment that I think I have learned, I have to remember that I have not understood anything at all. To learn is not to learn; not to learn is to learn; to think I have learned about not learning is to fall into the trap of thinking I have learned when I have not.

It hardly seems fortuitous that the queer vibes I initially got from "A Lover's Complaint" took the form of non-knowledge. I fell in love with queer theory because it held the promise of knowledge, but it can only ever break this promise and, in so doing, break my heart. But heartbreak, I am here to tell you, can be fun. Like a revolving door from which one cannot exit, queer theory enfolds its students *and* teachers in the unending movement of its critique. This persistent revolution, and the inability to stop this movement—

indeed, the desire to keep it going—has the structure of a compulsion. Queer theory urges me to spin through its revolving door, not so much holding me up by centrifugal force as pressuring me continually to fall.

One can attribute my falling (in love) to the fact that queer theory implicitly harbors its own critique. For every assertion that queer theory allows us to make about sexuality, a question exists that destabilizes the grounds of the assertion. Queer theory ensnared me by casting doubt on everything, including and especially itself. The young man in "A Lover's Complaint" persuades the maid to shed the "white stole of chastity" (297) in precisely the same way. He, too, produces self-critique: "When thou impressest, what are precepts worth / Of stale example? When thou wilt inflame, / How coldly those impediments stand forth / Of wealth, of filial fear, law, kindred, fame" (267–70). He might as well say to her, "I have given you no reason to trust me, but both you and I know this untrustworthiness makes me sexy." The "precepts" and "stale example[s]" of which he speaks refer to other women he also callously charms. The maid knows, because the young man in so many words tells her, that he has a "foul adulterate heart." However, not despite but *because of* these "impediments," her desire for him grows stronger, her movement toward him increasingly difficult to resist.

On How Not to Learn Your Lesson

If queer theory can be said to teach anything at all, it teaches the lesson of desire. One cannot learn this lesson by memorizing facts, imprinting them indelibly on one's mind. Rather, students have to enact this lesson as the compulsive activity of queer theory itself. That is, the movement that drives queer theory also crucially structures the uncontrollable desire in which it instructs us. "A Lover's Complaint" understands being out of control only too well, even as the poem may seem to disavow such understanding. The youth characterizes perfectly the activity of desire in an account of one of his many affairs, this one with a nun whom he leads astray: "But O, my sweet, what labour is't to leave / The thing we have not, mast'ring what not strives, / Planing the place which did no form receive, / Playing patient sports in unconstrained gyves!" (239–42). The final footnote for this passage parenthetically reminds us, "The entire sentence is ironic."[3] One might incline toward reading this sentence as suggesting the opposite of what it explicitly states. But if nothing else, queer theory insists that all statements, including editorial affirmations of irony, are suspect. Is this sentence really ironic?

Rather than reading the passage ironically, could we not take it literally? Is it not more plausible to read this sentence literally, as a comment on the nature of desire, than to understand it as ironically negating the apparent meaning of the statement?

In the oxymoronic lines I quote, Shakespeare describes the obsessive compulsive at her best (or worst, depending on your particular disposition). Take, for instance, the nagging example of someone "planing the place which did no form receive." This image refigures the intractable obsession with hand washing or the niggling suspicion that one has not locked one's door, even after checking it over and over again. This obsessive-compulsive insistence acts out the unruly project of queer theory and the structure of desire in which it participates. Just as one might smooth out a wrinkle on fabric where there is none, or spin endlessly through a revolving door, so, too, one chases relentlessly an object that forever recedes with the horizon. The refusal to abandon "the thing we have not," after all, imbues desire with all of its corruptive force.

Desire as corruptive: Most of us realize very early on that desire is not "good" for us. It pulls us in directions in which we ostensibly do not want to go and can push us to betray loved ones. Desire, we begin to think, does not have our best interests in mind. But the electric charge of being wronged by desire, of wronging someone else in desire; the pulsing exhilaration of taking a wrong turn, ending up somewhere way off the map: these make desire hypnotic. As if in a trance, ignoring all the warning signs by the side of the road, we blindly follow. No matter how many bad experiences one has—or better, *the more* bad experiences one has—the more the magnetic appeal of desire compels one to re-encounter such experiences. That is to say, in addition to being uncontrollable, desire is fundamentally repetitive. And Shakespeare insists with searing accuracy on the necessity of repetition, purchased by virtue of the inability to learn. "A Lover's Complaint" evokes at length the repetitive reverie of desire:

> But ah, who ever shunned by precedent
> The destined ill she must herself assay,
> Or forced examples 'gainst her own content
> To put the by-past perils in her way?
> Counsel may stop a while what will not stay
> For when we rage, advice is often seen,
> By blunting us, to make our wills more keen.

> Nor gives it satisfaction to our blood
> That we must curb it upon others' proof,
> To be forbod the sweets that seems so good
> For fear of harms that preach in our behoof.
> O appetite from judgment stand aloof!
> The one a palate hath that needs will taste,
> Though reason weep, and cry it is thy last. (155–68)

The young woman knows the trap into which she falls. "Precedent," previous "examples," "counsel," and seemingly undeniable "proof" speak of others' encounters with her seducer; their overwhelming message clearly asserts that nothing good can come of her giving into the desire for him. But she will not learn. "Satisfaction" cannot be purchased with caution. "Proof" is as nothing in the face of compulsion. "Advice" will not curb desire but make it "more keen." Repetition of others' "mistakes," in other words, is inevitable.

However, the poem briefly entertains the idea that, despite the inevitability of repeating others' mistakes, after a person has made her own she can put a stop to the repetitive pattern. Shakespeare sets up an opposition between youth and age, innocence and experience to suggest this idea of progress: "Thus, merely with the garment of a grace / The naked and concealed fiend he covered, / That th' unexperient gave the tempter place . . . Who, young and simple, would not be so lovered?" (316–20). The maid—"unexperient," "young and simple"—cannot help falling into her seducer's trap, but the fault is not her own because she does not know any better. Certainly, these lines unproblematically suggest this reading. But in the lines immediately following this, the opposition that the preceding passage sets up breaks down. The maid continues: "Ay me, I fell, and yet do question make / What I would do again for such a sake" (321–22). Her experience has not given her any insight that she did not already have. The affair reinvigorates her desire rather than weakens it.

Here, at the end of the poem, I find myself identifying most strongly with this woman. Her story ends where my love story starts to get interesting. I might as well also say of queer theory, "Ay me, I fell, and yet do question make / What I would do again for such a sake." This idea—in both Shakespeare's narrative and my own—marks the moment in which repetition becomes not just a necessity but *a wish*. One does not simply resign oneself to repetition but unfalteringly pursues it. I fell for and into queer theory, and now I want to fall again and again and again. The hunger for repetition erupts in the rhetoric of the poem's final stanza:

O that infected moisture of his eye,
O that false fire which in his cheek so glowed,
O that forced thunder from his heart did fly,
O that sad breath his spongy lungs bestowed,
O all that borrowed motion seeming owed
Would yet again betray the fore-betrayed,
And new pervert a reconciled maid. (323–29)

Apostrophe, the trope that stages the address of an abstract concept or inanimate object, clearly dominates here when the deceitful signifiers of the youth's feigned affections ("O that infected moisture of his eye") become the maid's addressees. And by repeating the figure of apostrophe, this stanza forcefully reiterates the desire for reiteration. Moreover, it seems no mistake that Shakespeare repeats apostrophe *in particular*. Barbara Johnson suggests that through apostrophe "the absent, dead, or inanimate entity addressed is thereby made present, animate, and anthropomorphic."[4] In other words, apostrophe makes present that which would otherwise be lost. By apostrophizing the qualities that seduced her, the maid does not simply wish for repetition but rather *experiences a repetition in the very moment of this utterance*. She revivifies her betrayal, returning to it as though it were taking place in the present of the poem, and relishes again her fall. Where Shakespeare writes that these qualities "would yet again betray," the conditional mood is not quite accurate. In the final stanza, apostrophe *actually does* "betray the fore-betrayed" and "new pervert[s]" a not-so-reconciled maid.

The New Pervert

Do we really long for heartache, for exploitation, for betrayal? I am suggesting that the answer to this question is yes, and that this answer issues straight from the heart of queer theory. Above all, queer theory suggests that the category of the "new pervert" does not exist. All perversions—which is to say, all articulations of desire—are old ones, products of a compulsion that predates and will postdate us. As Jonathan Dollimore says, ventriloquizing Freud, "One does not become a pervert, but remains one."[5] One might say, then, that when queer theory deflowered me, I was asking for it. And my romance, like the maid's with the beautiful youth, was and is doomed.

The betrayals for which we so yearn (de)form the foundation of queer theory in its capacity to deceive, to seduce, and to undercut everything, particularly itself. Queer theory promises to break my heart, and yet I continue to pursue it. Friends have counseled that I will get hurt, that the object of my affections will love me and leave me, that I would be better off settling down with a theory more reliable, less wayward. My response? "O appetite, from judgment stand aloof!" I cannot help myself. An enormous chocolate cake might as well sit before me, and I can do nothing but eat the whole thing. Queer theory may not be "good," but it *is* delicious.

And as I have taken the primrose path to the everlasting bonfire of queer theory, I invite you to do the same. Shakespeare, no doubt, would extend the invitation, as well. It is not going to be easy or simple or comforting, but it will be fun. So just try it; let yourself go. Or I might rather say, by way of persuasion: When thou impressest, what are precepts worth of stale example? When thou wilt inflame how coldly those impediments stand forth of wealth, of filial fear, law, kindred, fame. I am sure you will quickly find that queer theory reconfigures the texture of reality, ignites passion, makes the world more vibrant, inspires devotion, and breaks your heart. But on breaking your heart, if it gives you cause to complain, queer theory also fundamentally redefines the word "complaint." "A Lover's Complaint" turns out to be no complaint at all. It is, rather, an ecstatic encomium to desire, its necessary failures, and the erotic surcharge of failure itself. To complain, queer theory suggests, is to enjoy—to enjoy, that is, the fall.

Notes

1. "A Lover's Complaint," in Greenblatt et al., *The Norton Shakespeare*, 172–75. Citations in parentheses are to this edition.

2. "Sonnet 20," ibid., 2, 7, 3.

3. Greenblatt et al., *The Norton Shakespeare*, 1982 n. 8.

4. Johnson, *A World of Difference*, 185.

5. Dollimore, *Sexual Dissidence: Augustine to Wilde, Freud to Foucault*, 172.

The L Words

MADHAVI MENON

It is because we already have experience of that which makes
the present noncontemporaneous with itself that we can
actually historicise.

   —Dipesh Chakrabarty, *Provincializing Europe*, 112

Although it poses as a comedy, *Love's Labour's Lost* does not end happily. It
closets itself generically by appearing to be something—a comedy about love
—that it cannot actually bring itself to be. "Our wooing doth not end like an
old play. / Jack hath not Jill,"[1] laments Biron at the end when, instead of four
weddings, there is a funeral, and the men and women go their separate ways.
The play thus turns out to be a comedy in drag—its appearance lives up to all
the generic requirements of the comic form: four highborn men to match
four highborn women, low-brow humor, sexual innuendo, and a play that
moves toward heterosexual marriage. But this apparent compliance with
genre belies a resistance to its own form. The play looks like a comedy but it
does not act like one—or, rather, its desires appear to exceed, or fall short of,
its comic appearance. Instead of sexual gratification, the play only serves
sexual mystification. And instead of straight women—the Jills for whom the
Jacks pine—the play abounds with lipstick lesbians.[2]

   Not that there *are* any lesbians in this play, with or without lipstick—at
least, none that we would recognize as lesbians. But recognition is precisely
one of those fraught issues that trips us up in relation to this text, starting with
our recognition of the play as a comedy and extending to the fact that almost
everyone in it is continually in disguise.[3] The non-contemporaneity that Dipesh Chakrabarty sees as the hallmark of history is at work also in a Shakespearean play where nothing is but what is not. "The gallants shall be tested,"
the Princess announces before one of the many scenes of disguise in which
the men encounter the women, "For, ladies, we will every one be masked, /

And not a man of them shall have the grace, / Despite of suit, to see a lady's face" (5.2.127–30).

This specter of the masked lady, of the woman who cannot be identified at first glance, is also the specter of the lipstick lesbian who embodies the schism between an outside that "appears to be an integrated, stable subject according to the rules of normative heterosexuality," and an inside that gives the lie to such an appearance.[4] Rather than being suggestive of her sexual identity, the lipstick lesbian's desire is understood to be the opposite of the straight femininity she performs. This understanding is based on two assumptions: one, that identity should be transparent—you need to look like what you are; and two, that femininity in and of itself is putatively hetero—femme women are straight until proved otherwise. The lipstick lesbian does not coincide with herself, and the fear is that her appearance does not line up with her "reality." But what if the lipstick lesbian is all surface? What if the deceitful exterior is all we have by way of identity, with no internal "truth" to offset it? What if, rather than showing up the distinction between surface and depth, the lipstick lesbian insists on the depth of surfaces—she both is and is not a straight femme? Refusing to dive "beneath" her exterior, the lipstick lesbian presents herself as a problem of legibility *on the surface*. She is superficially difficult and provides no key with which to unlock her secrets. Instead of providing answers, she only poses troubling questions: Are our decisions about desire based on an exterior that is always deceitful? If so, then how do we ascertain the truth of desire? Would our regimes of fixing identity fail if there were no recognizable truth to desire?

These questions all hinge on the relation between exterior and interior, desire and truth. They also hinge on the lipstick lesbian, who seems to defy the stricture that desire be legible. Indeed, "lipstick" becomes a dangerous supplement to the "lesbian" whose internal identity is seen to be at odds with the femme stylishness of her surface. By using the lipstick lesbian to bear the burden of a disjunction between the so-called outside and in, normative sexuality protects itself from having to face up to the uncertainty of its own appearance.[5] But this uncertainty inheres in the very formulation of the relation between exterior and interior. On the one hand, identitarian sexuality suggests there is a *difference* between outside and inside, and on the other hand, it insists that the one should be indicative of the other. The outside is held to be both unreliable *and* a stable indicator of real identity; appearances both deceive *and* lead to truth. No matter what its superficial *relation* to the untruth, the inside is always understood to be the realm of truth. In a similarly phobic vein, the characters in *Love's Labour's Lost* continually stage the movement away from an unreliable outside to an internal truth. Starting with the men's search for knowledge at the expense of carnal pleasure, and ending with the women's dictate that the men need to learn true love, all the characters are in thrall to maintaining the distinction between outside and inside, which gets mapped onto appearance and truth, inferior and superior.

But the crime of the lipstick lesbian is that she deceives and she deceives — her surface is allegedly a lie in relation to her inside, and her inside is allegedly a lie in relation to her outside. She provides no safe space in which to articulate identity, no whorl within which fixity can emerge in full bloom. She embodies the very thing from which normativity recoils: the lack of truth in desire. And the play plays along with this lack, staying with the surface and probing its depths without succumbing to them. Indeed, *Love's Labour's Lost* has often been accused of being all surface, all rhetorical flourish and no substance, all lust and no love, "promoting verbal matter at the expense of signified matter," as James Calderwood puts it.[6] Unlike other Shakespearean comedies that focus on the epistemological conundrum posed by the cross-dressed body — the inside at odds with an outside — *Love's Labour's Lost* stays with the female body as the one that on the surface itself defies our regimes of knowing desire and identity. If femininity, like comedy, is meant to ensure internal compliance with an external norm, if it is meant to be what it looks like, then both *Love's Labour's Lost* and lipstick lesbians resist that compliance from within the form of compliance: their surface is both suggestive and destructive of themselves.

Such an assertion might suggest the universal falsity of femininity: all women belie the truth. This misogynistic conviction that women are not to be trusted, however, is a far cry from the situation that lipstick lesbians allow us to theorize. For Lisa Walker, the femme "both constructs the illusion of an interior gendered self (she looks like a straight woman) and parodies it (what you see is not what you get). Bringing the femme to the foreground elucidates the limitations of the expressive model of gender / sexual identity."[7] What *Love's Labour's Lost* does, however, is not only focus on the limits of representation for sexual identity but also highlights the schism within the surface of representation where identity is both produced and parodied. The play cannot end according to generic plan, because it cannot generate an identity where appearance will be coincident with essence. The problematic of the lipstick lesbian — that her appearance fails to signify in a stable manner — is also the problematic of *Love's Labour's Lost*. Both fail the first rule of identity, which insists that one has to look like one's desire and that one's desire has to be identifiable.

This is why the Princess, Rosaline, Catherine, and Maria are single at the end of the play—not because they have not been loved, but because this comedy cannot be comic. Instead, the play lingers on a luminous lot of lesbians who leave labels low in favor of what we may term "lipstick logos." The slippery knowledge of the glossy surface marks all four women in the play even and especially as they act lippy with the men who try and seduce them. The four women end up together after having actively rejected the men—or, what is worse, having put them on hold for the space of a year. This thwarting of the play's comic ends is also a thwarting of heterosexual identity, and Biron articulates that loss toward the end of the play when the four men, disguised as Russians, meet with a cold and cruel reception from the four women, themselves disguised to fool the men. Biron eventually figures out that the ladies' man-in-waiting, Boyet, had in fact given away their plan before the disguised Russians even came along to execute it:

[He] [t]old our intents before, which once disclosed,
The ladies did change their favours, and then we,
Following the signs, wooed but the sign of she. (5.2.467–69)

Like the lipstick lesbian, this alliterative "sign of she" trades on unreliable appearances. The ladies have "change[d] their favours" and disguised themselves so fully that the men quite happily woo the wrong women, convinced they are right about them. (I must note that these "full disguises" are nothing more than a string of pearls or a glove, so it is fairly amazing that the men are fooled by them.) What is particularly interesting is that the women seem to have no difficulty in recognizing the men, despite the full Russian drag. The threat for the men, then, retrospectively articulated by Biron, is not that they have been rejected by the women, but that they have been unable to read the women's exteriors as signifying their internal identities. The men have followed the signs, but the signs have not yielded signification. The Princess and her cohort, in the words of Lisa Duggan and Kathleen McHugh, are "not . . . performer[s] of legible gender transgression, like the butch and his sister the drag queen, but . . . betrayer[s] of legibility itself."[8] Women, Biron's shocked statement seems to imply, are all inscrutable, and if that is the case, then how is one to tell a lipstick lesbian apart from a straight femme, a comedy from the not so comic?

This question, of course, hinges on the question of difference itself. If identities are continually shifting, then how does one assign stability to difference? If straight women differ from lesbians because of X, then what happens if, far from marking the spot, X keeps shifting? What if the fond desire expressed in the play—"Immediately they will again be here / In their own shapes" (5.2.287–88)—can never be fulfilled as a demand for authenticity of appearance? Are lipstick lesbians the mirror into which we must all, as subjects of desire and regardless of sexual orientation, look? And if so, then does such a template serve to universalize lipstick lesbians while canceling their specificity as femme women desiring other women? For Alain Badiou, this alleged "universalism," far from flattening out difference, merely "presents itself as *an indifference that tolerates differences*."[9] Which is to say, the theorization of desire enabled by the lipstick lesbian does not universalize lipstick lesbians as the representative of all humanity and does not cancel the specific configuration of their desire. Rather, it allows us to be indifferent to the truth claim of different desires as being different from one another. This indifference allows us to isolate the lipstick lesbian as the figure most fully engaged with our *collective* fears about the untrustworthiness of desire and our *collective* fantasies about making desire meaningful. The "universality" of the lipstick lesbian, therefore, does not banish difference as much as it lives in / difference.

As Biron knows, this means one cannot always tell straight femme from queer, comedy from tragedy, and apparent from real. If, according to Cyrus Hoy, "the basic pattern of Shakespearian comedy . . . consists in a movement from the artificial to the natural, always with the objective of finding oneself,"[10] then *Love's Labour's Lost* doubly defies its comic status by moving from artifice to artifice and never allowing either its characters or its readers to "find" themselves. Instead, it problematizes the nature of the self by suggesting repeatedly that a face is meant to be outfaced—or, rather, that the face to which we have access both provides and thwarts our desire for a stable identity. It is in this sense that Biron banters with a dejected Holofernes who has been scorned for his role in the presentation of "The Nine Worthies":

> *Biron*: And now forward, for we have put thee in countenance.
> *Holofernes*: You have put me out of countenance.
> *Biron*: False, we have given thee faces.
> *Holofernes*: But you have outfaced them all. (5.2.607–11)

In *Love's Labour's Lost*, a face can exist only in multiple forms, and those forms can exist only in a state of perpetual unwriting. This resistance to deep legibility condemns a text about desire to play out without resolution. There is no relief in the play—even the dance with which most comedies vent their joy at having escaped nearly sodomitical experiences (*Twelfth Night*, for instance) is denied us. Instead, all we get is the announcement of a death and the postponement of desire's fulfillment. As far as the play is concerned, desire names the very thing that cannot be fulfilled even as it continually asks to be satisfied.

Lipstick lesbians thus name a problematic in our current day that resonates with the one explored in *Love's Labour's Lost* more than four hundred years ago. The non-coincidence of appearance and desire calls into question the status of identity formulated on the basis of desire; Shakespeare's play is filled with the hollowness of identifiable identity, and offers us instead a superficial depth that can never fully be plumbed. But we, writing about Shakespeare several centuries after the play, in a moment that we celebrate as being theoretically queer, remain attached to having identity positions legitimate our thoughts. One sees this repeatedly in essays and books in which critics provide their sexual credentials as a way to justify their critical concerns. But lipstick lesbians work precisely to undermine that justification. They do not provide us with a sexual identity so much as challenge the notion of an identity in which desires match and support acts that, in turn, match and support one's being in the world. Like *Love's Labour's Lost*, lipstick lesbians "offer a series of false bottoms" where the "truth" is indistinguishable from the surface and the surface is too stylish to match the truth.[11] The irony of "saying one thing and meaning another" marks both sets of "L" words, characterizing everyone and everything in a play where disguise is the norm and heterosexuality does not emerge triumphant at the end. The lesson of the lipstick lesbian, then, of women who "long, love, lust," to quote words from the title song of the hit television series *The L Word*, is to consider what it means to look the part and then to part that look from anything we might be tempted to call identity.

Notes

1. *Love's Labour's Lost*, in Greenblatt et al., *The Norton Shakespeare*, 5.2.851–53. Citations in parentheses are to this edition.

2. The term "lipstick lesbians" had its American heyday in the 1990s. Although it is not currently in vogue, the linguistic resonance of the term continues to reveal much about our desire to embody sexuality.

3. The riddles generated by disguise in this play extend even to characters' names. In the version of the text from 1598, many of Rosaline's lines are actually assigned to Catherine. This assignment prevents us from making sense of both Rosaline's and Catherine's roles in that version of the play, and a lot of work has gone into keeping its characters straight even, and especially, when the text has militated against it.

4. Walker, "How to Recognize a Lesbian," 884.

5. As Lisa Walker notes, "The femme's radical desire is understood to offset her normative external appearance, and so that desire is produced as internal": ibid., 885.

6. Calderwood, "*Love's Labour's Lost*," 318. Goldstein, "*Love's Labour's Lost* and the Renaissance Vision of Love," 347, suggests the play repeatedly enacts "the disavowal of spirituality in favor of sensuality." The introduction in the Norton edition asks in a similar vein: "How much do we stress the witty dialogue, with its link to wooing and wedding, as opposed to the ultimate repudiation of that wit, with its more somber assumptions about marriage and life?": Greenblatt et al., *The Norton Shakespeare*, 733.

7. Walker, "How to Recognize a Lesbian," 883.

8. Duggan and Kathleen McHugh, "A Fem(me)inist Manifesto," 167.

9. Badiou, *Saint Paul*, 99.

10. Hoy, "*Love's Labour's Lost* and the Nature of Comedy," 35.

11. Greenblatt et al., *The Norton Shakespeare*, 733.

Doctorin' the Bard: A Contemporary Appropriation of *Love's Labour's Won*

HECTOR KOLLIAS

Love's Labour's Won does not exist. Cited, as the editors of *The Norton Shakespeare* point out, in 1598 in Francis Mere's list of Shakespeare's comedies and believed to be a sequel to *Love's Labour's Lost*, it seems nevertheless not to have survived.[1] Gone, but, as the mere existence of this essay would indicate, not quite forgotten. As with other such lost works, it exists in conjecture, in the effort both of scholars to surmise what might have been and of creative writers to appropriate its lost existence for their own purposes. There is something both troubling and seductive in the idea that modern/contemporary writing and scholarship insist on conjuring up the ghost of a play with no material existence. In the age of the Internet and Wikipedia (which informed me of the existence of other plays with that title, whether they are regarded as taking their cues from Shakespeare or merely using "his" title for their own purposes),[2] it seems remarkably easy to conjure up words and plays from, as it were, thin air. The material existence of a body of texts that is thought of, as the editors of *The Norton Shakespeare* remind us, as "perpetually open" (72) is not sufficient, it would seem, for its "openness" is so radical that the mere ghost of a title can become the flesh of parasitic plays or conjecturing scholarly notes trying to edify the play from the ether of nonexistence, channeling it from some other dimension and waiting, hoping that it find flesh in this world.

It is not only the editors of *The Norton Shakespeare*, or those of the *Oxford Shakespeare* upon whose work the *Norton Shakespeare* is based and whose words in the notice to the play I am quoting, who are complicit in this conjuring plot—no less complicit is the editor of this volume for asking me to write about it, or am I for doing it. The *Norton* editors note that it would in no way be exceptional for a play of the time to be recorded, even printed, and then lost, and they also state that *"Love's Labour's Won* stands a much better chance of having survived, somewhere, than *Cardenio*: because it was printed, between 500 and 1,500 copies were once in circulation" (803). Nevertheless, in the only material sense of survival, the play *does not exist.* Any question of fidelity to the nonexistent immediately disappears, and any attempt to write about a nonexistent text immediately turns into a trick, a fakery. The most respectful one can be about such tricks is merely to assert their plausibility, as the editors do when they surmise that "conceivably the phrase [*Love's Labour's Won*] served as an alternative title for one of Shakespeare's other comedies" or that *"Love's Labour's Won* is the title of a lost play by Shakespeare" (803). The editors acknowledge the possibilities and judge that "none of these suppositions is implausible" (803). This still does not answer the question: What can be said of a lost play? What can I write about a text that does not exist?

Doctor in the House

This conundrum becomes much less taxing if one considers that a nonexistent play that nonetheless survives as a title and as the idea of a play is seemingly destined to acquire mythical status and, as such, to inspire writers to appropriate it, as a myth, in their own writings. For me, the most interesting appropriation is the one found in the popular BBC television science fiction series *Doctor Who*, in which *Love's Labour's Won* forms the kernel of the plot of an episode entitled "The Shakespeare Code," broadcast in the United Kingdom in early 2007.[3] The episode is one of several in which the time-traveling titular hero of the series visits the historical past and intervenes in it so as not, precisely, to change it. The overarching moral of *Doctor Who* would seem to be that human history is itself threatened and must be restored: Vesuvius must erupt and Pompeii must vanish, for example, lest the change in the historical fact produce a radical change in the whole "fabric of space–time" and humanity itself disappear. The doctor is himself an alien, of the race of the Time Lords, but he always has a human sidekick, and his overall concern is always the survival of the human race. If history is not to be changed then, *Love's Labour's Won*, which is meant to be performed on the re-created stage of Shakespeare's Globe Theater, must itself vanish; the foundling must be lost again after one fateful performance. This is one of several interesting twists in the fictional fate of the play, and one of several interesting queerings of the established order of what must, and what must not, survive. These twists and queerings will be what concern me here. As we shall see, these are queer twists not because they impose any kind of (homo)sexual content on the play that does not exist, but because of the very way in which the nonexistence of the play is attributed to a series of queer interventions, if we take "queer" in its broader and more disconcerting sense as that which troubles and distorts the transmission and the survival of a "humanity" always already conceived as heteronormative.

Before any analysis of the plot concerning Shakespeare and the conjuring tricks that resurrect and then kill off once and for all the ghost of *Love's Labour's Won*, a few words on the history and appeal of the series responsible for these tricks are called for. *Doctor Who* has been one of the longest-running successes of the BBC, having started in 1963 on a continuous run until 1989, when it was stopped until its triumphant revival in 2005. The early series were noted for frightening children with mechanical monsters and, later on, for their flimsy and low-budget settings. From 2005 onward, in the hands of Russell T. Davies and now Steven Moffat, the show has become flashier, sexier, more expensive, and its cult appeal transformed into a genuine wide-reaching television hit frequently cited as the BBC's most successful current television program. The figure of the doctor himself, once played as a middle-aged eccentric suited to the (predominantly British) stereotype of the asexual "boffin," has now been turned into a younger, cooler, and sultrier contemporary type who swapped Edwardian dress or multicolored, overlong scarves for a nicely tailored suit and Converse trainers. Although the doctor is hardly ever involved in sexual imbroglio, his sidekicks, to date always female, often find him an object of desire, and the show's sexiness and worldliness is accentuated by decisions such as having the pop singer, and European gay icon, Kylie Minogue star in a Christmas special episode. Part of the new charm of the resurrected show is its obvious knowing winks not just to its own history but also to a series of contemporary cultural contexts—it is, in other words, an exemplary postmodern exercise in fantasy storytelling.

In this more glamorous and knowingly self-referential context, it is hardly surprising that an episode constructed around the nonexistence of a Shakespeare play (with the already knowing reference to bestselling fiction in its title, "The Shakespeare Code") pitches its Shakespearean credentials halfway between light mockery and dutiful veneration. It is a fortuitous coincidence that a series that was canceled, in its first decidedly unsexy incarnation, around the time of the first blossoming of queer studies in the late 1980s, would come back to Shakespeare in a strikingly queer-informed manner.

Shakespeare himself is heard subtly to proposition the doctor, after which the doctor declaims: "Fifty-seven academics just punched the air with joy!" Shakespeare is read as unproblematically bisexual, having already greeted Martha, the doctor's attractive, young, black (human) companion, with the Elizabethan version of the construction worker's wolf whistle: "Hey nonny nonny!" Of course, the knowingness and playfulness also includes the inevitable confrontation with the past's markedly un-contemporary racial and sexual mores, with Martha becoming quite irate at William's exaltations such as "my ebony princess." At the same time, the writers are keen to stress Shakespeare's unique position among humans, having the doctor breathlessly exclaim: "Genius! *The* genius! The most human human that's ever been!" The oscillation between these poles of mockery and veneration is in itself seductive and makes for a television hour that can claim to be both playful and educational. After the doctor, on first seeing Shakespeare on the stage of the Globe, offers the opinion that his are "the most beautiful, brilliant words," William addresses the audience with an enthusiastic, "Shut your big fat mouths." As we shall see, the key interest in this postmodern appropriation of the Bard is precisely the queer power of words, their power to edify, resurrect, and kill—and their transformational power that can turn the human into the inhuman, "the world's greatest poet" into the puppet of unregenerate witches.

The Power of Words

The witches—three, of course—are the reason why, in the context of *Doctor Who*'s appropriation of the play, *Love's Labour's Won* has to be sacrificed. The story of the episode revolves around these three witches, members of an alien tribe lost in "the void" of space–time but who now return with the evil plan to conquer Earth and destroy the human race and whose plan involves using the Shakespearean stage to mount an elaborate conjuring of their "lost" sisters by having the final lines of his play dictated to Shakespeare while he is in a trance. Once these words (banal "cosmic coordinates" and definitely undeserving of the creator of "the most beautiful, brilliant words") are uttered on the stage, the army of demons begins to appear, and the mischievous plan is complete. These witches then, apart from being a rather obvious cipher for a queer inhumanity—an unregenerate sisterhood whose members live forever and do not, seemingly, reproduce sexually—are also entirely dependent for their existence on the power of words. Words conjure them up from the ether, and words destroy them. Queer theory has long been attentive to the power of the word of course, the power of identification and classification assumed by the insult, as discussed in seminal works such as Judith Butler's *Excitable Speech* and Didier Eribon's *Insult and the Making of the Gay Self*.[4] The parallelism between these inhuman sci-fi creations and real-life queers is hard to pass by. But what is perhaps more interesting is the power of words to edify, to resurrect, to bring life to creatures that do not materially exist—and the analogy this may have with the edification and resurrection, even for the purposes of prime-time family entertainment, of a lost Shakespeare play.

The power of words is essential to the witches' existence and, by extension, to the survival of humanity. It is the same power, in its synechdochical aspect as the power of the "mere" title, that has been able to keep the ghost of *Love's Labour's Won* alive. Words are in both cases properly *conjuring*, performing an ex nihilo creation or keeping ghosts alive. The writers of *Doctor Who* have even made this performative aspect of conjuring central to their conception of the "code" that the doctor has to break to solve the mystery, done, again, in a tone that playfully combines irreverence with veneration. The Globe *qua* building is a tetradecagon, and the importance of that architectural detail becomes apparent only when the doctor considers that a sonnet has fourteen lines. This curious yet spurious fact forms the venerable aspect of the treatment of words alongside the plot's central contention that words bring life. The irreverent aspect will appear, as we shall shortly see, as the solution to the problem posed by words. It is also apparent in the handling of Shakespearean scholarship in the episode. The writers clearly intend the audience to "know their Shakespeare stuff," as demonstrated in the several anachronistic attributions of famous Shakespearean lines, including, inevitably, "To be or not to be," to the doctor. William, always the pilferer, commends the doctor on his turn of phrase and asks for permission to use his words. The "genius" is playfully debunked as a borrower of alien verse. But the most playful, least reverent, and most interesting debunking of the Bard's words by another comes with the (obviously happy) resolution of the plot.

Conjuring (In)humanity

It should be obvious that the only man with the power to stop the witches' evil plan once the parasitically grafted end of the play has been spoken on stage is the Bard himself, using his own words to stop the damage that the witches' implanted words have done. The words he uses are not at all beautiful or brilliant, consisting mostly of the "cosmic coordinates" that need to be reversed, but the *coup de grâce* is not even his. The final utterance that sends the witches packing is: "I say to thee: Expelliarmus"—followed, of course, by the Doctor's amused, "Good old J. K." We are caught in an intertextual storm that superimposes Harry Potter's spell over the fictional words of the Bard over the fictional conjuring of the witches, on top of the existing remnant of the Shakespearean title. What is more, each one of these superimpositions has a cultural value ascribed tacitly or explicitly to the human and the inhuman. The world of the "inventor of the human," as Harold Bloom would have it, is threatened by the alien witches with destruction conjured by words; Shakespeare's words are the human weapon against this destruction, the labor that love wins by rescuing the entire human race. But this labor, although performed on stage by Shakespeare, is not authored by him. Rather, it is made up of borrowings from the alien Time Lord and the fictional wizard, so that finally the survival of humanity depends on the graft of a supplementary inhumanity that is only the flip side of the inhumanity that threatens it in the first place.[5] The survival of the play in this fantasy figures the death of the human itself, which also entails that the play's final disappearance, and the fact of its nonexistence is the gift of life to humanity by a certain kind of inhumanity, by something beyond the human. The fantasy shows that if the play *did* exist, if it had been allowed to be performed in the version perverted by the witches, then humanity would have disappeared. So the play is destroyed, in a gesture that is typical of the doctor's interventions in human history, *so that* humanity may have a future.

Quite apart from the amusing general tomfoolery on offer in this postmodern appropriation of "the most human human that's ever been," the culturally, even politically queer thrust of the episode lies with what it tells us of the conjuring and the survival of the human. In a playful yet deadly serious answer to the question of humanity's survival (and the survival of the lost play of humanity's greatest son), the writers of "The Shakespeare Code" present the inhuman, that which supplements and survives the human by helping humanity itself survive, the liminal figures of the Symbolic without which the Symbolic itself is not tenable. Humanity as it is today depends, the story tells us, on these interventions of the inhuman, those queer interventions made by bad witches, good aliens, and anachronistic wizards that form the extrahuman and extra-Shakespearean elements needed for the best story told about the nonexistent play. Not only do they tell a good story, but they also compel us to think about human survival and symbolic transmission in ways that implicate the presence—sometimes threatening, sometimes salutary, but always queer—of the inhuman. Thus, they compel us—us queers, at least—to consider our symbolic positions in relation to the heteronormative humanity that both includes and excludes us and that we variously threaten like unregenerate witches or help like well-meaning Time Lords. This is surely already much more than a title and a series of conjectures stemming from it. Where the editors of *The Norton Shakespeare* dutifully stop with conjuring a play's existence out of a title, the writers of "The Shakespeare Code" give us a dizzying and playful, yet serious, vision of a play's (non)existence symbolizing the future of humanity itself *and* show us the non-human invention of the human, the most alien alien that has ever been.

Notes

1. Greenblatt et al., *The Norton Shakespeare*, 803. Citations in parentheses are to this edition and are given by page number.

2. See http://en.wikipedia.org/wiki/Love's_Labour's_Won.

3. The episode can be found in the BBC's *Doctor Who*, series 3, vol. 1, DVD. It was written by Russel T. Davies and Gareth Roberts.

4. Butler, *Excitable Speech*; Eribon, *Insult and the Making of the Gay Self*.

5. See Bloom, *Shakespeare*.

Milk

HEATHER LOVE

Anything that is good will be experienced as though it was
already inside.
　—Adam Phillips, "On a More Impersonal Note," 101

Recently, critics have attempted to redefine queerness as a form of temporal
dislocation or asynchrony. Given the fact that the time of the family and the
time of the couple define time itself, we might understand deviations from
normative time—rather than any specifically sexual form of transgression—
as queer. *Macbeth* is extremely responsive to this approach. Paying attention
to questions of linearity, temporality, and succession in the play brings out the
queerness in the text in a way that paying attention to sexuality does not. In
particular, moments of temporal collapse—the collapse of past, present, and
future into a single instant—produce a situation that I think we might call
queer. "Ambition" designates a form of desire that does not respect temporal
sequence, and that produces situations of over-proximity. I will take these
uncanny moments of temporal and spatial collapse in the play as a guide for
my reading practice. With special attention to Lady Macbeth, I propose a
form of reading that is not merely close, but too close, claustrophobic, even
abject. Instead of getting critical distance on the text, or tracking its historical
context or ideological elements, I will get close to it and accept the intimacy
that it offers.

　The trouble starts when the Witches promise Macbeth a kingship without
succession. Posterity belongs to Banquo, who, "not so happy" as Macbeth,
"yet much happier," is fated to be "the root and father / Of many kings."[1] The
gap that opens between the two men in this early scene widens throughout
the play. Before he gives the order to murder Banquo, Macbeth reasons, "They
hailed him father to a line of kings. / Upon my head they placed a fruitless
crown / And put a barren scepter in my grip, / Thence to be wrenched with

an unlineal hand, / No son of mine succeeding" (3.1.60–64). In Macbeth's final encounter with the Witches he is treated to a harrowing vision of Banquo's line, "stretch[ing] out to th' crack of doom" (4.1.139). The king, though still nominally in power, is exiled from this royal pageant and from historical succession more generally. The tyrant has his day in the sun, his moment of bloody glory; because he cannot bestow his power, however, it has no meaning. The blood that should flow in his veins and in his sons' veins is on his hands instead.

Macbeth's inability to convert power into posterity is an effect not only of his excessive ambition but more specifically of his impatience. Banquo's original request to the Witches ("If you can look into the seeds of time / And say which grain will grow and which will not, / Speak then to me" [1.3.58–60]) suggests the long arc of his attention, which measures time in accord with generation and growth. Macbeth cannot wait for the Witches' prophecies to ripen; he lives in a time of "bloody execution" (1.2.18). A soldier king, Macbeth understands power as action; he has no time for the long durée of kingship but is ruled instead by a vision of history consummated in an instant. That vision is articulated as a fantasy in Macbeth's soliloquy as he contemplates killing Duncan:

> If it were done when 'tis done, then 'twere well
> It were done quickly. If th' assassination
> Could trammel up the consequence, and catch
> With his surcease success, but that this blow
> Might be the be-all and the end-all—here,
> But here upon this bank and shoal of time,
> We'd jump the life to come. (1.7.1–7)

Macbeth would rather have done not only with Duncan's murder and its potential consequences but also with life itself. To "jump the life to come" here suggests not only risking eternal damnation but also leaping across both life and the afterlife in an instant.

This "vaulting ambition" (1.7.27) is a form of contempt for the future that means that Macbeth can have no place in dynastic history. The king belongs instead in a different more "unlineal" succession—to that group of men known for their impatience and for their love of the barren scepter. Macbeth's eagerness to have done with life itself associates him with the figure that Lee Edelman has recently described as the *sinthomo*sexual, who "annuls the temporality of desire" by figuring "the unrestricted availability of jouissance."[2]

Macbeth plays the *sintho*mosexual in the scene immediately following the announcement of Duncan's death. The night before, Macbeth had murdered
Duncan and left the bloody daggers in the hands of his sleeping attendants.
When he hears that the king is dead, Macbeth feigns surprise and, in a trumped-
up rage, kills the grooms. When Macduff questions him, Macbeth responds:

Who can be wise, amazed, temp'rate and furious,
Loyal and neutral, in a moment? No man.
The expedition of my violent love
Outrun the pauser, reason. Here lay Duncan,
His silver skin laced with his golden blood;
And his gashed stabs looked like a breach in nature
For ruin's wasteful entrance; there, the murderers,
Steeped in the colors of their trade, their daggers
Unmannerly breeched with gore. Who could refrain
That had a heart to love, and in that heart
Courage to make's love known? (2.3.106–16)

Macbeth describes his impulsive murder not only as an act of rage, but also as
the result of an inability to hold in tension contradictory impulses. Even in
this moment of calculated and calculating spontaneity, Macbeth is remarkably consistent in his self-representation: he cannot allow time to unfold difference since he lives only in the moment. His way of making his love known
constitutes a "breach in nature" that allows for "ruin's wasteful entrance." In
contrast to Banquo, whose love begets kings, this love's only result is "daggers
breeched with gore."

Banquo is identified with what Edelman calls "reproductive futurity"—
the association between sexual reproduction, narrative and historical futurity,
and social meaning. The emblem of this notion of futurity is the Child who,
as Edelman writes, "has come to embody for us the telos of the social order."[3]
Edelman notes how difficult it is to challenge the ascendancy of the child in
contemporary political discourse. Given the symbolic investment in this figure, he wonders "What . . . would it signify not to be 'fighting for the children'? How could one take the *other* 'side' . . . ?"; he ultimately proposes that
we understand queerness as being on "the side of those *not* 'fighting for the
children.'"[4] By this definition, there are several figures in *Macbeth* we might
identify as queer—the Witches, for instance, cooking up the "finger of birth-
strangled babe" (4.1.30) in their brew. But if queerness means not fighting for
the children, then Lady Macbeth is the queerest character in the play.

Like her husband, Lady Macbeth is eager for eternity. Her two soliloquies in Act 1, Scene 5, concern her doubt about whether she and Macbeth will be up to acting on their desires. In the first, she worries that his "nature" is "too full o' th' milk of human kindness / To catch the nearest way" (1.5.15–17); in the second, she calls on "murd'ring ministers" to "stop up th'access and passage to remorse, / That no compunctious visitings of nature / Shake my fell purpose nor keep peace between / Th'effect and it" (1.5.43–46). For Lady Macbeth, as for her husband, getting what you want means closing the gap between intention and outcome. The problem is, this kind of consummation collapses time itself, so that the object of desire is delivered, enjoyed, and destroyed in one stroke. The structure of Lady Macbeth's desire is evident in first words to her husband:

> Great Glamis, worthy Cawdor,
> Greater than both, by the all-hail hereafter,
> Thy letters have transported me beyond
> This ignorant present, and I feel now
> The future in the instant. (1.5.53–57)

Lady Macbeth sees the hereafter in the present. In that sense, we might understand her ambition not as a desire in the traditional sense—a longing for an outcome located in the future—but as a constant enjoyment of the future in and as the present.[5]

The transformation of Lady Macbeth into a *sinthom*osexual is figured as a sex change. The spirits whom she asks to rid her of remorse she also asks to "unsex her": "Come, you spirits, / That tend on mortal thoughts, unsex me here, / And fill me from the crown to the toe topful / Of direst cruelty . . . Come to my woman's breasts / And take my milk for gall . . ." (1.5.39–42, 46–47). While Lady Macbeth urges her husband to be more of a man by emptying himself of milk, she aims to transform her own female nature by trading milk for poison. This exchange, wrought with the assistance of demonic spirits, brings on the chain of bloody events. It also nudges the play toward the all-male universe where it is already tending.[6] The Macbeths are virilized in part through Lady Macbeth's fantasies about the pleasures she and her husband might share as two men, acting together. First they will make sure that Duncan's grooms are drunk; then, she asks, "What cannot you and I perform upon, / Th'unguarded Duncan?" (1.7.70–71). Macbeth responds by saying that his wife should "bring forth men-children only" (1.7.73). The men-children that Macbeth conjures here are, presumably, not heirs in his line but walk-ons in the Macbeths' own personal *Salò*, their *120 Days of Sodom*. What could they not perform upon them?

Yet Lady Macbeth is not securely represented as masculine. Her queerness is bound up with her position as the king's wife and, more significantly, as mother. In overcoming her husband's reluctance to kill Duncan, Lady Macbeth makes it clear that, in his place, she would let nothing stand in her way. When he expresses his misgivings, she responds with a hypothetical that has the disturbing ring of truth.

> What beast was't then
> That made you break this enterprise to me?
> When you durst do it, then you were a man;
> And to be more than what you were, you would
> Be so much more the man. Nor time nor place
> Did then adhere, and yet you would make both.
> They have made themselves, and that their fitness now
> Does unmake you. I have given suck, and know
> How tender 'tis to love the babe that milks me:
> I would, while it was smiling in my face,
> Have plucked my nipple from his boneless gums
> And dashed the brains out, had I so sworn as you
> Have done to this. (1.7.47–59)

Lady Macbeth makes an argument not only about resolve but also about timing: Duncan sleeps beneath their roof this night; they should kill him before he leaves. If manliness demands courage, ruthlessly murdering a defenseless creature at the moment of greatest vulnerability demands a woman's touch. If she were to kill a child—just supposing—Lady Macbeth would choose just the right moment, while the baby is "smiling in her face." The event, imagined with fearsome specificity, punctures the tender stillness of a mutual regard; the plucked nipple and boneless gums and dashed brains recast her fantasy as a fait accompli.

We might understand Lady Macbeth as queer because of what Janet Adelman terms the "unnatural abrogation of her maternal function."[7] But Adelman suggest that Lady Macbeth's unsexing and cross-gendering demonstrate not only a departure from "natural" mothering but also "the horror of the maternal function itself."[8] Critics have long identified in the representation of both Lady Macbeth and the Witches a fear of maternal power and the mother's body. But before we identify these representations as merely examples of misogyny, or as a historically specific fear about the dangers of wet nurses or breast milk, we might want to compare it with another, quite different account of maternal ambivalence.

I am thinking of Adrienne Rich's description of what it was like to be the mother to three young sons in *Of Woman Born*. After quoting a diary entry written at the time ("My children cause me the most exquisite suffering of which I have any experience. It is the suffering of ambivalence: the murderous alternation between bitter resentment and raw-edged nerves, and blissful gratification and tenderness"[9]), Rich describes her ambivalence in detail:

> The bad and the good moments are inseparable for me. I recall the times when, suckling each of my children, I saw his eyes open full to mine, and realized each of us was fastened to the other, not only by mouth and breast, but through our mutual gaze: the depth, calm, passion of that dark blue, maturely focused look. I recall the physical pleasures of having my full breast suckled at a time when I had no other physical pleasure in the world except the guilt-ridden pleasure of addictive eating. I remember early the sense of conflict, of a battleground none of us had chosen, of being an observer who, like it or not, was also an actor in an endless contest of wills. This was what it meant to me to have three children under the age of seven. But I recall too each child's individual body, his slenderness, wiriness, softness, grace, the beauty of little boys who have not been taught that the male body must be rigid. I remember moments of peace when for some reason it was possible to go to the bathroom alone. I remember being uprooted from already meager sleep to answer a childish nightmare, pull up a blanket, warm a consoling bottle, lead a half-asleep child to the toilet. I remember going back to sleep starkly awake, brittle with anger, knowing that my broken sleep would make next day a hell, that there would be more nightmares, more need for consolation, because out of my weariness I would rage at those children for no reason they could understand. I remember thinking I would never dream again (the unconscious of the young mother—where does it entrust its messages, when dream-sleep is denied her for years?)[10]

Rich is not Lady Macbeth. But the rhythms of maternal ambivalence—if not literally murderous in this case—are strikingly similar: the stillness and beauty of a reciprocal gaze; the sudden rush of resentment, spiking into an event.

I think we might understand Lady Macbeth as queer not only because of her refusal of maternity but also because she lives out the queerness of motherhood. Maternity is composed of both mothering and anti-mothering. Despite the heavy policing of that line, it can be quite difficult to tell at any given moment who is fighting for the children and who is dashing their brains out. Adelman comments on the way that Lady Macbeth puts both mothering and anti-mothering to work for her with her husband:

> The fears of female coercion, female definition of the male, that are initially located cosmically in the witches thus find their ultimate locus in the figure of Lady Macbeth, whose attack on Macbeth's virility is the source of her strength over him and who acquires that strength . . . partly because she can make him imagine himself as an infant vulnerable to her. In the figure of Lady Macbeth, that is, Shakespeare rephrases the power of the witches as the wife / mother's power to poison human relatedness at its source; in her, their power of cosmic coercion is rewritten as the power of the mother to misshape or destroy the child.[11]

The uncanny effect of *Macbeth*—its ability to reach out and touch its readers—is produced by the encounter it stages with the body of the mother and with an active and potentially dangerous maternal ambivalence.[12] This relation to the reader might be understood as an example of what Joanna Levin calls "horrific maternal transmission."[13] The setting for the activity of fantasy in the play is the "first intimacy," the relation between mother and child.[14] Given the lack of distinction between self and other in this scene, it may not be possible for readers of *Macbeth* to position themselves securely outside the body of the mother. Neither can we distinguish once and for all between mother as maker and as unmaker.

Perhaps it is not accurate to say that we "read" Lady Macbeth at all. Instead we might say that, by stamping us with her will, desires, and fantasies, she gives birth to us as readers. Such threatening intimacy might lead us to distance ourselves from this representation of maternity, to sort out its elements of fantasy and its elements of ideology, to place it in its time. But the play invites us to get closer, to identify ourselves with the perverse mother and to drink her milk. Such a queer form of reading does not long for Lady Macbeth across a vast historical distance, but seeks to enjoy her right now, come what may.

Notes

Thanks to Melissa Sanchez for her generous reading of this piece.

1. Orgel, *Macbeth*, 1.3.66, 3.1.5–6. Citations in parentheses are to this edition.

2. Edelman, *No Future*, 86–87.

3. Ibid., 11.

4. Ibid., 3.

5. Ibid., 39, discusses this as the distinction between desire and enjoyment. The Lacanian term *"sinthome"* describes the subject's relation to enjoyment; the *sinthomo*sexual is defined by his association with "a fatal and even murderous jouissance."

6. The play ultimately "solves the problem of masculinity by eliminating the female": Adelman, *Suffocating Mothers*, 146.

7. Ibid., 135.

8. Ibid.

9. Rich, *Of Woman Born*, 21.

10. Ibid., 31.

11. Adelman, *Suffocating Mothers*, 137–38.

12. For another account of the uncanny effect of *Macbeth*, see the reading of the play's reception and performance history in Garber, *Shakespeare's Ghost Writers*, 87–123. Garber argues that the danger of the play is figured by Medusa, whose lethal power extends beyond the pages of the play's text and the borders of the stage.

13. Levin, "Lady Macbeth and the Daemonologie of Hysteria," 42

14. In his contribution to Bersani and Phillips, *Intimacies*, Adam Phillips speculates whether Bersani's model of "impersonal intimacy," usually associated with male–male erotic desire, might also be a way to describe the mother–child relation. He writes, "There is no relation more narcissistic, as Freud himself remarks, than the relation between mothers and children; and there is, by the same token, no relation more devoted to or more inspired by the virtual, the potential. The first intimacy is an intimacy with a process of becoming, not with a person": Phillips, "On a More Impersonal Note," 114. A relation of narcissistic mirroring that apprehends the child as a "process of becoming" might further extend the model of textual relations outlined above.

Same-Saint Desire

PAUL MORRISON

Were the course of true love ever in danger of running smoothly, Freud suggests, it would not run at all:

> An obstacle is required to heighten libido, and where natural resistances to satisfaction have not been sufficient men have at all times erected conventional ones so as to be able to enjoy love. . . . In times when there is no difficulty standing in the way of sexual satisfaction . . . love becomes worthless and life empty, and strong reaction-formations were required in order to restore indispensable affective values.[1]

Freud typically construes the social as a necessary check on the swellings of a libido that is itself pre-social. Here, however, the social is said to supplement the natural to produce those swellings. Love is, of necessity, hard, and when need arises, man erects conventional barriers in the way of satisfaction to get an erection.

Measure for Measure would seem to argue otherwise. The Duke fails to maintain conventional barriers in the way of satisfaction, but at apparently no cost to the free flowing of the Viennese libido. On the contrary. Lechery has become "too general a vice" in the city, "and severity must cure it."[2] The Duke thus delegates his authority to Angelo, who thereafter functions as a blocking agent, a socially authorized killjoy. Culture, however, is no match for nature, and natural desire will out. Even Angelo, whose urine is reputed to be "congealed ice" (3.1.355), experiences the promptings of the desire he would repress in others, and the blocking agent must himself be blocked. This is not to suggest, of course, that the play authorizes licentiousness. The grotesque anti-fornication statute that fuels the plot is simply dropped from the social order that emerges at the play's end, but a compulsory form of the aptly named "wed-lock," our culture's most effective check on the free flowing of libido, substitutes for it. And when every Jack is obliged to have his Jill,

we are clearly in the realm of the "problem" play: externally imposed obligations are not readily distinguishable from those freely chosen. The compelled
marriages of Angelo and Lucio, for example, totally vitiate the "affective
values" attached to love, which the freely chosen, if frankly surprising, union
of the Duke and Isabella does little to restore. Had Shakespeare any interest in
comedy as usual, he might have given us the reunion of Claudio and Juliet; at
the very least, an "I do" from Isabella, a gesture of consent to her "freely"
chosen marriage, would not have been amiss. But no: the eternity of having
and holding in *Measure for Measure* is either punishment imposed from without or an affectiveless capitulation, allegedly from within, to the conventions
of comic form.

"Make not impossible," Isabella pleads with the Duke in the final act of the
play, "that which but seems unlike" (5.1.52–53). Isabella is seeking to expose
Angelo for the cad that he is, but in the spirit of her logic, one might consider
another seemingly "unlikely," although not impossible, proposition: the Duke
as Friar appropriates a distinctly spiritual authority for the secular. Conventional
wisdom argues (or assumes) the opposite: the Duke delegates his secular authority to a religious fanatic. The only sacerdotal office that the Friar performs,
however, is the rite of penance, and as Michel Foucault has taught us, the secular
appropriation and dissemination of "the obligation to confess" underwrite
modern disciplinary regimes of the norm. True, there is something wildly
anachronistic in reading this "free" embrace of the compulsory back into *Measure for Measure*. The "Duke of dark corners" (4.3.145), as Lucio rather engag-
ingly calls him, is invested in gaining access to the recesses of his subjects' souls,
but his climactic exercise in Christian mercy is precisely that: *Measure for Measure*
construes the soul as a spiritual reality to be redeemed, not as a psychosexual
dispensation to be managed. An anachronistic reading of Shakespeare is, however, hardly the newest news in town, and *Measure for Measure*, in any case, is
remarkable primarily for its resistance to it. Shakespeare our contemporary is
Shakespeare the Whig—which is to say, the ideological construction that is
Shakespeare characteristically participates in the terms of a Whig debate in
which "self-governance," in every sense of the term, emerges triumphant.
What makes this the most problematic of "problem" plays—what positively
elevates it to the status of a perverse play—is its unabashed eroticization of
artificially constructed and externally imposed strictures.

A certain anachronism is, perhaps, inevitable. *Measure for Measure* flirts with a
modernity it never fully embraces. The manacled Claudio, for instance, perfectly expresses the logic of what will emerge, historically, as the disciplinary:

Lucio: Why, how now, Claudio? Whence comes this restraint?
Claudio: From too much liberty, my Lucio, liberty,
As surfeit is the father of much fast,
So every scope, by immoderate use,
Turns to restraint. (1.2.104–8)

The crucial moment of control is not the imposition of physical restraints from without, but the subject's own inner recognition, albeit after the fact, of the self-limiting nature of liberty, which is fully itself only when it is not full liberty at all.[3] Claudio's virility is clearly part of his charm, but even the hyper-butch concede the necessity (or heroism) of sexual self-regulation. Curiously, however, a faithful not-quite-wife does not: "This forenamed maid hath yet in her continuance of her first affection. His unjust unkindness, that in all reason should have quenched her love, hath, like an impediment in the current, made it more violent and unruly" (3.1.232–35). The maid is Mariana, whose passion for the unkind Angelo is all the more "unruly" for the barriers he willfully erects in its path. Claudio internalizes externally imposed strictures that are thus not experienced as strictures at all. Mariana eroticizes them. Claudio's free embrace of the compulsory anticipates the modern subject of disciplinary regimes. Mariana's passion remains stubbornly perverse.

"O cunning enemy," Angelo speculates after his initial interview with Isabella, "that, to catch a saint, / With saints dust bait thy hook!" (2.2.185–86). The erotics of same-saint desire are all the more intense for the impediments they presuppose, which readily available charms do not afford: "Never could the strumpet, / With all her double vigour—art and nature— / Once stir my temper, but this virtuous maid / Subdues me quite" (2.2.187–90). Same-saint desire does not participate equally in the dual dispensation: Angelo's sudden passion for Isabella seems wholly the product of prohibition, and so of "art" or culture (or whatever it is we choose to oppose to nature). Lucio thinks it monstrous that Claudio faces death for nothing more than "the rebellion of a codpiece" (3.1.359), but the problem with this problem play is knowing which comes first, the rebellious member or the codpiece. For Claudio, Lucio, and the sundry ne'er-do-wells of the play, it is the recalcitrant member. Sex is all mammalian warmth and spontaneity, and only the codpiece stands between it and the smooth workings of the social order. For Angelo, Isabella, and the Duke, however, the codpiece (or the chastity belt, as the case may be) is for the sake of the somatic insurrection. Isabella gets herself to a nunnery, which might seem obstacle enough, and psychoanalytically inclined critics tend to construe her desire for "a more strict restraint / Upon the sisterhood" (1.4.4–5) as a retreat from an unruly libido, a compensatory embrace of external prohibitions. But it is entirely possible—and infinitely more fun—to take her at her word: Isabella simply wants "more restraint," an eroticization of discipline, not a disciplined or disciplinary eroticism. "Ere I'd yield / My body up to shame" (2.4.103–4), she shamelessly decrees, "th'impression of keen whips I'd wear as rubies" (2.4.101). An absolute prohibition against sex occasions a particularly kinky form of it. Saint Isabella keeps company with Saint Genet.

Or consider the codpiece, an equivocal blocking agent if ever there was one. It conspicuously foregrounds the member (with or without the help of padding) it purports only to keep at bay. All blocking agents in *Measure for Measure*, however, are equivocal. Angelo initially seems well suited to the role, yet the anti-fornication statute does not originate with him, and there is a sense in which he merely runs sexual interference for his better. Yet if the Duke is the actual impediment behind the impediment, he is also the architect of the play's comic conclusion, which renders the blocking agent and the surrogate playwright functionally indistinguishable. Again, the impediments that allegedly inhibit the free expression of libido actually inaugurate and sustain it, at least for the likes of Angelo, Isabella, and the Duke. If sex is all mammalian warmth and spontaneity for the n'er-do-wells of the play, it is all reptilian craft and cunning for the saintly. It may be that history is to blame. English common law recognized two forms of "spousal"—the legally binding *Sponsalia per verba de praesenti* and the more ambiguous *Sponsalia per verba del futuro*—which historically minded critics are fond of invoking. The appeal to history, however, merely exacerbates the problem it is thus powerless to explain (away): the legitimacy of desire in *Measure for Measure* seems bound to technicalities and legalisms, which hardly seems compatible with our poet of nature. The Duke's notorious bed trick, in which Mariana substitutes for Isabella, has precedents in folklore and romance, but Shakespeare introduces a crucial complication into his source. In Whetstone's *Promos and Cassandra*, Cassandra, the Isabella character, does in fact sleep with the corrupt magistrate. The episode has generated considerable controversy—confusion over the identity of a bedmate is apparently less common than one might suppose —but it is the love of complication qua complication that is at least equally problematic. Lysander is no doubt right: the course of true love never did run smooth. In *Measure for Measure*, however, it seems perversely convoluted, mediated, dilatory. The play is too exquisite by half, too rarefied; too much given to art, too little to nature. Content infects form. The reptilian sexuality that the play represents (and purportedly condemns) is indistinguishable from the play itself.

The canonization of Shakespeare—the elevation of Shakespeare to the status of Canonicity itself—begins in earnest with the Restoration, which tended to be unapologetic about its ideological investments. Dryden is typical: "Though the fury of a civil war . . . had buried the Muses under the ruin of monarchy, yet, with the restoration of our happiness, we see revived poesy lifting up its head."[4] This is Whig history in full flower, and Dryden is eager to claim Shakespeare for it: if the canonization of the Bard begins in earnest with the consolidation of the liberal settlement, it is because Shakespeare always was an implicit apologist for it. The struggle against absolutism—Royalist or Republican—is clearly internal to England, yet the Whig narrative, in Dryden as elsewhere, tends to play itself out on an international stage. Shakespeare is all mammalian warmth and spontaneity; Racine is all reptilian craft and cunning, and Shakespeare is to Racine as the English constitutional settlement is to French absolutism. French plays, one character in Dryden notes, "are not so properly to be called plays, as long discourses of reasons of state."[5] But if anything bears testimony to the imbrication of the French stage and state— the authoritarianism in which they cohere—it is the former's adherence to externally imposed strictures, the so-called Aristotelian "unities." Shakespeare's stage may lack the suspect refinement of Racine's, but it is everywhere animated by the soul of a living, breathing man. What is merely mechanical and restrictive in the neoclassical reception of Aristotle (the unities of time and place), Shakespeare rejects; what is intrinsic to his craft (the unity of action), he naturally accepts. The aesthetic does not therefore escape the political—"Want of due connection" in a play, Dryden is quick to note, "is as dangerous and unnatural as in a state"[6]—but the cornucopian variety of the typical Shakespearean plot, the "parliamentary" unity-in-diversity, is not a dead symmetry. The French neoclassical stage labors under the equivalent of the absurd anti-fornication statute of *Measure for Measure*: more or less arbitrary strictures are imposed from without. Shakespeare, like Claudio, internalizes what is essential in the structures that he thus renders superfluous. The Bard is himself an example of the triumph of self-regulation and self-governance that his comedies promote.

And as with the political subject, so, too, with the sexual: the "irregular" plays of Shakespeare evince a "more masculine fancy and greater spirit in the writing, than there is in any of the French."[7] Our bard is a beef-eating Englishman. "Till eating and drinking be put down," Lucio quips, the anti-fornica-

tion statute does not have a prayer, and *Measure for Measure* consistently associates a mammalian sexuality with the body's untutored appetites. (The
French apparently find sustenance in daintier fare.) Shakespeare's reputation
is inextricably bound to his sexual precociousness. Anne Hathaway was pregnant when she marched down the aisle with Will, a fact that, if my own
experience can be considered typical, every schoolboy knows. In any contest
between the codpiece and the recalcitrant member it houses, Shakespeare
can be relied on to favor the latter. But Will and Anne, like Claudio and Juliet,
were also bound by a "true contract" (1.2.122), and sexual precociousness, as
every schoolboy is made to know, should not be confused with mere license.
Shakespeare's properly "masculine fancy" is part and parcel of his canonization. So, too, is the sexual self-regulation.

They order these things differently in France: There an anti-fornication
statute (or an inflexible application of aesthetic "laws") might well take hold.
Phèdre, for instance, explicitly dramatizes the force of prohibition, although it
is never quite certain which prohibition enjoys pride of place. The incest
taboo, and thus a psychosexual prohibition? Or the prohibition against touching on stage, and thus an aesthetic or cultural taboo? *Phèdre* exiles the object
of her incestuous desires, but the unity of place prohibits any Hamlet-like
departure for distant shores. There is no escape from physical proximity and
—as if to up the erotic ante—no possibility of physical contact, for if the unity
of place begets proximity, *les bienséances* prohibit contact. The play that dramatizes incestuous desire also produces it in and as the conditions of its
dramatization.

"Is't not a kind of incest," Isabella asks her brother, "to take life / From
thine own sister's shame?" (3.1.140–41), and *Measure for Measure*, like *Phèdre*, is
very much given to the logic of erotic substitution: a sister's maidenhead for a
brother's head; Mariana for Isabella in Angelo's bed. (Even Juliet, Claudio's
not-quite-wife, is said to be Isabella's adoptive "cousin" [1.4.45].) Freud, who
also has an interest in the logic of erotic substitution, argues that the successful negotiation of the Oedipus complex necessarily passes unnoticed. "Inhibi-
tions and disturbances" in the process of normal sexual development become
"recognizable to superficial observation" only in the perverse, which is our
primary use value: it is the inability to negotiate the system that renders its
(il)logic generally available.[8] Even normative man erects conventional barriers in the way of satisfaction to get an erection, and neither *Phèdre* nor
Measure for Measure subsumes those barriers under the gentlemanly decorum
of it-goes-without-saying-or-seeing. Such is the scandal of *Phèdre*, a play that

relentlessly translates form into content, content into form. And such is the
scandal of the same-saint desire thematized in *Measure for Measure*, the scandal
that is *Measure for Measure*. What is the Duke's bed trick, after all, other than
the mechanism of socially acceptable, socially compelled, erotic substitution
forced to speak its name? What is normative psychosexual development other
than an elaborate bed trick? Same-saint desire differs from its mammalian
counterpart only in this: the normative mistake the logic of self-regulation for
the experience of freedom; the heroic ingenuity of perversion finds erotic
opportunity even—or perhaps especially—in prohibition and restraint.

Notes

1. Freud, "On the Universal Tendency to Debasement in the Sphere of Love,"
187–88.

2. *Measure for Measure*, in Greenblatt et al., *The Norton Shakespeare*, 3.1.346. Citations in parentheses are to this edition.

3. On this theme, see Barker, *The Tremulous Private Body*.

4. Dryden, "An Essay of Dramatic Poesy," 250.

5. Ibid., 244.

6. Ibid.

7. Ibid., 247.

8. Freud, "Three Essays on the Theory of Sexuality," 7:211.

The Merchant of Venice

The Rites of Queer Marriage
in The Merchant of Venice

ARTHUR L. LITTLE JR.

The short reading of *The Merchant of Venice* is that Antonio wants to "marry" Bassanio—at least, if we define marriage as two people committing to sexual and civil rites with an intention to form an intimate union "so as to form one,"[1] and if, and only if, we do not grant heterosexuality any a priori or priority ownership of marriage as such, and we at least reflect on the possibility that the *rites* of heterosexual marriage have developed at least in part as a way to balance out a patriarchalist civil order seemingly driven and sustained by intense and intimate homosocial male union and communion. I want to suggest in this essay that the issue for Shakespeare in *The Merchant of Venice* is not same-sex unions in and of themselves but how such unions find themselves increasingly subjected to a heteroculturalist reading. As Alan Bray has cogently shown in his groundbreaking work on early modern friendship, same-sex intimate male couplings could either be celebrated as the pinnacle of civil order, caught up as they were "within the network of *obligation* and *kinship* that cemented the traditional society of England,"[2] or condemned as "sodomitical"—that is, as the quintessential embodiment of civil disorder—depending on the uses to which such unions were being put.[3] I see *The Merchant of Venice* as situated at a critical cultural point where the valuation of same-sex coupling is under siege by an encroaching heterofantasy world of marriage, capitalism, (re)production, and homophobia that pushes (for its own teleological ends) to reread the viability of same-sex intimate friendship in disruptive—suspiciously unproductive and sodomitical—terms. However, using Bray's work on early modern same-sex intimate friendship, Lee Edelman's critique of society's strategic deployment of reproduction in its cultural and political valuation of heterosexuality (and heterosexual marriage), and Didier Eribon's study of mourning (of loss) in the making of a gay subjectivity, I am arguing that *The Merchant of Venice* pushes back and insists not only on laying claim to the rites and rights of same-sex (I now want to say *queer*) coupling but challenges a heteroculturalist presumptuousness that hetero-normative culture has successfully emulated and replaced those rites.

Shakespeare's broader challenge to heteronormativity begins with Antonio's opening speech:

> In sooth, I know not why I am so sad.
> It wearies me, you say it wearies you;
> But how I caught it, found it, or came by it,
> What stuff 'tis made of, whereof it is born,
> I am to learn;
> And such a want-wit sadness makes of me
> That I have much ado to know myself.[4]

This is an extremely important instantiation of queer mourning (and speaking). Within the aggressively heteronormative worlds of Venice, and especially Belmont, queer speaking seems always necessarily an act of not only speaking about but performing queer "suffering,"[5] articulating and performing *lack* as a constitutive part of queer desire. Further, what I would call here Antonio's double act of speaking and not speaking seems to plot or plop him into a queer history of such double acts, from medieval and early modern variations on the "sin which is not to be named" to the late-nineteenth-century and early-twentieth-century "love that dare not speak its name." His speaking performs the impossibility of speaking and the imposition of a mournful silence; it also anticipates the fact that he is the titular character and will get to speak only one hundred and eighty-eight lines, almost half the number spoken by Bassanio or Shylock, not even a third of Portia's, and just ten more than either Gratiano or Launcelot.

Antonio mourns. To be sure, he mourns the impending loss of Bassanio, but he mourns, too, a loss of an affirmative language and knowledge of his social and institutional place. Given the dominance and pervasiveness of a heterocultural hegemony in the play worlds of the play, it is "impossible [for the queer subject] to finish" this work of mourning.[6] Antonio mourns how his own culturally unsanctioned desires, those of same-sex intimate friendship, push him outside the presumptions of what increasingly in early modern culture becomes *the* civil institution, *the* institution of valuation and belonging; he mourns because he sees the institution of heterosexual marriage working not only to displace but to replace same-sex communing. Notwithstanding anything I have said here, I will argue at the end of this essay that Antonio's mourning reaches far beyond either pathos or the personal.

As important as it is to note how significant mourning is to Antonio's performing his desire for Bassanio, it is important to note, too, how significant the heterosexual family (namely, the father-and-daughter bond) and mourning are to the performance of Portia's heterosexual desires. Portia's scene of mourning revolves around her dead father: "O me, the word 'choose'! I may neither choose who I would nor refuse who I dislike, so is the will of a living daughter curbed by the will of a dead father" (1.2.19–22), not only the father's last will and testament, but also the father's desire, his own intimate participation in his daughter's sexual life. What becomes striking about Portia's "weary" scene, as opposed to Antonio's (cf. 1.2.1 and 1.1.2), is how much her scene is about *not* mourning—or, to put it another way, how much it is about the father *not* being dead. After all, it is Portia, not her father, who is locked away in a casket, and it is her desire that is effectively dead until her father brings *her* will to life.

Hers is a fantasy world of heterosexuality and heterosexual marriage, and we cannot overemphasize how thoroughly and deliberately the play links heterosexuality and heterosexual marriage to the structurations of fantasy: "The four winds blow in from every coast / Renownèd suitors, and her sunny locks / Hang on her temples like a golden fleece . . . and many Jasons come in quest of her" (1.1.168–72). It is important to point out that, however fantastic, there is nothing really unrealistic or inconsequential (or fun) about Belmont's heterosexual marriage plot, driven not by Portia but by her father's global sexual and economic will, and its easy confluence of law, homosociality (the father with each suitor), heterosexuality, capital, and marriage. (The hetero-fantasy works most seamlessly when the daughter's will *is* the always present will of the father.) Fantasy in this context is serious business, and it is no mere convenience to compare the weightiness of this fantasy to that found in Edelman's brilliant analysis of what he calls the "fantasy of reproductive futurism,"[7] this fantasy that belongs as *consubstantially* to heterosexuality as does mourning to homosexuality. From this vantage, children not only become *the* sign of (heterosexual) civil order but a sign of the father's immortality: as long as the child produces, the father lives. Proper reproduction (through heterosexual marriage) effectively means that one never has to mourn the father's death. In this context, heterosexual marriage (and reproduction) comes to be seen as the ritualistic rejection of mourning. Portia's existence is evidence that the father—the father's desire—still reproductively lives.

Portia's father's casket games encapsulate not only in Belmont, but throughout Shakespeare's play, how economics is inextricably bound to sex and, more specifically, how sexual reproduction is bound to economic reproduction. To the extent that marriage works as an effective and affective conduit for the movement of capital, it is worth noting here how Portia's unsuccessful global suitors are restricted not only from breeding their own wealth by gaining access to Belmont's but are also restricted from reproducing their own flesh and blood. The commodifying of Portia through gold, silver, and lead caskets links her to the capitalism of Venice and, especially, to its raison d'être, the (re)production of wealth.[8] Marriage depends on a properly regulated heterosexuality—that is, a heterosexuality that polices and balances the relationship between sexual and material production. As much may be surmised, I believe, from the father's choice of the lead casket for Portia's portrait. Gold and silver are dangerously precious and seductive metals in themselves, and while Portia's hair may "hang on her temples like a golden fleece" (1.1.170), this similitudinary gold is no match for the real thing, and gold and silver are made more dangerous still, we learn from the Venetian storyline, by the fact that they may be made to breed so quickly that one may lose one's ability to count them (1.3.92). Sustaining the *fantasy* of reproductive futurism in the play's economic scheme depends on precisely regulating gold and silver, on putting them to use but not allowing them to outbreed or displace sexual production.

It all comes down to dowries and futures. Harry Berger Jr. puts it most succinctly when he argues in an essay on the play, "if fathers and children know that the world must be peopled, property handed down, and the status quo perpetuated, they also know that the price of this investment in the future is the acceptance of death."[9] But as I have been arguing, this future depends on the ritualistic *rejection* of death. Not surprisingly, Bassanio finds in the lead casket what he calls a "counterfeit" (3.2.115) of Portia, who, like Shakespeare's Falstaff, has only counterfeited death (5.4.111–17).[10] There is nothing arbitrary about Portia's father placing her image in a lead casket. As David Cressy has pointed out, lead caskets were enjoyed "only [by] the most privileged corpses,"[11] and according to Vanessa Harding, a lead casket could potentially "preserve the body inside it indefinitely, arresting the endogenous process of decay."[12] Portia's father flaunts his hold on the "fantasy of reproductive futurism" when he both exhibits his gold and silver *and* successfully competes with them through the emergence of his own reproductive will, his reproductive vessel, from death. In *The Merchant of Venice*, heterosexual marriage exposes death as only seeming to be real. The generic fantasy world of the "comedist Portia," as Marc Shell calls her,[13] relies heavily on this fantasy of outwitting death. Heterosexuality in *The Merchant of Venice* belongs decisively to the world of comedy.

The most speakable, and the most visible, threat to the play's comedic heterosexual marriage plot is usury, and it is important to turn to it, however briefly, to grasp how Shakespeare and Antonio promote the rites of queer marriage. Because usury has the potential to corrupt, its most expert practitioner suddenly finds himself shifted into a kind of revenge tragedy, where the vengeance against him comes in the form of his own marriage and mourning being desecrated and trivialized by his own daughter who has stolen his wedding ring, taken a portion of his wealth, and married a gentile. The social forces of the play revenge themselves on Shylock by using his sexual production—that is, his daughter—against his usurious ones. Usury, as Aristotle argued, and as many early modern writers repeated, was the "most hated sort" of wealth accumulation: "For money was intended to be used in exchange, but not to increase at interest. And this term interest, which means the birth of money from money, is applied to the breeding of money because the offspring resembles the parent. That is why of all modes of getting wealth this is the most unnatural."[14] In this economic context, usury does not differ profoundly from sodomy, and, in fact, as Jody Greene and Will Fisher have each argued in well-documented and wonderfully engaging studies, many early modern commentators made just this connection.[15] The connection between sodomy and usury is not a casual or merely comparative one, as Francis Meres makes evident in his *Palladis Tamia* (1598), one of many early modern examples: "As Paederastie is unlawful . . . so usurie and encrease by gold and silver is unlawful, because . . . nature hath made them sterill and barren, and usurie makes them procreative."[16] It makes sense to note, as have some critics, an affinity between Shylock and Antonio,[17] but I want to suggest that usury stands in for sodomy (not an early modern stretch) and becomes its public and indirect mouthpiece. However, Antonio conjures and rejects the ability of usury, of sodomy, to speak for queer friendship and desire. As Bray has made emphatically clear, sodomy does not and cannot speak for early modern unions and communions.

Early modern culture may have imposed heterosexual marriage as the model of dowries and futures, but despite the best efforts of comedists and "compulsory heterotemporal" critics,[18] *The Merchant of Venice* rejects granting heterosexual marriage any such fixed or transcultural status. Antonio challenges the system of marital normalcy and civility that relies so much on (defining itself against) sodomy and usury. The valuation of his desires depends on neither sexual nor economic production: coupling with Bassanio would bring him neither children nor wealth. His desires are not projected into reproductive futurisms but can be located in the present. In fact, Antonio does more than challenge this system, and my language of friendship does something of a disservice to the cultural and dramatic space Antonio occupies. After all, even as conservative an Anglican as Jeremy Taylor could argue more than a half-century later, in *Discourse of Friendship* (1657), that these close same-sex friendships "are marriages too," and he speaks to the ritualistic and pragmatic basis of these relationships when he argues that these "friendships are marriages of the soul, and of fortunes and interests, and counsels."[19] I would add (at least in some instances) "of the body," as well. While heterosexual marriage in the early modern period would increasingly become a "more formal and public act,"[20] I would submit that for wanting-to-commit-to-each-other same-sex friends, civil rites and rights would become increasingly personal and private.

Making his argument that friendship rites were not entered into lightly, Bray argues that, "given solemnly and before witnesses, its gestures gave to the obligations of friendship the objective character that made them indistinguishable from those of kinship."[21] Indeed, according to Bray, these rites culminated in the "gift of the body" itself.[22] Queer marriage is no mere abstraction in Shakespeare's play. If dowries, flesh, and blood are the most important markers of early modern heterosexual marriage rites and rights, then Antonio takes on heterosexual marriage at its most sacrosanct sites and proceeds to outstrip each of them. Unlike Portia's seemingly infinite dowry on display from her father's coffers, for example, Antonio's is not only from his own limited account but from a stash for which he has bartered his own body. And more important, while Portia's "counterfeit," her *representation*, lies locked away in a lead casket, Antonio's dowry lies corporeally vulnerable and accessible: "My purse, my person, my extremest means / Lie all unlocked to your occasions" (1.1.138–39), inside a body he would willingly have "racked even to the uttermost" (1.1.181).[23] Antonio's contract with Shylock only underscores the sincerity with which Antonio employs "the language of 'friendship'" (still very much alive in the late sixteenth century) to argue that his friendship with Bassanio is not limited to the linguistic realm.[24]

Naomi Tadmor has shown how the early modern English used the Bible to help formalize marriage and how the "biblical idiom" of making husband

and wife "one flesh" (Genesis 2:24) served as the centerpiece.[25] It is worth being reminded of the matrimonial flesh in the early modern *Book of Common Prayer*: "So men are bound to love their own wives as their own bodies. . . . For never did any man hate his own flesh, but nourisheth and cherisheth it, even as the Lord doth the congregation: for we are members of his body, of his flesh and his bones. For this cause shall a man leave father and mother, and shall be joined unto his wife, and they two shall be one flesh."[26] Antonio competes with this socially and religiously sanctioned speech act when he effectively offers his flesh as a testament, not so much conjoining his flesh to Bassanio but giving it to and for him.

The letting of blood (both a private and a public act) is the *coup de maître* of these economic and sexual matrimonial rites,[27] and it would not only complete these rites but sanction them were these rites to proceed without impediment. Antonio would effectively displace hymeneal blood with the very vitality of blood itself. This unseen bloodletting already serves, I would argue, as a *coup de théâtre*, successfully upstaging the play's other two unseen scenes of culturally laden bloodletting: Morocco's (2.1.6–7) and Shylock's (3.1.54). It makes sense that the patriarchally and homophobically empowered Portia would stop him, not only because Antonio would, figuratively, beat her to Bassanio's marriage bed, but because the entire fantastic and ritualistic structure of heterosexual marriage would collapse or, at least, be seriously compromised. The emphatic queer demonstration of this moment would only be further underscored by the fact that it is the older and more powerful of the two men who takes on the hymeneal, bloodletting position.

It is clear that in giving his dowry, flesh, and blood, Antonio gives his life (3.3.316–18, 4.1.116–17) and shows himself welcoming in the present as opposed to some hazily undefined future the ultimate proof of the endurance of the marital bond: "till death do us depart."[28] In other words, the queer friend may be the "weakest kind of [*reproductive*] fruit" (4.4.114), not the uxorial "fruitful vine" called for by the early modern *Book of Common Prayer*,[29] but neither does the valuation of its meaningfulness rely on promises and fantasies of reproductive futures. It is the anticipation of death, not of life, that proves the marital bond. It is important to understand, however, that queer mourning is not solely a personal or abject act. It is no less a ritualistically communal one—a social and political affirmative refutation of the demands of heterosexual comedists.[30] When Antonio says early in Shakespeare's play, "I hold the world but as the world . . . / *A stage*, where every man must play a part, / And mine a sad one" (1.1.77–79; emphasis added), Antonio and Shakespeare offer a highly refined and ritualized social and political indictment of a comedist culture that insists it has a right to insult us, to play out its fantasies (of not mourning) on and through our backs.

Notes

1. *Oxford English Dictionary*, s.v. "marry," def. 6c.

2. Bray, *The Friend*, 137; emphasis added.

3. Alan Bray talks about the use of sodomy as a weapon against same-sex relationships that were being challenged for any number of reasons: idem, "Homosexuality and the Signs of Male Friendship in Elizabethan England," esp. 53–57; see also idem, 217; Traub, "Friendship's Loss," 342.

4. *The Merchant of Venice*, in Greenblatt et al., *The Norton Shakespeare*, 1.1.1–7. Citations in parentheses are to this edition.

5. Didier Eribon argues that "surely homosexuality . . . is one of those social 'positions' that engenders a particular form of psychological 'suffering'": Eribon, *Insult and the Making of the Gay Self*, 37–38. Even though Pierre Bourdieu does not discuss gays and lesbians, Eribon takes the term "suffering" and "positional suffering" from "The Space of Points of View": the positional sufferer is one who "occup[ics] an inferior, obscure position in a prestigious and privileged universe." Bourdieu et al., *The Weight of the World*, 4.

6. Eribon, *Insult and the Making of the Gay Self*, 35.

7. Edelman, *No Future*, 46.

8. I am extending Marc Shell's argument that "generation or production is the principal topic" of Shakespeare's play: Shell, "The Wether and the Ewe," 107.

9. Berger, "Marriage and Mercifixion in *The Merchant of Venice*," 155.

10. *Henry IV, Part I* in Greenblatt et al., *The Norton Shakespeare*, 5.4.111–17.

11. Cressy, *Birth, Marriage and Death*, 434.

12. Harding, *The Dead and the Living in Paris and London, 1500–1670*, 143.

13. Shell, "The Wether and the Ewe," 120.

14. Aristotle, *The Politics*, bk. I, chap. 10, 15.

15. See Fisher, *Queer Money*; Greene, "You Must Eat Men."

16. Quoted in Fisher, *Queer Money*, 11.

17. Seymour Kleinberg, for example, has argued that "Shakespeare equates the sodomite and the Jew symbolically and psychologically, as they were already equated under Elizabethan law, which allotted the common fate of burning to witches, heretics, and sodomites": Kleinberg, "*The Merchant of Venice*," 120–21.

18. See Goldberg and Menon, "Queering History," 1616, passim, for a substantial and highly cogent discussion of heterosexism in early modern literary studies.

19. Quoted in Bray, *The Friend*, 142–43. Taylor does add that these same-sex marriages are "less indeed than the other, because they cannot, must not be all that endearment which the other is": quoted in ibid.

20. Tadmor, "Women and Wives," 12.

21. Bray, *The Friend*, 174.

22. Ibid., 158; see also chap. 4.

23. *The Norton Shakespeare* rightly annotates "racked" as "stretched," but Antonio alludes, quite corporeally, to be being stretched on a rack, a punishment one could be subjected to for not paying one's debt.

24. Bray, "Homosexuality and the Signs of Male Friendship in Elizabethan England," 53.

25. Tadmor, "Women and Wives," esp. 2, 15.

26. Booty, *The Book of Common Prayer, 1559*, 297. It is worth noting that *The Merchant of Venice* has at least twice as many references to flesh as any other Shakespeare play, and most of these refer to Antonio giving a pound of his flesh to settle Bassanio's debt.

27. I am suggesting a comparison here to the iconography of the bloody wedding-bed sheets, which would serve as public evidence of the private act of consummation.

28. Booty, *The Book of Common Prayer, 1559*, 292.

29. Ibid., 294.

30. The argument I am making here is reminiscent of Douglas Crimp's argument in his reading of queer mourning in "Mourning and Militancy." For example, Crimp argues, "Mourning, for Freud, is a solitary undertaking. And our troubles begin here, for, from the outset, there is already a social interdiction of our private efforts": Crimp, "Mourning and Militancy," 135.

What Do Women Want?

JONATHAN GOLDBERG

If Shakespeare had never existed we would not miss his works,
for there would be nothing missing.
— Richard Poirier, "Where is Emerson Now That We Need Him?," 1987

The current critical consensus on *The Merry Wives of Windsor* is that the wives, as embodiments of the sex / gender system that confines women's desire in marital propriety, want to protect their reputations against Falstaff's unwanted approaches and do so by exercising their domestic powers. The play thereby affirms middle-class monogamous marriage, a form of heterosexuality that the wives presumably want, although according to critics such as Natasha Korda, Wendy Wall, and David Landreth, it is not their sexuality that they affirm (married women apparently do not have any) but their domesticity—indeed, the domestication of their desires.[1] Korda, referring to "the open secret governing married women's property rights,"[2] transfers D. A. Miller's phrase "open secret" to apply not to the sexuality of the wives but to their possible status as having some claim to the property that they supposedly only manage for their husbands. Wall goes so far as to imagine that Mistress Quickly, not married to Dr. Caius, whose household she manages, cannot possibly arouse his sexual jealousy when he suspects she harbors a man in the closet. "The oddity is that Caius is a bachelor and his female roommate, Mistress Quickly, is his brewer, baker, launderer, and housekeeper rather than his paramour. Since he has no wife whose sexuality he can be interested in policing, Caius's anxieties seem to stem from a concern for *oeceonomia*."[3] Quickly, whose sexuality is a staple of asides at many moments in the play (Mrs. Ford refers to her, for example, as "foolish carrion"[4]), is assumed by Wall not to be in a sexual relation with her so-called roommate, for whom she performs the domestic services of a wife and servant at once. Wall thereby grants to Quickly what is presumed also to be the case about the married women in the play: that as exemplars of domestic virtue, they do not have sex lives. So, too, Landreth, taking this line of argument as far as possible, states, "There is plenty of focking and bucking in the play, but that doesn't mean there's any fucking. . . . The action never admits any of these hovering erotic possibilities, because the wives do not."[5]

The female domesticity celebrated in this criticism is virtually devoid of feminist critique about the limitations of women thereby represented. (Korda is somewhat more attentive to this issue but seems to conclude that, as long as women might hold on to some property as their own, their domestic situation is alleviated.)[6] Middle-class virtue is celebrated, part and parcel of the new materialism in early modern studies that extols as it documents in its study of objects and their consumption the blessings of capitalism.[7] The wives as exemplary are also assumed to be sexually domesticated, happily married were it not for Falstaff's advances or Ford's jealousy, what Korda calls "Ford's uncharitable suspicions" (for her, these include a mistrust of her handling of household goods).[8] It is unkind to assume the wives have any desire except to satisfy their husbands, who presumably also confine their desires to their wives. Since this is marital desire, it is presumed to be entirely normative, a virtual display case of what Michel Foucault termed the "legitimate couple, with its regular sexuality" that emerged as the "norm" in the eighteenth and nineteenth century. Aberrations are located elsewhere; the couple is the quiet site of "discretion," precisely the virtue that Korda and Landreth associate with the wives' disciplinary function.[9] Further supporting this picture, as Stephen Orgel has noticed, Mr. and Mrs. Page with their son and daughter are the only family unit of its kind in any Shakespeare comedy.[10] There is, in short, a heterosexuality in the play that is virtually devoid of sexuality. Certainly it is devoid of sex for Landreth (the Pages presumably did it twice some time ago), a condition, he assures the readers of *Shakespeare Quarterly*, that extends to the homoerotic titillation we might expect to find in a Shakespeare comedy: "We cannot look to homoeroticism to obliquely manifest a present desire," he claims, and then looks at the few examples he can muster in order to pronounce them "empty of any lingering erotic thrill."[11] In short, twenty-first-century critics of this play know all the lines that Eve Kosofsky Sedgwick rehearses in *Epistemology of the Closet*: "Don't ask; You shouldn't know. It didn't happen; it doesn't make any difference; it didn't mean anything; it doesn't have interpretive consequences. Stop asking here; stop asking just now; we know in advance the kind of difference that could be made by the invocation of *this* difference; it makes no difference; it doesn't mean."[12]

It is certainly the case that the wives intend to show that "wives may be merry, and yet honest too" (4.2.91). Falstaff has accosted them with the line, "You are merry, so am I" (2.1.7), and their plot involves the refusal of the identificatory collapse of "merry" and dishonest. (Dishonest means both unchaste and profligate with domestic goods, which also describes what, as wives, they are: their husbands' property.) But the implication of this parsing of merry and honest is that the wives are not usually both, that in being chaste they are not merry and that any chance for merriness lies outside the sphere in which they are honest—indeed, that their honesty precludes merriness. This is to say what the criticism has said but from a rather different angle. Do the Pages have sex? Page, unlike Ford, is not at all suspicious of his wife, certain that she will respond to sexual advances with "sharp words" (2.1.165). Is this something he knows from experience? Page allows his wife full run of the household; hers is not a life of labor but of leisure: "Never a wife in Windsor leads a better life than she does. Do what she will, say what she will, take all, pay all, go to bed when she list, rise when she list, all is as she will" (2.2.106–9). Such is the testimony of Quickly, made to Falstaff in the context of asking him to send his page to Mrs. Page: "Mistress Page would desire you send her your little page, of all loves; her husband has a marvelous infection to the little page; and truly Master Page is an honest man" (2.2.104–6). The implication of these propositions: Mrs. Page has all she will, all she wants, because her honest husband prefers boys, a situation that matches her disinclination for him. Much as Falstaff attempted to identify his merriness and hers, Page equals page. These are instances of what Laurie Shannon has located as Renaissance homonormativity.[13] Patricia Parker has noted that Falstaff's project of turning the wives' "honesty into English" (1.3.45) may house a pun on ingle that would lead to the page boy.[14] How exactly this chain of associations works is not clarified by Parker, but whatever the case may be, it appears that Mrs. Page's domestic pleasure depends on her husband being with a boy. Page is "honest" by having pleasure that does not take the form of having sex with his wife; he, too, separates mirth from honesty, sex from marriage.

Ford's case is different on several counts. The Fords have no children; aside from a reference to the page boy as a "pretty weathercock" (3.2.15), there are just about no lines suggesting Ford's involvement with boys. Unlike Page, Ford is plagued by jealousy; this could suggest that, not having sex with his wife (indeed, not having sex with anyone), he supposes she must be doing it with others behind his back. Ford's elaborate plan—to pay Falstaff to seduce his wife to make it easier for him to succeed with her—is as transparent as the pseudonym of Brook he takes (in the quarto that modern editions follow rather than adopting the Broom of the Folio). Ford becomes Brook to hatch what he prescribes "preposterously" (2.2.219), a condition doubly fulfilled, first when Falstaff thereby gets directly from Brook what he aimed to get from Ford's wife (his money), and again when the play concludes with Ford assuring Falstaff in its closing lines that his promise to Brook will be fulfilled "for he to-night shall lie with Mistress Ford" (5.5.229). Ford can have sex with his wife only if it is adulterous. He imagines her having sex with someone else, will even pay to make it happen, and then at the end of the play rewards himself by enacting his fantasy. In a rather invidious reading of what this male self-substitution involves, Ford is accused of effeminization (his Folio nomination of Broom makes him an instrument of his wife's domesticity). With textbook Freudianism, Peter Erickson announces that Ford and Falstaff have a homosexual relationship,[15] a reading from which Wall, fastening on the broom, demurs, translating any such sexuality into "perverse" domesticity.[16] A moment later, however, commenting on Falstaff's lament, "Mistress Ford? I have had ford enough; I was thrown in the ford; I have my belly full of ford" (3.5.31–33), Wall finds in his "affinity" with Ford what she had not in Ford: castration and sexual humiliation.[17]

These readings suppose that there is only one functional form of sex, marital heterosexuality, and that when it becomes fraught and anxious, it turns people gay. Landreth, for example, labels the final male–male couplings of Caius and Slender, the failed suitors of Anne Page who find themselves with boys at the end of the play, as examples of "male incompetence," sure as he is that "there really is only one way to use it correctly."[18] This is, in a way, a supposition that underlies Ford's jealous worry that he cannot trust his "wife with herself" (2.2.275), that if she ceases to be his, she becomes hers; it is as if sex outside of marriage is having sex with herself (just so, Ford turns the prospect of sex with his wife into sex as / with Brook). From this, it is but a short step to what he tells Mrs. Page: "I think if your husbands were dead, you two would marry" (3.2.12–13). Ford's suspicions are triggered because Mrs. Page has come to visit Mrs. Ford, who is at home and "idle," ready for female company and clearly not doing the laundry or scrubbing the floors the way critics such as Korda and Wall imagine her to be. These wives have servants to do domestic labor. Ford's line opens the prospect of female–female sociality in the play, forms of female solidarity that do not wed them to their brooms and laundry baskets. "Gossip Ford," Mrs. Page addresses Mrs. Ford; "sweetheart" is what she calls her (4.2.8, 10). "It is worth remembering," Foucault reminds us, "that the first figure to be invested with the deployment of sexuality, one of the first to be "sexualized," was the "idle" woman."[19] Fitting the bill, too, is the woman who visits the house, the servant's aunt that Ford cannot abide, "the old woman of Brainford; he swears she's a witch" and has threatened to beat her if he finds her there (4.2.73–74). "A witch, a quean, an old cozening quean. Have I not forbid her my house? She comes of errands, does she? We are simple men; we do not know what's brought to pass under the profession of fortune-telling. She works by charms, by spells, by the figure, and such daubery as this is, beyond our element—we know nothing" (4.2.149–54). Ford's outburst testifies to the sphere of women with women doing things that men do not understand and cannot do, things that are irrational and sexual, women engaged as go-betweens, trafficking among and with themselves.

The old woman then appears—or, rather, Falstaff does, dressed in her dress, which is conveniently to hand, presumably in a closet that Ford has not searched but that his wife knows. She appears and is addressed by Mrs. Page as "Mother Prat": "I'll 'prat' her. Out of my door, you witch, you hag, you baggage, you polecat, you runnion! Out, out! I'll conjure you. I'll fortune-tell you" (4.2.159–61). Why does a woman whose name ends in "ford" get renamed Prat? The editors squabble about what "I'll 'prat' her" means because of the possibility that "prat" might mean buttocks.[20] If that is what Ford prats, it matches the breeching that Evans promises Will in the language-lesson scene (4.1) that has been examined by Parker and Elizabeth Pittenger, who noticed how pederastic schooling is translated by Quickly into cross-gendered promiscuity.[21] The beating of Falstaff is another such cross-gender switch point. The scene is unique in Shakespeare, the only time when an adult male cross-dresses. Evans sees Falstaff's beard, but this does not mean he sees through the disguise and spies a man beneath. Rather, he sees a witch: "I think the 'oman is a witch indeed. I like it not when a 'oman has a great peard; I spy a great peard under his muffler" (4.2.166–68). We recall that the witches in *Macbeth* also sport beards. Are the wives women or not? (It is worth noting that "wife" can simply mean "woman" rather than "married woman.") Women accused of having sex with women in the period are frequently masculinized (an enlarged clitoris, men's clothing, or the use of the dildo are the usual accusations brought against tribades).[22] Here masculinization occurs by way of the beard—and the buttocks. That is, female–female sexuality is assimilated to male gender and to male–male sexuality. This can happen as well without all of the complexities involved in this moment of cross-dressing and cross naming. When Falstaff finally thinks he has Mrs. Ford, his term of endearment for her is "my doe with the black scut" (5.5.17). "Scut," the deer's tail, is close to cut. It is the anatomical equivalent of the back door through which Falstaff first entered Ford's house (3.3.19).[23]

Is there any normative marital heterosexuality in Merry Wives?, we might be asking at this point. The marriage system in the play is fueled by cupidity. Fenton's admission to Anne that what began as an attraction to her father's money, which he has transferred to "the very riches of thyself" (3.4.17), does not really distinguish true love as something else.[24] The shaming of Falstaff engineered by the wives in the final act serves as a cover for the coupling of Anne Page to her suitors, and the two plot lines are connected. In this instance, handing her daughter over to a man, female solidarity is broken: As Mrs. Page works on behalf of Dr. Caius's success, we see again that, for her, mirth and honesty are not meant to coincide in marriage. This is another instance of the policing that Korda discusses, the woman acting not merely against her own interests but against those of her sex more generally, mother betraying daughter. On the whole, men desire women in this play because other men desire them to do so. Slender woos Anne Page to oblige his uncle Shallow ("I will marry her, sir, at your request; but if there be no great love in the beginning, yet heaven may decrease it upon better acquaintance" [1.1.220–22]). He further obliges his uncle by supplying him with boys: "A Justice of the Peace sometime may be beholding to his friend for a man" (1.1.244–45). This match is further supported by Evans, whose desires seem to run to boys' buttocks; he has expressed his rivalry with Caius through it and celebrates their rivalrous union by obsessively recalling the poem by Marlowe inspired by Virgil's pederastic second eclogue. Anne urges Fenton to "seek my father's love" (3.4.19) if he wants to have her, and the only proof of her desire for him is a letter that Fenton claims to have, whose contents are never revealed. In the end, Caius is cozened, tricked, and robbed (the pattern is the object of Parker's essay) and has "married un garcon, a boy; un paysan, by gar, a boy" (5.5.194–95). So, too, has Slender wed "the postmaster's boy" (5.5.180), his letter-carrying function linking him with Quickly. ("This punk is one of Cupid's carriers" [2.2.123]—this is how Pistol affirms his desire for Quickly.) It also links him to the old woman of Brainford who bears messages incomprehensible to men. Their protests notwithstanding—"For all he was in woman's apparel, I would not have had him," Slender declares (5.5.184–85)—these unions reveal the homoerotic logic of desire in the play. (They also reveal that Caius and Slender had proceeded at least as far as the discovery of what lies beneath the boys' female attire.) It applies to Anne, as well: "I came yonder at Eton to marry Mistress Anne Page, and she's a great lubberly boy" (5.5.176–77). Slender's line does not merely remind us that her part was played by a boy. When he first heard of her, he commented, "Mistress Anne Page? She has brown hair and speaks small like a woman" (1.1.39–40). In speaking like a woman, she is not necessarily one. Contra Wall regards the ending of the play—the male–male coupling and the passing on of reproductive culture to "the whims of Anne Page, the only woman in the play not linked to *oeconomia*"[25]—as opening "a set of problems" that exceed the ruling domesticity of the play; the last act reveals how fully same-sex desire inhabits the domestic domain.

"The whims of Anne Page": What does a woman want? Early in the play, in Act 1, Scene 4, Quickly claims over and again to know what Anne wants, which is that she does not want Slender, Caius, or Fenton. The fact that Anne winds up with Fenton is not proof to the contrary. Late in the play, Quickly (who is neither wife nor maid, not a proper woman at all) takes on the part in the masque that Anne was to have played. A quean plays the queen. *Merry Wives* assumes that whatever women want, it is not men. There is scarcely a moment in the play when a woman voices a desire that is anything but the desire not to be with men. Mrs. Page's line, "I'll exhibit a bill in the parliament for the putting down of men" (2.1.26–27), could be their rallying call. And when a man wants a woman, as Falstaff claims he does, he tells Mrs. Ford: "What made me love thee? Let that persuade thee there's something extraordinary in thee. Come, I cannot cog and say thou art this and that, like a many of those lisping hawthorn buds that come like women in men's apparel and smell like Bucklersbury in simple-time. I cannot" (3.3.59–64). Falstaff would not mistake his erection (3.5.36), he is no woman in man's clothing. Such cross-dressing, he affirms, is what heterosexuality amounts to, a male effeminacy that he deplores. He does not want the wives insofar as they are women. The antipathy between the sexes; the strong confirmation of the usual homosocial triangle that suggests that women are not the objects of men's desire; the virulent antipathy to women and the hysteria that surrounds the possibilities of women with women—all of these further show how little comfort Shakespeare offers to the heterosexual norm that he has been taken to support, but also how hard won any queer reading of his plays must be. The prospect of same-sex desire that subtends sexual relations in *Merry Wives* is no less deplorable. Queer theory does not need Shakespeare.

Notes

This essay is an abbreviated version of "What Do Women Want? The Merry Wives of Windsor," *Criticism* 51.3 (Summer 2010): 367–83.

1. Korda, *Shakespeare's Domestic Economies*; Landreth, "Once More into the Preech"; Wall, *Staging Domesticity*. Richard Helgerson likewise reads the play as one in which "the local and the domestic, in the person of Windsor's merry wives, take control" and are then folded into a courtly solution; no questions of gender and sexuality are raised beyond the claim that the play first entails husbands' fears and fantasies and then secures the wives as avatars of the virgin queen: Helgerson, *Adulterous Alliances*, 71.

2. Korda, *Shakespeare's Domestic Economies*, 100.

3. Wall, *Staging Domesticity*, 91.

4. Bowers, *The Merry Wives of Windsor*, 3.3.169. Citations in parentheses are to this edition.

5. Landreth, "Once More into the Preech," 421.

6. For a feminist materialist critique, see Kegl, "The Adoption of Abominable Terms."

7. For a critique of this trend, see Bruster, "The New Materialism in Renaissance Studies"; Harris, "The New New Historicism's *Wunderkammer* of Objects."

8. Korda, *Shakespeare's Domestic Economies*, 90.

9. Foucault, *The History of Sexuality: An Introduction*, 38.

10. Orgel, *Impersonations*, 17.

11. Landreth, "Once More into the Preech," 423.

12. Sedgwick, *Epistemology of the Closet*, 53.

13. Shannon, "Nature's Bias."

14. Parker, *Shakespeare from the Margins*, 145–46, from a postscript added to an essay that originally appeared as "*The Merry Wives of Windsor* and Shakespearean Translation," *Modern Language Quarterly* 52.3 (September 1991): 225–62.

15. "His physical contact with the transvestized Falstaff provides a literal image of Ford's equivocal sexuality": Erickson, "The Order of the Garter, the Cult of Elizabeth, and Class–Gender Tension in *The Merry Wives of Windsor*," 132. Peter Erickson claims that, having been castrated by his wife, who, like Elizabeth I, provokes desires she does not fulfill, unmanned Ford becomes homosexual in his desire. Homosexuality is thus a failed heterosexuality, an equivocal sexuality that is not one. Erickson's views about sexuality and gender are also found in Korda, *Shakespeare's Domestic Economies*; Landreth, "Once More into the Preech"; Parker, *Shakespeare from the Margins*; Wall, *Staging Domesticity*. A source in Freud can be found in "Female Sexuality" (1931), in *Sexuality and the Psychology of Love*, 198.

16. Wall, *Staging Domesticity*, 118.

17. Ibid., 119.

18. Landreth, "Once More into the Preech," 424, 428.

19. Foucault, *The History of Sexuality: An Introduction*, 121

20. Bowers glosses the line as "*'prat' her* strike her buttocks"; T.W. Craik insists that "pratt her . . . is a nonceword. This idiomatic usage is incompatible with editors' interpretations of 'prat' as 'buttock'": Craik, ed., *The Merry Wives of Windsor*, 4.2.169n. H. J. Oliver shares this view. He says that the verb means simply to trick and does not even mention buttocks in his note: Oliver, ed., *The Merry Wives of Windsor*, p.114, glossing 4.2.170 in the Arden edition. Yet surely there is a link to "pratfall" that would make the connection.

21. Pittenger, "Dispatch Quickly," 406–7. Elizabeth Pittenger glances at the consequences of the sexuality that she finds in the grammar lesson that Evans administers and Quickly translates into a sex scene. My essay simply fills in what she indicates.

22. See, among others, Traub, *The Renaissance of Lesbianism in Early Modern England*, esp. chap. 5.

23. On this topic, see Daileader, "Back Door Sex."

24. In her brief for the quarto version of the play as an anti-courtly document, Leah Marcus fixes on Anne's more sentimental union with an uncourtly Fenton as the epitome of female desire in the play, the answer to the question Freud found unanswerable, "Was will das Weib?" That is the source of the epigraph of Marcus, "Purity and Danger in the Modern Edition," and of the title of this essay. For the text of the letter to Marie Bonaparte in which Freud remarked on that question, see Jones, *The Life and Work of Sigmund Freud*, 2:421.

25. Wall, *Staging Domesticity*, 124.

A Midsummer Night's Dream

Shakespeare's Ass Play

RICHARD RAMBUSS

Why, what an ass am I.
—*Hamlet*, 2.2.521

"I am your spaniel," Helena fawningly declares to Demetrius, whom she yearns (at least at this point in a play, where the strongest desires turn out to be the most mutable) to have as her master, if not husband.[1] Driven by his love of Hermia—who herself has feelings for the rival Helena—Demetrius flees before her into the forest, a dreamscape lush with sexual possibilities: not only the homoeroticism that sometimes encumbers, sometimes oils the marriage machine of Shakespearean comedy, but also child-love, anality, and bestiality. Helena, notably long-limbed and swift of foot (3.2.291–93, 343), shamelessly pursues him there, repeating, "Use me but as your spaniel" (2.1.205). I can well imagine how her saying so would rub many viewers the wrong way. But as for me, it is not perforce systems of women's subordination that I think of here. It is, rather, how the Duke of Buckingham—an athletic male beauty of the time, himself famous for his legs (figure 1)—signed his love letters to James, "Your majesty's most humble slave and dog." In one, he happily recalls a time they spent together at Farnham Castle, "where the bed's head could not be found between the master and his dog." In another, he discloses how his "thoughts are only bent of having my dear Dad and master's legs soon in my arms."[2]

I will suppose there is no need here to apologize for what may be a turn-on about role playing in variously conceived hierarchies, whether real or imagined (or real *and* imagined). Simply assuming, then, an erotics attendant upon the chains of command, I want to skew this short essay in a different direction by taking Helena's algolagnic profession of dogged devotion as a prompt for musing on human / animal relations in Shakespeare's forest play. Its vectors of same-sex attraction—the usual touchstone for queer readings of Shakespeare —no longer strike me as what is queerest about this comedy, which Hermia

FIGURE 1. Master of the Horse. *George Villiers, 1st Duke of Buckingham*, attributed to William Larkin, circa 1616; oil on canvas. Courtesy National Portrait Gallery, London

announces early on to be a classic story of crossed love: "If then true lovers have been ever crossed, / It stands as an edict in destiny" (1.1.150–51). This play's generic homoeroticism is routine for the form. Not that the all but compulsory homosexuality of Shakespeare's comedic plots is any less compelling for being pro forma. But what has now come to seem queerest to me about *A Midsummer Night's Dream* has more to do with its cross-species encounters, of which this play stages many, including human / fairy ones, to go along with the changes that it rings on human / animal relations (which sort into their own hierarchies). Those relations are my chief concern here, and they point to another, even more farfetched extra-textual free association lately triggered for me by Helena casting herself as a spaniel. It's the deep-throat kisses that Donna Haraway shares with her female canine companion to open *The Companion Species Manifesto*: *"Her red merle Australian Shepherd's quick and lithe tongue has swabbed the tissues of my tonsils. . . . We have had forbidden conversation; we have had oral intercourse." "How would we sort things out?"* wonders the cyborg theorist. *"Canid, hominid; pet, professor; bitch, woman; animal, human; athlete, handler."*[3]

Helena's spaniel dotage follows hard on the heels of jealous Oberon's unfolding of the bestial prank that he is to play on Titania, who has "forsworn his bed and company" (2.1.61–62). She has just angrily left the stage. The two fairies had been quarreling, each accusing the other of stealing from fairyland to cavort with their human counterparts: Titania with Theseus, himself hardly a model of fidelity; Oberon with Hippolyta, a virago in leather. But these immortal / mortal liaisons are treated in the play, as in myth, as a matter of course. What has really set Titania and Oberon at odds is the changeling boy. Titania holds on to the Indian prince, fetish-like, as a keepsake of his dead mother, pampering him in a precious, feminized world of flowers, sweets, and serenades, while Oberon wants to masculinize him as "Knight of his train, to trace the forests wild" (2.1.25). In the play as scripted, alas, the audience never sees the "lovèd boy" (2.1.26) whom each fairy desires to reserve as a private plaything. We are simply later told that Oberon has succeeded in getting him transferred offstage from Titania's bower to his own.

Oberon's means for gaining the child involves a potion from a special purple pansy. He came to learn of it while he sat listening to the strains of "a mermaid, on a dolphin's back" (2.1.150–68). The potion has similar siren-song qualities. "On sleeping eyelids laid," Oberon explains, it will make "or man or woman" forget himself or herself to desire and "madly dote / Upon the next live creature that *it* sees" (2.1.170–72; emphasis added). Shakespeare has stocked the woods bordering Athens with creatures: fairy, human, insect, animal. It is notable, then, that the play envisions nothing but an animal as a lover for Titania while she is under this spell. "Be it on lion, bear, or wolf, or bull, / On meddling monkey, or on busy ape / She shall pursue it with the soul of love" (2.1.180–82). In the next scene, Titania falls asleep to a lullaby addressed to Philomela—once a woman, now a songbird—that conjures up a woodland wonder-cabinet: "reremice [with] their leathern wings," "spotted snakes with double tongue," "thorny hedgehogs," "newts and blindworms," "weaving spiders," and "beetles black" (2.2.1–25). The song is meant to exorcize all kinds of noxious small creatures from Titania's resting place. But then Oberon appears, intoning, as he squeezes the pansy juice into her eyes, another incantatory roll call of forest beasts—larger, more nearly human-size ones:

> What thou seest when thou dost wake,
> Do it for thy true love take;
> Love and languish for *his* sake.
> Be it ounce or cat or bear,
> Pard, or boar with bristled hair,
> In thy eye that shall appear
> When thou wak'st, it is thy dear. (2.2.27–33; my emphasis)

Note how Oberon, in this catalogue of potential animal paramours for Titania, slips from the bestial "it" to the anthropomorphizing "his" of line 29—"Love and languish for *his* [that creature's] sake"—and then back to "it" for the rest of his speech. These pronominal shifts are intriguing theoretically. Is an animal a "he" (or "she"), or an "it"? What about a beloved pet or (as Haraway puts it) companion species? To what extent is "its" ontology altered by the domesticating processes (I won't say tyranny) of human love? Recall also the passage from Act 2 that I cited in the previous paragraph, where the "it" of line 172 refers to the madly doting "or man or woman," as if to say that there is something of the animal not only in the body, but also in the very "soul of love."[4]

Shakespeare's fairy queen takes a love object that is both a "he" and an "it," thing and person, human and animal. Puck gleefully reports midway through Act 3—making this amour the play's centerpiece—how "Titania waked, and straightway loved an ass" (3.2.34). He hereby adds another beast to the play's animal menagerie. Or, rather, what Titania falls for is part man, part ass. In casting herself under foot, Helena would be treated as Demetrius's spaniel:

238

"What worser place can I beg in your love— / And yet a place of high respect with me— / Than to be usèd as you use your dog?" (2.1.208-10). But with Bottom we move from a question of use or place to one of being. For beneath the unauthorized spell that Puck plies on top of Oberon's, Bottom is literally (the play repeatedly puts it) "translated"—changed, transported, enraptured —into something else: a hybrid genus that straddles species. The human-animal.[5]

Bottom is akin to the play's other border-crossing figures, such as Oberon's mermaid, a chanteuse who is half-woman, half-fish—or, more centrally, to the changeling who has likewise been carried over from the human realm (that of exotic India, no less) into an evocatively English fairyland. There, like the malleably gendered boy actor of the English stage, this "lovely," "lovèd" child (2.1.22, 26) serves as an especially transitive object of desire, crisscrossed by all kinds of homo and hetero investments, including more than a trace of inter-generational sexual interest. The play's eminently perverse erotic trajectories beg the question of its abiding place in the high-school curriculum. Then again, maybe such erotics are indeed the reason for the play's pedagogical popularity. Even so, I do not think that criticism has explicitly made enough of how Bottom and the changeling change places in Titania's bower and bosom. Maternal possessiveness shades there into erotic bondage. "Out of this wood do not desire to go. / Thou shalt remain here, whether thou wilt or no," she lovingly, domineeringly, instructs Bottom, who turns out to be game for this kind of thing. "Lead him to my bower," she commands at the scene's end. "Tie up my lover's tongue, bring him silently" (3.1.146–47, 192, 196). This is the very meaning of infantilization (*infans*: speechless). "Sleep thou," Titania coos to the adult baby Bottom, the next time that we see the amorous couple, "and I will wind thee in my arms." This, as she turns them both into inter-trussed plants: "So doth the woodbine the sweet honeysuckle / Gently entwist; the female ivy so / Enrings the barky fingers of the elm" (4.1.39–43).

This image of botanical bondage expresses a human (or quasi-human) relation in non-human terms. There is much of that in this play. But what Puck does to Bottom, we noted, transpires in another ontological register. (Compare Titania's designs, announced when she first lays eyes on the trans-formed Bottom, to transform him yet again: "I will purge thy mortal gross-ness so / That thou shalt like an airy spirit go" [3.1.154–55]. This purgative process would have made Bottom multiply interspecies: human-animal-fairy.) As for his animal metamorphosis, it is accomplished within the play by the fastening of a donkey's head (which we later watch Puck remove on stage)

FIGURE 2. Renaissance furry fandom: Ass's head worn by David Troughton as Bottom in John Caird's production of *A Midsummer Night's Dream* in 1989. Used with permission of the Royal Shakespeare Company

atop Bottom's own. That "ass's nole" (3.2.17), with its large, cuddly ears, is manifestly a stage prop: *"Enter Puck, and Bottom with the ass head"* (269). It is a piece of animal costuming, a part of a fur suit. Here, then, would be another way to think about this character's put-on animality: Nick Bottom, artisan and amateur actor, is a Renaissance proto-furry (figure 2).[6]

Bottom's name derives from the tools of his trade. A skein of thread is called a bottom, as is the core around which thread is wound. But Bottom's "ass's nole" also translates into asshole.[7] "I am such a tender ass," he adduces after his asinine transformation (4.1.25). (It is hard here to resist the allure of assonance.) The mooning Titania follows suit, caressing his "amiable cheeks" and "stick[ing]" thereabouts musk roses (4.1.2–3). This kind of dulcet pillow talk carries over into Act 5, when, during the play within the play, Bottom (as Pyramus) asks Tom Tinker (impersonating a non-human wall) to show him his crack: "O sweet and lovely wall, / Show me thy chink, to blink through with mine eyne" (5.1.175–76). Then Thisbe (played by Francis Flute) enters on the wall's other side. Spying her via that chink, Pyramus beseeches: "O, kiss me through the hole of this vile wall!" Thisbe instead lays an arse-kiss on Wall himself: "I kiss the wall's hole, not your lips at all" (5.1.199–200).

Several things, which I can here only touch on, stand out about the anal erotics of *A Midsummer Night's Dream*, Shakespeare's ass play. The first is that here anal desire is principally female in issue, if not aim. "Methought I was enamored of an ass," Titania declares, coming to from what she thinks was but a dream (4.1.76). Second, little scope is allotted to that desire. The space the play magically opens in Act 3 for interspecies sodomy (a redundancy to which I will return) is closed off in Act 4 when the spell is lifted and Titania returns, tail between her legs, to her proper mate, the bullying Oberon. This is also to say that while anality, as I have argued elsewhere, can be ennobling in certain male (especially military) contexts, here it redounds to Titania's degradation. Indeed, anality is the play's chief strategy for shaming, even as it supplies the play's erotic core. "This is to make an ass of me," complains Bottom, though he speaks for Titania, too (3.1.116–17). Her phobically repudiated anal eroticism instances the ready translation of an affect into its opposite that I earlier remarked. "O, how I love thee! how I dote on thee!" thus becomes "O, how mine eyes do loathe his visage now!" (4.1.44, 78).

The sense of shame is compounded by the fact that the piece of ass Titania falls for is no better than a horse's—worse, a donkey's—ass. Shakespeare plays this beastly lowliness for broad comic effect. But there is also a darker underbelly to it, for bestiality equates with sodomy in the Renaissance.[8] And "bully Bottom," Titania's lover, is associated with the animal world even before he crosses over into it himself (3.1.7). An "acting animal" who wants all the roles for himself, Bottom insists, "Let me play the lion too," while boasting in a strange figure of cross-species cross-voicing that he can "roar . . . as gently as any sucking dove, . . . [or] any nightingale" (1.2.64, 75–76). In Act 3, his entrance as an ass is cued by Thisbe's line about a horse (3.1.98). Having then scared off his fellows by his beastly visage, Bottom renders by way of a bawdy song yet another of the play's animal catalogs, this one of birds, from "ouzel cock" to "cuckoo gray" (3.1.120–31).

Human interest in seeing someone perform or be treated—abjected, disciplined, coddled, desired, feared—as an animal is widely reflected throughout *A Midsummer Night's Dream*. The play is a specimen case of human-animals and animalized human expression. Bottom may be its densest transfer point for cross-species fantasies, but he is hardly the only one. Helena, would-be spaniel, despairs, "I am as ugly as a bear" (2.2.94). She also muses on how Demetrius's flight from her advances rewrites (and re-genders) the classic narrative of the amorous hunt: "The story shall be changed: / Apollo flies and Daphne holds the chase, / The dove pursues the griffin, the mild hind / Makes speed to catch the tiger" (2.1.230–33). She later calls Hermia a vixen, or she-fox (3.2.323–24). Hermia, for her part, fondly recalls a time when the two were as harmonious songbirds—even lovebirds—"Both warbling of one song, both in one key" (3.2.206). This figure harks back to Lysander's casting Hermia and Helena as birds in the previous act, though there it was to distinguish them by complexion: "Who will not change a raven for a dove?" (2.2.114). This avian imagery anticipates Theseus's question later in the play, when, with his hunting party, he comes upon the four lovers sleeping in the woods: "Begin these wood birds but to couple now?" (4.1.139). Back in Act 3, Hermia had drawn Demetrius into the round robin of bestial put-downs by ironically making him out to be the real dog here—"Out, dog! out, cur!"—before mixing animal metaphors and denouncing him as a serpent (3.2.65–73). Speaking of serpents (which are unnervingly numerous in this forest comedy), Hermia has an erotic nightmare involving Lysander and a snake (2.2.145–51). When Lysander's love for Hermia shifts to hate in Act 3, he likewise mingles species, first calling her a cat and then threatening to shake her off like a serpent (3.2.260–61). More than one production has begun with Hippolyta (named for "horse" in Greek) in a cage, as though the Amazon were a captured wild animal or zoo specimen.[9]

And then there is Puck. He introduces himself in terms of a scatological joke he plays on an old woman: "Sometime for three-foot stool mistaketh me: / Then slip I from her bum, down topples she" (2.1.52–53). Puck amuses Oberon by assuming the "likeness of a filly foal" to tease the horses (44–46). The hobgoblin also shifts shape among various animal forms—"Sometime a horse I'll be, sometime a hound, / A hog, a headless bear"—in chasing around Bottom's mates (3.1.104–5). But most pertinent is Puck's assertion that "those things do best please me / That befall prepost'rously" (3.2.120–21). "Preposterous," notes Patricia Parker, shows up in period denunciations of sodomy.[10] It means ridiculous, reversed, perverse—ass-backward. I have just suggested

242

FIGURE 3. Aristotle, the first ponyboy: *Aristoteles and Phyllis, or the "Power of the Womane,"* Hans Baldung Grien, 1513; woodcut. Bildarchiv Preussischer Kulturbesitz / Art Resource, New York

that here love of the ass is gendered female. In hindsight, that claim may need to be revised, given what Puck, the play's chief comic operator, puts forward as the pleasure principle of all of his horsing around. Consider thus the "country proverb" he offers by way of promising that everything will come out right in the end: "Jack shall have Jill, / Nought shall go ill, / The man shall have his mare again, and all shall be well" (3.2.461–63).

Puck's interspecies adage—which reinscribes animality into the play's happy ending, not to say the "soul of love"—instigates me to venture afield and conclude by setting Shakespeare's *Dream* in something of a predictive relation to ponyplay: a highly theatricalized, specialty form of contemporary BDSM role-playing. Ponyplay casts the bottom in the role of human pony (in contrast to real or here so-called "bio" horses) and costumes "it" accordingly, just as this play does its Bottom. These play ponies come in different kinds. There are mares, stallions, cart ponies, wild ponies, and show ponies. They may be harnessed, ridden, groomed, and sometimes even branded by their masters or handlers. Mouth bits make speech impossible. Like other BDSM sexualities, ponyplay turns on the surrender or exercise of control, but it also (like furry fandom) offers an escapist release from the burdens of being simply human.

I have rendered Shakespeare's comedy as prescient in its sense of the perverse. But some enthusiasts of ponyplay bestow on it the prestige of a Renaissance pedigree by referring it back to sixteenth-century England and the use of ponygirls to haul coal out of mineshafts. Another strand of ponyplay lore dates it even further back to Aristotle, who wore a bridle and let himself be ridden by Phyllis, making him the first ponyboy (figure 3, above).

And let us not forget the expressively animalized relations between James and Buckingham, his loving subject, son, friend, dog. Among the titles the king lavished on his favorite was that of Master of the Horse. Buckingham may himself have become a horse master, but that did not keep James, his own master, from summoning his pet, in one especially passionate letter, to "come galloping hither."[11]

Notes

1. *A Midsummer Night's Dream*, in Orgel and Braunmuller, *William Shakespeare*, 2.1.203. All citations in parentheses are to this edition.

2. Bergeron, *King James and Letters of Homoerotic Desire*, 179, 199. The king, for his part, addressed his letters to Buckingham "Sweet heart" and signed them, "Your dear dad and husband."

3. Haraway, *The Companion Species Manifesto*, 2, 1. Recall that for Haraway, cyborg theory starts with an animal: a Space Age white lab rat implanted with an osmotic pump that dispenses controlled doses of chemicals to modify its physiological parameters.

4. Compare Foucault's "entomologization" of sex in the first volume of *The History of Sexuality*. The passage that famously declares that "the sodomite had been a temporary aberration; the homosexual was now a species" exotically continues, "So too were all those minor perverts whom nineteenth-century psychiatrists entomologized by giving them strange baptismal names: there were Krafft-Ebing's zoophiles and zooerasts, Rohleder's auto-monosexualists; and later, mixoscopophiles,

gynecomasts, presbyophiles, sexoesthetic inverts, and dyspareunist women": Foucault, *The History of Sexuality*, Volume 1, 43.

5. See *A Midsummer Night's Dream* 3.1.114–15, 3.2.32, 4.2.4. The rapture that Bottom experiences in his foray across ontologies—human, animal, fairy—registers in his "The eye of man hath not heard" speech (4.1.199–217), which jumbles I Corinthians 2:9–10 on the ineffability of ecstatic experience.

6. Furry fandom (which sometimes but not always has an explicitly sexual component) takes off from anthropomorphized animal characters in animated films, cartoons, comics, art, and literature. Some "furries" create their own personal animal characters ("fursonas") and dress up in costumes ("fursuits") to impersonate them. The companion term "plushies" refers to both stuffed animals and adults attracted to them.

7. It has been noted by some nay-sayers that the *Oxford English Dictionary* does not record any pre-nineteenth-century usages of "bottom" as "buttock" or "ass" as "arse." But the play nonetheless provides several lexical routes through Bottom's figure to the behind, including "cheeks," which the *Oxford English Dictionary* does allow as period slang for the buttocks. Bottom's craving for hay—"Good hay, sweet hay, hath no fellow" (4.1.33)—evokes the bawdy "sweet bottom grass" (1. 236) of *Venus and Adonis*, which I read as an animal companion poem to this play. "Bottom" also means not just the lowest or deepest part but also "foundation," which Jeffrey Masten brilliantly reminds us is etymologically related to "fundament": Masten, "Is the Fundament a Grave?," 133–37.

8. See Foucault, *The History of Sexuality*, Volume 1, 43.

9. Peter Holland notes a production in San Francisco in 1966 in which Hippolyta appears "as a captive animal wearing black body make-up and a leopard-skin bikini in a bamboo cage": Holland, *A Midsummer Night's Dream*, 51, 131.

10. Parker, *Shakespeare from the Margins*, 11, 26–27.

11. Bergeron, *King James and Letters of Homoerotic Desire*, 150.

Closing Ranks, Keeping Company:
Marriage Plots and the Will to be Single
in *Much Ado About Nothing*

ANN PELLEGRINI

Act I: Side by Side by Side

It took Stephen Sondheim four attempts to write the finale to *Company*, his
musical meditation on marriage, its relations and refusals. Directed by Harold
Prince, the play opened to critical acclaim in New York, in April 1970, and went
on to win six Tony Awards, but not before experiencing some major out-of-
town hiccups. The play revolves around the unmarried Robert—"Bobby
Buby" to his friends—and the five married couples that make up his social
world, and whom he in some way completes. In the world of *Company*, "One's
impossible, two is dreary," but "three is company." Officially billed as a musical comedy, *Company* strains the form: it is effectively plotless, composed of a
series of vignettes depicting Robert with his married friends, Robert on dates,
and the married couples talking and worrying about Robert's unmarried
state. This plotlessness derives from Robert's own evasion of the marriage
plot. He is emplotted in the lives of his married friends, to be sure, yet himself
remains skeptical of marriage as destination. His one half-hearted marriage
proposal to his friend Amy on her wedding day—to another man—issues not
out of romantic love or jealousy or some newfound commitment to coupling
but as a kind of self-preservation. "Marry me," he pleads, "and everybody will
leave us alone." Success! His proposal clears Amy of her marital ambivalence;
she promptly races off to marry her fiancé.

As Kay Young states the matter in her own elegant analysis of *Company*, "If
the pre-Sondheim musical designed itself around the frame of the call and
response between lovers—as his feed line set up her punch line, her lyric
inspired his song, his dance step challenged her tapped response—*Company*

recasts the musical's fundamental frame. The female lover is replaced by five marriages and the male lover is replaced by Bobby who acts as passive questioning audience to them. His attempts to reproduce what he witnesses, to find the girl and do the marriages, lead him to find the girls and do *nothing*."[1]

But this is not precisely a nothing, either. One may be impossible, but single is not alone—or does not have to be. Bobby wants to be "side by side by side," a geometric tripling that exceeds the couple form. His sideways approach to relationality constitutes a kind of willful and also potentially lush laterality. His failure to forge the right sort of intimacies thus opens onto alternative social horizons. This is no small thing, which may be why there was so much ado about Bobby's "nothing."

In Sondheim's own words, "A lot of the controversy about *Company* was that up until *Company* most musicals, if not all musicals, had plots. In fact, up until *Company*, [Sondheim himself] thought that musicals had to have very strong plots. One of the things that fascinated [him] about the challenge of the show was to see if a musical comedy could be done without one. Many of the people who disliked the show disliked it for that reason."[2] Reactions to the play's refusal of plot or, more precisely, to its questioning of the *marriage* plot as the definition of what plot means took an openly phobic form. Reviewing *Company*'s pre-Broadway tryout in Boston, *Variety* sneered its contempt: "Who cares what happens to 'Bobby Buby' is only one of the problems affecting Harold Prince's unconventional-form musical. . . . The songs are for the most part undistinguished. . . . As it stands now it's for ladies' matinees, homos and misogynists."[3] Evidently, indistinction is dangerously catchy; the danger is less that *Company*'s "unconventional-form" and "undistinguished lyrics" will not find their audience, but that they will.

Ladies' matinees is a reference to the show's most famous song, "The Ladies Who Lunch," now indelibly associated with Elaine Stritch, who originated the role of the thrice-married and twice-divorced "Joanne." As much a snarl as a song, "The Ladies Who Lunch" pays mock tribute to "the girls who stay smart, . . . who play wife, . . . who follow the rules and meet themselves at the schools, too busy to know they are fools." This is Betty Friedan with a vodka stinger in hand. In a pitch of homophobic panic, *Variety*'s nameless reviewer converts a nascent or, perhaps, proto-feminist protest into evidence of gay male hatred of women. Ladies who lunch, men who love men, and those women and men who reject the narrow options held out to women—in such company as this "invincible crew," no one is safe. Well, I'll drink to that. "Strike up, pipers!"

The Boston version of *Company* ended with "Happily Ever After," which Prince later described as "the bitterest, most unhappy song ever written."[4] Personally, I think it is a toss-up with "Have Yourself a Merry Little Christmas," surely the gloomiest holiday song ever composed. ("Someday soon, we all will be together, if the fates allow / Until then, we'll have to muddle through somehow / So have yourself a Merry Little Christmas now." Now *there's* holiday cheer for you. But it is still an improvement over the original draft of the lyrics, which commanded, "Have yourself a merry little Christmas / It may be your last / Next year we may all be living in the past.") But, I digress, with a queer song in my heart. In any case, digression is all to the point of this shapeless musical that refuses the designated happy ending of the musical as such. This is Young's point in observing that, in *Company* and in other plays, Sondheim "unmusicalizes" marriage.[5] For Bobby, who has spent the play observing his friends' marriages, "Happily Ever After" is not all it is cracked up to be. With all eyes on him—his married friends' and the audience's—he sings:

Someone to hold you too close,
Someone to hurt you too deep,
Someone to love you too hard,
Happily ever after.
Someone to need you too much,
Someone to read you too well,
Someone to bleed you of all
The things you don't want to tell—
That's happily ever after,
Ever, ever, ever after
In hell.

This bitter song "scared" the audience, Prince reports, "and it scared us [the play's creative team] because it was too complicated. . . . If I heard that song I wouldn't get married for anything in the world."[6] And that was precisely the problem. What kind of "happily ever after" is that?

The hostility of the Boston critics and audience led Prince to push for a different ending, a more optimistic one. Sondheim obliged, in a Stephen Sondheim sort of way. Since its premiere in New York in April 1970, the play has ended with the tour de force, "Being Alive." The song records Robert's emotional growth. After rejecting marriage and the promise (and the prem-ise) that there is a particular someone for him, he now seems ready to risk being for another. This risk is posed as the risk of life:

> But alone
> is alone,
> Not alive.
> Somebody crowd me with love,
> Somebody force me to care.
> Somebody let me come through,
> I'll always be there
> As frightened as you
> To help us survive
> Being alive,
> Being alive,
> Being alive!

Critics and audiences have embraced "Being Alive" as the better song; for his part, Sondheim has called the new ending of the show a "cop-out. When Bobby finally realizes that he shouldn't be alone at the end of the scene, it's too small a moment and you don't believe it."[7]

The suggestion seems to be that the grand insight Bobby has is out of scale; we are not convinced that Bobby is convinced. But what if the problem here is the scale itself? Perhaps, just perhaps, the smallness of the moment is due to a narrowing in relational possibilities, from company to the couple. Indeed, the pleasure audiences take in the play's new ending depends, in large part, on their *un*-knowing what they have just seen. Bobby's social world has been peopled—crowded—all along with friends who nudge and nurture. And yet, the new ending seems to equate finding that one special someone not just with growing up, but with life itself. Against the zero sum of the couple form, to be single is to be no thing at all.

I am not here scolding audiences who leave performances of *Company* humming "Being Alive." I did. The song has an irresistible pull to it. However, for queer audience members, the song's pleasures are complicated by the curtain it drops on alternative endings and alternative social horizons.[8] Re-marking these other ways of being for and to each other seems all the more necessary at a historical moment animated by vitriolic debates over same-sex marriage.

Interlude: As if

In a dazzling analysis of the social force of performative utterances, Eve Kosofsky Sedgwick introduces the nonce category "periperformative" to get at "a powerful class of negative performatives—disavowal, demur, renunciation, depreciation, repudiation, 'count me out,' giving the lie." Because they are unconventional responses, periperformatives require "a high threshold of initiative," she continues.[9] Periperformative utterances are a way of falling out of alignment with such utterly conventional and conventionalized performatives as "I do" and "I now pronounce you man and wife." Sedgwick lays stress on the spatial arrangements of the performative, the way audiences are called as witnesses to and "around" it. It is these "periperformative vicinities," their neighborly and, sometimes, deeply un-neighborly relations, that Sedgwick moves to chart.

Another word for this spatializing dynamic is "theater": "Like a play, marriage exists in and for the eyes of others. . . . Like the most conventional definition of a play, marriage is constituted as a spectacle that denies its audience the ability either to look away from it or intervene in it."[10] As Sedgwick underscores, it is far easier to forever keep your peace than to say just why it is that John and Mary should not be joined in matrimony, holy or otherwise. Moreover, in the face of renewed efforts legislative, judicial, and populist to block marriages between John and Peter and between Mary and Bea, there remains scarcely any room to protest same-sex marriage—or, at least, to express skepticism of it as the end game of LGBTQ "rights" without being drafted onto the side of those who see in gay marriage the end of Western civilization as we know it.[11] As if.

Act II: Doubling Down

Against such a backdrop, *Much Ado About Nothing*'s villainous Don John emerges as something of a queer anti-hero. After scowling his way through Hero's and Claudio's first wedding—and setting in motion Claudio's performative un-performance of the wedding vow—he skips town and skips out (or tries to) on the re-do of "I dos." If his periperformative ultimately fails to derail the "happy" ending, it does temporarily stun the marital plot, starkly illuminating—in or as a kind of freeze frame—not just marriage as theater, but marriage as a closing of ranks.

Theatricality is both obstacle to and instrument of the linked marriage plots of *Much Ado About Nothing*. Much of the play's wit derives from watching Beatrice and Benedick, sworn marriage resisters each, succumb to the desire to marry. At the beginning of the play, Beatrice would rather her dog bark at crows than that any man swear love for her. She sings a different tune by play's end. *Much Ado About Nothing* ends with a double wedding—Hero's to Claudio, Beatrice's to Benedick—and an invitation to dance. Hero and Claudio may be bores, but who could resist the charms of Beatrice and Benedick? Benedick, long a holdout to marriage and now its champion, gets the play's last words: "Strike up, pipers!"[12] The music begins, and the play ends on a joyous and joyously theatrical note. The final stage directions read, simply, "Dance. Exeunt." As Claire McEeachern notes in her commentary on the scene, "This is the only play of Shakespeare's explicitly to end with a dance for the general company."[13] It is the social choreography of marriage and the worlds it irresistibly makes. "The world must be peopled" (2.3.233).

Indeed. For all the shining wit of Beatrice's and Benedick's tirades against marriage, and for all the undeniable pleasure we take in watching their temporary revolt, in the end the will to be single cannot hold against the call to be married or be no one at all. If Benedick and Beatrice are "gulled" to their happy ending, so, too, are the audiences who laugh their delight. The pleasures of the audience "outside" the play are aligned with the desires of the friends and family within it, who orchestrate the love match. All dance. All exit. Worlds are harmonized anew. But at what cost? On the other side of this happy ending, when the dance is done, the bastard Don John awaits his punishment. Caught in flight, he has been dragged back to Messina and now lurks just off-stage, witnessing by his absence to the community that exists by simultaneously conjuring and excluding bastards like him. In full, Benedick's and the play's final cue to celebration is: "Think not on him [Don John] til tomorrow; I'll devise thee brave punishments for him. Strike up, pipers!" (5.4.125–26). The strike of music portends the blow of violence to come.

Don John is half brother to Claudio's lord prince, Don Pedro of Aragon. Earlier in the play, Don John stalled the forward motion of the marriage plot by a different feat of gulling. He convinced both Claudio and Don Pedro of Hero's infidelity, first with words of accusation—"the lady is disloyal" (3.2.93) —and then with the promise of visual evidence: "I will disparage her no farther till you are my witnesses: bear it coldly but till midnight, and let the issue show itself" (3.2.16–18). The showing is a cunning bit of theater contrived for their consumption. At the appointed hour, Don John's henchman, Borachio, appears in Hero's bedroom window with Hero's chambermaid

Margaret. Margaret is dressed in Hero's clothes, and Borachio calls her by that name, "Hero." Watching from a distance, Claudio and Don Pedro mistake "Hero" for Hero and take the bait.

In *Shakespeare After All*, Marjorie Garber names *Much Ado About Nothing* Shakespeare's "great play about gossip. Everything is overheard, misheard, or constructed on purpose for eavesdropping."[14] Throughout the play, gossip functions as an engine of social engineering, for better and for worse. Bad gossip stops ("crosses") a marriage; good gossip sets one in motion. The trick played on Claudio leads to tragedy for an innocent young woman. In apparent contrast, when friends and family stage their set pieces within earshot of Benedick and Beatrice, they do so to comic—which is to say, to *happy*—ends. The company bands together "to bring Signor Benedick and the Lady Beatrice into a mountain of affection th'one with th'other" (2.1.337–39). It is proposed as a wry diversion, something to pass the time in the week between Hero's and Claudio's betrothal and the wedding ceremony. The trick is played for laughs and for love: "The sport will be when they hold one an opinion of another's dotage, and no such matter. That's the scene I would see, which will be merely a dumb-show" (2.3.208–11). And yet, we do not need Freud to remind us of the aggression that is the beating heart of humor. Benedick and Beatrice find themselves ensnared in the marriage plottings of a larger social world that would teach them the value of the marriage bed. This is ultimately no sporting matter—as Hero's social death, when she is denounced at the altar by Claudio, testifies.

"This looks not like a nuptial," reports a puzzled Benedick, witness to the un-wedding (4.1.67). Crucially, this "not" in no way undoes, unknots, conventional alignments of women's chastity with men's honor. Instead, around the performative, and even against it, this little theatrical scene reinstates the asymmetrical terms of "being alive" in the eyes of one's community. Scenes such as these thus underscore the destructive power of gossip, the way it mobilizes and feeds off profoundly gendered concerns over how one stands in the eyes of others. This is not the "deep gossip" celebrated by the poet Allen Ginsberg in his eulogy for Frank O'Hara and so beautifully analyzed by Henry Abelove.[15] Social anxieties about women's sexuality and the prospect of cuckoldry are the frame through which the witnessing community understands what is given to be heard and made to be seen. Gossip thus insinuates itself into social relations as a kind of theater. *Much Ado About Nothing* is equally, then, one of Shakespeare's great plays on the power of theatricality to convert nothing into something. Another way to put this: Gossip theatricalizes social relations. It does its poisonous work—and its wickedly pleasurable work, as well—because people imagine themselves into its scenes / seens. Marriage as theater constitutes, and is constituted by, a community of witness, and it is no easy work to sit on your hands when all around you are standing and cheering.

What other scenes and what other pleasures might we imagine? This is a question pursued, in slightly different form, by Michel Foucault in "The Social Triumph of the Sexual Will." In what has become the most quoted passage in the interview, Foucault poignantly calls for an expanded "relational fabric": "In effect, we live in a legal, social, and institutional world where the only relations possible are extremely few, extremely simplified, and extremely poor. There is, of course, the relation of marriage, and the relations of family, but how many other relations should exist!"[16] But the passage that arrests my attention happens somewhat later in the interview. Close your eyes and you can hear the steady pulse of the political and ethical questions Sondheim negotiates in his four attempts to conclude *Company*. Let us call this the fifth ending, the one that has not happened yet. Asked to address the status of the single person, Foucault responds:

> The single person must be recognized as having relations with others quite different from those of a married couple, for example. We often say that the single person suffers from solitude because he is suspected of being an unsuccessful or rejected husband. . . . When in reality the life of solitude is often the result of the poverty of possible relationships in our society, where institutions make insufficient and necessarily rare all relations that one could have with someone else and could be intense, rich— even if they were provisional—even and especially if they took place outside the frame of marriage.[17]

To its last breath, *Company* pushes against this frame, or seeks to. After pledging himself to "Being Alive" and to wanting something, anything, Bobby stands alone on stage and blows out his birthday candles. In the brief flash before the stage goes dark, as Bobby wills his breath towards the candles, there is a space of possibility in which we are invited—dared, even—to wish with him for different and as yet unscripted finales and to reach towards other ways of being in and desiring company.

Notes

1. Young, "Every Day a Little Death," 79.
2. Quoted in Zadan, *Sondheim and Co.*, 139–40.
3. Quoted ibid., 139.
4. Quoted ibid., 140.
5. Young, "Every Day a Little Death," 80.
6. Quoted in Zadan, *Sondheim and Co.*, 140.
7. Quoted ibid., 140.
8. For an important argument about the possible disjuncture between the marriage and the wedding, see Freeman, *The Wedding Complex*. Freeman contrasts the verticality of marriage, which binds the couple to the state, to the horizontal ties that exceed the couple form and that the wedding may make visible, if only for an instant. This essay is indebted to her work. My thoughts about the side by side of Sondheim's *Company* have also benefitted from far-ranging conversation with H. N. Lukes, Molly McGarry, and Matthew Trachman, with whom I saw the 2006 Broadway revival of *Company*.
9. Sedgwick, "Around the Performative," 70.
10. Ibid., 72.
11. For an illuminating analysis of this longstanding accusation-cum-wish, see Jakobsen, "Can Homosexuals End Western Civilization As We Know It?," 49–70.
12. McEachern, *Much Ado About Nothing*, 5.4.126. Citations in parentheses are to this edition.
13. Ibid., 318, n. to 5.4.126.
14. Garber, *Shakespeare After All*, 375.
15. Abelove, *Deep Gossip*, xi–xiii.
16. Foucault, "The Social Triumph of the Sexual Will," 158.
17. Ibid., 159. Although in this passage Foucault seems to present solitude as a form of privation, his real brief is with depictions of the single life as "lonely" and with social arrangements that would force someone to choose between being in a couple or being alone. Around the edges of Foucault's argument there thus emerges a version of solitude as a practice of the self that intensifies sensation and relational possibilities by producing and preserving spaces for imagining all the things one does *not* have to be or want. I am grateful to Jill H. Casid for pushing me to think more sharply about the space of solitude for Foucault.

Othello

Othello's Penis: Or, Islam in the Closet

DANIEL BOYARIN

The primal scene of queer theory is the epistemology of the closet.[1] In open-ing the doors of that closet, much has been made, of course—not least by Sedgwick herself—of the figure of Esther, that closet-queen Jew. In this very brief essay, I want to think about another open secret in another work of literature, the secret of Othello's penis, to adumbrate the notion that the open secret at the heart of the play is the secret of Islam in Europe and that the structure of this secret shares in the structure of the open secret of the closet of a later Europe's "homosexual."[2]

One wonders whether Othello (like Daniel Deronda) ever looked at his penis. It is notorious that Deronda never "looked down":[3]

> The text's insistent reference leads relentlessly to the referent—to *la chose*, in fact: the hero's penis, which must have been circumcised, given what we are told of his story. . . . Deronda must have known, but he did not: other-wise, of course, there could be no story. The plot can function only if *la chose*, Deronda's circumcised penis, is disregarded; yet the novel's realism and referentiality function precisely to draw attention to it.[4]

I offer this only to set off the much less studied question of Othello's penis, which seems just as much a mystery (to him) as Deronda's is to him, for if a child raised for two years among orthodox Jews was surely circumcised, so surely was a Muslim man grown to adulthood among Muslims.

Looking for such a Muslim man, as Julia Lupton has written, we "look east, toward Arabia and Turkey, and to the northern parts of Africa, [where] Othello would become a Muslim-turned-Christian, . . . inheritor of a mono-theistic civilization already marked by frequent contacts with Christian Eu-rope and hence more likely to go renegade."[5] Of course, northern Africa and Islam is where we are bound to look, for Muslim is what a Moor is and North Africa where a Moor comes from. I would only slightly refocus the point by

remarking that it is not only that the Moor is the inheritor of such a mono-
theistic civilization in contact with Christian Europe but that Moors had been
ruling much of "Christian" Europe for centuries—not only in Spain—and the
anxiety about the Christianness of Christian Europe itself is at stake in Othello's penis: that "old black ram" tupping/topping your white you.[6] Has he
really been Christianized, and if so, did his prepuce grow back miraculously?
Has Europe really been Christianized, purged of its Muslim color?

One wonders whether Othello was somehow miraculously de-circum-
cised at the time of baptism. Is it this miracle that has left his penis in such
obscurity? I suggest that the ambiguous fleshly sign in this play provides an
exemplary early instance of the queering of the very identity markers that
form our contemporary mantras of race, gender, religion—or, better put, by
letting the categories of the play form themselves before our reading eyes, we
open our eyes to the constructedness of our most naturalized of differences.

It is by now notorious that modern criticism and performance practice of
Othello are driven by a profound and tenacious feeling that the play is about
"race" as we experience it. The exciting generalization about this text of
Shakespeare's is that in it we encounter a system of differences that are not
racial or generated by sexuality or even quite gendered or religious as an independent variable, but all of these aggregated, laid on one another in ways that
make nonsense of (or, rather, demonstrate the recent construction of) our
own social and critical litanies. Oddly, Othello's alleged "thick lips" and dark
skin seem less significant a marker of his indelible identity than his hidden
penis. I am going to offer the notion that the figure of Othello's ambiguously
circumcised penis is as important—or even a more important—as a signifier of
his "race" than the color of his skin.[7] The first few times we meet Othello's
"race," it is his blackness (and notoriously his "thick lips") that are in evidence:

> *Iago*: 'Zounds, sir, you're robb'd; for shame, put on
> your gown;
> Your heart is burst, you have lost half your soul;
> Even now, now, very now, an old black ram
> Is tupping your white ewe. Arise, arise;
> Awake the snorting citizens with the bell,
> Or else the devil will make a grandsire of you:
> Arise, I say.[8]

"Race" in its modern sense seemingly could not be clearer here, and miscegnation, the monstrous image of the rampant black penis entering the lily-

white female body (as well as the specter of a grandchild with horns and black skin) is raised with all of its fascinating, arousing, horror.

However, when linked with another, related image, we can see that Shakespeare is not playing, at any rate, the nineteenth-century and twentieth-century race card:

> *Iago*: 'Zounds, sir, you are one of those that will not serve God, if the
>   devil bid you. Because we come to
> do you service and you think we are ruffians, you'll
> have your daughter covered with a Barbary horse;
> you'll have your nephews neigh to you; you'll have
> coursers for cousins and gennets for germans. (1.1.118–24)

Othello and his sex have thus been figured as bestial in two ways within the space of a few lines. But the African has now moved from sub-Saharan black Africa to Muslim North Africa and done so, I think, quite decisively for the play. Shakespeare—and, indeed, Iago—are not confused as to the placing of a Moor. He is from Barbary, North Africa (the word "Moor" refers, at least originally, to Mauretania), a Barbary stallion. For Iago, his Barbar/ian "nature" figures Othello as bestial other, despite whatever "baptism" he has been known to undergo.

We need to pay some attention to the differential force of these images, let them play out their different logics of miscegnation. In the first, Desdemona is herself bestialized through her bestial intercourse. (As Cassio says: "Reputation, reputation, reputation! O, I have lost my reputation! I have lost the immortal part of myself, and what remains is bestial. My reputation, Iago, my reputation!" [2.3.266–69]). If Othello is ramified, then she is rendered sheepish, as well. Her fantasized monstrous child, spawn of the devil, is so not because his father is a sheep and his mother a human but because they are sheep of different colors. The Barbary horses, however, are an entirely different kettle of fish. Here it is only Othello who is rendered a stallion; Desdemona remains a human woman. It is equine nephews, cousins, germans whom Brabantio will acquire through this marriage, not even a mule for a grandchild. This (ungrammatical) detail suggests strongly that we look to an allusion to delve more deeply into Shakespeare's design here. For equine barbarian penises, we need look no further than Ezekiel 23:20: "There she lusted after her lovers, whose penises were like those of donkeys and whose emission was like that of horses."

The context of Ezekiel 23 will provide, in fact, a rich and important clue for the reading of *Othello*, for the entire chapter is a graphic and vivid and horrifying depiction of miscegnation as bestiality with such appalling outcome that the passage in the play becomes a *mise en abîme* and thus hermeneutic key. The chapter tells a parable of two sisters, Aholah and Aholibah, who both went whoring after foreign lovers (one in, as we are told, Samaria, and the other, Jerusalem). Their lovers, in both cases, were profoundly attractive young military men: "She doted upon the Assyrians her neighbours, captains and rulers clothed most gorgeously, horsemen riding upon horses, all of them desirable young men [Ezekiel 23:12]." It is of these young men that it is said their penises are like the penises of asses and their ejaculations like those of horses. And the consequences are predictable (at least for Ezekiel): "Therefore, O Aholibah, thus saith the Lord GOD; Behold, I will raise up thy lovers against thee, from whom thy mind is alienated, and I will bring them against thee on every side [Ezekiel 23:22]." While Shakespeare certainly does not allow the punitive moralizing tone of the biblical passage to creep into his text, this intertextual reading does open up a significant moment in the play, a reading of Desdemona as tragic heroine in her own right. It is her desire, her very falling in love, it would seem, with the religious and racial other who so attracts with his stories of derring-do that dooms her to her tragic fate. No more a punishment than the downfalls of any other tragic heroes and with equal (if not greater) admiration of and deep sympathy for the tragic hero whose flaw causes his downfall, Desdemona's loving not wisely but too well is the author of her destruction, for as in the biblical text, it is the very male partner in an "improper" love who becomes the enemy that destroys the female lover. She loves the Barbary horse, whose penis is a horse's. But he is a Barbary horse, not just any horse, and hence a circumcised one. The figure thus works within the Shakespearean text very closely, *mutatis mutandis* (as already noted) to the biblical co-text, for there sex is a figure for religious infidelity, and so here, too. The Othellan figure of Desdemona's desire for the other is thus a representation of the nearly sexual attractiveness of Islam.[9]

Moors are Muslims; Muslims are circumcised. Yet Othello, famously ends his life with the following speech:

> *Othello*: Soft you; a word or two before you go.
> I have done the state some service, and they know't. . . .
> Set you down this;
> And say besides, that in Aleppo once,
> Where a malignant and a turban'd Turk

> Beat a Venetian and traduced the state,
> I took by the throat the circumcised dog,
> And smote him, thus.
> *Stabs himself.* (5.2.389–406)

I focus on the last line but one—"I took by the throat the circumcised dog"—that posits circumcision as the very sign and emblem of a "malignant and a turban'd Turk." In denying his own circumcision, as it were, Othello's project here is constructing himself as a Christian, Venetian patriot—"muscular Christian"—one of "us," not one of the (feminized and bestialized) others and, hence, it would seem, a fit sexual partner for Desdemona. Othello's own penis then becomes a site unseen of ambiguity with regard to the components of an identity (sexualized) of both the European "white" self and the components of its own constructed otherings. In tracing a moment in the play that focuses on this ambiguous organ as the very marker of self and other, I hope, repeating Lupton but with a difference, to at least limn out the imbrication of sex(uality), religion, and race.

The passage is itself a conflicted, almost logically tortured one (and I do not think this is mimesis of Othello's own internal state of unrest). On the one hand, Othello explicitly demands that the author of his biography, the historian of the sad events, retell only that which relates to his unhappy sexual history, his relation with Desdemona and its tragic end, and explicitly not mention the service he has done the state, especially not to "extenuate" him. But then, at the very end of the speech, he insists that the narrator of the events must indeed make mention of the events in Aleppo when, in defending Venice's honor against the Muslim Turk, he stabbed him as he stabs himself now. The contradiction says (as the Hebrew expression has it): Interpret me! Let us take Othello at his word. The reason that Othello wants his Aleppan exploit spoken of is not to extenuate his circumstances but only to make us understand that he dies a Christian, a proper Venetian—he is not a circumcised pagan murderer but a Christian who killed his wife for honor (an irony in the present moment in which "honor killing" has become one of the very things with which to vilify Islam). He is asserting his status as Christian and non-Turk, as European—but also, I would add, as an un-erasable scar on the white surface of Christendom. And, of course, there is that other circumcised penis haunting Christendom always, un-erasably, an indelible stain on humanity. The original circumcised dogs are the Jews, called, indeed, "the circumcision," according to Paul: "Beware of dogs; beware of evil-doers; beware of the circumcision" (Philippians 3:2).

What, then, of Othello's own penis? Is he (still) of "the circumcision" or no? To the best of my memory, there is only one place in the play where Othello is marked at all as Christian—namely, when Iago says:

> For 'tis most easy
> The inclining Desdemona to subdue
> In any honest suit: she's framed as fruitful
> As the free elements. And then for her
> To win the Moor—were't to renounce his baptism,
> All seals and symbols of redeemed sin,
> His soul is so enfetter'd to her love,
> That she may make, unmake, do what she list,
> Even as her appetite shall play the god
> With his weak function. (2.3.335–50)

So Othello has been baptized but would renounce his own baptism for the sake of Desdemona, and, indeed, in the end he does, as it were, renounce his baptism, revert to his violent "Moorish" (equals Muslim) ways, and kill her.[10] The changeability of the Moor in his will signals also his changeability with respect to Desdemona, but also, and even more importantly, perhaps, with respect to religion. There is more than a hint already in the beginning of the play that his conversion, his Christianity, is very much in question among the Venetian signory:

> *Brabantio*: How! the duke in council!
> In this time of the night! Bring him away:
> Mine's not an idle cause: the duke himself,
> Or any of my brothers of the state,
> Cannot but feel this wrong as 'twere their own;
> For if such actions may have passage free,
> Bond-slaves and pagans shall our statesmen be. (1.2.110–15)

Here, at any rate, it seems clear that Othello is not a "Christian." If his action in kidnapping or "magicking" Desdemona goes unpunished by the duke or the state's council, then Venice is in danger of being ruled by "bond-slaves" (Othello) and "pagans" (Othello). This passage calls up a biblical allusion: "Under three things the earth trembles; under four it cannot bear up: / a slave when he becomes king, and a fool when he is filled with food; / an unloved woman when she gets a husband, and a maidservant when she displaces her mistress" (Proverbs 3.21–23). Othello is the slave who would be king. Othello is both bondsman and "pagan," hence not Christian in Brabantio's eyes, for all his conversion. "Pagan" here is not in contradistinction to Muslim but signifies Muslim; the mark of Cain is not Othello's blackness but the hidden / not hidden evidence of his not quite Christianity. There is no evidence that I know of to the contrary and—at least, in the *Merchant of Venice*—good reason to understand Shakespeare's "pagan" as any non-Christian: "Adieu! tears exhibit my tongue. Most beautiful pagan, most sweet Jew! if a Christian did not play the knave and get thee, I am much deceived. But, adieu: these foolish drops do something drown my manly spirit: adieu" (2.3). If a sweet Jew be a beautiful pagan, then it would seem almost *a fortiori* that a Muslim is a pagan, too, for Shakespeare. This general view is supported by multiple medieval representations of Muslims as idolaters. If further proof were needed, let the famous poem by James I on the battle of Lepanto, in which the Venetians, after their battle with the Turks, thank God for having "redeemd" them "from cruel Pagans thrall" be my witness.[11] *Willing*, then (in his changeable will), perhaps to renounce all signs and seals of his redeemed sin for the sake of Desdemona, he cannot, however, renounce (but only denounce) the signs and seals of his sin; they are inscribed on his penis.

Lynda Boose observes that "once his Ensign has raised the flag inscribing Othello within the difference of skin color, all the presumably meaningful differences Othello has constructed between himself and the infidel collapse."[12] But there is more, for beside the turban (which can be doffed), there is the mark on his penis, which cannot. As a preacher only slightly later than Shakespeare argued:

> Many, and as I am informed, many hundreds, are Musselmans in Turkie, and Christians at home; doffing their religion as they do their clothes, and keeping a conscience for every harbor they shall put in. And those Apostates and circumcised Renegadoes.[13]

If such anxieties attend the Christian converted and reconverted back from Islam, *a fortiori* they attend the Muslim convert, too. Clothes (turbans) can be doffed but circumcised penises cannot so easily. Boose writes, "Clothes, or rather cultural signifers, make the man and cultural and theological alignments—unlike biological ones—can always be changed."[14] There is, however, a theological alignment, a theological orientation of the flesh, that cannot always be changed, as he is fated to kill the Muslim, who is indelibly marked in his penis as such and who plausibly, so plausibly, enters Europe in the guise of a convert to Christianity. Not surprising, then, that the Muslim Moor seeks, even—or, rather, precisely—at the very end, to erase the ineradicable mark (at least discursively) by cursing and stabbing the circumcised Turk. But he cannot. Indeed, far from turning away from his "pagan" past, he himself "turns Turk," as he himself has warned (in yet another *mise en abîme*):

> Why, how now, ho! from whence ariseth this?
> Are we turn'd Turks, and to ourselves do that
> Which heaven hath forbid the Ottomites?
> For Christian shame, put by this barbarous brawl:
> He that stirs next to carve for his own rage
> Holds his soul light. (2.3.169–78)

"For Christian shame," indeed. "Are we turn'd Turks?" indeed. Although much further historical research and presentation would be necessary to make this point fully in a scholarly way, my reading of Othello's hidden penis suggests that a certain epistemological structure, an epistemology of the "open secret," is already adumbrated in *Othello*. Othello's occluded circumcision, hidden and denied, represents the Christian shame—namely, that Christendom is not Christian. Muslims have been inside it for nearly a millennium. When Othello kills his own Muslim while alluding to Paul against the Jews, the structure of the modern open secret is already in place. Daniel Deronda is Othello's grandson, and not so incidentally, Elliot's solution is to banish him to Zion. Europe must be Christian as society must be heterosexual. All that was needed was the invention of "homosexuality" for the epistemology of the closet to be complete.

Notes

I thank both Janet Adelman [Her memory for a blessing] and Madhavi Menon for their generous comments on an earlier version of this essay. Neither ought take any responsibility, however, for its flaws other than aiding and abetting after the fact.

1. Sedgwick, *Epistemology of the Closet* (2nd. ed., 2008).

2. Cf. Vitkus, "Turning Turk in Othello," 146, who does not quite get or make the point of the sexualization of this anxiety.

3. Marcus, "Human Nature, Social Orders, and Nineteenth-Century Systems of Explanation," *Salmagundi* 28 (1975): 20–42, 41.

4. Chase, *Decomposing Figures*, 169.

5. Lupton, "Othello Circumcised," 74.

6. For this pun, see Adelman, "Iago's Alter Ego," 129. For a very different approach to Othello's circumcision, see Lupton, "Othello Circumcised," who considers Othello's Islam an ambiguous proposition, a reading with which I implicitly disagree.

7. Cited in Vitkus, "Turning Turk in Othello," 150. For Muslims explicitly marked as Pagans, see ibid., 163, n. 67.

8. *Othello*, 1.1 92–98. Citations are from the Arden edition (1996), edited by E. A. J. Honigmann.

9. Vitkus, "Turning Turk in Othello," 145–46.

10. Ibid., 159

11. See n. 7 above.

12. Boose, "The Getting of a Lawful Race," 38.

13. Henry Byam, from a sermon preached 16 March 1627, cited in Vitkus, "Turning Turk in Othello," 152. Boose makes a related claim: "The Getting of a Lawful Race," 40. I am thus not arguing against her but with her and amplifying certain points. Boose's main arguments lie elsewhere.

14. Boose, "The Getting of a Lawful Race," 37.

"Curious Pleasures":

Pericles beyond the Civility of Union

PATRICK R. O'MALLEY

Marriage, the Book of Genesis suggests, is predicated on the transformation of alterity into identity, of difference into coherence. It is due to the formation of Eve from Adam's own body that a man comes to "leave his father and his mother, and . . . cleave unto his wife: and they shall be one flesh" (Genesis 2:24). Indeed, the linguistic structures that constitute the continuing national conversation around the rights of members of the same sex to legally formalize their (binary and implicitly monogamous) partnerships have continued to turn on the notion of identity. That means not only the "identity" of sexual orientation—fewer mainstream politicians are publicly making the argument that gay people as a class simply should not have rights—but also the yet older understanding of the term, what the Oxford English Dictionary calls "the quality or condition of being the same in substance, composition, nature, properties, or in particular qualities under consideration; absolute or essential sameness; oneness."[1] Both the language of "*same*-sex marriage" and "marriage *equality*" (the latter largely favored by the pro-marriage queer community) turns on this invocation of sameness, of identity, and both proponents and opponents of gay people's right to access the privileges and responsibilities of state-sanctioned marriage rely on it.

It is, it seems, an uncanny doubling that not only defines the same-sex couple but also constitutes both the possibility and the threat of that union. Thus, for example, a gay writer for the *Times* of London quipped in July 2004, "I've got nothing against them, but heterosexuality is unnatural, isn't it? People of two different sexes who have nothing in common and don't even speak the same emotional language shacking up."[2] The feature was illustrated with the image of a wedding cake topped with the figures of two identically dressed and styled men. And in March of that same year, *Maclean's* magazine noted the identical clothing of a lesbian wedding in Toronto: "The brides were radiant in their black tuxes." The article's headline similarly highlighted sameness, coyly announcing the new mirror of nomenclature: "Mrs. and Mrs. in a Gay Mecca."[3] The June 6, 2006, issue of *The Advocate* did the *Times* one better with its cover story "Polygamy and Gay Men," presenting its readers with the image of a wedding cake topped with three identical figurines of blandly Caucasian, tuxedoed men, their plastic hands folded demurely across their midsections. This is how *The Advocate* imagines polygamy?

It might seem, then, that an epistemology of gay relationships that privileges sameness would tend to understand those relationships as ideal versions of what heterosexual relations can only imperfectly or metaphorically mimic. Whatever the intended irony of these pieces—and *The Advocate* has its tongue more fully planted in its cheek than does *Maclean's*—they nonetheless rely on the visual and rhetorical coherence of the partners as a metaphor for their union—as do, of course, the ads for matching same-sex-union rings that underwrite *The Advocate*'s publication. And yet opponents of gay marriage have themselves also generally emphasized the identity of same-sex partners; in fact, especially from the religious opposition, the language of sameness underwrites the ontological impossibility of gay marriage in the first place. In November 2003, the U.S. Conference of Catholic Bishops released a statement arguing that "for several reasons a same-sex union contradicts the nature of marriage." The first of these reasons lies not in the radical alterity of gay people but in the irredeemable *sameness* of same-sex partners: "[The same-sex union] is not based on the natural complementarity of male and female."[4] Quoting Luce Irigaray's claim in *An Ethics of Sexual Difference* that "Man and woman, woman and man are always meeting as though for the first time because they cannot be substituted one for the other,"[5] Dennis O'Brien argued in the conservative *Christian Century* that the fundamental alterity that putatively constitutes heterosexuality is the very basis of its exclusive claim to marriage: "Why heterosexuality? Because the human spirit can expand as it moves toward the different. . . . The final fact is that the bodily, biological difference between men and women is the urtext of the heterosexual narrative."[6] Indeed, with no apparent irony, the California Court of Appeals initially held that "California law does not literally prohibit gays and lesbians from marrying; however, it requires those who do to marry someone of the opposite sex."[7]

In entering this debate on these terms, queer people have already lost. By acceding to a logic that privileges sexual differentiation as the primary system of categorization, we not only obstruct potentially powerful relationships and coalitions between non-heterosexual men and women; we also simultaneously surrender to a progressive (in the sense of evolutionary) paradigm within which queer desires and interactions are necessarily constructed as a simple and primitive version of the more realized and complex modes of heterosexuality. Freud's rhetoric of homosexuality as a "slip[ping] back to auto-eroticism" makes this point all too clearly.[8] The challenge of gay marriage is not, I think, to form unions that continue to sentimentalize a fantasized sameness, unions whose picturesque internal identity is matched only by their attempts to mirror heterosexual conventions in as many ways as possible.[9] It is, rather, to re-imagine the crucial role of alterity itself in a multifarious array of legitimate relations. The challenge is to reimagine queer life and love as structured fundamentally on difference without falling to the Scylla of hierarchy or the Charybdis of a mushy liberal diversity. Can we articulate queer relationships without fetishizing the notion of *oneness* that underwrites both the "idem" of identity and the "mono" of monogamy?[10] It is the problem that Leo Bersani has identified as existing at the root of the quest to imagine a generalized homosexuality: "To recognize universal homo-ness can allay the terror of difference, which generally gives rise to a hopeless dream of eliminating difference entirely. A massively heteroized perception of the universal gives urgency to a narcissistic project that would reduce—radically, with no surplus of alterity—the other to the same."[11] Indeed, the legalization of same-sex marriage in Massachusetts led some employers to *eliminate* benefits for non-married domestic partners.[12] Marriage here starts to look like the collapsing of options into a single authorized version rather than an expansion of the possibilities for people's relationships and commitments, in all of their variety. Can we escape from the matrix of the received gay marriage plot without relying on the One: the myth of unfractured identity and the fantasy of a coherent comic narrative that ends—with bridesmaids or boutonnieres—with union with "the one," happily ever after into an undifferentiated future? What alternative versions can we use to revise what has begun to look like a master narrative of marriage that might collapse rather than open the potential range of human interaction and desire? Is there room for difference in our romantic and erotic relations, for some delay to figure out where the shotgun in our weddings might be pointed—that is, for the diffidence of a Derridean *différance*?

It is here that I take a truly perverse pleasure in offering *Pericles: Prince of Tyre* as a rhetorical model that, in its display of a romance always and already hopelessly collapsed back onto itself, might offer a vision of queer relationships precisely as opposition to identity, coherence, and sameness. For it is these same crises of coherence, the same desire to rewrite the messiness of alterity as identitarian unity, that marks much of the critical response to *Pericles*, the queer sheep of the Shakespearean flock. To the extent that this text can resist its own normalizing readership, we might imagine a way out of the ideology of union as only exogamous and monogamous dualism. Missing from the First Folio and Second Folio, the play's early textual history is recorded only in the Quarto of 1609 and its reprints, a text (represented in textual notes by the defiantly singular "Q") that is almost uniformly declared "corrupt." And well it might be. As Alexander Leggatt has observed, "To touch for a moment on the question of authorship: few believe *Pericles* to be entirely Shakespeare's; the writing is so inconsistent, not just in quality but in kind. There is, on the other hand, no general agreement about the identity of the other author, or authors, or about the nature of Shakespeare's involvement. . . . The play does not seem to me fully coherent."[13] A lot of hands and touches are at play in those sentences, promiscuously (and anonymously) mingling, even without the oddly oblique allusion to the "nature" of Shakespearean "involvement."

No wonder, then, that Roger Warren, in his updating for the new millennium of the Oxford edition of 1986, edited by Gary Taylor and MacDonald P. Jackson, entitles a long section of his introduction, "The Text: Corruption and Reconstruction." The rather startlingly rehabilitative rhetoric accords well with the dominant Straight-Eye-for-the-Queer-Text practices that continue to characterize editorial responses to this play. Nor is it a wonder, in a play that returns again and again to wonder itself, that in the case of the Oxford edition (first under Taylor and Jackson, and then under Warren) this primarily involves the collapsing of promiscuity into a binary structure. As Warren notes, "This edition presents *Pericles* as a collaboration between Shakespeare and George Wilkins, Wilkins writing scenes 1–9, Shakespeare scenes 11–22."[14] By emphasizing the largely separate (and never equal) partnership of Shakespeare and Wilkins (both of whom are listed as authors on the title page), the Oxford edition fails to escape the troubling image of two sets of men's hands meeting across the text's multifarious gaps. But at least, with the proper emendations, there are only two major sets, and the gap between them for the most part is wide and distinct enough to imagine chastity. Oddly, this same quest for coherence on the part of the Oxford editors occasionally (as at 21:23 and 21:195) involves the importation of phrases or cadences from entirely different plays (*The Winter's Tale* and *Twelfth Night* in these cases). That might seem to increase rather than decrease the proliferating multiplicities (of sources, hands, influences) that mark this text, but that is less of a concern, it seems, if you know where the hands have been.

But all of this "corruption"—and the anxiety about corruption—finds its roots in the text itself with its insistent excesses, redundancies, absences, and queer resistances to the very normalizing teleologies that constitute this strangest of romances *as* (heterosexual) romance. The doublings pile up, rhetorically and narratively, in seemingly unnecessary repetition: multiple shipwrecks; the loss of Thaisa and of Marina, neither of whom is actually dead; two successive recognition scenes to reconstitute the fractured family; the double narration of the fates of Antiochus and his daughter, one told by Helicanus ("a fire from heauen came and shriueld / Vp those bodyes euen to lothing" [916–17]), the next rather less dramatically by Gower ("To'th Court of King Symonides, / Are Letters brought, the tenour these: / Antiochus and his daughter dead" [1095–97]). And then there is the surprising way that both Thaisa and her father imagine Pericles as an eroticized substitute for food: "These Cates resist mee, hee not thought vpon," Simonides muses (820), and Thaisa almost immediately chimes in with, "All Viands that I eate do seeme vnsauery, / Wishing him my meat" (822–23).

As those lines suggest, *Pericles* repeatedly invokes (if only to abjure) a sort of incest that quickly threatens to become a type of ménage à trois, the problem of too many hands (and mouths) obtaining here, as well. Those incestuous engagements have attracted much critical attention, and incest itself becomes in this play a sexual practice that—like homosexuality—involves participants who are both too similar and too different. Neither masturbation nor conjugality, it partakes of both. It is no accident that Antiochus and his daughter suffer the same fate as the cities of the plain (as, in their own way, do Cleon and Dionyza). Like those meddling hands and mouths, they don't *fit*—or, rather, perhaps they fit too well with each other for the normalizing imperatives of heterosexual and marital closure to contain them comfortably. Dramatic resolution is often, like Bersani's "massively heteroized perception of the universal," a reduction of alterity into identity, of resistant otherness into the coherence of marriage. Resolution is in fact precisely what this play refuses even as it moves inexorably toward what looks like the stability of the coherence of heterosexual monogamous romance. There is a reason that Gower, in his epilogue, describes Pericles's family in parallel with Antiochus's. One way to subsume that excess alterity would be to marginal-ize it as romantically charged homosociality—the figure of Antonio in *The Merchant of Venice*, for example, or the friendship of Demetrius and Lysander in *A Midsummer Night's Dream*. But rather than displacing its queer energy even onto same-sex affectionate or rivalrous bonds (as we see, in various ways, in *Hamlet*, in *Henry IV*, in *Twelfth Night*, in *Coriolanus*, in *Othello*), *Pericles* for the most part rejects even the comforting conventions of binary homosociality, let alone homosexuality.

Instead, and despite the putative move toward the closure of marriage, the threatening weirdnesses of the text continually end up shoved toward the surface, toward the promiscuous play of language itself—that is, toward jagged difference rather than reparative coherence as its structuring principle. Indeed, it is telling how many textual cruxes of this play actually revolve around identity and difference as they underwrite—or fail to underwrite—the conventions of romance. In the Oxford edition, for example, Pericles escapes the "rapture of the sea" (5.193), a phrase wet with erotic desire, its etymological similarities to rape transformed into plunder.[15] But in the Quarto, we find not "rapture" but "rupture" (718), not delight—or wealth—but an interruption, not a coming together (however violent) but a breach. Rapture might belong somewhere along the way of the marriage plot; rupture is its end.

"I doe beseech you," Gower declares, as the play nears its final scenes, "To learne of me who stand with gappes / To teach you" (1745–47). The Oxford editors—like those of the Riverside and Norton editions—take the normalizing reading of these lines in terms both of meter and sense: "I do beseech you / To learn of me, who stand i'th' gaps to teach you" (18.7–8). That is, in the Quarto, Gower stands "with" gaps; in the later editions, he stands *in* them, and his educational value derives from that positioning. But that difference—indeed, the *gap* between the Quarto and the modern editions—is the very question of what gaps are good for and what we can learn from them. For the Oxford edition, Gower fills in the space of the gaps, providing coherence and, ultimately, meaning. In the Quarto, corrupt as it may be, the gaps gape wide between us and the possibility of comprehension. Gower is not there a bridge but himself a mystery, the confederate of gaps and not their conqueror. His lesson is a matter not of superseding gaps but of engaging with them. He stands with the gaps.

And there stand I, as well: with gap and rupture, with redundancy and excess, with the queerness of the text and the way that it undermines its own marital fantasies of coherence. As Paula Ettelbrick has rightly noted, "The concept of equality in our legal system does not support differences. It only supports sameness."[16] It is not necessary to be insistently anti-relational to critique the relational imperative that underwrites our conversation about gay rights and rites. D. A. Miller has observed of Jane Austen's *Emma* that closure corrects the possibility of "a radical picaresque: an endless flirtation with a potentially infinite parade of possibilities."[17] In similar language, but a very different politics, Christopher Rice, the son of the vampire novelist Anne Rice and a writer in his own right, closed an essay for (again) *The Advocate* with a sort of paean to monogamy: "I can't enjoy the ocean with a single partner if I keep heading back to the pond for a dip with the guy I met five minutes ago."[18] Never mind the false dichotomy. In light of *Pericles*, the maritime imagery is striking. For Rice, the ocean stands for the vast undifferentiated expanse of sameness, of monogamy, of identity, of resistance precisely to picaresque possibility; in Shakespeare's unruly Quarto, it is "rupture." In contrast to a politics that insists on the union of two people in a coherent and stable couple as the basis of civic value and the condition of rights and privileges, *Pericles* insists on the gaps, the resistance to the imperative of choosing the One: the one relationship, the one lover, the one label, the one sense of identity. What it offers us is a chance to suspend our quest for the civility of civil union or marriage for the cheekier—and, thankfully, less coherent—incivility of queerness.

Notes

1. *Oxford English Dictionary*, 2nd. ed., s.v. "identity," def. 1a.

2. Robbie Millen, "Heterosexuality? It's Unnatural," *Times* (London), July 22, 2004, T2: 3.

3. Ken MacQueen, "Mrs. and Mrs. in a Gay Mecca," *Maclean's*, March 29, 2004, 30.

4. Quoted in Alan Cooperman, "Catholic Bishops Oppose Legalizing Gay Marriage," *Washington Post*, November 13, 2003, A2.

5. Irigaray, *An Ethics of Sexual Difference*, 12–13.

6. O'Brien, "A More Perfect Union," 203.

7. *In re Marriage Cases*, 143 Cal. App. 4th, 918 (2006).

8. Freud, "Leonardo da Vinci and a Memory of His Childhood," 100.

9. In its opinion of October 2006, the New Jersey Supreme Court bases the emotional appeal of its demand that same-sex couples have the same rights—although not the same nomenclature—as opposite-sex couples in the fact that the gay couples just seemed so similar to the straight couples, an observation that the majority opinion cites almost immediately: "In terms of the value they place on family, career, and community service, plaintiffs lead lives that are remarkably similar to

those of opposite-sex couples." See *Harris v. Lewis*, 2006 N.J. Lexis 1521, 19 and 20 (2006).

10. As Amy Brandzel has noted, in *Goodridge*, the Massachusetts State Supreme Court approvingly "reference[d] here the ways in which same-sex-marriage advocacy has not attacked the 'binary nature[s]' of marriage. While it is true that same-sex-marriage advocates have critiqued the male / female and homosexual / heterosexual binaries latent in marriage, they have not attempted to undermine the sanctity of the domestic couple" (193). Indeed, although the 2008 Supreme Court of California's decision that legalized same-sex marriage in that state—and was overturned at the polls by Proposition 8—begins by declaring that marriage is the right of an individual, it quickly shifts to locate that right in the *couple*, thus necessarily stressing the binary (and implicitly monogamous) unit. The slippage between a rhetoric of the rights of an "individual" and those of a "couple" characterize the entire opinion. While that move would seem to largely moot the question of identity itself (the court's opinion using the term "gay" only about 50 times, including in quotations and names of organizations and "same-sex couple(s)" over 170 times), the court also insists that sexual orientation, like race, is a stable classification subject to strict scrutiny: see *In re Marriage Cases* 43 Cal. 4th, 757 (2008).

11. Bersani, *Homos*, 146. But see also Bersani's later repudiation of difference per se as the animating characteristic of desire in "Sociality and Sexuality," where he ultimately argues that "we love, in other words, inaccurate replications of ourselves," a claim that uncannily echoes the genealogy of "corrupt" reproductions that mark *Pericles*'s textual history: idem, "Sociality and Sexuality," 656. Compare the critique of the privileging of alterity that underwrites historicism in Menon, *Unhistorical Shakespeare*, 1–4 and passim, in favor of a "homohistory" that embraces (without fetishizing) sameness.

12. See Jesse Noyes, "Gays at *Globe* Told to Marry or Lose Benefits," *Boston Herald*, July 8, 2006, 2.

13. Leggatt, "The Shadow of Antioch," 167.

14. Warren, "Introduction," in idem, *Pericles, Prince of Tyre*, 4. Unless indicated otherwise, citations in parentheses are to this edition, usually from the "Diplomatic Reprint of The First Quarto of 'Pericles,'" which is not divided into scenes or acts and reproduces original spelling, punctuation, and capitalization. Occasionally, for comparison, I also quote the "Reconstructed Text," which closely follows the earlier Oxford edition and divides the text into scenes but not acts.

15. See *Oxford English Dictionary*, 2nd. ed., s.v. "rapture," defs. 1, 3b.

16. Ettelbrick, "Since When Is Marriage a Path to Liberation?," 259.

17. Miller, *Narrative and Its Discontents*, 15.

18. Christopher Rice, "Monogamy and Me," *Advocate*, March 29, 2005, 72.

Number There in Love Was Slain

KARL STEEL

Shakespeare's elegy for the Phoenix and Turtledove opens by demanding that an unnamed "bird of loudest lay" herald a funeral procession comprising only those birds who possess "chaste wings."[1] It forbids from the "troop" (8) the "shriking harbinger" (5) and "every fowl of tyrant wing" (6). The prohibitions against eros, death, and tyranny suggest an incipient Boethian stoicism that would disdain love, thanatophobia, and any external compulsion. But the herald has in fact banished only those aspects of these forces that might embarrass, rather than support, the coming of Reason. All tyrants have been proscribed, "save the eagle, feather'd king" (11), which the ritual demands to "keep the obsequy so strict" (12). Into this solemnity also enters the "death-divining" (15) swan priest, a creature naturally aware that time and death bind itself and all creatures. The crow, clothed in "sable" (18), follows as the chief mourner. With its "breath," it "givest and takest" life (19), echoing, as H. Neville Davies observed, the Burial Rite in the Book of Common Prayer.[2] Since such pomp properly concludes whatever life the crow offers, the crow's presence does not so much give life as call on the already living to recall that death permeates the past, present, and future of the time the "treble-dated" (17) crow offers. What life this procession recognizes has been regulated by the powers of eagle, swan, and crow, the state, church, and mortality itself; they encompass life in a ceremony that, rather than challenging or scorning death, gives the community over to death. In place of unchaste wings, we have thanatophilia. If, as Herbert Marcuse argued, the ideology of death promotes death as more than a merely technical, biological impediment, but as the great terminus that "gives 'meaning' to life, or is the precondition for the 'true' life of man,"[3] the funeral ceremony aims to re-socialize the Phoenix and Turtledove and their eros by binding them in death's order. According to the rite, the community's most suitable response to the lovers is not enthusiasm, imitation, wonder, or inspiration, but neither is it noisy grief, the resentment of death's injustice or meaninglessness, or a refusal of the sacrifice.

The only appropriate response is the dutiful tribute of sighed prayer (67), offered as an anthem by the avian mourners:

> Here the anthem doth commence:
> Love and constancy is dead;
> Phoenix and the turtle fled
> In a mutual flame from hence.
>
> So they lov'd, as love in twain
> Had the essence but in one;
> Two distincts, division none:
> Number there in love was slain.
>
> Hearts remote, yet not asunder;
> Distance, and no space was seen
> 'Twixt the turtle and his queen;
> But in them it were a wonder.
>
> So between them love did shine,
> That the turtle saw his right
> Flaming in the phoenix' sight:
> Either was the other's mine. (21–36)

With this anthem, the carefully plotted ritual goes awry in wonder, and the intended confinement of eros fails. Encountering the avian mourners' inability or unwillingness to make the Phoenix and Turtledove fall into line, Property is "appalled" (37) and Reason, "confounded."

Acting as an agent of Property, whose purpose is to sort things into distinct entities, Reason first characterizes the birds' love as one in which division "gr[e]w together" (42) so that two "simples" (44), the most basic of elements, became "well compounded" (44). Reason then exclaims that the birds are a "true . . . twain" (45), devoted to one another as two birds, uncompounded and separate but at the same time also a "concordant one" (46). These two descriptions are not so much a contradiction as a call for proper classification. The birds *should* be either one or two, which would result in the following straightforward effects: If the birds grew together into one, their two loves would collapse into concord, a homogeneous compound; their contact would be no contact at all but only the self-satisfaction of a single being containing its all in itself. If the birds remained two, they would be separated into two nodes, locked apart in a relationship, straining for impossible fulfillment. It is one or the other only, according to Reason.

Reason continues its correction of the avian anthem with its threnos. Like the anthem's avowal that "love and constancy is dead," the threnos mourns what the world has lost with the passing of the Phoenix and Turtledove: Truth, Beauty, Rarity, and Grace. Reason seeks to deny the lovers' independent existence by rarifying them into abstractions. By substituting abstractions for the Phoenix and Turtledove, and by announcing that these rational concepts have passed from the world, Reason attempts to assimilate the two birds to itself and to hollow out a melancholy in devotees of the Phoenix and Turtledove. Reason demands that devotees recognize the Phoenix and Turtledove only as rational truths, even the greatest of truths, but they must also recognize that because the two birds are lost to the world; they can be experienced only as an absence to be longed for, so that longing itself is the experience of truth. When all are made to desire the Phoenix and Turtledove, while being made to comprehend themselves in the impossibility of fulfilling that desire, grief becomes a necessary condition of being.

Reason's threnos allows the Phoenix and Turtledove a marginal physical presence, "here enclosed" in "cinders" (55), which functions as a kind of "urn" (65). Reason preserves the lovers as a monument, a hardened site around which the mourners should cluster in loss. Yet the cinders of the Phoenix can never be understood simply as a grave, for they are not "merely an infertile, dead substance, but on the contrary a breeding-ground of new life."[4] And since both birds have "fled / in a mutual flame from hence" (23–24), the fertile remains must belong not only to the Phoenix but also to the Turtledove, who has clearly picked up some tricks. Thus, despite Reason's designation of the cinders as a grave, the cinders defy finality and the promise of mere iteration or reproduction. After all, the Phoenix, typically *the* self-sufficient, singular creature, now has a partner; if it comes back, or if it has gone off somewhere, it has not done so alone. Here, before the mourners, the cinders witness that something has been *left behind*: what remains after everything else has been enclosed by Reason, what signals that the Phoenix and Turtledove must be occurring elsewhere, what attests to the efforts of a ceremony by which something too difficult to observe, too troubling to experience, too titillating, too immediately *present*, is deliberately misplaced—or, more pointedly, shut up.

We must, then, return to the middle, wondering stanzas, to hold open what Reason tried to close. The love that has so confounded Reason shows the Phoenix and Turtledove having "hearts remote, yet not asunder" (29), "two distincts, division none" (27), in which "either was the other's mine" (36) and in whose contact "number . . . in love was slain" (28). Their ecstasy invokes what Shakespeare offers as a non-teleological cluster of possibilities, which I present as four different models of contact or desire, none predominating, in a trajectory toward complete dissolution. In what I present as the first model, of "hearts remote, yet not asunder," the Phoenix and Turtledove enjoy a relationship as two separate birds that are nevertheless perfectly contiguous. This kind of touching or being beside is described in Cary Howie's *Claustrophilia* as "a relationship of contiguity or juxtaposition that would not be reducible to either an antagonism, on the one hand, or simple collapse, on the other."[5] This touching allows the Phoenix and Turtledove to embrace but not to be absorbed into each other, disappeared, or assimilated. Their mutual touching also describes a related mode of contact—Sara Ahmed's queer phenomenology[6]—in which our contact with something, or someone, is reciprocated, in which what we touch touches us back, in which our own touch touches us with the palpable certainty that we are not alone. Touching transforms us by conjuring us into a mutual, mobile being within which, as long as the touch persists, the self is not "the same" (38) as it was prior to contacting the other but in which the self persists as something that can touch, and be touched, by another. This is a relationship of intimate surfaces, a relationship of selves that hold something of themselves, or that are allowed to hold something, in reserve.

"Two distincts, division none" (27) suggests a second mode, where the two birds pass through the borderings, however intimate, of the contact described by Howie and Ahmed without losing their distinct existences. This is less a touching than a disaggregation of boundaries, but not one in which the two selves disappear. Surfaces have been permeated, or have opened up. Here any certainty about the precise borders of self—or, indeed, about self-presence itself—gives way to what Tom Boellstorff calls the "copresence without incorporation" of a queer "meantime."[7] Certainty has yielded, but distinctiveness persists; selves might prove more reluctant to be located, but they can still be found. This is coincidence, co-spatiality, not complete mutual assimilation. It can also be considered through what Howie, drawing on Kaja Silverman, calls "participation,"[8] a merging rather than a mutual touching that proceeds without reduction into one being. This is the intermingling of *being together* rather than the contact of *being with*.

A third model is suggested by "either was the other's mine," a co-presence

in which the Phoenix and Turtledove render inadequate the concept of relationship and, indeed, the spatial relations of interiority and exteriority.[9] Here
there can be no talk of touching, or of the stimulated contact of phenomenology, of surfaces. Nor can there be talk of being together: the "co-" of co-
presence must be deleted, for the birds are entirely with each other, spread
through each other's being, reserving only that property that allows each self
to be given over to the other.

With the passivity of the declaration that "number there in love was slain"
—slain by whom? slain by what?—the two birds model a fourth characterization of eros and its effects, in which self is altogether obliterated. This is a
"radical disintegration and humiliation of the self,"[10] by which the Phoenix
and Turtledove "reject personhood, a status that the law needs [for] discipline"[11] —or, indeed, a status needed for touching, for co-presence, for giving
oneself over. In this utter dissolution, the birds slip away altogether from
Reason's categorization, from the funeral progress, and from the possibility
of death itself. Directed neither at community, conjugality, nor, for that matter, posterity   the very image of the future as child that Edelman has decried
—the birds aim at and preserve nothing. In refusing contact, refusing to maintain even the minimal presence that would either permit or upstage death,
unconcerned with what the flow of beings into each other might bring, and
without even mutual recognition, the birds "trace . . . the untraversable path
that leads to no good and has no other end than an end to the good as such."[12]

Whatever the model of desire, of contact, of presence, of abandonment, of
refusal—though my uncertainty among these requires that I stop speaking of
desire, contact, or presence and write, instead, "whatever is being modeled"
—the truth of the Phoenix and Turtledove is one of neither unification nor
loss. If Reason succeeds in fixing the birds into a coherent single or separated
double existence, then it gives them over to the cinders before which the birds
of death sigh their prayer; if Reason abstracts the Phoenix and Turtledove out
of the flux of this world, Reason will have put them away. Reason requires that
life and its pleasures be conjoined to death and that all existence be sorted into
two realms: for the birds, the mortal, grieving, and supersessionary, and for
Reason, the eternal, transcendent, and static.

But without Reason, confounded, another kind of truth occurs. Having
fled "hence" from Reason, but still being present *on their own terms*, the birds
experience a truth of the moment, continually emerging in different forms,
pressures, and contacts, in being with, being together, or even in the absolute
abandonment of being. This truth in the moment is without lack because it

disorients itself from the dream of fulfillment and from the promise of a future to come when desire might cease in mutual assimilation. This truth defies the absolute; it is not to be anticipated or reasoned; it is here, *now*, in the crowdings of bodies in contact and may even emerge, as in the middle stanzas of the lyric, in the ecstatic participation of watching. Defying fixed being, defying the exclusive adoption of any single mode of eros, the poem provides only one united image: that of pure constancy and pure motion, the emblematic traits of the Turtledove and Phoenix, one always wending undeterred toward the other, and one always coursing toward self-obliteration and unceasing renewal. One present in the world as an actual bird, one present only as a fable, each now is with the other in a conjunction that enacts the impossibility of the fabulous within the mundane itself. Such birds need no posterity, neither the melancholic community that coalesces around the cinders nor children to supplant them and then to arrive in turn at their own deaths. If they have posterity, it is themselves,[13] or this record witnessing both their passion and Reason's attempts to reduce them to oblivion, witnessing, perhaps, even their refusal to witness to anything. Together, the Phoenix and Turtledove create not simply a unity, a duality, or a form fixed in eternity but, rather, an ever shifting, a dedicated, perpetual falling—or soaring—into one another.

Wondering, I return to the opening line to imagine—certainly not to *identify*—the unnamed "bird of loudest lay" as the purportedly dead birds within the other, the singing dove, and the perpetually presencing Phoenix. I refuse to give this bird over to allegory. I want to imagine it becoming with the "sole Arabian tree" (2), whose name in Greek, as Christine Gilham points out, is *"phoinix."* Outside the procession, outside Reason's command, yet still within the poem, I want to imagine this bird at the beginning as a presence that attests to life disoriented away from death's powers and devotees. I want to imagine this bird, this erotic assembly, as the first great refuser of Reason, as being present throughout the procession. I want to imagine this ever shifting, singing structure, whatever it is, as having slipped the confines of Property, as singing at its own funeral, and as finally putting down the ideology of death itself. I want to imagine this being as unknowable but not unheard by a procession that would rather give Reason the last word.

Notes

1. Roe, *The Poems*, 1, 4. Citations in parentheses refer to this edition. The poem first appeared in 1601 in Robert Chester's *Love's Martyr*. Because the dedicatee of the volume, Sir John Salusbury, had ten children, and because both he and his wife, Ursula, were alive when the anthology appeared, it has been usual to try to identify the childless, dead couple of "The Phoenix and Turtle" with other historical figures —for example, Elizabeth and Essex or, more recently, the Catholic martyr Ann Line and her husband, Roger: see Finnis and Martin, "Another Turn for the Turtle." I have preferred to take advantage of the lack of correspondence between the poem and Salusbury to abandon historical allegory entirely.

2. Davies, "The Phoenix and Turtle," 529.

3. Marcuse, "The Ideology of Death," 64.

4. Gilham, "Single Natures Double Name," 127.

5. Howie, *Claustrophilia*, 149.

6. Ahmed, Sara, "Orientations," 551.

7. Boellstorff, Tom, "When Marriage Falls," 243.

8. Howie, *Claustrophilia*, 33.

9. Here I echo Bersani, "Psychoanalysis and the Aesthetic Subject," 170.

10. Idem, "Is the Rectum a Grave?," 217.

11. Idem, *Homos*, 129.

12. Edelman et al., "Conference Debates," 822.

13. Sims, "Shakespeare's *Phoenix and Turtle*," 65.

The Rape of Lucrece

Desire My Pilot Is

PETER COVIELLO

I am willing to concede that this may be little more than my own poverty of imagination talking—of *historical* imagination not least—but it seems to me there is not all that much in "The Rape of Lucrece," Shakespeare's little-cherished narrative poem of 1594, to startle even an ordinarily well-versed latter-day scholar of desire and its queerer errancies. The story the poem tells, in a detail that it is fair at moments to call excruciating, is about the rape and subsequent suicide of the fair and virtuous Lucrece. Or, rather, it tells of the villainous Tarquin's plot to rape Lucrece, of whose beauty and chastity her unwise husband Collatine had bragged; of his agonized deliberation over whether actually to rape her; of Lucrece's pleading with Tarquin and its eventual failure; and of her anguished guilt and horror-stricken consciousness in the aftermath of her rape, which leads her finally, after having secured a vow of revenge from her husband, to suicide. Not, perhaps, the stuff of Wednesday Night Book Group, but neither, in a corpus that includes *Titus Andronicus* and *Troilus and Cressida* (to name only near-to-hand instances of sexual violence), all so out of the ordinary.

I want to suggest here, though, that "The Rape of Lucrece" also rings subtle and, I think, usefully unsettling changes on some of the familiar stories queer studies has been telling itself over the past few decades about *desire*— stories about what, after Leo Bersani, is commonly called desire's "self-shattering" force and about the uses and, especially, the consequences of thinking about desire as that in the self which shatters or exceeds or escapes or otherwise confounds it. This version of desire has been at the core of many of the most exciting, energizing, and incisive sorts of queer critique and queer imagination and, in truth, I have no wish to belittle it. I do think, though, that "The Rape of Lucrece," in its idiosyncratic fashion, asks us to think hard about the story of desire as self-shattering and about what we take it to mean, since a desire in which the familiar and valorized versions of the self all are put to rout is, for the poem's purposes, no good or happy thing. Perhaps most oddly, I want to take this poem and, in particular, the figure of Lucrece—loquacious pleader for her own virtue, loquacious mourner for her lost purity, and a woman bragged about for her beautiful chastity—and use them to make a brief argument, inflected by Freud, about the possible compatibility of self-shattering desire and one of the most seemingly normative forms of sexual regulation, which is also an implied topic of the poem. I mean *monogamy*, the limiting of the self to a single sexual partner, a social practice that, as critics like Laura Kipnis argue with some gusto, tends to asphyxiate the self-renovating force of desire more than otherwise. Shakespeare's brutal and largely joyless poem may offer us one way to think about monogamy—of all unlikely things—as something other than brutal and joyless, and even as something not necessarily not queer.

To begin, then. By now almost everybody knows something about the story of sexuality as "self-shattering." It seems, indeed, if not a cliché of contemporary queer scholarship, then at the very least a notion no longer young. We might trace the idea back to Bersani's extended reading of Freud, particularly of the *Three Essays*, in *The Freudian Body* (1986), although the idea of sex, and especially of gay men's sex, as "self-shattering" would get a more polemical, finally more famous articulation in the essay "Is the Rectum a Grave?" In Bersani's reading of Freud, "sexuality" is the name for a mysterious impulse in the self to pursue intensities of sensation that are not only, for long moments, unpleasurable but in their very intensity are averse to the sustaining of that self's egoic coherence. *"Masochism serves life,"* Bersani asserts, because desire is elementally self-assaulting. Sex in this reading is the turning of the self's erosion, the violent deterioration of its coherence and consistency, into *pleasure*.[1] In "Is the Rectum a Grave?" Bersani extends this reading and links gay men's sex, in its self-shattering aspects, to the radicality of a sex without selves, a sex in which, as Bersani says following Bataille, "the self is exuberantly discarded." Coherent selves are the condition for and of internecine sexual warfare. Since it is *"the degeneration of the sexual into a relationship that condemns sexuality to becoming a struggle for power,"* sex is to be celebrated not as something bucolic and tender but as the violent disruption of the proud selfhood on which *interpersonal* violence depends.[2]

Such, at any rate, is Bersani's story. A perhaps less formally Freudian way into the question comes to us from Adam Phillips, who sees in the unconscious, in its perseverance in dream work and in the errancy of language and in the waywardness of our ever surprising desires, vivid testament to the self's inexhaustible *multiplicity*. The unconscious, that is, stands for Phillips as the storehouse for all of the versions of ourselves that we cannot quite bear to become, or have ceased to be, or that are in too dire conflict with other cathected versions of ourselves to gain conscious audition. Desire in this vein is self-shattering less because of sensory intensities that corrode the ego's boundaries than because it is in sex that we are most powerfully, often terrifyingly *strange* to ourselves. It is in our desire, in other words, that we find ourselves confronted with the aspects of ourselves that most forcefully traduce our deeply invested daylight versions of who we are. Sex, then, is where our most cherished versions of ourselves go to die—or, at least, to be subjected to transgressions and depravities that, if they are not always easy to countenance, nevertheless have the virtue (for Phillips, following Freud) of reminding us how various, how internally various, we are; of keeping the story of ourselves from becoming too complacent, too settled, too entrapping. Desire, in this key, is queer—necessarily the enemy of heteronormativity and its rituals and routines, anchored as they are in marriage, reproduction, and, of course, *monogamy*, that effortful delimiting of the desiring self's rich multiplicity.[3]

"The Rape of Lucrece" sketches out, in an almost diagrammatic way, precisely this version of desire as that which confounds, and puts to pitiful rout, all of the self's sanctioned roles. This is clear enough at the outset of the poem when the narrator describes Tarquin as he plots his assault on Lucrece:

> Such hazard now must doting Tarquin make,
> Pawning his honor to obtain his lust;
> And for himself himself he must forsake.
> Then where is truth if there is no self-trust?
> When shall he think to find a stranger just,
>> When he himself himself confounds, betrays
>> To sland'rous tongues and wretched hateful days?[4]

His plot to rape Lucrece figures here as a kind of self-forsaking, a bitter self-alienation, legible not least in the stuttered locution "himself himself confounds." The specificity of these self-transgressions only grows clearer as his internal debate continues:

> Oh shame to knighthood and to shining arms!
> O foul dishonour to my household's grave!
> O impious act including all foul harms!

> A martial man to be soft fancy's slave!
> True valor still a true respect should have.
>   Then my digression is so vile, so base,
>   That it will live engraven in my face. (197–203)

Tarquin here recognizes himself *as* himself, as knight, as gentleman, as son, as valorous military man. But all of these versions of himself, he comes to see, are traduced by what he *desires*, what he is unable to prevent himself from doing.

Indeed, it is on precisely this point that Lucrece herself pleads with Tarquin, endeavoring in her pleas to recall to him, in effect, the selves he *is*, none of which can accommodate the rape he threatens:

> She conjures him by high almighty Jove,
> By knighthood, gentry, and sweet friendship's oath,
> By her untimely tears, her husband's love,
> By holy human law and common troth,
> By heaven and earth, and all the power of both,
>   That to his borrowed bed he make retire,
>   And stoop to honour, not to foul desire. (568–74)

Or again, more pointedly still:

> In Tarquin's likeness I did entertain thee.
> Hast thou put on his shape to do him shame?
> To all the host of heaven I complain me,
> Thou wrong'st his honour, wound'st his princely name;
> Thou art not what thou seem'st, and if the same,
>   Thou seems not what thou art, a god, a king:
>   For kings like gods should govern everything. (596–602)

Desire interrupts the selves Tarquin knows he should be and of which Lucrece does her terrified best to remind him. In his desire, Tarquin is strange to himself—estranged from himself, Lucrece insists ("To thee, to thee, my heav'd up hands appeal, / Not to seducing lust, thy rash relier . . . / Let him return, and flatt'ring thoughts retire" [638–41])—in a way that, for the purposes of the poem, is a matter of horror and, eventually, tragedy.

But it is desire, finally, that wins the day. Here is how Tarquin settles his argument with himself:

> Then childish fear avaunt, debating die!
> Respect and reason wait on wrinkled age!

> My heart shall never countermand mine eye:
> Sad pause and deep regard become the sage;
> My part is youth, and beats these from the stage.
>   Desire my pilot is, beauty my prize;
> Then who fears sinking where such treasure lies? (274–80)

Desire my pilot is: Knighthood, royal lineage, honor, chivalry, military cama-raderie, filial duty, all perish, or are suspended and held in abeyance, as desire pilots Tarquin (possessed now of a vision of himself as acting the part of an impetuous youth whose *future* might partake of reason and propriety) into the act from which the multiple succeeding tragedies emerge.

There is much to say about this scripting of desire. We might note, before anything else, that it is not a valedictory account of desire as a sort of heroic endeavor or godlike passion. Although not, perhaps, as entirely monitory as it appears in my recounting, the poem nevertheless is not (like *Romeo and Juliet*, say) a nominal condemnation of desire's dangerous impetuosity, beneath which is sustained a complex, in some ways tender, even admiring regard for love's daring or for the breadth and force of its inspiration. Tarquin, here, is a rapist, and what the pursuit of his desire produces, most tangibly, is a veritable ecstasy of anguish in his victim, as Lucrece's hundreds of lines of minutely atomized horror make painfully evident. This, I think, gives a kind of pause, for here is an account of desire as, in ways that have become familiar to us, *queer*—as self-shattering, as that which introduces us to our radical self-vari-ance and to the alarming errancy of the wishes and aims by which we are constituted. But the force of the poem's counter-emphases is hard to miss. First, this is a vision, the poem implies, less of Desire than of specifically *male* desire and, indeed, of a violent patriarchal (and monarchically tyrannical) desire. And there is, too, the unsettling proximity in the poem of a notion of desire as queer—as elementally self-transgressing—and the strong reading of such desire as necessarily conducing toward violence and, finally, rape. To transgress the self is also potentially to transgress any of its ethical entail-ments, which, as the poem takes pains to show, is a state of affairs that does not typically bode well for any of the near-to-hand vulnerable, particularly women. If "The Rape of Lucrece" is in all a poem about desire and its self-shattering force, it is also, I think, a powerfully unconsoling one.

Unconsoling, perhaps, but not necessarily discrediting. Tarquin, after all, is no Everyman. (Indeed, his rapacity is in some ways simply a figure for the illegitimacy of his relation to authority. One does not strain to hear antimonarchical notes in the account of Tarquin's violence and over-reaching avarice.) Neither does the poem begin and end with Tarquin himself—or, for that matter, with his desire. There is, too, Lucrece.

Consider how strange a figure Lucrece cuts in the poem—strange despite the seemingly rote conventionality of her virtuous beauty ("This heraldry in Lucrece' face was seen, / Argued by beauty's red and virtue's white" [64–65]) and of her pleading, then grief, all in the name of one or another species of strict propriety. Indeed, it is not hard to see her as the poem's spokesperson for all of the principles of order, the socially mandated conventionalities, that desire threatens to rupture or damage: feminine chastity, marital duty, duty to heredity, duty to reputation, and so on. She seems to embody nothing so much as the virtues of an almost impossibly comprehensive female social compliance. And yet the preface to the poem tells so odd a story about her. In Ovid's version, on which Shakespeare bases his account, Lucrece is in Tarquin's sights at all not because Collatine has bragged of her surpassing beauty but because she has won, of all Ovidian peculiarities, something like a chastity contest. From Shakespeare's preface:

> The principal men of the army meeting one evening at the tent of Sextus Tarquinius, the King's son, in their discourses after supper everyone commended the virtues of his own wife; among whom Collatinus extolled the incomparable chastity of his wife Lucretia. In that pleasant humor they all posted to Rome, and, intending by their secret and sudden arrival to make trial of that which everyone had before avouched, only Collatinus finds his wife, though it were late in the night, spinning amongst her maids; the other ladies were all found dancing and reveling, or in several disports. Whereupon the noblemen yielded Collatinus the victory, and his wife the fame. (65)

What could it mean to win at chastity? To be bragged about, by a husband, as a wife incomparably chaste? If this is a boast about Lucrece's deep-seated resistance to the errancies of the life of desire, does not that glancingly imply (along with the swaggering confidence of Collatine's *possession* of his wife) something like marital tedium? Can you boast of a desire so anchored in propriety? Is a desire so committedly non-transgressive *desirable*?

By her stark opposition to undutiful Tarquin, that is, Lucrece might seem to us, if not simply sexless, at the very least insulated from the transgressive force of desire in its queerer registers—available to sex, that is, only through compliance, subservience, normative duty, or, finally, violation. In this dutiful, resolutely non-transgressive desire of hers we might find a familiar emblem of monogamy itself as, precisely, sexless, acquiescent, *deadening*. Kipnis, in her riffs on adultery, rises to just this conclusion: Adultery is a kind of heroism for her because monogamy is the most immediate index of the self's paralyzing immiseration by the interlocking routines of heteronormative late-capitalist life. Whatever else it might entail, monogamy stands finally in Kipnis's indictment as a brutal, socially mandated *reduction* of the great swarming variety of selves we are, to which sex is always unsettlingly, life-givingly introducing us.[5] Monogamy for her is the refusal, or evasion, or cancellation of the self-renovating force of desire, desire conceived as elementally self-transgressing.

That is Kipnis's story. But I am not sure it is Shakespeare's, just as I am not sure monogamy and the sorts of self-shattering desire we have been considering are necessarily so opposed, so elementally incompatible. What if, by a different logic, we take seriously the possibility that their bitter expansive grief testifies less to the violation of a cherished social propriety than to the depth of Collatine's and Lucrece's mutual devotion; that Lucrece's boasted-of chastity speaks not of sexlessness but of some other, more obscure relation to desire — desire even in its most forcefully errant, self-displacing, self-multiplying forms? In this admittedly speculative reading, what the poem's boasted-of monogamy might entail is not the evasion of self-variance through strict social compliance, but the finding of a person who somehow countenances both one's cherished and one's indecent selves, who lessens the sense of sharp or unbearable conflict between them; a person who can accept versions of ourselves that we find difficult to bear, who can make room for them, *on our behalf*, among the other versions of self that we hold dear. Monogamy, in this figuring, might be less the deadening de-pluralization of the self Kipnis encourages us to see than the lucky discovery of a person who makes the wildest kinds of internal variance *liveable*, a person who can cherish — as we perhaps cannot — errant, frightening versions of ourselves. So the happiness visible to us in the poem only in its destruction may not represent the opposite or cancellation of Tarquin's experience of desire as self-transgressing. It may speak instead to a monogamy anchored in the mutual ratification of the other's errancy, that thrilling, scary multiplicity each makes *habitable* for the other.[6]

If someone wants to call this a queerer version of monogamy, that is fine by me, though I have no real investment in any such a designation. It seems to me more a mild corrective to a commonplace, oddly sanctimonious theoretical dismissal of monogamy — a corrective that recalls Elizabeth Freeman's wonderful comments about taking seriously "people's longing for [the] relief, the privilege of being ordinary," and her trenchant reminder that "that desire is a powerful one, can take honorable forms, and sometimes results in extraordinary outcomes despite itself."[7] Shakespeare's grim poem, I have tried to suggest, intimates the possibility of a relation between monogamy and desire —desire even in its queerer registers—that is somehow other than fundamentally antagonistic. That, to me, is a little extraordinary.

Notes

1. Bersani, *The Freudian Body*, 39. There is of course a Lacanian back story here as well for those interested in pursuing it, one that would be rooted in the notion of *jouissance*. The work of Lee Edelman and Tim Dean might be cited as prominent in the working out of this Lacanian strand of the story of desire as the scene of the self's dissolution.

2. Idem, "Is the Rectum a Grave?," 218.

3. This vision of desire and the self's multiplicity appears across the range of Adam Phillips's work. Some of its most trenchant articulations appear in *Terrors and Experts*, especially in the chapters "Sexes" and "Authorities," in the latter of which he writes, "When Freud asserted, in his *New Introductory Lectures*, that the patient's symptoms *were* his sexual life, he was speaking up for the inventiveness, the resourcefulness of his patient's sexuality; that we are at our most articulate in our sexuality, because we are at our most puzzling : Phillips, *Terrors and Experts*, 30.

4. Prince, "The Rape of Lucrece," lines 155–61. The page and line numbers cited in parentheses are from this edition.

5. Kipnis, "Adultery."

6. Here the speculativeness of this reading, perhaps even the *fanciful* speculativeness, comes to the fore. We would have to believe, on precious little textual evidence beyond his lacerating grief, that Collatine is as monogamous in his relation to Lucrece as Lucrece is in her relation to him.

7. Freeman, "Still After," 497.

Richard II

Pretty Richard (in Three Parts)

JUDITH BROWN

First Part: I (Aesthetics, Tongues, History)

Pater loved him, as did Yeats; Auden less so, although he acknowledged that Richard of Bordeaux was gifted with poetry, if not with brains. Most critics have agreed that what makes Richard II great is his lyricism, his escape, as Auden puts it, into language. Richard is best a poet, not a king. Richard speaks in gorgeous verse, unusual in itself for a history play, yet his word-fondling tongue has also made him an object of some suspicion: as one mid-twentieth-century critic complained, he "calls out the latent homosexuality of critics."[1] The play does not pussyfoot around the homosexuality the king calls out in his court. Bolingbroke (who speaks in a more butch prose) suggests sodomy in the "foul wrongs" of Richard's courtiers that "made a divorce betwixt his queen and him."[2] But is there more to these "sinful hours" (3.1.12) shared between men? Was the homophobic critic right? Does Richard call out to the critically queer? And what does he say? Richard's verse lends itself to ears attuned to alternative narratives, to hidden spaces of desire, to bent history, and to tales pulled out of standard temporality. This essay argues that Richard speaks less to his contemporaries than to those who would listen in time out of order, who share Richard's "daintiness of ear" (5.5.45) and predilection for pretty phrases and who thus confirm his rule over their critical senses.

Perhaps Pater knows best. Father of sorts to queer aesthetics, Pater writes that Richard, of all of Shakespeare's kings, "is the most sweet-tongued of them all." "What a garden of words!" he exclaims and, with a flourish that rivals Richard's own, claims that lyric poetry "preserves the unity of a single passionate ejaculation."[3] Richard's poetry delivers just that through the play's most highly ranked organ, that vital instrument of Richard's reign: the tongue. If there is a part that stands for the whole in this play, it is the tongue, and it is Richard's tongue as it shapes, forms, fondles, and luxuriates over the words that have, for centuries, excited his critics. At times eager, daring, double, and moving, the tongue is an active agent, although it can also be care-tuned, unwilling, and finally silent. The tongue is queer, as Carla Mazzio suggests without saying so explicitly in her history of the "sinful organ," and it plays across the surface of this particular history. The tongue encodes "crises of logic, of language, and of sense" and is, in its early modern representations, argues Mazzio, "disruptive" and a site of "collective self-estrangement."[4] The tongue is particularly attuned to surfaces—whether through texture, heat, taste, or the shaping of smooth syllables—and thus is the site of eroticized pleasure and of power as the instrument of language. The very queerness of the tongue is located in its unboundaried demand, its refusal to accede to the limits of form, its traversing of thresholds in the name of desire. The law has no place in the language of the tongue; instead, the mobile organ reorganizes law, creates for itself a world open to and thirsting for new realms of possibility.

One might indeed wax poetic on the many possibilities of the tongue, that purest organ of sensuality. After all, it is the tongue over which one rolls one's wine, sucks one's sweets, creates a garden of sensory pleasure. It delivers the surface in surprising and tactile ways, it shapes, it fondles, it dishes up a world of superficial pleasures. The tongue, for Richard, is the site of rich complication: It delivers his pleasures, and shapes ours, through the lyric words, the delicious lines, he offers us. It is the pleasure of form itself, after all, that the tongue provides, of beautifully rendered rhetoric, the black marks on the page lifting themselves into our mouths, demanding reshaping, rehearsing, through our tongues. For who does not read Richard aloud, enjoying not just the pleasure of speech but the pleasure of sound, of form, as those gorgeous words take shape once more, as if Richard lives anew in his reader? Richard's tongue forges our most passionate connection to the king, our enduring pleasure in the words he so sweetly mouths.

That sweet tongue is thus the shared sign of pleasure—sensual, poetic, rhetorical, formal—and yet, and yet this is the complication, it will also be the instrument of Richard's demise as king, his untimely commands, his disproportionate demands. Richard's unguarded tongue will lead to his unguarded reign, a reign more thoroughly, openly, and delightedly sensual than it is cautious, abstemious, or juridical. Richard is many things in this play, not all of which are defined by the roving interest of his tongue, yet he is defined by his tastes in drink, in men, in gay apparel, in gorgeous surroundings, in jewels, in pretty words. Indeed, he is the superficial king, the king of glam. All Richard wants is a world tailored to his desires, an Earth that will support him in this, that will rise up against any who might take his pleasures away.

In fact, the play only just *alludes* to Richard's pleasures—what it actually narrates is their loss and Richard's painful struggle to understand, then inhabit, this loss. As his monarchal power dissipates, his rhetorical power increases—the tongue gains ground as it becomes the sole site of pleasure even as it mouths the pain of dissolution, of the unmaking of a king. This, then, is the tongue untied as it negotiates a magnitude of loss that defies understanding. The tongue is untied as the king is undone; in fact, Richard forgoes his place in history so that he may speak without the constrictions of identity: "Ay, no; no, ay: for I must nothing be. / Therefore no, no, for I resign to thee. / Now, mark me how I will undo myself" (4.1.200–2). To enter Richard II is to enter negative space, a queer cavity of undoing. Unkinged, undecked, unmanned, undone, Richard floats free of history, in all of its baseness, and into the more fitting sovereignty of queer aesthetics. Queer aesthetics thus hinges on undoing, on the mobility of form, on the making and remaking of boundaries that it might mouth its desires, making them come alive with the force of a beautiful utterance.

If Richard's language becomes progressively more beautiful as he struggles with loss—that of his crown, his identity, his place—it is the beauty of disjuncture, of difficulty, of struggle, and of negation. The king seems to recognize this—his beauteous face becomes his beauteous verse—when he demands a mirror:

> Give me the glass, and therein will I read.
> No deeper wrinkles yet? Hath Sorrow struck
> So many blows upon this face of mine,
> And made no deeper wounds? O, flatt'ring glass! . . .
>   [throws glass down.]
> For there it is, cracked in a hundred shivers.
> Mark, silent king, the moral of this sport:
> How soon my sorrow hath destroyed my face. (4.1.275–78, 288–90)

Richard marks his continued prettiness in the face of sorrow, a false relation between inside and outside, a disjuncture between seen and unseen with an intervening layer of flattery. The unseen carries the power, and he theatrically smashes the glass to the floor, cracking it into a hundred shivers, the shivers that mark the undoing of a body, the convulsions that interrupt its coherence and provide a visual form of disjuncture. It is a virtual exercise, a remaking himself into the reflected image, destroying one with the other. Richard finds his tongue in the mirror's shattered pieces and gathers himself up from the space of disjuncture, speaking in the face of his broken face, now multiplied, incoherent, and poetic. The shattering of Richard is figured against the stolid silence of Bolingbroke, a multiplicity figured against a unity. Yet the broken lines of glass present the exquisite lines of poetry, the formal intervention that seeks aesthetic solace from sorrow.

Second Part: –I (Sovereignty, Pleasure, Dissolution)

This is all very poignant—the shattered glass, Richard's performance of sorrow—but it is Richard's dissolution in the form of drunken carousing that leads to his Dissolution, the deposing of the king in this play. Is this a Just Dissolution or just dissolution, upper and lower case, high court or base, the realm of abstract ideals or that of physical pleasures? Richard's impulses, we know, are for a gratification of the senses. Once challenged, he dissolves into self-pity, self-indulgence, theatricality, and fear, and who could blame him, knowing what he is up against? The play understands the artifice of king, the show that the office demands, the performance of divine right even in the face of overwhelming odds. As Richard unwinds into fear, he is encouraged to play more convincingly the part he was born into: Act as king and you will be king. Aumerle will counsel "remember who you are," and his queen will sadly chastise, "Wilt thou, pupil-like, / Take the correction mildly, kiss the rod" (5.1.31–32). When the queen says this, however, Richard's last "fair show" (3.3.70) has already been staged on a balcony at Flint Castle. This is his last convincing act as king, speaking out to his audience assembled below and using the rich plural of royal prerogative before he is called to the base court where he is debased—unbased, as it were—having already lost his base as king, and soon as Richard. He understands this, even as he commands his audience from the balcony: "[to Aumerle] We do debase ourselves, cousin, do we not, / To look so poorly and to speak so fair?" (3.3.126–27). Thus begins the descent; the fair words here will lead to another language of unremembering:

> O God! O God! that e'er this tongue of mine,
> That laid the sentence of dread banishment
> On yon proud man, should take it off again
> With words of sooth! O, that I were as great
> As is my grief, or lesser than my name!

> Or that I could forget what I have been!
> Or not remember what I must be now! (3.3.132–38)

The six exclamations here remind us of the difficulty of his task, to unremember. Richard recognizes the closing circle as his tongue delivers the words "O God! O God!" The tongue, both victim and perpetrator in this passage, must become the passionate instrument of negation, of undoing, of movement away from what was and into a far less determinate space.

It is sad, of course, for the fair king to fall from the hearts of his public, to lose so big to Bolingbroke. Yet it is not unjust—he has not just ordered murders but wasted vast sums and compensated by raising taxes and stealing property to fund his profligacy. But can we find another kind of justice in Richard: a justice of the tongue, a justice out of time, a relation to the ear that demands re-hearing or rehearsing in another time and place? Or perhaps to combine the two meanings of just dissolution, one might see that the dissolution—the giving over to pleasure—is Just, an abstract ideal, a commitment to something beyond the power of sovereignty. Richard's garden of words in Pater's frothy estimation is justice served, a justice of the tongue delivered to later generations of aesthetes. Here we might find a kind of productive anachrony in time out of joint, something Jacques Derrida spins out in his work on Marx, asking: "Is not disjuncture the very possibility of the other?"[5] Derrida's question, hardly directed to questions of aesthetics, still might illuminate the question of justice in *Richard II*. "Is not disjuncture the very possibility of the other?" Richard seems hardly a model for the other, drunken with luxury, in the seat of power, with a star-laden lineage. And he is no obvious model for justice. But in his struggle to give it all up, to give himself up, to undo identity, to "undeck the pompous body of a king" (4.1.249), Richard attempts something significant, even if it comes about by force. To undeck. This is to divest of ornaments first, but also to remove something fundamental: the floor, his base, the foundations of not just a king but of a man in time. Richard is removed, one might say, from his lineage and from a justice bound up in the enforcement of royal power. Instead, he finds his home in the disjuncture of time, the removal from one moment in time—the time of history—and into an unboundaried, shattered time, a time that plays across history and into the willing ears of those who would hear differently.

Undecking, undoing, unmaking: These are the verbs that at this point in the play frame Richard. In the pain of solitude of his final imprisonment at

Pomfret Castle, Richard plays through a variety of roles, trying to find himself and, therefore, some quick exit from his present humiliation:

> Thus play I in one person many people,
> And none contented; sometimes am I king,
> The treasons make me wish myself a beggar,
> And so I am. Then crushing penury
> Persuades me I was better when a king.
> Then am I kinged again and, by and by,
> Think that I am unkinged by Bolingbroke,
> And straight am nothing. (5.5.31–38)

Richard may play I but cannot sustain the one or the many. None of the roles will fit, and he struggles to accept his status as nothing. "And straight," he says, "am nothing," removing the "I" itself from the formulation. He may put on new roles, but he is inevitably reminded of his fate, becoming nothing straightaway. And if straight he is nothing, he leaves room for a queer something. He will find that something on the tip of his tongue, as words of despair unfurl to signal a different layer of power that will not aid him in his descent and will not hold off his imminent murder. The words shed no power, then, within Richard's string of time but offer themselves up to the disordered string where we might also benefit from this monarch's undoing. Time might waste Richard, the man, but time out of order offers more to us. And what might that be? Certainly, he offers beauty over heroism, frailty over brute strength, passion over armored indifference. But nothing here commends Richard to history; nothing endures. And in that nothing, we have Richard's greatest offering.

Third Part: – –I (Identity, Negation, Justice)

Richard throws the mirror down in an act of negation. The mirror images of negation—two negatives, "ay, no; no, ay"; therefore, "no, no"—create a vast and timeless universe of virtual nothing and a transformation by way of form. "The shadow of your sorrow," offers Bolingbroke, hath destroyed the shadow of your face" (4.1.291–92). Negative on negative, shadow on shadow, Richard has formally been undone, removed from office, denied his freedom, reduced thus in one sense but opening out in another. Just as Derrida searches for the site of radical possibility in the other, Richard achieves a kind of otherness in his human unmaking, his movement into nothing:

> But whate'er I be,
> Nor I, nor any man that but man is,
> With nothing shall be pleased, till he be eased
> With being nothing. (5.5.38–41)

Pleased and eased in rhyming relationship that requires nothing, the un-grounding of this or any man, the easing into a different relation with the self, with experience, with historical circumstance. In Derrida's inquiry into the possibilities for justice, the disadjustment he situates in the other that I cited earlier, he asks: "How to distinguish between two disadjustments, between the disjuncture of the unjust and the one that opens up the infinite asymme-try of the relation to the other, that is to say, the place for justice?"[6] That space might be tiny, as tiny as two letters: "ay, no; no, ay; no, no." Also as tiny as the prefix that negates in two letters Richard's life: the "un" that marks dissolu-tion. This is the sovereign prefix that makes up one quarter of all prefixes in English,[7] undoing nouns and their adjectives, creating verbs and participles in negative form. "Un" signals opposition, contrariness, negation, privation, and absence. In his undoing, unkissing, undecking, and unkinging, Richard opens up a place for justice, perhaps, a radical asymmetry between what was and all that remains. One must appreciate the disjunctures to appreciate Richard as poet, Richard as another kind of sovereign. Ethics here are located not in any reciprocal exchange, in some version of winged Justice, but in the asymmetrical gaps, the pinpricks opened up, for example, by *Richard II's* sovereign prefix, "un."

Aesthetics play a role in that space, in that asymmetrical gap. The queer tale of the "disordered string" in its movement away from the norms of chronology, of history, of narrative opens up by way of disjuncture, by way of the nothing whose form itself wafts across the centuries. Richard finds this form in the poetic line, tuned to a pitch or frequency particularly suited to queer readings that look to the not yet of history, to queer potential, to alter-native endings. Ay, no; no, ay. Therefore no, no. Double negatives produce a positive, critically positive in their excess of negativity, and mark a move that is necessarily less determined. Deck, kiss, king (the stems) are not neutralized but made potent with the addition (really a subtraction) of "un." The tongue is master of this move, unkissing and reordering its relations with the world. Time out of joint here is time attuned to queer criticism, to justice newly aligned with aesthetics, to the possibilities of form broken free from the con-straints of the law.

The transcendence of Richard's final scene begs a few questions: Is Richard's transformation by way of the "un" a mark of transcendence? Does "queer" itself become a transcendent term, lifted away from bodies, sexualities, conventional histories? Richard's dying words, to be sure, mark his rise to a seat on high, undone as human, achieving something un-human or extra-human, his place as virtual king:

> Mount, mount, my soul; thy seat is up on high,
> Whilst my gross flesh sinks downward here to die. (5.6.111–12)

Richard, in his last moments, recognizes another last act and another final performance. Is this transcendence or an artful bow by a master actor in rhyming couplets? The transcendent, in its movement away from pain, guilt, and various sordid realities, has its appeal, of course. First, it is so clean. But Richard's sweet tongue, the tongue that ungrounds the play, also maintains its ground, maintains a relation to the sensual, the erotic, the articulated pleasures Pater so exuberantly associated with the play. Richard, in ways, still holds on to the mirrored pieces, finding a reflection that suits. And straight he is nothing. And straight, nothing. In his final words, Richard performs multiple feats. He bows to history and offers up his death; he performs a vision of greatness as he transcends the base Earth and its gross flesh; and he reminds us of that flesh and its extraordinary command of pleasure—particularly our pleasure—as we listen, daintily, to Richard's last and lasting words.

Notes

1. A. P. Rossiter, quoted in Muir, *Richard II*, xxviii.
2. Ibid., 3.1.12, 14–15. Citations in parentheses are to this edition.
3. Pater, "Shakespeare's English Kings," 191, 198.
4. Mazzio, "Sins of the Tongue in Early Modern England."
5. Derrida, *Specters of Marx*, 26.
6. Ibid., 26.
7. The count of prefixed words appears in Carroll et al., *The Word Frequency Book*.

Richard III

Fuck the Disabled: The Prequel

ROBERT MCRUER

The queer pleasures of Richard Loncraine's film version of William Shakespeare's *Richard III* (1995) might be said to originate in the men's toilets.[1] Or, rather, in Loncraine's jump cut to the toilets from a lavish ballroom packed with people. Loncraine's *Richard III*, while retaining Shakespeare's plot and language, is stylized to evoke a proto-fascist Britain in the 1930s. With big band music in the background, peace, harmony, and their correlates—the joys of heterosexual communion and family life—are being celebrated in the ballroom scene with laughter, children playing, and ladies and gentleman dancing. There are, of course, no necessary links between peace and harmony and heterosexual and familial bliss, but in this setting as in so many others the former are represented as natural outcomes of the latter. With the stage thus set, Loncraine splits Richard's famous opening soliloquy: Instead of using the Shakespearean stage directions that would have Richard entering and speaking alone, Loncraine makes half of the lines public (in the ballroom) and half of them private (in the toilets). Lee Edelman has characterized the men's room as "the site of a particular heterosexual anxiety about the potential inscriptions of homosexual desire,"[2] and Loncraine queerly exploits that anxiety, implying that something perverse emanating from the toilets will indeed disrupt all that is happy, harmonious, and heterosexual.

Before the jump cut, Richard of Gloucester (played by the gay actor Ian McKellan, who co-wrote the screenplay with Loncraine) commemorates, to a room delighted by his urbane wit, the fact that "the winter of our discontent" has ended and been made "glorious summer" by a son ("sun") of York. Richard's brother King Edward IV (John Wood), in other words, has emerged victorious from the hostilities between the warring houses of Lancaster and York.[3] Richard's seduction of his audience in this speech culminates with a wink toward Edward's heterosexual prowess:

And now, instead of mounting barbèd steeds
To fright the souls of fearful adversaries,
He capers nimbly in a lady's chamber
To the lascivious pleasing of a lute. (1.1.10–13)

As this section of Richard's famous speech concludes, however, Loncraine cuts to the toilets, and in that private or semiprivate space (no one is present, but, of course, another man could enter at any time and be privy to what Richard has to offer), Richard reveals what we knew or suspected all along: Perversions of the heterosexual and familial excess we have just witnessed are afoot, even if not immediately legible in the lines we have just heard. A few of Richard's remaining lines are delivered as he stands speaking over his shoulder at the urinal, and the rest are spoken directly into the camera. Although Richard's disability—a misshapen back and paralyzed arm—has been visible before this moment (as he moves through the crowds at the dance), at the urinal it is centralized. With his one functional arm, Richard unzips his fly and begins to piss. As he does so, he continues to speak, and his back is, for the first time, positioned center screen.

For most scholars in disability studies, perhaps only Charles Dickens's pitiful Tiny Tim is a more universally hated figure. Richard III is thus, from a certain critically disabled perspective, one of the two most despised characters in literature. Even though it paradoxically redoubles the hatred an ideal audience is already supposed to have for Richard, this distaste for Richard in disability studies is not particularly difficult to comprehend, given the ways in which his "monstrous" body logically explains his monstrous deeds. His "deformity," in other words, is generally causally connected to his evil machinations.

At the urinal and to the camera in Loncraine's *Richard III*, McKellan amplifies that two-dimensional causal connection, with very little revision of Shakespeare's lines:

But I, that am not shaped for sportive tricks,
Nor made to court an amorous looking glass;
I, that am rudely stamped. . . .
Deformed, unfinished, sent before my time
Into this breathing world scarce half made up,
And that so lamely and unfashionable
That dogs bark at me as I halt by them—
Why, I, in this weak piping time of peace,
Have no delight to pass away the time,

> Unless to espy my shadow in the sun
> And descant on mine own deformity. . . .
> And therefore, since I cannot prove a lover . . .
> I am determinèd to prove a villain
> And hate the idle pleasures of these days. (1.1.14–31)

Because of his disability, Richard is a misfit in a time that apparently delights in beautiful and fashionable images. Richard thus hates the future portended by the son of York on the throne and villainously chooses to eschew the vacuous sunny disposition—and tiresome celebrations of heterosexuality in general— that the times demand.

David T. Mitchell and Sharon L. Snyder provide the most complete disability studies analysis of *Richard III*, arguing that, over and over, actors and scholars have approached the play in ways that "express a compulsion to verify or disprove a psychology of disability."[4] Mitchell and Snyder, for instance, cite Constance A. Brown's analysis of Laurence Olivier's *Richard III* (1954). For Brown, Olivier demonstrates that Richard's "quest for power is a substitute for normal sexual behavior," which his deformity has of course precluded.[5] Mitchell and Snyder read McKellan's Richard differently; in a recognizable and yet indispensable disability studies vein, they emphasize that McKellan's interpretation, as he emphasizes in an interview, demonstrates that "Richard's wickedness is an outcome of other people's disaffection with his physique."[6]

Brown's analysis conserves both normalcy and the facile equation of disability and wickedness. McKellan, as Mitchell and Snyder see it, provides a reparative interpretation; McKellan, in other words, puts forward an essentially liberal interpretation that demonstrates that it is not the individual, but an ableist society, that is responsible for Richard's evil. Neither the conservative nor the liberal interpretation of Richard, however, does justice to the queer pleasures of the men's room, to Richard's sneering at the compulsory heterosexuality he has just witnessed in the ballroom. These queer pleasures, I argue, are crip pleasures as well, with "crip" signifying not simply an identitarian complement or alternative to dominant forms of embodiment but, rather, the will to undo compulsory able-bodiedness. Liberal deployments of "disability" generally position it not simply as ability's diminished, inauthentic, or invalid twin but as a positive, substantive, *authentic* alternative to able-bodiedness. Crip perspectives are not as invested in substance or authenticity as in processes that unsettle, unravel, and unmake straightness, broadly conceived. Thus, if compulsory able-bodiedness calls for sportive tricks, nimble dancing, and amorous heterosexual cruising, it is hard—from a queer / crip vantage point—not to be seduced by the promise of Richard's "lamely and unfashionable" deflation of all of that. If, even for an orgasmic moment, he can expose the ways in which the marriage of compulsory heterosexuality and compulsory able-bodiedness has no future, it is hard not to find him kind of hot.

From a liberal perspective, then, McKellan may be justified in his Disability Studies 101 argument, relocating the "problem" of disability from the impaired body to an unaccommodating society. Yet in his dutiful reproduction of that argument, McKellan misses or sacrifices what is most seductive about his own performance. A liberal recognition of poor Richard's exclusion from society sacrifices the pleasures emanating from his anti-futural plots in the toilets or from his unrepentant and ecstatic (perhaps even mad) laughter at the end as he falls to a fiery death after being shot by Richmond (Dominic West). Academics "often miss," McKellan goes on to insist in the interview, "what actors discover, that Shakespeare fleshed out those types and made them human."[7] Yet perhaps even disabled or gay actors like McKellan, when they are essentially making a plea for inclusion in the category "human," often miss what is delightfully queer and crip about the figures they must represent and about the destructive (yet compelling) processes those figures set in motion.

The antisocial thesis in queer theory has no clear analogue in disability studies as it is currently constituted, even though crips, like queers, are in fact figures "phobically produced precisely to represent," as Edelman puts it, "the force that shatters the fantasy of Imaginary unity."[8] Wherever and whenever able bodies project themselves into a future, imagining both that their health, beauty, and ability will last forever and that their children will somehow guarantee this, a crip will be phobically produced to threaten that happy future. Everyone, after all, wants a "healthy baby"—"little pretty ones," as Queen Elizabeth describes her own boys (4.2.109). But that fantasy of the healthy baby, made eerily literal through the "healthy baby" contests that first emerged during the *actual* proto-fascist era of eugenics, is always threatened by the crip child who comes into the world scarce half made up. Authentic disabled people, of course, can and should make claims for inclusion in that world, but inauthentic crips, "lumps of foul deformity . . . inhuman and unnatural," to borrow Lady Anne's words right before she is temporarily captivated by Richard's inauthenticity, cannot (1.2.59, 62).

One dominant line of disability theorizing would place contemporary dis-ability performance in direct opposition to the legacy of characters such as Richard III and Tiny Tim, offering proud (and substantive) disability identi-ties in place of pitiful or evil figurations. As Carrie Sandahl and Philip Aus-lander argue, in an award-winning and indispensable anthology on disability and performance, "Disabled performers and theater artists have rejected these [stereotypical] scripts and created work based on their own experiences, challenging both tired narrative conventions and aesthetic pratices."[9] Yet cer-tain crip performances, McKellan's among them (even if he does not always avow it), embrace the antisocial and accept what Edelman terms, in an image that provocatively calls to mind a back bent over or crippled, the "figural burden" we have inherited and are compelled to occupy.[10]

The performance artist Greg Walloch's "Fuck the Disabled" is one exam-ple, and I want to put forward two arguments in a brief consideration of it, arguments that I hope contribute to the ongoing queering of disability studies and the necessary cripping of queer theory.[11] First, reading the figures con-jured up in "Fuck the Disabled" through *Richard III* makes it possible to see crip processes at work whenever any body is phantasmatically figured as healthy, able, and normal. Second, blasphemously reading *Richard III* as a sort of prequel to "Fuck the Disabled" allows crips and queers to take pleasure in representations of any and every normal body's undoing. Neither conserva-tive fantasies about disabled bodies nor liberal refutations of those fantasies allow for that pleasure.

"I was sitting at brunch with a friend of mine," Walloch begins. "She said, 'Greg, can I ask you a personal question? . . . Is the reason that you're gay due to the fact that you're crippled and you can't get lucky with women, so you had no other choice but to sleep with men for sex?'" Walloch pauses briefly and then continues:

> I looked at her and was like: "Are you reading my mind? I was just thinking about that! Yes, that is *exactly* the reason I sleep with men. It's a sad story, my life. You see, underneath it all I'm actually a heterosexual man, but because of my unfortunate, grotesque disfigurement I was shunned by women and polite society and forced into the depravity of the under-ground world of man-to-man sex. I never much cared for sucking dick, but if I wanted any action I had better get used to it."
>
> I never wanted to be gay. I tried to fight it, but soon I found I'd devel-oped a strange addiction to crack . . . a different kind of crack. You know,

the sacrifices the disabled have to make in this country today because of lack of acceptance are unbelievable! If you're disabled, don't make the same mistakes I did. Don't let this happen to you.

Like Richard, Walloch "cannot prove a lover" and is therefore unfit for "the idle pleasures of these days." And although he inhabits the figure of the pitiful crip rather than the evil crip ("It's a sad story, my life," "Don't let this happen to you"), Richard can easily be positioned here as Tiny Tim's evil twin. Both are figures from polite society's worst nightmare; both are spatially positioned—in the toilets, in the depravity of the underground world of man-to-man sex—apart from that society. And perversions, for both, are causally connected to their monstrous bodies or "grotesque" disfigurements.

Yet both, the straight fantasy suggests, might be cured, rehabilitated, or—if necessary—eliminated. Walloch thus responds to the sad state of affairs he has described by establishing his own foundation, Fuck the Disabled. "If you're a woman eighteen to thirty-five," he suggests, "call us at 212-DIS-ABLE":

> Are you attracted to subservient men? Well, crippled guys can barely stand up. Have you had bizarre sexual fantasies involving a midget or several midgets? We can help. And you know what they say about mentally retarded men? Small intellect, big . . . you know what I'm talking about.
>
> So call us: 212-DIS-ABLE. Fuck the disabled [pause] to keep the disabled from turning gay.

Was ever woman in this humor wooed? Was ever woman in this humor won? Momentarily, at least, yes, as the DVD version of "Fuck the Disabled" cuts to a woman arriving at Walloch's apartment, claiming that she is there because of the advertisement. With the New York artist Cottonhead singing, "Fuck me, 'cause it makes me think you love me," in the background, Walloch and the woman have sex as part of Walloch's reparative therapy ("Nope, still gay," Walloch says at the end).

Richard's lines following his successful wooing of Lady Anne seem so appropriate for Walloch's sketch because both performances position heterosexuality, naturally linked to able-bodiedness, as a laughable ruse. As Richard suggests after Anne has fallen for his fabricated declarations of true love, amorous heterosexual relations seem to be more appropriate for men like Anne's late husband Edward (whom Richard murdered):

> A sweeter and a lovelier gentleman,
> Framed in the prodigality of nature,

> Young, valiant, wise, and, no doubt, right royal,
> The spacious world cannot again afford. (1.2.263–66)

Both performances, moreover, present audiences with faces of inauthenticity; as both crips turn toward their interlocutors, they appear to acquiesce to the normative, rehabilitative desire for a world without perversion. The pleasure audiences experience in the performances, however, comes from the knowledge that "irrefutable, organic, and material deviance" nonetheless remains right beneath the surface.[12] Lady Anne might not express a desire to fuck the disabled to keep the disabled from turning gay, but her effusive, "Much it joys me too / To see you become so penitent" (1.2.238–39) is almost as ridiculous, and audiences know it.

Although, at least as far as Loncraine's *Richard III* would have it, even if Anne *did* plan to pity fuck Richard to keep him from turning gay, or simply to keep him straight in the most far-reaching sense of the word, her strategy is bound to fail. Just two scenes later, in a passage revised from Shakespeare's text (some of the lines are Shakespeare's but they are moved forward in the drama), Richard approaches James Tyrell (Adrian Dunbar), who will serve not just as the murderer of the princes (as in Shakespeare's version) but of Clarence and, indeed, of pretty much anyone Richard wants to have eliminated (in a faithfulness unparalleled in *Richard III*, the male–male pairing that commences in this scene lasts through the entire film). A palpable erotic energy hangs in the air between the two men, and the lines they exchange are made to drip with sexual innuendo (fueled both by McKellan's brilliant performance and, no doubt, by what audiences think that they know about his off-screen sexual desires). After seeing Tyrell and saying, "I partly know the man," Richard ambles over to a pen where Tyrell is feeding apples to the boars. (The boar is Richard's symbol.) The dialogue is essentially Shakespearean, even if it would be as appropriate at the Eagle or the Ramrod. And it proceeds without any of the pretense that characterized Richard's "wooing" of Lady Anne—no declarations of undying love here, and no confusion about who is the top:

> *Richard*: Is your name Tyrell?
> *Tyrell*: James Tyrell [pause]. And your most obedient servant.
> *Richard* [clearly pleased, and smiling lasciviously]: Are you, indeed?
> *Tyrell* [slowly]: Prove me, my gracious Lord.

Tyrell then hands Richard an apple, perhaps—since this couple's origins are so clearly satanic—in an antisocial embrace of the right-wing, homophobic chest-

nut that God did not create Adam and Steve. In and through that damning
exchange, and the knowing glances that accompany it, their bond is sealed.

Fuck Richard III, scholars and activists have essentially told us. Fuck the
disabled figures we have inherited from an ableist literary tradition. This
essay, in the end, takes that injunction a bit more literally and risks finding
Richard sexy and queer—in and through the deformity that has made him
evil. It also suggests that the crip processes of refusal most famously figured
by Richard III, determined to prove a villain and hate the idle pleasures of
dull, straight days, are inevitably at work in a range of queer performances
that do not simply counter conservative ideas about disability or humanize
those most affected by them (as important as those well-established critical
projects might be), but that instead sneer at or piss on the unnatural (and
always doomed) union of heterosexuality and able-bodiedness.

Notes

1. Richard Loncraine, dir., *Richard III*, DVD, United Artists, Los Angeles, 1995.

2. Edelman, *Homographesis*, 160.

3. Mowat and Werstine, *The Tragedy of Richard III*, 1.1.1–2. Cites in parentheses are
to this edition.

4. Mitchell and Snyder, *Narrative Prosthesis*, 113.

5. Quoted ibid.

6. Quoted ibid., 116.

7. Ibid.

8. Edelman, *No Future*, 22.

9. Sandahl and Auslander, "Introduction," 4.

10. Edelman, *No Future*, 22.

11. Eli Kabillio, dir., *Fuck the Disabled*, DVD, Mad Dog Films, New York, 2001.

12. Snyder, "Unfixing Disability in Lord Byron's *The Deformed Transformed*," 272.

Romeo and Juliet

Romeo and Juliet Love Death

CARLA FRECCERO

If the project of queering Shakespeare entails the effort to confront, analyze, challenge normativities of form, method, ideology, sexuality, and reception, where better to go a-queering than *Romeo and Juliet*? It is a peculiar play, one that simultaneously ironizes and idealizes youthful romantic heterosexual love. Its citations—citabilities—and traces infiltrate our radios and iPods, not to mention our love affairs, whether gay or straight, with ideological injunctions to submit to Jacques Lacan's characterization of the superegoic commandment—all too often these days adopted by restaurant waitstaff—to "enjoy!" It is against this imperative that my efforts to dislocate *Romeo and Juliet* are directed.

Over a decade ago, Jonathan Goldberg engaged in some serious queering and crux cracking when he tackled the "open Rs" of the texts of *Romeo and Juliet*.[1] My commentary builds on his work. I also owe a debt to Lee Edelman, whose *No Future* helped me figure out why this play—and the *Romeo + Juliet* (1996) that Baz Luhrmann directed—so overwhelmingly captures the driving negativity of teen spirit while masquerading as a story about the tragic interruption of idealized romantic heterosexual love across barriers of social difference.[2] Madhavi Menon's argument about the anti-normative teleological force of Shakespeare's *Venus and Adonis* and that poem's formal and thematic investments in failure also shapes my thinking.[3]

The modern romantic reading of *Romeo and Juliet*, enshrined, for example, in movies such as *West Side Story* and Franco Zeffirelli's 1968 film, understands it to be a story about youthful love as a force that resists the demands of the social in the name of pure absolutes, demonstrating—didactically, sacrificially—the triumph of heterosexual love (construed here, unusually, as sameness) over social "difference."[4] Likewise, it is a story about the transcendence of the individual over the interests of the group and kin. Modernity's reading of this play also stages the political in order, precisely, to oppose love to it and thereby mystify love as beyond and elsewhere than politics.

Sexuality studies scholars and queer theorists, focusing on early modern homoerotics, pave the way for a reading of this tale as a romantic comedy gone awry, a story about a young man struggling to leave the homosocial pack whose bonds of blood (-sport) militate against the normative demands of adult heterosexual marriage. This reading has received its analytics from the work of Eve Kosofsky Sedgwick on homosociality among men; from Valerie Traub's study of female homosociality in Shakespeare; and from Michael Rocke's historical discussion of youthful aristocratic homoerotic male communities in Renaissance Florence, among others.[5] Some postmodern interpretations, such as Luhrmann's, attuned to these homoerotics, extend the "sameness" implicit in the play's take on love to sexual difference, setting up in oppositional and asymmetrical (yet equally sacrificial, equally tragic, equally romantic) relations same- and opposite-sex love in the couples Mercutio–Romeo and Romeo–Juliet. Alan Bray's *The Friend*, a study of early modern enduring and amorous bonds of male same-sex friendship, seems written to describe the relationship between Mercutio and Romeo, right down to the moment where Mercutio takes offense at Tybalt's suggestion that he is Romeo's consort, since such friendships suffer grievously—that is, result in death—when named sodomitic.[6]

Thus, we might say, in the domain of sexuality, that heteronormative romantic readings of *Romeo and Juliet* are themselves historically anachronistic in their extraction of the couple from a network of relations that delineate a field of differences and samenesses. Desire here is not, as Goldberg points out, "determined by the gender of its object," and "the coupling of Romeo and Juliet is not a unique moment of heterosexual perfection and privacy but part of a series whose substitutions do not respect either the uniqueness of individuals or the boundaries of gender difference."[7] Mercutio–Romeo, the same-sex romanticized friendship, is replaced by, and foreshadows, the nexus of idealizing love and death realized more explicitly toward the end of the play by Romeo and Juliet.

But to indict modern heteronormative readings in favor of more "accurate" or "authentic" sexual and gendered understandings of the play, as I've just done, is not necessarily to queer it. Accuracy and authenticity are often disciplinary mechanisms operating in the service of "straightening out" the perversity of other possibilities. What is queer in this play is not its homoeroticism, although this is relevant for studies of the history of sexuality. Nor is it only the substitutability of the objects of love, although this comes closer to queer theory's de-normativizing aims. Changing the (gender of) objects of desire can easily leave intact the grand mystified romance of star-crossed lovers struggling (and failing) to surmount insuperable social impediments to their love. So, for instance, Romeo and Juliet can remain in tragically romantic dire straits even when it's an (Indigo) girl-on-girl song.[8] (Although, to digress for a moment, Dire Straits gets at something about the queerness of *Romeo and Juliet* by imagining the disappointing futurity of a Romeo discarded by his once ecstatically dazzled, now jaded Juliet-turned-girl-group singer of a song about replacement boyfriends, which makes her one of the Angels, as she is when Luhrmann has her standing at her balcony after the costume ball—"O, speak again, bright angel!" [2.1.68]).[9] Melissa Etheridge can be Romeo, too, if she wants, and even scramble gendered subject and object up so much you can't tell which one's Romeo and which, Juliet. In her song, the lyric couple's been whittled down to the bare bones of you and I—another understanding of the situation that gets at something queer about this sonnet-infested play.[10]

Queer theory, suspicious of ideological normativities in *all* of their manifestations, whether "gay" or straight, can be said, in its deconstructive reading, to rejoin even more forcefully the pre-romantic, premodern analytics of this narrative by attending to the death drive at the heart of erotic politics. For this play refuses both futurity and maturity to its youthful protagonists who, like teenagers all over the United States, kill themselves and each other, again and again, in the name of a fantasy that wards off the meaninglessness of the void it harbors. In this way, *Romeo and Juliet* undoes and indicts, even as it constructs, the modern myth of romantic love.

The play's contradictions and ironies provide a path to deconstruction: relentless and restless negativity at the site of newfound love and life; seriality at the site of the one and only ("one fire burns out another's burning" [1.2.43]); convention and cliché at the site of the unique ("O brawling love, O loving hate . . . O heavy lightness, serious vanity" [1.1.169–71]); intensive social investment in the very thing prohibited by social constraints; transgression in the service of normativity; absolute loss that is simultaneously and necessarily recuperable, and with interest ("But I can give thee more; / For I will raise her statue in pure gold, / That whiles Verona by that name is known, / There shall no figure at such rate be set / As that of true and faithful Juliet. / As rich shall Romeo's by his lady's lie" [5.3.297–302]); valorized particularity sacrificed for the sake of the communal ("A pair of star-crossed lovers . . . Doth with their death bury their parents' strife" [prologue, 6–8]); marriage as death; death as life; life as death; politics in the bosom of the apolitical; the preciousness *and* dispensability of youth (Romeo, we know, must die).[11] Narrative inhabits the static lyric moment ("The fearful passage of their death-marked love, / . . . Is now the two hours' traffic of our stage" [prologue, 9–12]); lyric inhabits narrative; sonnets are interrupted, fragmented, truncated; there is a breaking down or failure of form in the midst of poetic form's most formal performance; and, finally, time is out of joint, untimely (as Dire Straits put it, "When you gonna realize it was just that the time was wrong?").[12] The queerness of *Romeo and Juliet* is, then, that it celebrates—if it can be called celebration—the drive. Or rather, *Romeo and Juliet* makes legible the insistence of the drive. That insistence devastates each idealizing fantasy's fiction of meaning even as it invests it with an excess of enjoyment: Repetition, substitution, death are the results of desire, not singularity, futurity, issue. Romeo and Juliet say no to every form of social viability that threatens to compromise their desire, from the "time will tell" patience counseled by sympathetic adults and friends, to exile ("banishèd / is death mistermed" [3.3.20–21]), to a proper alternative marriage ("Delay this marriage for a month, a week, / Or if you do not, make the bridal bed / In that dim monument where Tybalt lies" [3.5.199–201]), to the law itself that would administer justice in their stead. The name of this refusal, this no, this drive, is Death. In the face of every ideological apparatus—parents, the church, the law—striving to inculcate a politics of reproductive futurity, Romeo and Juliet insist that there is no time; the time is now; it is sonnet / lyric time, not narrative time; there is no future. This is the meaningless, absolute, irrational queer force, the drive that drives them to their tombs.

Both like and unlike Judith Butler's Antigone, these teenagers "emblematize a certain heterosexual fatality."[13] We might also ask, with Butler, "to what other ways of organizing sexuality might a consideration of that fatality give rise?"[14] "Antigone," she writes,

> fails to produce heterosexual closure for [the] drama. . . . She does seem to deinstitute heterosexuality by refusing to do what is necessary to stay alive. . . . If the tomb is the bridal chamber, and the tomb is chosen over marriage, then the tomb stands for the very destruction of marriage, and the term "bridal chamber" represents precisely the negation of its own possibility. The word destroys its object . . . performs the destruction of the institution.[15]

Or, in the heroic terms of Edelman's Lacanian Antigone, "Political self-destruction inheres in the only act that counts as one: the act of resisting enslavement to the future in the name of having a life."[16]

But does the convergence of wedding and burial destroy the institution that forced the choice? And does Romeo's and Juliet's fatality give rise to other ways to think the organization of sexuality—or, for that matter, the political? Yes and no. Shakespeare is having it both ways, it seems, for the couple takes care to get married before it gets enshrined in a Capulet memorial. The political irony here is the irony of the political (and a propos, is chiasmus the privileged trope of irony?). *Romeo and Juliet* deconstructs reproductive futurism nowhere more than in killing those children in the name of whose futurity the social order of the play is organized. And this destruction has a logic, a rationale, a telos, even—a telos with productive consequence, the "burial" of the parental strife, so that strife comes in retrospect to seem to be the very passionate *jouissance* of the star-crossed lovers themselves. In the place of living flesh and blood, two golden statues; in the place of obstinate and wasteful refusal, valuable and perduring memorials. Isn't this what "politics," by which here we understand a certain social order, wants? Death is a "social institution," and "compliance with death," Herbert Marcuse reminds us, "is compliance with the master over death: the polis, the state, nature, or the god."[17] "The inculcation of the acceptance of death," Louise Fradenburg adds, "has been the ground for all forms of domination," and the elegiac recuperation that offers reparation for loss also teaches us "submission to the rule of law, a subjection for which we are to be compensated by figures that transcend mortality and individuality."[18] Although the play does not stress that recuperation at its end, its futurities arouse my suspicion.

Do we not in some way—and perhaps especially in a time of such widespread and violent political conflict—risk sharing a mystified attachment to this tale: to have been able to eternalize the moment, to have died young and beautiful and become monumentalized by a city and a history? To be remembered beyond the grave? To escape, to exit?

On the other hand, I want to think with infernal irony on that other text that glorified the romance of two unknowns, Paolo and Francesca, caught in *amor interruptus*. Like the discarded Romeo of Dire Straits, but from another angle, Francesca finds herself on the other side disgustedly attached for all eternity to that nobody who stood in and substituted, for the briefest of moments, for the object-cause of her desire ("Yeah, you know, I used to have a scene with him").[19]

The greatest irony of all may reside, finally, in the work of memorialization and perpetuity performed not by the thematics of the play, but by its endurance as literature. A condition of the drive's representation, of the *frisson* generated in *Romeo and Juliet*'s death-driving readers, of the text's seemingly endless infernal ability to breed new iterations of the myth of heterosexual love—as well as counter-narratives to this myth—is its monumentalization as literature. Perhaps that is what literature is, then, after all: the grand performance of the sign's illusory meaningfulness, its ability to craft generative fantasy—about the fantasy of generation—from beyond the grave, not as the triumph of literature over death, but, rather, as the triumph in death of literature over life.[20]

Notes

1. Goldberg, "*Romeo and Juliet*'s Open Rs."

2. Edelman, *No Future*; Baz Luhrmann, dir., *Romeo + Juliet*, Bazmark Films, 1996.

3. Menon, "Spurning Teleology in *Venus and Adonis*."

4. Jerome Robbins and Robert Wise, dirs., *West Side Story*, Mirisch Corporation, 1961; Franco Zeffirelli, dir., *Romeo and Juliet*, BHE Films, 1968. Normally, sexual difference is construed as difference per se; here, however, true to a medieval tradition of perfect courtly lovers, the two young people strikingly resemble each other to establish "the social" as the arena of agonistic difference.

5. Rocke, *Forbidden Friendships*; Sedgwick, *Between Men*; Traub, *Desire and Anxiety*.

6. Bray, *The Friend*; *Romeo and Juliet*, in Greenblatt et al., *The Norton Shakespeare*, 3.1.44–45. Citations in parentheses are to this edition.

7. Goldberg, "Romeo and Juliet's Open Rs," 222.

8. Dire Straits, "*Romeo and Juliet*," on *Money for Nothing*, Warner Bros., 1988; Mark Knopfler, "Romeo and Juliet," performed by Indigo Girls, on *Rites of Passage*, Epic Records, 1992.

9. Richard Gottehrer, Robert Feldman, and Jerry Goldstein, "My Boyfriend's Back," performed by the Angels, *My Boyfriend's Back*, Collectables, 1963.

10. Melissa Etheridge, "No Souvenirs," on *Brave and Crazy*, Island Records, 1989. For a reading of the song, see Freccero, *Queer / Early / Modern*, 26–28.

11. Andrzej Bartkowiak, dir., *Romeo Must Die*, Silver Pictures, 2000.

12. Peter Holland's introduction to the Pelican Shakespeare edition of *Romeo and Juliet* discusses the sonnets in the play; it also has an excellent discussion of time compression and untimeliness in *Romeo and Juliet*: see Holland, "Introduction."

13. Butler, *Antigone's Claim*, 72.

14. Ibid.

15. Ibid., 76.

16. Edelman, *No Future*, 30.

17. Marcuse, "The Ideology of Death," 73, 76.

18. Butler, *Antigone's Claim*, 184; Fradenburg, "Voice Memorial."

19. Alighieri, *The Divine Comedy*, Canto V.

20. I thank Jody Greene for asking me to think about the place of the literary in this argument.

More or Less Queer

JEFFREY MASTEN

As you will already know, the play *Sir Thomas More* is queerer than any of the other texts addressed in this volume. Queerer than *The Merchant of Venice*, *Twelfth Night*, *The Two Gentlemen of Verona*, *The Two Noble Kinsmen*, *As You Like It*, certainly *Hamlet*, or any of your other run-of-the-mill Shakesqueerean plays, texts that (it should be obvious by this point in the volume) a serious queer critic could hardly be bothered with. In *Sir Thomas More*, by contrast, the cross-class homoeroticism of the title character's immortal line near the hour of his death—"Sirrah fellow, reach me the urinal"[1]—has been evident to most discerning readers. As hardly bears mentioning, More's eloquent soliloquy in Act 3, including his self-admonition to "Fear their gay skins" (3.1.18), has presented a rich vein for critics anatomizing the complexities of early modern queer embodiment and homophobia. Needless to say, More's culminating aphorism in that speech has become a touchstone for early modern queer work: "[L]et this be thy maxim: . . . / *A bottom great wound up, greatly [is] undone*" (3.1.19–21; emphasis added).

"As you will know," "needless to say," "hardly bears mentioning": in the Shakespearean and Shakesqueerean canons, *Sir Thomas More* is not the familiar play I have invoked. If you are not a Shakespearean, and possibly even if you are, you likely have not read the play, even the bits of it—the allegedly Shakespearean pages of this rare, collaborative play manuscript—often reproduced in current complete-works editions. In this sense, the play could hardly be less queer: hardly noticed.

The play's aberrance, however, is well established. It is the only play associated with Shakespeare that survives in manuscript. Unlike every other play now in the canon, it was not published in the sixteenth or seventeenth century. Like *The Two Noble Kinsmen*, *Cardenio*, and possibly *Henry VIII*, it is collaborative, but unlike those plays, its collaboration is no mere monogamous arrangement of Shakespeare and John Fletcher. At least six people seem to have collaborated in its writing and revision, among them potentially actors and copyists as well as playwrights.[2] *More* is, further, "the only surviving play indisputably marked" by Edmund Tilney, Master of the Revels, the royal censor.[3]

In modernity, the play is so queer as hardly to be extant. The only free-standing, modern-spelling edition, the Revels edition of 1990, is only recently back in print. The last complete-works edition to include the full text was C. J. Sisson's in 1954.[4] There is not yet an Arden edition, and, of the prominent U.S. teaching editions, the Riverside and Norton editions include only "The Additions" and "Passages" ascribed to Shakespeare. The "RSC Shakespeare" (2007) includes only "A Scene for *Sir Thomas More*," presented after the collection's genre-based organization of plays and poems.[5]

Further signs of aberrance: since the case first began to be built for including *More* in the Shakespearean canon in the early years of the twentieth century—its biggest boost came from a volume in 1923 with essays by key figures in what would become the dominant movement in twentieth-century Shakespearean editorial practice[6]—Shakespeare's participation in the play's manuscript has been continually under dispute. The second edition of *The Norton Shakespeare* asserts that "a small minority [of scholars] denies" the attribution of part of the play to Shakespeare,[7] but, as Paul Werstine notes, the originally adduced evidence of uniquely Shakespearean spellings (e.g., "scilens") and handwriting features has been discredited: "[T]he case for Shakespearean authorship of the Hand D pages rests chiefly on the analogies that scholars have drawn between the fictional More's plea for civil order" and Shakespeare's imagined political views.[8] What, then, could be Shakesqueerer than a Shakespeare play not written in whole or in part by Shakespeare? (I hesitate to note that my play begins to unravel the whole enterprise in this volume. Nevertheless, if Shakesqueer, why not Jonsqueer, Websqueer, Beaumont-and-Fletchqueer? Why all this bother with queering at the level of the "author" in the first place? Doesn't this mode of organization simply reproduce the notions of the bounded individual and unitary subjectivity that have been central to queer critique since its advent? Doesn't queering thus organized reproduce the "completeness" fetish of the most traditional complete-works volume?)

In this sense, *Sir Thomas More* is either or both more and / or less queer than other Shakespeare plays. On the one hand, possibly—even probably—the play is not by Shakespeare. On the other, passages from it are now routinely included in complete-works volumes. Indeed, the manuscript, closely held at the British Library, has achieved a totemic significance, functioning as the "missing link"—the only extant manuscript that potentially connects the writer with playwriting. As such, its function in complete-works editions seems to be as much about providing a photogenic (if not exactly legible) example of Shakespeare's ostensible handwriting as about providing an actual play. Where, in the case of *The Two Noble Kinsmen* and *Henry VIII*, the whole collaborative play is included, with *More*, we read only the "Shakespeare" bits, plus photographs of the manuscript (and sometimes Shakespeare's few signatures). As Werstine has noted, the manuscript of the play is "the site upon which the metaphysics of authorship has been centred for most of [the twentieth] century."⁹ Marginal, fragmentary, present as absent, dubious but essential: perhaps this can serve as a provisional working definition of "Shakesqueer."

One of the queerer aspects of *More* is an almost complete absence of critical analysis. Metaphysically central to the conception of Shakespeare as a working playwright and to a twentieth-century editorial practice that seeks to found its treatment of early printed texts on Shakespeare's otherwise hypothetical manuscripts—the basis, that is, for every modern edition quoted in this volume—the play has nevertheless evaded commentary in a field that annually cranks it out. With few exceptions, critical discussion of the play has been occluded by, or in the service of, discussions of authorship, manuscript bibliography, and attribution. There is, to my knowledge, no queer criticism of this play. Which is to say, in this case, that "scilens" equals death.

Incorporated into the structures of socialized desire,
Amazons expose that desire as a system of roles that might
always be detached from the bodies they exist to regulate.
—Kathryn Schwarz, *Tough Love*, 45

"Whither wilt thou hale me?" says Doll Williamson to the foreigner Francis de Bard in the opening line of *Sir Thomas More* (1.1.1), which in its first set of scenes stages the "Ill May Day" riots of 1517, adapting the chronicle histories of Henry VIII's reign. A response of urban Londoners to their grievances against immigrants in their midst, the riots stage the "strangers" stealing various forms of what the play presents as English property: jobs, commerce, food, wives. (The strangers are sometimes specified as "Frenchmen" or "Lombards," on which more later.) "How now, husband?" says Doll. "What, one stranger take thy food from thee, and another thy wife?" (1.1.31–32).

If one point of the play is to portray the resistance of the English to strangers (analogous to the xenophobic "libels" circulating in London around the likely date of the play's first composition),[10] it simultaneously stages—from its first line, as we have seen—a specifically female resistance that exceeds the anti-alien movement. Even earlier, the play's opening stage direction describes Doll as "*a lusty woman*" (1.1.s.d.), and it is worth noting that *Sir Thomas More* is one of only three plays associated with Shakespeare that begins with a woman / boy actor speaking.[11] The opening scenes of the play return relentlessly to Doll's militancy—a resistance described as resolute marital fidelity to her English husband but also repeatedly threatening female rule and the world upside down: "Hands off proud stranger. . . . if men's milky hearts dare not strike a stranger, yet women will beat them down, ere they bear these abuses" (1.1.56–58). Doll imagines an unruly female army supplying male lack:

> I'll call so many women to mine assistance, as we'll not leave one inch untorn of thee. If our husbands must be bridled by law, and forced to bear your wrongs, their wives will be a little lawless, and soundly beat ye. (1.1.63–68)

At the end of the scene, Doll vows to "make [herself] a captain among ye, and do somewhat to be talk of for ever after" (1.1.134–35). If the allusion to being talked of in the chronicle histories sets up Doll as an over-reacher—she is not named in the multiple historical accounts of these events—she does become a captain in the play: the later scene staging the riots begins with a stage direction for "DOLL *in a shirt of mail, a headpiece, sword and buckler, a crew attending*" (2.1.s.d.).

The play thus represents what Kathryn Schwarz has called an "amazon encounter," but Doll stages not precisely Schwarz's Amazons brought from afar and domesticated—in all of the queerness such an encounter unleashes in Schwarz's readings—but, instead, an already English Amazon whose overturning of patriarchal pieties of silence and obedience is itself produced out of the encounter with strangeness. "I have no beauty to like a husband," she says—and the text probably means "please a husband," though it is ambiguous—"yet whatsoever is mine scorns to stoop to a stranger" (1.1.5–7). Doll's militantly faithful rebellion threatens to change May Day into "midsummer," instituting what we might call "queer time," revising the ecclesiastical calendar to install a new red-letter saint's day of riot: "We'll alter the day in the calendar, and set it down in flaming letters" (2.1.36–38). If Doll ultimately seems re-domesticated by the events of the play—she is nearly hanged for her role in the insurrection but pardoned as she concludes her scaffold speech— she nevertheless seems to replay the "double move" Schwarz sees in Amazon narratives,

> which project an image into an antisocial condition of sexual identity only to bring it back again. Back, that is, into articulations of male homosocial power and its perpetuation through domesticated heterosexuality, articulations that the intervention of 'Amazon' can only disconcert.[12]

"Now let me tell the women of this town," she says on the scaffold, "[N]o stranger yet brought Doll to lying down" (2.4.127–28). Stressing fidelity to her husband and children, Doll nevertheless raises the specter of female sexual resistance.

And even earlier, female *penetration*: In the riot scene, Doll threatens, "We'll drag the strangers out into Moorfields, and there bombast them till they stink again" (2.1.42–43). The Revels edition glosses "bombast" as "lit[erally] 'to stuff,' " and this meaning derives from the noun "bombast," meaning "cotton-wool used as padding or stuffing for clothes."[13] But, in the period, "bombast" is spelled interchangeably with "bumbast(e)"[14]—indeed, "bumbast" is the spelling in the manuscript, which the Revels edition "modernizes" to "bombast." The interchangeable spellings, together with the Oxford English Dictionary's additional period meaning of "bumbast," suggest that Doll's threatened action against the strangers might run the gamut from spanking to stuffing or fucking; for *bumbast*, the *OED* gives: "to beat on the posteriors; hence, to flog, beat soundly, thrash."

Pardon my bombasted philological detail, but the *OED*'s queer etymology for "bumbast" is irresistible:

> app. f. *BUM n.*[1] [i.e., buttocks] + *BASTE v.*[3]: [i.e., beat] but *bum* might be a meaningless intensive or reduplicative prefix.

To whom, Shakesqueerean readers, is "bum" a "meaningless intensive"? Furthermore, "bum" as "reduplicative prefix"—*bum* as a *poster*ior that (re)doublingly *pre*fixes something—seems only to reinscribe the inversions of before and behind, the "preposterous" trope of *hysteron proteron*, the beast with two backs, associated with sodomy discourse in this period.[15] Doll's threat is to take the strangers out beyond the city walls and stuff or spank them, or double-spank them before and behind, bumbast them rhetorically and otherwise, until, it seems, they shit themselves.[16]

Doll's lines moments later seem only to emphasize these sexual possibilities, as well as the underlying threat to husband, domestic heterosexuality, and patriarchy: "If thou beest afraid, husband, go home again and hide thy head, for by the Lord *I'll have a little sport now I am at it*" (2.1.60–62; emphasis added). "Sport" sometimes means "sex" in the period,[17] and, though it also means "fun" here, Doll's line efficiently collapses riot with female sexual availability, the issue around which the riot (dis)organized itself in the first place. "No stranger yet brought Doll to lying down," but the play may well imagine the reverse.

Further, whether the play was ever acted or not, Doll's part was designed to be played by a boy actor, and the specter here of a boy bumbasting foreigners is an additional reversal of the period's usual hierarchies, whether in pedagogical beating of schoolboys or in the stock positionings of pederasty. The play does not evade this potential homoeroticism; in the later allegorical play within the play, one boy player plays three female roles, "Dame Science, Lady Vanity, / And Wisdom," to which Sir Thomas More comments: "And one boy play them all? By'r Lady, he's loaden" (3.2.75–77). The bawdy flirtation of the male character Wit and Lady Vanity, played by the boy, follows, as Wit comes to her "a stranger" who (encouraged by the Vice-character Inclination) quickly becomes "familiar" (3.2.211–16): "I could find in my heart to kiss you in your smock," Wit says. Lady Vanity's / the boy's rhyming reply is even more explicit: "My back is broad enough to bear that mock" (3.2.237–38). The doubling of actors' parts makes it likely that the same boy would have played Doll and Lady Vanity.[18]

Beyond these anti-patriarchal and sodomitical resonances around Doll and the boy who may have played her, there is another way in which queer discourses might cohere in their incoherence in the play. As I noted, the play sometimes uses the term "Lombards" to refer to "strangers"; indeed, this has been a fine point in the discussion of the censorship of the play, since at one point in the manuscript Tilney crosses out the words "straunger" and "ffrencheman" and replaces them with "lombard."[19] In the scholarship on the play, Tilney's manuscript intervention here is typically understood to depoliticize the text: the crown would not have wanted to offend the French ambassador, and there would likely have been fewer Lombards than French in London in the 1590s.[20] But Lombards in the cultural imaginary may have loomed larger, or at least differently. In his systematic seventeenth-century description of English felonies, Edward Coke gives an instructive xenophobic etymology to "Buggery, or Sodomy": "*Bugeria* is an Italian word . . . , and it was complained of in Parliament, that the Lumbards had brought into the Realm the shamefull sin of Sodomy."[21] Doll, resisting a Lombard, imagines "bumbasting" the Lombards, who brought in sodomy—which always arrives from elsewhere. In a contemporaneous pamphlet by Robert Greene, "abhominable" "sodomie," "self-love," and "bumbast" arrive (together) from a distinctly Italian elsewhere. The Englishman Cloth-breeches says to Velvet-breeches ("borne in *Italy*"), "[T]hou [hast] beene the ruine of the *Romane* Empire, and nowe fatally art thou come into *Englande* to atempte heere the like subuersion."[22]

Buggery, says Coke, "is . . . committed by carnall knowledge against the ordinance of the Creator, and order of nature, by mankind with mankind, or with brute beast, or by womankind with bruite beast."[23] Doll, fighting a Lombard, responds "Compel me, ye dog's face?" (1.1.8–9). In its engagement of these discourses and its simultaneous xenophobic celebration and near-hanging of Doll, the play teeters between Doll as sodomite, rape target, and anti-royal subversive; for sodomy, a "crime of majesty, against the heavenly King, . . . the judgement . . . is that the person attainted be hanged by the neck, untill he, or she be dead."[24] The condensation of these discourses in the opening scenes of the play is made more resonant through the very structure of Coke's attempt to encode the law, suggesting the culture's associative logic for these crimes. Among his enumeration of English felonies, "Of Buggery, or Sodomy" is followed directly by "Of Rape" and "Felony for carying away a woman against her will." Doll, resisting being carried away against her will ("Whither wilt thou hale me . . . ye dog's face?"), later imagines carrying away and bumbasting the beasts.

What are the dangers of consorting with strangers and Lombards? "Freres des Lombards," Randle Cotgrave notes in his French–English dictionary of 1611: "*Moles, Moonecalues, monstrous birthes; tearmed so, because the women of Lombardie by much feeding on hearbes, fruites, and other crudities, bring forth sometimes those monsters in stead of children.*"[25] Or, as the play has it, cataloguing the allegations against the strangers and the effects of their diet of roots, potatoes, parsnips: "They bring in strange roots" (2.3.10). Are we now speaking of vegetables, of monstrous crossbreeds; of sodomy, brought by the Lombards from elsewhere; or of etymological roots? "*Bugeria* is an Italian word."

Perhaps it goes without saying that there will be no easy alignment in this play and, more generally, between queerness, feminism, class struggle, and anti-xenophobic and anti-nationalist critique, a fact made starkly clear to me as I watched the Royal Shakespeare Company perform *Sir Thomas More* on August 1, 2005. Three weeks after the subway bombings in London, the attendant attention to "strangers" among "us," and reaction that included the killing of an unarmed Brazilian immigrant living in London by the police, it seemed impossible not to feel progressive politics drawn in multiple directions by a production in which Doll led a working-class riot against foreigners played by black, if not visibly Muslim, actors.[26]

To see this fracturing (reading the overlaps rather than the chapter divisions in Coke's account) is to resist the default treatment of *More* as one man's tragedy and the riot scenes as merely in the service of More's progress from Sheriff to Sir Thomas and eventual martyrdom in defying Henry VIII. Like the work of the play's revisers, who, for reasons we do not understand at a date we cannot pinpoint, seem to have ignored the demands of censorship, a queer reading would dwell in the complexities of the riot rather than delete or submerge them, as Tilney requires in his edict on the manuscript's first page:

> Leave out . . . the insurrection wholly with the cause thereof and begin with Sir Thomas More at the Mayor's sessions, with a report afterwards of his good service done, being Sheriff of London, upon a mutiny against the Lumbards—only by a short report and not otherwise, at your own perils.[27]

The play, even in its later focus on More's life, itself resists a reduction to great-man history in its many re-doublings (even "queerings") of More, played in one scene by his servant to fool Erasmus, in More's acting as Good Counsel in the play within, and in his frequent punning on the supplementarity of his own name. Forgoing office near the end of his life, he says, "my title's only More" (4.2.71).

Queer theory might, further, help us to critique the bibliographical and attributive work that, as I have noted, has occluded discussion of the play, where Doll scarcely makes an appearance. There is not space to perform such a critique here, but queer theory's interrogation of identity, identification, and identity over time could help us develop a more critical account of authorial attribution in *More* and of what it means for something to be "by Shakespeare" more generally, ideas that have rested on a number of imbricated essences—for example, the notion of an author whose political attitudes do not change over time and who is thus identifiable. "It is thus no accident," writes Alfred W. Pollard, stating the early case for Shakespeare's participation in *More*, "that in these three pages we find the attitude to mobs, the attitude to the crown, and the deep humanity, which are recurrent features in the work of William Shakespeare."[28] Or the essence of Shakespeare said to inhere in widely shared and variant spelling habits, in a linguistic system prior to standardization. Or the ostensible essence of handwriting: "The problem" in identifying handwriting, writes Pollard,

> is thus first to visualize how a handwriting after a lapse of some twenty years and in totally different circumstances will show the *natural effects* of these and yet *preserve its identity,* and secondly, to make the process thus visualized intelligible to others not specially equipped to deal with it.[29]

Queer theory can at least help us draw attention to what goes under the sign of "natural effects," to the ostensible continuities of identity, and to criticism's habit of visualizing things both into and out of intelligibility, providing, as well, a possible vantage point for those ostensibly not "specially equipped."

At the same time, Pollard's words may carry an uncannily productive reminder for a queer theory that would, after a lapse of several centuries, produce a queer Shakespeare somehow separate from, or queerable without reference to, the detailed peculiarities of historical evidence that may themselves lead to a queer re-theorization of the period, its authors, and its texts— here represented by my admittedly shorthand analysis of complexly intertwined discourses around sodomy, insurrection, and rape. How else will we, not necessarily "specially equipped" in these later times to inhabit the queerness of these earlier intersections, account for what is, in *More*, Shakesqueer? These questions—for Shakespeare studies and for queer theory—are, more or less, where I would want to begin if I were not at my own peril in going beyond a short report.

Notes

This essay is dedicated to the memory of Scott McMillin, whose brilliant book on this play, *The Elizabethan Theatre and The Booke of Sir Thomas More* (1987), first led me to engage with it. Thanks also to Anston Bosman and Jay Grossman.

    1. Gabrieli and Melchiori, eds., *Sir Thomas More,* 5.3.22. Citations in parentheses are to this edition.

    2. McMillin, *The Elizabethan Theatre and The Booke of Sir Thomas More*; Werstine, "Close Contrivers."

    3. Dutton, *Mastering the Revels,* 81.

    4. Sisson, ed., *William Shakespeare.*

    5. Bate and Rasmussen, eds., *The RSC Shakespeare.*

    6. Pollard, ed., *Shakespeare's Hand in the Play of Sir Thomas More*; Werstine, "Shakespeare *More* or Less."

7. Cohen, "Introduction to *Sir Thomas More*," 2031.

8. Werstine, "Close Contrivers," 17–18.

9. Ibid., 7.

10. Levine, "Citizens' Games," 41; Gabrieli and Melchiori, *Sir Thomas More*, 11, 19, 45, 48.

11. See *All's Well That Ends Well* (Countess) and *Macbeth* (First Witch).

12. Schwarz, *Tough Love*, 5.

13. *Oxford English Dictionary*, s.v. "bombast" (*n.*), "bombase" (*v.*), and "bombace."

14. Ibid., s.v. "bumbaste" (*v.*), "bombast" (*n.*).

15. Goldberg, *Sodometries*, 180–81; Parker, "Preposterous Reversals," 435–36.

16. I am indebted to Ryan Friedman, who first brought the potential sodomitical resonances of rhetorical "bombast" to my attention: Friedman, "Bombastic Subjects."

17. *Oxford English Dictionary*, s.v. "sport" (*n.¹*), def. 1c.

18. McMillin, *The Elizabethan Theatre and The Booke of Sir Thomas More*, 78–79.

19. Greg, ed., *The Book of Sir Thomas More*, 13 (lines 364, 368). Tilney does not always delete Frenchmen; see ibid., 13 (line 359).

20. Dutton, *Mastering the Revels*, 83, 97; Scouloudi, *Returns of Strangers in the Metropolis*, 84–85.

21. Coke, *The Third Part of the Institutes of the Laws of England*, 58.

22. *A Qvip for an Vp-start Courtier*, sig. B1v–B2v.

23. Coke, *The Third Part of the Institutes of the Laws of England*, 58.

24. Ibid.; in part my translation.

25. Cotgrave, *A Dictionarie of the French and English Tongues*, s.v. "Lombard."

26. Robert Delamere, dir., *Thomas More*, performed by the Royal Shakespeare Company, Swan Theatre, Stratford-upon-Avon, August 1, 2005.

27. Gabrieli and Melchiori, eds., *Sir Thomas More*, 17; my modernization.

28. Pollard, *Shakespeare's Hand in the Play of Sir Thomas More*, 5–6.

29. Ibid., 12; emphasis added.

Momma's Boys

ARANYE FRADENBURG

Lo! As a careful housewife runs to catch
One of her feather'd creatures broke away,
Sets down her babe and makes an swift dispatch
In pursuit of the thing she would have stay,
Whilst her neglected child holds her in chase,
Cries to catch her whose busy care is bent
To follow that which flees before her face,
Not prizing her poor infant's discontent;
So runn'st thou after that which flies from thee,
Whilst I thy babe chase thee afar behind;
But if thou catch thy hope, turn back to me,
And play the mother's part, kiss me, be kind:
So will I pray that thou mayst have thy Will,
If thou turn back, and my loud crying still.
　　—Shakespeare, Sonnet 143

No doubt there are shameful practices undeserving of the term "queer." But once retrieved by the sexual minorities it was formerly used to insult, it has become a generous term. It is a counter-humiliant insofar as it no longer isolates, but now *links*, many sexual practices some prefer to keep asunder.[1] It is particularly loyal to those who have been shamed for loving in ways that appear to contravene gender but extends itself to many abjected desires, even to the abjection of unending desire, fatal to self-possession. This essay addresses love that is infantile, incestuous, dependent. I would say Oedipal love, except that it is not a consequence of either a "successful" or "failed" heterosexuality. It is the love you feel for inappropriate objects: for someone thirty years older, thirty years younger. The kind of love that makes a fool, a pervert, a stalker out of you.

Time, mortality, aging are always around in Shakespeare's Sonnets because when we are infants, we are in love with people a lot older than we are, and they with us, and we all "know" it, if not consciously. We cannot become a human subject without taking in how our parents feel about us; the adult's passionate love for the child is also in the child and in the adult she will become. This love is readily eroticized, on both sides.[2] It is not just "tenderness" but "in-loveness"; it has a passional quality and is manifested through extraordinary bodily intimacy.

We are told repeatedly that this kind of love will never work. Transgenerational love is something we must sacrifice. It is regularly featured in cautionary tales. It is regularly featured in the mainstream media as the chief danger facing children today. It is sometimes ascribed to sexual minorities, because it frightens the general population—for example, it is gay men and psycho killers who love or hate their mothers too much, not 40-plus percent of us. But the shaming power of this kind of love is boundless.

In comparison even with other kinds of "undesirable" behavior (such as aggression), children's erotic gestures are rarely mirrored or "mentalized" by adults.[3] This is not simply a matter of what can and cannot be spoken. It means that eroticism will be attended to obliquely at best in the parent–child communions *on which becoming human depends.* Because eroticism is poorly marked in the exchanges that create the social self, we "plead for love" through books (Sonnet 23), regularly seeking media-tion. People use sonnets to express their feelings, as if the sonnet stood between, or linked, our (infantile) wordlessness and the words to say it. Sonnets are go-betweens—public relations, perhaps, for growing boys. They are transitional (and transitioning) objects.[4] So sonnets turn up everywhere.

Sonnet 143 serves as the epigraph for an article titled, "The Separation–Adaptation Response to Temporary Object Loss."[5] The studies reported in the article showed that children have separation anxiety when they first go to school. Children do well if their parents stay with them until they are ready to let them go, however long that takes. Looking over my notes on this article, I see that I was especially struck by two points: A study of suicide rates in the Scandinavian countries showed that "prolonged dependence permitted by the Danish mother results in . . . acknowledgment of dependency needs without shame on the part of the adult" (I wrote "do not be ashamed of wanting to depend on others" in the margin); another researcher, linking separation anxiety and suicidal tendencies, says, "A child loves the mother so much that he feels separation from her as death."[6]

Nothing about the Sonnets seems over the top if you imagine them to be expressing the matter-of-life-and-death quality of the feelings of infants, of parents, of boys and girls passionately attached to men and women, or vice versa. The helplessness of infantile love, the intense focus of parental love (really, they are versions of each other), the awesome importance of it all: It is all there. The Sonnets have been regularly elevated as the mode of (mature) subjectivity and interiority; many of my students, however, find Will childish and narcissistic (he whines endlessly, he should get over it, he's a loser). We are often not comfortable when we see the infantile in the grown-up. But I would argue that this is exactly the view the Sonnets permit.[7] Though easily adopted one at a time, the Sonnets' overall effect can strike readers as queer, and not just because they are about a man as well as a woman, or maybe the other kind of ass kissing. The unquestionable polish and vast reflectiveness of the Sonnets are yoked to an infantile aesthetic, an aesthetic for the infant in all of us, for all adults who can all be driven to creepy behavior. That is why we have restraining orders (and incest taboos).

Freud pointed out long ago that disgust screens something once deeply pleasurable. The shame we feel about infantile attachment inhibits our thinking across the board, even among people whose lifework is devoted to the very young, even in psychoanalysis and affect theory. What about agency, we ask? Isn't consumption just so passive? Isn't it better to produce rather than lack? Even affect has to have autonomy. It is not easy these days to speak for going nowhere—for wanting (things) to stay (the same). The cravings of confabulated subjects embarrass us. If only, as Teresa Brennan suggests, we could stop worrying about our objects (and our selves).[8] Well, maybe Kierkegaard is right that there is no absolute finitude, and it does feel good sometimes to be part of the stream of life, but there *is* dissolution.

I do not mean to oppose anything exactly—certainly not critiques of the subject that do not just want to point out that it is a construct but also want to put that construct in its place, as an effect, a derivation, of the workings of living matter. I am not opposed to the notion of strange attractors, or autonomous regions resonating at a distance.[9] On a more quotidian level, developmentalists agree that the more effectively children's needs are met, the more they are likely to initiate and enjoy independent action. (Traumatic feelings of helplessness are not suited to the internalization of "self-soothing" strategies.) I wonder, however, what "independent" means when we are talking about a head crammed full of internalized experiences / fantasies of reassurance and rescue. That "autonomy" and "independence" are the words used for the ability to *remember* momma (procedurally or otherwise) when she is not there is a symptom of the shame we feel about attachment and our difficulty mourning it. My concern is that the discourse of the post-human invites melancholia. What to do about the finitude of particular expressions (e.g., people)? Re-frame that finitude in the context of infinite finitudes. Re-connect the human to matter and energy. De-sublimate the subject. Absolutely—as long as we do not imagine this will exempt us from the work of mourning.

As the human goes, so goes language, insofar as it has been held to be one of our distinguishing marks. I am troubled by the way language gets positioned these days in relation to preverbal and non-verbal experience. There is a *cathecting*, not simply a consideration, of the idea that language cannot reach non-conscious preverbal memories and affects. But I have to ask: Have we ever been preverbal? Fetuses can hear. Infants understand language long before adults have thought they did. Infants get to work on phoneme coding very early. People are constantly talking to them. Infants know when something is being *said* to them. Their interactions with caregivers are "proto-conversational" (e.g., turn taking).[10] These days, their parents teach them sign language. (A father remarked to me recently how uncanny it was to see his baby angrily making the sign for "more.") When babies make signs, their parents say the corresponding words: More? You want more? Locomotion is, and indicates, linking. When disturbed by insecure or disorganized attachment (e.g., in the presence of the parent, the child goes around in circles or walks toward the parent and then away), disturbances in communication will be there, too (in "haunted" vocalizations, stammering).

It is true that much, even most, of a human life form is alien to the subject it artifices. But we are never not "in" language. Language happens in the brain, not just in the mind; the brain puts affects and symbols together. Language reaches out to affect, and affect reaches out to language; from the neuroplastic standpoint, this is because timing is everything. If neurons that fire together wire together, if "operators" link disparate kinds of sensory (and more) information together at higher levels of abstraction (without which we could not perceive "objects"), then language will be linked to the affects that accompany either its utterance or its reception. The memorial re-alignment of language with affect, when it happens, is transformative. These are the moments that interest me—in Kristeva's terms, the convergence of the semiotic and the symbolic.

Anecdote 1: I am presenting an informal paper on neuroplasticity to the

"Literature and the Mind" Symposium at the University of California, Santa Barbara. We are discussing the chapter on psychoanalysis in Norman Doidge's *The Brain That Changes Itself*.[11] I focus on terms such as "transcription," "transduction," and "activation." The problem is one of linkage—between preverbal and verbal experience, procedural and episodic memory, right brain and left brain. Arguably, psychoanalysis supports crossover between these different places and modalities. It does so in part by reactivating attachments, which are memorial but not necessarily explicit: procedural memory includes patterns of interaction with attachment figures. Interpersonal attachments are processed by the limbic system. But attachment is also the means whereby the orbitofrontal system speaks to the limbic system. (Among other things, the orbitofrontal system enables us to "manage" impulses.) The "attuned mother" helps the infant's orbitofrontal system to develop by naming emotions, triggers, and consequences and by linking these names "cross-modally" to sounds, visions, smells, and tactile sensations. "Wow" is usually said loudly, accompanied by gestures connoting vitality and intensity—such as clapping hands. Infants show surprise when these concordances vary.[12] So attachment facilitates the development of the brain and learning.[13]

Learning is, at first, learning how to interpret and endure what we feel and sense, with someone's *help*. (For one thing, if my caregiver takes the time to symbolize an event for me, it is probably not a dire emergency.) Love is the context. This is what makes it possible for us to become subjects with unfolding histories. So, I ask: What are the implications for literary study of the notion that "affect regulation" (awful term) and attachment are the primary contexts in which preverbal and verbal modes of communion and communication are linked? Literature foregrounds the ongoing relationship between preverbal and verbal language—between tone, intensity, rhythm, on the one hand, and the self-operating system of abstract symbols known as language on the other. Does literature always and foremost reactivate the bonds between us and our caregivers (make us feel or seek attachment or its absence) —and therefore also our histories of desire, safety, and danger?

And someone attending the Symposium says: "Well, yes, but I don't know that it needs to be the *mother*."

Anecdote 2: I am dining with two analysts who specialize in the treatment of children. I mention that one of my analysands can remember breastfeeding. For this analysand, the preparation of solid food is disenchanting. In fact, density in any form—like land masses—means heartbreak and abandonment (her artwork is always of water). I say, "How sad ever to have to give anything up." The two analysts exchange glances and say, briskly, how different it is for different infants. I think: "What? Are there infants who like giving things up? You know, when they still want them?"

It is true that infants give things up all the time—when they are ready. The infant-mother pair I observed last year *choreographed* the consumption of solids, dispersing blockage through flows of artful movement. Not everyone feels betrayed by alteration. In fact we do (learn to) enjoy it. I just want to speak for the momma's boys and crybabies in our midst; for the addicted, the insecurely attached, the people who beg, plead, and make you wonder how anybody can get so lost.

But it is the Sonnets that lead me to this position. *They* speak for the insecurely attached. It is not the only thing they do, but they do plenty of it. There are people—children, for example—who are shy, tongue-tied, who need us "to hear with eyes" (Sonnet 23). For me it is a relief, a thawing, to feel something for them / me. Maybe attachment is such a powerful force that we know at some level how desperate we might have become if things had not gone well for us: "Hold me up afloat" (Sonnet 80). The Sonnets regularly allude to the fact that attachment is a learning field, a field of difficulty and striving to articulate. This is one meaning of the convention whereby the sonneteer disclaims verbal capacity. Sonnets seem to know they are transitional objects and thus thematize the effortfulness of language acquisition, our need of help when we try to say what we feel.

Attachment happens whether or not children are well treated. Abused kids often defend their parents and fear being taken from them. Attachment may ensure survival, but like any evolutionary mechanism (if such it be), it is not designed to make us *happy*. In fact it gets crazy all too easily: "Thy adverse party is thy advocate" (Sonnet 35). The world of the Sonnets is an intersubjective one—Sonnets are about the way others live in our minds—and the focus on attachment in the Sonnets is (of course) unrelenting: "But if the while I think on thee, dear friend, / All losses are restored, and sorrows end" (Sonnet 30). As in earliest infancy, "love's face" is endlessly there, old and young, mine and yours, "thy mother's glass" (Sonnets 3, 93): bright-eyed, fair-browed, unpainted, furrowed, "chapped with tanned antiquity" (Sonnet 62), the dwelling place of sweet love, white and deep vermilion, or neither white nor deep vermilion, but still "as rare" (Sonnet 130). Even amid the flurry described in Sonnet 143, we glimpse the face of the mother: the bird "flies before" it. It is as if the Sonnets were recording the internalization of "active quiet"—the short periods of time in which infant-mother pairs focus on each other's faces, open-

mouthed, looking, looking away and back again, smiling, imitating, recipro-
cating, talking and listening, and then some rest. This is "phatic" communion,
the purpose of which is not to communicate information but, rather, to create
intersubjectivity. This means, also, the experience of aliveness.

So "you" occupy my mind, "and this gives life to thee" (Sonnet 18). Fine, if
you are alive in my mind—or, rather, if that is where I have to talk to you, you
probably are not around. But this is not just about controlling the locomo-
tions of the other by incorporating them; it is about the way representation
allows us to maintain and create *links* with people we cannot be with. Like
mothers who are at work. Like inappropriate objects whose presence would
call our judgment into question. The Sonnets foreground how thinking
about you, caring for you, attending to you spells life for me, and vice versa.
Attention can go wrong (e.g., it can become aggressive), but giving and receiving it stirs up our vitality affects. When attention is refused or distracted,
we cry, we follow our beloved's followings: "Whilst her neglected child holds
her in chase, / Cries to catch her whose busy care is bent / To follow that
which flees before her face." It is insofar as the Sonnets engage us in the
process of *attending* that they vivify and intensify our felt experience; so you
"gave my heart another youth" (Sonnet 110). How could we *not* fall in love
with those who give us life—as we seek in turn to vivify those we love? This is
why "still-face" experiments—when the caregiver is asked to keep his or her
face still—induce anxiety in babies. In the presence of an expressionless
mother, babies will start crying in short order.

The world of the Sonnets is a simple one. Mostly we just feel the seasons,
whether it is day or night, warm or cold. Besides plants and flowers there are a
few objects, but not many: clock, mirror, plough, ink, the occasional fancy
tomb. And the only thing I am doing with my mind is thinking about you,
trying to express how I feel about you, how you make me feel. Others are
pretty vague, however powerful to intrude. We do not notice much about
what they look like or do. (Except for the inevitable third. When the Dark
Lady arrives on the scene, everything changes.) The *thought* of you, on the
other hand, "thy sweet love *remembered*," restores losses, ends sorrows; thinking and feeling have agency in the Sonnets, we attend to their doings. Attachment consists of this kind of (inter)subjective activity and concentration. Arguably, sonnets follow the intersubjective workings of attachment more
closely than any other literary genre. When do we ever witness in greater
detail the vital role of symbol formation and memory in helping us survive an
absence, bear anxiety, fend off panic? Is the timing of a sonnet sequence—

engagement-pause, engagement-pause, on and on—not also the timing of symbol formation?

A sonnet sequence is a sequence of moods. Its time and timing are (inter)-subjective, processual and associational. As a sequence, it foregrounds link-ing.[14] There are disturbances (advent of Dark Lady) and opportunities for linkage. There is the feeling of needing to *absorb* change or of getting stuck in some really bad affect ("For I have sworn thee fair, and thought thee bright, / Who art as black as hell, as dark as night" [Sonnet 147]). The speaker is always in the middle of loving: "My love is as a fever, longing still" (Sonnet 147). The sequence foregrounds specifically the linking of language to affect: the link-ing power of metaphor, the deepening resonance of repeated words, the rhythm of the heartbeat, disturbed by "busy care" and two instances of en-jambment in the opening lines (Sonnet 143), signaling flurry, shift in focus, attention diverted; then, the rhythmic reassurance of "Play the mother's part, kiss me, be kind," reinforced by alliteration, reassurance given us by the form of the poem if, on the level of content, only hoped for; a sonorous scheme repeated, over and over again. The intricacy of the sonnet form is about "preverbal" communion, the feeling of *attunement* that can be solicited by a complex, tight little rhyme scheme or disrupted; the brevity as well as the intensity of attention. Rhythm is about continuity and its disruption. Meta-phor is based on the cross-modal communication of infants and caregivers and on the pattern recognition we are born with. Rhyme, rhythm, and meta-phor link things and signs that are different from each other. Or signal discor-dance. Everything about the form of the sonnet sequence evokes the intensity of actively quiet attention, its attention to detail, to responsiveness.

Speaking of psychoanalysis, Marcio Giovanetti has suggested that "the quality of an analysis depends upon the capacity of both the analyst and the analysand . . . to create what in poetry is called 'rhyme.'"[15] The queer effect of the Sonnets' engrossment derives from the linking of elaborate language about feeling to wordless infantile experience: linguistic virtuosity and in-tense "preverbal" communion; age and youth; youth and age. "Thou art thy mother's glass, and she in thee / Calls back the lovely April of her prime: / So thou through windows of thine age shall see, / Despite of wrinkles, this thy golden time" (Sonnet 3). This heteronormative command to reproduce not-withstanding, the Sonnets make us feel the queerness of the loves, lives, and letters generated by generation. "Help" links the generations with strong bonds, with *jouissance*. We need the incest taboo because generation *generates* transgenerational love. We all grow up on Queer Street.

Notes

1. All citations to Shakespeare's Sonnets are from http://www.Shakespeares-Sonnets.com.

2. Recall, e.g., Julia Kristeva on maternal *jouissance*, in *Desire in Language*, 191.

3. Fonagy, "A Developmental Theory of Sexual Enjoyment."

4. Winnicott, "Transitional Objects and Transitional Phenomena."

5. Van Leeuwen and Pomer, "The Separation-Adaptation Response to Contemporary Object Loss."

6. Ibid., 715–16.

7. See, e.g., Hackett, "Was Shakespeare Gay?"; Halpern, *Shakespeare's Perfume*; Rothenberg, "Infantile Fantasies in Shakespearean Metaphor."

8. Brennan, *The Transmission of Affect*, 143.

9. Massumi, *Parables for the Virtual*, 14, 38.

10. Bateman and Fonagy, *Psychotherapy for Borderline Personality Disorder*, 64.

11. Doidge, *The Brain That Changes Itself*.

12. See the discussion of "Amodal Perception" and "Vitality Affects" in Stern, *The Interpersonal World of the Infant*, 47–61.

13. Bateman and Fonagy, *Psychotherapy for Borderline Personality Disorder*, 79.

14. Bion, "Attacks on Linking."

15. Smith, "Creating the Psychoanalytical Process, Incorporating Three Panel Reports," 224.

The Sonnets

Speech Therapy

BARBARA JOHNSON

"I fell and broke my hip," I repeated. "My room is too hot." I took deep breaths, articulated slowly, and didn't break the flow of sound coming out of my mouth. But the words felt heavy and lumbering. Each one demanded a separate effort and called up images I fought against in the middle of the night. A missed connection, a step miscalculated, a loss of balance. My condition had been diagnosed a year before. So far, the only signs were losing my voice occasionally and periodic difficulty in articulating words. These episodes were accompanied by a flood of images generated by the doctor's list of possible developments.

"I fell and broke my hip," I repeated, looking into the face of the speech therapist, who made encouraging movements with her head. I wondered what she had read on my chart, whether her objective was to help me articulate that "I had fallen and broken my hip" or to help me develop another connection for converting thoughts into words.

I focused on her face, looking as if I wanted her approval. But her smile and her cheery turquoise shirt distracted me. She looked young and dedicated, focused on the short-term objective. Encourage the subject to talk. Change topics if indicated. Body language important. Lean toward subject in a supportive mode.

She would say each sentence, and I would copy her pronunciation. She looked encouraged. But the sentences, and my resistance to hearing them, grew heavier. They were depressing. They evoked a hospital room, a cranky patient, a catastrophic event. Couldn't I repeat something worth memorizing instead? "Sure," she said. "What would you like to try?"

"Shakespeare's Sonnets," I answered without thinking. Her question had caught me off guard. I had assumed anything I suggested would be hypothetical.

She whirled to her computer, clicked three or four times, and lo and behold! Shakespeare's Sonnets started emerging from her printer. She was clearly pleased to oblige: she knew who Shakespeare was, and she knew where to find him. "Pick one," she said triumphantly.

"Number 73," I responded, choosing the one everyone knew.

> That time of year thou mayst in me behold
> When yellow leaves, or none, or few do hang
> Upon those boughs which shake against the cold,
> Bare ruin'd choirs, where late the sweet birds sang.
> In me thou see'st the twilight of such day
> As after sunset fadeth in the West;
> Which by and by black night doth take away,
> Death's second self, that seals up all in rest.
> In me thou see'st the glowing of such fire,
> That on the ashes of his youth doth lie,
> As the death-bed whereon it must expire,
> Consum'd with that which it was nourish'd by.
>> This thou perceiv'st, which makes thy love more strong,
>> To love that well which thou must leave ere long.[1]

She held the page, looked down at it, and read. "That time of year thou may'st in me behold, When yellow leaves, or none, or few do hang. . . ."

"Wait a minute," I stopped her. "Maybe this is too hard." "Look in thy glass," I thought, "and tell the face thou viewest, Now is the time. . . ." She was trying too hard to put me at ease, staring too intently at my mouth as I articulated the words. She simulated what she thought was a teacherly tone. "Let's look at the whole poem, then, just to get our bearings. It has fourteen lines," she concluded, smiling to elicit a response from me.

"All sonnets have fourteen lines; that's what a sonnet is." I watched as she processed the information. But was she noting the form of a sonnet or the spacing between the words I uttered? I couldn't read her face.

"So do all sonnets have fourteen lines? It's a form, like a haiku?" Connection made. She had left her track and looked to me for an answer.

"Yes, but actually there are two main kinds: the Petrarchan, with two quatrains and two tercets, and the Shakespearean, with three quatrains and a couplet."

"Who was Petrarch?" she asked. Was she waiting to hear how my words would come out or whether he was a Shakespearean? Petrarch's name included two aspirated consonants that would indicate whether the subject was breathing, articulating, and connecting. I had spoken his name so quickly that she hadn't caught any hesitation.

"Er, ah, an Italian writer from about the same time as Dante." Now I was caught up in the game, seduced by the temptation to see how long I could keep her on content instead of my pronunciation.

But she was counting. "OK, then, there are three quatrains in this and a couplet," she responded.

"Not only does it have three quatrains, but each one is a separate grammatical unit and a different metaphor, and the couplet, as here, is supposed to comment on what has gone before." I was on home territory, and she had crossed over. I had offered the bait, and she had gone for it. I leaned back in my chair and asked her quietly, "What's wrong with this picture, by the way":

When yellow leaves, or none, or few do hang . . . ?

She leaned forward. When I didn't answer, she offered, "Well, it's Fall." I smiled in an effort to get her to elaborate. Encourage the subject to talk. Change topics if indicated. Body language important. Lean toward subject in a supportive mode. I tried another question: "But why does he put 'few' after 'none'?"

She remained quiet. "I give up," she said. The printout of the sonnet folded between her hands as she leaned back into her chair. She had been keeping the rhythm, articulating the answers, and concentrating on the questions. Now she looked disoriented. The rules of the game had been switched; the lines of demarcation blurred and the roles reversed. Teacher and student, form and content, fear and reassurance.

"So," I said, "why does he put 'few' after 'none'? Because the logic of the poem leads you to expect that you are going toward the worst, but here, there is a moment of hope just when you least expect it."

I sat as still as I could to avoid sending any signals. She had come all the way from "repeat after me" to quatrains and metaphors. If I had led her there, it meant we had both gone the distance. I didn't want to go back.

In the moment before she answered, I could see her debating several responses. I recognized relief from the way she relaxed her cheek muscles as she retreated from the logic of the poem to her own territory.

"I'm afraid time's up for this week," she said. "Here's a little paragraph I cut out that some people stick up by their mirror," she added, handing me a little square photocopied passage cut from something. "In the course of this week, I'd like you to look at this poem in a new way. Use different color magic markers to indicate where in the mouth the consonants are, and try to bring everything forward as much as possible." Homework. She knew how to make me feel comfortable.

When I got home, I photocopied the Sonnets in *The Norton Anthology of Poetry* and sat down to do the assignment. At first I could see only the words. *"Consum'd with that which it was nourish'd by."* Looking for consonants in a text that was still living was like performing an autopsy on a warm body. *"That time of year thou mayst in me behold . . . Bare ruin'd choirs . . . Sweet birds sang.* "M," "F," "B," and "P" were clearly in the front. And where were "D," "N," and "C"? And "L"?

My eyes dropped to the end of the sonnet. "To love that well which thou must leave ere long." Love well, leave ere long. "Verb plus one-syllable adverb, verb plus two-syllable adverb." In the back of my mind, I was somewhere between the warm body and the autopsy, but I didn't want to leave that place. "Leave . . . It's the same consonant as leaves!" My heart was beating faster, but I didn't forget to breathe. "The end says 'you love me even if you know I'm going to die'—your love is that positive thing that comes suddenly when the worst is predicted. The same logic as 'When yellow leaves, or none, or few do hang'! 'Leave'—the verb, mortality—echoes 'leaves,' the noun, the substance of that hope." I would never have made that link (note the "I") without taking note of the consonants. The exercises suddenly seemed less absurd to me.

I looked at the little square of instructions. The size and shape of it resembled a sonnet. I read:

> Compensation requires that speech production become conscious: Darley, Aronson, and Brown (1975) included the notion of purposeful activity among their basic principles of treatment. They stressed the need to make speech highly conscious, recognizing that doing so requires a major shift in the speaker's orientation to the speech act, one in which being heard and understood takes precedence over quick and emotive expression. Conscious control requires constant monitoring and self-criticism, at least during the early stages of therapy, as well as recognition by the clinician and patient that maximum effort rarely can be maintained constantly.

I smiled. This was hardly advice any self-respecting academic needed.

The next week I arrived with my own text of the poems, properly highlighted, with the consonants in the front colored in bright yellow and those from the back of the mouth in lime green. In the elevator, I closed my eyes for a moment to center myself. It's just a matter of breathing in and breathing out. The door swung open a few seconds after the sound of the bell.

"Guess what I have," I said, showing her the multicolored sonnets on which I had been working. "No," she replied, "guess what I have." I looked down as she pulled out the small, hardback, pocket-size 1929 edition of Shakespeare's sonnets she had just bought at a friend's moving sale. "I thought it might be easier to read from a book than from a printout," she said.

"This is fantastic!" I said, fingering the little book. "This will show what they were thinking in 1929."

"I never thought of that. The sonnets stay the same, but the editions change. What would be a modern edition?"

"Actually, the sonnets don't stay exactly the same either, but you're right— the apparatus changes far more." (After all, it was Shakespeare who asked, "Why write I still all one, ever the same?") I gave her some references.

"I have to get used to this language," she said. "So ''ere' means 'before,' 'bark' means 'boast,' 'time's scyth' means 'mortality.' . . ."

Meanwhile I repeated to myself, "Compensation Requires. Purposeful activity. Speech must be highly conscious and constantly monitored, but this type of effort could rarely be maintained constantly." Suddenly my eye fell on Sonnet 85. "Listen to this!" I shouted:

> My tongue-tied muse in manners holds her still,
> While comments of your praise, richly compiled,
> Reserve their character with golden quill
> And precious phrase by all the muses filed.
> I think good thoughts, whilst others write good words,
> And like unlettered clerk still cry amen,
> To every hymn that able spirit affords,
> In polished form of well-refinèd pen.
> Hearing you praised, I say, "'tis so," "'tis true,"
> And to the most of praise add something more.
> But that is in my thought, whose love to you,
> Though words come hindmost, holds his rank before.
>> Then others for the breath of words respect,
>> Me for my dumb thoughts, speaking in effect.

"I'm afraid I don't understand much," she sighed. "What does 'in manners holds her still' mean?"

"It means, 'This is why we need speech therapy,' " I replied.

Note

1. Sonnet 73, and all quotations are from Ferguson, *Norton Anthology of Poetry*.

More Life: Shakespeare's Sonnet Machines

JULIAN YATES

Will we one day be able, and in a single gesture, to join the thinking of the event to the thinking of the machine? Will we be able to think . . . *both* what is happening (we call that an event) *and* the calculable programming of an automatic repetition (we call that a machine)? Will we be able in the future (and there will be no future except on this condition) to think *both* the event *and* the machine as two compatible or even indissociable concepts, although today they appear to us to be antinomic? Antinomic because we think that what happens ought to keep, so we think, some non-programmable and therefore incalculable singularity. . . . No thinking of the event, therefore, without an aesthetic and some presumption of living organicity.

—Jacques Derrida, "Typewriter Ribbon," 277

Moments of disorientation are vital.

—Sara Ahmed, *Queer Phenomenology,* 157

One of the characteristics of our collective moment is the confusion as to what constitutes life or the appearance of "life." The distinction between organism and machine, between the organic and inorganic, "event" and "repetition," is no longer clear.

Following Michel Foucault and Giorgio Agamben, we may attribute this erosion of clear distinctions between a more freely distributed *zoë,* "bare life," and a human *bios* to the biopolitics of the modern state, liberal and totalitarian, and its processing of citizen-subjects.[1] We could also, following historians and sociologists of techno-science, attribute this confusion of categories to the de-territorialization of life as "code" effected by microbiology's remodeling of the organism as an encoding of genetic information.[2] "No longer a sovereign site of interiority, a vital inside that struggles with an inanimate outside," observes Richard Doyle, "organisms in the contemporary life sciences become moments in an evolutionary syntax, nodes in a network not of 'vitality' but of information." This becoming-code enables life to travel to "milieus other than carbon." It makes life the effect of a particular network of actors, human and not, rendering some of those actors more and less "lively." The machine / organism opposition is reduced, in his words, to a "smudge." "More than a becoming-machine of the organism, this retooling or 'refiguring' of life," continues Doyle, "provokes double-takes on the becoming-lively of the machine."[3] Are you and I simply "wetware," the necessary occasion or prostheses by which our machines simulate life or our genetic codes are made mobile? "Our machines are disturbingly lively," is how Donna Haraway frames this confusion, "we ourselves frighteningly inert."[4]

My aim in this short essay is to provoke a series of readerly disorientations or reorientations to William Shakespeare's 154 Sonnets that treats them as an exercise in a mode of thinking that troubles the distinctions between "event" and "machine," "organic" and "inorganic," "life" and "liveliness." It is usual to locate in Shakespeare's Sonnets (1609) a variously modeled account of a sometimes transhistorical, sometimes historically bounded human desire, sexuality, or personhood, figured as retrievable content. In what follows, I model the Sonnets and the critical apparatus they have acquired in the editing as an "event machine": a series of programs or routines that produce affective "events" in and for readers, who recursively attribute their processing of and by those routines to an "incalculable singularity" that goes either by the name of the historical person-qua-referent "Shakespeare" or to the Sonnets themselves as repository of value. The Sonnets offer rhetorical software that renders their readers and the historical worlds those readers posit "lively."

To this end, it may be useful to recall that in England in the 1590s and in the first decades of the seventeenth century, the word "sonnet" was both a noun and a verb, designating a constitutive process by which a person might be translated into poetic praise.[5] As emitters of sonnet objects or sonnet matter, Renaissance poets served both as purveyors of a cult of immortality and as relays in a grand mechanism of cultural translation by which those people named "English" entered into a "becoming Italian," or "becoming Petrarch." Within this economy of translation, "sonneteering" or "sonnetizing" figured quite clearly as a set of techniques for creating new orders of "life effects" as the dedication page to Shakespeare's Sonnets (1609) attests:

To. The. Onlie. Begetter. Of.

These. Insuing. Sonnets.

M^r. W. H. All. Happinesse.

And That Eternitie.

Promised.

By.

Ovr. Ever-living. Poet.

Wisheth.

The. Well-Wishing.

Adventurer. In.

Setting.

Forth.

T. T.[6]

Here, at the very moment the text of the Sonnets appears to allude to a possible identity for the simulacral young man they address, "Mr. W. H.," the literary speculator Thomas Thorpe engages in a little typographical self-congratulation that it is he who has served as faithful intermediary, making good on the promises made by "our ever-living poet," which are realized in the here and now of you gazing at the dedication page to this "sonneted" eternity of a book.

But what exactly is the product of this "begetting?" What order or forms of life issue forth? My title, "More Life," frames one answer—an answer that asks you to hear the word "life" as a collective noun referring to an abundance of forms or, to use the Renaissance word, "kinds." Heard this way, "More Life" manifests not as the demand for a continuance on the linear state of being (my life, your life) but stages an ontological slide as types of beings and ways of being multiply. The phrase emerges in the course of an iconic scene in Ridley Scott's film *Blade Runner* (1982) that may serve as a staging ground for the kind of reorientation I propose.[7] In this scene, a figural machine or inorganic, Roy Batty, addresses its maker and does so in a manner that suspends the script of filial piety and fatherhood that typically codes invention. In doing so, Batty offers an inhuman model of desire, a replicant reading of the human.

More Life, Replicant Reading

"What seems to be the problem?" asks Elden Tyrell, founder of the Tyrell Corporation, which manufactures replicants, or "skin jobs," so lively that they pass as "organic," "human," and "alive." "More Human than Human" is the company's motto. "Death" replies Roy Batty, who has returned to Earth with three of his kind to discover whether it is possible to prolong their lives beyond the fixed four-year terminus the company engineers. "Well," Tyrell temporizes, "that seems a little out of my jurisdiction." But Batty interrupts. "I want more life, fucker," he says, pronouncing "fuck-er" slowly, accenting the syllables so that an audience may hear the trace of the eroded sound "father," haunting the word that now signifies as curse.[8]

As Doyle notes in his inspired reading of the film, "Replication is the simulacrum's habit and habitat. 'Fucker' is therefore not a term of abuse, but an empirical observation about the differing modes of proliferation deployed by simulacra and sexually reproducing organisms respectively; simulacra are not heterosexual kin, they threaten to float free of their economies or ecologies of 'origin.' As replicators and not reproducers, the skin jobs of *Blade Runner* threaten not to fuck." Simulacra, Doyle adds, "emerge out of an ecology of neither sex nor death" and so figure "a desire not anchored in any reproductive economy." The demand, "I want more life, fucker!" anticipates "the contingency of a machine that would float free of the constraints suffered and enjoyed by its creators"[9]—hence, the necessity within the logic of the film of implanting death effects, a final, abusive, deadly mimesis of the human, that will produce not death, for the machine has never been "alive," but a simulated ending that is nevertheless final.

It is tempting, then, to read Batty's "More Life" as the machine's desire for more "life," plural, more bodies to render it more "lively." "More users," "more readers" is perhaps the cast of Thomas Thorpe's pitch to the patron-cum-begetter of the Sonnets, he whose refusal to "fuck" brings about the proliferation of sonnets that Thorpe presents—a pitch made more successfully still by the editors of the First Folio (1623). Read this way, like "fuck-er," the word "begetter" signifies an occasion or "event" whose singularity is a product of its proliferation in so very many sonnets. In this guise, you and I become "read-ers," those who lumber into view as potential hosts to the routines and programs that the simulacral young man the Sonnets beget. Sonnet 55 sees us coming. Pitting the linguistic materiality of its "pow'rful rhyme" against "the gilded monuments / of princes" (48), it describes the viral process by which the beloved object "live[s] in this, and dwell[s] in lovers' eyes" (51)—as the poem installs itself via the "eies" of its readers.

Sonnet 122 depicts the process via the uncertain status of a "gift" that hovers uncertainly within and without the speaker:

Thy gift, thy tables, are within my brain
Full charactered with lasting memory,
Which shall above that idle rank remain
Beyond all date ev'n to eternity—
Or at the least, so long as brain and heart
Have faculty by nature to subsist—
Till each to razed oblivion yield his part
Of thee, thy record never can be missed.
That poor retention could not so much hold,
Nor need I tallies thy dear love to score.
Therefore to give them from me was I bold
To trust those tables that receive thee more.
    To keep an adjunct to remember thee
    Were to import forgetfulness in me. (104)

But what exactly is the gift the speaker has received? Were these "tables" a type of commonplace book filled with fine words and memories written by the giver? Were they a blank set of pages that the speaker dutifully filled with descriptions of the person he observes? Were they a table-book in which phrases have been written on wax sheets and so subject to easy or ready erasure and reuse?[10] In the course of the first eight lines, the orientation between the speaker and "thy tables" shifts, casting speaker as both reader and writer. We know that he has "thy tables" or their contents memorized— "charactered" away. To have kept them would have been to "keep an adjunct" to the "adjunct" that the speaker has himself already become. "Thy tables" are gone—given away, "razed," perhaps, and ready for re-charactering in the hands of others. What the sonnet imagines, then, is an enlivening circuit, an on-going set of modifications to both the speaker and the "tables," as their giver's memory winks in and out of being.

The demand "more life" signals a mode of reading that attends to the way the Sonnets might be said to "seduce" or recruit readers by and with representing "life," or its appearance, to their "wetware."[11] In this sense, the vast language of poetic repair and maintenance that the Sonnets describe, as in the concluding couplet of Sonnet 15—"And all in war with time for love of you / As he takes from you, I engraft you new" (16)—trades on a discourse of anticipation, a liveliness with regard to death, that transforms "life" into the repetition of a series of routines. Time appears here as a reversible and contingent effect of a particular technology, making the historical referent "Shakespeare" or his

Sonnets more intensely "present" *here, today*, in the eternal present of the copy you hold in your hands.

But is it clear that this is the kind of "life" the Sonnets want? The discourse of lack, of human desire still animates this model of what organisms and machines may be said to demand. Surely, "more life" speaks not of linear duration or of fixed quantity but, instead, of inexhaustible surplus or multiplicity. Just "more," "more" forms of "life," enacting, perhaps, Elizabeth Grosz's modeling of insect mimesis and mimicry as "always in excess of their survival value" and always revealing "the captivation of a creature by its representations of and as space."[12] Read this way, Batty's demand for "more life" asks for more programs, more routines, more ways to be lively—more sonnets, please, more ways to feel, to see off the terminal death effects that approach.

More Lively, Replicant Editing

Some way into appendix 1 of Stephen Booth's edition of the Quarto of 1609 (1977), you can read the follow summation of inquiries as to the sexual orientation of William Shakespeare and his *Sonnets*: "HOMOSEXUALITY: William Shakespeare was almost certainly homosexual, bisexual, or heterosexual. The sonnets provide no evidence on this matter. See 126.4, note" (548).

However tempting it may be to write off Booth's dry dismissal of the "matter" of Shakespeare's sexuality as a bad-tempered attack of the editorial grumps, or worse, there is something in the cast of his syntax that disorients, threatens, or even aims to proliferate. Even as Booth closes off the question of a finite sexual identity—"William Shakespeare was almost certainly homosexual, bisexual, or heterosexual"—the studied nonchalance of the self-canceling "almost certainly" renders any closure of the "matter" premature. The insistence on a fundamental disconnect between the linguistic materiality of the Sonnets and the referential "William Shakespeare" introduces the possibility that the historical person named "Shakespeare," not to mention the legion of variously historical people named "readers," might factor their desires and take their pleasures in ways that defy the logic of any reproductive economy. It is not simply that by his syntax Booth renders the "matter" of Shakespeare's sexuality indeterminate but that, even as his sentence seems to close on a finite possibility, it renders that sexuality multiple or as multiplicity.

Clearly, Booth is having fun. He is out to deep-six what he regards as the biographical excesses of those critics he chooses to confine to appendix 1. For the hyper-formalist Booth, we might say that the error of bio-graphy or life writing is that the "life" or *bios* it writes is, in truth, the "liveliness" of a reader mistakenly attributed to the defunct historical referent, "Shakespeare," whom the reader now resuscitates to live out a zombified existence in the reader's own writing project du jour. In Jacques Derrida's terms, we might say that readers who deduce from the Sonnets a sexual "event" indexed to an organic being—"Shakespeare"—are instead caught in a series of routines or "automatic repetitions" that they attribute to an "incalculable singularity" rather than to the programs of the text. Viewed this way, from the perspective provided by Booth's hyper-formalism, the Sonnets assume the status of a machine, a calculable program of routines that seek to produce the effect of an "incalculable singularity," a "life" or series of lively "life effects." Where do these "life effects" occur? Not merely in the organic host body of the reader but in the circuit or network that forms between Sonnets and readers.

That Booth calls foul when it comes to biography does not mean that his edition aspires to exit the predicament he reveals. On the contrary: Where biographers find life enduring in and among the Sonnets, treating them as fossilized affect, Booth lets the Sonnets be. He exchanges the "bad fetish" of bios writing for the "good fetish," or "incalculable singularity" of "the sonnets we have"—or that he will make (ix). His editorial practice then constitutes a mode of zoography, an attempt to map the inhuman matrix of the Sonnets without reference to the supposed human bios, Shakespeare. Of course this zoography is itself indexed to a moral imperative and a moral philosophy of his own. The jocular hit of hyper-formalism he deploys prepares the ground (surprise, surprise) for his own machinic operation, his own relays for producing forms of "life" from a reading of the Sonnets. As Booth tells us in his preface, "My primary purpose in the present edition is to provide a text that will give a modern reader as much as I can resurrect of a Renaissance reader's experience of the 1609 Quarto" (ix). "I have adopted no editorial principle," he continues, "beyond that of trying to adapt the modern reader—with his assumption about idiom, spelling, and punctuation—and the 1609 text to one another."

Open this edition, then; work your way through the facing facsimile reproduction of the 1609 edition of the Sonnets and Booth's lightly edited and regularized versions; and you, the reader, are the bios being written, the life being produced. Stick with it, and you will find yourself "becoming 1609"—or, more accurately, "becoming Booth in 1977 (or thereabouts) as he 'becomes 1609.'" Almost immediately, then, Booth's ostensible historical or historicist project reveals itself to be closer to a grafting or splicing of different time frames, stabilized by the empty reference that derives from Booth's continual, symptomatic use of the personal pronoun. "I think it will be profitable if I demonstrate the problems inherent in this sort of commentary" (xi); "I fear that much of what I say will look mad to a reader who forgets that when I say 'suggestion,' or 'overtone,' and when I talk about ideas and echoes that merely cross the reader's mind, I mean only what I say." Booth worries that his fidelity to the textual machine will lead his readers to think that he has become too lively, too animated, listing, as he sometimes does, "peripheral, rhyme-like repetitions of stock words . . . in different meanings . . . possible puns" (xi), and that readers will become frustrated or angry with him as his "notes can seem dedicated not to doing what the commentary should do—clarify the sonnets—but to transforming lines that are simple and clear into something complicated and obscure" (x). Like Grosz's camouflaging insect, the mimicking historicist of Booth's hyperbolic formalism gets the better of him. The "mutual adaptation" of reader and Sonnets on which Booth embarks figures a mode of life lived as liveliness merely, a giving of oneself to the role of "fuck-er" / "read-er" as demanded by the figural machine Roy Batty. And in doing so, like the "mimicking insect," Booth "lives a camouflaged existence as not quite [him]self, as another."[13] So also do his read-ers.

Repair

Sonnet 16 is a special case. "This is Sonnet 16" (xi), writes Booth, eventalizing the poem:

> But wherefore do not you a mightier way
> Make war upon this bloody tyrant time?
> And fortify yourself in your decay
> With means more blessed than my barren rhyme?
> Now stand you on the top of happy hours,
> And many maiden gardens yet unset,
> With virtuous wish would bear your living flowers,
> Much liker than your painted counterfeit.
> So should the lines of life that life repair
> Which this time's pencil or my pupil pen
> Neither in inward worth nor outward fair
> Can make you live yourself in eyes of men.

> To give away yourself keeps yourself still,
>
> And you must live, drawn by your own sweet skill. (ix, 16)

In the minute mapping of potential readings that follows, Booth treats this poem as an inexhaustible fund or site of linguistic fecundity. The poem rehearses a language of "repair," asking the simulacral young man to draw out his own "lines of life," children, in place of the "lines of life" that spring from the speaker's pen. Only they will enable him to live "in eyes of men," for indeed his children will be those "men." And "his" life will be lived as theirs.

Booth notes the potential for an intra-lingual pun on *père* in "repair" (159), but this pun represents an uncertain signal. Like Roy Batty's emphatic dissyllabic "fuck-er / fath-er," the pun subsumes the stable discourse of paternity into a larger discourse of replication. It will be the "lines of life," after all, children and sonnets, that "repair" or re-*père* (re-father) the young man—the anticipation of some putative future installing itself in his actions, disciplining his present, even now. At the core of Sonnet 16's ostensible subordination of its "barren rhyme" to the "lines of life" subsists a modeling of human reproduction from the position provided by the machine, reversing the genealogical cast of the phrase "lines of life" so that those "lines" represent the security that will render the putatively dead young man "lively," if not alive. No father, then; just as Batty might put it: some "fuck-er."

If, as I have argued, Sonnet 16 stages a modeling of human reproduction from the vantage point provided by poetic or machinic replication, then, as Booth's edition shows us, we have it always in our power to refuse such paternal ghosts as haunt these lines. It is possible always, in other words, to give oneself over to the zoë of the text and so "to think *both* the event *and* the machine as two compatible or even indissociable concepts." Stick with the Sonnets, then; steer clear of the urge to invest in this or that remnant of a "life" or a "bios" that you think you find there, and perhaps we will find ourselves closer to understanding Batty's demand and wake to find ourselves not wanting or lacking anything but embarked, instead, on a quest for "more life."

Notes

I thank Carolyn Dinshaw for giving me the title of this essay; Karl Steel for sending me to Sara Ahmed; Jeffrey Cohen for his "inhuman art"; Madhavi Menon for the inspiration and the occasion; and Richard Burt for his joyful provocations.

1. Agamben, *Homo Sacer*, 1–2, 3–12.

2. It is not possible here to offer an exhaustive bibliography, but key studies

would include Doyle, *On Beyond Living*; Hayles, *How We Became Posthuman;* Squier, *Liminal Lives.*

3. Doyle, *Wetwares*, 121.

4. Haraway, "A Cyborg Manifesto," 152, also quoted in Doyle, *Wetwares*, 121.

5. *Oxford English Dictionary*, s.v. "sonnet."

6. Booth, *Shakespeare's Sonnets*, 3. Citations in parentheses refer to this edition.

7. Ridley Scott, dir., *Blade Runner*, Warner Brothers, June 23, 1982.

8. Hampton Fancher and David Peoples, screenplay for the film *Blade Runner*, February 23, 1981, available online at http://scribble.com/uwi/br/script_19810223 .txt (accessed January 11, 2009).

9. Doyle, *Wetwares*, 121–31, esp. 122, 123.

10. On the technology of erasable wax tables and table-books, see Peter Stallybrass, Roger Chartier, J. Franklyn Mowery, Heather Wolfe, "Hamlet's Tables and the Writing Technology of Shakespeare's England," *Shakespeare Quarterly* 55:4 (2004): 379–419.

11. Doyle, *Wetwares*, 29.

12. Elizabeth Grosz, "Libido as Desire and Death," in idem, *Space, Time, and Perversion*, 190.

13. Ibid.

Latin Lovers in *The Taming of the Shrew*

BRUCE SMITH

Except for necrophiliac philologists, a dead language will not strike most readers today as a sexy subject. More than once in Shakespeare's scripts, however, a student learning Latin provides the occasion for energetic sexual joking. Take, for example, the tutoring scene in Act 3, Scene 1, of *The Taming of the Shrew*, when Hortensio disguises himself as a music tutor and Lucentio disguises himself as a Latin tutor to gain access to the seemingly un-shrewish of the play's two sisters, Bianca:

> [Hortensio *tunes his lute.* Lucentio *opens a book*]
> *Bianca*: Where left we last?
> *Lucentio*: Here, madam.
>   [*Reads*] "*Hic ibat Simois, hic est Sigeia tellus,*
>   *Hic steterat Priami regia celsa senis.*"
> *Bianca*: Construe them.
> *Lucentio*: "*Hic ibat*," as I told you before—"*Simois*," I am Lucentio—"*hic
>   est*," son unto Vincentio of Pisa—"*Sigeia tellus*," disguised thus to get
>   your love—"*hic steterat*," and that Lucentio that comes a-wooing—
>   "*Priami*," is my man Tranio—"*regia*," bearing my port—"*celsa senis*,"
>   that we might beguile the old pantaloon.
> *Hortensio*: Madam, my instrument's in tune.
> *Bianca*: Let's hear. [Hortensio *plays*] O fie, the treble jars.
> *Lucentio*: Spit in the hole, man, and tune again.
> [Hortensio *tunes his lute again*]
> *Bianca*: Now let me see if I can construe it. "*Hic ibat Simois*," I know you
>   not—"*hic est Sigeia tellus*," I trust you not—"*hic steterat Priami*," take
>   heed he hear us not—"*regia*," presume not—"*celsa senis*," despair not.
> *Hortensio*: Madam, 'tis now in tune.
> *Lucentio*: All but the bass.
> *Hortensio*: The bass is right, 'tis the base knave that jars.[1]

No footnotes are needed to catch the double entendres on "my port" (or is it "my part"?), "my instrument," "spit in the hole," and "the bass." So far, so funny. But maybe not so queer. Sexy puns were, after all, to be expected: They were sixteenth-century playwrights' stock in trade. What is queer about this scene—queer in the more fundamental sense of querying orthodoxies of all sorts—is its conjoining of sex and syntax in such a way that the rules that govern both cases are called into question.

But why the conjunction of sex and syntax? For Shakespeare and his contemporaries there were several good reasons. For a start, what else should be on boys' minds after age twelve or so as they studied Latin? In *Taming*'s original performances, the bawdy puns may have been spoken by adults, but the humor is strictly puerile and would have appealed to the memories of everybody in the audience who had studied Latin. Then and now, Latin teaching is all about gender, declensions, conjugations, and couplings—in fine, about what goes *with* what, *by* what, *on* what, *in* what. Ultimately, sex and syntax go together because language articulates where body (and what is going on within, on, and through the body) becomes word. Sex and syntax compose what might be called "bio-psycho-philology," in itself a queer idea.

Ordinarily, biology, psychology, and philology are thought to belong to separate discourses. There is language or *logos* in each case, but that language operates within boundaries that have been heavily policed, at least within universities. Language about language (philology) and language about the entity that knows (psychology): An overlap there seems possible. But what could language about language (philology) possibly have to do with language about living bodies (biology)? Queer theory calls off the border police. Shakespeare and his original audience did not need postmodern theory, however, to tell them that the conjunction of sex and syntax was funny. The schoolroom scene in *Taming* takes its place in a play that calls into question the naturalness of sexual positions from start to finish. Standard classroom practice directed teachers and students to consider five aspects of the Latin language that positively invite playfulness on the part(s) of students: gender, declension, conjugation, coupling, and articulation. Let's play.

Gender

Anyone who wants to know where Queen Elizabeth's favorite playwright, John Lyly, got his knack for learned erotic innuendo might do well to consult his father's school textbook *A Short Introduction of Grammar*, which went through 285 printings between 1543 and 1800. Twenty-first-century queer theorists should be pleased by Lily's opening: "Genders of nouns be seven: the masculine, the feminine, the neuter, the common of two, the common of three, the doubtful, and the epicene." Subtle (we would say subconscious) links among "gender," "engender," "genitals," "generate," and "generations" seem to be present in the examples Lily chooses: a man (*hic vir*) for masculine gender, a woman (*haec mulier*) for feminine, a stone (*hoc saxum*) for neuter ("stone" was a slang term for testicles), a father or a mother (*hic* and *haec parents*) for the common thing among two genders, "happy" (*hic*, *haec*, and *hoc foelix*) for the common thing among three, a day (*hic vel haec dies*) for doubtful gender, and an eagle (*haec aquila*, "both he and she") for the epicene.[2] The last example in particular demonstrates how gender is not a naturally occurring thing but an artificially imposed classifying system. Biologically, an individual *aquila*, or eagle, can be male or female; grammatically, it is always feminine. And so, by implication, with humans.

Aficionados of classical mythology might have appreciated in the last example a gesture toward Jupiter in the guise of an eagle whisking Ganymede to Olympus. Just who was "epicene" in this episode was not really open to question. "Ganymede" was the common slang term for the boy favorite of an (often) older male lover, and all-consuming lusts like Jupiter's were thought to render a man effeminate. By these lights, Jupiter and Ganymede were both epicene.

Gender is subject to the same disjunctions in Act 3, Scene 1, of *The Taming of the Shrew*, as Hortensio and Lucentio play the effeminate suitors and trade sexually loaded insults with each other. Add Bianca's penis to the picture (in the play's original performances) and you have a situation to send Philip Stubbes and other moralistic enemies of theater into a paroxysm of spleen. Syntax is upset. Lucentio "jars," in Vicentio's final jab, because he wrecks the hoped for conjunction of *hic* and *haec*, he and she. Lucentio, who can go with Hortensio as easily as with Bianca, makes for loose syntax.

Declension

The verse that Lucentio chooses for his flirtatious dialogue with Bianca is, ironically, part of a letter the chaste Penelope writes to her husband, Ulysses, in Ovid's *Heroides*, a passage in which she quotes back to him his own words. Literally, the passage means, "Here flowed the Simois; here is the Sigeian land; here stood old Priam's lofty palace."[3] Lucentio, however, declines the verse otherwise. In doing so, he dusts off words to be found in a Latin dictionary and applies them to the living English flesh right there on the stage: *riami regia*, "Priam's palace." When Lucentio mistranslates that phrase to mean "bearing my part," he exploits the word's associations with both "king (*rex / regis*)" and "rule (*regula*, rule, pattern, model, what a king *does*)" even as he wrests Latin syntax to his own immediate ends. Bianca, who seems to be less adept at Latin than her teacher, does worse when she hears in *regia* the English word "rage" and translates it as an off-putting "presume not." What the two speakers attempt to do here, in Bianca's word, is "construe" the Latin passage, to deconstruct it by breaking it up into its parts and fitting those parts together according to standard rules of syntax. Having fun with language—making puns, for example—involves breaking those rules, but the schoolroom is not supposed to be a place for fun. And, besides, you have to know the rules before you can break them. John Brinsley sets the agenda in *The Posing of the Parts* (1615). Why are nouns, pronouns, verbs, and participles declined, Brinsley's student is scripted to ask the teacher. Answer: "They may be varied or changed from their first ending into diverse endings, as *magister, magistri, magistro* [teacher, of the teacher, to the teacher], *amo, amas, amat* [I love, you love, he / she / it loves]." The loving teacher. As with Lily, one wonders what was really on Brinsley's mind, or beneath it. From declining in the presence of the master to declining on a bed was an easy step, at least in the minds of schoolboys who had studied Latin under the likes of Brinsley's teacher.

Conjugation

To take a verb through all its persons, moods, and tenses was to *conjugate* it. *Amo, amas, amat*—at least, that would be the conjugation in Lucentio's case. In Bianca's case, it would be the passive-voice *amor, amaris, amatur*. If it is Bianca's case, and you take seriously the promise of her "despair not," it would be future tense: *amabo, amabis, amabit*. If you are not sure how serious she is, it would be the subjunctive *amem, ames, amet*. Enough! The conjugations that Lucentio and Vicentio have in mind do not have to be learned. All three participants in this Latin exercise seem to realize full well the etymological linkages among "conjugate," "conjugal," "conjoin," and "conjoint," all involving the fundamental idea of yoking two things together, as in the Latin "*conjungere* (to marry)."

Coupling

The queerest of the conjunctions between sex and syntax involves couplings, the agreements of nouns and adjectives and of nouns and pronouns with respect to gender and the coordination and subordination of clauses vis-à-vis each other. In *Taming*, in Hortensio's apt phrase, the couplings jar. Brinsley's dialogue on "construction" is particularly interesting in this regard. "What mean you by 'construction'?" the student asks. The teacher's answer sets in place three criteria of correctness: "The due joining or right ordering and framing together of words and speech. Or the right joining of the parts of speech together in speaking according to the natural manner, or according to the reason and rule of grammar."[4] Nature, reason, and rule supply the principles to be applied.

As in syntax, so in sex. At least that is the reasoning that informs the paired pamphlets *Hic Mulier* and *Haec Vir*, both from 1620. Lily's category of the epicene is not accepted by the pamphleteer, who wants women to look and behave like women and for men to behave like men. According to nature, reason, and rule, the epithets should be *Haec Mulier* (This Woman) and *Hic Vir* (This Man). The pamphleteer's reasoning in *Hic Mulier* starts from a grammatical point and invokes the father of grammar: "*Hic mulier*—how now? Break Priscian's head in the first encounter? But two words, and they false Latin? Pardon me, good Signor Construction, for I will not answer thee as the Pope did, that I will do it in despite of the grammar. But I will maintain, if it be not the truest Latin in our kingdom, yet it is the commonest. For since the days of Adam, women were never so masculine."[5] Man-like women break every syntactical rule. They are masculine in gender and generation ("from the mother to the youngest daughter"), in number ("from one to multitudes"), in case ("even from the head to the foot"), in mood ("from bold speech to impudent action"), in tense ("for without redress they were, are, and will be still most masculine, most mankind, and most monstrous.")[6] Bianca may not be dressed like a man, but her sauciness with her tutors / suitors flouts all the rules. Lucentio's construings of the Latin text are amusingly plausible, as well they might be for a man who has received a standard Latin education; hers fly wider of the mark. Bianca's behavior in Act 3, Scene 1, agrees (in gender, mood, and tense, if not in number and case) with Kate's far more audacious challenge of the syntactical rules of society in the rest of the play.

Kate's behavior is, in a word, preposterous. In *The Art of English Poesy*

(1589), George Puttenham provides a syntactical definition of "preposterous" as a strategy that poets might choose in certain situations: "Ye have another manner of disordered speech, when ye misplace your words or clauses and set that before which should be behind, & *è converso*. We call it in English proverb 'the cart before the horse.' The Greeks call it *histeron proteron*. We name it 'the preposterous,' and if it be not too much used is tolerable enough, and many times scarcely perceivable, unless the sense be thereby made very absurd."[7] So much for syntax. When it comes to sex, "preposterous" is altogether less tolerable. Jonathan Goldberg, Patricia Parker, and Jeffrey Masten have made "preposterous" a key word in queer philology.[8] Lucentio's and Bianca's macaronic exchanges in Act 3, Scene 1, shape up, at least for listeners who know Latin, as preposterous speech of just the sort that Puttenham describes: disordered, words and clauses misplaced, posterior elements in English ("as I told you before") put before anterior elements in Latin (*"Hic ibat,"* "here flowed"). And sex is the subtext.

With respect to sexual behavior, preposterous syntax, according to Brinsley, can mean two things: (1) "the concords of words" and (2) "the governing of words."[9] In her forwardness, Kate—and to a certain extent, her sister Bianca—upsets the concords of words by seizing the masculine *hic* and eschewing the feminine *haec*. Also at issue in their actions is a disruption in the governing of words, whereby the stronger controls the weaker, as, for example, the noun controlling the verb; the substantive, the adjective; the antecedent, the relative pronoun. When Bianca takes over Lucentio's Latin verse and turns it to her own ends, the verb governs the noun; the adjective, the substantive; the pronoun, the antecedent. All preposterous. "Take heed he hear us not," "presume not," "despair not": In the three commands that conclude her construal, Bianca turns the usually governing masculine "I" into an acted-on "you."

Articulation

The conjunction of sex and syntax in *Taming* and elsewhere in Shakespeare's plays points up the way language, literally, *articulates* the body. The word "articulate" in this connection carries a double meaning. Language joins together the body's parts at the same time that it divides vocal sound into the distinct parts that we know as words. This coupling of flesh and words is ultimately arbitrary, as the scene of Princess Catherine's learning English in *Henry V* makes uproariously clear:

Catherine: D'elbow, de nick, et de sin. Comment appelez-vous les pieds et
la robe?

Alice: De foot, madame, et de cown.

Catherine: De foot et de cown? O Seigneur Dieu! Ils sont les mots de son
mauvais,corruptible, gros, et impudique, et non pour les dames
d'honneur d'user. Je ne voudrais prononcer ces mots devant les
seigneurs de France pour tout le monde. Fuh! De foot et de cown!
Néanmoins, je réciterai une autre fois ma leçon ensemble. D'hand, de
fingre, de nails, d'elbow, de nick, de sin, de foot, de cown.

Alice: Excellent, madame![10]

The deconstructive effect of this scene—after all, the body part on which we
walk can just as readily be *"les pieds"* as "the feet"—is all the greater when the
governing noun is *pes / pedis*. Every educated man in early modern England in
effect knew *two* languages: the "mother tongue" he learned at his mother's
knee and the Latin lingua franca that he learned at the hands of a schoolmaster. Often enough, those hands were on the boy's posterior. Walter Ong has
called attention to the corporal punishment that was often involved in initiat-
ing boys into the all-male fraternity of Latin letters.[11] Learning Latin was, for
most boys, quite literally a pain in the butt. "Nouns and pronouns, I pronounce you traitors to boys' bottoms," quips the clown Will Summer in
Thomas Nashe's play *Summer's Last Will and Testament*. "Syntaxis and pros-
odia, you are tormentors of wit."[12] The word becomes flesh, indeed.

The consequence of this regime of corporal punishment was not only a
vocabulary of sexuality (we know all about that from Foucault) but a *syntax* of
sexuality, a set of rules for articulating the body. It was this queer form of
double consciousness—two vocabularies, two forms of syntax, one in English
and one in Latin—that created the room for slippage that Hortensio, Lucentio, and Bianca love to occupy. The humor they generate as they use Latin and
English words to play around with each other might seem to be culture-
specific. After all, you have to know at least something about Latin to appreciate the bawdy body puns that Lucentio and Bianca trade with each other.
Since learning Latin was one of the things that shaped boys into men, you
might say the sense of humor here is "puerile." The player who acted Bianca
in the play's original performances was, after all, just such a boy as might have
been found in a schoolroom if he were not apprenticed as an actor. Something more fundamental is going on, however. Every application of the pronoun "she" to the boy was an aural and visual illustration of Lily's "epicene"

gender and an abomination to the likes of the pamphleteer who wrote *Haec Vir*. The play of bodies in *The Taming of the Shrew* (the comedy is much more physical than in, say, *Love's Labour's Lost*) is accompanied by a play with language about bodies. The net result is an act of *disarticulation* that separates language from bodies and opens up room for imaginative play in between two languages. The schoolroom scene in *The Taming of the Shrew* gives new meaning to the epithet "Latin lover."

Notes

I thank Chris Pye, Reeve Parker, Ellis Hanson, Madhavi Menon, and the participants in the Shakesqueer Symposium at Cornell University.

1. *The Taming of the Shrew*, in Greenblatt et al., *The Norton Shakespeare*, 3.1.26–45. Citations in parentheses are to this edition. Other instances of erotic pedagogy are Hugh Evans's attempt to show off young William's Latin skills to Mistress Page in Act 4, Scene 1, of *The Merry Wives of Windsor* and (albeit in quick English, not dead Latin) Princess Catherine's learning from her lady-in-waiting Alice the English names for body parts in Act 4, Scene 1, of *Henry V*.

2. Lily, *A Short Introduction of Grammar*, sigs. C5–C5v; spelling and orthography modernized.

3. As cited and translated in Greenblatt et al., *The Norton Shakespeare*, 197.

4. Brinsley, *The Posing of the Parts*, sig. H3. In the first edition of *The Posing of the Parts* (1612), Brinsley cites only one criterion: "the natural manner."

5. *Hic Mulier, or The Man-Woman*, sig. A3; spelling and orthography modernized.

6. Ibid.

7. Puttenham, *The Art of English Poesy*, sig. V1; spelling modernized.

8. Goldberg, *Sodometries*, 180–81; Masten, "Is the Fundament a Grave?," 129–45; Parker, *Shakespeare from the Margins*, 20–55.

9. Brinsley, *The Posing of the Parts*, sig. H3.

10. *Henry V*, in Greenblatt et al., *The Norton Shakespeare*, 3.4.44–54.

11. Ong, *Fighting for Life*, 81.

12. Nashe, *Summer's Last Will and Testament*, sig. G3v; spelling and orthography modernized.

Forgetting *The Tempest*

KEVIN OHI

For many queer writers, to imagine scenarios of literary and cultural transmission is to confront the ways precious knowledges and forms have been
consigned to oblivion: writings lost or made forever uncertain by their equivocal provenance, by fragmentation, by adulterating translation, by illegible
or missing historical contexts, by charismatic misreading, by incompetent
teachers, or by dull or distracted students. There are reasons enough for gay
writers to be particularly attuned to temporal discontinuity. The more or less
active disregard for gay histories and knowledges (to say nothing of gay lives)
that makes for curiously resonant silences in official history means not only
that gay history, however conscientiously researched, is inevitably riddled
with blanks but also that, for the individual gay person, a dawning awareness
of same-sex desire cannot but mark a rupture in one's personal history. To
discover a world that fosters such desires is often to discover all the many ways
one's life did not lead there; such is the discontinuity of development called
"coming out." Lost texts can be found; lost histories can be recovered. Gay
people can cultivate an obliviousness to life's asynchronicity and can easily —
and, moreover increasingly, do—find ways to be reproductive. Yet the circumstances that force gay people to confront the discontinuities of conscious life
and of historical transmission are salutary to the degree that they make visible
one aspect of literary and cultural knowledge: its non-transmissibility. "How
splendid it would be, Agathon," says Socrates in *The Symposium*, "if wisdom
was the sort of thing that could flow from the fuller to the emptier of us when
we touch each other, like water, which flows through a piece of wool from a
fuller cup to an emptier one."[1] If Alcibiades's riotous interruption of the
celebrated banquet does not undermine, by de-sublimating, the defense of
boy love as a step toward ideal beauty that precedes it so much as undermine
the possibility of reading that passage itself as a form of sublimation, the
fantasy that knowledge could be passed by a touch is troubled not by the

teacher's compromising desire for such communion but by the compromising assumption that knowledge is a thing that can be contained, conveyed, or, in the jargon of twenty-first-century pedagogues, "assessed."

"How splendid it would be": The realization of knowledge's embodiment in a touch is less denied than consigned to a potentiality that preserves it.[2] Scenarios of lost knowledges and vanished texts in queer writings ask what it means to lose what cannot be possessed.[3] Queer imaginings of failed or thwarted transmission make perceptible the potentiality of literary "objects": Thus to meditate on what has been forgotten or lost is to bring out the interruption that writing shelters within it to the precise extent that is actualized.[4] These imaginings of lost texts enact the "remembrance" that, in Agamben's gloss of Benjamin, has the power to "redeem" the past: "Remembrance is neither what happened nor what did not happen but, rather, their potentialization, their becoming possible once again."[5] This is the context, to my mind, for understanding what is queer about *The Tempest*.

A curious scene has Prospero repeatedly, even obsessively, interrupting his narration to Miranda of the circumstances of their exile from Milan with injunctions to pay attention: "Dost thou attend me? . . . thou attend'st not . . . dost thou hear?" (1.2.76, 87, 105).[6] Reading Prospero's weird, almost paranoiac, fear that Miranda's attention will lapse just as he is telling her (as he would have it) who she is, we should, perhaps, before "explaining" it psychologically, attend to its strangeness, which links it to the play's recurrent concern with forgetfulness.[7] Miranda here confesses amnesia and absorption: "I not remembering how I cried out then / Will cry it o'er again" (1.2.133–34). A strange "I" that, "not remembering," can, nevertheless, cry "it o'er *again*," its gesture of encompassing its own oblivion throws into question its coherence while also asserting a kind of mastery. One is led to suspect that in rendering the histories of a daughter and a state, it is as important for Prospero to establish Miranda's forgetfulness as it is for the play to establish her capacity for sympathy.[8] And his ostensible desire to inform Miranda of her origins stalls on the seemingly more interesting question of locating one's birth, on the untraceable threshold that separates one from oblivion by constituting a beginning to memory. While Prospero's fascination with Miranda as *his* history might invoke an equivocal (or equivocated) separation (garden-variety parental narcissism), it also registers his fascinated inability (at least partially acknowledged) to compass her memory: "How is it / That this lives in thy mind? What sees thou else / In the dark backward and abyss of time?" (1.2.48–50). The interest of that general question overwhelms the more particular question of what she remembers of their exile, and at issue is less exposition—for us, for Miranda—than a fathomless forgetting.[9] This amnesia by fiat seems an effort to fashion a plummet to sound a memory—it the abyss as much as "time" is—suspected, likewise, to be fathomless, to render it a knowable oblivion: "Canst thou remember / A time before we came unto the cell? / I do not think thou canst" (1.2.38–40). That formulation—"canst thou remember / A *time*"—recalls "the dark backward and abyss of time" and evokes what Stephen Orgel reminds us about the word *Tempest*: its root is *time*.[10] According to the pun, to forget a *time* is to forget nothing short of the play itself. Indeed, Act 1, Scene 2, frames the play with a series of narratives—to Miranda, to Ariel, and to Caliban—where Prospero insists that each has forgotten origins that he, vicariously, can then recall. "Dost thou forget," he asks Ariel, "From what a torment I did free thee? . . . Thou dost" (1.2.250–53). "I must / Once a month recount what thou hast been, / Which thou forget'st," he adds (2.2.262–63). These narratives rehearse the play's larger political narrative, which, curiously, reminds the shipwrecked usurpers of their misdeeds so that they can, by Prospero's decree, be forgotten. "There, sir, stop," he says to Alonso, who is in the middle of an apology. "Let us not burden our remembrances with / A heaviness that's gone" (5.1.198–200).

The amnesty that founds the play's political reconciliation may be founded on amnesia;[11] that amnesia is bound up with the enchantment that Prospero calls his "art." At another famously weird moment, Prospero interrupts the wedding masque for Miranda and Ferdinand to profess that he has—dangerously, it seems—forgotten the mutiny he has baited as a restaging of the plot that left him exiled: "I had forgot that foul conspiracy / Of the beast Caliban and his confederates / Against my life" (4.1.139–41). Awakening from it to leave his goddesses floating, mid-masque, somewhat awkwardly in the rafters, Prospero in his forgetfulness also replays what originally marooned him: his absorption in the "volumes / I prize above my dukedom" (1.2.167–68). To Prospero, moreover, his brother's usurpation is something he, Prospero, did to himself: "I pray thee mark me: / I thus neglecting worldly ends . . . in my false brother / Awaked an evil nature, and my trust, / Like a good parent, did beget of him / A falsehood in its contrary as great / As my trust was, which had, indeed, no limit, / A confidence sans bound" (1.2.88–97).

There would be any number of ways to read this curious assertion of mastery, where neglect seems less an abdication of control than another form of it. (One also hesitates over "like a good parent"—hesitates about whether parenting is a principle of replication or a principle of symmetrical inversion.)

For my purposes, I would stress that mastery is made curiously indistinguishable from relinquishment. Indeed, Prospero's power is above all a power to make others lose track of themselves; his is an art of forgetfulness. Striking, then, is the contrast between his anxious demands that Miranda mark his words and the magisterial tone with which he dispenses with her curiosity: "Here cease more questions: / Thou art inclined to sleep. 'Tis a good dulness, / And give it way—I know thou canst not choose" (1.2.185–86). Whatever his power over the natural world—to conjure up storms and shipwrecks, to bedim the noontide sun—his power to compel attention seems less secure than his power to compel sleep.

It may be, however, that absorption in the play is a form of forgetfulness, even self-forgetfulness, that looks a lot like slumber. "I forget," says Ferdinand as he performs Caliban's labor in hopes of marrying Miranda; "i.e., to work at my task," glosses Orgel's edition, but the statement of forgetfulness floats, ungrounded—as if forgetting were, simply, what one does here. ("Ferdinand," says Gonzalo, "found a wife / Where he himself was lost" [5.1.210–11].) Ferdinand is echoed by Miranda a few lines later: "But I prattle / Something too wildly, and my father's precepts / I do forget" (3.1.57–59). True love is cast as complementary forgetting.[12] "The latter end of his commonwealth," remarks Antonio of Gonzalo's paraphrase of Montaigne, "forgets the beginning" (2.1.155), which leads to Gonzalo's being dubbed a "lord of weak remembrance" (2.1.230). Prospero's imperatives often command Ariel to restate what has, on- or off-stage, already been said: "Say again, where didst thou leave these varlets? / [Ariel:] I told you, sir, they were . . ." (4.1.170–71). Prospero's repeated assertions of others' forgetting, this makes clear, is a form of command: "Hast thou forgot / The foul witch Sycorax . . . Hast thou forgot her? . . . Where was she born? Speak; tell me" [1.2.256–60].) That everything in the play, it sometimes seems, must, by the displaced Duke's command, be retold or reenacted seems to compel the forgetfulness it also aims to forestall. In Prospero's restaging of the initial conspiracy, the would-be usurpers are done in by their forgetfulness—not only by Prospero's soporific charms, but also by their tendency to forget their plot, to be distracted by tangential opportunities for thievery. And the relation of the original usurpers to their later incarnations or parodists is likewise one of forgetting: "There are few yet missing of your company / Some few odd lads that you remember not" (5.1.254–55). Prospero's interruption of the wedding masque thus literally makes manifest his getting caught up in his own plot: "I had forgot" marks the moment where control and its relinquishment become indistinct.

This is one reason why the imperative of the epilogue—which could be paraphrased as (almost indifferently) "don't forget me" or "forget me"— seems less to relinquish than to repeat the claims made for art's power to absorb. Indeed, the play's gestures of relinquishment are striking not only for the beauty of their poetry but also for the frequency with which they are repeated. The epilogue; Prospero's promise to break his staff and bury his book; the valedictory close to the masque: Prospero's renunciation of his art is troubled less because he fails to renounce convincingly than because he convincingly renounces so often. Renunciation has constituted his art from the beginning. "Lie there, my art," he says after the pyrotechnics of storm and shipwreck (1.2.24); the gesture with which he puts aside his robe anticipates the "final" renunciation and links it to the forgetfulness he demands from his listeners. "I have done nothing but in care of thee," he tells Miranda just before these lines: "Of thee, my dear one, thee, my daughter, who / Art ignorant of what thou art" (1.2.15–19). The tortured syntax ("of thee, my dear one, thee, my daughter, who") seems performatively to put in question the identity of the daughter whose attributed distraction just after this therefore seems the less surprising (and whose identity, seen from his perspective, might be paired with his, from hers: "Sir, are you not my father?" [1.2.54]). That syntax, and the paired self-loss, seem linked, further, to the seeming pun on art. "Lie there, my art"; "thou art ignorant of what thou art." The circularity of the latter formulation—to cease to be ignorant of what one is is to learn that one is ignorant of what one is, and to fill in the ignorance could only be to repeat the condition it diagnoses, to constitute an ignorance therefore at once dispelled and perpetuated—means that it, like Prospero's renunciation, can only be repeated.

Repeated, the gesture of renunciation is nevertheless unlocatable in the play:

> "Our revels now are ended. These our actors,
> As I foretold you, were all spirits, and
> Are melted into air, into thin air,
> And, like the baseless fabric of this vision,
> The cloud-capped towers, the gorgeous palaces,
> The solemn temples, the great globe itself,
> Yea, all which it inherit, shall dissolve,
> And, like this insubstantial pageant faded,
> Leave not a rack behind. We are such stuff

As dreams are made on, and our little life
Is rounded with a sleep. (4.1.148–58).

One in a series of dry runs at relinquishment (where, moreover, the well-established *topos* linking the ephemeral masque to life's ephemerality makes the vanishing theatrical spectacle itself a rehearsal for the more encompassing disappearance to come), it is temporally strange. The actors, as "foretold," *were* spirits, and Prospero and Ferdinand hover somewhere between the revels announced as "ended" and the world catastrophe, the dissolution, that "shall" occur. (One notes a similar wavering in the redoubled simile: "like the baseless fabric of this vision . . . like this insubstantial pageant faded." "Faded" opens the possibility—however momentarily—that the pageant was not insubstantial before it faded and thus opens up a gap—temporal, among other things—between "baseless fabric" and "insubstantial pageant," a gap also enacted by the tension between adjectival [function] and verbal [form] in the past participles: ended, foretold, melted, faded, rounded.) The disconcerting number of "ands" further locates the repetition of relinquishment within this gesture of renunciation. Likewise, his later renunciation—"this rough magic / I here abjure" (5.1.50–51)—is equivocated by the verb tenses that follow it: "When I have required / Some heavenly music—which even now I do— / To work mine end upon their senses that / This airy charm is for, I'll break my staff, / Bury it certain fathoms in the earth, / And deeper than did ever plummet sound / I'll drown my book" (5.1.51–57). By the epilogue, the renunciation has already occurred: "*Now* my charms are all o'erthrown" (5.1.319). The renunciation is suspended in a *now* that, never present, can only be posited between a future to come and a past accomplished. The epilogue's repeated gestures of deixis at once bring the play into the temporal and spatial presence of its performance and make that presence curiously unlocatable.

The long history of the play's reception as Shakespeare's own renunciation is not to be resolved—or corrected—by any more accurate account of the historical circumstances of its initial performance or chronological place in Shakespeare's oeuvre—because it responds to a renunciation that is unlocatable even within the play. As Mary Crane notes, the island, somehow both Mediterranean and Caribbean, varies so much according to who describes it that it seems meta-theatrical, its indeterminate space determinable (only) as a stage.[13] For Henry James, the play presents a "torment scarcely to be borne" —the torment of how the "supreme master of expression" could *stop* writing: "*How* did the faculty so radiant there contrive, in such perfection, the arrest of its divine flight"; "the fathomless strangeness of his story, the abrupt stoppage of his pulse after The Tempest is not, in charity, lighted for us by a glimmer of explanation."[14] For James, the torturous fact is that Shakespeare's lapse into silence does not coincide with his death. The problem posed by Shakespeare's silence is thus less the contingent historical question of the particular writer's career, less that, even, of his unaccountable decision willingly to renounce his gift, than that the lapse into silence appears not as a boundary to human life but as internal to it—internal, indeed, to the greatest capacity for linguistic expression the world has ever seen.

Strikingly, James renders this problem as one of cultural transmission, collocating the torment of our inability to compass Shakespeare's silence with the torment of historical inquiry's failure to shed any but the most meager of lights on the circumstances of his life. Intimated is a forgetting central to literary transmission, one that brings together the passage of time with the silence at the heart of an infinite potential for expression. One thinks, in this regard, of a particular overdetermined moment: the citation of Virgil's *Aeneid* when Ferdinand first sees Miranda. "Most sure, the goddess / On whom these airs attend," he says, recalling Virgil's "O dea certe" (1.2.421). The cited moment—to modern eyes, anyway—is one of the stranger ones in *The Aeneid*. A shipwrecked Aeneas encounters a woman he is sure is a goddess, but his cited certainty does not extend to the more crucial fact that she is the particular goddess who happens to be his mother.[15] "Knowing her for his mother, he called out / To the figure fleeing away": Aeneas recognizes his mother only after the fact, only as she walks away, and shrouds herself in mist.[16] Whatever the various ways to read the play's citation of this moment of (maternal) non-recognition (the various mothers not present—Sycorax, Miranda's mother, and the grandmother whose virtue Miranda wryly refuses to impugn—come to mind), it also figures a relation to a literary tradition: the play's relation to *The Aeneid* or *The Metamorphoses*, for example, which can be recognized, perhaps, as they recede and shroud themselves in mist. The moment renders, too, with particular economy, the play's dynamic of forgetfulness—the non-recognition might thus stand in for the forgetfulness that Prospero extorts from his listeners that they might be absorbed. Prospero's obsessive concern with his daughter's distractedness, like the repeated scenes of self-forgetting that at once repeat the play's political plot and point "outward" to the author's renunciation, to the author—in Agamben's terms—as a "gesture" of self-subtraction, as the originating absence at the threshold of the work that, put into play, makes reading possible and marks where it must come to an end,[17] collocates the play's psychological and political plots with a particular model of literary transmission.

Forgetting in *The Tempest* could thus be read as an instance of a forgetting that Daniel Heller-Roazen suggests is internal to language, and to the literary tradition.[18] It also makes *The Tempest* queer. There are certainly queer moments enough, even if "queer" is understood to mean, simply, gay sexuality—one thinks of Trinculo crawling under Caliban's cloak and the play on anal parturition it enables,[19] or, indeed, of the repeated severing of parenting from any visible heterosexuality—an eclipse as much of normative sexuality as of maternity. (Prospero's fantasies of giving birth to himself—and to nearly everyone else—are, in this register, queer in addition to being megalomaniacal.) Yet I have risked attenuating the sexual content, and risked generalizing the term "queer" almost to the point of desexualizing it to link *The Tempest* to what I see as a queer current in the English literary tradition—or simply the queerness of that tradition, which is to say not its homoerotic content but its persistent understanding of transmission as synonymous with failed or thwarted transmission. Queer transmission produces knowledge but does not pass material—genetic or literary—to future generations.[20] The relation to explicit sexual content seems attenuated because "queer transmission" marks a site of erotic intensity that is, at the same time, what is most essentially "literary" about the tradition.[21] Partly because it invokes an understanding of the homoerotic basis of cultural transmission dating at least to *The Symposium*, the play takes shape in a tradition where it would be difficult to argue for the "sublimation" of homoerotic desires "into" literature because the literary has been so thoroughly saturated with homoerotic energy. Whatever other contexts it invokes, Prospero's equivocal art of forgetting also asks to be read in this context of queer literary transmission.

Notes

1. I am grateful to Rob Odom for pointing me to this formulation in *The Symposium*. Elsewhere, I discuss this passage in relation to Oscar Wilde's imagining, in *De Profundis*, of "how splendid it would be," not, as Wilde is often read to assert, to affirm a gay identity, but to denounce oneself: see Ohi, "Erotic Bafflement and the Lesson of Oscar Wilde."

2. The argument here is indebted to Heller-Roazen, *Echolalias*; idem, "Tradition's Destruction."

3. See Agamben, "Bartleby, or On Contingency." See also Heller-Roazen, "Editor's Introduction," which traces the concept of potentiality through the history of

philosophy and allows one to see why the "actualizing" of writing also entails its potentialization. I discuss potentiality in greater detail, and spell out its relation to the queer erotics of Pater's historiography, in Ohi, "Queer Atavism and Pater's Aesthetic Sensibility."

4. Agamben, "Bartleby, or On Contingency," 267.

5. Citations in parentheses are from Orgel, *The Tempest*.

6. Orgel, for example, writes: "Prospero's expostulations take the form of demands for attention and reassurance. Miranda makes it clear that her attention is in no danger of wandering, but her father's violence is retrospective, the playing out of an old rage, and Miranda is not really its object": Orgel, *The Tempest*, 6.

7. "Attend me": As the echo of the French "*attendre*" might suggest, the imperative is to pay attention but also to wait—on or for—him, to give oneself over to the vacant time (which Ariel might know) between commands.

8. In an essay about Wordsworth's *The Borderers* suggesting, among other things, that "Wordsworth's fascination with the motif of forgetfulness derives . . . in large part from *The Tempest*," Reeve Parker traces the forgetfulness of *The Tempest* in relation to a disavowed parricidal wish—a wish to escape a bondage to memory and narrative encoded in an ostensibly protective paternal embrace—itself predicated, for Prospero, on forgetting his own self-usurpation: Parker, "Reading Wordsworth's Power," 317. For Parker, the sympathy generated at this moment of *The Tempest* is not unrelated to the forgetfulness. "Pity is the fiction that displaces the truth of self-usurpation": ibid., 321.

9. For Christopher Pye, the insistence in this scene on establishing Miranda as tabula rasa ("a pure, groundless ground situated in the nevertheless determinate interval between matter and spirit") is linked to the play's exploration of the self-generating, autochthonous structure of the aesthetic: "How does the self-inclusive work mark its own marking?" That problem of the aesthetic, he suggests, is at once that of subjectivity as culturally inscribed and that of historical inscription. History does not intervene from the "outside" of the play; it is internal to the play's meditation on its self-constituting grounds. More generally, Pye's argument, the complexity of which is much greater than my summary here indicates, underlines the stakes of forgetfulness in the play—in the movement between absorption and distraction: Pye, "First Encounter / Missed Encounter" (part of his forthcoming book on early modern political aesthetics).

10. "*Tempestas* . . . has as its root *tempus*": Orgel, *The Tempest*, 49–50.

11. Loraux, *The Divided City*.

12. The lovers are likewise paired in their capacity for repeated mourning: "Sitting on the bank, / Weeping *again* the King my father's wreck, / This music crept by me upon the waters" (1.2.390–92).

13. Crane, *Shakespeare's Brain*, 190–200.

14. James, "Introduction to *The Tempest*," 1207, 1215–16, 1219. For a more detailed discussion, see Kevin Ohi, "Hover, Torment, Waste: Late Writings and the Great War," in idem, *Henry James and the Queerness of Style*.

15. The strangeness of this moment was pointed out by Carl Phillips during a reading at Boston College in 2004.

16. Virgil, *The Aeneid*, book 1, 11.406–7.

17. Giorgio Agamben, "The Author as Gesture," in idem, *Profanations*, 61–72. It is perhaps because of this dynamic of a mastery that is indistinguishable from a relinquishment and self-forgetting, and because of the difficulty of distinguishing Prospero's renunciation from the absorption that has constituted his art, that Prospero provides an epigraph to Agamben's essay on "Genius," in *Profanations*, 9–18. Most fascinatingly, that essay's final turn to a letting go of genius itself is compared to Prospero's at last setting Ariel free.

18. See Heller-Roazen, *Echolalias*; idem, "Tradition's Destruction."

19. See the brilliant reading of this scene in Goldberg, *Tempest in the Caribbean*, 54.

20. See Edelman, *No Future*.

21. This essay forms a part of a larger project that will give flesh to these claims, exploring the queer allure of thwarted transmission in writing ranging from Plato to Wilde, Pater, James, and Faulkner: see Ohi, "Queer Atavism and Pater's Aesthetic Sensibility."

Skepticism, Sovereignty, Sodomy

JAMES KUZNER

Why discuss *Timon of Athens* in terms of queer theory? Jody Greene has already told us why, and it has been some time since she did. To rehearse: She has shown, at length, that the "economy" of *Timon* can be seen as a queer or sodomitical one, defined by an "unnatural" expansion and consumption of wealth that is metaphorically linked to excessive, dangerously wasteful, non-normative sexual exchange.[1] This claim—that although the play could seem to single out Timon as sodomitical, it in fact does nothing of the sort—is a familiar one, developing as it does Jonathan Goldberg's account of "sodometries." In tracing the relational structures that cluster around the utterly confused category of sodomy, Goldberg shows how "sodomy" could, by definition, be performed by just about anyone yet somehow also "fully negates the world, law, nature"—how it is somehow everywhere and nowhere, "always mobilizable" for just this reason.[2] Like Goldberg, Greene writes that because the confused category of sodomy continues to do cultural work, "The task of tracing out the history of that cultural work and of exposing the 'confusions' surrounding the definition of the sodomitic is a pressing and a timely one."[3] So that is why *Timon* ought to be discussed alongside queer theory. It permits us to think queerness well beyond directly sexual contexts; in presenting economic figurations of sodomy, it broadens our sense of how this category can be used to stigmatize.

Discussing *Timon* in terms of queer theory, from this point of view, means tracing the pernicious potential of confused categories. The play surely engages with queer theory in the manner outlined earlier, and yet we could question whether giving and taking, as the play represents them, are always as "grim" as Greene claims.[4] Greene justifies her claim as follows: Unlike life as Shakespeare might imagine it within a more moderate order, Timon's giving (until there is nothing left to give) and others' taking (all that he gives) produce a paradoxical economy—excessive consumption that is somehow never enough, "insatiability . . . which constantly but never adequately feeds the appetite of 'covetous men.' "[5] This economy is "threatening"—its waste so dire —because the world of Athens is one of limited resources, which everyone (but Timon) knows but does nothing to respect, instead taking advantage of his generosity in bloodthirsty fashion. Timon cannot keep giving, his "friends" cannot keep taking; his case shows that resources run out, that his generosity has no chance.[6] Timon fails to listen to those (Flavius, Apemantus, so many others) who insist that the rapacity of Athens is structured by manipulating distinctions—between surfaces of friendship and depths of indifference, between possessive subjects and the objects they would like to possess—distinctions that Timon seems not to grasp and that Athenians exploit at his expense.

But this world—of scarcity—is not the only one offered by *Timon*. The play also suggests that excessive, wasteful economic behavior need not have catastrophic consequences, were Athenians to adopt Timon's giving outlook. Indeed, one economy evident in *Timon* (if not in Athens) resembles that in Georges Bataille's thinking about general economy. For Bataille, the world is defined not by scarcity but by surplus, by resources that must be wasted. Exorbitance, accordingly, becomes anything but "unnatural."[7] Early in the play, Timon holds the seemingly childlike belief that his world is just this way—inexhaustible—and while *Timon* could be read as his painful correction on just this point, once he banishes himself he finds himself in a wilderness that offers him all that he needs and more. "Within this mile break forth a hundred springs," he remarks. "Want? Why want?"[8] The gold that ran out in Athens, he discovers, is everywhere out in the wild; the notion of the precious, scarce object is an Athenian invention, as empty a fabrication as the cynic Apemantus's claim that the "bleak air" and "cold brook" cannot possibly sustain Timon, cannot serve as the page and chamberlain that could support him in the human world. Out here, matter is superabundant, and resources cannot possibly be exhausted. It is people who fabricate scarcity— people who create the need for calculation, dividing the world into sets of subjects and objects to be manipulated and stockpiled. Accordingly, *Timon* shows how "wasteful" relations can be pathologized only within fabricated social space, only within the walls that Timon would have "dive in the earth / And fence not Athens" (4.1.2–3), only when we impose an economy not dictated by the resources of the non-human world. The play suggests that the sodomitical aspect of the world—now understood as plenitude—loses its appeal only if we insist that that world is essentially ungenerous.

To the extent that the world outside Athens is defined by surplus, not scarcity, the play occupies another terrain of queer theory—on which we might find Leo Bersani's gay outlaw or, more pertinently, Bataille's sovereign man.[9] While Greene exposes the *confusions inherent in the application of sodomy as a category*, here *Timon*'s utility resides in how it embraces the *confusion of categories* that sodomitical practice can accomplish. Insofar as this practice can be made legible, it cannot quite negate "world, law, nature." Rather, it undoes some of their structuring distinctions. In ways that Bataille regards as salutary, sovereign man refuses some of these distinctions, including those on which the acquisitive, rapacious individuals of *Timon*'s Athens depend (such as ones mentioned, between subject and object, surface and depth, and between human and animal, present and future, and so on). For Bataille, the experience of sovereignty offers a therapeutic exit from the world of precious things easily lost, freedom from the anguish that is anticipation (of what we do not have, of what we are not yet). This is far different from the form of sovereign selfhood we might associate with self-possession: we no longer cling to ourselves as possessive subjects with protected interiors, stop longing for missing objects and forms of self-fulfillment. Indeed, we stop thinking in terms of separations between subjects and objects, self and the world we might manipulate. In Bataille's account, experiences of sovereignty offer just the opposite of bounded selfhood: the embrace of useless expenditure, the refusal to unlock ourselves from our environment or divide ourselves into a present and a dreamed-for (or dreaded) future. Sovereignty offers an existence in a pure present that excludes the wish for life and the fear of death alike.

In the wild, Timon finds a kind of sovereignty. Although the social *does* intrude on him time and again (to name a few, Apemantus, the Painter and Poet, bandits, Alcibiades, and Flavius all turn up), he finds a possible exit from the world of duplicity, the monstrous world of humankind. Apemantus may be right to say that Timon "has cast away thyself, being like thyself" (4.3.247), but by the end of the play, this is not a problem. "My long sickness / Of health and living now begins to mend," Timon says, "and nothing brings me all things" (5.1.213–15). Within a present not subjected to the demands of the future, he finds what he never could inside Athens. Of his death, he asks Flavius to say that

> Timon hath made his everlasting mansion
> Upon the beached verge of the salt flood,
> Who once a day with his embossed froth
> The turbulent surge shall cover . . .

> Graves only be men's work, and death their gain.
>
> Sun, hide thy beams. Timon hath done his reign. (5.1.246–55)

Bataille writes that when sovereign man erodes distinctions, he—like the sodomite, like Bersani's gay outlaw, like the radical queer theorist—comes to have a peculiar relationship to death. Sovereign man may still die, but he does not die humanly inasmuch as he does not die in anguished anticipation (whether of dissolution or of final fulfillment).[10] For Timon, similarly, to be "done his reign" is sovereignly to do himself in. On the verge between land and sea, Timon imagines himself as a human subject becoming non-human, indistinct from the world of natural objects. Indeed, Timon becomes unlocatable. (Does he exist in the mansion that will be covered by the tide? Is he the embossed froth itself?) He imagines himself always returning, existing nowhere precisely, instead within a cycle that repeats endlessly. Anticipating nothing, Timon does not, cannot, die humanly.

From this perspective, *Timon's* relationship to queer theory appears quite different. From here, the play fuses Bersani's theories of shattered selfhood with the generativity and abundance that Jeffrey Masten associates with the anus or "fundament" (and that supposedly serves as the very foundation, not the death, of the self).[11] Timon engages with queer theory not, or not only, by showing how sodomy is an utterly confused category, but by confusing the categories that structure queer theory and queer selves.

My essay was supposed to end here. Greene's account of how *Timon* speaks to queer theory is partial; mine moves beyond the threateningly sodomitical world and economy of scarcity in Athens to describe the general economy that the play urges on its audience. But alas, I no longer believe the argument I set out to make. I just do not think that the play really warrants accepting one consideration of how *Timon* relates to the queer, my account over Greene's; the world of Athens over the world in the wild. To be sure, Athens is an unhappy, unappealing place, where people conceal their excess, the possibility (exposed by Greene) that they are sodomites. It is arguable that Timon ought to have seen this and, still more, ought to have adjusted to the imposition of an economy of scarcity, the structuring distinctions that separate subjects from, and should make them wary of, one another. Besides, while he seems to have found in the wild an outside—a place of salutary excess and distinctions undone—the Athenians who show up over and over cast doubt on whether a world of surplus and dissolved selfhood can actually be obtained. The play presents a pair of worlds at odds with each other. In one, there are distinctions in place that can and should be acknowledged insofar as they mask a dangerous excess, a rapacity that should be unmasked. In the other, these distinctions can and should be escaped, should give way to a more salutary form of sodomitical practice. The play gives us no reason to want to live in the first world; nor does it give full realization (or full plausibility) to the second. In this sense, we could say that Timon's position with respect to queer theory, not unlike the category of sodomy, feels utterly confused.

But "confused," inasmuch as it carries negative valences, may be the wrong term to describe the play's competing economies. I thus want to end by charting a third route leading from *Timon* to the present and possible futures of queer theory. This way incorporates the first two. Forget for a moment the practice of Lucian's *Timon the Misanthrope* (the most commonly cited source of the play); forget, more crucially, the logic that views opposition in terms of antagonism, that would oppose argument to counterargument, Greene's to mine, as Timon opposes himself to the human world that he would like to split apart with his spade. There is, I believe, another Timon behind *Timon*: Timon of Phlius, pupil of Pyrrho, part of the skeptical tradition that led to Sextus Empiricus's *Outlines of Pyrrhonism*. "Scepticism," Sextus writes, "is an ability to place in antithesis, in any manner whatever, appearances and judgements, and thus—because of the equality of force in the objects and arguments opposed—to come first of all to a suspension of judgement."[12] The principle by which we suspend judgment and do not dogmatize, according to classical skepticism, is this setting of things in opposition. Skeptics such as Sextus and Timon of Phlius believe that this is always possible; there is never a given argument, a single account of the world, that does not have a strong, equally evidenced counter—so long as we are willing to seek it out. This in turn forces us to suspend judgment, unable to dogmatize. And this is precisely what *Timon of Athens* asks us to do. In defining the modes of doubt, Sextus writes that nothing "appears to us singly but in conjunction with something else," just as Athens does not appear to us except alongside the wild beyond Athens.[13] Sextus also emphasizes the effect of positions and perspectives on how the world looks to us. Depending on where we find ourselves in *Timon*, similarly, we might believe that its world is one defined by scarcity or by surplus, by sodomitical excess that is dangerous on the one hand or salutary on the other.[14] In opposing arguments about what the world is, and in equipping us with no sure method to adjudicate between them, the play holds those arguments in what seems a perfect equipollence, one that cannot be resolved. The play thus urges us to suspend judgment about which world is the one that we can inhabit.

This being so, *Timon* can be said to develop "queer" skepticism. Surely, forms of skepticism, if not classical ones, underwrite the queer theory I have discussed. For Goldberg and Greene, skepticism entails challenging supposed justifications for marking certain individuals as sodomites and not others; this skepticism means fully appreciating the constructed nature of social categories. For Bataille or Bersani, it means casting a skeptical eye toward pictures of selfhood that supposedly go without saying: for instance, those for which bounded selfhood and possessive individualism ought to be our preferred form of life. *Timon*, by contrast, asks for what would be less radical (in terms of concrete political consequences) but at least as wrenching (in terms of how we look at the world). Were we to practice skepticism in the form urged on us by *Timon*, we would enter the state that, according to Timon of Phlius, the otherwise accomplished Xenophanes wanted to enter but could not:

> Would that I had attained my share of shrewdness,
> To look two ways at once; on a treacherous path
> I was led astray, an old man, and still innocent
> Of Doubt! For wherever I turned my mind,
> All was resolved into one and the same, and all that exists,
> However weighed, was always of one same nature.[15]

What if the interest of *Timon* to queer theory resided not only in an unveiling, in seeing the utterly, perniciously confused (and confusing) category of sodomy to be found there? Equally, what if it resided not only in the salutary confusion that comes from a sovereign shattering of the self? What if it were not only those things, but also the effort to look in more than one direction? What if queer skepticism meant entering a state of non-assertion, of neither affirming nor denying anything, of appreciating difference and distinction without ascribing final value to them? What if it were to acknowledge the different worlds that—depending on where we are, which way we face—we all inhabit and move between, but also to admit that there is no reliable way for us to make sense of or order them, to choose one over the other?

Suspension of judgment, the classical skeptics claim, coming after so much frustration about the world's resistance to consistent pictures of it, opens onto an experience of tranquility or "unperturbedness" (*ataraxia*). Leaving *Timon* with such suspension, readers might be frustrated, for instance, that its world seems to contain bounded subjects and scarce objects, or sovereign, open subjects and superabundance, excess and waste that are pathologized or excess and waste that are praised. Readers might be frustrated that identity and ontology appear one way at one moment and another at another, but, then, they might also consider that the question of what existence *is*, for this play, may be less important than its multiple and contradictory appearances. We might inhabit the contradiction rather than attempt to argue our way out of it, entertain the idea that we do not know how the world, selves, and sexualities are constructed—do not know how any come to be—and that the appearances from which we might form judgments simply do not add up. *Timon*, that is, allows us to view queer theory through the lens of classical skepticism. The play undermines not only notions of normative sexuality—if we do not know how the world is, the notion of proper orientation becomes nonsensical—but also ideas about how sexuality emerges. *Timon* forecloses accepting either the strong theory of psychoanalysis or the theory that sexual identity is a construction that must be exposed, revealed, denaturalized, and so on.

The play urges us to instead cope with the utter queerness of what the world presents to us, from without as from within. This is so whether or not *ataraxia* ever arrives. At the least, we would end with a strong counterweight to the dogmatic thinking to which we are so often inclined. Such a counterweight would force us not to draw the boundary that would make one queer reading more correct or authoritative than another, and it would force us to consider whether producing queer readings means producing incoherent ones.

Of course, Timon of Phlius and *Timon of Athens* suggest that this route may not be one that we can see to its end. These Timons ask for what seems nearly impossible but is worth taking very seriously: they ask us to look two ways *at once*. Not (as I have done here) to consider in turn two sides of a contradiction, two parts of a play, but to consider both at one and the same time, to feel, and perhaps learn to respect, the full import of this incoherence and the suspension of all judgment to which it leads. These Timons ask us to yearn for the sudden illumination that this "confusion"—if that is what we want to call it—could yield, although this would be an illumination that discourse, unfolding over time, would not be able to bear. I have to believe that this is part of what a theorist such as Goldberg has in mind when he explores (and asks that we explore) the "terrains of confusion."[16] But perhaps this exploration, however incomplete, would lead somewhere that is not quite, or not utterly, confused—or, at least, not defined by meaningless incoherence. Quite the contrary. Trying to look two ways at once would end in a surfeit, in rich, multiple meaning that at once fills and threatens to overwhelm us. Were this—this not unintelligible incoherence that appears in the world and in ourselves—to end in *ataraxia*, it could be as a kind of *jouissance*, the bliss that for Bersani both makes and mars us, seeming to grant us a place only to immediately undermine the integrity of that place. I do not know. I do not know if I could ever accomplish *Timon*'s imperative, even for a single moment, let alone if I could turn looking two ways into twenty, or two hundred. I do not know how to go about it, or that it would even lead to *ataraxia*. I cannot say exactly what the consequences for looking and thinking would be. But I do think that trying to grasp all that *Timon* offers us—and trying to practice a fully queer form of skepticism—means trying to find out, means wishing to look two ways at once.

Notes

1. Greene, "You Must Eat Men."
2. Goldberg, *Sodometries*, 18–19.
3. Greene, "You Must Eat Men," 191.
4. Ibid., 196.
5. Ibid., 174.
6. Ibid., 176.
7. See Bataille, *The Accursed Share*.
8. Mowat and Werstine, *Timon of Athens*, 4.3.468–73. Citations in parentheses are to this edition.
9. See Bersani, *Homos*.
10. Bataille, *The Accursed Share*, 3:219.
11. See Masten, "Is the Fundament a Grave?"
12. Hallie, *Sextus Empiricus*, 33.
13. Ibid., 64
14. Ibid., 63.
15. Ibid., 93.
16. Goldberg, *Sodometries*, 8.

A Child's Garden of Atrocities

MICHAEL MOON

What sounds as though it may have been one of the most memorable twentieth-century performances of *Titus Andronicus* has been almost entirely forgotten and never made it to a theater or before a paying audience. It took the form of an amateur theatrical mounted in college rooms at Oxford in 1924 by a cast that, if it was not quite yet recognized as stellar by the wider world, was already so to its respective members: Harold Acton, Cecil Beaton, Brian Howard, Oliver Messel, George "Dadie" Rylands, Stephen Tennant, and Rex Whistler. Dadie Rylands played Titus in a short toga designed for him by Messel to show off the panto-worthy "principal boy" legs for which Rylands was loved and long remembered by his contemporaries. Stephen Tennant made a languid, Firbankian Tamora, Queen of the Goths, playing her as an even bitterer and more irascible Miss Havisham, and Brian Howard proved an overly lively Lavinia, who is said to have kept slapping and screaming imprecations at fellow cast members, despite repeated reminders that she was now mute and handless. The champagne-and-gauze-driven production made it as far as the beginning of Act 4, when the last players standing yielded to necessity, and the evanescent production passed into oblivion ("history").

All right, OK, I admit it: that was all made up. Not the male luminaries of the Bright Young Things of the 1920s, of course, but their *Titusnacht*.[1] I offer my account of an imaginary performance of the play as homage to the sci-fi novelist and sometime theater critic Tom Disch, who, faced with the unacceptable fact of Charles Ludlam's death of AIDS in May 1987, published a review (in the *Nation* of June 20, 1987) of his own entirely imaginary version of the production of *Titus Andronicus* that Ludlam was to have presented in the New York Shakespeare Festival that summer (the production had been canceled because of Ludlam's illness). Disch believed that Ludlam's *Titus* would have been a genuine political as well as artistic event in a country living in "a state of plague masquerading as business as usual." Disch imagines Ludlam eschewing the Noh-derived aestheticizations of violence that Peter Brooks's staging (with Laurence Oliver and Vivien Leigh in 1955) had popularized, long scarlet ribbons emanating from Lavinia's violated mouth and wrists, in favor of *Texas Chainsaw Massacre*–level gore effects. Disch also imagines Titus's helpers aggressively serving the front rows of spectators generous helpings of the giant "beef"-and-cheese calzones on offer at the "banquet-of-horror" climax of the play.

But in a sense, Ludlam had already "had his say" about *Titus*, early in his career, in his second play, *Conquest of the Universe; or, When Queens Collide* (1968), in which he channeled the modes of theatrical excess and bombast that had previously been most intensively mined in plays such as *Tamburlaine* and *Titus* and some classics of the Spanish Golden Age known in the Anglophone world only to a handful of aesthetes such as Ludlam. Stylistic elements of *Flash Gordon* serials, tabloid-style headlines, and late-night television advertising added an American modern piquancy to the stew. Still, while taking some satisfaction in his early absorption of *Titus Andronicus* as a key ingredient in the art of the textual-and-stylistic pastiche that he was to spend his career in cultivating, I nonetheless find myself wanting twenty years after the fact to mark and mourn once more the absence of Ludlam's full-scale interpretation of the play. He still seems to me to have had the highest potential among recent directors and performers for delivering an optimal version of *Titus*, because he and the company he had formed and trained were of recent performers (at least in the United States) the ones in closest living contact with the widest range of theatrical traditions and performance styles out of which plays such as *Titus* emerged and to which it has in turn contributed.

Ludlam was a connoisseur and a skilled reanimator of what Susan Stewart has called "distressed genres"—in his case, a host of theatrical forms ranging from fairground comedy and raunchy burlesque to such supposedly archaic forms as martyr and morality play. As certifiably the very last of the great Victorian actor-managers, Ludlam had given his strongest performance in his most widely acclaimed production, his overhauling of that warhorse of well-made plays, *Camille*. Famously, Ludlam's Marguerite's décolletage revealed an expanse of the actor's undisguised furry chest, but audiences wept anyway —because, despite the low-comedy high jinx constantly going on around her, Ludlam played Marguerite absolutely "straight"—that is, with complete actorly sincerity. Having laughed uproariously at all the circumstances leading Marguerite to her deathbed reconciliation with her lover, audience members tended to realize only as she was dying onstage that Ludlam had *not* been camping it up all evening but had made his character the still center of things who gradually but inexorably brought all the raucous fun going on around her to a point of absolute quiet. Deprived of his *Titus*, admirers of Ludlam's art flocked to the revival of *Camille* that his company staged in posthumous tribute to him. In this production, the play revealed its full capacity to serve, in the wake of Ludlam's brilliant and short-lived reanimation of the theatrical, as *Trauerspiel*—play of mourning, of lamentation, of sorrow—not only for him but for many others felled by AIDS and political indifference.

As if in belated compensation for our loss of his version, Ludlam-esque productions of *Titus Andronicus* have proliferated in the two decades since his death, many in styles related, through punk, exploitation film, and drag and queer performance, to his. Of these, one entitled *Mondo Andronicus* was staged in 1997 by the Thrillpeddlers, a horror-and-fetish troupe in San Francisco that specializes in the classics of Grand Guignol (along with Victorian "spanking plays" with titles like *A Visit to Miss Birch*). The Shakespearian "script" was for this production translated into "youth-speak" for the younger characters ("Demetrius, *dude!*"), while the elder generation of characters tended to speak in the bland and banal accents of 1950s sitcoms, at least until the shock begins to register. Titus greets Lavinia, "Hi, Kitten, how's Daddy's little princess," before he realizes what has happened to her.

Several versions of the inevitable *Titus Andronicus: The Musical* have emerged in the past decade. One of them, entitled *Titus X* (written by Shawn Northrip), enacts the main actions of the play over a deafening punk-rock score ("Death Pie" to bring the play to a rousing close) and features brawny and pierced soldiers in kilts; it was performed at the Kennedy Center in 2002 and in New York in 2006. Another, more Broadway-derived musical version staged in Colorado in 2005 emphasized the spunky resourcefulness of both characters and performers: The actors playing Titus and Lavinia brought down the house by doughtily leading the company in a rollicking rendition of "(Let's Do) the Hand-Jive" at a point in the play when their characters had only one hand left between them. As I write in the summer of 2007, a group of young performers is taking yet another version of the play—this one titled *Tragedy! A Musical Comedy* (written by Mike Johnson)—to New York City's Fringe Festival.

In 2001, Trey Parker and Matt Stone presented a full-out Senecan / Andronican episode of their popular and highly acclaimed animated television series *South Park* titled "Scott Tenorman Must Die." In the episode, Eric Cartman, a fat, tyrannical fourth-grader, seeks revenge on Scott Tenorman, a "mean" eighth-grader from whom Eric has bought a baggie of pubic hairs (naïvely believing that "getting" pubic hairs, even from some other guy, will make him the first boy in his cohort to "become a man"). Eric tries several times to get his ten dollars back from the older boy, who embarrasses him in increasingly elaborate and humiliating ways. Driven into a kind of fury, Cartman first tries to train a horse to, as he puts it, "bite off Scott Tenorman's wiener." When this feint fails, Cartman tricks a cantankerous local rancher into mistakenly shooting and killing Scott's parents for trespassing. Eric then invites the community to a "Chili con Carnival" he has organized, at which he finally wreaks his revenge on the older boy by tricking him into eating what turns out to be the special "Mr. and Mrs. Tenorman Chili" that Eric has prepared for him. When Scott realizes that Cartman has tricked him into eating the flesh of his own dead parents, he collapses in horrified tears. Still not absolutely satisfied with his revenge, Cartman leans over and begins to lick the tears on Scott's cheeks. "Oh, let me taste your tears, Scott," he croons, "Mmm, your tears are so yummy and sweet. Oh, the tears of an *unfathomable sadness*."

The official line is, of course, that no children watch *South Park*—it is obviously highly unsuitable for them. But, of course, its reputation for "foul language" and "outrageously twisted humor" among the middle-school set (Scott Tenorman's crowd) has made it required viewing for some third- to fifth-graders (the age of its four protagonists) who either have very "liberal" parents or who know how to use TiVo. It is easy to imagine some children finding it "cool," even exhilarating, to watch a relentless fourth-grader ultimately triumph (in an absurdly bizarre way) over a "mean" eighth-grader. But can we imagine what they may make of his last line, "Oh, the tears of an unfathomable sadness"? Who or what is speaking when Cartman utters (with relish, with wonder) the phrase "tears of unfathomable sadness"? If some of the older kids understand that "unfathomable" may mean both "unmeasurable" and "incomprehensible," it should be easy for them to relate this feeling to the possible loss of a parent, or worse, both parents—not to mention having been tricked into eating bits of them in chili. Adult audiences with some knowledge of cultural or theatrical history may bring to the phrase a parallel sense (also ultimately unfathomable, perhaps) of how long audiences have been shuddering—with horror, with some weird pleasure or satisfaction, even possibly with laughter—at the spectacle of someone feeding an unsuspecting enemy the flesh of his murdered loved ones. Aegisthus tells the story of Atreus feeding his hated brother Thyestes the flesh of two of

Thyestes's sons in Aeschylus's *Agamemnon*, early in *The Oresteia*. It is no "ancient myth" for him; Aegisthus himself is the only surviving son of the hapless Thyestes, and those were his brothers who were fed to his father. Agamemnon, in whose murder Aegisthus participates, is the son of Atreus, the "boycooker."[2]

As we have seen, Parker and Stone in *South Park* invert the Aeschylean and Senecan and Shakespearean trope of sons fed to parent by showing us parents being fed to son. The joke may be a kind of long overdue revenge of the younger generations of revenge tragedy itself on the parental generation who have for millennia of theater been the ones butchering, stewing, baking, and serving up to their parents the offspring of their enemies. From the perspective of some of the younger generation in the audience, the crimes of Titus, not those of Tamora or her vicious sons, may seem the most heinous of all. Deprived of most of his tribe of sons by warfare, Titus (early in the play) nevertheless strikes down one of his handful of surviving sons for momentarily thwarting his will, and he dispels much of whatever sympathy one might be able to muster for him at the climactic "banquet" near the play's end by making it the occasion for murdering his daughter Lavinia—for having been raped? To "put her out of his [Titus's] misery," so to speak?

Long considered unperformable, or not worth performing, *Titus Andronicus* has attracted phenomenal amounts of theatrical energy and attention in recent years. In the publicity surrounding the release of Julie Taymor's film version of the play, *Titus* (1999), the director, as well as many of the reviewers, opined that the history of the genocidal twentieth century had transformed the play from what had long been taken to be a barbaric-seeming curiosity into an indispensable text for our times. Taymor presents her film as though it is all being seen through the eyes of a child. In doing so, she emphasizes the formative, initiatory character of the heroics and the horrors that the play presents for us to witness. The film's opening scene shows a little boy in a stark, vaguely modern domestic interior playing with toy (Roman) soldiers. Sounds of war break out outside, and the boy is somehow abducted into an ancient world of bellicose Romans and Goths. In the action that ensues, the same boy enacts the key child role in the play of Young Lucius, Titus Andronicus's grandson, whose school text Ovid helps his elder male relatives unlock the mystery of who has violated his young aunt Lavinia and helps her tell her story, despite her attackers' supposedly having deprived her of the physical means of doing so. After witnessing and surviving a host of atrocities, the boy is shown fleeing the culminating mass violence of the play at the very end of the film. As he does so, Taymor shows him taking "the Moor" Aaron's newborn son with him.

I began with one imaginary performance; let me end by evoking at least some of the elements of such another. It may be just possible to descry some of the contours of the lines of flight into some future (or futurity) along which Young Lucius and Aaron's unnamed infant son are moving at the end of Taymor's *Titus*. Can we imagine the play of Young Lucius and, let us call him, Young Aaron? I mentioned earlier that I believe the production of *Titus Andronicus* Ludlam did not live to direct would have been a great *Trauerspiel*—a play of mourning, lamentation, and sorrow—for its time. Would this "new play" be another *Trauerspiel*, or would it be some other kind of drama? Despite all the emphasis in our own recent versions of the play on "deranged" humor, on embracing what has become a pop-punk version of "theater of cruelty" that threatens at this point to dwindle into a cozy cliché, perhaps the most radical departure in interpreting the play through performative means is none of the punk-rock, sado-fetish productions of our own time but one very different, lone, outlying production that has still not been assimilated into our understanding of *Titus Andronicus* and its theatrical and political potential. That is the great nineteenth-century African American actor Ira Aldridge's production of the play, in which he performed the role of Aaron all over Europe, from London and Edinburgh to Germany, Poland, and St. Petersburg. A review of a performance in London in 1857 provides a succinct description of the changes Aldridge imposed on the play to make it a worthier star vehicle for himself (he was a celebrated Othello and Shylock) and more acceptable to his audiences:

> Aaron is elevated into a noble and lofty character. Tamora, the Queen of Scythia, is a chaste though decidedly strong-minded female, and her connection to the Moor appears to be of a legitimate description; her sons Chiron and Demetrius are dutiful children. . . . Old Titus himself is a model of virtue and the only person whose sanguinary character is not toned down much is Saturninus the Emperor, who retains the impurity of the original throughout.[3]

Imagine a recension of *Titus* in which Tamora and Aaron, Chiron and Demetrius have all been purified of their villainy and "Old Titus" himself of his mad lust for revenge, one in which the distinctly secondary character of Saturninus bears the whole burden of evildoing. Leslie Fiedler argues that in such lines of Shakespeare's Aaron as, "Let fools do good, and fair men call for grace; / Aaron will have his soul black like his face," Aaron's repeated descriptions of himself "in such stereotypical[ly racist] terms" eventually make him "come to seem more an allegorical figure in a speaking pageant than the real antagonist of a tragedy."[4] The dissemination of Walter Benjamin's early treatise on *Trauerspiel* and tragedy has taught us much about the aesthetic and political implications of allegorical and emblematic theater. When the role of Aaron is lampooned into a "Shaft," a hyper-phallic figure of "Blaxploitation" fantasy, as he routinely is these days, he is no less allegorical and emblematic a figure than Ira Aldridge's revision of him into a "noble Moor." Is there a producer, director, playwright, or acting company today that can enact for us the high stakes of allegorizing and de-allegorizing the figures of the emergent world that "Young Lucius" and "Young Aaron" may yet inhabit? Is it imaginable that a "Young Tamora" and a "Young Lavinia" could also make their way there?

Notes

1. The 1923–24 season actually saw two new productions of *Titus Andronicus*, the first to be mounted in decades. The redoubtable Lilian Baylis produced one as part of her "complete" cycle of Shakespeare plays at the Old Vic, and the Alpha Delta Phi fraternity at Yale presented what it at the time claimed to be "the first performance of the play ever seen by an American audience, and . . . probably the last." Reviews of both productions are reprinted in Kolin, *Titus Andronicus*, 381–83, 385–87.

2. The relevant passage is in Shapiro and Burian, *The Oresteia*, 203, lines 1830–40.

3. "A Review of Ira Aldridge's *Titus* at the Britannia, Huxton," reprinted in Kolin, *Titus Andronicus*, 378.

4. Fiedler, *The Stranger in Shakespeare*, 180. For a more recent appraisal of the significance of race in the play, see Smith, *"Titus Andronicus."*

Troilus and Cressida

The Leather Men and the Lovely Boy:
Reading Positions in *Troilus and Cressida*

ALAN SINFIELD

You get a lot of interesting correspondence if you work in a program about sexual dissidence. Siddeek Bakr Tawfeek, an Iraqi living in Qatar, has kindly written to me, recalling a lecture delivered by George Wilson Knight, titled "Masturbation and Mysticism," at the University of Leeds in 1972:

> Professor Sinfield, apart from a magazine called THE MASTURBATOR, I have always found that sexuality as a cultural and academic subject included gay and lesbian sex, but not masturbation. Therefore, I, Siddeek Bakr Tawfeek, hereby claim that I am introducing masturbation as part of sexuality, and by way of promoting my claim, I humbly suggest to you, Professor Sinfield, to please consider to include masturbation in your [master's in] Sexual Dissidence in Literature and Culture, on basis of the fact that I put in the form of this rhetorical question: Isn't masturbation, after all, a sexual dissidence?[1]

Knight told Siddeek that solitary masturbation involves inflicting cruelty on oneself instead of on others. If Israelis and Arabs therefore sat and masturbated together, they would resolve all their conflicts and come to peace and understanding. Compare the sexual charge that suffuses the meeting of the warriors in *Troilus and Cressida*.

In the mid-twentieth century, the queerness of *Troilus and Cressida* was so manifest that hardly anyone was bold enough to mention it, for fear of betraying insider knowledge. Yet the topic could not be entirely effaced. Knight is valuable to me because he offers a progressive, twentieth-century view of *Troilus and Cressida* and queerness. In *The Mutual Flame*, he ponders "the feminine aspect of Shakespeare's own self, or soul"; the bisexuality of the "creative consciousness" and "that blend of sexual attributes [that] male youth naturally attracts." He argued that the emotions of Shakespeare's Sonnets are "Homosexual"—but not including "physical intercourse"; just "physical and sexual attraction."[2] So the sensitive is demarcated from the sodomitical.

This demarcation informs Knight's innovative essay on *Troilus and Cressida*, where he gathers all virtues into one camp and all vices into the other. The Greeks stand for "the bestial and stupid elements of man, the barren stagnancy of intellect divorced from action": in a word, sodomy. So Achilles is "a lumbering giant of egotism, lasciviousness and pride," in contrast to Hector, who is "symbol of knighthood and generosity."[3] This binary model—matinee hero versus squalid ruffian—is now customary among directors and critics of the play. Yet it is scarcely plausible. Hector's superiority cannot be maintained; the first we hear of him is chiding his wife and striking his armorer; the last we see is of him killing an unworthy opponent to get his armour. The affinities between the two camps are more striking and are remarked by the characters (4.7.120–38).[4]

Queer Reading Positions

So which of Knight's readings are, or were, queer? My concern is less with a definition of queer than with the process of reading. But I believe he gets high points for visibility and low points for moralizing the vanilla sodomitical boundary.

A queer reading activates those textual cues that make sense in a queer context. This does not suppose an innate gay sensibility; anyone may occupy a queer position. Neither the text nor the position is unitary, fixed, or unavailable to others. However, LGBT people may find that it comes easily to us, especially with texts that have been worked over already from a queer concern.

Why, then, is a reading position necessary? Can we not just read the text? Briefly, the answer is no. Writers, directors, and readers who like to claim their work to be universal are usually defaulting to the prevailing ethical, social, and political ideology. That is why reading is always political.

I mean to discuss four fault lines: points where the aspiration of the writer to squeeze something like characters into something like narratives enforces distinctive and awkward encounters with history and ideology, both for initial audiences and for readers today.[5] I discuss the Greek and Trojan leathermen, the partnership of Achilles and Patroclus, Pandarus as scene queen, and Troilus as lovely boy. I will claim that a reading of *Troilus and Cressida* conducted from a queer position makes for a more subtle, historicized, contemporary, and wise reading. Nor are the outcomes limited to individual productivity. The cumulative insights of LGBT readers and writers may contribute to queer subcultural self-understanding.

Leather Boys

Wilson Knight's characterization of the Hector and Achilles in terms of their (ascribed) sexualities was developed in John Barton's production for the Royal Shakespeare Company in 1968. Alan Howard's Achilles "danced in full drag with Hector, and exuded menace. More or less naked bodies (dressed in leather straps and codpieces) were silhouetted against a black backdrop."[6] The warriors flaunt their bodies to each other like modern leathermen in a narcissistic sadism-masochism routine. Thersites offers leathers as the suitable garment for a scenario riven by volatile opinion. "A plague of opinion! A man may wear it on both sides, like a leather jerkin" (3.3.254–56). The fashion was set: "Homoeroticism and leather kit were de rigueur, as were a variety of attempts to polarize the Greek and Trojan forces."[7]

Not all representations of same-gender passion are progressive. In Barton's production, Achilles's sinister sexuality appeared continuous with his treachery in securing the death of Hector. Same-gender attraction, one might deduce, was sexy but bad.

A queer reading position may generate a further dimension to the violent imagery among the warriors. In the manner cultivated by gay novelists such as John Rechy and Larry Kramer, it may figure a yearning for intimacy. Achilles is more keen to know Hector's body than actually to fight with him:

Now Hector, I have fed mine eyes on thee;
I have with an exact view perused thee, Hector,
And quoted joint by joint. (4.7.114–16)

Hector is riled: "Why dost thou so oppress me with thine eye?" Achilles persists: "Tell me, you heavens, in which part of his body / Shall I destroy him —whether there, or there, or there?" (4.7.125–27). Notice also how the round of embracing introductions of Hector to the Greeks is like the compulsory personal welcome party that greeted Cressida. The warriors, too, might kiss.

Achilles apprehends his more amiable feelings for his fellow person as a kind of queer sickness. It involves an excursion into the feminine; but perhaps a real warrior (compare Antony and Coriolanus) has to cope with that.[8] He has

> a woman's longing,
> An appetite that I am sick withal,
> To see great Hector in his weeds of peace,
> To talk with him and to behold his visage
> Even to my full of view. (3.3.230–34)

They might masturbate together. At least in these "weeds of peace," no one gets killed.

Civil Partnerships

Nowadays, everyone can see a homosexual couple in Achilles and Patroclus, and many will recognize, or believe they recognize, a "Greek" mode of homosexual activity: a boy being escorted through adolescence by an older lover. "With him Patroclus / Upon a lazy bed the livelong day," Ulysses reports (1.3.146–47). Patroclus is spoken of as a boy—Achilles calls Hector "boy-queller" (5.5.47). According to the scurrilous Thersites, Patroclus is Achilles's "male varlet," "his masculine whore" (5.1.15–16). "Your great love to me," Patroclus prefers to call it (3.3.214). These might be a typical range of opinions in our own time.

Yet queer people know that same-gender relations are more various. Is Patroclus inevitably the younger, for instance? In *The Iliad*, though of lower rank, he is the elder of the two and is entrusted with the mentoring of Achilles. David Halperin has pointed out that the gendering and sexuality of the warrior, and of Achilles in particular, seem not to have been a problem for the Homeric Greeks. It is the later, classical Greeks and Romans who expected a dominant (active) and subordinate (passive) pairing. They were perplexed when they tried to map their model onto texts from the Homeric period.[9]

In any case, it is not Achilles's same-gender attachment that makes him hold back. Patroclus has been urging him to fight, though he has himself "little stomach to the war." "Sweet, rouse yourself," he urges (3.3.213, 215). Achilles does risk being interpreted as effeminate:

> A woman impudent and mannish grown
> Is not more loathed than an effeminate man
> In time of action. (3.3.210–12)

However, the impediment is not Patroclus but Achilles's devotion to Hector's sister, Polyxena:

> Here is a letter from Queen Hecuba,
> A token from her daughter, my fair love,
> Both taxing me, and gaging me to keep
> An oath that I have sworn. I will not break it. (5.1.34–37)

And this "love" is uttered not by Achilles as some kind of exculpation. He is surprised and annoyed that his private arrangement ("privacy") has become known to Ulysses (3.3.185–88).

It is excess of cross-gender passion that makes a warrior effeminate. That, after all, is how Paris caused the war, and he is despised for his uxorious devotion; besotted on his sweet delights, Priam says (2.2.142–43). Paris is not fighting because he is detained by Helen: "I would fain have armed today, but my Nell would not have it so" (3.1.127–28). The point is that effeminacy does not particularly signal homosexuality, and love of a spouse need not preclude queer passion.[10]

A psychoanalytic critic, such as Deborah Hooker, may try to absorb Achilles and Patroclus into a modern paradigm (straight is to butch as gay is to effeminate). But she can do so only by flatly contradicting the text. Polyxena "is obviously not his prime motivation for withdrawing from the warfare," she asserts, and his "pleasure in Patroclus" is "effeminate."[11] Hooker seeks to justify Luce Irigaray's homophobic idea of gays as the essential embodiment of patriarchy. For Hooker and Irigaray, the same-gender attachment between Achilles and Patroclus "threatens the homosocial order," not because it challenges the limits of straight sex, but because "it openly interprets the law according to which society operates."[12] These are provoking ideas; a queer reading may quarrel with them.

My elaboration of the sexual potential of various scenarios in *Troilus and Cressida* fits loosely with historicist theories of Michel Foucault, Alan Bray, and Jeffrey Weeks, who maintain that a man who engaged in (what we think of as) homosexual acts need not mark himself out as a certain kind of person, unfit for marriage and reproduction. Patroclus also is sexually interested in women. He kisses Cressida enthusiastically, and Thersites reports his eagerness to hear of promising whores (4.6.28–35, 5.2.190–91). Consider the relaxed sleeping arrangements in Achilles's hut, according to Homer: Achilles and Patroclus sleep in diagonal corners, while their female partners sleep in the alternate corners. Patroclus's companion was given to him by Achilles.[13]

Scene Queen

Generally, Pandarus is taken at face value. He is a voyeur, rather distasteful but necessary to the action. He is also a recognizable type: the court butterfly. See him as Osric (*Hamlet*); as the popinjay who is said to have appeared inappropriately at Hotspur's victory:

> He was perfumed like a milliner,
> And 'twixt his finger and his thumb he held
> A pouncet-box, which ever and anon
> He gave his nose, and took't away again . . .
>> (*Henry IV Part 1*, 1.3.36–39)

Helen and Pandarus have created at her court a stronger fussy, camp clique than we expect to see until *The Importance of Being Earnest*. Pandarus is in his element. "What's that? What's that?" he asks as he bustles in, afraid of missing any gossip. "What were you talking of when I came?" (1.2.37, 44). Pandarus cruises like a queer. Notice how he encourages Paris's Boy to be cheeky, repeatedly calling him "friend":

> *Pandarus*: Friend, know me better. I am the Lord Pandarus.
> *Servant*: I hope I shall know your honour better.
> *Pandarus*: I do desire it. (3.1.11–13)

In male queer subculture today, the extravagant queen has an uncertain role. Some sectors recognize and celebrate her, while others dispute her relevance in a postmodern world. Little of this contemporary debate will be heard from a straight reading position.

Pandarus's obsession with getting Cressida and Troilus into bed is not explained by marrying his niece into the royal family. Since Priam had upward of fifty sons, that is not such a big deal. To a queerly positioned reader it is obvious: Pandarus is infatuated with Troilus. In the guise of recommending him to Cressida, he is able to tell his love (like Viola in *Twelfth Night*). As with Antonio financing Bassanio's expedition to Belmont, Pandarus must support the cause he hates (the liaison between the boy and the woman)—it is the only way to stay in the game. Observe how he engineers a tiff with Troilus in the opening scene, forcing the boy to plead with him, keeping the scene going by storming out.

The Lovely Boy

The displaced, proxy liaison, founded in differences of class and age, evidently figures some imaginative intensity in Shakespearean texts. Compare Venus wooing Adonis, the cross-dressed Rosalind sweet-talking with Orlando, the compulsory courting of Princess Katharine in *Henry V*, the edgy role playing between Falstaff and the Prince in *Henry IV, Part 1*? It is, of course, the pattern of the Sonnets, published in doubtful circumstances, like *Troilus*, in 1609. The most outrageous displacement is Pandarus's. He calls out to Cressida, "If my lord get a boy of you, you'll give him me" (3.2.94–95).

Troilus, then, is the most generous representation of the aristocratic lovely boy who tantalizes the older, working writer. The sonneteer, fancifully and ruefully to be sure, locates himself as Pandarus—the mentor who urges marriage on his student while conceiving a same-gender passion for him. Knight, uniquely, speaks up for Pandarus: His "fussy interest in his young friends' love-adventure is truly delightful."[14]

For it is the play that, steadily, is in love with Troilus. Cressida and Pandarus speak for his sexual attractions. Observe the scarcely called-for encomium, spoken by Ulysses to Agamemnon on the authority of Aeneas (4.7.98–115). It reads like an expansion of Hamlet's Stoic appreciation of Horatio (*Hamlet* 3.2.59–79). Troilus has Hector's affection and respect. He is suitably skeptical about the war but loyal to his comrades. His boyishness protects him, for the time being, from an imputation of effeminacy and corrupt unmanly behavior (though he already believes it is "womanish" for him not to be in today's battle [1.1.103]).

"Lovely boy" is Puck's term for Oberon's much desired Indian boy (*A Midsummer Night's Dream*, 2.1.26). It is used also in Sonnet 126, the last of those addressed to the youth: "O thou my lovely boy, who in thy power / Dost hold time's fickle glass" (Sonnet 126.1–2). Troilus is the best case that can be made for the addressee of the Sonnets, presumably at a happy moment in the liaison. The danger area is his sexuality, which is willful and self-absorbed. Thwarted, it seems, by Cressida and Pandarus, his sexuality has become inward-looking. At the moment that Cressida is being made available, his thought is of his own performance:

> I am giddy. Expectation whirls me round.
> Th' imaginary relish is so sweet
> That it enchants my sense. (3.2.16–18)

In Sonnet 4, the poet upbraids the boy:

> Unthrifty loveliness, why dost thou spend
> Upon thyself thy beauty's legacy? . . .
>
> For having traffic with thyself alone,
> Thou of thyself thy sweet self dost deceive. (Sonnet 4.1–2, 9–10)

Troilus and the lovely boy, presumably, are Knight's destructive kind of mas-turbator.[15]

But is it what Shakespeare meant?, asks the traditional critic. I should be very surprised if it were. At points, the Shakespearean text appears to offer an amazing collusion with myself as queer-positioned reader. I experience the privilege of bardic ratification.

At other points, I am provoked to reach for a purposefully queer reading— against the grain, raiding the text, creative vandalism. Thersites is not actu-ally using the idea of leathers in the same way as a modern sadism-masochism scenario: you and I know that. It is an amusing link, with an element of figurative truth, and no one is deceived; to the contrary, the intervention of the commentator is manifest. Effeminacy still figures in formations of class and sexual orientation but differs in subtle ways. Masturbation is not silenced in these texts, but we do not really know how it signified. But then, as I indicated near the start of this essay, I am looking not for ideal harmonies in texts but for fault lines that disclose the operations of power.

One advantage of an explicit reading position is that it licenses playful interpretations while maintaining a criterion of relevance. Another is that it is able to address its own constructedness in history. Explicit queering of the text may remind us all that meaning is made by people in determinate situa-tions, and that the elaboration of this reading rather than that is, ultimately, a political action.

Notes

1. Personal e-mail correspondence on May 21, 2007; quoted with permission.

2. Knight, *The Mutual Flame*, 30, 33, 35.

3. Knight, *The Wheel of Fire*, 47, 71.

4. Burrow, *Troilus and Cressida*. Citations in parentheses for *Troilus and Cressida* are to this edition. Citations for other Shakespearean texts are to Craig, *The Oxford Shakespeare*.

5. Sinfield, *Faultlines*, 47. In *Faultlines*, my aim was to theorize the sources of

dissidence, and my conclusion was that they arise out of the conflict and contradiction (the fault lines) that the dominant itself produces. "Any position supposes its intrinsic *op*-position. All stories comprise within themselves the ghosts of the alternative stories they are trying to exclude": ibid., 47.

6. Burrow, "The Play in Performance," lxx. See Hammond, *Figuring Sex between Men from Shakespeare to Rochester*, 58–61; Mallin, *Inscribing the Time*, 47.

7. Burrow, "The Play in Performance," lxxi.

8. See Sinfield, *Shakespeare, Authority, Sexuality*, 86–111; Spear, "Shakespeare's 'Manly' Parts."

9. Halperin, *One Hundred Years of Homosexuality*, 75–87.

10. See King, "Queer Pride and Epistemological Prejudice"; Shepherd, "What's So Funny about Ladies' Tailors?"; Sinfield, *The Wilde Century*.

11. Hooker, "Coming to Cressida through Irigaray," 914–15. See O'Rourke, "Rule in Unity."

12. Irigaray, quoted in Hooker, "Coming to Cressida through Irigaray," 915.

13. Homer, *The Iliad*, 162.

14. Knight, *The Wheel of Fire*, 60.

15. Sonnet 4 is read by the editors Stephen Booth and Katherine Duncan-Jones as a complaint that the Boy is masturbating instead of using his semen to reproduce himself: Booth, *Shakespeare's Sonnets*, 142–43; Duncan-Jones, *Sonnets*, 118. John Kerrigan comments, "Some readers find in *traffic with thyself* a hint of masturbation; but the innuendo can be nothing more": Kerrigan, *Sonnets and A Lover's Complaint*, 177.

Is There an Audience for My Play?

SHARON HOLLAND

I saw my first production of Shakespeare's *Twelfth Night* at the Globe Theatre in London in the summer of 2002.[1] Having been disappointed by the city's other theatrical offerings—we were living in Chicago at the time, and its fantastic theater scene had spoiled us for the offerings of other cities, no matter how compelling—we decided to visit the re-creation of the historic theater at the foot of the new Tate Modern and to see the last of Shakespeare's comedies. I had not been to a Shakespeare production across the Atlantic; I felt as if we were in for a real treat. We were not disappointed, as mischief and mayhem ruled the stage for the two-hour play. The twist here was that this production might have pleased even Shakespeare himself—one reviewer with the *Guardian* of London notes that the Globe's program calls Tim Carroll's production the "most historically authentic to date."[2] In keeping with tradition, most of the roles for women were played by men, leading Ben Brantley, theater critic for the *New York Times*, to dub it "The Male *Twelfth Night*."[3] What captured my attention, and prompts this essay's query as title, is the audience—or what I prefer to call the "constituency." An audience can be a number of instruments: an assembly of listeners, the readership of a book, or the whole group of spectators or viewers of a play. In contrast, a constituency is a politically represented group or a body of customers or supporters. In other words, an audience is an always already captivated *entity*, whereas a constituency has to be worked—massaged into its allegiance. This latter group—this constituency—makes for an interested and interesting reading of high art. Since much of our love of Shakespeare is cultivated—either by the high-school curriculum or the culture wars of the 1980s and the *end* of Western civilization as we knew it—so much of what we see and our attention to it is formed by the discourse that supports its timeless greatness. Since the groundbreaking work of Kim F. Hall and Patricia Parker, among others, we have come to understand that naming a constituency is as much about the "greatness" or genius of a work as it is about its interpretation.[4]

But I digress. Worried more about our theater garb than authenticity, my partner and I were housed stage left, high above the rabble—then and now—but nonetheless with a perfect view of the "audience." This afternoon, most of the theatergoers were lazy tourists like us in the upper seats or throngs of middle-school and high-school students in the gallery, undaunted at the prospect of spending two hours on their feet watching Shakespeare. At the opening scene, the group of gallery watchers were a bit nonplussed by the men in drag. There were questioning looks as a few savvy students pointed to their programs and spread the word—the parts of women were being played by men! Some nodded with understanding, others frowned, still others seemed to rise to the challenge of the play, and the kids from the United States seemed to say, "Bring it on!" In any event, the performances by Mark Rylance (Olivia) and Michael Brown (Viola / Cesario) were impeccable, and I began to remember, as I watched the high-school crowd watching Olivia swing effortlessly from one end of the almost barren stage to the other, how easily a good performance can awaken one's desire; that in the end, it is not the object of our gaze but its performance of itself—whatever it is—that so captures our imaginations. In truth, those students were transfixed, and as the play progressed to its inevitable end where love's labor was not lost, the students were draped over the partition that marked the end of the stage and the beginning of the gallery, rapt and hanging on to the old Bard's every word. I, too, was transfixed and remembered the genesis of Maria's intrigue where she announces: "I will drop in his way some obscure epistles of love; wherein, by the colour of his beard, the shape of his leg, the manner of his gait, the expressure of his eye, forehead and complexion, he shall find himself most feelingly personated."[5] Maria's intent is figuratively and literally to capture Malvolio—her bit of chicanery is meant to make Malvolio believe that he is in the act of procuring Olivia's affections when he is actually being prepared to play the mad fool, a role for which he will be imprisoned. But what are the components, noted in this quote, that enable Maria's successful ruse? "The colour of his beard, the shape of his leg, the manner of his gait, the expressure of his eye, forehead and complexion" all serve to *personate* the lover. At this point in the play, we are led to believe that love is merely a personation; that object choice is a mere indifference in the game of love.

Twelfth Night then becomes as much a play about how to play at love as it is about the fact that whom we love is of little consequence. Maria's note to

Malvolio dictates who he should be(come) to be recognized by the object of his affection. What he does not know is that he is the dupe in all of this, as Maria's skillfully wrought letter seals his imprisonment—the *play* on appearances proves the letter to be a mirror—it reflects the tiny world that Malvolio inhabits back on him and ensures his demise.

In another scene of similar personation, Viola, disguised as Cesario, recounts to the Duke (Orsino) a description that fairly fits him, but this fit goes unrecognized by the Duke, who is a stereotypical and unimaginative lover, at best:

> *Duke*: How dost thou like this tune?
> *Viola*: It gives a very echo to the seat Where Love is throned.
> *Duke*: Thou dost speak masterly:
> My life upon't, young though thou art, thine eye
> Hath stay'd upon some favour that it loves:
> Hath it not, boy?
> *Viola*: A little, by your favour.
> *Duke*: What kind of woman is 't?
> *Viola*: Of your complexion.
> *Duke*: She is not worth thee, then. What years, I' faith?
> *Viola*: About your years, my lord.
> *Duke*: Too old, by heaven: let still the woman take
> An elder than herself: so wears she to him,
> So sways she level in her husband's heart:
> For, boy, however we do praise ourselves,
> Our fancies are more giddy and unfirm,
> More longing, wavering, sooner lost and worn,
> Than women's are.
> *Viola*: I think it well my lord.
> *Duke*: Then let thy love be younger than thyself. (2.4.20–39)

These two scenes play together well, and are mirrors for each other, as the aspect of the lovers is revealed to us most directly in each scene. Yet a comic obtuseness—or, rather, a stubborn insistence on a *masculinized* vanity—Malvolio's vain attempt to rise to the occasion of the intended lover's eye and the Duke's misguided knowledge of what women want—drives the two scenes. Moreover, the audience members become keepers of the gendered *truth* of the play: that all is not what it seems, since they know who the "real" men are. Things are and will be, *What You Will*. But in this case, gender cannot be performed without the appropriate apparatus on which to hang it, and through-out the play, even though we are gender fucked again and again, we are still indebted to the structure of heterosexual romance that rights the gendered wrongs at play in *Twelfth Night*.

No other line brings us to our queer knees better than Viola's pronounce-ment: "I am all the daughters of my father's house, And all the brothers too" (2.4.123–25). When Viola utters these lines, the audience, I want to argue, becomes a *constituency*. It is at precisely this moment that we become con-vinced of the rightness of our own version of events. But I will also argue that something else is happening here, as a gendered or feminist reading under-stands the emphasis on the "father's house" as pointed. In this play, boys will be men, and men will be boys, and women do not amount to much in the long run—for it is the father's house that counts here. Shakespeare's sleight of hand is heightened when Malvolio, in another scene that completes Maria's ruse and reflects on the Duke's previous obtuseness, observes on receiving his lover's letter: "By my life, this is my lady's hand: these be her very C's, her U's and her T's; and thus makes she her great P's. It is in contempt of question, her hand" (2.5.95–98). If another woman can easily impersonate a female lover's hand, then what does this say about the authenticity of the female part? Women's love can be made and unmade, while men's attraction is al-ways already solidified and even engendered not only in the father's house but also by the audience's belief that this is the only "house" that counts. It is a man's world over and over again as the play unfolds—one hand mistakenly exchanged for another until, surprise, surprise, all is righted in the world in the play's penultimate scene. In this scene we are reminded that the players will "strive to please you every day" (2.5.557), a playful nod from our Bard that we have been keepers of the flame once again. What I am offering here is rather obvious: What the play shores up in us, what it inspires in us, is the kernel that keeps it afloat: the promise of heterosexual love fulfilled *despite* the mistakes and the constant wandering (in that Steinian sense) behavior. The brilliance of Shakespeare's play is its ability to cajole us into believing that *What You Will* actually has been subverted by come what may. Ultimately, *Twelfth Night* is not the *quand même* of Sarah Bernhardt's generation.

What I am also getting at here is the sense that all desire seeks an object, and critics do, too. When the audience of Carroll's *Twelfth Night* becomes a constituency, it holds on to the truth of the personation: the very possibility that the marriage plot is a dialogue between men for whom women are the language, to paraphrase Simone de Beauvoir in *The Second Sex*. What the all-

male production does is solidify this arrangement much more faithfully than
another production might do. My question here is simple: Does the presence
of men playing women, often playing men, alter the landscape of desire? Can
men playing women playing men be adequate conduits of "lesbian" desire?
My purpose here is not to rehash an old debate about whether or not lesbian
desire is or can be properly *gendered*. Eve Kosofsky Sedgwick, Teresa de Lau-
retis, Barbara Johnson, and other early queer studies entrepreneurs have
taken that bull by the horns. My central question is one with personal implications: Can a woman playing a man playing a woman, or a man playing a
woman playing a man, achieve the goal of wooing an *audience* into becoming
potential *lovers* of Shakespeare, thereby making them a constituency? It is
clear that the use of male actors to play the female parts (no pun intended) is
intended to produce the feeling of authenticity inspired in critics like the
Guardian reviewer. The more interesting question here is how at the same
time a production like Carroll's can woo a potentially "gay" audience—or, at
least, *reinvigorate* a queer constituency. My next query then is how the wooing
of this particular demographic is achieved and over whose (dead) body it
happens. Is there a role for lesbian desire in the cross-casting that served a
more utilitarian purpose in Shakespeare's time but actually codes for something else in ours?

I have now articulated two purposes here: first, the objectives of this play's
producers; and second, the more subtle structure of desire, longing, and identification that a sexuality studies critic like me finds interesting. In any event,
it can be said that the goals of the play's producers might be at odds with the
goals of my essay's central query. If the action of the play were to *fashion* queer
(male) desire, then how does that action work to solidify that desire? In the
principal scenes between Malvolio and the Duke, is gay desire always already
heterosexual desire? Is desire a marriage between two men for whom women
are the language (marked by absence or presence, in the Lacanian sense)?
While it is difficult to return to that moment in London six years ago, it is
possible to speak of its meaning in the context of the play's successful run in
London and in the United States.

As noted earlier, several of the critics in the United Kingdom thought
Carroll's production one of the most "authentic" to date. Several reviewers in
the United States thought so, too. As Rick Reed, reviewer for Chicago's pre-
mier LGBT newsweekly, noted, "[This is] one of the finest interpretations of
Shakespeare I've ever seen. Mark Rylance as the widow Olivia, is astonish-
ingly good. Rylance glides across the stage as if he has casters hidden beneath

his flowing black dresses, dignified and comical all at the same time."[6] Reed also noted that "the company [had] opted to stage it as closely as possible as it would have been in Shakespeare's time. Handmade costumes, a sextet of Elizabethan musicians, and an all-male cast of 13 harken back to its original production before Queen Elizabeth I at the Middle Temple Hall in 1602. If that production was anything like this shimmering jewel, the Queen and the crowds who came to see Twelfth Night must have been pleased indeed." Reed's assumption that the crowd in 1602 must have been as pleased as he is from his twentieth-century vantage point is important indeed. This play is a crowd pleaser, no doubt, and "crowd" here moves us in the direction of the universal—to the kind of appeal that Shakespeare is known to have in his modern incarnation.

But what *part* of the crowd keeps Shakespeare on the stage? If theatergoers are overwhelmingly white and privileged, then what is the point of such universal appeal? I am well aware of the violently speculative nature of my claims here, but I want to try to locate the play's success in a constituency that is believed to be a universal audience when, in fact, it is nothing of the kind. The Shakespeare theatergoers I know are of three kinds: those queers who also often love opera; those feckless hordes of undergrads who flock to Shakespeare as part of their early British literature courses; and those academics who go to every play every year and manage to either write it off on their taxes or have the research budgets to accommodate such theatergoing. In fact, one could argue that the largest *market* constituency of Shakespeare is its academic audience. Each time Shakespeare is produced somewhere outside its comfort zone—in a prison, as with Curt Toftleland's documentary *Shakespeare behind Bars* (2006), for example—we are reminded that Shakespeare's constituency is still narrowly defined. Jeannette Catsoulis of the *New York Times* reviewed Tofleland's documentary and observed, "In the Luther Luckett Correctional Complex in Kentucky, inmates enjoy a wealth of educational programs supported by a warden who believes that prisons should be more than warehouses. 'Shakespeare Behind Bars' follows one of those programs, an all-male acting troupe that over the course of one year will rehearse and perform Shakespeare's final play, *The Tempest*."[7] In the final analysis, the inmates in Toftleland's documentary become human through the power of Shakespeare to transform incarcerated male bodies into legible bodies for those on the outside to see. The prisoners can never be keepers of the tradition, only its recipients. Furthermore, the all-male show inside fails to have the same *gendered* look as its counterpart on the outside (Carroll's *Twelfth*

Night). The irritating truth of gender and desire here is that queer play and politics are not the same inside and out; the all-male crew at Luther Luckett will not serve as the "authentic" or true-to-the-original cast. They will always already be playing themselves: *prisoners* doing Shakespeare. Since the popular view in the United States of sex in prison (where same-sex desire[?] could be called normative) is articulated by shows such as *Oz* and understood as violence, *not* sex, the space of the prison makes it very difficult for an audience to see the liminality of male bodies. In this setting, "play" is all but impossible.

Coda: A Night at the Opera

Before I wrote this brief essay, my partner and I went to the Lyric Opera in Chicago to see Handel's *Giulio Cesare*. It was to be a momentous night. I had not been to an opera since my youth, and I specifically chose David McVicar's version (originally created for the Glyndebourne Festival in 2005) because I have been in love with counter-tenors since I was in high school, and David Daniels was to play the role of Cesar. Moreover, the reviews in the *Tribune* and *Chicago Reader* stated that the direction was flawless—campy, outrageous, and fun. The opera was indeed lovely—filled with that simultaneous soul-crushing feeling and sublime textured movement that the opera of my childhood seemed to offer. And it was also one of the most "diverse" crowds on stage: a cross-dressing singer from Spain playing the son of Pompey and the first female conductor ever at the Lyric. Yes, I liked my return to the opera, indeed, but not its constituents. Let me explain. As we neared curtain time, a gentleman approached our row and, on finding that we were in fact seated in the wrong place, grunted: "You people are in the wrong seats." We moved—gracefully, I might add—but not before I said rather audibly: "I'm glad my mother wasn't here to hear that man say 'you people'—she would have read him the riot act!" Lucky for him, he missed one of my mother's free indirect discourses on manners and "white people." When Senator John McCain addressed Senator Barack Obama in their next-to-last debate as "that one," I was reminded of how phrases such as "you people" diminish both the speaker and the intended. This was a form of speech that Toni Morrison so aptly called "race talk." In any event, the evil queen in me wanted to throw a little shade and say, "You're wearing khakis to the opera on a Saturday night. Now you tell me: Which one of us is in the wrong seat?" But instead, I folded my vintage cape, retrieved my walking stick, and settled into reading the program notes.

At the first curtain, and with great anticipation, we trotted off to retrieve our "boxed lunch" on the third floor. Many of the tables on that level were taken, so we went back up to the fifth floor, where we proceeded to shovel food into our mouths with all the dignity we could muster in anticipation of the first bell. We were perched along the side of the staircase, as were many of the people around us. After about five minutes, the crowd thinned on our side of the stairs, leaving us and another couple on that side of the staircase. An usher came along and barked: "You two have to move; you're blocking the aisle"—so we moved for the *second* time during that night at the Lyric Opera and finished our meal. As we finished, we were approached by another visibly queer couple, and the gentleman said: "Did that man tell you to move?" We said in unison: "Yes." He responded, "Doesn't he have something better to do? I'm so sorry about that." What was that man apologizing for? He was not wearing a Lyric Opera badge indicating that he was in charge of something. He need not have felt responsible for the unconscious act of a stranger. Or did he? If you feel responsible for something, or felt as if you had invited someone who was different into your home for the evening, wouldn't you feel responsible? So here we hover between liberal guilt and white supremacy. Therein lies the rub. Why was that man on the stairs bothering *us*? There were enough breaches in opera etiquette, not to mention plain fashion mistakes, to occupy his time for the entire night. Why pick on a black girl playing a man playing a dandy fag? I had an audience, no doubt, but did I have the same kind of presence I would have if I were tied to a constituency—as either its member or its object? In other words, what would have happened in that scene if I had not been so readily misread as a black subject? How was this gentleman to know that it was my skin, and not my dress, that was unwelcome? In truth, how was I to know?

By way of conclusion, I will be brief. As I reflect on my Lyric Opera experience and listen to David Daniels sing a few arias, I am thinking of the nature of box seats and how I have always enjoyed them. After being with the constituencies of both the opera and the theater, I would like again to wade into the depths, but only if I can be assured my own box seat, with its convenient separate entrance and exit. In addition, I will point out that the minute I try to join the crowd and become the cross-dressing player, I am put in my place by a constituency who still believes in the rightness of the heterosexual romance—a romance always decked out in racial drag.

Notes

1. The production ran from Wednesday, May 22, through Saturday, September 28, 2002.

2. Maddy Costa, "Twelfth Night," *Guardian*, May 24, 2002.

3. Ben Brantley, "The Male 'Twelfth Night' Is a True Masquerade," *New York Times*, October 19, 2003.

4. See Hall, *Things of Darkness*; Parker, *Shakespeare from the Margins*.

5. *Twelfth Night*, in Rowse, *The Annotated Shakespeare*, 525. Citations in parentheses are to this edition.

6. Rich Reed, review of *Twelfth Night*, *Windy City Times*, December 3, 2003.

7. Jeannette Catsoulis, "Inmates as Actors, Transformed by Art," *New York Times*, March 10, 2006.

The Two Gentlemen of Verona

Pageboy, or, *The Two Gentlemen from Verona: The Movie*

AMY VILLAREJO

In this essay, I read Shakespeare's early, cliché-ridden, marginal, infrequently performed romantic comedy as a movie. By that I mean that, without too much work, the play could lend itself to becoming, rather specifically, a lesbian romantic comedy film, even if its titular men and their pursuit of female love interests supply the bulk of the action. Lesbian romantic comedies, as any queer filmgoer will tell you, are the only commercially successful "lesbian" films (the scare quotes are necessary not least because some of these films are made by straight men, such as Kevin Smith's *Kissing Jessica Stein*). In their generic constraints, they differ little from their putatively straight predecessors, often merely substituting girl for boy in prefabricated plots. This is likely the key to their success: Once the action gets going, we pretty much know its destination. You know them as well as I do.

   Two Gentlemen, a text that might enjoy the same lowly status in the Shakespearean canon as *Kissing Jessica Stein* does in queer cinema, engages such a substitution in a plot device not uncommon, as Shakespeare's readers and watchers will know, to Elizabethan drama but perhaps equally familiar to queer filmgoers: cross-dressing. I want to stress its *action* as crossing, in which a (someone thinks) woman is disguised textually but also in "her" appearance and behavior as a (someone thinks) man, creating sexual frisson difficult to determine as homo- or heterosexual. Cross-dressing as a dramatic device, that is, requires crossing something previously given (even if obliquely or implicitly) and yet remaining somehow the same. This results in a Mendelian experiment in gender and sexuality, much as Shakespeare's satire in *The Two Gentlemen* results in a burlesque of a romantic comedy while nonetheless remaining one. *Queen Christina, Sylvia Scarlet, Yentl, Boys Don't Cry, Hu-Du-Men, Tipping the Velvet, By Hook or by Crook, Butch Jamie*: Whether proto-trans,

trans, or queer (and without meaning to stuff these all into a convenient Latinate drawer), these films exploit *visual* undecidability and its pleasures, moving across or against knowing. Someone—a character or the spectator—sees a woman in a man, a man in a woman, a trannie boi in a man, a dyke in a boi, or some variation thereof. In such seeing lies pleasure and possibility, not (only) narrative pleasure but ineffable, evanescent, momentary or fleeting crossing; in that crossing flickers, in turn, a kind of desire or ambition that the romantic comedy generically cannot quite contain. In *Two Gentlemen*, there is double crossing (literally and figuratively). Proteus crosses (and may love) Valentine, and the pining Julia dons the garb of a pageboy to travel to court to pursue her love, Proteus.

What is queer about these substitutions in this romantic comedy? For one thing, hair. To bind the titular two gentlemen together in love visually seems to require the feminization of one; to fracture that bond requires the intervention of a woman in disguise as a man. For in *Two Gentlemen*, Julia transforms into a minor character, one who is (as a character) already present in the text, the page, who is in turn the structural bridge between the homosocial world occupied by the initial two young gentlemen and the mature hetero destination of the dual couples that resolves the action. Binding and fracture—both might be figured through the pageboy, a hairstyle summoned for the BBC's filmed version of the play that functions in fascinating ways, first, to make visible some of the playful queerness of the play, to feminize the actor who plays Proteus; and second, as a figuration for a disguise that actually renders a woman into a boy (that is, turning Julia *into* a page and a boy).

This rendering is generic. It is what romantic comedies do. They move, they give, and then they give back. They (lightly) jumble and toss, mix and move glances and banter, attraction and barriers, overheard whispers and I-wish-I-could-have-known-all-along deceptions, just so that we can (lightly) exhale at a pleasing union at the end. Here, though, to defend my emphasis on the pageboy, the page really is *the* figure in the play, the character written by Shakespeare who structurally facilitates this movement. He is called Speed. He propels not just the action but also the language, ratcheting up the rhythms and the rhymes, the puns and the alliteration. He calibrates the pace of the play, but he also is *the* pivotal figure of movement. Speed, in sum and by definition, moves: between the world of gentlemen and that of their servants, the laws of the civilized court and the forest of outlawry where justice paradoxically lies, the needs of men and the desires of women. Because he embodies this crossing, this movement between the play's carefully delineated spaces and social spheres, this page / boy becomes for Shakespeare a figure for other crossings (splittings, fractures) in the play.

That Julia's crossing into a page and boy is enabled by a specific prop, a hat, adds further incentive to a line of investigation following pages and hair. In what follows, then, I elaborate an argument for a queer reading of the play (and, if not more important, its performance) through this unstable figuration of the pageboy.

Visuality on Television

I have found a friend in Arthur Holmberg, who argues in a wonderful article on *The Two Gentlemen of Verona* that to appreciate the play is to value its performance, the theatrical (or televisual or filmic) experience of it. Citing the disdain of those intellectuals who consider "going to the theater intellectually irrelevant," Holmberg observes, too, that the Shakespearean plays' translation to film and television is similarly considered vulgar:

> Not long ago I overheard one of the leading authorities on Shakespearean texts express chagrin over the fact that U.S. Public Television in collaboration with the BBC would screen all thirty-seven Shakespearean plays. "Shakespeare's plays should be read," he contended. "In production they seem silly and vulgar."[1]

What impresses Holmberg about the unembellished student production in Edinburgh that he sets at the center of his reflections—aside from its intimacy, simplicity, and buoyant spirit—is the youth and beauty of its adolescent cast, which heightens the specifically visual character of Shakespeare's burlesque treatment of the romantic comedy. "If the models of Petrarchan love [in the main male characters of Valentine and Proteus], however, are destroyed visually, the verbal and dramatic irony no longer has any point."[2] Holmberg further seems alone in observing, even if too disdainfully for my taste (repeating the gesture he scorns), that audiences will come to Shakespeare *as a movie*: "The modern public, conditioned and pacified by movies and television, tends to fidget unless it is entertained visually."[3] It is in the visual insistence of this student production on the characters' adolescence (their youth and beauty) that brings to life the very stuff of the play, its (to Holmberg's mind, Eriksonian) themes of adolescence's "vocational anxiety, intimacy, and the dual problem of competition and competency."[4] He is finally astute in noticing Julia's crossing: "Julia's disguise as a page raises the questions of sexual ambiguity and gender identification."[5]

In fact, both sexual ambiguity and gender identification spill over as problems and as titillations beyond the figure of Julia into the characterizations of the male leads, Valentine and Proteus (with John Hudson as Valentine and Joanne Pearce as Silvia), in the very BBC production that Holmberg's leading Shakespearean dismisses as silly and vulgar. Let me spend a moment on the boys, then, before turning to Julia, since in this production they remain at center stage (as much as they are displaced in the Chinese film adaptation I discuss later). Produced in 1983 and circulated first on video and now on DVD, these *Two Gentlemen* are almost as gay as those played by Peter Egan and Ian Richardson in Robin Phillips's production for the Royal Shakespeare Company in 1970 (in which the divine Helen Mirren played Julia—how I wish I could have seen it!—and Patrick Stewart played Lance). Like Phillips's production, the BBC, to put it soberly, "puts a heavy emphasis on adolescence."[6] But instead of Phillips's modern-day clone costuming (with the boys in leather shorts with half-inch inseams), the homo-bond between Valentine and Proteus is here articulated through Protcus's hair.[7]

The term "pageboy" refers to a haircut, sometimes called a Prince Valiant, defined by its smooth jaw-length line and bangs. Related but not identical to the bob of the 1920s and the blunt cut popularized by Vidal Sassoon in the 1960s, the pageboy appears to have been popularized by Twiggy. As in her case, it frequently appears boyish on women and feminizing on men. (A recent film by the Coen brothers, *No Country for Old Men*, exploits the uncanny effects of a pageboy-like haircut by the Oscar-winning hair stylist Paul LeBlanc for Javier Bardem's character, Anton Chigurh, for whom it signifies simply "crazy.") As Dylan Jones notes, "Though particular haircuts have always affected the mainstream, it is in the area of youth culture that their significance is most obvious."[8]

In the BBC production, John Hudson's Valentine sports a modified mullet: short on top, long in the back, with enough layers around his face to conjure images of soft rock icons of the late 1970s. Tyler Butterworth's Proteus, come to think of it, *is* Andy Gibb, with just the fourth Bee Gee's combination of queer appeal and 'tween idol possibility; his pageboy strikingly combines wispy curls with a smooth line of hair, curled under, encircling his head. (The pageboy on the actual page Speed, by contrast, is as classical an instantiation of the cut as one could find.) Proteus's and Valentine's love for each other is coded in submerged sexuality from their first scene together, in which Valentine bids Proteus goodbye as he leaves for court. These two play it for the BBC by throwing punches where kisses otherwise would be.

If Valentine and Proteus present themselves as the couple that will trump heterosexual love as closure (for it is not Valentine's hetero desire but, instead, his feelings for Proteus, his capacity to forgive Proteus's deception, that seal the four-way marriage at the play's end), Julia similarly underscores just how queer this play might become and does so similarly through her hair. Here the homosocial bond is between Julia and her "waiting woman," Lucetta, and it is played, by Tessa Peake-Jones and Hetta Charnley, respectively, as a giggly-girl love fest with lots of hand clasping and conspiratorial touching. Shakespeare's dialogue helps to emphasize the sexual significance of hair, as in this discussion plotting Julia's disguise:

> *Lucetta*: But in what habit will you go along?
> *Julia*: Not like a woman, for I would prevent
> The loose encounters of lascivious men.
> Gentle Lucetta, fit me with such weeds
> As may beseem some well-reputed page.
> *Lucetta*: Why then your ladyship must cut your hair.
> *Julia*: No, girl, I'll knit it up in silken strings
> With twenty odd-conceited true-love knots.
> To be fantastic may become a youth
> Of greater time than I shall show to be.
> *Lucetta*: What fashion, madam, shall I make your breeches?
> *Julia*: That fits as well as "Tell me, good my lord,"
> What compass will you wear your farthingale?
> Why, ev'n what fashion thou best likes, Lucetta.
> *Lucetta*: You must needs have them with a codpiece, madam.
> *Julia*: Out, out, Lucetta, that will be ill-favoured.
> *Lucetta*: A round hose, madam, now's not worth a pin
> Unless you have a codpiece to stick pins on.
> *Julia*: Lucetta, as thou lov'st me, let me have
> What thou think'st meet and is most mannerly.[9]

The dialogue lingers initially on hair, perhaps signaling its importance for the deception the women plan. If fashion provides the most fun for sexual banter in the dialogue, however, hair remains the key *visual* element in staging the movement of cross-dressing. In the BBC production, sans codpiece, Tessa

FIGURE I. Cross-dressing, 1970s-style: Helen Mirren in the Royal
Shakespeare Company's production, 1970. Image provided by and
used with the permission of the RSC

Peake-Jones piles her hair up into a cap and off she goes, thus morphing into
the page character called Sebastian. Julia / Sebastian and Silvia recognize—
with a hint of lesbo possibility—noble grace in one another with much heaving of bosoms and dabbing of tears (in Act 4, Scene 4), a scene staged in the
production with Helen Mirren in full proto-dyke gear of vest, jeans, boots,
and a leather cap to hide Mirren's own locks (see figure 1).

It is here, too, that Don Taylor's production in 1983 renews its even queerer
interest in the boys: Proteus is most visibly smitten with Sebastian. Although
we "know" that he is seeing Julia in "him" ("Chiefly for thy face, and thy
behaviour / Which, if my augury deceive me not, / Witness good bringing
up, fortune and truth" [4.4.57–59]), Proteus moons over Sebastian with the
same dreamy rapture he had displayed for both Julia and Silvia. If Julia's cap is
all that is necessary to disguise her from her beloved, all that is required to
restore order is her hair's unveiling when she "discovers herself" in the final
act (5.4.95).

What I see at work through the figure of the page / boy, then, is obviously
both movement and containment: moments of queer desire and queer dis-

placement articulated through visual cues, most prominent among them the hiding and unveiling of hair, that both are and are not recuperated in the play's overt dialogue and closure. *Plus ça change*, yet we must not simply dismiss this generic form from a highbrow position that disdains its visual fun. If Shakespeare's play has been read as a burlesque of the genre of romantic comedy, it might, in other words, be understood just as helpfully as a lesbian romantic comedy that has been queered through further play with the male leads' trajectories of desire and identification. Substituting girls for boys, in other words, at the very least calls attention to the delicious possibilities the generic form seeks to constrain, and it is for this reason that romantic comedies appeal. The pageboy—character and hairstyle, multiple and modal—comes to signal the space this play's visuality offers for queer crossing. I want to think further about this veiling and unveiling as practices that might be more socially located, situated, and contextualized rather than functioning mostly, as they do in these British performances, as narrative propellers. That is, I see the queer dimensions of the BBC production as teasing out visual tropes that remain relatively unmoored in terms of their socio-historical forces. To dig more deeply into the consequences of these tropes, I turn to another film version of *Two Gentlemen* that offers a more clearly articulated vision of what this queerness might *mean*, in addition to how it might *look*.

A Spray of Plum Blossoms

In *A Spray of Plum Blossoms* (1931), a Chinese film adaptation of *Two Gentlemen*, the lovely Julia is played by none other than Ruan Lingyu, an icon—if not *the* icon—of the Shanghai cinema of the 1930s. She committed suicide at twenty-four (on International Women's Day, March 8, 1935) at the height of a career in silent cinema.[10] Most accounts appear to agree that her suicide was precipitated by ongoing antagonism with her first husband, Zhang Damin, and the magnification of those scandals in the tabloids. In what Zhang Zhen calls a "startling, reverse mimesis," Ruan's final film (also a cause of scandal), *New Woman*, was based on the story of an actress who commits suicide.[11] Maggie Cheung played Ruan in Stanley Kwan's biopic about the actress, *Centre Stage* (*Yuen Ling-yuk*, 1992), steeping her in a complicated nostalgia, "the experience of loss for something already gone."[12] This tragic dimension was essential to Ruan's screen persona.

Ruan Lingyu's astonishing androgynous screen presence in *The Spray of Plum Blossoms* supports comparisons of her with Greta Garbo, another figure who invokes nostalgia, luminosity, and sexual ambiguity and another figure who left the screen at a relatively young age, freezing her persona in a fusion of biography and screen image. Ruan's films from Shanghai in the 1930s reveal a complicated nexus of gender politics, ambiguous sexual allure, national-popular concerns, and cinematic density—a nexus too rich to treat with sufficient depth here. What I want to emphasize in introducing this adaptation, however, is the very extent to which it offers itself as neither a definitive production nor an exemplary production *of the play*, as is very clearly the case with the BBC's desire to give Shakespeare to the great unwashed masses. With the Chinese film, we have a play that serves as the vehicle for (1) one of the brightest stars in the pantheon of the Shanghai cinema; (2) a national-political essay on gendered militarization; and (3) a specific confluence of gendered and sexualized images in the figure of the "New Woman." I want to read all three within the space of two shots: the setup for Ruan's cross-dressing and the image of its allure. The latter, for me, is the film's *punctum*.

Initially giggly and controlling, Ruan's Julia develops complexity and depth as she leaves Shanghai to pursue Proteus in Canton. At Silvia's direction, Julia initially *hides*, tucking herself behind a screen in Silvia's room to overhear Proteus's cuckolding denial that she, his fiancée, exists. A moment later, his scoundrel behavior confirmed, Silvia recommends disguise.

A medium shot frames the back of a young guard, in military uniform, in intimate conversation with Silvia on the couch in her rooms around which dialogue has tended to revolve. Dark hair hides underneath a military cap, and the film's spectator is invited to gaze on a lovely neck on which the camera lingers (thereby and surprisingly sexualizing an inert body presumed to be male). The reverse shot, in which Ruan's face is revealed as the military guard, is stunning. Much longer in duration, I think, than its Hollywood counterpart would be, the disclosure of Ruan's face allows time to savor the pleasure of butch allure; the audacity, itself delightful, of the women taking action together; and the developing bond between Julia and Silvia that is the product of that audacity. It is in this shot that the *power* of this crossing is first made plain, and that power then becomes woven through the resolutely social questions of national power the film raises. As Zhang Zhen further observes, in an article that provides rich context for the film, which, again, is too capacious to sketch here,

> Ruan's Julia and Lin Chuchu's Sylvia attain far stronger androgynous qualities than their counterparts in the play. Romance in the film is not so

much the end as the means by which the two modern Chinese girls learn more about themselves and forge an alliance with one another. In much of the film we see the two leading ladies flaunt their male attire or, to be precise, military garb. [Shi] Luohua [the alliteration for Sylvia], the daughter of the Governor-general, is no love-starved maiden locked away in the deep recesses of an aristocratic palace but an officer with rank. An early intertitle card describes her as "a maiden with a spirit of masculinity." (She does, however, retain her long hair.)[13]

I like the parenthetical clause, obviously, as an aside about hair, but it does more. It highlights how indebted the bond between these women is—again, to place emphasis on this—to that *movement* of crossing as it is framed in the film (in a litany of lesbian clichés, no less): of normative gender signifiers (hair), of normative gendered behavior (horseback riding, military uniforms, and military rituals of power), of normative expectations (to marry, especially the one chosen by the father), and of normative social bonds (hetero versus homo, but also based on region, class, and so on). In this text, the work of veiling and unveiling becomes, in other words, embedded in a richer tapestry of queer life than the BBC production allows precisely because the BBC production refuses any careful consideration of history (preferring love-starved maidens in overwrought scenery of aristocratic palaces to these modern Chinese women). In noticing how *A Spray of Plum Blossoms* makes of *The Two Gentlemen of Verona* a film that returns historical texture to the play, I am also obliged to remark how much more *modern* a text is the Chinese film of 1931 than the BBC television adaptation of 1983 insofar as the BBC production evacuates questions of national power in favor of a bid for a more "timeless" televisual image.

That is to say, *A Spray of Plum Blossoms* is a very different *kind* of movie than the "made-for-television" Shakespeare our cranky scholar dismisses, insofar as it enters explicitly into the discourse of modern sexualities—"modern" here signaling some inquiry into historicity. It helps us to give what Tze-lan D. Sang calls, in her wonderful monograph on Chinese lesbianism, "temporal depth to transnational processes."[14] The film offers a fascinating glimpse into a queer vernacular forged via Shakespeare in Republican China involving a fusion of feminism and female same-sex desire. As Sang puts it, we may see here an "alternative modern discourse on homosexuality" rather than "a deformed, deficient, and uninformed version of Western sexology."[15] In this film, I think, we see for a moment what queer wants to name: fleeting sexual dissidence, the precarious hold of gender, and the possibilities of powerful and sexy women joining in laughter. It is better than the play.

Notes

1. Holmberg, *"The Two Gentlemen of Verona,"* 33.
2. Ibid., 37.
3. Ibid., 39.
4. Ibid., 40.
5. Ibid.
6. Schlueter, "Introduction," 44.
7. If we need to gloss the term "clone," something has gone awry in passing along our queer history: a kind of urban gay men's uniform that originated in the Castro district of San Francisco and Greenwich Village in New York, of which the prototypical elements would include Levi's 501 jeans, work boots, and a tight-fitting T-shirt.
8. Jones, *Haircults*, 8.
9. *The Two Gentlemen of Verona*, in the Riverside Shakespeare, second ed., G. Blakemore Evans, General Editor, 2.7.38–58. Citations in parentheses are to this edition.
10. Although the transition to sound was under way.
11. Zhen, *An Amorous History of the Silver Screen*, 265.
12. See the taut characterization of Ackbar Abbas's work in Nedham, "The Post-colonial Hong Kong Cinema."
13. Zhen, "Cosmopolitan Projections," 154.
14. Sang, *The Emerging Lesbian*, 11.
15. Ibid, 124.

The Two Noble Kinsmen

Philadelphia, or, War

JODY GREENE

for the birds . . .

His brutalized body lies crumpled in a filthy lot outside the city walls, dust under him, dust around him, but no dust to cover his exposed flesh and bones. It is *the law*. The ground under him is blackened, fire-hardened, war torn. Even the weeds cannot survive here. Handkerchiefs covering their faces, bandit-style, the sentries shoot craps, keeping their eyes averted from the armor-plated piles of presumptively human remains punctuating the stark blankness of the plain. They scrupulously ignore the steady stream of supplicants, some winged, some furred, who bow and feed in droves, in a parodic office for the dead. A ritual is being meticulously enacted here, a ritual of disincorporation from the human collectivity and reincarnation into the most benighted of animal ones. "You shall watch him chewed up by birds and dogs and violated," Creon promises—or, perhaps, exhorts—the citizens.[1] But they do not watch; they cannot. They will not. They hope, by refusing to witness the ritual, to inoculate themselves somehow against its inevitable ill effects.

Still, there is one who watches, obsessively watches, creeping out periodically past the traumatized sentries and into the open to monitor the progress of these outcast rites, patiently awaiting her moment. She has figured out how to move among the corpses like, or even as, one of those lean, hungry dogs feeding on the dead. In fact, she takes a perverse pleasure in witnessing the frenzy, in training her eyes on the spectacle of her brother's bones being painstakingly stripped of flesh by the birds and then carried off, one by one, by the howling pack. She has developed a kind of grudging respect for the relish with which these carrion eaters treat his remains. "A dainty treasure for the birds," she calls what is left of her brother, "their feast's delight."[2] They certainly know how to appreciate the dead. Above all, though, she sees, or thinks she sees, this in the spectacle of the birds' ravenous visitations: they do justice to her brother by making use of his remains, ensuring their own survival by digesting the body he no longer needs. "For myself, *I* myself will bury him," she repeats like a mantra. "It will be good to die, so doing."[3]

is this winning?

This same filthy, stinking lot plays a starring role in the opening scene of Shakespeare's and Fletcher's *The Two Noble Kinsmen*, although, of course, we do not see a lot onstage.[4] Tricky, tricky, tricky, all those putrefying corpses. And while the dogs might be possible, how to pull off that thing with the birds? No, all of that has to take place offstage. The opening obscene, let us call it. And obscene is just the word for it, really, because this is supposed to be a wedding party—the wedding of Theseus and Hippolyta, to be exact—and all of a sudden we are being asked to turn our attention to a bunch of corpses, three kings who "I' th' blood-sized field [lie] swollen, / Showing the sun [their] teeth, grinning at the moon" (1.1.99–100). Swollen corpses at a wedding? Nasty. No wonder this play has been called an "embarrassment" to the Shakespeare canon, when it is allowed as a member of that canon at all.[5]

Take the first scene, for instance. Theseus and his Amazon war captive—make that fiancée—Hippolyta are on the way to their wedding. The play opens with an epithalamium, a sweet song in praise of the incipient nuptials, sung by a cute boy dressed as Hymen. The song details the flowers strewn in front of the happy couple as they walk and then moves on to the wedding's avian invitees, which is where things start to head south:

> Not an angel of the air,
> Bird melodious or bird fair,
>   Is absent hence.
> The crow, the sland'rous cuckoo, nor
> The boding raven, nor chough hoar,
>   Nor chatt'ring pie,
> May on our bride-house perch or sing,
> Or with them any discord bring,
>   But from it fly. (1.1.16–24)

What's with the double negative? Who is not absent? The song oddly enumerates all of the birds who will not get an invitation to this event, the birds of death and sorrow, of discord and ill omen. When three weeping queens

dressed in little black dresses burst in and start chattering like magpies immediately after the conclusion of the not so happy couple's not so happy song,
we do not even have time to be surprised, let alone relieved at the wedding's
delay. These queens have come from Thebes, where the war between Eteocles and Polynices has just ended. Like Polynices himself, the defeated kings
remain unburied, rendering them tasty pickings, not coincidentally, for the
very birds about whom we just heard: "We are three queens whose sover-
eigns fell before / The wrath of cruel Creon," the first queen explains, "who
endure / The beaks of ravens, talons of the kites, / And pecks of crows, in the
foul fields of Thebes" (1.1.139–42). The queens beg Theseus to go to war to
avenge the dishonor done to their husbands, and after a suitable delay, including some rather suspicious prompting and begging from Hippolyta herself,
he abandons his wedding plans and heads off to do the deed. No big surprise,
given that "wars, and this sweet lady" (3.6.203) are all Theseus cares about,
apparently in that order. He gallantly steps up to be the queens' "undertaker"
(1.1.74), to complete the mission they cannot, as women, accomplish for
themselves, which involves a rather literal form of under-taking: the trans-
position of the bodies to an appropriate resting place under the earth. That's
right: Antigone's mission exactly. It is hard not to wonder if they ran into each
other out there.

The Two Noble Kinsmen, then, opens by staging an impossible possibility, a
wrinkle in literary historical time: a meeting between Theseus and Antigone
on a field outside the walls of Thebes, where both have come to defy Creon
by laying to rest Polynices and his followers. The meeting, of course, never
happens. It never could happen. These two miss each other entirely, occupying, as they do, fundamentally different if uncannily overlapping orders of
fictional existence. Anamorphosis: by the time Theseus arrives, Antigone
must already be dead, having failed in her undertaking and strangled herself
in the tomb in which Creon has had her imprisoned, "death's stone bridal
chamber."[6] Theseus, by contrast, will return home triumphant, having vanquished Creon, freed Thebes from tyranny, and made it back from the battlefield in plenty of time to take his place next to Hipployta in their own, no
doubt equally carceral "bride-house," a feat he chillingly describes as "greater
than any war" (1.1.171).

But wait, not so fast. Among the trophies Theseus brings back from
Thebes are the bodies of Creon's nephews Palamon and Arcite. Yes, you heard
right: Doppelgängers of Eteocles and Polynices. Moreover the wounded boys
hover, like Antigone herself, "neither with the living nor the dead."[7] Unlike

Antigone, however, these spectral visitors will rise again to bring a new war into the very heart of Athens, re-creating what René Girard calls the "stupid reciprocity of reprisals between undifferentiated antagonists" they grew up with back home.[8] This war will once again interrupt Theseus's wedding festivities but, in exchange, will give him free rein to exercise his other passion, the one for war, a war being fought—ostensibly, at least—on behalf of a "sweet lady" this time.

Theseus tells Emilia, the flimsy pretext for the latest "stupid" war, "You are the victor's meed, the prize and garland / To crown the question's title" (5.3.16–17). "Of this war / You are the treasure" (5.3.30–31). Thanks, but no thanks, responds Emilia. She wants to stay out of it, "guiltless of election" (5.1.154) concerning the identity of the one who is going to win her hand. But no one is listening. And anyway, she asks, trying another tack, "is this winning?" (5.3.138). She offers this query after one noble kinsman defeats the other and secures her hand in marriage—an outcome that will be reversed before the play is over through a series of events so absurd as to be unworthy of rehearsal. What kind of winning is this for the kinsman who must lose his friend, and what kind is it for the Amazon who must marry to cement a series of political alliances in which she bears no interest? The Amazons were defeated and dispossessed long before the play even began. "Arm your prize," Theseus jokes to the winning kinsman, as if to immunize against the threat that she might remember she, too, was a soldier once and try to escape becoming a trophy wife by arming herself, *for herself* (5.3.135). Yet Emilia need not worry. This peace will be short lived. Another armed conflict is just around the corner. "Tragic carnage." That is how Jacques Derrida, in *Glas*, describes the kind of human relations depicted in *Antigone* and beyond, from the ridiculous, blood-soaked pact for mutual destruction of the warring kinsmen that founds and maintains the state and its will to violence, to the "union of opposites" called marriage, which perpetuates the family as a counterbalance to and collaborator with that masculine state.[9] The war between these domains, like that within them, is unending. "This war is not one war among others," Derrida writes. "It is *the* war."[10]

eleven, or, singular singularity

"Union." "Opposites." Not particularly appealing alternatives, are they? Is there not some outside, some crack in the carapace, some tiny nugget of relief from the ubiquitous bellicosity that afflicts dramatic and, let's face it, lived scenes in which fratricidal mirroring and amatory possession emerge as the only models for love? Is there another kind of *philos*, one that is neither an unstable and potentially lethal narcissistic "twyning" (1.1.178) nor an act of appropriation, a question of title and entitlement? Is that so much to ask?

As it happens, *The Two Noble Kinsmen* does gesture—obscenely, once again —at one twosome that does not seem to have collapsed into or even teetered on the brink of carnage, perhaps because the participants were separated at age eleven. These were Emilia and her childhood "play-fellow" Flavina (1.3.50), who died, as Emilia makes a point of noting, when Hippolyta was already grown up and "at wars" (1.3.51). Not yet ready for *the* wars, the Amazonlets remained in peace at home, expressing their love for and through each other by mutual emulation, in a kind of syncopated bliss. "What she liked / Was then of me approved," Emilia remembers, "what not, condemned— / No more arraignment" (1.3.64–66). These girls are a law unto themselves— autonomous, as it were, a word also famously applied to Antigone,[11] although here, rather than being wholly atomized, as it is in Antigone's case, the law-making is mutual, a shared "arraignment." Nonetheless, these practices of mutual mirroring ought, at the very least, to raise suspicion in the attentive reader of this play. "The hand of war hurts none here" (2.2.87), Arcite confidently announces to his "twyn" (2.2.64) less than a hundred lines before declaring war on Palamon in the following, unrelenting terms: "Friendship, blood, / And all the ties between us, I disclaim" (2.2.174–75).

We know, then, where such mirroring gets you. Yet this is not the only way Emilia parses her love for Flavina, and the other version is intriguing. "Loved for we did," she remembers, "and like the elements / That know not what nor why, yet do effect / Rare issues by their operance; our souls / Did so to one another" (1.3.61–64). There is an elementary agnosticism at the heart of this mutual and mutually productive affection, which nonetheless *effects* something new in the "operance." The image here is intentionally vague but seems to suggest chemical elements that react together to produce some critical third term, without themselves being wholly consumed by the interaction—more catalytic conversion than amatory alchemy. This involuntary chemical reaction apparently leaves the souls, if not untouched, then at least intact; there is still "one" and "another" at the end of the day, as well as something new. It is as though the very age beyond which their relationship could not progress—eleven—is a kind of cipher for their relational stance: one, and another one. Unlike the kinsmen who hop on the ancient bandwagon of masculine friendship by fantasizing that their "two souls . . . in two noble bodies" will "grow together" (2.2.63–65) into a single soul, these girls maintain a separation, and a mysteriously productive one at that.

In the love of Emilia and Flavina, then, *The Two Noble Kinsmen* offers something like an alternative to homo-narcissistic sociality or proprietary appropriation. We have to ask what kind of alternative is really held out here, however, given that the love in question is immature, truncated, and retrospective—the girls were separated by death at an early age, and no analogous love appears within the time of the play itself. Indeed, it seems to be part of the point of the rest of the play to relentlessly obliterate any further hope of non-pathological relating. "I am extinct" (5.3.20), Emilia laments late in the play, as though when Flavina died the "rare" species to which the two of them, perhaps alone, had belonged, died, too. Separation without opposition is not so easy to replicate, after all. That the memory of this dead love lives on and even haunts Emilia—and with her, the play as a whole—suggests, however, that a space may have been left open in *The Two Noble Kinsmen*, an impossible space that memorializes and in so doing keeps alive the possibility of a less toxic mode of relating, one that cannot simply be written over or replaced by another love—least of all, one that fits the mold of a martial victory or land grab.

This model of loving is not unprecedented in the history of literature. Indeed, it resonates uncannily with one left open in *Antigone* itself, in the form of the relationship between Antigone and the brother she is trying to bury, Polynices. Unlike in the case of *The Two Noble Kinsmen*, however, *Antigone* offers almost no information concerning what is distinctive about Antigone's relationship with Polynices—nothing on the order even of Emilia's brief ode to Flavina. Antigone's deep bond to her brother appears to have nothing to do with his particularity and everything to do with his position.[12] She repeatedly defends her decision to defy Creon by invoking the duties one holds to one's family, and to one member of the family in particular. "How could I win a greater share of glory / than putting my own brother in his grave?,"[13] she asks. The word for brother here, "*autadelphos*," means one born from the same womb, whether a brother or a sister. In her calculation of family values, then, Antigone endorses the pre-eminent significance of the love that comes from having originated from the same maternal matrix, a love so distinctive it was known in Greek by its own term, "*philadelphia*."[14] The term appears only once in the play, bridging what it means both to love and to grieve for a womb mate. "Here before the gates comes Ismene," the Chorus sings, "shedding tears for the love of a brother."[15] *Philadelpha dakrua*—tears for the love of a womb mate—does not, in fact, specify whether the sibling grieved for is male or female, and the translation appears to miss the fact that Ismene is grieving for at least two and possibly more of her siblings in this scene, given that her sister has just been condemned to death and both of her brothers have recently been killed—by each other.

Of course, the play's repeated references to same-wombedness constitute a kind of obsessive pointing back to Antigone's paternal legacy, Oedipus's own overvaluation *and forgetting* of the maternal womb. His children should remember what womb they came from, the play seems to suggest, since he apparently could not. Yet over and above this hortatory aim, Antigone offers a more positive rationale for why same-wombedness should be important and at times pre-eminent among intrafamilial relationships—why, that is, being a brother, or a sister, ought to matter. Her argument runs as follows:

> Had I been a mother
> Of children, and my husband been dead and rotten,
> I would not have taken this weary task upon me
> Against the will of the city. What law [*nomos*] backs me
> When I say this? I will tell you:
> If my husband were dead, I might have had another,
> And child from another man, if I lost the first.
> But when father and mother both were hidden in death
> No brother's life would bloom for me again.[16]

Most commentators on the play, ancient and modern, have frowned on this passage; Goethe, for instance, famously called it a "blemish" on *Antigone's* beautiful face.[17] Yet Derrida follows Hegel in endorsing Antigone's vision of siblinghood's "singular singularity."[18] Hegel, Derrida notes, was almost nonsensically unstinting in his praise for the love of one *autadelphon* for another—and specifically, of the same-wombed brother and sister: "unique example in the system," he writes, of a relationship—a "recognition"—that "passes through no conflict, no injury, no rape."[19] Just try to find *that* on the relational battlefield of *The Two Noble Kinsmen*, at least in living form. Try to find it anywhere, for that matter. Re-scripting the usual story of one consciousness seeking recognition and overcoming the other in the process of securing it, these two, unique consciousnesses appear to work in tandem. "The for-(it)-self of one does not depend on the other," Derrida writes.[20] In sacrificing herself for the irreplaceable *autadelphon*, Antigone is also acting on her own behalf—"For myself, *I* myself will bury him"—by being her own undertaker, as well as his.

Hegel, of course, never adequately explains why or how the brother and sister are able to be "for" each other in this way. "Empirically," Derrida announces, deadpan, "it seems false."[21] And yet Derrida follows Hegel in insisting on what makes this relationship unique: its immunity to violence. The brother–sister relation is the only one "that does not know the horizon of war."[22] Hegel takes as a precondition for this pacifism the absence of desire, which he banishes from the scene of *philadelphia* simply by announcing that it is not there. As Derrida parses it, Hegel merely decides that the sexual difference that holds between a brother and a sister is not sexual difference per se. What holds in its stead is something Derrida calls "diversity": "Diversity is a moment of difference, an indifferent difference, an external difference, without opposition."[23] This natural diversity is unsustainable, of course. Even here, the lack of differentiation is fragile and eventually will be overcome. With this overcoming, moreover, there will be loss—worse, extinction. "In overcoming the natural difference as *diversity* of the sexes," Derrida writes, "we pass on to difference as *opposition*."[24] But for a moment there, we glimpsed, or thought we glimpsed, the possibility of something different: symbiosis without parasitism; co-constitution without a tearing of the flesh; one, and then another, here again.

. . . to the dogs

A filthy lot outside the walls of Thebes. Enter a tyrant, another tyrant, a young girl, some dogs. Birds everywhere, circling, some flying in from offstage; others leaving through a wormhole in literary space, a tear in the fabric of fictional time. Or would it be a seam?

Try this on for size: one tyrant dies at the hands of the other tyrant and is buried in his multipurpose bridal chamber and charnel house. Better yet, they both die. Better yet, they both lie out there as fodder for the birds. While their stupid battle rages, the girl quietly buries her brother and, her work done, goes off in search of another singular love, for the living promise of one, and then another. The dogs get fat on what remains. The birds have plenty to sing about.

Counter-factual? Counter-fictional, more like. Impossible, really. This is the trouble with being fascinated by "a figure inadmissible in the system," as Derrida puts it.[25] The relationship is irreplaceable; that is the whole point.

And anyway, even a tyrant is somebody's brother.

Derrida seems convinced not only of the "vertiginous" appeal but also of the critical benefits of "focusing, in a text, around an impossible place."[26] We must do so, he insists, because what cannot be admitted—"the absolute indigestible,"[27] as he calls it—may well be the key to the workings of the system as a whole. This seems right, as far as it goes. But at the end of the day, we are left with the following problem: Once we have established a critical practice based on foreclosed possibilities, operances rare in their origin and extinct in their actuality, how might we use that practice not only to better understand the workings of the system but to dismantle it? Such a critical practice is worth having only if the "dainty treasures" we find in the forgotten corners of literary works turn out, in some fashion, to be digestible, after all, food for others and not just food for thought.

Notes

1. Grene, *Antigone*, 205–6. For the Greek, I have used Shuckburgh, *The Antigone of Sophocles*. I am extremely grateful to Karen Bassi and Daniel Selden for their assistance with the Greek text.

2. Ibid., 29–30.

3. Ibid., 78–79.

4. See Potter, *The Two Noble Kinsmen*. Citations in parentheses are to this edition.

5. For the notion of the play as an embarrassment, see Charles H. Frey's introduction to idem, *Shakespeare, Fletcher, and* The Two Noble Kinsmen, 1.

6. Grene, *Antigone*, 1206.

7. Ibid., 850.

8. Girard, "Lévi-Strauss, Freud, Derrida, and Shakespearean Criticism," 34.

9. Derrida, *Glas*, 170–71.

10. Ibid., 146.

11. Grene, *Antigone*, 821.

12. For a detailed exploration of the dynamic of kinship position in *Antigone*, as well as the Hegelian treatment of this theme, see Butler, *Antigone's Claim*.

13. Grene, *Antigone*, 502–3.

14. The significance of the term *"autadelphon"* is discussed in Miller, *Postmodern Spiritual Practices*, 85–96; Tyrrell and Bennett, *Recapturing Sophocles'* Antigone, 31–36.

15. Grene, *Antigone*, 526–27.

16. Ibid., 904–12.

17. Oxenford, *Conversations of Goethe with Eckerman and Soret*, 227–28.

18. Derrida, *Glas*, 163.

19. Ibid., 150.

20. Ibid., 149.

21. Ibid., 165.
22. Ibid., 150.
23. Ibid., 168.
24. Ibid.
25. Ibid., 151.
26. Ibid.
27. Ibid.

Venus and Adonis

Venus and Adonis Frieze

ANDREW NICHOLLS

My practice is concerned with the twentieth-century conflation of "sentimental" and "kitsch," where both terms currently seem to point to a perverse imitation of "authentic" culture. It is equally concerned with the way gay subjectivity is cast as an artificial, self-indulgent imitation of the plenitude of heterosexuality. As a gay visual artist, my ethical response to this legacy is to flaunt appropriation: practically everything that I draw is stolen from other sources. I most commonly reference china designs and etched illustrations from Victorian texts, including children's books, pulp novels, and scientific and religious publications. More recently, I have also begun to reference classical and religious artworks spanning the Renaissance through the twentieth century. Stealing from these texts (many of which espouse a conservative morality) to create my own ideal compositions can be considered a queering.

The *Venus and Adonis* drawings reference a number of historical artworks, in particular paintings by Jacob Jordaens (*Venus and Adonis*, ca. 1630) and John William Waterhouse (*The Awakening of Adonis*, ca. 1900). They deviate from the majority of historical paintings inspired by the poem by obscuring Venus's body and exposing Adonis's. The drawings follow Shakespeare's narrative fairly closely. Venus appears in a glorious surfeit of desire to sweep Adonis from his steed, attended by a collage of pig cherubs and celestial blooms, but fails to arouse his interest. By the final panel, the pigs have come to represent Venus's failed seduction, turning on the object of her unrequited passion. Sprouting from the dead Adonis's mouth is *Swainsona formosa*, Sturt's desert pea, a wildflower from arid central Australia whose alien beauty displaces Venus's Eurocentric blossoms.

Producing this work has provided the opportunity to explore aesthetically what a queer drawing practice may entail. The artificiality of the process is highlighted through the explicit layering of different drawing styles, different line weights, and different decorative motifs. There was also pleasure in reinterpreting a text historically associated with heterosexual titillation for my own erotic enjoyment. The drawings take queer pleasure in the failure of heterosexual desire, but no malice is intended.[1]

Notes

Archival ink pen on Arches Aquarelle paper, eight from a series of ten panels, each measuring 84 by 58 centimeters, 2008–9.

   1. I thank the artist Nalda Searles for this elegant disclaimer.

Andrew Nicholls, *Venus and Adonis Frieze*, archival ink pen on watercolor paper, eight from a series of ten panels, each measuring 84 by 58 cm, 2008–9

Lost, or "Exit, Pursued by a Bear":
Causing Queer Children on Shakespeare's TV

KATHRYN BOND STOCKTON

We were as twinned lambs. . . .

Had we pursu'd that life. . . .

Too hot!

Commend it strangely to some place.

The sea mocked them . . . the bear mocked him.

   The Winter's Tale, 1.2.68, 72; 1.2.109; 2.3.181; 3.3.96–97

Kings, who are lambs, together cause a bear. A bear bespeaks a child connected to these lambs. The lambs can't breed –not with each other. What has caused the child? Now, suspend this question.

It is only obvious. *The Winter's Tale* was written with TV in mind. Shakespeare knew that his drama in the future would be written from its middle, focusing on the story's outcasts, and that its name could only be *Lost*. (There would be seacoasts, survivors, bears. . . . It would play primetime on ABC. . . .) Likewise, he must have sensed there is a story inside reproduction not getting told—that would stay untold, even through the "gayby boom" centuries later. Children, as he might put it bluntly, do not issue solely from parental intercourse or parental love. Children bodily, shockingly, profoundly, just as forcefully are the result of parents' lost and castaway attractions: all of the people one has not had sex with, or has slept with but not bred with, or has stopped pursuing. (My ex-girlfriend would not have had her specific children had our relationship not broken up.) Strangely, your child is the fertility of your negativity. Your specific child, whoever she may be, is caused by each of your lost attachments, all of your prior failed attractions and your other unpursued pursuits. Put positively, Nothing *causes* her. Aristotle's invert, she, as much as anything, is the effect of non-prime moving. She is the cessation of certain motions, the sum of blocked relations, is *lost* found. She is queerly caused.

It is obvious, therefore, and Ovidian. Two transformations tantalize Shakespeare, tempting him to render them; falling hard to these temptations, he appears to realize both. One involves television, which, of course, Shakespeare invented. The other involves TV's special devotee, the Child. Shakespeare transforms Drama and Children. Moreover, he does so through a stage direction that we must view at first in the negative. The liveliest stage direction in Shakespeare tells things exactly as they are not. Cause in *The Winter's Tale* is not anywhere near so simple, so succinct, or lacking in liquid effects as implied by *"Exit, pursued by a bear."*[1] In this early version of *Lost*, with its castaways on remote seacoasts, the bear is just one effect of a cause that spreads across the play. The cause is a crush that cannot be consummated, though its nothingness causes a child. This is the crush of a king on a king (who, together, "were as twinned lambs") that becomes embodied by a daughter *named* "Lost" (hence, her name "Perdita"), she who is a castaway left among bears. ("For the babe / Is counted lost forever, Perdita, / I prithee, call't," we are told [3.3.31–33].) Since she inherits the effects of this crush—Loss writ large—but grows beside them, Perdita is a *queer form of growth inside perdition*. She is the child of a queer fertility. She is launched from a couple's being dashed.

Not that this is the usual way to understand *The Winter's Tale*. Rather, the standard summarizing of the play might go like this: Two kings extremely fond of each other since their boyhood—he of Sicilia, he of Bohemia—must now part. Polixenes of Bohemia must go home, since his kingdom needs its king; Leontes of Sicilia cannot accept this parting, longing to make "Bohemia" stay. Trying to make Polixenes linger, Leontes importunes his wife to beg his friend to tarry among them; when she obliges, Leontes, out of some mad fancy, accuses them, wife and friend, of wanting each other and, indeed, of producing a child (who is Leontes's). As a result, Polixenes flees; the wife, Hermione, goes on trial and seemingly dies (along with her son); and the baby girl is abandoned on a seacoast frequented by bears, one of whom chases and eats the man who leaves her. Here is where the story now becomes suspended. As we are told by Time, appearing in the guise of a Chorus, sixteen years go rolling by, during which Perdita is nurtured by a shepherd (who nurtures lambs). Only when she is pursued by Florizel, Polixenes's son, who has cast himself from Bohemia, do her storied origins unfurl. It becomes revealed to Florizel, Leontes, Polixenes, *and* Perdita that this shepherd girl is a lost daughter, truly the embodiment of Leontes's losses. With Lost found, Leontes is united with Polixenes, and Hermione's statue, inert but growing all this time, somehow comes alive. The living suspense of sixteen years and the lives of outcasts (some left growing on deserted seacoasts; some still growing in stopped motion, all away from the reader's eyes) are now opened from the inside out.

But could this tale have been *told* from its insides? Inside loss? In my delusions, as you may have guessed, *Lost* is this experiment. *Lost*'s ingredients owe themselves to Shakespeare. As the series commences on its island, one eye blinking and flickering open, as if the story emerges from interiors, suspension begins. We are hung in time. The story *is* suspension. Duration is waiting (albeit active waiting), the actions of outcasts waiting to be found. And, as one might picture, characters' back stories start to spill out from this expanding feeling of hanging. Why was each of them on the plane that wrecked? What not only happened but also didn't happen that put each of them on that flight? (The strings of causality are both serpentine and centered on parents as the cause of *Lost*: Jack's drunk dad; Locke's paternal fraud; Sawyer's suicidal, ripped-off father; Kate's abusive patriarch, along with Sun's, who affects Jin; Clare's own act of becoming a mother.) And, intriguingly, there is a polar bear in an early episode, scaring everyone nearly to death when it gives chase, but, more compellingly, indicating there are strange causalities no one fully grasps. (What can cause a polar bear to live at this latitude?) Slyly, the bear is an early clue to the time abyss—not the climate—central to the island. Time passes strangely, with magical propensities, as it stretches laterally, as much as anything. Viewers find it hard to track the time that's passed. There is more than a hint of suggestion that the island is lost in Time.

So is Leontes temporally lost before he is birthing his losses in Perdita. Leontes himself is lost in a childhood he had wanted to delay forever, "to be boy eternal" with Polixenes, on an entranced island of time. Temperature, however, is not beside the point. He feels hot about Polixenes, however you slice it. Funny enough, Harold Bloom has called this play "the story of Leontes, an Othello who is his own Iago," as if this hotheaded king has a couple burning on his brain.[2] Indeed, Leontes does. He has a frisky couple of boys, himself and Polixenes, on his mind, inside himself, they whose "mature dignities and royal necessities made separation of their society," so that they have "embraced, as it were, from the ends of opposed winds" (1.1.25–26, 30–31). How does Leontes think of this "embrace," especially with Polixenes in his presence, about to leave as the play begins? He regards it as imperiled, as just about to be lost (again). (Otherwise, why would so many lines at the drama's start fixate, emotionally, on this parting?) As I will show, he "commend[s] it strangely" (2.3.181) to two places. First, he locates this embrace-as-lost in his wife—but perhaps not as the play, on its surface, makes us think. Maybe his jealousy is not standard issue. In fact, as I will argue, it makes as much sense that he is unconsciously projecting his feelings for Polixenes onto Hermione—making his own heat for Polixenes supposedly hers ("Too hot, too hot!")—as it makes sense that he could consciously believe his wife and friend betray him. Indeed, he has ordered Hermione, in her words, to echo strongly his own pleadings; hence, Hermione's words speak his. Hermione's supposed lust for Polixenes is nothing but his own. (Even in the standard take on his jealousy, her hot feelings are only his fantasy.) And, in an almost Wildean exchange, a lord puzzles Polixenes by telling him, "I cannot name [Leontes's] disease, [but] it is caught / Of you that . . . are well." "A sickness caught of me, and yet I well?," Polixenes queries. "How should this grow?" (1.2.385–86, 397, 430). Second, as I have implied all along, Leontes puts his loss of Polixenes *in* his daughter. When he falsely imagines that Perdita "issues" from his friend, he makes *her* the loss of *him* (especially since Polixenes flees). She is Leontes's castaway love. And because Perdita becomes suspended in time—with her childhood as an island of Time afloat, hidden where the story is lost and *Lost*—she is a version of the queer childhood that Leontes lost with Polixenes. Yet Perdita is queer growth, sideways growth, for sixteen years: Leontes beside himself in sorrow, in the growing form of his daughter. Perdita is a moving suspension in this play (echoed by her mother's movement as a statue). She is the motion of loss between men, the blocking of relation kept in (e)motion, and a growth inside delay. No wonder the child and bear bespeak each other as the effects of a father's man crush (with its roots in boyhood). Both are creatures of hibernation, growing while suspended in a winter's tale.

Of course, my fantastic engagement with this play is no surprise. In my work, I limn the elegant, often unruly contours of growing that defy the usual sense of "growing up," in its false and neatened formulations.[3] I stake a different kind of claim for growth and for its intimate relations with queerness. Overall, I prick (deflate or just delay) the vertical, forward-motion metaphor of growing "up" and do so by exploring the many kinds of growing sideways depicted by twentieth-century texts. I even coin "sideways growth" to refer to something related but not reducible to the death drive; something that locates energy, pleasure, vitality, and (e)motion in the back and forth of connections and extensions that aren't reproductive in a standard way. These I theorize as moving suspensions and shadows of growth, both of which abundantly appear in *The Winter's Tale*. Even more intensely, estranging, broadening, darkening forms of the child as idea are my pursuit, with a keen eye on the ghostly "gay" child as a figure hovering in the twentieth century—and a figure braiding with other forms of children who are broadly strange. A "gay" child illuminates the darkness of the Child. To be sure, many queer adults report, even without being prompted by Shakespeare, that they remember desperately feeling (when they were children) there was simply nowhere to grow, feeling a frightening, heightened sense of growing toward a question mark. Or growing up in haze. Or hanging in suspense—even wishing time would stop, or just twist sideways, so that they wouldn't have to advance to new or further scenes of trouble. Far from a simple, sentimentalized plea for children's rights to come out "gay," my thoughts scout the conceptual force of ghostly gayness in the figure of the child. When it surfaces as an idea, this child outlines, in shadowy form, the pain, closets, emotional labors, sexual motives, and sideways movements that attend all (people whom we call) children, however we deny it.

I am not suggesting that Leontes is a "gay" child. But Leontes's childhood wish to arrest the clock on his love with Polixenes to live inside that state, to curl up in it, adumbrates a pattern that would emerge as "gay" child suspensions centuries later. More to the point, the vicissitudes and losses of his early longings rear up again with his friend's departure, which will make his daughter his loss of his friend, spawning the queerness of her own childhood. How does the play put these matters into words? Precisely, wryly, through its fertile negatives. Through a supreme, almost astonishing, oddly multiplying language of the negative. By these means, Shakespeare conveys the depth of a love ripe with Perdition—but, through losing and loss, alive and strangely growing in a child.

The bond between the kings, as grown in suspension and separation, is where the play begins, fittingly talked of in their absence by their go-betweens: "Sicilia cannot show himself overkind to Bohemia. They were trained together in their childhoods, and there rooted betwixt them then such an affection which cannot choose but branch now"; "with interchange of gifts, letters, loving embassies . . . they have seemed to be together, though absent; shook hands, as over a vast; and embraced, as it were, from the ends of opposed winds. The heavens continue their loves!" (1.1.21–24, 27–31). But the play continues with departure, not continuance. Having spent a pregnant nine-month interval with Leontes ("nine changes of the watery star hath been / The shepherd's note since we have left our throne" [1.2.1–2]), Polixenes aims to leave. This place of parting is where we enter, not having seen what togetherness looked like. What follows now, what we hear and see, are cascading, replicating "nos" back and forth between the men: no, you cannot leave; no, I cannot stay; "I'll no gainsaying"; "Press me not. . . . There is no tongue that moves, none, none i' th' world, / So soon as yours could win me" (1.2.2.20–22). Each "no," each "not," actually showcases their affection, delivers their passion to listening ears, along with the wrenching of their parting. Thus, in their linguistic repetitions (the most direct reproduction between them) is to be found what is birthed between men—love lost—which takes dramatic material forms. Even their slipping Hermione's tongue and ears between them multiplies negatives, as if Hermione were no condom against the reproduction of "no."

At first, Hermione is employed to hear the story of their boyhood feelings so that the audience also can hear it. Polixenes tells her, "We were, fair queen, / Two lads that thought there was no more behind / But such a day tomorrow as today, / And to be boy eternal" (1.2.63–66). Then he continues, strongly conveying their young devotion as a perfect, unfallen state that did not cause them to know perdition until their time together was lost, "We were as twinned lambs that did frisk i' th' sun, / And bleat the one at th' other. . . . we knew not / The doctrine of ill-doing, nor dreamed / That any did. Had we pursued that life . . . we should have answered heaven / Boldly 'Not guilty'" (1.2.68–75). Hermione delightfully responds sarcastically, referring to their relations with women: "By this we gather / You have tripped since" (giving bold meaning to men and women "falling" in love [1.2.76–77]). Fascinating, then, how the play continues by making Hermione speak the man crush, turn up the temperature on the relation that her wifehood structurally blocks. Leontes makes her be his tongue that would be touching the ears he would reach: "Tongue-tied our queen? Speak / you" (1.2.28)—which she does at length. He interrupts her only to spur her: "Well said, Hermione." "Is he won yet?" "Hermione, my dearest, thou never spok'st / To better purpose" (1.2.34, 87, 89–90). ("Never?" she asks, recalling her wedding vows.) Perversely, her acts of speaking for him, speaking *as* him to Polixenes, make it seem as if she is betraying him—"Too hot, too hot! / To mingle friendship far is mingling bloods" (1.2.109–10), cries Leontes—whereas she is allowing him, through his jealous fantasies, to imagine how it would sound to address Polixenes in heat. Finally, Leontes, explosive with rage, reaches his climax in negativity: "Is whispering nothing? / Is leaning cheek to cheek? Is meeting noses? . . . Is this nothing? / Why, then the world and all that's in't is nothing. . . . Bohemia nothing, / My wife is nothing, nor nothing have these nothings, / If this be nothing" (1.2.284–85, 292–96). He needs "nothing" to signify something so he can feel that he did not have nothing when he was having something (nothing but delay) with Polixenes. This is why Perdita, seen by her father as the "issue" of his friend, is the tautology of her father's man crush, as if she were saying, "Before you ever had it, you lost it" — which could be said of Leontes with her.

Can what is lost, then, ever be found? The oracle announcing Leontes's guilt had explicitly proclaimed, "The king shall live / without an heir if that which is lost be not found" (3.2.133–34). But if your heir *is* Lost, is Perdita? According to *The Winter's Tale*, what is found is *Lost*: a story of outcasts and outcastness; love cast out. In other words, one can't lose that Loss. Not even a bear, for instance, can devour it. (Point of fact: A bear does not eat Perdita.) What Leontes finds, therefore, is love-lostness, from his childhood, *as* his child. This is why the pairing of Florizel (Polixenes's son) and Perdita is the blocked relation on which the play ends, echoing, I would say, their fathers' blocked connection. Florizel knows Polixenes will not accept his marriage to a supposed shepherd girl, so not surprisingly, his and Perdita's speaking of their love is laced with negativity and put at sea. Florizel says, "To this I am most constant, / Though destiny say no"; "I am put to sea / With her who here I cannot hold on shore"; Perdita says to him: "I cannot speak / So well, nothing so well; no, nor mean better" (4.4.45–46, 379–80, 497–98). The play's reunions, quite importantly, issue ironically from this blockage. As these children importune Leontes, seeking haven from Polixenes, Leontes bends back in time to his friend, saying to Florizel: "Were I but twenty-one, / Your father's image is so hit in you . . . I should call you brother, / As I did him, and speak of something wildly / By us performed before" (5.1.126–30). Most intriguingly, reunion among them—the fathers and their children—occurs offstage, completely out of view, making the finding of what is Lost out of sight, even if it is, says the play, "most true, if ever truth were pregnant by circumstance" (5.2.31–32). "Did you see the meeting of the two kings?," says one gentleman to another, who simply answers, "No." "Then," replies the other, "have you lost a sight which was to be seen, cannot be spoken of" (5.2.40–43).

Here is where *Lost* is Shakespeare's heir, his TV. As the final episode of Season Four ended, viewers were greeted by a strange scene: the sudden, utter vanishing of the story's island, as six characters (the Oceanic Six) were being helicoptered off to being found. It had been suggested that two outcasts (Locke and Ben) were going "to move the island" by some mysterious, unexplained means. Now, however, here it was happening, just as the six were glancing back. What does it suggest? So far, only this: The loss you think you've lost, while something lost is found, is only on the move; has been moved; is moving still. Like a queer child, you are heir to this delay—growing, nonetheless, inside your perdition, your hibernation.

Or as Florizel says to Perdita: "I wish you / A wave o' th' sea, that you might ever do / Nothing but that, move still, still so" (4.4.140–42).

Notes

1. Dolan, *The Winter's Tale*, 3.3.57 s.d. Citations in epigraph source note and within parentheses are to this edition. Let me also note that this essay was written just after Season Four of *Lost* concluded. Therefore, my piece does not take account of any developments in the series beyond this point. Whether the ultimate ending of *Lost* will confirm or contradict the reading I give here is not clear as my essay goes to press.

2. Bloom, *Shakespeare*, 639.

3. See Stockton, *The Queer Child*.

Abelove, Henry. *Deep Gossip.* Minneapolis: University of Minnesota Press, 2003.

Adelman, Janet. "Iago's Alter Ego: Race as Projection in Othello." *Shakespeare Quarterly* 48, no. 2 (Summer 1997): 125–44.

———. *Suffocating Mothers: Fantasies of Maternal Origin in Shakespeare's Plays:* Hamlet *to* Tempest. New York: Routledge, 1992.

Aeschylus. *The Oresteia,* translated by Alan Shapiro and Peter Burian. Oxford: New York: Oxford University Press, 2003.

Agamben, Giorgio. "Bartleby, or On Contingency." In *Potentialities: Collected Essays in Philosophy,* edited and translated by Daniel Heller-Roazen, 243–71. Stanford: Stanford University Press, 1999.

———. *Homo Sacer: Sovereign Power and Bare Life,* translated by Daniel Heller-Roazen. Stanford: Stanford University Press, 1998.

———. *Profanations,* translated by Jeff Fort. New York: Zone Books, 2007.

Ahmed, Sara. "Orientations: Toward a Queer Phenomenology." *GLQ* 12, no. 4 (2006): 543–74.

———. *Queer Phenomenology: Orientations, Objects, Others.* Durham: Duke University Press, 2006.

Alighieri, Dante. *The Divine Comedy: Inferno,* reprint ed., edited and translated by John D. Sinclair. New York: Oxford University Press, 1961 (1939).

A Qvip for an Vp-start Courtier. London: Iohn Wolfe, 1592.

Aristotle, *The Politics,* edited by Stephen Everson. Cambridge: Cambridge University Press, 1997.

Badiou, Alain. *Saint Paul: The Foundation of Universalism,* translated by Ray Brassier. Stanford: Stanford University Press, 2003.

Bacon, Francis. *The Advancement of Learning,* edited by William Aldis Wright. Oxford: Clarendon, 1885.

———. *New Atlantis; a Work Unfinished, Written by the Right Honorable Francis, Lord Verulum, Viscount St. Alban.* London: Thomas Newcomb, 1659.

Baker, Herschel. "Introduction to *The Life and Death of King John*." In *The Riverside Shakespeare,* edited by G. Blakemore Evans and J. J. M. Tobin, 765–68. Boston: Houghton Mifflin, 1997.

Barker, Francis. *The Tremulous Private Body: Essays on Subjection.* London: Methuen, 1984.

Barthes, Roland. *A Lover's Discourse: Fragments,* translated by Richard Howard. New York: Hill and Wang, 1978.

——. "La Musique, la voix, la langue." In *L'obvie et L'obtus*, 246–52. Paris: Le Seuil, 1982.

Bataille, Georges. *The Accursed Share: An Essay on General Economy*, translated by Robert Hurley. New York: Zone Books, 1988.

Bate, Jonathan, and Eric Rasmussen, eds. *The RSC Shakespeare: The sComplete Works*. London: Palgrave Macmillan, 2007.

Bateman, Anthony, and Peter Fonagy. *Psychotherapy for Borderline Personality Disorder: Mentalization-based Treatment*. Oxford: Oxford University Press, 2004.

Bennet, Josephine Waters. "New Techniques of Comedy in *All's Well That Ends Well*." *Shakespeare Quarterly* 18, no. 4 (Autumn 1967): 337–62.

Berger, Harry, Jr. "Marriage and Mercifixion in *The Merchant of Venice*: The Casket Scene Revisited." *Shakespeare Quarterly* 32, no. 2 (Summer 1981): 155–62.

Bergeron, David Moore. *King James and Letters of Homoerotic Desire*. Iowa City: University of Iowa Press, 1999.

Berlant, Lauren, and Michael Warner. "What Does Queer Theory Teach Us about X?" *PMLA* 110, no. 3 (May 1995): 343–49.

Berry, Philippa. *Of Chastity and Power: Elizabethan Literature and the Unmarried Queen*. London: Routledge, 1989.

Bersani, Leo. *The Freudian Body: Psychoanalysis and Art*. New York: Columbia University, 1986.

——. *Homos*. Cambridge: Harvard University Press, 1995.

——. "Is the Rectum a Grave?" *October* 43 (Winter 1987): 197–222.

——. "Psychoanalysis and the Aesthetic Subject." *Critical Inquiry* 32, no. 2 (Winter 2006): 161–74.

——. "Sociality and Sexuality." *Critical Inquiry* 26.4 (Summer 2000): 641–56.

Bersani, Leo, and Adam Phillips. *Intimacies*. Chicago: University of Chicago Press, 2008.

——. "On a More Impersonal Note." In Bersani and Phillips, *Intimacies*. Chicago: University of Chicago Press, 2008, 89–117.

Betteridge, Tom, ed. *Sodomy in Early Modern Europe*. Manchester: Manchester University Press, 2002.

Bevington, David, ed. *The Complete Works of Shakespeare*, 5th ed. New York: Pearson Longman, 2004.

——. *The Complete Works of Shakespeare*, portable ed. New York: Pearson Longman, 2007.

Bion, W. R. "Attacks on Linking." *International Journal of Psychoanalysis* 40 (1959): 308–15.

Bloom, Harold. *Shakespeare: The Invention of the Human*. London: Fourth Estate, 1998.

Blount, Thomas. *Glossographia, or a Dictionary Interpreting All Such Hard Words of Whatsoever Language Now Used in Our Refined English Tongue*. London: Thomas Newcombe, 1661.

Boellstorff, Tom. "When Marriage Falls: Queer Coincidences in Straight Time." *GLQ* 13, no. 23 (2007): 227–43.

Boose, Lynda E. "'The Getting of a Lawful Race': Racial Discourse in Early Modern England and the Unrepresentable Black Woman." In *Women, "Race," and Writing in the Early Modern Period*, edited by Margo Hendricks and Patricia Parker, 35–54. London: Routledge, 1994.

Booth, Stephen, ed. *Shakespeare's Sonnets*. New Haven: Yale University Press, 1977.

Booty, John E., ed. *"The Book of Common Prayer, 1559": The Elizabethan Prayer Book*. Folger Shakespeare Library. Charlottesville: University of Virginia Press, 2005 (1976).

Bourdieu, Pierre. "On Symbolic Power." In *Language and Symbolic Power*, edited by John B. Thompson, translated by Gino Raymond and Matthew Adamson, 163–70. Cambridge: Harvard University Press, 1991.

Bourdieu, Pierre, et al. *The Weight of the World: Social Suffering in Contemporary Society*, translated by Priscilla Parkhurst Ferguson, Susan Emanuel, Joe Johnson, and Shoggy T. Waryn. Stanford: Stanford University Press, 1999.

Bowers, Fredson T., ed. *The Merry Wives of Windsor*. New York: Penguin, 1963.

Bray, Alan. *The Friend*. Chicago: University of Chicago Press, 2003.

———. "Homosexuality and the Signs of Male Friendship in Elizabethan England." *History Workshop Journal* 29 (1990): 1–19.

———. "Homosexuality and the Signs of Male Friendship in Elizabethan England." In *Queering the Renaissance*, edited by Jonathan Goldberg, 40–61. Durham: Duke University Press, 1994.

———. *Homosexuality in Renaissance England*. New York: Columbia University Press, 1995.

Brennan, Teresa. *The Transmission of Affect*. Ithaca: Cornell University Press, 2004.

Brinsley, John. *Posing of the Parts*. London: Humphrey Lownes for Thomas Man, 1612.

Brockbank, Philip, ed. *Coriolanus*. Arden Shakespeare: 2nd Series. London: Methuen, 1976.

Bruster, Douglas. "The New Materialism in Renaissance Studies." In *Material Culture and Cultural Materialisms in the Middle Ages and Renaissance*, edited by Curtis Perry, 225–38. Turnhout, Belgium: Brepols, 2001.

Burger, Glenn, and Steven F. Kruger, eds. *Queering the Middle Ages*. Minneapolis: University of Minnesota Press, 2001.

Burke, Kenneth. *Language as Symbolic Action: Essays on Life, Literature, and Method*. Berkeley: University of California Press, 1966.

Burrow, Colin. "The Play in Performance." In *Troilus and Cressida*, edited by Colin Burrow, lxiv–lxxiv. Harmondsworth: Penguin, 2006.

Burrow, Colin, ed. *Troilus and Cressida*. Harmondsworth: Penguin, 2006.

Butler, Judith. "Against Proper Objects." *Differences* 6, nos. 2–3 (1994): 1–26.

———. *Antigone's Claim: Kinship between Life and Death*. New York: Columbia University Press, 2000.

———. *Excitable Speech: A Politics of the Performative*. New York: Routledge, 1997.

———. "Imitation and Gender Insubordination." In *Inside / Out*, edited by Diana Fuss, 13–31. New York: Routledge, 1991.

———. "Is Kinship Always Already Heterosexual?" *Differences* 13, no. 1 (2002): 14–44.

431

Calderwood, James. "*Love's Labour's Lost*: A Wantoning with Words." *Studies in English Literature 1500–1900* 5, no. 2 (Spring 1965): 317–32.

Carroll, J. B., P. Davies, and B. Richman. *The American Heritage Word Frequency Book.* New York: Houghton Mifflin, 1971.

Case, Sue-Ellen. "Toward a Butch–Femme Aesthetic." In *The Lesbian and Gay Studies Reader*, edited by Henry Abelove, Michèle Aina Barale, and David M. Halperin, 294–306. New York: Routledge, 1993.

Casey, Charles. "Was Shakespeare Gay? Sonnet 20 and the Politics of Pedagogy." *College Literature* 25, no. 3 (Fall 1998): 35–52.

Cavitch, Max. *American Elegy: The Poetry of Mourning from the Puritans to Whitman.* Minneapolis: University of Minnesota Press, 2007.

Chakrabarty, Dipesh. *Provincializing Europe: Postcolonial Thought and Historical Difference.* Princeton: Princeton University Press, 2000.

Chambers, E. K. *Shakespeare: A Survey.* London: Sidgwick and Jackson, 1925.

Chase, Cynthia. *Decomposing Figures: Rhetorical Readings in the Romantic Tradition.* Baltimore: Johns Hopkins University Press, 1986.

Cohen, Walter. "Introduction to *Sir Thomas More*." In *The Norton Shakespeare: Based on the Oxford Edition*, 2nd ed., edited by Stephen Greenblatt, Walter Cohen, Jean E. Howard, and Katharine Eisaman Maus, 2011–14. New York: W. W. Norton, 2008.

Coke, Edward. *The Third Part of the Institutes of the Laws of England.* London: M. Flesher, 1644.

Colie, Rosalie L. *The Resources of Kind: Genre-Theory in the Renaissance.* Berkeley: University of California Press, 1973.

Copjec, Joan. *Imagine there's no Woman: Ethics and Sublimation.* Cambridge: MIT Press, 2002.

Corum, Richard. "Henry's Desires." In *Premodern Sexualities*, edited by Louise Fradenburg and Carla Freccero, 71–97. New York: Routledge, 1996.

Cotgrave, Randall. *A Dictionarie of the French and English Tongues.* London: Adam Islip, 1611.

Craig, W. J., ed. *The Oxford Shakespeare: Complete Works.* London: Oxford University Press, 1962.

Craik, T. W., ed. *The Merry Wives of Windsor.* Oxford: Oxford University Press, 1990.

Crane, Mary Thomas. *Shakespeare's Brain: Reading with Cognitive Theory.* Princeton: Princeton University Press, 2001.

Crawford, Julie. "The Homoerotics of Shakespeare's Elizabethan Comedies." In *A Companion to Shakespeare's Works*, vol. 3, edited by Richard Dutton and Jean Elizabeth Howard, 137–58. Oxford: Blackwell, 2003.

Cressy, David. *Birth, Marriage and Death: Ritual, Religion, and the Life-Cycle in Tudor and Stuart England.* Oxford: Oxford University Press, 1999.

Crimp, Douglas. "Mourning and Militancy." In *Melancholia and Moralism: Essays on AIDS and Queer Politics*, 129–49. Cambridge: MIT Press, 2002.

Cvetkovich, Ann. "Public Feelings." *South Atlantic Quarterly* 106, no. 3 (Summer 2007): 459–68.

Daileader, Celia. "Back Door Sex: Renaissance Gynosodomy, Aretino, and the Exotic." *ELH* 69, no. 2 (Summer 2002): 303–34.

Daniell, David, ed. *Julius Caesar*. Arden Shakespeare: 3rd Series. Walton on Thames: Thomas Nelson and Sons, 1998.

Davies, H. Neville. "The Phoenix and Turtle: Requiem and Rite." *Review of English Studies* 46 (1995): 525–30.

Dean, Tim. "Lacan and Queer Theory." In *The Cambridge Companion to Lacan*, edited by Jean-Michel Rabaté, 238–52. Cambridge: Cambridge University Press, 2003.

De Grazia, Margreta. "The Scandal of Shakespeare's Sonnets." *Shakespeare Survey* 46 (1994): 35–49.

Deleuze, Gilles. *Foucault*, translated by Seán Hand. Minneapolis: University of Minnesota Press, 1988.

De Man, Paul. "The Concept of Irony." In *Aesthetic Ideology*, edited by Andrzej Warminski, 163–84. Minneapolis: University of Minnesota Press, 1996.

Derrida, Jacques. *Apprendre à vivre enfin: Entretien avec Jean Birnbaum*. Paris: Galilée, 2005.

——. *Archive Fever: A Freudian Impression*, translated by Eric Prenowitz. Chicago: University of Chicago Press, 1996.

——. *Glas*, translated by John P. Leavey Jr. and Richard Rand. Lincoln: University of Nebraska Press, 1990.

——. "Plato's Pharmacy." In *Dissemination*, translated by Barbara Johnson, 63–171. Chicago: University of Chicago Press, 1981.

——. *Specters of Marx: The State of the Debt, the Work of Mourning, and the New International*, translated by Peggy Kamuf. New York: Routledge, 1994.

——. "Typewriter Ribbon: Limited Ink (2) ('within Such Limits')," translated by Peggy Kamuf. In *Material Events: Paul de Man and the Afterlife of Theory*, edited by Tom Cohen, Barbara Cohen, J. Hillis Miller, and Andrzej Warminski, 277–360. Minneapolis: University of Minnesota Press, 2001.

Derrida, Jacques, and Maurizio Ferraris. *A Taste for the Secret*, edited by Giacomo Donis and David Webb. Malden, Mass.: Polity Press, 2001.

Descartes, René. *Meditations and Other Metaphysical Writings*, translated by Desmond M. Clarke. New York: Penguin, 2000.

DiGangi, Mario. *The Homoerotics of Early Modern Drama*. Cambridge: Cambridge University Press, 1997.

Dinshaw, Carolyn. *Getting Medieval: Sexualities and Communities, Pre- and Postmodern*. Durham: Duke University Press, 1999.

——. "Queering the Shakespearean Family." *Shakespeare Quarterly* 47, no. 3 (Fall 1996): 269–90.

Doidge, Norman. *The Brain that Changes Itself: Stories of Personal Triumph from the Frontiers of Brain Science*. New York: Viking, 2007.

Dolan, Frances E., ed. *The Winter's Tale*. Pelican Shakespeare Series. New York: Penguin, 1999.

Dollimore, Jonathan. *Sexual Dissidence: Augustine to Wilde, Freud to Foucault*. Oxford: Oxford University Press, 1991.

Doyle, Richard. *On Beyond Living: Rhetorical Transformations of the Life Sciences*. Stanford: Stanford University Press, 1997.

———. *Wetwares: Experiments in Postvital Living*. Minneapolis: University of Minnesota Press, 2003.

Dryden, John. "An Essay of Dramatic Poesy." In *Critical Theory since Plato*, edited by Hazard Adams, 214–40. New York: Harcourt Brace Jovanovich, 1971.

Duggan, Lisa. "The New Homonormativity: The Sexual Politics of Neoliberalism." In *Materializing Democracy: Toward a Revitalized Cultural Politics*, edited by Russ Castronovo and Dana Nelson, 175–94. Durham: Duke University Press, 2002.

Duggan, Lisa, and Kathleen McHugh. "A Fem(me)inist Manifesto." In *Brazen Femme: Queering Femininity*, edited by Chloe Tamara Brushwood Rose and Anna Camilleri, 165–70. Vancouver: Arsenal Pulp Press, 2002.

Duncan-Jones, Katherine, ed. *The Sonnets*. Arden Shakespeare. Walton-on-Thames: Thomas Nelson, 1997.

Dutton, Richard. *Mastering the Revels: The Regulation and Censorship of English Renaissance Drama*. Iowa City: University of Iowa Press, 1991.

Eccles, Ambrose, ed. *Cymbeline: A Tragedy*. London: G. G. and J. Robinson, C. Dilly, and T. Payne, 1794.

Edelman, Lee. *Homographesis: Essays in Gay Literary and Cultural Theory*. New York: Routledge, 1994.

———. *No Future: Queer Theory and the Death Drive*. Durham: Duke University Press, 2004.

Edelman, Lee, Robert L. Caserio, Tim Dean, Judith Halberstam, José Esteban Muñoz. "Conference Debates: The Antisocial Thesis in Queer Theory." PMLA 121, no. 3 (2006): 819–28.

Eigen, Michael. *The Electrified Tightrope*, edited by Adam Phillips. Northvale, N.J.: Jason Aronson, 1993.

Eng, David L., Judith Halberstam, and José Esteban Muñoz, eds. "What's Queer about Queer Studies Now?" *Social Text* 23, nos. 84–85 (2005): 1–17.

Eribon, Didier. *Insult and the Making of the Gay Self*, translated by Michael Lucey. Durham: Duke University Press, 2004.

Erickson, Amy Louise. *Women and Property in Early Modern England*. London: Routledge, 1993.

Erickson, Peter. "The Order of the Garter, the Cult of Elizabeth, and Class–Gender Tension in *The Merry Wives of Windsor*." In *Shakespeare Reproduced*, edited by Jean E. Howard and Marion F. O'Connor, 116–42. Abingdon, Oxon: Routledge, 1987.

Erzen, Tanya. *Straight to Jesus: Sexual and Christian Conversions in the Ex-Gay Movement*. Berkeley: University of California Press, 2006.

Ettelbrick, Paula. "Since When Is Marriage a Path to Liberation?" In *Same Sex Marriage: The Moral and Legal Debate*, edited by Robert M. Baird and Stuart E. Rosenbaum, 164–68. Amherst, N.Y.: Prometheus Books, 2004.

Evans, G. Blakemore, ed. *The Riverside Shakespeare*. Boston: Houghton Mifflin, 1997.

Ferrand, James. *Erotomania, or, a Treatise Discoursing on the Essence, Causes, Symptoms,*

Prognostics, and Cure of Love or, Erotique Melancholy. Oxford: Edmund Forrest, 1645.

Ferguson, Margaret, et al., eds. *Norton Anthology of Poetry*. 4th ed. New York and London: W. W. Norton and Company, 1996.

Fiedler, Leslie. *The Stranger in Shakespeare*. New York: Stein and Day, 1972.

Finnis, John and Patrick Martin. "Another Turn for the Turtle: Shakespeare's Intercession for Love's Martyr," *Times Literary Supplement*, April 18, 2003: 12–14.

Fisher, Will. "Queer Money." *English Literary History* 66, no. 1 (1999): 1–23.

———. "The Renaissance Beard." *Renaissance Quarterly* 54, no. 1 (Spring 2001): 155–87.

Fonagy, Peter. "A Developmental Theory of Sexual Enjoyment." *Journal of the American Psychoanalytic Association* 56 (2008): 11–36.

Foster, Thomas, Carol Siegel, and Ellen E. Berry, eds. *The Gay '90's: Disciplinary and Interdisciplinary Formations in Queer Studies*. New York: New York University Press, 1997.

Foucault, Michel. *Abnormal: Lectures at the Collège de France, 1974–1975*, edited by Valerio Marchetti and Antonella Salomoni, translated by Graham Burchell. New York: Picador, 2003.

———. "Different Spaces." In *Essential Works of Foucault, 1954–1984*. 3 vols., edited by Paul Rabinow, 2:175–86. New York: New Press, 1998.

———. *History of Madness*, translated by Jonathan Murphy and Jean Khalfa. London: Routledge, 2006.

———. "Madness, the Absence of an Oeuvre." In *The History of Madness*, translated by Jonathan Murphy and Jean Khalfa, 541–49. London: Routledge, 2006.

———. *The History of Sexuality: An Introduction*, translated by Robert Hurley. New York: Pantheon, 1978.

———. *The History of Sexuality*, vol. 1, translated by Robert Hurley. New York: Vintage, 1990.

———. *The Order of Things: An Archeology of the Human Sciences*, translated by A. M. Sheridan Smith. London: Tavistock, 1970.

———. "The Social Triumph of the Sexual Will." In *Ethics: Subjectivity and Truth*, edited by Paul Rabinow, 157–62. New York: New Press, 1997.

Fradenburg, Louise O. "'Voice Memorial': Loss and Reparation in Chaucer's Poetry." *Exemplaria* 2, no. 1 (1990): 169–202.

Fradenburg, Louise, and Carla Freccero. *Premodern Sexualities*. New York: Routledge, 1996.

Freccero, Carla. "Practicing Queer Philology with Marguerite de Navarre: Nationalism and the Castigation of Desire." In *Queering the Renaissance*, edited by Jonathan Goldberg, 107–23. Durham: Duke University Press, 1994.

———. *Queer / Early / Modern*. Durham: Duke University Press, 2006.

Freeman, Elizabeth, ed. "Queer Temporalities." GLQ 13, nos. 2–3 (2007): 159–421.

———. "Still After." *South Atlantic Quarterly* 106, no. 3 (2007): 495–500.

———. *The Wedding Complex: Forms of Belonging in Modern American Culture*. Durham: Duke University Press, 2002.

Freud, Sigmund. "Civilization and Its Discontents." In *The Complete Psychological*

Works of Sigmund Freud in 24 Volumes, vol. 21, edited and translated by James Strachey. London: Hogarth Press and the Institute of Psycho-Analysis, 1966.

——. "Leonardo da Vinci and a Memory of His Childhood." In *The Standard Edition of the Complete Psychological Works of Sigmund Freud in 24 Volumes*, vol. 2, edited by James Strachey, 57–137. London: Hogarth Press, 1957.

——. "On the Universal Tendency to Debasement in the Sphere of Love." In *The Complete Psychological Works of Sigmund Freud in 24 Volumes*, vol. 21, edited and translated by James Strachey, 177–90. London: Hogarth Press and the Institute of Psycho-Analysis, 1966.

——. *Sexuality and the Psychology of Love*, edited by Philip Rieff. New York: Collier, 1963.

——. "Three Essays on the Theory of Sexuality." In *The Complete Psychological Works of Sigmund Freud in 24 Volumes*, vol. 21, edited and translated by James Strachey, 130–243. London: Hogarth Press and the Institute of Psycho-Analysis, 1966.

——. *The Uncanny*, translated by David McClintock. New York: Penguin, 2003.

Frey, Charles H., ed. *Shakespeare, Fletcher, and* The Two Noble Kinsmen. Columbia: University of Missouri Press, 1989.

Friedman, Ryan. "Bombastic Subjects: Inauthenticity and Disorder in the Discourse of Renaissance Humanism." Unpublished ms., 2001.

Frye, Northrop. *The Anatomy of Criticism: Four Essays*. Princeton: Princeton University Press, 2000 (1957).

——. "The Tragedies of Fortune and Nature." In *Stratford Papers on Shakespeare*, edited by B. W. Jackson, 38–55. Toronto: W. J. Gage, 1961.

Furtwangler, Albert. *Assassin on Stage: Brutus, Hamlet, and the Death of Lincoln*. Urbana: University of Illinois Press, 1991.

Gabrieli, Vittorio, and Giorgio Melchiori, eds. *Sir Thomas More, by Anthony Munday and Others*. Revels Plays. Manchester: Manchester University Press, 1990.

Garber, Marjorie. *Coming of Age in Shakespeare*. London: Methuen, 1981.

——. *Shakespeare after All*. New York: Pantheon Books, 2004.

——. *Shakespeare's Ghost Writers: Literature as Uncanny Causality*. New York: Methuen, 1987.

——. *Vested Interests: Cross-Dressing and Cultural Anxiety*. New York: Routledge, 1992.

Gibbons, Brian. "Romance and the Heroic Play." In *The Cambridge Companion to English Renaissance Drama*, edited by A. R. Braunmuller and Michael Hattaway. Cambridge: Cambridge University Press, 1990.

Gil, Daniel Juan. *Before Intimacy: Asocial Sexuality in Early Modern England*. Minneapolis: University of Minnesota Press, 2006.

——. "Avant-garde Technique and the Visual Grammar of Sexuality in Orson Welles's Shakespeare Films." *Borrowers and Lenders* 1, no. 2 (Fall 2005): 1–27.

Gilham, Christine. "'Single Natures Double Name': Some Comments on Phoenix and Turtle." *Connotations* 2 (1992): 126–36.

Girard, René. "Lévi-Strauss, Frye, Derrida, and Shakespearean Criticism." *Diacritics* 3, no. 3 (Fall 1973): 34–8.

Goethe, Johann Wolfgang von, Johann Peter Eckermann, and Frédéric Jacob Soret.

Conversations of Goethe with Eckerman and Soret, translated by John Oxenford. London: G. Bell and Sons, 1901.

Goldberg, Jonathan. "The Anus in Coriolanus." In *Historicism, Psychoanalysis and Early Modern Culture*, edited by Carla Mazzio and Douglas Trevor. London: Routledge, 2000.

———. "Desiring Hal." In *Sodometries: Renaissance Texts, Modern Sexualities*, 145–75. Stanford: Stanford University Press, 1992.

———. "The History that Will Be." In *Premodern Sexualities*, edited by Louise Fradenburg and Carla Freccero, 3–21. New York: Routledge, 1996.

———. "Lucy Hutchinson Writing Matter." *ELH* 73 (2006): 275–301.

———. "Romeo and Juliet's Open Rs." In *Queering the Renaissance*, edited by Jonathan Goldberg, 218–35. Durham: Duke University Press, 1994.

———. *Shakespeare's Hand*. Minneapolis: University of Minnesota Press, 2003.

———. *Sodometries: Renaissance Texts, Modern Sexualities*. Stanford: Stanford University Press, 1992.

———. "Sodomy and Society: The Case of Christopher Marlowe," *Southwest Review* 69 (1984): 371–78.

———. *Tempest in the Caribbean*. Minneapolis: University of Minnesota Press, 2003.

Goldberg, Jonathan, and Madhavi Menon, "Queering History." *PMLA* 120, no. 5 (2005): 1608–17.

Goldstein, Neal. "*Love's Labour's Lost* and the Renaissance Vision of Love." *Shakespeare Quarterly* 25, no. 3 (Summer 1974): 335–50.

Graham, Walter, ed. *Double Falsehood*. Cleveland: Western Reserve University Bulletin, 1920.

Greenblatt, Stephen "Invisible Bullets." In *Shakespearean Negotiations: The Circulation of Social Energy in Renaissance England*, 21–65. Oxford: Clarendon Press, 1988.

Greenblatt, Stephen, Walter Cohen, Jean E. Howard, and Katharine Eisaman Maus, eds. *The Norton Shakespeare: Based on the Oxford Edition*. New York: W. W. Norton, 1997.

Greene, Jody. "'You Must Eat Men': The Sodomitic Economy of Renaissance Patronage." *GLQ* 1 (1994): 163–97.

Greg, W. W., ed. *The Book of Sir Thomas More*. Malone Society Reprints. Oxford: Oxford University Press, 1911.

Grene, David, ed. and trans. *Antigone*. In *Sophocles I*, 2nd ed. Chicago: University of Chicago Press, 1991.

Gross, Gerard J. "The Conclusion of *All's Well That Ends Well*." *Studies in English Literature 1500–1900* 23, no. 2 (1983): 257–76.

Grosz, Elizabeth. *Space, Time, and Perversion*. New York: Routledge, 1995.

Gurr, Andrew. *Playgoing in Shakespeare's London*, 3rd ed. Cambridge: Cambridge University Press, 2004.

Halberstam, Judith. *In a Queer Time and Place: Transgender Bodies, Subcultural Lives*. New York: New York University Press, 2005.

Haldane, J. B. S. *Possible Worlds and Other Essays*. London: Chatto and Windus, 1928.

Hall, Kim F. *Things of Darkness: Economies of Race and Gender in Early Modern England*. Ithaca: Cornell University Press, 1995.

Hallie, Philip P., ed. *Sextus Empiricus: Selections from the Major Writings on Scepticism, Man, and God*, translated by Sanford G. Etheridge. Indianapolis: Hackett, 1985.

Hallword, Peter. *Badiou: A Subject to Truth*. Minneapolis: University of Minnesota Press, 2003.

Halperin, David M. *One Hundred Years of Homosexuality: And Other Essays on Greek Love*. London and New York: Routledge, 1989.

Halpern, Richard. *Shakespeare's Perfume: Sodomy and Sublimity in the Sonnets, Wilde, Freud, and Lacan*. Philadelphia: University of Pennsylvania Press, 2002.

Hamilton, Charles. *Shakespeare with John Fletcher—Cardenio—or—The Second Maiden's Tragedy*. Lakewood, Colo.: Glenbridge, 1994.

Hammond, Paul. *Figuring Sex between Men from Shakespeare to Rochester*. Oxford: Oxford University Press, 2002.

Haraway, Donna. *The Companion Species Manifesto: Dogs, People, and Significant Others*. Chicago: Prickly Paradigm Press, 2003.

Harbage, Alfred, ed. *William Shakespeare: The Complete Works*. Baltimore: Penguin Books, 1974.

Harding, Vanessa. *The Dead and the Living in Paris and London, 1500–1670*. Cambridge: Cambridge University Press, 2002.

Harris, Jonathan Gil. "The New New Historicism's *Wunderkammer* of Objects." *European Journal of English Studies* 4, no. 2 (2000): 111–23.

Hayles, Katherine N. *How We Became Posthuman: Virtual Bodies in Cybernetics, Literature, and Informatics*. Chicago: University of Chicago Press, 1999.

Helgerson, Richard. *Adulterous Alliances*. Chicago: University of Chicago Press, 2000.

Heller-Roazen, Daniel. *Echolalias: On the Forgetting of Language*. Brooklyn: Zone Books, 2005.

——. "Tradition's Destruction: On the Library of Alexandria." *October* 100, no. 1 (2002): 133–54.

Heller-Roazen, Daniel, ed. "Editor's Introduction: 'To Read What Was Never Written.'" In Giorgio Agamben, *Potentialities*, 1–23. Stanford: Stanford University Press, 1999.

Herndon, William Henry and Jesse William Weik. *Herndon's Lincoln*. Eds. Douglas L. Wilson and Rodney O. Davis. Chicago: University of Illinois Press, 2006 (1895).

Hic Mulier, or The Man-Woman. London: I. Trundle, 1620.

Hocquenghem, Guy. *Homosexual Desire*. Durham: Duke University Press, 1993.

Hodgdon, Barbara. "The Making of Virgins and Mothers: Sexual Signs, Substitute Scenes and Doubled Presences in *All's Well That Ends Well.*" *Philological Quarterly* 66, no. 1 (1987): 47–71.

Holland, Peter. "Introduction." In *Romeo and Juliet*, reprint ed., edited by Peter Holland, xxxi–xliv. New York: Penguin, 2000 (1960).

Holland, Peter, ed. *A Midsummer Night's Dream*. Oxford Shakespeare Series. Oxford: Clarendon Press, 1995.

Holmberg, Arthur. "*The Two Gentlemen of Verona*: Shakespearean Comedy as a Rite of Passage." *Queen's Quarterly* 90, no. 1 (Spring 1983): 33–44.

Homer. *The Iliad*, rev. ed., translated by E. V. Rieu, edited by Peter Jones. Harmondsworth: Penguin, 2003.

Hooker, Deborah A. "Coming to Cressida through Irigaray." *South Atlantic Quarterly* 88 (1989): 899–932.

Hooker, Richard. *Of the Laws of Ecclesiastical Polity*, edited by Arthur McGrade. Cambridge: Cambridge University Press, 1989.

Howard, Jean Elizabeth, and Phyllis Rackin. *Engendering a Nation: A Feminist Account of Shakespeare's English Histories*. New York: Routledge, 1997.

Howie, Cary. *Claustrophilia: The Erotics of Enclosure in Medieval Literature*. New York: Palgrave Macmillan, 2007.

Hoy, Cyrus. "*Love's Labour's Lost* and the Nature of Comedy." *Shakespeare Quarterly* 13, no. 1 (Winter 1962): 31–40.

Humphries, A. R., ed. *King Henry IV, Part 2*. Arden Shakespeare: 2nd Series. New York: Methuen, 1966.

Hunter, G. K., ed. *All's Well That Ends Well*. London; New York: Methuen, 1959; Arden, 2006.

Irigaray, Luce. *An Ethics of Sexual Difference*, translated by Carolyn Burke and Gillian C. Gill. Ithaca: Cornell University Press, 1993.

Jagose, Annamaric. *Inconsequence: Lesbian Representation and the Logic of Sexual Sequence*. Ithaca: Cornell University Press, 2002.

———. *Queer Theory: An Introduction*. New York: New York University Press, 1996.

Jakobsen, Janet R. "Can Homosexuals End Western Civilization as We Know It? Family Values in a Global Economy." In *Queer Globalizations: Citizenship and the Afterlife of Colonialism*, edited by Arnoldo Cruiz-Malavé and Martin Manalansan, 49–70. New York: New York University Press, 2002.

James, Henry. "Introduction to *The Tempest*." In *Literary Criticism*, Library of America, vol. 1, 1205–20. Originally published in *The Complete Works of William Shakespeare*, vol. 16, edited by Sidney Lee. New York: George D. Sproul, 1907.

Jankowski, Theodora A. "'Where There Can Be No Cause of Affection': Redefining Virgins, Their Desires, and Their Pleasures in John Lyly's *Gallathea*." In *Feminist Readings of Early Modern Culture*, edited by Valerie Traub, M. Lindsay Kaplan, and Dympna Callaghan, 253–74. Cambridge: Cambridge University Press, 1996.

———. *Pure Resistance: Queer Virginity in Early Modern English Drama*. Philadelphia: University of Pennsylvania Press, 2000.

———. "Pure Resistance: Queer(y)ing Virginity in William Shakespeare's *Measure for Measure* and Margaret Cavendish's *The Convent of Pleasure*." In *Shakespeare Studies*, vol. 27, edited by Leeds Barroll, 218–55. Madison, N.H.: Fairleigh Dickinson University Press, 1998.

Jarman, Derek. *Dancing Ledge*, edited by Shaun Allen. London: Quartet Books, 1984.

Johnson, Barbara. *A World of Difference*. Baltimore: Johns Hopkins University Press, 1987.

Johnson, E. Patrick, and Mae G. Henderson, eds. *Black Queer Studies: A Queer Anthology*. Durham: Duke University Press, 2005.

Johnson, Nora. "Shakespearean Melodramas: Edwin Booth and Cultural Hierarchy." Unpublished ms., podcast online at swarthmore.edu / faculty_lectures.

Jones, Dylan. *Haircults: Fifty Years of Styles and Cuts*. London: Thames and Hudson, 1990.

Jones, Ernest. *The Life and Work of Sigmund Freud*, Vol. 2. New York: Basic, 1955.

Kahn, Coppelia. *Man's Estate: Masculine Identity in Shakespeare*. Berkeley: University of California Press, 1981.

——. " 'Passions of Some Difference': Friendship and Emulation in Julius Caesar." In *Julius Caesar: New Critical Essays*, edited by Horst Zander, 271–83. New York: Routledge, 2005.

Kastan, David Scott. "*All's Well That Ends Well* and the Limits of Comedy." ELH 52, no. 3 (1985): 575–89.

Kegl, Rosemary. " 'The Adoption of Abominable Terms': Middle Classes, Merry Wives, and the Insults That Shape Windsor." In *The Rhetoric of Concealment*, 77–126. Ithaca: Cornell University Press, 1994.

Kerrigan, John, ed. *The Sonnets and A Lover's Complaint*. Harmondsworth: Penguin, 1986.

King, Thomas A. "Queer Pride and Epistemological Prejudice." In *The Politics and Poetics of Camp*, edited by Moe Meyers, 23–50. London: Routledge, 1994.

Kipnis, Laura. "Adultery." In *Intimacy*, edited by Lauren Berlant, 9–47. Chicago: University of Chicago Press, 2000.

Kleinberg, Seymour. "*The Merchant of Venice*: The Homosexual as Anti-Semite in Nascent Capitalism." *Journal of Homosexuality* 8, nos. 3–4 (1983): 113–26.

Knight, G. Wilson. *The Mutual Flame: On Shakespeare's Sonnets and the Phoenix and the Turtle*. London: Methuen, 1955.

——. *The Wheel of Fire: Interpretations of Shakespearian Tragedy*. London: Routledge, 1986.

Kolin, Philip C., ed. *Titus Andronicus: Critical Essays*. New York: Garland, 1995.

Korda, Natasha. *Shakespeare's Domestic Economies*. Philadelphia: University of Pennsylvania Press, 2002.

Kristeva, Julia. *Desire in Language: A Semiotic Approach to Literature and Art*, edited by Leon S. Roudiez, translated by Thomas Gora, Alice Jardine, and Leon S. Roudiez. New York: Columbia University Press, 1980.

Kurtz, Martha A., "Rethinking Gender and Genre in the History Play." *Studies in English Literature, 1500–1900* 36, no. 2 (Spring 1996): 267–87.

Lacan, Jacques. "Seminar on the Purloined Letter." In The *Purloined Poe: Lacan, Derrida, and Psychoanalytic Reading*, edited by John P. Muller and William J. Richardson. Baltimore: Johns Hopkins University Press, 1988.

Lamon, Ward Hill. *Recollections of Abraham Lincoln 1847–1865*, edited by Dorothy Lamon. Chicago: A. C. Clurg, 1895.

Landreth, David. "Once More into the Preech: The Merry Wives' English Pedagogy." *Shakespeare Quarterly* 55, no. 4 (Winter 2004): 420–49.

Lefort, Claude. "The Death of Immortality?" In *Democracy and Political Theory*, translated by David Macey, 256–82. Minneapolis: University of Minnesota Press, 1988.

Leggatt, Alexander. "Introduction." In *All's Well that Ends Well*, edited by Russell Fraser, 1–43. Cambridge: Cambridge University Press, 1985.

———. "The Shadow of Antioch: Sexuality in *Pericles, Prince of Tyre*." In *Parallel Lives: Spanish and English National Drama, 1580–1680*, edited by Louise and Peter Fothergill-Payne, 167–79. Lewisburg, Pa.: Bucknell University Press, 1991.

Levin, Joanna. "Lady Macbeth and Daemonology of Hysteria. *ELH* 69, no. 1 (2002): 21–55.

Levin, Richard A. "Did Helen Have a Renaissance?" *English Studies* 87, no. 1 (2006): 23–34.

Levine, Nina. "Citizens' Games: Differentiating Collaboration and Sir Thomas More." *Shakespeare Quarterly* 58 (2007): 31–64.

Lezra, Jacques. "Cervantes' Hand." In *Unspeakable Subjects: The Genealogy of the Event in Early Modern Europe*, 177–256. Stanford: Stanford University Press, 1997.

Lily, William. *A Short Introduction of Grammar, 1549*. Menston: Scolar Press, 1970.

Lincoln, Abraham. "Address at the Dedication of the Gettysburg National Cemetery." *Heath Anthology of American Literature*, Vol. B. Boston: Houghton Mifflin, 2009, 2234–35.

Lochrie, Karma. *Heterosyncracies: Female Sexuality When Normal Wasn't*. Minneapolis: University of Minnesota Press, 2005.

Loraux, Nicole. *The Divided City: On Memory and Forgetting in Ancient Athens*, translated by Corinne Pache and Jeff Fort. New York: Zone Books, 2002.

Lotringer, Sylvère, ed. *Foucault Live: Collected Interviews, 1961–1984*, translated by Lysa Hochroth and John Johnston. New York: Semiotext(e), 1989.

Lucey, Michael. *The Misfit of the Family: Balzac and the Social Forms of Sexuality*. Durham: Duke University Press, 2003.

Lupton, Julia Reinhard. "Othello Circumcised: Shakespeare and the Pauline Discourse of Nations." *Representations* 57 (Winter 1997): 73–89.

Mallin, Eric Scott. *Inscribing the Time: Shakespeare and the End of Elizabethan England*. Berkeley: University of California Press, 1995.

Marcus, Leah S. "Purity and Danger in the Modern Edition: *The Merry Wives of Windsor*." In *Unediting the Renaissance*, 68–100. London: Routledge, 1996.

Marcus, Steven. "Human Nature, Social Orders, and Nineteenth-Century Systems of Explanation: Starting in with George Elliot." *Salmagundi* 28 (1975): 20–42.

Marcuse, Herbert. "The Ideology of Death." In *The Meaning of Death*, edited by Herman Feifel, 64–76. New York: McGraw-Hill, 1965.

Marshall, Cynthia. *The Shattering of the Self: Violence, Subjectivity and Early Modern Texts*. Baltimore: Johns Hopkins University Press, 2002.

Massumi, Brian. *Parables for the Virtual: Movement, Affect, Sensation*. Durham: Duke University Press, 2002.

Masten, Jeffrey. "Is the Fundament a Grave?" In *The Body in Parts: Fantasies of Corporeality in Early Modern Europe*, edited by David Hillman and Carla Mazzio, 129–46. London: Routledge, 1997.

——. *Spelling Shakespeare, and Other Essays in Queer Philology.* (forthcoming).

442

Mazzio, Carla. "Sins of the Tongue in Early Modern England." *Modern Language Studies* 28, nos. 3–4 (1996): 95–124.

McDonald, Russ, ed. *A Midsummer Night's Dream.* New York: Penguin Putnam, 2002.

McEachern, Claire Elizabeth, ed. *Much Ado About Nothing.* Arden Shakespeare: 3rd Series. London: Thomson Learning, 2006.

McMillin, Scott. *The Elizabethan Theatre and the Booke of Sir Thomas More.* Ithaca: Cornell University Press, 1987.

Menon, Madhavi. *Unhistorical Shakespeare: Queer Theory in Shakespearean Literature and Film.* New York: Palgrave Macmillan, 2008.

——. "Spurning Teleology in Venus and Adonis," *GLQ* 11, no. 4 (2005): 491–519.

Metz, Harold. *Sources of Four Plays Ascribed to Shakespeare*: The Reign of King Edward III, Sir Thomas More, The History of Cardenio, The Two Noble Kinsmen. Columbia: University of Missouri Press, 1989.

Miller, D. A. *Narrative and Its Discontents: Problems of Closure in the Traditional Novel.* Princeton: Princeton University Press, 1989.

Miller, Paul Allen. *Postmodern Spiritual Practices: The Construction of the Subject and the Reception of Plato in Lacan, Derrida, and Foucault.* Columbus: Ohio State University Press, 2007.

Mitchell, David T., and Sharon L. Snyder. *Narrative Prosthesis: Disability and the Dependencies of Discourse.* Ann Arbor: University of Michigan Press, 2000.

Montaigne, Michel de. "Of Experience." In *Essayes of Montaigne: John Florio's Translation,* edited by J. I. M. Stewart. New York: Modern Library, 1933.

Moss, Ann. *Printed Commonplace-Books and the Structuring of Renaissance Thought.* Oxford: Oxford University Press, 1996.

Moulton, Charles Wells, ed. *The Library of Literary Criticism of English and American Authors,* vol. 1. Buffalo: Moulton, 1901.

Mowat, Barbara A., and Paul Werstine, eds. *Cymbeline.* Folger Shakespeare Library. New York: Washington Square Press, 2003.

——. *Timon of Athens.* New York: Simon & Schuster, 2006.

——. *The Tragedy of Richard III.* Folger Shakespeare Library. New York: Washington Square Press, 2004.

Muir, Kenneth, ed. *Richard II.* Shakespeare Signet Classic. New York: Signet, 1963.

Nashe, Thomas. *Pierce Penniless His Supplication to the Devil.* 1592. London: Shakespeare Society, 1842.

——. *Summer's Last Will and Testament.* London: Simon Stafford, 1600.

Needham, Gary. "The Post-colonial Hong Kong Cinema." In *Asian Cinemas: A Reader and Guide,* edited by Dimitris Eleftheriotis and Gary Needham, 62–71. Edinburgh: Edinburgh University Press, 2006.

Neely, Carol Thomas. *Broken Nuptials in Shakespeare's Plays.* New Haven: Yale University Press, 1985.

O'Brien, Dennis. "A More Perfect Union: Reservations about Gay Marriage." In *Same-Sex Marriage: The Moral and Legal Debate,* edited by Robert M. Baird and Stuart E. Rosenbaum, 23–68. Amherst, N.Y.: Prometheus Books, 2004.

Ohi, Kevin. "Erotic Bafflement and the Lesson of Oscar Wilde." *Genre* 35, no. 2 (Summer 2002): 309–30.

——. *Henry James and the Queerness of Style*. Minneapolis: University of Minnesota Press (forthcoming).

——. "Queer Atavism and Pater's Aesthetic Sensibility." In *Victorian Aesthetic Conditions: Pater Across the Arts*, edited by Elicia Clements and Lesley Higgins. Basingstoke: Palgrave Macmillan, 2010.

Oliver, H. J., ed. *The Merry Wives of Windsor*. Arden Shakespeare Series. London: Methuen, 1971.

Ong, Walter J. *Fighting for Life: Contest, Sexuality, and Consciousness*. Ithaca: Cornell University, 1981.

Orgel, Stephen. *Impersonations*. Cambridge: Cambridge University Press, 1996.

Orgel, Stephen, ed. *The Tempest*. New York: Oxford University Press, 1987.

O'Rourke, James. "'Rule in Unity' and Otherwise: Love and Sex in *Troilus and Cressida*." *Shakespeare Quarterly* 43, no. 2 (Summer 1992): 139–58.

O'Rourke, Michael. "Introduction: Siting Queer Masculinities." In *Queer Masculinities, 1550–1800: Siting Same-Sex Desire in the Early Modern World*, edited by Katherine O'Donnell and Michael O'Rourke, xx–xxix. New York: Palgrave Macmillan, 2006.

Ostovich, Helen, and Elizabeth Sauer, eds. *Reading Early Modern Women: An Anthology of Texts in Manuscript and Print, 1550–1700*. London: Routledge, 2004.

The Oxford English Dictionary, 2nd ed., 20 vols., prepared by J. A. Simpson and E. S. C. Weiner. Oxford: Clarendon Press, 1989.

Park, Katharine. "The Criminal and Saintly Body: Autopsy and Dissection in Renaissance Italy." *Renaissance Quarterly* 47 (1994): 1–33.

——. "The Life of the Corpse: Division and Dissection in Late Medieval Europe." *Journal of the History of Medicine and Allied Sciences* 50, no. 1 (1995): 111–32.

Parker, Barbara L. "The Whore of Babylon and Shakespeare's Julius Caesar." *Studies in English Literature* 35, no. 2 (Spring 1995): 251–69.

Parker, Patricia. "*All's Well That Ends Well*: Increase and Multiply." In *Creative Imitation: New Essays on Renaissance Literature in Honor of Thomas M. Greene*, edited by David Quint, Thomas Greene, et al., 355–90. Binghamton, N.Y.: Medieval and Renaissance Texts and Studies, 1993.

——. "Preposterous Events." *Shakespeare Quarterly* 43, no. 2 (1992): 186–213.

——. "Preposterous Reversals: *Love's Labor's Lost*." *Modern Language Quarterly* 54, no. 5 (1993): 435–82.

——. *Shakespeare from the Margins: Language, Culture, Context*. Chicago: University of Chicago Press, 1996.

Parker, Reeve. "Reading Wordsworth's Power: Narrative and Usurpation in *The Borderers*." *ELH* 54, no. 2 (July 1987): 299–331.

Paster, Gail Kern. *The Body Embarrassed: Drama and the Disciplines of Shame in Early Modern England*. Ithaca: Cornell University Press, 1993.

Pater, Walter. "Shakespeare's English Kings." In *Richard II*, edited by Kenneth Muir, 151–58. Shakespeare Signet Classics. New York: Signet, 1963.

Phillips, Adam. *Terrors and Experts*. Cambridge: Harvard University Press, 1995.

444

Pittenger, Elizabeth. "Dispatch Quickly: The Mechanical Reproduction of Pages." *Shakespeare Quarterly* 42, no. 4 (Winter 1991): 389–408.

Plato. *The Symposium*, translated by Christopher Gill. London: Penguin Books, 1999.

Plutarch. *Plutarch's Lives of the Noble Grecians and Romans, Volume 5 (1579)*, translated by Thomas North. London: David Nutt, 1896.

Poe, Edgar Allan. "William Wilson." In *The Complete Tales and Poems of Edgar Allan Poe*, 626–41. New York: Vintage Books, 1975.

Poirier, Richard. "Where is Emerson Now that we Need Him? Or, Why Literature Can't Save Us." *New York Times* (Feb. 8, 1987).

Pollard, Alfred W., ed. *Shakespeare's Hand in the Play of Sir Thomas More*. Cambridge: Cambridge University Press, 1923.

Potter, Lois, ed. *The Two Noble Kinsmen*. Arden Shakespeare: 3rd ed. Walton on Thames: Thomas Nelson and Sons, 2002.

Prince, F. T., ed. "The Rape of Lucrece." In *The Arden Shakespeare: The Poems*, 63–149. New York: Routledge, 1960.

Puttenham, George. *The Art of English Poesy*. London: Richard Field, 1589.

Pye, Christopher. "First Encounter / Missed Encounter: *The Tempest* in History." Unpublished ms.

——. "The Theater, the Market, and the Subject of History." *ELH* 61, no. 3 (Autumn 1994): 501–22.

Quiller-Couch, Arthur. "Introduction." In *All's Well That Ends Well*, edited by Arthur Quiller-Couch and John Dover Wilson. Cambridge: Cambridge University Press, 1929.

Quint, David. *Cervantes's Novel of Modern Times: A New Reading of Don Quijote*. Princeton: Princeton University Press, 2003.

Radway, Janice. *Reading the Romance: Women, Patriarchy, and Popular Literature*. Chapel Hill: University of North Carolina Press, 1991 [1984].

Rambuss, Richard. "After Male Sex." *South Atlantic Quarterly* 106, no. 3 (Summer 2007): 577–88.

——. *Closet Devotions*. Durham: Duke University Press, 1998.

Ranald, Margaret Loftus. "The Betrothals of *All's Well That Ends Well*." *Huntington Library Quarterly* 26, no. 2 (1963): 179–92.

Reynolds, Reginald. *Beards: Their Social Standing, Religious Involvements, Decorative Possibilities, and Value in Offence and Defense through the Ages*. Garden City, N.Y.: Doubleday, 1949.

Rich, Adrienne. *Of Woman Born: Motherhood as Experience and Institution*. New York and London: W. W. Norton & Company, 1986 [1976].

Roach, Joseph. *Cities of the Dead: Circum-Atlantic Performance*. New York: Columbia University Press, 1996.

Rocke, Michael. *Forbidden Friendships: Homosexuality and Male Culture in Renaissance Florence*. New York: Oxford University Press, 1996.

Roe, John, ed. *The Poems*. New York: Cambridge University Press, 2006.

Rollins, Hyder Edward, ed. *The Letters of John Keats 1814–1821*. Cambridge: Harvard University Press, 1958.

Rothenberg, Alan B. "Infantile Fantasies in Shakespearean Metaphor: III. Photo-phobia, Love of Darkness and 'Black' Complexions." *Psychoanalytic Review* 64 (1977): 173–202.

Rowse, A. L., ed. *The Annotated Shakespeare: Volume I: The Comedies*. New York: Clarkson N. Potter, 1978.

Rubin, Gayle. "The Traffic in Women: Notes on the 'Political Economy' of Sex." In *Toward an Anthropology of Women*, edited by Rayna Reiter, 157–210. New York: Monthly Review Press, 1975.

Sandahl, Carrie, and Philip Auslander. "Introduction: Disability Studies in Commo-tion with Performance Studies." In *Bodies in Commotion: Disability and Perfor-mance*, edited by Carrie Sandahl and Philip Auslander, 1–12. Ann Arbor: Univer-sity of Michigan Press, 2005

Sang, Tze-lan D. *The Emerging Lesbian: Female Same-Sex Desire in Modern China*. Chi-cago: University of Chicago Press, 2003

Schlueter, Kurt. "Introduction to *The Two Gentlemen of Verona*." In *The New Cam-bridge Shakespeare*, 2–17. Cambridge: Cambridge University Press, 1990.

Schneider, Rebecca. "Patricidal Memory and the Passerby." *Feminist Scholar and Critic Online* (2003). Available online at http://www.barnard.edu/sfonline/ps/schneide.htm.

Schwarz, Kathryn. "'My Intents Are Fix'd': Constant Will in *All's Well That Ends Well*." *Shakespeare Quarterly* 58, no. 2 (2007): 200–27.

——. *Tough Love: Amazon Encounters in the English Renaissance*. Durham: Duke Uni-versity Press, 2000.

Scouloudi, Irene. *Returns of Strangers in the Metropolis 1593, 1627, 1635, 1639*. London: Huguenot Society, 1985.

Sedgwick, Eve Kosofsky. "Around the Performative: Periperformative Vicinities in Nineteenth-Century Narrative." In *Touching Feeling: Affect, Pedagogy, Performativ-ity*, 67–92. Durham: Duke University Press, 2003.

——. *Between Men: English Literature and Male Homosocial Desire*. New York: Colum-bia University Press, 1985.

——. *Epistemology of the Closet*. Berkeley: University of California Press, 1990.

——. "A Poem Is Being Written." *Representations* 17 (Winter 1987): 110–43.

——. "Swan in Love: The Example of Shakespeare's Sonnets." In Sedgwick, *Between Men: English Literature and Male Homosocial Desire*, 28–48. New York: Columbia University Press, 1985.

——. *Tendencies*. New York: Routledge, 1994.

Shannon, Laurie. "Nature's Bias: Renaissance Homonormativity and Elizabethan Comic Likeness." *Modern Philology* 98, no. 2 (2000): 183–210.

——. *Sovereign Amity: Figures of Friendship in Shakespearean Contexts*. Chicago: Uni-versity of Chicago Press, 2002.

Shaw, George Bernard. *Two Plays by Bernard Shaw: Geneva, Cymbeline Refinished, and Good King Charles*. New York: Dodd, Mead, 1946.

Shaw, John. "Fortune and Nature in *As You Like It*." *Shakespeare Quarterly* 6, no. 1 (Winter 1955): 45–50.

Shell, Marc. "The Wether and the Ewe: Verbal Usury." In *Modern Critical Interpretations: The Merchant of Venice*, 107–20. New York: Chelsea House, 1986.

Shepherd, Simon. "What's So Funny about Ladies' Tailors? A Survey of Some Male-(homo)sexual Types in the Renaissance." *Textual Practice* 6, no. 1 (Spring 1992): 17–30.

Shuckburgh, E. S. *The Antigone of Sophocles, with a Commentary, Abridged from the Large Edition of Sir Richard C. Jebb*. Cambridge: Cambridge University Press, 1992 (1902).

Sims, James H. "Shakespeare's *Phoenix and Turtle*: A Reconsideration of 'Single Natures Double Name.'" *Connotations* 3, no. 1 (1993–94): 64–71.

Sinfield, Alan. *Faultlines: Cultural Materialism and the Politics of Dissident Reading*. Berkeley: University of California Press, 1992.

——. *Shakespeare, Authority, and Sexuality: Unfinished Business in Cultural Materialism*. London: Methuen, 2006.

——. *The Wilde Century: Effeminacy, Oscar Wilde, and the Queer Moment*. New York: Columbia University Press, 1994.

Sisson, C. J. ed. *William Shakespeare: The Complete Works*. New York: Harper, 1954.

Smith, Henry F. "Creating the Psychoanalytical Process, Incorporating Three Panel Reports: Opening the Process, Being in the Process and Closing the Process." *International Journal of Psychoanalysis* 83 (2002): 211–27.

Smith, Ian. "*Titus Andronicus*: A Time for Race and Revenge." In *A Companion to Shakespeare's Works, Volume 1: The Tragedies*, edited by Richard Dutton and Jean E. Howard, 284–302. New York: Blackwell, 2003.

Snyder, Sharon L. "Unfixing Disability in Lord Byron's *The Deformed Transformed*." In *Bodies in Commotion: Disability and Performance*, edited by Carrie Sandahl and Philip Auslander, 271–83. Ann Arbor: University of Michigan Press, 2005.

Snyder, Susan, ed. "Introduction." In *All's Well that Ends Well*, xii–xxxix. Oxford: Oxford University Press, 1993.

Spear, Gary. "Shakespeare's 'Manly' Parts: Masculinity and Effeminacy in *Troilus and Cressida*." *Shakespeare Quarterly* 4, no. 4 (Winter 1993): 409–22.

Spicksley, Judith M. "To Be or Not to Be Married: Single-Women, Money-Lending, and the Question of Choice in Late Tudor and Stuart England." In *The Single Woman in Medieval and Early Modern England: Her Life and Representation*, edited by Laurel Amtower and Dorothea Kehler, *Medieval and Renaissance Texts and Studies* no. 263, 65–96. Tempe: Center for Medieval and Renaissance Studies, 2003.

Squier, Susan Merrill. *Liminal Lives: Imagining the Human at the Frontiers of Biomedicine*. Durham: Duke University Press, 2004.

Stanivukovic, Goran V. "Between Men in Early Modern England." In *Queer Masculinities, 1550–1800: Siting Same-Sex Desire in the Early Modern World*, edited by Katherine O'Donnell and Michael O'Rourke, 232–51. New York: Palgrave Macmillan, 2006.

Stern, Daniel. *The Interpersonal World of the Infant: A View from Psychoanalysis and Developmental Psychology*. New York: Basic, 1985.

Stewart, Alan. *Close Readers: Humanism and Sodomy in Early Modern England*. Princeton: Princeton University Press, 1997.

Stockton, Kathryn Bond. "Growing Sideways, or Versions of the Queer Child." In *Curiouser: On the Queerness of Children*, edited by Steven Bruhm and Natasha Hurley, 277–315. Minneapolis: University of Minnesota Press, 2004.

——. *The Queer Child, or Growing Sideways in the Twentieth Century*. Durham: Duke University Press, 2009.

Sumner, Charles. *The Promises of the Declaration of Independence: Eulogy on Abraham Lincoln, Delivered before the Municipal Authorities of the City of Boston*. Boston: Ticknor and Fields, 1865.

Tadmor, Naomi. "Women and Wives: The Language of Marriage in Early Modern English Biblical Translations." *History Workshop Journal* 62 (2006): 1–27.

Théberge, Paul. *Any Sound You Can Imagine: Making Music / Consuming Technology*. Hanover, N.H.: Wesleyan University Press, 1997.

Tillyard, E. M. W. *Shakespeare's History Plays*. London: Chatto and Windus, 1948.

Traub, Valerie. *Desire and Anxiety: Circulations of Sexuality in Shakespearean Drama*. London: Routledge, 1992.

——. "Friendship's Loss: Alan Bray's Making of History." *GLQ* 10, no. 3 (2004): 339–65.

——. "The Homoerotics of Shakespearean Comedy." In *Desire and Anxiety: Circulations of Sexuality in Renaissance Drama*, 117–44. New York: Routledge, 1992.

——. *Mapping Embodiment in the Early Modern West: The Prehistory of Normality*. (forthcoming).

——. "The Renaissance of Lesbianism in Early Modern England." *GLQ* 7, no. 2 (2001): 245–63.

——. *The Renaissance of Lesbianism in Early Modern England*. Cambridge. Cambridge University Press, 2002.

Tripp, C. A. *The Intimate World of Abraham Lincoln*. New York: Simon and Schuster, 2005.

Turner, Henry. *Shakespeare's Double Helix*. London: Continuum, 2007.

Tyrrell, William Blake, and Larry J. Bennett. *Recapturing Sophocles' Antigone*. Lanham, Md.: Rowman and Littlefield, 1998.

Van Leeuwen, Kato, and Sydney L. Pomer. "The Separation-Adaptation Response to Contemporary Object Loss." *Journal of the American Academy of Child Psychiatry* 8 (1969): 711–33.

Virgil. *The Aeneid*, translated by Robert Fitzgerald. New York: Vintage, 1990.

Vitkus, Daniel J. "Turning Turk in *Othello*: The Conversion and Damnation of the Moor." *Shakespeare Quarterly* 48, no. 2 (Summer 1997): 145–76.

Walker, Lisa. "How to Recognize a Lesbian: The Cultural Politics of Looking like What You Are." *Signs* 18 (Summer 1993): 866–90.

Wall, Wendy. *Staging Domesticity*. Cambridge: Cambridge University Press, 2002.

Walloch, Greg. "Fuck the Disabled." In *Queer Crips: Disabled Gay Men and Their Stories*, edited by Bob Guter and John R. Killacky, 4–5. New York: Harrington Park Press, 2004.

Warren, Roger, ed. *Pericles, Prince of Tyre*. Oxford: Oxford University Press, 2003.

Wells, Stanley, and Gary Taylor, eds. *William Shakespeare: The Complete Works*. Oxford: Oxford University Press, 1999.

Werstine, Paul. "Close Contrivers: Nameless Collaborators in Early Modern London Plays." In *The Elizabethan Theatre XV*, edited by C. E. McGee and A. L. Magnusson, 3–20. Toronto: P. D. Meany, 2002.

———. "Shakespeare *More* or Less: A. W. Pollard and Twentieth-Century Shakespeare Editing." *Florilegium* 16 (1999): 125–45.

Whitman, Walt. *The Collected Works of Walt Whitman*, edited by Floyd Stovall. New York: New York University Press, 1964.

———. *Leaves of Grass: Facsimile Edition of the 1860 Text*, edited by Roy Harvey Pearce. Ithaca: Cornell University Press, 1961.

Whitney, Charles. *Early Responses to Renaissance Drama*. Cambridge: Cambridge University Press, 2006.

Wilde, Oscar. *De Profundis*, edited by Robert Ross. London: G. P. Putnam and Sons, 1902.

Wilson, Glenn, and Qazi Rahman. *Born Gay*. London: Peter Owen, 2004.

Wilson, Richard. "Unseasonable Laughter: The Context of *Cardenio*." In *Secret Shakespeare: Studies in Theatre, Religion and Resistance*, 230–45. Manchester: Manchester University Press, 2004.

Winnicott, D. W. "Transitional Objects and Transitional Phenomena—A Study of the First Not Me Possession." *International Journal of Psychoanalysis* 34 (1953): 89–97.

Winthrop, John. "A Modell of Christian Charity." *Winthrop Papers, Volume 2: 1623–1630*, edited by Stewart Mitchell, 282–95. Boston: Massachusetts Historical Society, 1931.

Wolin, Richard. *The Seduction of Unreason: The Intellectual Romance with Fascism from Nietzsche to Postmodernism*. Princeton: Princeton University Press, 2004.

Young, Kay. " 'Every Day a Little Death': Soundheim's Un-musicaling of Marriage." In *Reading Stephen Sondheim: A Collection of Critical Essays*, edited by Sandor Goodhart, 77–88. New York: Garland, 2000.

Zadan, Craig. *Sondheim and Co.* New York: Macmillan, 1974.

Zhen, Zhang. *An Amorous History of the Silver Screen: Shanghai Cinema, 1896–1937*. Chicago: University of Chicago Press, 2005.

———. "Cosmopolitan Projections: World Literature on Chinese Screens." In *A Companion to Literature and Film*, edited by Robert Stam and Alessandra Raengo. London: Blackwell, 2004.

Zimmerman, Susan. *The Early Modern Corpse and Shakespeare's Theatre*. Edinburgh: Edinburgh University Press, 2005.

Žižek, Slavoj. *Looking Awry: An Introduction to Jacques Lacan through Popular Culture*. Cambridge: MIT Press, 1991.

———. *The Plague of Fantasies*. New York: Verso, 1997.

All Is True (Henry VIII)

Frye, Susan. "Queens and the Structure of History in Henry VIII." In *A Companion to Shakespeare's Works*, edited by Richard Dutton and Jean Elizabeth Howard, 427–44. Malden, Mass.: Blackwell, 2003.

Goldberg, Jonathan. "The Making of Courtly Makers." In *Sodometries: Renaissance Texts, Modern Sexualities*, 29–62. Stanford: Stanford University Press, 1992.

McMullan, Gordon. "'Thou Hast Made Me Now a Man': Reforming Man(ner)liness in *Henry VIII*." In *Shakespeare's Late Plays*, edited by Jennifer Richards and James Knowles, 40–56. Edinburgh: Edinburgh University Press, 1999.

Menon, Madhavi. "After Words: *Henry VIII* and the Ends of History." In *Wanton Words: Rhetoric and Sexuality in Renaissance Drama*, 157–71. Toronto: University of Toronto Press, 2004.

Phillippy, Patricia. "The Body of History: Embalming and History in Shakespeare's *Henry VIII*." In *Women, Death, and Literature in Post-Reformation England*, 54–80. Cambridge: Cambridge University Press, 2002.

All's Well That Ends Well

Adelman, Janet. "Bed Tricks: On Marriage as the End of Comedy in *All's Well That Ends Well* and *Measure for Measure*." In *Shakespeare's Personality*, edited by Norman N. Holland, Sidney Homan, and Bernard J. Paris, 151–74. Berkeley: University of California Press, 1989.

Berkeley, David S., and Donald Keesee. "Bertram's Blood Consciousness in *All's Well That Ends Well*." *Studies in English Literature 1500–1900* 31 (1991): 247–58.

Engle, Lars. "Shakespearean Normativity in *All's Well That Ends Well*." *Shakespeare Studies* 4 (2004): 264–78.

Harmon, A. G. "'Lawful Deeds': The Entitlements of Marriage in Shakespeare's *All's Well That Ends Well*." *Logos* 4, no. 3 (Summer 2001): 115–42.

Harris, Jonathan Gil. "All Swell That End Swell: Dropsy, Phantom Pregnancy, and the Sound of Deconception in *All's Well That Ends Well*." *Renaissance Drama* 35 (2006): 169–90.

Menon, Madhavi. "First Night: Metalepsis, *Romeo and Juliet*, *All's Well That Ends Well*." In *Wanton Words: Rhetoric and Sexuality in English Renaissance Drama*, 68–93. Toronto: University of Toronto Press, 2004.

Antony and Cleopatra

Cixous, Hélène, and Catherine Clement. "Sorties: Out and Out: Attacks / Ways Out / Forays." In *The Newly Born Woman*, 63–129. London: I. B. Tauris, 1996 (1975).

Conkie, Robert. "Constructing Femininity in the New Globe's All-Male *Antony and Cleopatra*." In *Shakespeare Re-dressed*, 189–209. Cranbury, N.J.: Associated University Presses, 2008.

Dollimore, Jonathan. "*Antony and Cleopatra* (c. 1607): *Virtus* under Erasure." In *Radical Tragedy: Religion, Ideology, and Power in the Drama of Shakespeare and His Contemporaries*, 204–17. Durham: Duke University Press, 2004 (1984).

Harris, Jonathan Gil. "'Narcissus in Thy Face': Roman Desire and the Difference It Fakes in *Antony and Cleopatra*." *Shakespeare Quarterly* 45, no. 4 (1994): 408–25.

Little, Arthur, Jr. "(Re)posing with Cleopatra." In *Shakespeare Jungle Fever: National-Imperial Re-visions of Race, Rape, and Sacrifice*, 143–76. Stanford: Stanford University Press, 2001.

As You Like It

Bulman, James. "Bringing Cheek by Jowl's *As You Like It* Out of the Closet: The Politics of Queer Theater." In *Shakespeare Re-dressed*, 79–95. Cranbury, N.J.: Associated University Presses, 2008.

Crawford, Julie. "The Homoerotics of Shakespeare's Elizabethan Comedies." In *A Companion to Shakespeare's Works: The Comedies*, edited by Richard Dutton and Jean Elizabeth Howard, 137–58. Oxford: Blackwell, 2003.

Di Gangi, Mario. "Queering the Shakespearean Family." *Shakespeare Quarterly* 47, no. 3 (Fall 1996): 269–90.

Masten, Jeffrey. "Textual Deviance: Ganymede's Hand in *As You Like It*." In *Field Work: Sites in Literary and Cultural Studies*, edited by Marjorie Garber, Paul Franklin, and Rebecca Walkowitz, 153–63. London: Routledge, 1996.

Tvordi, Jessica. "Female Alliance and the Construction of Homoeroticism in *As You Like It* and *Twelfth Night*." In *Maids and Mistresses, Cousins and Queens: Women's Alliances in Early Modern England*, edited by Susan Frye and Karen Robertson, 114–30. Oxford: Oxford University Press, 1999.

Cardenio

Frey, Charles. "'O Sacred, Shadowy, Cold, and Constant Queen': Shakespeare's Imperiled and Chastening Daughters of Romance." In *The Woman's Part: Feminist Criticism of Shakespeare*, edited by Carolyn Ruth Swift Lenz, Gayle Greene, and Carol Thomas Neely, 295–313. Urbana: University of Illinois Press, 1983.

The Comedy of Errors

Fineman, Joel. "Fratricide and Cuckoldry: Shakespeare's Doubles." *Psychoanalytic Review* 64 (1977): 409–53.

Freedman, Barbara. "Reading Errantly: Misrecognition and the Uncanny in *The Comedy of Errors.*" In *Staging the Gaze: Postmodernism, Psychoanalysis, and Shakespearean Comedy*, 78–113. Ithaca: Cornell University Press, 1991.

Jankowski, Theodora A. "Queer: The Desired Trajectory from Virgin to Wife." In *Pure Resistance: Queer Virginity in Early Modern English Drama*, 113–35. Philadelphia: University of Pennsylvania Press, 2000.

Parker, Patricia. "Transfigurations: Shakespeare and Rhetoric." In *Shakespeare: An Anthology of Criticism, 1945–2000*, edited by Russ McDonald, 880–907. Oxford: Blackwell, 2004.

Wyric, Deborah Baker. "The Ass Motif in *The Comedy of Errors* and *A Midsummer Night's Dream.*" *Shakespeare Quarterly* 33, no. 4 (Winter 1982): 432–48.

Coriolanus

Adelman, Janet. "Escaping the Matrix: The Construction of Masculinity in *Macbeth* and *Coriolanus.*" In *Suffocating Mothers: Fantasies of Maternal Origin in Shakespeare's Plays*, Hamlet to The Tempest, 130–64. New York: Routledge, 1992.

Jagendorf, Zvi. "*Coriolanus*: Body Politic and Private Parts." *Shakespeare Quarterly* 41, no. 4 (1990): 455–69.

Marshall, Cynthia. "Wound-man: *Coriolanus*, Gender, and the Theatrical Construction of Interiority." In *Feminist Readings of Early Modern Culture: Emerging Subjects*, edited by Valerie Traub, M. Lindsay Kaplan, and Dympna Callaghan, 93–118. Cambridge: Cambridge University Press, 1996.

Riss, Arthur. "The Belly Politic: *Coriolanus* and the Revolt of Language." *English Literary History* 59, no .1 (1992): 53–75.

Smith, Bruce. "Combatants and Comrades." In *Homosexual Desire in Shakespeare's England*, 31–78. Chicago: University of Chicago Press, 1994.

Cymbeline

Menon, Madhavi. "Facts: *Cymbeline* and the 'Whore' of Historicism." In *Unhistorical Shakespeare: Queer Theory in Shakespearean Literature and Film*, 51–72. New York: Palgrave Macmillan, 2008.

Mikalachki, Jodi. "*Cymbeline* and the Masculine Romance of Roman Britain." In *The Legacy of Boadicea*, 96–114. London: Routledge, 1998.

Parker, Patricia. "Romance and Empire: Anachronistic *Cymbeline.*" In *Unfolded Tales: Essays on Renaissance Romance*, edited by George M. Logan and Gordon Teskey, 189–207. Ithaca: Cornell University Press, 1989.

Shapiro, Michael. "From Center to Periphery: *Cymbeline.*" In *Gender in Play on the*

Shakespearean Stage: Boy Heroines and Female Pages, 173–98. Ann Arbor: University of Michigan Press, 1994.

Stallybrass, Peter. "Worn Worlds: Clothes and Identity on the Renaissance Stage." In *Subject and Object in Renaissance Culture*, edited by Margreta De Grazia, 289–320. Cambridge: Cambridge University Press, 1996.

Hamlet

Blum, David. "Closet Hamlet." *Time*, September 22, 1997, 88–90.

Howard, Tony. *Women as Hamlet: Performance and Interpretation in Theatre, Film, and Fiction*. Cambridge: Cambridge University Press, 2007.

Lacan, Jacques, Jacques Alain-Miller, and James Hulbert. "Desire and the Interpretation of Desire in *Hamlet*." *Yale French Studies* 55, no. 56 (1977): 11–52.

Rosenblatt, Jason P. "Aspects of the Incest Problem in *Hamlet*." *Shakespeare Quarterly* 29, no. 3 (1978): 349–64.

Stone, James. "Androgynous 'Union' and the Woman in *Hamlet*." In *Shakespeare Studies*, vol. 23, edited by Leeds Barroll, 71–99. Cranbury, N.J.: Associated University Presses, 1995.

Henry IV, Part 1

Chedgzoy, Kate. "Successors to His Name: Shakespearean Family Romances." In *Shakespeare's Queer Children: Sexual Politics and Contemporary Culture*, 7–48. Manchester: Manchester University Press, 1995.

Hall, Jonathan. "Carnival and Plot in *Henry IV, Parts 1 and 2*." In *Anxious Pleasures: Shakespearean Comedy and the Nation State*, 215–34. Cranbury, N.J.: Associated University Presses, 1995.

Knowles, James. "*1 Henry IV*." In *A Companion to Shakespeare's Works*, vol. 2, edited by Richard Dutton and Jean Elizabeth Howard, 412–31. Oxford: Blackwell, 2003.

Lewis, Alan. "Shakespearean Seductions, or, What's with Harold Bloom as Falstaff?" *Texas Studies in Literature and Language* 49, no. 2 (2007): 125–54.

Traub, Valerie. "Prince Hal's Falstaff: Positioning Psychoanalysis and the Female Reproductive Body (*Henry IV, Parts 1 and 2, Henry V*)." In *Desire and Anxiety: Circulations of Sexuality in Shakespearean Drama*, 50–70. New York: Routledge, 1992.

Henry IV, Part 2

Barnaby, Andrew. "Imitation as Originality in Gus Van Sant's *My Own Private Idaho*." In *Almost Shakespeare: Reinventing His Works for Cinema and Television*, edited by James R. Keller and Leslie Stratyner, 22–41. Jefferson, N.C.: McFarland, 2004.

DiGangi, Mario. "The Homoerotics of Favoritism in Tragedy." In *The Homoerotics of Early Modern Drama*, 100–33. Cambridge: Cambridge University Press, 1997.

Gil, Daniel Juan. "Avant-garde Technique and the Visual Grammar of Sexuality in Orson Welles's Shakespeare Films." *Borrowers and Lenders* 1, no. 2 (Fall 2005): 1–27.

Goldberg, Jonathan. "Hal's Desire, Shakespeare's Idaho." In *Shakespeare's Hand*, 222–52. Minneapolis: University of Minnesota Press, 2003.

——. "Desiring Hal." In *Sodometries: Renaissance Texts, Modern Sexualities*, 145–78. Stanford: Stanford University Press, 1992.

Henry V

Altman, Joel B. "'Vile Participation': The Amplification of Violence in the Theater of *Henry V*." In *Shakespeare: The Critical Complex*, edited by Stephen Orgel and Sean Keilen, 401–32. New York: Garland, 1999.

Corum, Richard. "Henry's Desires." In *Premodern Sexualities*, edited by Louise Fradenburg and Carla Freccero, 71–98. New York: Routledge, 1996.

Goldberg, Jonathan. "Desiring Hal." In *Sodometries: Renaissance Texts, Modern Sexualities*, 145–78. Stanford: Stanford University Press, 1992.

Hedrick, Donald. "Advantage, Affect, History, *Henry V*." *PMLA* 118, no. 3 (2003): 470–87.

Sinfield, Alan, and Jonathan Dollimore. "History and Ideology, Masculinity and Miscegenation: The Instance of *Henry V*." In Alan Sinfield, *Faultlines: Cultural Materialism and the Politics of Dissident Reading*, 109–42. Berkeley: University of California Press, 1992.

Henry VI, Part 1

Howard, Jean Elizabeth, and Phyllis Rackin. "Weak Kings, Warrior Women, and the Assault on Dynastic Authority: The First Tetralogy and *King John, Henry VI, Part 1*." In *Engendering a Nation: A Feminist Account of Shakespeare's English Histories*, 43–64. London: Routledge, 1997.

Jankowski, Theodora A. "Queer(y)ing Virginity: Virgins, Lesbians, and Queers of All Types." In *Pure Resistance: Queer Virginity in Early Modern English Drama*, 1–30. Philadelphia: University of Pennsylvania Press, 2000.

Kurtz, Martha A. "Tears and Masculinity in the History Play: Shakespeare's 1 *Henry VI*." In *Grief and Gender: 700–1700*, edited by Jennifer C. Vaught, 163–76. New York: Palgrave Macmillan, 2003.

Paxson, James J. "Shakespeare's Medieval Devils and Joan la Pucelle in 1 *Henry VI*: Semiotics, Iconography, and Feminist Criticism." In *Henry VI: Critical Essays*, edited by Thomas Pendleton, 126–56. New York: Routledge, 2001.

Pye, Christopher. "The Theater, the Market, and the Subject of History." In *The Vanishing: Shakespeare, the Subject, and Early Modern Culture*, 17–37. Durham: Duke University Press, 2000.

Henry VI, Part 2

Barasch, Frances K. "Folk Magic in *Henry VI, Parts 1 and 2*: Two Scenes of Embedding." In *Henry VI: Critical Essays*, edited by Thomas Pendleton, 113–26. New York: Routledge, 2001.

Howard, Jean Elizabeth, and Phyllis Rackin. "Weak Kings, Warrior Women, and the Assault on Dynastic Authority: The First Tetralogy and *King John, Henry VI, Part 2*." In *Engendering a Nation: A Feminist Account of Shakespeare's English Histories*, 65–82 London: Routledge, 1997.

Schwarz, Kathryn. "Fearful Simile: Stealing the Breech in Shakespeare's Chronicle Plays." In *Tough Love: Amazon Encounters in the English Renaissance*, 79–108. Durham: Duke University Press, 2000.

Vanhoutte, Jacqueline. "Defining the 'True-born Englishman': Monarchy, Motherland, and Masculinity in Shakespeare's History Plays." In *Strange Communion: Motherland and Masculinity in Tudor Plays, Pamphlets, and Politics*, 135–75. Cranbury, N.J.: Associated University Presses, 2003.

Williamson, Marilyn L. "'When Men are Rul'd by Women': Shakespeare's First Tetralogy." *Shakespeare Studies* 19 (1987): 41–59.

Henry VI, Part 3

Bach, Rebecca Ann. "Manliness before Individualism: Masculinity, Effeminacy, and Homoerotics in Shakespeare's History Plays." In *A Companion to Shakespeare's Works*, vol. 2, edited by Richard Dutton and Jean Elizabeth Howard, 220–45. Oxford: Blackwell, 2003.

Forker, Charles. "Royal Carnality and Illicit Desire in the English History Play of the 1590s." In *Medieval and Renaissance Drama in England*, vol. 17, edited by John Pitcher and S. P. Cerasano, 91–131. Cranbury, N.J.: Associated University Presses, 2005.

Howard, Jean Elizabeth, and Phyllis Rackin. "Weak Kings, Warrior Women, and the Assault on Dynastic Authority: The First Tetralogy and *King John, Henry VI, Part 3*." In *Engendering a Nation: A Feminist Account of Shakespeare's English Histories*, 83–99. London: Routledge, 1997.

Liebler, Naomi C., and Lisa Scancella Shea. "Shakespeare's Queen Margaret: Unruly or Unruled." In *Henry VI: Critical Essays*, edited by Thomas Pendleton, 79–97. New York: Routledge, 2001.

Schwarz, Kathryn. "Vexed Relations: Family, State, and the Uses of Women in *3 Henry VI*." In *A Companion to Shakespeare's Works*, vol. 2, edited by Richard Dutton and Jean Elizabeth Howard, 344–60. Oxford: Blackwell, 2003.

Julius Caesar

Kahn, Coppelia. "Mettle and Melting Spirits in *Julius Caesar*." In *Roman Shakespeare: Warriors, Wounds, and Women*, 77–109. London: Routledge, 1997.

——. " 'Passion and Some Difference': Friendship and Emulation in *Julius Caesar*." In *Julius Caesar: New Critical Essays*, edited by Horst Zander, 271–86. New York: Routledge, 2005.

Paster, Gail Kern. " 'In the Spirit of Men there is no Blood': Blood as Trope of Gender in *Julius Caesar*." *Shakespeare Quarterly* 40.3 (Autumn 1989): 284–98.

Pearson, Robert E., and William Uriccho. "How Many Times Shall Caesar Bleed in Sport? Shakespeare and the Cultural Debate about Moving Pictures." *Screen* 31, no. 3 (1990): 243–61.

Willbern, David. "Constructing Caesar: A Psychoanalytic Reading." In *Julius Caesar: New Critical Essays*, edited by Horst Zander, 213–26. New York: Routledge, 2005.

King John

Campana, Joseph. "Killing Shakespeare's Children: The Cases of *Richard III* and *King John*." *Shakespeare* 3, no. 1 (April 2007): 18–39.

Candido, Joseph. "Blots, Stains, and Adulteries: The Impurities in *King John*." In *King John: New Perspectives*, edited by Deborah T. Curren-Aquino, 114–25. Cranbury, N.J.: Associated University Presses, 1989.

Howard, Jean Elizabeth, and Phyllis Rackin. "Weak Kings, Warrior Women, and the Assault on Dynastic Authority: The First Tetralogy and *King John*." In *Engendering a Nation: A Feminist Account of Shakespeare's English Histories*, 119–36. London: Routledge, 1997.

Menon, Madhavi. "Cast in Order of Appearance: Catachresis, *Othello*, *King John*." In *Wanton Words: Rhetoric and Sexuality in English Renaissance Drama*, 94–123. Toronto: University of Toronto Press, 2004.

Vaughan, Virginia M. "*King John*: A Study in Subversion and Containment." In *King John: New Perspectives*, edited by Deborah T. Curren-Aquino, 62–75. Cranbury, N.J.: Associated University Presses, 1989.

King Lear

Aebischer, Pascale. "En-gendering Violence and Suffering in *King Lear*." In *Shakespeare's Violated Bodies: Stage and Screen Performance*, 151–89. Cambridge: Cambridge University Press, 2004.

Chedgzoy, Kate. "Wise Children and Foolish Fathers: Carnival in the Family." In *Shakespeare's Queer Children: Sexual Politics and Contemporary Culture*, 49–93. Manchester: Manchester University Press, 1995.

Hammond, Paul. "James I's Homosexuality and the Revision of the Folio Text of *King Lear*." *Notes and Queries* 47 (March 1997): 62–64.

Shannon, Laurie. "Poor, Bare, Forked: Human Negative Exceptionalism, Animal

Sovereignty, and the Natural History of *King Lear.*" *Shakespeare Quarterly* 60, no. 2 (Summer 2009): 168–96.

Thompson, Ann. "Are There Any Women in *King Lear?*" In *The Matter of Difference: Materialist Feminist Criticism of Shakespeare*, edited by Valerie Wayne, 117–28. Ithaca: Cornell University Press, 1991.

A Lover's Complaint

Bates, Catherine. "Feminine Identifications in *A Lover's Complaint.*" In *Masculinity, Gender and Identity in the English Renaissance Lyric*, 174–215. Cambridge: Cambridge University Press, 2008.

Harned, Jon. "Rhetoric and Perverse Desire in *A Lover's Complaint.*" In *Critical Essays on Shakespeare's* A Lover's Complaint, edited by Shirley Sharon-Zisser, 149–64. Hampshire: Ashgate, 2006.

Roberts, Sasha. "Textual Transmission and the Transformation of Desire: The Sonnets, *A Lover's Complaint,* and *The Passionate Pilgrim.*" In *Reading Shakespeare's Poems in Early Modern England*, 143–90. Hampshire: Macmillan, 2003.

Sharon-Zisser, Shirley. " 'True to Bondage': The Rhetorical Forms of Female Masochism in *A Lover's Complaint.*" In *Critical Essays on Shakespeare's* A Lover's Complaint, edited by Shirley Sharon-Zisser, 179–90. Hampshire: Ashgate, 2006.

Wall, Wendy. "Impersonating the Manuscript: Cross-Dressed Authors and Literary Pseudomorphs." In *The Imprint of Gender: Authorship and Publication in the English Renaissance*, 227–78. Ithaca: Cornell University Press, 1993.

Love's Labour's Lost

Breitenberg, Mark. "The Anatomy of Masculine Desire in *Love's Labor's Lost.*" In *Anxious Masculinity in Early Modern England*, 128–49. Cambridge: Cambridge University Press, 1996.

Hall, Jonathan. "War, Wit, and Closure in *Love's Labour's Lost.*" In *Anxious Pleasures: Shakespearean Comedy and the Nation State*, 87–97. Cranbury, N.J.: Associated University Presses, 1995.

Henderson, Diana. "Shakespeare's Laboring Lovers: Lyric and Its Discontents." In *Passion Made Public: Elizabethan Lyric, Gender, and Performance*, 167–213. Urbana: University of Illinois Press, 1995.

Hopkins, Lisa. "What Makes a Marriage?" In *The Shakespearean Marriage: Merry Wives and Heavy Husbands*, 66–84. New York: St. Martin's Press, 1998.

Parker, Patricia. "Preposterous Estates, Preposterous Events: From Late to Early Shakespeare." In *Shakespeare from the Margins: Language, Culture, Context*, 20–55. Chicago: University of Chicago Press, 1996.

Macbeth

Alfar, Cristina Léon. "'Blood Will Have Blood': Power, Performance, and the Trouble with Gender." In *Fantasies of Female Evil: The Dynamics of Gender and Power in Shakespearean Tragedy*, 111–35. Cranburry, N.J.: Associated University Presses, 2003.

Freud, Sigmund. "Some Character-Types Met with in Psycho-Analytic Work." In *The Standard Edition of the Complete Psychological Works of Sigmund Freud, Volume XIV (1914–1916): On the History of the Psycho-Analytic Movement, Papers on Metapsychology and Other Works*, translated by James Strachey, eds. James Strachey, Anna Freud, Alix Strachey, and Alan Tyson, 309–33. London: Hogarth Press, 1957.

Goldberg, Jonathan. "Speculations: *Macbeth* and Source." In *Shakespeare Reproduced*, edited by Jean E. Howard and Marion F. O'Connor, 242–64. Oxford: Routledge, 1987.

Keller, James R. "'Naught's Had, All's Spent': Shakespeare, Queer Rage, and *The Talented Mr. Ripley*." In *Queer (Un)friendly Film and Television*, 68–81. Jefferson, N.C.: McFarland, 2002.

Wilton, Tamsin. "On Not Being Lady Macbeth: Some (Troubled) Thoughts on Lesbian Spectatorship." In *Immortal, Invisible: Lesbians and the Moving Image*, edited by Tamsin Wilton, 113–30. London: Routledge, 1995.

Measure for Measure

Blank, Paul. "The Lesbian Rule of *Measure for Measure*." In *Shakespeare and the Mismeasure of Renaissance Man*, 153–90. Ithaca; Cornell University Press, 2006.

Crane, Mary Thomas. "Male Pregnancy and Cognitive Permeability in *Measure for Measure*." *Shakespeare Quarterly* 49, no. 3 (Fall 1998): 269–92.

Dollimore, Jonathan. "Transgression and Surveillance in *Measure for Measure*." In *Political Shakespeare: New Essays in Cultural Materialism*, edited by Jonathan Dollimore and Alan Sinfield, 72–87. Ithaca: Cornell University Press, 1985.

Drouin, Jennifer. "Diana's Band: Safe Spaces, Publics, and Early Modern Lesbianism." In *Queer Renaissance Historiography: Backward Gaze*, edited by Vin Nardizzi, Stephen Guy-Bray, and Will Stockton, 85–110. Burlington, Vt: Ashgate, 2009.

Shell, Marc. "Incest in Pardon and Marriage." In *The End of Kinship: "Measure for Measure," Incest, and the Ideal of Universal Siblinghood*, 139–74. Stanford: Stanford University Press, 1988.

The Merchant of Venice

Belsey, Catherine. "Love in Venice." In *Shakespeare and Gender: A History*, edited by Deborah Barker and Ivo Kamps. 196–213. London: Verso, 1995.

O'Rourke, James. "Racism and Homophobia in *The Merchant of Venice*." ELH 70, no. 2 (2003): 375–97.

Patterson, Steve. "The Bankruptcy of Homoerotic Amity in Shakespeare's *Merchant of Venice*." *Shakespeare Quarterly* 50, no. 1 (Spring 1999): 9–32.

Pequigney, Joseph. "The Two Antonios and Same-Sex Love in *Twelfth Night* and *The Merchant of Venice*." In *Shakespeare and Gender: A History*, edited by Deborah Barker and Ivo Kamps, 178–95. London: Verso, 1995.

Sinfield, Alan. "How to Read *The Merchant of Venice* without Being Heterosexist." In *Shakespeare, Authority, Sexuality: Unfinished Business in Cultural Materialism*, 53–67. London: Routledge, 2006.

The Merry Wives of Windsor

Neely, Carol Thomas. "Confining Madmen and Transgressing Boundaries: *The Comedy of Errors, The Merry Wives of Windsor*, and *Twelfth Night*." In *Distracted Subjects: Madness and Gender in Shakespeare and Early Modern Culture*, 136–66. Ithaca: Cornell University Press, 2004.

Theis, Jeffrey. "The 'Ill Kill'd' Deer: Poaching and Social Order in *The Merry Wives of Windsor*." *Texas Studies in Literature and Language* 43, no. 1 (2001): 46–73.

Tiffany, Grace. "Experimental Androgynes: Falstaff, Ursula, and *The New Inn*." In *Erotic Beasts and Social Monsters: Shakespeare, Jonson, and Comic Androgyny*, 136–69. Cranbury, N.J.: Associated University Presses, 1995.

Wall, Wendy. "'Household Stuff': The Sexual Politics of Domesticity and the Advent of English Comedy." *ELH* 65, no. 1 (1998): 1–45.

A Midsummer Night's Dream

Freedman, Barbara. "Dis / Figuring Power: Censorship and Representation in *A Midsummer Night's Dream*." In *Staging the Gaze: Postmodernism, Psychoanalysis, and Shakespearean Comedy*, 154–91. Ithaca: Cornell University Press, 1991.

Girard, René. "'O Teach Me How You Look': Helena and Hermia in *A Midsummer Night's Dream*." In *A Theatre of Envy: William Shakespeare*, 40–49. New York: Oxford University Press, 1991.

Paster, Gail Kern. "Covering His Ass: The Scatological Imperatives of Comedy." In *The Body Embarrassed: Drama and the Disciplines of Shame in Early Modern England*, 113–62. Ithaca: Cornell University Press, 1993.

Schwarz, Kathryn. "Tragical Mirth: Framing Shakespeare's Hippolyta." In *Tough Love: Amazon Encounters in the English Renaissance*, 203–35. Durham: Duke University Press, 2000.

Weller, Barry. "Identity Dis-Figured: 'A Midsummer Night's Dream.'" *Kenyon Review* 7, no. 3 (Summer 1985): 66–78.

Much Ado About Nothing

Cook, Carol. "'The Sign and Semblance of Her Honor': Reading Gender Difference in *Much Ado About Nothing*." In *Shakespeare and Gender: A History*, edited by Deborah E. Barker and Ivo Kamps, 75–103. London: Verso, 1995.

Hall, Jonathan. "From Double Words to Single Vision: Patriarchal Desire in *Much Ado About Nothing* and *Othello*." In *Anxious Pleasures: Shakespearean Comedy and the Nation State*, 170–96. Cranbury, N.J.: Associated University Presses, 1995.

Howard, Jean E. "Renaissance Antitheatricality and the Politics of Gender and Rank in *Much Ado About Nothing*." In *Shakespeare Reproduced*, edited by Jean E. Howard and Marion F. O'Connor, 163–87. Oxford: Routledge, 1987.

Menon, Madhavi. "Citation: Bollywood Quotes *Much Ado*." In *Unhistorical Shakespeare: Queer Theory in Shakespearean Literature and Film*, 73–94. New York: Palgrave Macmillan, 2008.

Neely, Carol Thomas. "Broken Nuptials in Shakespeare's Comedies: *Much Ado About Nothing*." In *Broken Nuptials in Shakespeare's Plays*, 24–57. New Haven: Yale University Press, 1985.

Othello

Belsey, Catherine. "Desire's Excess and the English Renaissance Theatre: *Edward II, Troilus and Cressida, Othello*." In *Erotic Politics: Desire on the Renaissance Stage*, edited by Susan Zimmerman, 84–102. New York: Routledge, 1992.

Dollimore, Jonathan. "*Othello*: Sexual Difference and Internal Deviation." In *Sexual Dissidence: Augustine to Wilde, Freud to Foucault*, 148–68. Oxford: Oxford University Press, 1991.

Little, Arthur. "'An Essence That's Not Seen': The Primal Scene of Racism in *Othello*." *Shakespeare Quarterly* 44, no. 3 (Fall 1993): 304–24.

Matz, Robert. "Slander, Renaissance Discourses of Sodomy, and *Othello*." *ELH* 66, no. 2 (1999): 261–76.

Pechter, Edward. "'Have You Not Read of Some Such Thing?': Sex and Sexual Stories in *Othello*." *Shakespeare Survey* 49 (1996): 201–16.

Pericles

Adelman, Janet. "Masculine Authority and the Maternal Body: The Return to Origins in *Pericles*." In *Pericles: Critical Essays*, edited by David Steele, 184–90. New York: Garland, 2000.

Kim, Han. "Endless Story, *Pericles*: Words and Open Ending." *Shakespeare Review* 29 (1996): 71–104.

Newcomb, Lori Humphrey. "The Sources of Romance, the Generation Story, and the Patterns of the Pericles Tales." In *Staging Early Modern Romance: Prose Fiction, Dramatic Romance, and Shakespeare*, edited by Mary Ellen Lamb and Valerie Wayne, 21–46. New York: Routledge, 2009.

Thorne, W. B. "Pericles and the 'Incest-Fertility' Opposition." *Shakespeare Quarterly* 22, no. 1 (Winter 1971): 43–56.

The Phoenix and the Turtle

Bock, Philip. " 'Neither Two nor One': Dual Unity in 'The Phoenix and the Turtle.' " *Journal of Psychoanalytic Anthropology* 10, no. 3 (1987): 251–67.

Green, Andre. "To Love or Not to Love: Eros and Eris." In *Love and Its Vicissitudes*, edited by Andre Green and Gregorio Kohon, 1–40. New York: Routledge, 2005.

The Rape of Lucrece

Breitenberg, Mark. "Publishing Chastity: Shakespeare's 'Rape of Lucrece.' " In *Anxious Masculinity in Early Modern England*, 97–127. Cambridge: Cambridge University Press, 1996.

Enterline, Lynn. " 'Poor Instruments' and Unspeakable Events in *The Rape of Lucrece*." In *The Rhetoric of the Body from Ovid to Shakespeare*, 152–97. Cambridge: Cambridge University Press, 2000.

Kahn, Coppelia. "Publishing Shame: *The Rape of Lucrece*." In *A Companion to Shakespeare's Works*, edited by Richard Dutton and Jean Elizabeth Howard, 259–74. Malden, Mass.: Blackwell, 2003.

Little, Arthur. "Picturing the Hand of White Women." In *Shakespeare Jungle Fever: National-Imperial Re-vision of Race, Rape, and Sacrifice*, 25–67. Stanford: Stanford University Press, 2000.

Sanders, Eve Rachele. "Writes in His Tables." In *Gender and Literacy on Stage in Early Modern England*, 138–64. Cambridge: Cambridge University Press, 1998.

Richard II

Goldberg, Jonathan. "Rebel Letters: Postal Effects from *Richard II* to *Henry IV*." In *Shakespeare's Hand*, 189–211. Minneapolis: University of Minnesota Press, 2003.

Hopkins, Lisa. "The King's Melting Body: *Richard II*." In *A Companion to Shakespeare's Works*, vol. 2, edited by Richard Dutton and Jean Elizabeth Howard, 395–411. Oxford: Blackwell, 2003.

Klett, Elizabeth. "Many Bodies, Many Voices: Performing Androgyny in Fiona Shaw and Deborah Warner's *Richard II*." *Theatre Journal* 58, no. 2 (2005): 175–94.

Logan, Robert. "*Edward II, Richard II*, the Will to Play, and an Aesthetic of Ambiguity." In *Shakespeare's Marlowe: The Influence of Christopher Marlowe on Shakespeare's Artistry*, 83–116. Burlington, Vt.: Ashgate, 2007.

Menon, Madhavi. "*Richard II* and the Taint of Metonymy." *ELH* 70, no. 3 (2003): 653–75.

Richard III

Hogdgon, Barbara. "Replicating Richard: Body Doubles, Body Politics." *Theatre Journal* 50, no. 2 (1998): 207–25.

Howard, Jean Elizabeth, and Phyllis Rackin. "Weak Kings, Warrior Women, and the

Assault on Dynastic Authority: The First Tetralogy and *King John, Richard III.*" In *Engendering a Nation: A Feminist Account of Shakespeare's English Histories*, 100–18. London: Routledge, 1997.

Kurtz, Martha. "Rethinking Gender and Genre in the History Play." *Studies in English Literature 1500–1900* 36, no. 2 (Spring 1996): 267–87.

Rackin, Phyllis. "Engendering the Tragic Audience: The Case of *Richard III.*" In *Shakespeare and Gender: A History*, edited by Deborah E. Barker and Ivo Kamps, 263–82. London: Verso, 1995.

Romeo and Juliet

Burt, Richard. "No Holes Bard: Homonormativity and the Gay and Lesbian Romance with *Romeo and Juliet.*" In *Shakespeare without Class: Misappropriations of Cultural Capital*, edited by Donald Hedrick and Bryan Reynolds, 153–88. New York: Palgrave Macmillan, 2000.

Derrida, Jacques. "Aphorism / Countertime." In *Acts of Literature*, edited by Derek Attridge, 414–33. New York: Routledge, 1992.

Goldberg, Jonathan. "'What? in a Names That Which We Call a Rose': The Desired Texts of *Romeo and Juliet.*" In *Shakespeare's Hand*, 253–70. Minneapolis: University of Minnesota Press, 2003.

Kristeva, Julia. "*Romeo and Juliet*: Love–Hatred in the Couple." In *Tales of Love*, translated by Leon S. Roudiez, 209–33. New York: Columbia University Press, 1987.

Reynolds, Bryan, and Janna Segal. "Fugitive Explorations in *Romeo and Juliet*: Transversal Travels through R&Jspace." *Journal for Early Modern Cultural Studies* 5, no. 2 (2005): 37–70.

Sir Thomas More

Fisher, Will. "'His Majesty the Beard': Beards and Masculinity." In *Materializing Gender in Early Modern English Literature and Culture*, 83–128. Cambridge: Cambridge University Press, 2006.

Masten, Jeffrey. "*More* or Less: Editing the Collaborative." In *Shakespeare Studies*, vol. 29, edited by Leeds Barroll, 109–31. Cranbury, N.J.: Associated University Presses, 2001.

Stallybrass, Peter. "The World Turned Upside Down: Inversion, Gender, and the State." In *The Matter of Difference: Materialist Feminist Criticism of Shakespeare*, edited by Valerie Wayne, 201–20. Ithaca: Cornell University Press, 1991.

The Sonnets

Fineman, Joel. *Shakespeare's Perjured Eye: The Invention of Poetic Subjectivity in the Sonnets*. Berkeley: University of California Press, 1988.

Pequigney, Joseph. "The Bisexual Soul." In *Such Is My Love: A Study of Shakespeare's Sonnets*, 81–101. Chicago: University of Chicago Press, 1985.

Sedgwick, Eve Kosofsky. "Swan in Love: The Example of Shakespeare's Sonnets." In *Between Men: English Literature and Male Homosocial Desire*, 28–48. New York: Columbia University Press, 1985.

Smith, Bruce R. "Shakespeare's Sonnets and the History of Sexuality: A Reception History." In *A Companion to Shakespeare's Works*, edited by Richard Dutton and Jean Elizabeth Howard, 4–26. Malden, Mass.: Blackwell, 2003.

Traub, Valerie. "The Sonnets: Sequence, Sexuality, and Shakespeare's Two Loves." In *A Companion to Shakespeare's Works*, edited by Richard Dutton and Jean Elizabeth Howard, 275–301. Malden, Mass.: Blackwell, 2003.

——. "Sex without Issue: Sodomy, Reproduction, and Signification in Shakespeare's Sonnets." In *Shakespeare's Sonnets: Critical Essays*, edited by James Schiffer, 431–54. New York: Garland, 2000.

The Taming of the Shrew

DiGangi, Mario. "The Social Relations of Shakespeare's Comic Households." In *A Companion to Shakespeare's Works*, edited by Richard Dutton and Jean Elizabeth Howard, 90–113. Malden, Mass.: Blackwell, 2003.

Fineman, Joel. "The Turn of the Shrew." In *Shakespeare: An Anthology of Criticism, 1945–2000*, edited by Russ McDonald, 399–416. Oxford: Blackwell, 2004.

Freedman, Barbara. "Taming Difference and *The Taming of the Shrew*: Feminism, Psychoanalysis, Theater." In *Staging the Gaze: Postmodernism, Psychoanalysis, and Shakespearean Comedy*, 114–53. Ithaca: Cornell University Press, 1991.

Jaster, Margaret Rose. "Controlling Clothes, Manipulating Mates: Petruchio's Griselda." In *Shakespeare Studies*, vol. 29, edited by Leeds Barroll, 93–108. Cranbury, N.J.: Associated University Presses, 2001.

Taunton, Nina. "Patterns of Sadomasochism and Fashion-Fetishism in *Taming of the Shrew*." *Erfurt Electronic Studies in English* 8 (1996). Available online at http://webdoc.gwdg.de/edoc/ia/eese/artic96/taunton/8_96.html. Accessed May 15, 2010.

The Tempest

Ellis, Jim. "Conjuring *The Tempest*: Derek Jarman and the Spectacle of Redemption." *GLQ* 7, no. 2 (2001): 265–84.

Goldberg, Jonathan. "Under the Covers with Caliban." In *Shakespeare's Hand*, 286–308. Minneapolis: University of Minnesota Press, 2003.

Menon, Madhavi. "Encore! Allegory, *Volpone*, *The Tempest*." In *Wanton Words: Rhetoric and Sexuality in English Renaissance Drama*, 124–56. Toronto: University of Toronto Press, 2004.

Starrs, D. Bruno. "A Queer New World: Adaptation Theory and the Zeugma of Fidelity in Derek Jarman's *The Tempest* (1979)." *American* 4, no. 1 (2006): 71–91.

Zabus, Chantal. "Flaunting *The Tempest*: From 'Insubstantial Pageant' to Celluloid Frescoe." In *Tempests after Shakespeare*, 243–64. New York: Palgrave Macmillan, 2002.

Timon of Athens

Adelman, Janet. "Making Defect Perfection: Imagining Male Bounty in *Timon of Athens* and *Antony and Cleopatra*." In *Suffocating Mothers: Fantasies of Maternal Origin in Shakespeare's Plays, from* Hamlet *to* The Tempest, 165–92. New York: Routledge, 1992.

Charney, Maurice. "Love and Lust: Sexual Wit." In *Shakespeare on Love and Lust*, 181–208. New York: Columbia University Press, 2000.

Graham, Kenneth John Emerson. "The Performance of Pride: Desire, Truth, and Power in *Coriolanus* and *Timon of Athens*." In *The Performance of Conviction: Plainness and Rhetoric in the Early English Renaissance*, 168–89. Ithaca: Cornell University Press, 1994.

Kahn, Coppelia. "'Magic of Bounty': *Timon of Athens*, Jacobean Patronage, and Maternal Power." In *Shakespearean Tragedy and Gender*, edited by Shirley Nelson Garner and Madelon Sprengnether, 135–70. Bloomington: Indiana University Press, 1996.

Schalkwyk, David. "'More than a Steward': The Sonnets, *Twelfth Night*, and *Timon of Athens*." In *Shakespeare, Love, and Service*, 115–63. Cambridge: Cambridge University Press, 2008.

Titus Andronicus

Detmer-Goebel, Emily. "The Need for Lavinia's Voice: *Titus Andronicus* and the Telling of Rape." In *Shakespeare Studies*, vol. 29, edited by Leeds Barroll, 75–92. Cranbury, N.J.: Associated University Presses, 2001

Kesler, R. L. "Subjectivity, Time, and Gender in *Titus Andronicus, Hamlet*, and *Othello*." In *Enacting Gender on the English Renaissance Stage*, edited by Viviana Comensoli and Anne Russell, 114–34. Urbana: University of Illinois Press, 1999.

Little, Arthur. "Picturing the Hand of White Women." In *Shakespeare Jungle Fever: National-Imperial Re-vision of Race, Rape, and Sacrifice*, 25–67. Stanford: Stanford University Press, 2000.

Menon, Madhavi. "Origins: *Titus Andronicus* and the Source of Desire." In *Unhistorical Shakespeare: Queer Theory in Shakespearean Literature and Film*, 95–114. New York: Palgrave Macmillan, 2008.

Wynne-Davies, Marion. "'The Swallowing Womb': Consumed and Consuming Women in *Titus Andronicus*." In *The Matter of Difference: Materialist Feminist Criticism of Shakespeare*, edited by Valerie Wayne, 129–52. Ithaca: Cornell University Press, 1991.

Troilus and Cressida

Belsey, Catherine. "Desire's Excess and the English Renaissance Theatre: *Edward II, Troilus and Cressida, Othello*." In *Erotic Politics: Desire on the Renaissance Stage*, edited by Susan Zimmerman, 84–102. New York: Routledge, 1992.

Charnes, Linda. "The Two Party System in *Troilus and Cressida*." In *A Companion to Shakespeare's Works*, edited by Richard Dutton and Jean Elizabeth Howard, 302–15. Malden, Mass.: Blackwell, 2003.

Cook, Carol. "Unbodied Figures of Desire." *Theatre Journal* 38, no. 2 (March 1986): 34–52.

McCandless, David Foley. "*Troilus and Cressida*." In *Gender and Performance in Shakespeare's Problem Comedies*, 123–66. Bloomington: Indiana University Press, 1997.

Traub, Valerie. "Invading Bodies / Bawdy Exchanges: Disease, Desire, and Representation (*Troilus and Cressida*)." In *Desire and Anxiety: Circulations of Sexuality in Shakespearean Drama*, 71–90. London: Routledge, 1992.

Twelfth Night

Ake, Jami. "Glimpsing a 'Lesbian Poetics' in *Twelfth Night*." *Studies in English Literature 1500–1900* 43, no. 2 (Spring 2003): 375–94.

Crewe, Jonathan. "In the Field of Dreams: Transvestism in *Twelfth Night* and *The Crying Game*." *Representations* 50 (1995): 101–23.

Elam, Keir. "The Fertile Eunuch: *Twelfth Night*, Early Modern Intercourse, and the Fruits of Castration." *Shakespeare Quarterly* 47, no. 1 (Spring 1996): 1–36.

Jardine, Lisa. "Twins and Transvestites: Gender, Dependency, and Sexual Availability in *Twelfth Night*." In *Erotic Politics: Desire on the Renaissance Stage*, edited by Susan Zimmerman, 27–38. New York: Routledge, 1992.

Traub, Valerie. "The Homoerotics of Shakespearean Comedy (*As You Like It, Twelfth Night*)." In *Desire and Anxiety: Circulations of Sexuality in Shakespearean Drama*, 117–44. London: Routledge, 1992.

The Two Gentlemen of Verona

Friedman, Michael. "'Were Man but Constant, He Were Perfect': *The Two Gentlemen of Verona*." In *The World Must Be Peopled*, 41–75. Cranbury, N.J.: Associated University Presses, 2002.

Girard, René. "Love Delights in Praises: Valentine and Proteus in *The Two Gentlemen of Verona*." In *A Theater of Envy*, 8–20. Oxford: Oxford University Press, 1991.

Shannon, Laurie. "The Early Modern Politics of Likeness: Sovereign Reader-Subjects and Listening Kings." In *Sovereign Amity: Figures of Friendship in Shakespearean Contexts*, 17–53. Chicago: University of Chicago Press, 2002.

Shapiro, Michael. "Bringing the Page Onstage: *The Two Gentlemen of Verona*." In *Gender in Play on the Shakespearean Stage: Boy Heroines and Female Pages*, 64–92. Ann Arbor: University of Michigan Press, 1994.

Simmons, J. L. "Coming Out in Shakespeare's *The Two Gentlemen of Verona*." *ELH* 60, no. 4 (1993): 857–77.

The Two Noble Kinsmen

Abrams, Richard. "Gender Confusion and Sexual Politics in *The Two Noble Kinsmen*." In *Drama, Sex, and Politics*, edited by James Redmond, 69–76. Cambridge: Cambridge University Press, 1985.

Roberts, Jeanne Addison. "Triangulations of Desire." In *The Shakespearean Wild: Geography, Genus, and Gender*, 125–40. Lincoln: University of Nebraska Press, 1991.

Schwarz, Kathryn. "Epilogue: Via *The Two Noble Kinsmen*." In *Tough Love: Amazon Encounters in the English Renaissance*, 236–38. Durham: Duke University Press, 2000.

Shannon, Laurie. "Professing Friendship: Erotic Prerogatives and 'Human Title' in *The Two Noble Kinsmen*." In *Sovereign Amity: Figures of Friendship in Shakespearean Contexts*, 90–124. Chicago: University of Chicago Press, 2002.

Sinfield, Alan. "Intertextuality and the Limits of Queer Reading in *A Midsummer Night's Dream* and *The Two Noble Kinsmen*." In *Shakespeare, Authority, Sexuality: Unfinished Business in Cultural Materialism*, 68–85. London: Routledge, 2006.

Venus and Adonis

Belsey, Catherine. "Love as Trompe-L'Oeil: Taxonomies of Desire in *Venus and Adonis*." In *Venus and Adonis: Critical Essays*, edited by Philip Kolin, 261–86. New York: Routledge, 1997.

Menon, Madhavi. "Spurning Teleology in *Venus and Adonis*." GLQ 11, no. 4 (2005): 491–519.

Rambuss, Richard. "What It Feels Like for a Boy. Shakespeare's *Venus and Adonis*." In *A Companion to Shakespeare's Works*, edited by Richard Dutton and Jean Elizabeth Howard, 240–58. Malden, Mass.: Blackwell, 2003.

Schiffer, James. "Shakespeare's *Venus and Adonis*: A Lacanian Tragicomedy of Desire." In *Venus and Adonis: Critical Essays*, edited by Philip Kolin, 359–75. New York: Routledge, 1997.

Stanivukovic, Goran. "'Kissing the Boar': Queer Adonis and Critical Practice." In *Straight with a Twist: Queer Theory and the Subject of Heterosexuality*, edited by Calvin Thomas, 87–108. Urbana: University of Illinois Press, 1999.

The Winter's Tale

Guy-Bray, Stephen. "Idylls and Kings." In *Homoerotic Space: The Poetics of Loss in Renaissance Literature*, 176–215. Toronto: University of Toronto Press, 2002.

Johnson, Nora. "Ganymedes and Kings: Staging Male Homosexual Desire in *The Winter's Tale*." In *Shakespeare Studies*, vol. 29, edited by Leeds Barroll, 187–217. Cranbury, N.J.: Associated University Presses, 1998.

Neely, Carol Thomas. "Incest and Issue in the Romances: *The Winter's Tale*." In *Broken Nuptials in Shakespeare's Plays*, 166–210. New Haven: Yale University Press, 1985.

Shannon, Laurie. "Friendship's Offices: True Speech and Artificial Bodies in *The Winter's Tale*." In *Sovereign Amity: Figures of Friendship in Shakespearean Contexts*, 185–222. Chicago: University of Chicago Press, 2002.

Traub, Valerie. "Jewels, Statues, and Corpses: Containment of Female Erotic Power (*Hamlet, Othello, The Winter's Tale*)." In *Desire and Anxiety: Circulations of Sexuality in Shakespearean Drama*, 25–49. London: Routledge, 1992.

Matt Bell is an assistant professor in the English Department at Bridgewater State College. His essays have appeared in GLQ: *A Journal of Lesbian and Gay Studies and American Literature*. He is working on a book project that exposes a tension between gay sexuality and the narrative framework of the gay liberation movement.

Amanda Berry is visiting assistant professor in the Literature Department at American University. Her research considers literary representations of the public and publicity as they intersect with the figuration of the sexualized body and sexual identities. Her recent work analyzes canonical British Romantic-era texts that problematize sexual expression and representation. She is also interested in comic books and graphic novels and is working on a manuscript about masculinity and trauma provisionally entitled *No Man on Earth*.

Daniel Boyarin is Hermann P. and Sophia Taubman Professor of Talmudic Culture, Departments of Near Eastern Studies and Rhetoric, University of California, Berkeley, and a member of the core faculty in the minor in gay and lesbian studies. His publications include "Foucault's History of Sexuality—The Fourth Volume, or, a Field Left Fallow for Others to Till," the introduction to a special issue of the *Journal of the History of Sexuality*, which he co-edited. Other publications include *Sparks of the Logos: Essays in Rabbinic Hermeneutics* (2003) and *Border Lines: The Partition of Judaeo-Christianity* (2004).

Judith Brown is associate professor of English at Indiana University, Bloomington. Her publications include *Glamour in Six Dimensions: Modernism and the Radiance of Form* (2009) and essays in *Modernism / Modernity*, *Modernist Cultures*, and the *Journal of Modern Literature*.

Steven Bruhm is Robert and Ruth Lumsden Professor of English at The University of Western Ontario, London, Ontario. He is the author of *Gothic Bodies: The Politics of Pain in Romantic Fiction* (1994) and *Reflecting Narcissus: A Queer Aesthetic* (2001) and numerous articles on the queer gothic and co-editor of *Curiouser: On the Queerness of Children* (2004). He is currently working on the temporalities of queer choreography.

Peter Coviello is associate professor and chair of English at Bowdoin College, where he has also chaired the programs in Africana Studies and Gay and Lesbian Studies. He is the editor of Walt Whitman's *Memoranda During the War*, and the author of *Intimacy in America: Dreams of Affiliation in Antebellum Literature* and of essays that have appeared in GLQ, ELH, *American Literature*, and elsewhere.

Julie Crawford is associate professor of English and comparative literature and women's and gender studies at Columbia University. Her work on early modern literature and culture includes essays on Sapphic versification and women readers in Sidney's *Arcadia*, Lady Anne Clifford's queer family values, and, most recently, female same-sex counsel in Shakespeare. She is the author of *Marvelous Protestantism: Monstrous Births in Post-Reformation England* (2005) and is completing a book on women and literary production in early modern England.

Drew Daniel is an assistant professor of English at Johns Hopkins University. He is the author of *Twenty Jazz Funk Greats*, (2007) on the English occult industrial group Throbbing Gristle. His published reviews, catalogue essays, and articles range across Elizabethan drama, queer theory, psychoanalysis, contemporary film, and the musical avant-garde. He is currently completing a book manuscript entitled *The Melancholy Assemblage: Affect and Epistemology in the English Renaissance*. He is also one-half of the electronic duo Matmos.

Mario DiGangi is professor of English at Lehman College and the Graduate Center, City University of New York. He is the author of *The Homoerotics of Early Modern Drama* (1997) and of essays in collections such as *Ovid and the Renaissance Body* and *Love, Sex, Intimacy and Friendship between Men, 1550–1800*. He has edited *The Winter's Tale* for Bedford's Texts and Contexts series and *Romeo and Juliet* and *A Midsummer's Night Dream* for the Barnes and Noble Shakespeare. He recently completed a book on sexual types in early modern drama.

Lee Edelman is the Fletcher Professor of English Literature and chair of the Department of English at Tufts University. He is the author of *Transmember-* *ment of Song: Hart Crane's Anatomies of Rhetoric and Desire* (1987), *Homographe-sis: Essays in Gay Literary and Cultural Theory* (1994), and *No Future: Queer Theory and the Death Drive* (2004). He has published numerous essays on topics in poetry, theory, film, and cultural analysis. His latest book project, *Bad Education*, uses queer theory to question the value of survival and the survival of value in the ideology of the Humanities.

Jason Edwards is senior lecturer in nineteenth-century and early-twentieth-century art history at the University of York. He is the author of *Alfred Gil-bert's Aestheticism: Gilbert Amongst Whistler, Wilde, Leighton, Pater, and Burne-Jones* (2006) and *Eve Kosofsky Sedgwick* (2008). He has also been the guest editor of the "Anxious Flirtations: Homoeroticism, Art and Aestheticism" special issue of *Visual Culture in Britain* (2007), and is the editor (with Stephanie L. Taylor) of *Joseph Cornell: Opening the Box* (2007).

Aranye Fradenburg is professor of English and comparative literature at the University of California, Santa Barbara. She is also a clinical associate at the New Center for Psychoanalysis in Los Angeles and the director of the UCSB English Department's specialization "Literature and the Mind." By trade, she is a medievalist who has written on premodern sexuality and edited (with Carla Freccero) *Premodern Sexualities* (1996).

Carla Freccero is director of the Center for Cultural Studies at the University of California, Santa Cruz, and a professor in the departments of Literature, Feminist Studies, and History of Consciousness. Her most recent book is *Queer / Early / Modern* (2006).

Daniel Juan Gil is associate professor of English at Texas Christian University. He is the author of *Before Intimacy: Asocial Sexuality in Early Modern England* (2006), and articles on sexuality and social theory that have appeared in *Common Knowledge, Shakespeare Quarterly, ELH*, and *Borrowers and Lenders: The Journal of Shakespeare and Appropriation*.

Jonathan Goldberg is Arts and Sciences Distinguished Professor at Emory University where he directs Studies in Sexualities. His books that further queer work include *Sodometries, Desiring Women Writing, Willa Cather and*

Others, Tempest in the Caribbean, and *The Seeds of Things*, as well as the edited volumes *Queering the Renaissance* and *Reclaiming Sodom*.

Jody Greene is associate professor of literature and feminist studies at the University of California, Santa Cruz. She is the author of *The Trouble with Ownership: Literary Property and Authorial Liability in England, 1660–1730* (2005). She has edited a special issue of *GLQ* in memory of Alan Bray (2004) and a special issue of *Eighteenth-Century Studies* honoring the work of Jacques Derrida (2007).

Stephen Guy-Bray is professor of English at the University of British Columbia. His most recent books are *Against Reproduction: Where Renaissance Texts Come From* and the co-edited collection *Queer Renaissance Historiography: Backward Gaze*, which were both published in 2009. He has just finished a study of difference and sameness in the Renaissance.

Ellis Hanson is professor and department chair of English at Cornell University. He is the author of *Decadence and Catholicism* (1997), the editor of *Out Takes: Essays on Queer Theory and Film* (1999), and most recently the editor of *Digital Desire* (2010), a special issue of the *South Atlantic Quarterly*.

Sharon Holland is associate professor of English at Duke University. She is the author of *Raising the Dead: Readings of Death and (Black) Subjectivity* (2000) and co-author of *Crossing Waters, Crossing Worlds: The African Diaspora in Indian Country* (2006). She is now at work on a second monograph, entitled *The Erotic Life of Racism*.

Cary Howie is an assistant professor in the Department of Romance Studies at Cornell University. He is the author of *Claustrophilia: The Erotics of Enclosure in Medieval Literature* (2007) and co-author (with William Burgwinkle) of *Sanctity and Pornography in Medieval Culture: On the Verge* (2010).

Lynne Huffer is professor of women's studies at Emory University. She is the author of *Mad for Foucault: Rethinking the Foundations of Queer Theory* (2010), *Maternal Pasts, Feminist Futures: Nostalgia and the Question of Difference* (1998), and *Another Colette: The Question of Gendered Writing* (1992).

Barbara Johnson taught courses at Harvard University in nineteenth- and twentieth-century English literature, French literature, American (especially Afro-American) literature, and literary theory. Her books include *The Feminist Difference* (1998), *The Wake of Deconstruction* (1993), *A World of Difference* (1987), and *The Critical Difference* (1981).

Hector Kollias is lecturer in French at King's College, University of London. He has published articles on Jean Genet, Guillaume Dustan, Jean-Luc Nancy, Jacques Rancière, and Maurice Blanchot. He is writing a book-length study on the psychoanalytic concept of perversion and its uses and misuses in queer theory.

James Kuzner is assistant professor of English at Case Western Reserve University. An article of his—on political community, queer theory, and *Coriolanus*—has appeared in *Shakespeare Quarterly* and another article, on Milton, pleasure, and public reason, has appeared in *Criticism*.

Arthur L. Little Jr. is associate professor of English at the University of California, Los Angeles, where he teaches and conducts research on Shakespeare as well as contemporary LGBTQ literatures and cultures. He is the author of *Shakespeare Jungle Fever: National-Imperial Re-Envisions of Race, Rape, and Sacrifice*, and is working on a book-length cultural study of *Hamlet*.

Philip Lorenz is an assistant professor of English at Cornell University, where he teaches courses on Renaissance and modern drama. His research focuses on political theology and sovereignty in early modern English and Spanish drama. He is completing his first book, *The Tears of Sovereignty: Perspectives of Power in Renaissance Drama*.

Heather Love is an associate professor of English at the University of Pennsylvania, where she teaches twentieth-century literature, film, gender studies, and critical theory. She is the author of *Feeling Backward: Loss and the Politics of Queer History* (2007) and is working on a book on the source materials for Erving Goffman's *Stigma: On the Management of Spoiled Identity*.

Jeffrey Masten is Herman and Beulah Pearce Miller Research Professor in Literature at Northwestern University, where he teaches in the English Department and the Gender Studies Program. He is the author of *Textual Inter-*

course: Collaboration, Authorship, and Sexualities in Renaissance Drama (1997) and is completing a book entitled *Spelling Shakespeare, and Other Essays in Queer Philology.*

Robert McRuer is professor of English at George Washington University, where he teaches queer studies, disability studies, and critical theory. He is the author of *Crip Theory: Cultural Signs of Queerness and Disability* (2006) and co-editor (with Abby L. Wilkerson) of "Desiring Disability: Queer Theory Meets Disability," a special issue of GLQ.

Madhavi Menon is associate professor of literature at American University and the author of *Wanton Words: Rhetoric and Sexuality in English Renaissance Drama* (2004) and *Unhistorical Shakespeare: Queer Theory in Shakespearean Literature and Film* (2008).

Michael Moon is the author of *A Small Boy and Others: Imitation and Initiation in American Culture from Henry James to Andy Warhol* (1998), *Disseminating Whitman: Revision and Corporeality in Leaves of Grass* (1991), and a forthcoming study of the "outsider artist" Henry Darger. He has taught LGBTQ studies at Duke, Johns Hopkins, and Emory.

Paul Morrison is professor of English and American literature at Brandeis University. His publications include *The Explanation for Everything: Essays on Sexual Subjectivity* (2001) and *The Poetics of Fascism: Ezra Pound, T.S. Eliot, and Paul DeMan* (1996).

Andrew Nicholls is an artist, writer, curator, and designer in Perth, Western Australia. He has exhibited across Australia as well as in Italy and the United Kingdom and has curated exhibitions for numerous galleries in Perth and Sydney. Nicholls writes for a number of Australian arts publications. In his art practice, he explores how the sentimental has functioned as an often under-acknowledged force driving mainstream culture. In 2009 he published the first major catalogue documenting his practice, *Love Andrew Nicholls, Drawn Works 1998–2008.*

Kevin Ohi is associate professor of English at Boston College. He is the author of *Innocence and Rapture: The Erotic Child in Pater, Wilde, James, and Nabokov*

(2005) and *Henry James and the Queerness of Style* (forthcoming, 2011). His articles on Victorian literature, American literature, and film have appeared in
*ELH, Camera Obscura, GLQ, Victorian Literature and Culture, Genre, African Ameri-
can Review, Cinema Journal*, and elsewhere.

Patrick R. O'Malley is associate professor of English at Georgetown University. He is the author of *Catholicism, Sexual Deviance, and Victorian Gothic Culture* (2006) and of essays on the representation of religion and sexuality in the
works of John Henry Newman, Oscar Wilde, and James Joyce.

Ann Pellegrini is associate professor of Performance Studies and Religious
Studies at New York University, where she also directs NYU's Center for the
Study of Gender and Sexuality. She is the author of *Performance Anxieties:
Staging Psychoanalysis, Staging Race* (1997), co-author of *Love the Sin: Sexual
Regulation and the Limits of Religious Tolerance* (2004), co-editor of *Queer Theory
and the Jewish Question* (2003), and co-editor (with Janet R. Jakobsen) of *Secu-
larisms* (2008). She is currently completing a new book on queer structures of
religious feeling.

Richard Rambuss holds a joint appointment in the departments of English
and Comparative Literature at Emory University, and is chair of the English
Department. He teaches courses in early modern literature, gender and sexuality studies, and film. He is the author of *Closet Devotions* (1998) and a con-
tributor to *Queering the Renaissance* (1994).

Valerie Rohy is an associate professor of English at the University of Ver-
mont. She is the author of *Anachronism and Its Others: Sexuality, Race, Temporality* (2009) and *Impossible Women: Lesbian Figures and American Literature* (2000),
and editor (with Elizabeth Ammons) of *American Local Color Writing, 1880–
1920* (1998).

Bethany Schneider is assistant professor of English at Bryn Mawr College.
With Daniel Heath Justice and Mark Rifkin, she edited *Sexuality, Nationality,
Indigeneity*, a special issue of *GLQ* (Volume 16, numbers 1–2, 2010), and her essay
"Oklahobo: Following Craig Womack's Queer and Native American Studies"
appeared in the "After Sex" special issue of the *South Atlantic Quarterly*.

Kathryn Schwarz is associate professor of English at Vanderbilt University. She is the author of *Tough Love: Amazon Encounters in the English Renaissance* (2000). Her most recent articles on early modern gender and sexuality have appeared in *Renaissance Drama*, *differences*, PMLA, *Shakespeare Quarterly*, and ELH. Her new book, *What You Will: Feminine Volition and Shakespearean Social Contracts*, will be published by the University of Pennsylvania Press in 2011.

Laurie Shannon is associate professor of English at Northwestern University. Her first book, *Sovereign Amity: Figures of Friendship in Shakespearean Contexts* (2002), concerns affect, gender, sexuality, and sovereignty in early modern visions of utopian counterpolitics. Her current project, *The Necessary Animal: Zootopian Politics in the Environs of Shakespeare* (forthcoming) considers animal claims in a period credited (and discredited) with an invention of the human.

Ashley T. Shelden is an assistant professor of English at Kennesaw State University. Her areas of specialization include twentieth-century British literature, psychoanalysis, and queer theory. Her essay on Freud's "The Psychogenesis of a Case of Homosexuality in a Woman," was published in *Straight Writ Queer* (2006). She is working on her first book project, *Making Love: Sexuality and the Construction of Modernism*.

Alan Sinfield teaches in the Sexual Dissidence and Social Change Master's Program at the University of Sussex. His recent publications include *Out on Stage: Lesbian and Gay Theatre in the Twentieth Century* (1999), *Gay and After* (1998), *On Sexuality and Power* (2004), and *Shakespeare, Authority, Sexuality* (2006).

Bruce Smith is professor of English at the University of Southern California. His selected publications include *Shakespeare and Masculinity* (2000), *The Acoustic World of Early Modern England: Attending to the O-Factor* (1999), and *Homosexual Desire in Shakespeare's England: A Cultural Poetics* (1991).

Karl Steel is an assistant professor of English at Brooklyn College, CUNY. His work concentrates on the discursive relationship of humans to animals in the Middle Ages. His first book, *How to Make a Human: Animals and Violence in the Middle Ages*, will be published by Ohio State University Press in 2011.

Kathryn Bond Stockton is professor of English and director of gender studies at the University of Utah, where she teaches queer theory and nineteenth-

and twentieth-century literature. She is the author of *Beautiful Bottom, Beautiful Shame: Where "Black" Meets "Queer"* (2006) and *God between Their Lips: Desire between Women in Irigaray, Bronte, and Eliot* (Stanford University Press, 1994). Her newest book is *The Queer Child, or Growing Sideways in the Twentieth Century* (2009).

Amy Villarejo holds a joint appointment in film studies and the Feminist, Gender, and Sexuality Studies Program at Cornell University. She is the author of *Lesbian Rule: Cultural Criticism and the Value of Desire* (2003). She is also the co-editor of *Capital Q: Marxism after Queer Theory* (forthcoming) and the author of other books and articles on queer theory, cinema, and media.

Julian Yates is associate professor of English and material culture studies at the University of Delaware. He is the author of *Error, Misuse, Failure: Object Lessons from the English Renaissance* (2003). His current work addresses questions of ecology and ways to address the agency of inhuman actors in social networks.

Note: Page numbers in italics indicate illustrations.

Madhavi Menon is associate professor of literature
at American University and the author of *Wanton
Words: Rhetoric and Sexuality in English Renaissance
Drama* (2004) and *Unhistorical Shakespeare: Queer
Theory in Shakespearean Literature and Film* (2008).

∼≥

Library of Congress Cataloging-in-Publication Data
Shakesqueer : a queer companion to the complete
works of Shakespeare / edited by Madhavi Menon.
   p. cm. — (Series Q)
Includes bibliographical references and index.
ISBN 978-0-8223-4833-7 (cloth : alk. paper)
ISBN 978-0-8223-4845-0 (pbk. : alk. paper)
1. Shakespeare, William, 1564–1616—Criticism
and interpretation. 2. Queer theory.
I. Menon, Madhavi. II. Series: Series Q.
PR2976.S346 2011
822.3'3—dc22   2010035884